Circling Marx

Historical Materialism Book Series

The Historical Materialism Book Series is a major publishing initiative of the radical left. The capitalist crisis of the twenty-first century has been met by a resurgence of interest in critical Marxist theory. At the same time, the publishing institutions committed to Marxism have contracted markedly since the high point of the 1970s. The Historical Materialism Book Series is dedicated to addressing this situation by making available important works of Marxist theory. The aim of the series is to publish important theoretical contributions as the basis for vigorous intellectual debate and exchange on the left.

The peer-reviewed series publishes original monographs, translated texts, and reprints of classics across the bounds of academic disciplinary agendas and across the divisions of the left. The series is particularly concerned to encourage the internationalization of Marxist debate and aims to translate significant studies from beyond the English-speaking world.

For a full list of titles in the Historical Materialism Book Series
available in paperback from Haymarket Books, visit:
https://www.haymarketbooks.org/series_collections/1-historical-materialism

Circling Marx

Essays 1980–2020

Peter Beilharz

Haymarket Books
Chicago, IL

First published in 2020 by Brill Academic Publishers, The Netherlands
© 2020 Koninklijke Brill NV, Leiden, The Netherlands

Published in paperback in 2021 by
Haymarket Books
P.O. Box 180165
Chicago, IL 60618
773-583-7884
www.haymarketbooks.org

ISBN: 978-1-64259-602-1

Distributed to the trade in the US through Consortium Book Sales and
Distribution (www.cbsd.com) and internationally through Ingram
Publisher Services International (www.ingramcontent.com).

This book was published with the generous support of Lannan
Foundation and Wallace Action Fund.

Special discounts are available for bulk purchases by organizations and
institutions. Please call 773-583-7884 or email info@haymarketbooks.org
for more information.

Cover art and design by David Mabb. Cover art is a detail of *Long Live
the New! no. 38*, Kazimir Malevich drawing on Morris & Co. design, paint
and wallpaper on canvas (2016).

Printed in the United States.

10 9 8 7 6 5 4 3 2 1

Library of Congress Cataloging-in-Publication data is available.

Contents

Third Circle

Acknowledgements

Forty years is a long time in a life – a long time to read, to listen, to write. These essays span a series of hopes, dreams, disappointments; and we carry on. I cannot thank by name all those who helped make all this possible across such a long time. I thank all my teachers and mentors, and all my friends. We could shorthand this as thanks to *Thesis Eleven*, but that would not get it all either.

Sian Supski, Andrew Gilbert and Tim Andrews helped make the collection work. Peter Thomas had the kindness to suggest it. Danny Hayward and the HM cell turned it into a book. Alonso Casanueva Baptista performed magic with the Index. Hilde Kugel was a wonderful desk editor. Dor, Nikolai and Rhea, Sian and Savannah lived with me across all this. I am grateful to all, and hope that these results might be of some use-value to those who follow. For those who might be interested, some parallel paths are tracked in my *Intimacy in Post-Modern Times – A Friendship with Zygmunt Bauman*, Manchester University Press, 2020, in my introduction to *Alastair Davidson – Gramsci in Australia*, Brill, 2020, and in forthcoming memoirs on Castoriadis, and the first forty years in *Thesis Eleven*.

To my past readers, friends and colleagues, thank you. To my new readers, welcome.

Peter Beilharz
Sichuan University, PRC/Curtin University, WA

Copyright Notices

1. 'Karl Marx', from Peter Beilharz (ed.), *Social Theory*, Sydney, Allen and Unwin, 1992.
2. 'Marxism and History', *Thesis Eleven* 2, Sage, 1981.
3. 'Negation and Ambivalence: Marx, Simmel and Bolshevism on Money', *Thesis Eleven* 46, Sage, 1996.
4. 'Marx, Modernity and Motion', from Ghassan Hage and Emma Kowal (eds.), *Force, Movement, Intensity*, Melbourne, Melbourne University Press, 2011.
5. 'The Marxist Legacy, from Gerard Delanty and Stephen P. Turner' (eds.), *Routledge International Handbook of Contemporary Social and Political Theory*, London, Routledge, 2011.
6. 'Socialism: Modern Hopes, Postmodern Shadows', from George Ritzer and Barry Smart (eds.), *Handbook of Social Theory*, London, Sage, 2001.
7. 'Social Democracy: Kautsky and Bernstein', from *Labour's Utopias*, London, Routledge, 1992.
8. 'Edward Bellamy: Looking Back at American Socialism in the Nineteenth Century', unpublished paper, presented to ASA Proceedings, Atlanta, 2003.
9. 'The Other Trotsky', *Thesis Eleven* 3, Sage, 1982.
10. 'The Young Trotsky', *Political Theory Newsletter* 3/2, Canberra, ADFA, 1991.
11. 'Isaac Deutscher – History and Necessity', *History of Political Thought* 7/2, Imprint Academic Ltd, 1986.
12. 'Political Economy and Transition: Ernest Mandel', from *Trotsky, Trotskyism and the Transition to Socialism*, London, Croom Helm, 1987.
13. 'Daniel Bell – American Menshevik', *Thesis Eleven* 118, Sage, 2013.
14. 'Nicos Poulantzas and Marxist Theory', *Australian Left Review* 73, Sydney, CPA, 1980.
15. 'Louis Althusser', from Beilharz, *Social Theory*, Sydney, Allen and Unwin, 1992.
16. 'Prehistoric Modes of Textual Production, or, Books Begat by Other Books: Hindess and Hirst', *Alternatives*, Sage, 36/1, 2011.
17. 'The Decline of Western Marxism: Trotsky, Gramsci, Althusser', *Thesis Eleven* 75, Sage, 2003.
18. 'Cornelius Castoriadis, Political and Social Writings', *Thesis Eleven* 22, Sage, 1989.
19. 'Budapest Central: Agnes Heller's Theory of Modernity', *Thesis Eleven* 75, Sage, 2003.

Circling Marx: An Introduction

Across the path of my life there has been a great deal of motion, global and local, and there have also been some constants. A child of the fifties, I have never recovered from the formative influence of the British blues wave of the sixties. I have not been able to shake off a sense of comfort, release and belonging when I am on the beach or in the bush in Australia. The cities have changed rather more, and the suburbs continued to sprawl. And I have never got past Karl Marx, even though so many other things have moved on in terms of intellectual fads and fashions. The famous definition of what constitutes a classic includes the notion that each reading brings something afresh. I have spent more time reading Marx over fifty years than any other, though of course I also return to Gramsci, to Bauman and Heller, to Shakespeare and to Goethe, to the Russians and to Australian and New World fiction. Just now I am back to Kafka and Beckett. Like Baudelaire, I still also lust for something new. But Marx is the perennial, for me. There is always something new to learn there, and something fresh to pass on.

My formation as a Marxist carried me from the seventies into the eighties. At that moment, it seemed to me, one attraction of Marxism was that its sources were so rich and diverse, and its implications so manifold – in literature and art, in geography and urban studies, history and world systems analysis, in language and culture, popular and high and in between. There was simply so much going on. The point is not that marxism was a universal system of knowledge, so much that it opened up onto so many human and social concerns. Marxism was not an ideology, or a self-contained system for me; rather it was a point of carriage into so many other worlds and ways of thinking. You could leave, or leave and return, or you could circle. This may well be what Marx intended when he denied that he was a Marxist. His project was not to sell a truth-system or a franchise, a brand name, though he was also obsessed with the possibility of getting it right. His was, rather, a point of entry to the discourse of modernity, which necessarily also implied transcendence. The language may jar, but the issue is moot: Marxism, as an historicism, also opens into postmarxism. Marxism necessarily came from elsewhere, and takes us somewhere else again.

I began publishing as a Marxist in the middle seventies. My initial forays were into the work of those who were then received as the new giants, from Mandel to Poulantzas, Hindess and Hirst, Hall and Thompson. I had some intuitive sense that those who came in between, such as Gramsci and Lukács, were a cut above. But my initial compass was provided by Marx, and by those who, like Heller and Markus, wanted to take him seriously and yet, as above, to move on.

I came to understand that there was no way around Marx, and that many of his followers were not only less interesting but lazy, driven by formulae rather than by curiosity. I was convinced of the value of the hermeneutic approach to close reading, but I was also sufficiently given to historicism to sense that there were never just two people involved in those close readings. As Freud had it, there were always more than two people in the room. All the history and debates of and around marxism also intervened when you read Marx, or any other such classic. There were ghosts everywhere.

The essays collected in this volume reflect these tensions in text and reception. They are grouped in three circles, an historical rather than strictly autobiographical sequence. The first circle, closer to Marx, is not presented in the order of writing but grouped thematically. The second circle takes in the immediate legacy, including Social Democracy and Bolshevism, that great parting of ways in the Marxist tradition. There are necessarily some blurred boundaries here. The Trotskyist tradition, for example, plainly extends into the third circle, into the 1970s. Thematically, I think it belongs to the culture and frame of the World Wars. The third circle was opening as I came to what is called maturity. Heller, Feher, Bauman and Castoriadis and Bernard Smith belong here, as does Althusser as a period prominence in the history of more recent Marxism. Gramsci also belongs here, as appropriated by the seventies revival; and Critical Theory, with especial reference to the Frankfurt School, also travels across these times. Lastly, for the purposes of this volume, *Thesis Eleven*, our own project, also belongs here, although it is also possible that it spreads into the fourth circle, which is left here as an anticipation for others to catalogue and evaluate.

1   My Road to Marxism

1966 was a good year. Cream, *I Feel Free*; Hendrix, *Hey Joe. Gimme Some Lovin*, and *Friday On My Mind*. I was twelve going on thirteen, finding my way into life and my first year of high school. Girls suddenly became very interesting. 1967 was also good. I discovered the Bluesbreakers, via an older girl, *A Hard Road* first, then back to the Clapton Beano album. The first Canned Heat album showed up in the antipodes: I fell in love again, and then I caught up with Paul Butterfield, and began to play drums. The first time I played in public was a track off *East/West*. There came to be inspiring local bands like Wild Cherries and then Chain and Spectrum, and all this was cooked up in a kind of hippy soup, where opposition to the war in Vietnam and Conscription were vital and radical politics and rock music seemed to be all of a piece. Under the influence of my elder brother and his mates, we went back, to the black man's blues,

Lead Belly, Elmore James, John Lee Hooker, Sonny Boy Williamson, Sonny and Brownie. In between, John Hammond Jr, Koerner Ray and Glover and Dylan, and the 1965 compilation *The Chicago Blues Today*. There was a great deal of turbulence, though perhaps more beyond Australia than within. In Australian cities, the global connect was less Paris 1968 than Vietnam, this connected directly to us by the bitter thread of Conscription. Protest seemed as natural to me as it looked ridiculous to my parents.

The regress principle was a good one; I have followed it ever since. So that when I discovered Marxism, I was bound to want to go back to Marx, and then to his own sources in turn. I tried to read excerpts from *Capital* in 1969, but there were other more interesting things going on; I was fifteen. My brother was my dealer for music, but my intellectual appetites were to be piqued by my year 12 teacher and mentor, Doc Saffin. So now I am 17, going on 18. Saffin bid me to read Edward Bellamy, and his local antipodean follower, William Lane. Socialism, like utopia, presented itself to me as a good idea. And the Year 12 curriculum was amazing: Huxley and Orwell, Koestler and Camus, Wilde and Beckett, Shakespeare, Marx's favourite, and then the Russians. No Marx in sight, as far as the curriculum was concerned, but it wasn't too hard to work out where to go: existentialism, humanism, then Marcuse and his mates.

1972: I am eighteen. I have left home, and am a secondary teacher in training at Rusden College in the suburbs of Melbourne, living in Lilydale, commuting to Clayton, hours on bus and train, lots of time to read. The culture at Rusden is small, benign, encouraging without being pushy. Likely it was exactly what I needed at the time, an arts college. I had a fine teacher in Colin Duncan, an Anglican canon, who encouraged me to read Marx and Hegel and on Marx and humanism. Don Gibb gave me license to research the local and transnational utopian William Lane more thoroughly. Others, like Alan Rice, suggested I read Althusser. Perhaps it was because Althusser was looking to usurp the position I was just arriving at. I read *For Marx* and couldn't work out what the fuss was about. Later I read *Reading Capital* annually, for years on the bus; it also made little sense till I was taught it, later, by Alastair Davidson.

The Whitlam Government is elected 2 December; interesting times begin. I am reading voraciously, guided on by Saffin, but indiscriminately. In effect, these years are autodidactic, and promiscuous. I am reading Marx in Easton and Guddat, Fromm, Marcuse, Mattick, Mandel, Dunayevskaya. I have worked out that I can walk across the road to Monash University on Fridays and get the best of both possible worlds, small and big culture, music and marxism. Friday lunch at Monash there are amazing free bands like Chain and Spectrum. Before and after, I go to a place new to me called the library stacks, where the periodicals are held; or else to 335.4 in the open shelves, where there is a cornucopia of stuff on Marx and Marxism. So ignoring the catalogue, I just work my way through the shelves, carrying pile after pile of heavy books to my carrel, checking out what the other, smarter or more commanding hippies are reading or pretending to read.

There were some weird psychodynamics here, more than a little pretence and posturing, and it is likely no accident that most of the punters were boys rather than girls. But as with music, you get to know folks, and they pass it on. Like music, left politics in Melbourne and at Monash was capable of machismo and arrogance but also of generosity, help and friendship. Both scenes, music and marxism, I have come to realise, were little countercultures. Others were always ready to tell you what you should be listening to or reading, who you could talk to, where the action was. Sometimes their advice was dubious, but it was a world opening up to me.

Under the influence of my youthful cartoon image of Gramsci, I begin to collect and work out of my own notebooks, exercise books carefully annotated and indexed for future reference. I have an early brush with Trotsky, but contrary to rumour, never become a follower; there seems to be a standard prejudice that anyone interested in Trotsky must at some stage have signed up. I never did; in fact I never signed up at all, though I did take out subscriptions to all the local left press, read all the local periodicals as well as those from the USA and the UK, and became a regular less at the staid Communist Party Rooms in Lonsdale Street than at its wonderful bookshop, the International, in Elizabeth Street, which was another standard stop in my weekly counterculture routine. These days, I guess, you would call it a network, or a resource or drop-in centre. Some other Fridays I would meet up with Saffin there, to see the latest, to meet new friends and scour through the second hand section on the sixth floor. There were always connections.

1971 was a big year for those of us on the left and trapped largely or exclusively within the English language. There arrived the International Publishers edition of the *Selections from the Prison Notebooks*, and the Merlin edition of *History and Class Consciousness*. I was so happy about the latter that I told my mother the good news in *Hausdeutsch*; she seemed unimpressed, both by my German and by my left-wing enthusiasms. Gramsci and Lukács were to figure prominently in my formation, not least in connection with the carriers and currents of cultural traffic that advantaged me. I came to work closely both with Alastair Davidson, who had already published a book on Gramsci in Sydney in 1968, when I was in third form and busy with Rory Gallagher, Ten Years After and Cream's *Wheels of Fire*. And later I came to work closely with the students of Lukács, who took up the period of their Australian exile from 1978, though they were like my mum by this stage well past any enthusiasm for the Lukács of *History and Class Consciousness*.

Earlier I am distracted by libertarian Marxism, and anarchism. I read Kropotkin, Malatesta, Berkman; I can do without Bakunin, though I do read him, and likely fail to take Proudhon too seriously because Marx has already dismissed him. I have met Rosa Luxemburg, and I have encountered the story of Kronstadt (as Daniel Bell said to me much later, that is the breaker, the point of no return). I am learning about council communism, reading Cardan or Castoriadis via the London Solidarity pamphlets, discovering Pannekoek and the fact that his book on workers' councils was first published in Melbourne. With my friend Steve Wright I am reading Isaac Rubin, Victor Serge, Rosdolsky, Cleaver, Rachleff, and discovering the *Autonomista*, Negri before he was Negri. I admire the libertarian and emancipatory spirit of these thinkers, but I am also taken by the Gramscian common sense that what might be necessary would be less dreams of utopia and more claims about a new order. If socialism is to be made from below, it needs more than the politics of impossibilism. But I do not like political parties, and I never joined one, not of any kind.

As to Trotsky, my mission was rather to get him off the stage, no small arrogance on my part, but one from which I do not resile. I was puzzled and concerned as to the magnetic attraction of Trotsky for those on the left who could not abide Stalin. It was as though the halfway house away from Stalinism had become a prison house of its own. My initial research interest, in the history of Trotskyism in Australia, became an interest in Trotskyism as a language or system of thought, and its power to hold those of such intelligence in the face of other facts. Two basic facts, it seemed to me, were that revolutions could no longer work at all, that the emergent scale and complexity of what we would later call modernity would make the very idea of revolution impossible. The other was moral, or ethical – revolutions involved one group of people killing another. Revolution became the repetition of domination. If revolutions occurred, then the Revolution would devour its own children as well as those of others. In other words, I was attracted to the tradition of Classical Marxism, to the Marxist culture of the Second International, and to the Western Marxist tradition which came to follow it. I could not abide Bolshevism, and never have.

In 1975 the Whitlam Government was dismissed by the Vice Regal, and arguments for reform became much more difficult. I completed my teacher training in Politics and History and stepped sideways into Monash Politics. Despite, or perhaps because of the enthusiastic support of Alastair Davidson and Herb Feith, my four-year Rusden degree was granted the credit equivalence of one year's achievement by the higher ups. I was wounded, but even so the challenge was too good to pass on: I would have to do well in eight units over two years before entering fourth year as an MA Preliminary candidate. My young wife, Dor, was prepared to support me in this excursion; neither of us knew how long it would take or where it would end up. The upside for me was that I kind of knew my way by now, and had some sense of who I was; and I was to be treated to a veritable smorgasbord of theory delivered by some of the finest minds in the world and certainly in my backyard in Melbourne: Alastair Davidson, Zawar Hanfi, and Harry Redner. I had found my orientation. These years were to become my apprenticeship.

With Alastair I studied, and then taught Revolutionary Theories and Movements, from Marx to Althusser, and Comparative Communist Systems, Italy and France in the years of ascendant Eurocommunism. Reformism, it seemed, was not quite dead yet, at least not yet in Europe. These were wonderful days of discovery that I have discussed elsewhere, in my introduction to the Brill volume of Davidson's own collected essays. Alastair was my guiding light, licensing my folly and gently educating it. With Zawar, there was the natural and necessary regress of Marxism as Critical Theory – No Marx Without Aristotle! His was a verse and line close reading of Marx from the *1844 Manuscripts* to the *German Ideology*, the *Grundrisse* and *Capital*. Zawar gave me a textual grounding which I still rely on today: what, for example, is the meaning of *Naturwüchsigkeit* in the *Grundrisse*? This came together with the fundamental insight that Marx's entire project could indeed be read as a life's instalments in the critique of political economy, and the optic that Marx was good at diagnosis, less good at prognosis. Zawar had translated Feuerbach; he was a serious textual scholar in the Germanic tradition. He introduced me to Karl Loewith, whose essay on Weber and Marx together with Lukács' *Reification* essay became fundamental points of my orientation. I began to understand that read together, Marx and Weber could make up the basis of what would later emerge as Critical Theory in the hands of the Frankfurt School. Zawar taught us much else, from Parmenides to Aristotle, to Hegel and Heidegger, and finally to Gadamer and Habermas. Zawar worked at a level of sophistication that also made me appreciate the fact that I had some previous experience in these fields; I am not sure how some of my undergraduate peers can have coped. I guess they tuned out.

So we devoured the early Habermas, we devotees, especially *Theory and Practice*, and later, with Boris Frankel, read *Legitimation Crisis* and all else that came up in the period enthusiasm for the critique of the state, from Horkheimer to Offe, O'Connor, Poulantzas and Erik Wright. With Harry Redner we read Orwell and Huxley, a timely revisit, Nietzsche and Adorno, Spengler, Sorel, Arendt and Ortega y Gasset, and especially the work of Harry's own champion, Max Weber. Harry also had timely meditations on the Marx of the *Eighteenth Brumaire*, and Alastair and Harry together took us through the structuralist labyrinth, from Marx and Freud through the Russian formalists, and Saussure to Levi-Strauss, the Annales, Barthes and Foucault. Alastair also introduced me more thoroughly to Lefebvre, both textually and in person, and to Laclau, in the same dual dimension. The fact of embodiment became an important dimension of knowing, of understanding theory and its artists.

So we had our local Gramsci, so to speak, in Davidson. Davidson taught us a great deal, some of which is illustrated in the accompanying Brill volume which collects his essays, *Gramsci in Australia*. He also taught us to read, and how to stake a claim, but he also taught us that theories were like language games; you could inhabit a theory, or visit it, without becoming a signed up member or enthusiast. And you should do your best to read everything, not least the views that you expected to disagree with. The work of theory was necessarily agonistic and open-ended. So we read Gramsci but also Althusser or Lefebvre or Braudel, and we read widely in what I would now call historical sociology or historical materialism. This meant taking historicity or everyday life seriously, as a vital antidote to philosophy. It also meant grappling with the tensions between the global and the demands of the national popular. As Davidson understood, with Gramsci you could go either way, and perhaps we in the antipodes had it as our fate forever to keep moving.

There were some very fine teachers, but there was also some autonomous activity here. After that early youthful false start with *Capital* at Croydon High School, we began at Monash to organise Capital Reading Classes. They were fantastic, thorough, democratic but self-disciplined. Up to twenty of us, undergraduates and postgraduates would meet upstairs in the higher echelons of the Menzies Building and take turns at leading, suggesting interpretations, disagreeing when necessary, but learning together. Then there were Sunday afternoon discussions, sometimes with the Hungarians at their soirees, sometimes with Johann Arnason at his Max Weber Circle, sometimes on a book or topic, sometimes reading a text like *Discipline and Punish* over some several weeks or months. This was formative for the culture of *Thesis Eleven*, which from the beginning was also to become an organiser.

I was no longer quite so carefree or young, and music had begun to recede from its hitherto central place in my life. Marxism and theory and history gobbled me up. This was the cultural moment in which Athol Vitzdamm-Jones, Julian Triado and I began to discuss the idea of a journal, which became *Thesis Eleven* from the end of 1980. The Hungarians had arrived in 1978. There were many things that we shared, including a reliance on or comfort with the lan-

guage of Marxism. And there were many new things to learn from the Hungarians, as there were from Johann Arnason, who had arrived in Melbourne three
years earlier, who also knew everything and was happy to be passing it on. Marx
was a constant presence in all this. As regards the Hungarians, the marxology
came at that time from Agnes Heller, but especially, behind or alongside her,
from George Markus. Like Hanfi, Markus was the most extraordinary hermen-
eut. He literally knew everything, and could explain it even on the telephone, as
I discovered once when I made a call to Sydney to talk to him, or him to me, on
the idea of Second Nature. Markus combined a kind of personal modesty with
an intellect without parallel. The quality of his work, in *Marxism and Anthropology* and *Language and Production*, and in smaller pieces like 'Four Forms of
Critical Theory', which we published in the debut issue of *Thesis Eleven*, left a
deep mark on my thinking, both in terms of the content and the method of
thinking involved.

The emergent culture of *Thesis Eleven* formed us, just as it was also formed
by us. Its ambitions reflected the open canopy around us. Growing also meant
growing out of Marxism. In its earliest years the journal contained many tensions, including those which involved the illusions that we might be changing
the world. We were, of course, but in smaller and more personal ways than the
Theses on Feuerbach might have suggested. Here the invisible leading thinker
was likely the structuralist Freud as much as Marx. We had to learn about the
irrationality of our lives and those of others. We had to learn how important
it was just to look after each other, how fragile our relations were in the midst
of the incredible transformations of our time, not least those that impacted so
deeply on the universities. For we had overinvested in the potential of universities, which were often good hosts to the practice of thinking into the eighties.
But this was all about to change.

Agnes Heller and Ferenc Feher left Melbourne for the New School in New
York in 1986. This eight-year sojourn was deeply formative for us, an experience
I have discussed in my essay on the Budapest School in Australia.[1] Together with
many others I applied for Agnes' position at La Trobe, and picked it up in 1988.
This was an honour and a challenge. I was to teach, among other things, her
course on Socialist Ideas. I was keen to be panoramic, and this opened the door
to my study of *Labour's Utopias*, but I also needed to deliver on Marx.

Labour's Utopias was my second book, the sequel to my critique of Trotskyism. I stand by the argument and still admire the structure of my first book,
which was modelled on that of *Capital*, after a fashion ... to begin with the single

---

1   Beilharz 2018a.

cell unit, Trotsky, and think this out through his followers in history, philosophy and political economy, and then into the expanded arguments of the various chapters of the Fourth International. I was much taken at the time by the idea of generative metaphor, that pattern of thinking which generates its conclusions automatically out of its premises. The idea of automatic Marxism was also in the air. I wanted to understand how thinkers of this calibre could so persistently be mistaken in their insistence on the impending imminence of socialist revolution. The critiques of Mandel and Deutscher, some of them reprinted in this volume, I also stand by, though in retrospect it is possible that I failed sufficiently to register the extent of Mandel's achievement, especially in *Late Capitalism*;[2] it is not surprising that a thinker of the calibre of Jameson should have come to rely on his theses.[3] But I was young, at this formative point, and the tasks of critique were calling me. The hopes of socialism seemed so important, and the quality of much of what passed for socialist argument seems so mediocre or just wrong. It was easier to criticise than to build, especially after the disaster of the Russian Revolution.

Trotskyism certainly shared something with the milieu of classical Marxism. The Marxism of the Second International was a clear political failure, but the achievement of its intellectual culture, as indicated for example in the pages of *Die Neue Zeit*, remain monumental. The project of *Labour's Utopias* was to expand the optic, by taking in Bolshevism, Fabianism and Social Democracy. Written under the influence of Stuart Macintyre and Ian Britain in the year I spent at Melbourne History in 1987, it was later to crack Stuart's acute observation that the order was a little too obvious. Bolshevism bad, Fabianism better, Social Democracy just right. My new post at La Trobe gave me access for the first time to travel and to travel funds. So I travelled, especially to the Amsterdam Institute of Social History. I made friends there with good people like Mino Carchedi and Marcel Van der Linden, and in London with Paul Hirst and Michele Barrett, as I did the LSE Archives and those at Nuffield. Other, more complicated and elongated relationships opened with figures like Zygmunt Bauman in Leeds.

Back home, I came to the conclusion that I had spent too much of my time looking to discredit the revolutionary tradition, which had already done quite a good job of this without my help. The new illusion on the left involved the hopes invested in Antipodean New Labour, this well before the later arrival of Blair in the north. During my time working at Phillip Institute, before La Trobe,

---

2   Beilharz 1976.
3   Beilharz 1991a, 1992b.

I had garnered some reputation, working together with Rob Watts, as a critic of labourism. This resulted in *Transforming Labor*, published in 1994; and then turned into *Postmodern Socialism*, in the same year. Things were looking grim. Bolshevism had lost its allure for the broad left, only to give way to new fantasies about the prospects of the new social contract. Communism in the Soviet Union and its satellites had gone, good riddance. In the meantime many of my friends had run to the other side of the boat, and were now keen new labourists. I needed a line out of this labyrinth, without giving up on the socialist norms and values that had oriented my life to this point.

It, or he, arrived in the form, the work and person of the Australian Marxist art historian, Bernard Smith. Bernard described himself as a cultural historian with a primary interest in the visual. Since the publication of his first, Marxist history of Australian painting in 1945, he had consistently sought to explain culture, among other things, with reference to technology. Already in 1945 he was discussing postmodernism. Closer to home, Smith also had an acute interest in the world system of imperialism, and in the flows of cultural traffic that ran both north and south as well as sideways. I spent years working on and with Bernard, then to turn my view towards Leeds. There, I found that Bauman, too, defined his interest then as dual, in culture and socialism. Well beyond Marx, as we both differently were, Bauman still had Marx's image on his study wall. (Bernard, if I recall, had the face of William Morris on his.) As Bauman liked to put it, our vocation was to ask questions, rather than ourselves look to answering them on behalf of others. I visited him annually in Leeds for more than twenty years, and we became both collaborators and friends, to the extent that some identified us as a three-legged man. Our views and our life paths were not the same, though I am proud to have been his interpreter. As he said to me more than once, my job was to put order into the chaos of his work. It was my privilege to do this both with Bauman and with Bernard Smith, though Smith's work had its own clarity of purpose. My purpose in writing about Smith was not to reduce chaos but to show continuity, and to show that social theory in the antipodes might also live somewhere else than in sociology as a disciplinary field. And for both these exemplary thinkers, Marx was a point of departure rather than arrival. These were both vital lines out, in different ways.

My road to Marx, and to Marxism has evidently involved some circling; this is an issue to which I shall return. Let me now turn to another question. Why Marx? What was the source of this attraction?

2   **Why Marx?**

In 1971, in year 12, my first great mentor N.W. Saffin said to me, in class but *sotto voce*, 'Mr Beilharz, I see in you the seeds of a socialist'. It was the first time anybody called me mister. It was also the first time anybody called me a socialist. Saffin was right about the incipient socialism, I think, though he was a positivist himself, a critical mind and teacher though never a preacher for any particular cause, except perhaps that which had radicalised him so much earlier: the Spanish Revolution. I came quickly to understand, and to want to argue, that marxists had no monopoly on the claim to socialism or to socialist argument. Marxism was not the only fruit. My curiosity took me also to anarchism, to council communism, to Guild Socialism, *The New Age*, to the rich streams of socialism that ran from below. And yet my attraction to Marx was almost immediate.

I began by successfully reading the *1844 Manuscripts*, solo, then to be taught these rich texts again by Hanfi, along with *The German Ideology*, the *Grundrisse*, and *Capital*. We ran our Capital Reading Classes independently. What, then, was the fascination? To start at the end of the story, *Capital* seemed to me to offer the most extraordinary optic on the phenomenon of capital itself. It is a flawed book, but unlike Gareth Stedman Jones, I would not say that it was a failure, except if we shift that optic to regard all intellectual activity as a matter of successive approximations, and all brainwork as therefore failure-bound.[4]

Capital remains a desert island book for me. Its ambitions, its attempt to construct an intellectual architectonic of capitalism, remain for me deeply impressive. Marx was plainly obsessed with the question of what is the best, or if you insist, the most privileged way to explaining capitalism. This is not the way I work; for me, it is rather Montaigne, and the approach of the *essai* or attempt, which is better, or at least it is closer to what I am capable of. Marx's architecture is closer to that of the Crystal Palace; I prefer Gehry, or Liebeskind, or Fender Katsilidis. Yet Marx's attempt, his own grand *essai*, remains for me astonishing. Capital itself, the phenomenon to be explained, is a system, or a structure, and this invites an approach which is systematic or structural. Yet capital also has its mysteries; it is a form which is elusive. Value has a form, which calls for explanation. If it invites a systematics, it also calls out a poetics.

How did Marx pursue his grand narrative? Why begin with the commodity? Plainly Marx was persuaded that there was a best possible way to understand capital, beginning not with its emergence or history, as say the later Weber tells

---

4   Beilharz 2017; Stedman Jones 2017.

it in *The Protestant Ethic*, but with its logic, and in fact with its ethics. So we begin with the single commodity, the cell form: this is an exercise in making sense of the logic of capital. But it is also an ethics. Its prelude, in the *1859 Contribution*, introduces Aristotle already in opening the optic of the study. And for Marx, the classical ethic remains: a shoe is made for wearing, not for sale. Things have their essential, or use value; it is only when they are inserted into systems of exchange that they take on the aura of exchange value or compulsory equivalence. But more importantly, and more important than any particular claims about the plausibility of the labour theory of value, this is what makes all things under capitalism commensurable. Everything now is for sale, love, sex, landscape, nature, beauty, they all have their price, and they are made to be commensurable. Marx, in other words is a classicist or a pre-modern here, but he is also and at the same time a postmodernist, because he wants to insist on the centrality of difference. Capital makes the incommensurable commensurable. It elides difference, by making all things actually or potentially exchangeable.

And so *Das Kapital* unfolds, through the intellectual prism of the value form, and to the fantasy world of the fetishism of commodities. Here Marx revives his earlier spin on Feuerbach, via his reading of the French explorer and ethnographer Charles De Brosses. This is the familiar romantic trope of inversion inserted into the harder critique of political economy, for Marx's remains a world of ghosts and spirits. It is Gothic and Victorian, Enlightenment and Romantic all at once. It enchants, itself. And this is one of the reasons why I still find the text so compelling – not for its outcome, in the contrived revolutionary rhetoric of Chapter 32, but for the spirit of its engagement with capital itself. Its choreography is astonishing; it is, I think, a great work of literature. Marx exits the realm of the commodity via Dante, to descend into the hell of the factory itself; he is still, with Engels, in Manchester in 1844. Earlier, in the *1859 Preface*, he has heralded his own arrival with Dante: 'Here must all distrust be left ...' *Capital* also opens with Dante – 'Follow your road, and let the people talk'.

The figure of the worker arrives later, in *Capital*, and this is both a strength and a weakness. For the proletariat is the object, and not only the subject or agent of this story. And while it is true that Marx's narrative is carried by his own image of the proletariat as a necessarily revolutionary class, anticipating Lukács' image of the ascribed revolutionary consciousness, it also bears cameos of faces like those of the girl labourer Mary Ann Walkley, which are enough to make you cry. This is, truly, the descent into hell that is for Marx the capitalist mode of production, here in its factory form. And for Marx, it is also the theatre of everyday life.

Is *Capital* then a failure? It seems to me that it is more accurate to describe it as radically incomplete, this not least because Marx himself was unable to finish it. Perhaps the very task that he set himself was impossible. Structurally, and Marx liked the architectural metaphor, it may be something of a folly. As Tomba puts it in his study of *Marx's Temporalities*, Marx's favoured style is often sarcasm, and his favourite trope is tragicomedy. The tragicomic model in Marx is, as Tomba puts it, not descriptive but performative.[5] But there is more, and it is also in a sense performative, or at least it is informed by choreography. As an antipodean, I take some pride in the fact that while *Capital* Volume I formally closes its theatre with the imminence of assured revolution, the text finally issues in our part of the world, per the story of Mr Peel in Western Australia in Chapter 33. *Capital* actually has a double, or a false ending. Does Mr Peel fit Marx's Grand Plan, or any other philosophical desideratum concerning logical coherence? Absolutely not. The issue of the double or false ending has largely eluded scrutiny; Jameson cues it as a tolling of bells, heroic and comic.[6] This version of the tragedy/farce couplet is suggestive, but less than entirely convincing. For there is a last word, and it resounds here through the antipodes.

Marx had a strong interest in surplus population, which follows on from Enclosure and the primitive accumulation of capital, and grows into migration out and colonisation, here in the form of the project of systematic colonisation associated with Wakefield and acted out after a fashion in South and Western Australia and New Zealand. What this suggests, as a final conclusion to *Capital*, is that there is no readily forthcoming end to capital. Gifted as it is at exporting the capital relation (and this is the passage where Marx best explains this: capital is not a thing, it is a social relationship), Chapter 33 of *Capital* leaves open the door to the further development of capitalism. The prospect here is that it is globalisation, and not revolution, which will rule.

Was Marx's project, to seek to explain the mysteries of capital, not itself a kind of maniacal fantasy? Maybe. The dialectics of essence and appearance still appear. But as the preceding discussion suggests, there was also a deep curiosity driving his critique of political economy. Half an hour spent perusing the *Grundrisse* or the *Ethnological Notebooks*, or the correspondence or the journalism will be enough to convince of this. What these writings suggest is that while Marx's own theoretical ambitions were set high and stubborn, his was also a life of the seeking of wisdom. Zawar Hanfi had taught

---

5   Tomba, Thomas and Farris 2013, p. 39.
6   Jameson 2011, p. 88.

me, I still think usefully, that Marx could be read as having had a single over-arching project: his purpose was to engage in and advance on the critique of political economy, as this was both a science and a philosophy and an ethics. But Zawar was also fond of words like propadeutics, and maieutics, and that is how he encouraged us to encounter Marx's project at Monash in the seventies. To read Marx in this way was to engage in a reading, or to open a hermeneutic circle. This could only ever be one way of reading Marx; the circles feed on themselves, or expand upon one another. In this way of think-ing we work by way of introductions, or successive approximations. We circle. This is to concern ourselves with textual logics rather than with intentions, and in this it agrees with Marx; never judge an epoch by what it thinks of itself.

It took me years to learn to read Marx in this way, and I am not finished yet, ergo the desert island image, my own private Robinsonade. While I was attrac-ted to the image of the soft, or *Wissenschaftlich* image of science, I was I think even from early on taken by the claims to rigour in Marx. This could be con-densed under the image popularised by Althusser, of the *problematique*, which I take to be a theoretical claim that presumes a constellation of concepts, as for example in the idea of modes of production as a combination of elements, though the thinking of Gramsci, his *bête noire*, might be an even better work-ing example – hegemony, coercion/consent, passive revolution, conjuncture, common and good sense, war of position and manoeuvre, Fordism/American-ism and so on. In any case, with Marx, Gramsci or even Althusser, we were here somewhere beyond the simple moral outrage or lazy utopianism of many on the left, where the bleating of refusal or empty denunciation seemed to suf-fice instead of interpretation or argument. It could not suffice to declaim the unfairness of the world; this was nothing new. Capital did, in fact, still need to be explained.

It seems plain, at the same time, that Marx's *Capital* has an ethics, which underpins the entire edifice. Yet there is a shift of mood and emphasis from the *1844 Manuscripts*, which as a text does not rely on moral outrage but on an ethical argument concerning human capacity and its own enclosure. (And let's not forget, these were after all manuscripts, rich and fecund but written not for us, who came so much later, but for Marx's self-clarification.) The strength and limit of the argument concerning alienation is that it values labour over all other forms of human activity, while it also fails sufficiently to locate the worker as subject/object in a new, modern world where division of labour and exchange would always rule. Marx was, as I have argued, always utopian, though the nature of his utopia becomes industrialised and shifts into the mar-gin of free time that might go alongside necessary labour or technology. If we are to be honest, then we must confess that we are all utopians, even those who believe that less is more.[7]

The key text here, alongside others, remains the Fourier reverie or spoof in the *German Ideology*. As James Furner has argued, what is most salvageable from the utopia of huntman-herdsman-fisherman-critic is the dimension of the multiplicity of individual identities, which is in fact as modern and as pressing today as it is romantic in origin for Marx and Fourier.[8] This position is in counterpoint to the implicit anthropology of the *1844 Manuscripts*, where labour is all, the primeval category and value, where labour stands as a kind of proxy for creativity and human power. By 1845 Marx is rather taken by the image of the human individual as a suffering, sentient, sensual being. Contrary to the claims of reams of antimarxist gush over the decades, Marx was an individualist in his anthropology. The imaginary unit of his thinking is the suffering, sentient, creative human being; only he, or she, is not alone. Collectivism might be the shadow presence in the idealised image of the proletariat, but class remains a sociological or prophetic rather than an anthropological category for Marx. What Marx's political critics from the right have never been able to accept is that Marx was not a liberal. For Marx, that is to say, the individual is also always socially constituted, formed by the sociability in which everyday life is saturated. The rich individual, as Agnes Heller earlier argued, was the character rich in needs, many of which would be needs for other people. When it comes to actually existing societies, there are only social individuals. It is this sociability, rather than the property rights of possessive individualism, which makes it possible for individuals to coexist, and even perhaps flourish.

In Marx, then – and this was in a sense the main issue in the Young/Mature Marx debate of the sixties – there is an anthropological and ethical continuity of thinking which runs underneath the shift from actor or individual to structure or system. In early works the subject dominates; by *Capital* the frame of thinking is rather in terms of the character-masks of labour and capital, or the Trinity Formula of land, labour and capital, and what each agent is compelled to do by the rules of capital's game. The play of capital now dominates its actors. The figure of Mary Ann Walkley is still there, in the pages of *Capital*, as the flowers still decorate the chains of domination and exploitation. She is not a cartoon proletarian. She is a sentient, suffering human being. She represents Manchester, not Moscow, not the heroic iconography of Soviet imagery, but

---

7   Beilharz, 1992b, 2015.
8   Furner, 2011.

rather the tragedy and pathos of early industrial life in England. She lives on, wherever capital takes itself, these days, I suppose, in China.

There remains one major text here yet to appear in my narrative: *The Communist Manifesto*. My early response to this document was that it was propaganda at worst, a pamphlet at best. Likely it is both, and as with many other keywords like party and communist and communist party, the word propaganda meant something less troubled before the twentieth century. I came to understand the importance of the *Communist Manifesto* only later, through my own teaching at La Trobe.

My initial disinterest in the *Manifesto* may have had to do with its dramaturgy, and with its military reading of class warfare. At worst, it looked to me like poor sociology, read across into my own place and time, as vulgar marxists were wont to do. It failed to place the middle class, losing it in the broad sweep of class bipolarisation. This looked like cartoon Marxism to me, more so as my fellow student radicals took it for an accurate diagnosis and prognosis of life in Australia in the eighties.[9] It presumed what needed rather to be established; that there were only two dominant classes, and that class struggle led to the historic victory of the proletariat. This was the scenario of automatic revolution which Marx then transposed into Chapter 32 of *Capital*, dropping it into the theatre of *Capital* from unseen mechanisms high above the stage. When I came to verse and line the *Manifesto*, in order to teach the text, rather more nuance was to appear. For if writing is one way to understand, alongside reading, then teaching can be another thing altogether, this not least because repetition reveals. It is another form of circling.

Now generally recognised to be the prose of Marx, rather than Engels, the *Manifesto*'s popularity in recent radical culture is also a symptom of mistranslation. A single phrase has returned Marx to radical eyes. You can search high and low in the German original, but you will not find a phrase that is the equivalent of 'all that is solid melts into air', Marx's translator made it up, echoing Shakespeare. The German original is a smaller and more historically specific image, suggesting more that all that is standing and estate-like will evaporate under the pressure of capitalist development. The power of the original German image is that it is more compressed, referring to the age of steam, the technology and culture of steam power and locomotion. The larger, or inflated message is more evocative, but it has also come to be more ontological, as in the brilliant riff by Marshall Berman, *All That is Solid Melts into Air*, though the message for today is here rendered more like Bauman's liquid modernity

---

9   Beilharz 1985.

than Marx's closer phrasing suggests. All this is food for thought, though it is also possible that in the process the message of the *Communist Manifesto* has not only been scrambled but also reduced to a single phrase. The other lasting image, submerged in the process, is that of the Sorcerer's Apprentice. This latter is consonant with Marx's hymn of praise for the bourgeoisie, this most revolutionary of classes, which temporarily harnesses the powers of Prometheus and Proteus but in the process also becomes the object acted upon rather than the leading subject of modern times. Like that of most enduring thinkers, Marx's work is contradictory. The discrepancy between his desire and the logic of his argument is powerfully suggestive. It suggests that the permanent revolution is motored by capitalism, not by its self-styled opponents. It suggests a political economy that is out of control.

Circling Marx

So for forty years and more I have been circling Marx, or he has been circling me. What becomes apparent on consideration of my best essays on Marx and Marxism, as gathered in this volume, is that the circles have also expanded outwards. They are not necessarily the many circles of Dante's inferno. There may be no hope of redemption here. For these circles are also generational, as each generation has made its own Marx, one, or more at a time.

The traditions of Marxism have their own histories and stories. Starting with Marx, or even with his predecessors, there follow the major waves of Social Democracy, Bolshevism, Stalinism, Trotskyism, Western Marxism, Critical Theory, East European Marxism, Althusserianism, Eurocommunism, and so on. At some point in this unfolding the image of circles is swamped by that of bifurcation. There are, then, two major streams of Marxism.[10] One embraces the state and state power: the other stakes its claim against the Behemoth.

It seems to me that there are two long lines out of Marx and into critical theory, construing the latter in the broadest sense in terms of the critical and emancipatory legacy of Marx into our own times.

The first echoes the Critical Theory of the Frankfurt School, though my own preference is for the long tail that goes out through Eastern Europe rather than the stricter lineage which remains Frankfurt-city bound. As I have mentioned in this essay, I take the key mediators of this lineage to be Lukács and Loewith. Though it is Simmel rather than more precisely Weber who shadows the *Reific-*

---

10   Beilharz 2018b.

ation essay, the younger Lukács offers the most resplendent prospect for the fusion of Marx and Weber's ways of thinking. Loewith for his part likely assimilates Marx and Weber too much, but the sympathy is there, even if they were not exactly diagnosticians of exactly the same social trends, as he puts it, in alienation and rationalisation. Yet what this thinking makes possible is the kind of Weberian Marxism then followed through by Adorno and Horkheimer, into the work of the Budapest School and Bauman. Viewed in this way, the key texts following *Dialectic of Enlightenment* and *The Authoritarian State* are *Modernity and the Holocaust* and *Dictatorship Over Needs*. After Weber, bureaucracy and the state come into clearer focus as fundamental problems of modernity. Marxism here becomes the critique of rationalisation of the world.

The second line out of Marx follows the interest in historical materialism, and in this it is continuous with the critique of the rationalisation of the world. It follows the clue of historical specificity, identified by Korsch in his book on *Karl Marx*, and it might be traced through into the work of Markus on Marxism and anthropology. It connects up to historical sociology in the manner of Barrington Moore, to the sociology of states and revolutions, and all this is shadowed by the thinking of Gramsci. But it also recalls the Marx of the *Eighteenth Brumaire*, where the logic evokes not socialist revolution so much as repetition. It would be too much to read Freud back into Marx, but there is nevertheless something going on here, some few small sparks in the dark. As Marx explains it, when serious historic actors set out to change the world they still persist in summoning the ghosts of their pasts in order to legitimise what they do. Jacobins and Bolsheviks alike, through to the Great Helmsman, they all take on the lineaments of the ghosts of the past. Revolutionary ideology, in this way, never breaks free of religion. Or to put it more bluntly, we never break free of our own pasts. Freud is the elephant in the room. This means that we are also ever creatures of repetition. This is the psychic reason why wilful, or political revolution cannot work. Revolution in the economy, the permanent revolution of capital is another thing. The past otherwise weighs down on us like a nightmare on the living.

Repetition, circling; perhaps they are the same thing. Years of teaching, reading and writing have served to convince me that at the same time repetition is a good thing, because like playing music it is never quite the same. Mimesis is also a creative process. Or as wiser heads might have it, repetition is the precondition of all historical action.[11] To say that we are creatures of repetition is not to say that we are incapable of learning; to the contrary. But contra Haber-

---

11   Deleuze 1994, p. 91.

mas, we cannot simply project the image of the single individual onto social learning processes. As the new authoritarian populism shows, public learning processes are open to reversal and transformation through appeals to nostalgia and claims less to repetition, exactly, than to some proclaimed imaginary return. What we now witness, among other things, is a proclaimed return to the protectionist legacy of social democracy, claims to revive the old national industry policy without the legacy of socialism or democracy as it was hitherto understood.

As to my own circles, I nestle them here as follows. To anticipate, in a manner which is less than completely exhaustive: In the first circle, I assemble more closely textual encounters with Karl Marx. These begin with the 1989 task I set myself, and others, to condense our favoured thinkers into capsules of 2,500 words (the most amusing knockback was from a colleague who thought I had asked for 25,000 words; he could not tithe). Here I am working, as I still do, under the influence of Zawar Hanfi, though the insistence that there are many Marxes might indicate a bit more historicism, or even the gentle influence of the postmodern. The early essay on 'Marxism and History' enters the field of debate concerning modes of production, but also looks to loosening up the terms of reference. So often it is the followers of Marx who ossify what are more flexible ideas in Marx, including the very notion of mode of production itself. Marx and Simmel are then brought to bear upon each other in a way that suggests productive friction; Simmel was the more modern, and is here the figure whose influence needs usefully to be brought to bear upon Marx. The essay on Marx and motion updates my encounter with *The Communist Manifesto*. It resulted from a highly productive team writing project with Ghassan Hage and his colleagues at the University of Melbourne, a kind of turbocharged revisitation of those distant Capital Reading Classes all those years ago. Here, we were reading Newton rather than Marx, and taking turns in a manner almost like the utopia of *The German Ideology*, where we acted both as writers and variously as each others' readers and critics. There remain so many ways to learn, even thus later in life.

Having been raised by historians, from Saffin to Davidson and Macintyre, I knew that there were many marxisms as well as many Marxes. Though my physical capacity for archives has declined, I spent many happy years in them, to the extent that I wrote postcards from each as I worked. These were published in the Australian journal *Labour History*. As I have mentioned, I initially began work on the history of Australian Trotskyism, which immediately took me out, to the Internationals, to the world system and its patterns of hegemony and traffic. Mapping came to me as a natural metaphor for the kind of work I was doing. I also became committed to exposing what I would now call cartoon

Marxism, the lazy and easy reliance on caricatures for example of Kautsky or the Webbs as some kind of idiots. I read the work of these reformers closely, and set out to defend them in different ways in *Labour's Utopias* and elsewhere.

Though the views in my book on Trotskyism were described by one reviewer as unremittingly negative, I also took a more positive view for example of the Young Trotsky, Trotsky before and against Bolshevism. Others, such as Deutscher and Mandel, I took to be more compromised in their views. I met Mandel in Melbourne in 1983 and was certainly impressed by his intellect and cosmopolitanism, though at the end of the day the arguments of this most sophisticated of Trotskyists were still unconvincing. Even the most elaborate versions of revolutionary Marxism in the twentieth century seemed world denying. Much later, when I was working at Harvard, I got to know Daniel Bell, and interviewed him for *Thesis Eleven* twenty years after interviewing Mandel for our journal.[12] Bell's was a kind of old world charm, when it came to Marxism; he knew the language of the tradition but no longer could speak it with conviction, except in jest. He could perform Marxism but no longer believed in it, inasmuch as that might be possible. He now appeared to me as a kind of American Menshevik. If it was worth taking Kautsky seriously, then this was also an optic worth taking on, opening up onto the cultural contradictions of capitalism. Ex-marxists are also more than interesting. The ex- might sometimes be necessary, even if only as a thought experiment. For some others, of course, it would become necessary to leave.

Marxism, as I have had cause to argue elsewhere, could also be viewed as the concurrence of broader trends before Marx, which returned to the mainstream after Marx, becoming part of everyday commonsense ('it's the economy, stupid!')

My third circle, more generational than strictly chronological, spreads out further again, though it is also a constant dialogue with the ghost of Marx. Some of my own ghosts figure here: Althusser, and differently Poulantzas. The cult of Althusser, as I have implied here, was I think on the whole a generational mistake. This is not to say that his work was without interest, or that his attack on humanism was without merit; Marxism also needs its contrarians. Ihab Hassan, who befriended me twenty years ago, said to me once, 'Peter, you need to learn to think against yourself!', and while it stung, he was of course correct. Intellectual life depends on doubt, if not an excess of self-doubt; but likely not self-criticism, which is another Stalinist tic, or jolt, altogether. I suppose my advice for a young Marxist arriving just now, today, might be simply to keep moving.

---

12   Beilharz and Mandel 1983; Beilharz 2006a.

When I was a young marxist Poulantzas arrived and looked like a way through Althusser, though again, a half hour spent now with the texts makes me wonder. There seems to be much of a prospectus suggested in his work. Perhaps that was the promise: an engaged and critical mind that in other circumstances would have been capable of taking us further. The exit, in his last book, *State, Power, Socialism*, was suggestive, but seemed to revive the best of western Marxism rather than to vindicate the promise of structuralist Marxism. The early essay on Poulantzas carried here got me stick; its critics saw it as a 'deplorable article' evincing an interesting condition on my part, what they called 'slight hysteria'. These may have been ideologically overcharged times, into the eighties, but the choice of term, with all its period gender baggage, was nevertheless unfortunate. Possibly I was ahead of the wave; like many of us then on the left, I wanted more of structuralist Marxism, perhaps more than either Marxism of this kind or structuralism could politically give. All of which, *in toto*, makes for something of a puzzle, as I am arguing here that Marxism is a major tradition for critical thinking, and this is also true for structuralism, whose rise and fall remains something of an enigma. Whatever exactly happened to structuralism, including its eclipse and extension into poststructuralism, it remains useful to align two of the greatest modern thinkers, Marx and Freud, with its impulse. Structuralism remains a powerful way of thinking, even if the movement itself collapsed under the weight of its own contradictions. The work of Foucault, I suppose, remains its richest and most suggestive legacy.

Melbourne and especially Sydney were full of Foucauldians in the eighties. Some of them were super-smart, especially the close readers and translators on the Harbour, but there was also a Foucult, a weakness for the lazy spray-ons earlier exercised by orthodox marxists. From Davidson I had learned to read Foucault contextually, as one of a number of fascinating French thinkers, with equally fascinating precedents from Aries to Canguilhem. But I did not join this party either. I learned a great deal from Paul Hirst, in London, and from Barry Hindess in Canberra. Paul became a kind of boosterist for all kinds of good ideas, and Barry became something of a sceptic. In these earlier times, before we had met either of them, they made up a team of mythic proportions, HindessandHirst. The legacy of their work in the middle seventies is now also less clear, but at the very least they then also made us think. Hindess, Hirst, Hassan; think outside the box, or turn it upside down and see what falls out.

In these years I also learned a great deal from feminists, though more often Anglo than French or German: Carole Pateman, Carol Gilligan, Iris Marion Young, Dorothy Smith. And if I was unable to shake off Marxism, it is likely no accident that the second great love of my life, Sian, is a feminist. Earlier I had entered these circles together with Chris Nyland, in a book called *Fabianism and Feminism*. There we sought to defend what we called an ordinary feminism. For me, this reached back to an earlier La Trobe Sociology Paper, called *Heroes and Pedestrians*. I was always taken by the image of the *quotidienne*, of everyday socialism and feminism. My sense is that I learned much more from feminist historians than from feminist philosophy. Probably I learned much more in general from historians than philosophers on the Anglo left. In this regard it is also no accident that I learned a great deal from Marxist anthropologists such as my colleague at La Trobe, the late Joel Kahn.

The more lasting legacies for me were the circles that rippled put from Western Marxism and critical theory. Habermas was the most passing of these interests, for me. His work became far too systematic and ambitious for my taste or preference. I followed the early work with enthusiasm, from *Theory and Practice* to *Legitimation Crisis*. I was honoured when my first critique of Trotsky appeared in the Habermas 50th Birthday issue of *Telos* in 1979; in this context he was the great thinker, I was the imposter.[13] But then there came *The Theory of Communicative Action*, a project which seemed to involve shifting from his earlier claim to the reconstruction of historical materialism to something of even more grandeur, like the reconstruction of social theory itself. And yet it felt like Parsons, or at least like Luhmann. But I was 25, and doubtless out of my depth. I retain a strong sense of admiration and respect for Habermas, coupled with an abiding affection for the early work. Perhaps our formative tastes in theory, after all, are like our formative influences in music. I still listen to Paul Butterfield.

Others among my earlier influences have also changed in tenor and direction, and yet my commitments here have been more sustained. The key figures here for me are Castoriadis, Feher, Heller and Markus, and then Smith and Bauman. As it happens, there were all my friends in some capacity or other. I have always had reason to think of ideas as embodied. This proximity has been my great good fortune. There are so many different ways to learn, and I am still learning.

All these last thinkers are also ex-marxists of some kind or another. Yet there the ex- also signals some kind of continuity. For many thinkers, this is as the cliché tells – once a Marxist, always under the influence. Castoriadis wanted to be more revolutionary than Marx. The Hungarians have carried on the critical legacy in other ways, yet their life's works and their projects would make no sense if Marx was pulled out. Bauman, for his part, refused to let socialism go.

---

13   Beilharz 1979b.

Socialism, as he long was given to argue, is the counterculture of modernity. As the conversation shifted from capitalism, or economy, to the broader horizons suggested by modernity, the post or even the liquid modern, the popular significance of socialism here has receded, but not its urgency or capacity for critical insight. Perhaps it is not too much to say of these thinkers that having come of age in worlds where Marxism was inseparable from Marx, it took some time to unhook the two. Then, as Castoriadis liked to say, it was a matter of making peace with Hegel, at least the Hegel of '*Weltgeschichte ist Weltgericht*', for Heller of returning to Kant or entering the zone of the postmodern.

The fact remains that there are many different ways to do Marxism, or to apply the power of its insights. In terms of the thinkers I have worked with, the best example of this practical legacy may be the figure of Bernard Smith. As I have argued repeatedly, Bernard wears his Marxism lightly over his many years, but the touch is always there. Art matters, here, but culture and technology are correlated rather than held apart. World-systems also frame our lives, but this in terms of the uneven flows of cultural traffic. If, as Marx puts it in Chapter 33 of *Capital*, capital is a relationship, then so is the antipodes a relationship rather than a place or thing. Art, creativity, exploitation and exchange all take place in terms of the world system and its cultural traffic. Bernard Smith was a Marxist, and this is one factor explaining the persistence and veracity of his work and legacy. For Bernard it was unnecessary to take a distance from Marxism because his relationship to Marx was non-doctrinal. Marxism was a compass rather than a map. He left the Communist Party of Australia in the early fifties after an instructive encounter with actually existing socialism. Unlike the early Hungarians and Bauman, he was as an antipodean able to enter and to leave Eastern Europe and orthodox Marxism without persecution. His intellectual activity was inductive and historical rather than philosophical. His approach and his frame of reference was, if you like, closer to Hobsbawm or to Jameson or perhaps John Berger than to Lukács. His was less the Hegel endorsed by Castoriadis, than the Hegel who sat with the Owl of Minerva.

And now the circle of this introduction is closing. The volume closes with two editorials from *Thesis Eleven*, the first, in 1980, and the countereditorial from 2005, after 25 years. Does *Thesis Eleven* remain a Marxist journal? I would say, rather, postmarxist, in all of its ramifications. For in all this we are also after Marx. These editorials indicate something of the distance travelled. The larger, more challenging question might be, not what in the journal or our thinking has changed, but what has changed in the cultures that inform it and us. After, ex-, and arriving sideways, the fluxus anticipated by Marx still absorbs us. Modernity is motion. The circles spread outwards. With the passing of time, some of those are also closing, completing revolutions of their own. We repeat, we revolve, we discover and learn anew. This is our own historicity, and in small ways it also represents progress. If only we could have more, please. Some new circles or openings, some new sources of hope, some new ways forward in these great and terrible times.

First Circle

∵

CHAPTER 1

Karl Marx (1992)

One Marx, or many? Both, or all of the above. The work of Marx can be interpreted in various different ways, including the early romantic critique of the 'Paris Manuscripts', Marx the philosopher, the historical anthropology of *The German Ideology*, the critical history of the *Eighteenth Brumaire* or *The Civil War in France*, Marx the historian, the private brainstorming of *Grundrisse*, the later critical economy of *Capital*, Marx the economist, and so on. And there is a panoply of interpretations, and the subsequent 57 varieties of Marxism – Bolshevism, social democracy, Trotskyism, Maoism, critical theory, Western Marxism, council communism, and so forth – all of which pick up one theme or other in Marx's writing – too much to make sense of.

One way to argue the unity of Marx's thought, rather than its fragmentation and subsequent proliferation into various Marxes, is to read his project as possessing a single over-arching theme: the critique of political economy. Marx's theoretical work began as romantic critique, subsequently to become ensnared within political economy itself. It was only after Marx's death in 1883 that his work was to become widely influential, but in the truncated forms of propaganda developed by the Soviets in the East and in the models of society encouraged by professional sociologists in the West. Like Weber's thought, Marx's theory lost much of its critical impact in the hands of stratification theorists. But the trajectory of Marx's own theory was also one which became progressively less critical and more fully locked into the logic of industrialism.

The Paris Manuscripts

The question of the relationship between the young and the 'mature' Marx was a major motif in the Marx renaissance that spread from the 1960s on. It was not just a spectacle organised by publishers and academics. The fundamental question involved was whether Marx's theory was continuous or whether there was some kind of qualitative shift in his work. Whatever the continuity, the path of Marx's own work is one from praxis to structure, from action to system.

Marx set out in his *Paris Manuscripts*, published in German in 1932 and in English only in the 1960s, to put political economy to the test. Classical political economists such as Smith and Ricardo had recognised the central economic contribution which labour made to the production of wealth or value, but they would not give labour its proper place in politics or in society. Partly they did this by fudging the nature of the *process* of the production of wealth, as though property preceded labour, whereas property was actually the result of creative labour or *praxis*, the sensuous human activity through which humanity constituted itself. Labour thus expended its lifeblood in creating capital which (to use a later image) turned on labour like a vampire.[1] This critique of political economy took Marx to the philosophical critique of the division of labour. His early work echoes the German romantics, such as Schiller; the orientation is to cast backward, and to contrast a postulated image of humanity as a whole before industrialism, a species which does not know alienation, to its dismembered, dethroned condition under capitalism. Alienation, the division of humans and their individual subdivision: these only arrive with capitalist civilisation.

The undercurrent in this argument is the necessity of human or proletarian redemption, which Marx progressively redefines as he enters the labyrinth of economy itself. By redemption Marx imagines the simultaneous supersession of private property (capital) and the recovery of human integrity. The issue here is that while Marx chooses to identify human suffering as a central social and theoretical problem, he also ascribes a central status to labour as the suffering and redemptive agent. The bearer of socialism, Marx tells, is the proletariat, the 'last class' – he portrays it as a mythical actor, inserting a teleology in history but also imputing the historic task of socialism to a particular class, as though a general cause could be pursued by a particular agent.[2] The image of socialism in Marx's early work is thus that of a society of craft-labourers. By *The German Ideology* Marx's image of the socialist future is closer to the Renaissance.[3]

In *The German Ideology* Marx and Engels also began to address the question of ideology, criticising – ironically, given the privileging of the proletariat in their theory – the pretensions of the bourgeoisie that their own interests were the popular and general interests. In 1848 Marx and Engels published their most famous work, *The Communist Manifesto*, a brilliant polemic sketching one key dimension of Marx's project: the profoundly *ambivalent* assessment of capitalist civilisation, which made everything possible, as it were, and simultaneously denied humanity its potential for self-realisation. It was a brilliant achievement, anticipating Tonnies, Simmel, Seabrook and Berman, and drawing on inspiration such as Carlyle ('the cash nexus') and on Goethe's image of the sorcerer's apprentice. The bourgeoisie conjured up an economic spell of manic

---

1   Marx, 1965, 1975, pp. 322–34.
2   Marx 1975, pp. 333–48.
3   Marx and Engels 2004, p. 47.

growth which it could not control; Marx simply sidestepped the question of whether this was a problem for which the proletariat was the solution.

The *Manifesto* also returned to the theme of history, discussed in *The German Ideology*. Here came the axiom that all history was the history of class struggle. For the young Marx, class struggle was the pivot; for the later Marx, it was class structure, labour and capital as formal categories. Here Marx planted the two-class model which sociologists and historians were later to seize upon and which also became concepts central to *Capital*. History was not merely the history of struggling classes – modern history was the titanic struggle between the two fundamental classes: bourgeoisie and proletariat.

The *Grundrisse*

Marx's shift from action to structure was politically determined by the defeat of the 1848 revolutions. If the world did not change, the obvious question was why not. How did it reproduce itself?[4] This was to become the essential logic of *Capital*, a systems logic, an explanation of capitalist production, how it functioned and how it would allegedly dysfunction, collapse and inaugurate socialism. Marx's major transitional work here was the *Grundrisse*, the Notebooks for *Capital*. There are three major themes worth indicating here. First, in the '1857 Introduction' Marx discussed questions of epistemology and methodology.[5] Marx's views were not novel, but his canvassing of the issues enabled the English readers of the *Grundrisse*, sometimes under the influence of Althusser, to begin to pose questions about claims to knowledge and premises of the construction of knowledge. Certainly the logic of Marx's approach was that knowledge is constructed and not 'discovered', and though Marx sometimes claimed the status of science for his work, this suggested that human science was a qualitatively different kind of endeavour to natural science. Thus Marx implicitly aligned his project back to Vico's proposition that humans know best that which is unique to them: human history itself.

This brings us to the second theme. Marx also discusses here the question of the transition from feudalism, in a passage much discussed in the *Science and Society* debate of the 1950s.[6] The point here is less the content of Marx's views than the fact that his project was still governed by a sense of what apparently

---

4   Korsch 1936, p. 114.
5   Marx 1973, pp. 100–8.
6   Marx 1973, pp. 471–98; Hilton 1976.

had happened in history; by *Capital*, history was marginalised, being introduced only into chapter 10. By *Capital*, then, Marx returned to his earlier sense
that History was necessity, a necessary process leading from feudalism to capitalism to socialism rather than a contingent process in which masses of men and
women *chose* socialism. This problem of automatism or teleology also under-
lines the third pertinent theme of the *Grundrisse*. In a passage picked up later
by Marcuse,[7] Marx shifted to the proposition that the technological revolution
and not the class struggle might inaugurate socialism. The internal developmental logic of capitalism was such that automation would pull the rug out
from under class relations.[8] The agent of history again became mythologised:
the actors were not the sensuous, suffering human beings who populated the
pages of Marx's early work, but the forces of history, or now, of economy, and
even technology.

The *Grundrisse* has left us some of the most fascinating evidence of Marx's
intellectual process, that twenty-year long labour which eventually culminated
in the final publication of *Capital* Volume One in 1867. In 1859, however, Marx
published another signpost to *Capital*, his 1859 *Contribution to the Critique of
Political Economy*. Partly because of the codification of Marxism by his followers into the twentieth century, the book was less frequently read than the
preface was. It was in the 1859 *Preface* that Marx, in passing, offered a thumb-
nail sketch of his project: to find the secret of bourgeois society in political
economy. This was necessary, Marx claimed, because economy was the fundamental determinant, upon which there arose a legal and political superstructure and definite forms of social consciousness. In broad outline, humanity
progressed from Asiatic, ancient and feudal to bourgeois modes of production, as productive forces came into conflict with existing class relations.[9] This
relatively innocent sketch of an intellectual agenda subsequently became catechism for generations of socialists and communists: base-determined superstructure; explain economy and all else is explained; socialism is inevitable,
and so on. Marx, for his own part, may not have subscribed to all these clichés,
but he did provide elaborate reasons for viewing capitalism as the central phenomenon of modernity, simultaneously the agent of its own self-promotion
and its own downfall.

---

7   1964, p. 42.
8   Marx 1973, pp. 740–6.
9   Marx 1970, pp. 20–1.

Capital

The culmination of Marx's science and of his mythology is *Capital*. Chapter 1, 'Commodities', is the most theoretically significant part of the work and also the most difficult. Marx provides a devastating critique of capitalist and utilitarian ethics. He sets the cue on the opening page of the 1859 *Contribution*, where he refers to Aristotle's *Politics*: a shoe is made for wearing, not for exchange – things have their own reasons for being, they are not commensurable. Yet commodification makes everything commensurable – two books are 'worth' one coat, four meals – everything, lamentably, has its price. Bourgeois society, in short, reduces human value to economic value, and it levels out the differences which ought to be characteristic of everyday life. Our labours disappear into things, which then come to dominate us, appear to precede us and, fetish-like, we fall into praise of this artificial world. Thus Marx begins the carefully constructed narrative of *Capital*, leading us from the surface or end of the process into the Dante's inferno of production.

The substance of the book concerns a critical analysis of capitalist production; it is, in a sense, a pioneering sociology of the modern factory. It is not a *history* of capitalism, although history is discussed – the history of labour legislation, primitive accumulation: the bloody emergence of capitalism via the enclosure acts – and it reappears in the penultimate chapter, where socialist revolution steps unexpectedly on the stage: negations are negated, the expropriators expropriated, etc. Here, at least, there is one element of continuity with the *Paris Manuscripts*: the inevitability of socialism as redemption is again asserted, and the struggle is still primarily that between the two fundamental classes and the concepts they represent – labour and capital. What, then, happens to the class struggle, which Marx earlier viewed as the central fact of history? One response would be that *Capital* is not a work of history, but of theory; but the obvious response would be, what happens to history in Marx's theory? Where have the actors gone? What has happened to the other classes?[10] Such is the objection raised, in different ways, by Castoriadis and Touraine; and there are numerous other criticisms such as Pateman's refusal of Marx's category labourpower as disembodied. For if Marx, in a sense, leaves the class struggle out, he also leaves the sex struggle out (except that he makes one important point: capitalism as a system itself is indifferent to gender: it will happily exploit anyone and everyone).

---

10   Beilharz 1985; Rundell 1989.

Capital remains, in all, one of the most extraordinary of works in social theory. Its architecture is splendid, and its narrative compelling and replete with insight. Its difficulty, by contemporary standards, lies in its attempt to produce the proper general theory of capitalism. Consequently, everyday life and the world system, the endless peculiarities and complexities of particular experience, are left out. The obvious response to such criticism is that it is a general work, but this is to beg the question whether it is better to shift from the general to the particular or the other way round. Certainly the idea of discussing capital today outside the world system is less than persuasive. The more general issue remains, however, whether this is an economic theory or a social theory; whether a theory of capitalist production can claim to comprehend all that is social and cultural; whether, in plainer terms, life can be reduced to labour. Marx himself was no enthusiast for the centrality of economy – he directed the first chapter of *Capital* against it. Yet he also came to accept industrialism as fate, and to reconstruct his image of socialism in the grey colours of the city rather than the shades of the countryside. At the same time, his longing was always for the past, as well as the future.[11] In terms of social theory, he is arguably still best read as a critic of capitalist culture rather than as a system builder for, like Weber, Nietzsche and Freud, he was nothing if not critical.

Marx's reception has been complicated, in Australia as elsewhere, both by his political and scholarly followers. Marxism has a long tradition of influence through the labour movement. With the expansion and radicalisation of the tertiary education system into the 1960s, Marcuse (and Gramsci) became popular, along with the writings of the young Marx. Marxism became influential in sociology via the work of Connell and Irving,[12] via Habermas in Theophanous[13] and Frankel[14] and Pusey,[15] via Althusser in cultural studies and political economy, as well as through the influence of Europeans and North Americans such as Braverman,[16] Mandel,[17] and Carchedi.[18] Enthusiasm for Marx's early works was also fuelled by the Australian sojourn of Agnes Heller. We are left with a situation in which, thanks to postmodernism, Marx is not even read

---

11   Prawer 1978.
12   1980.
13   1980.
14   1983.
15   1991.
16   1974.
17   1975a.
18   1977.

to be 'forgotten', let alone remembered. This is unfortunate, because the end of Marx's own grand narrative also represents a potential beginning for many smaller, more local stories which remain to be told, heard, argued about and acted upon.

Marxism and History (1981)

The bifurcation of marxism into theory and history reflects the division of labour and knowledge in bourgeois society and in its universities. In bourgeois society itself, practical knowledge and theoretical knowledge are generally separate practices. As the product of bourgeois society marxism often mirrors its worst values (on the one hand, the fetish of Science, on the other, the fetish of common sense) and its worst practices (on the one hand, intellectual élitism, on the other, anti-intellectualism). In universities philosophers and historians love to hate each other. Their differences mirror, among other things, different systems of proof: for philosophers, a logical mode of argument wins the case, for historians, the weight of empirical evidence. Marxism finds itself compromised here: for its claims rest on its practical nature, yet the bourgeois society which resists change also necessitates that marxism have a strong critical and therefore theoretical position. The contradiction between theory and practice is clear in Marx's work if we contrast, for example, *Capital* with the *Theses on Feuerbach*. But this is a necessary contradiction, for the claim of marxism to have a primary interest in *changing* the world necessitates the *understanding* of the forces, structures and psychologies which work against social change. The difficulties involved in both dimensions of marxism are clear: the practical dimension lapses too easily into pragmatic struggles and imperatives, inducing a reformist logic and losing sight of the end-goal, that of generalised radical change; while the critical practice often engenders a distance from, and cynicism for, the monolithic bourgeois society which seems to plod on so mercilessly. The activist mode, simplifying our problems, engenders pragmatism; the exclusively theoretical mode, exaggerating our problems, induces the condition called 'theoreticism'.

Thesis Eleven has set itself the task of attempting to foster the combination of these modes or dimensions of marxism. Sad to say, a situation which demands the *combination* of theory and practice sees their increasing severance. After the Althusserian era, it is now fashionable to simply equate theory with theoreticism, and to justify all historical or empirical work as belonging to the realm of 'historical materialism'. In this conjuncture we can only reinstate Marx's jibe, that theoretical ignorance never yet helped anybody. But in its tragic replays, the history of marxism itself is a history of the battle between history and theory, with now one, now the other dominant and its opponent discredited. The recent feud between Thompson and Althusser is merely the most recent refiguration of the battle between 'history' and 'science'. The end of the Althusserian era sees the discrediting of theoretical discourse and the growing hegemony of its historical opponent. The new historical turn in British marxism signals the revival of a humanistic, historical marxism repressed since the earlier debate between Thompson and *New Left Review* in the mid-sixties.[1] However, the new turn does not seem to distinguish itself from the long-existing tradition of inversion. The present situation suggests rather a return, a denial of the theoretical-political significance of the Althusserian episode, a mere repetition or return to history with little suggestion of synthesis or progress. The realisation of a necessary *synthesis*, the realisation that in a sense both Althusser and Thompson were *half-right*, is the greatest contribution of Perry Anderson's new book, *Arguments Within English Marxism*.[2]

It will be argued below that the historical revival is not without problems. Nor is it necessarily healthy: for the apparent relief of many marxists at the glimpse of a possible liberation from tiresome theoretical considerations coincides with a revived orthodoxy, especially apparent in a revived technological determinism, the forces-relations of production theorem performing a miraculous comeback as a fixed and general theory of history. In this context, the 'back to history' plea is less innocent than it looks. Anderson's plea for synthesis and with it, for an honest and principled debate, is not without its own problems. As will be seen, Anderson himself despite the synthetic argument seems to endorse the reinstatement of the determinist view of history presented in Cohen's *Karl Marx's Theory of History: A Defence*.[3] The importance of the synthetic message, however, overrides the deterministic inclination, making Anderson's book perhaps his most important political statement yet: for here we have a reconsideration of past dogmatism, a plea for a new openness, and a recognition that there can be no monopoly of truth in marxist debate. The return to history, the denial of the positive lessons of Althusser which *themselves* deny any simple return to an historical practice, indicate a tragic example of socialist amnesia. Anderson's study highlights this irony: the tragedy can only be extended if his arguments go unnoticed, swept aside in the rush back to history.

---

1   See e.g. Thompson 1978a.
2   1980.
3   1978.

1

Readers of *New Left Review* could not help but notice some changes of late. The most striking occurrence was registered in Raphael Samuel's study, 'British Marxist Historians'.[4] Its opening words demolished, in the *Review* itself, much of the conventional wisdom associated with its project (and well-articulated in Anderson's own *Considerations on Western Marxism*).

Samuel argued that marxism was not a closed or pure discourse or system uncontaminated by the springs of bourgeois ideas; that fundamentalist appeal to texts would not do as the substance for argument; that marxism could not be reduced to philosophy, let alone epistemology, but was marked by historical and political determinations which gave it its distinct character. At the same time Samuel suggested, if implicitly, that history without historiography was no solution to the existing impasse. The implication was that questions about the development of marxism, its relation to bourgeois society and bourgeois culture, could not be answered by historical work alone: debate about the *meaning* of the practice of history linked history to theory.[5] Though notions of a monolithic '*NLR* line' were exaggerated in the past,[6] this kind of contestation within the *Review* was hardly the norm. It signalled a change in tenor, a different attitude to the posing of fundamental questions.

The most striking immediate features of Anderson's *Arguments* are in its balanced and reasonable treatment of contending arguments, manifested above all in its plea for *diversity*.[7] Anderson begins with the problem of historiography and historical materialism as such. This is a vital beginning point, for it has become apparent in Australia as elsewhere that in the shifting lexicon of Marxism, theory is now a dirty word, whereas the practice of history is coextensive with historical materialism. Thompson's history is shown to be a history without structures, allowing sliding notions of human agency to blur the difference between the limited everyday autonomy of individuals and their united collective strivings for socialism.[8] *Experience* is the crucial category for Thompson, particularly in his opus *The Making of the English Working Class*: to the virtual exclusion of the development of the capitalist mode of production,

---

4   Samuel 1980.
5   Samuel 1980, p. 31.
6   Anderson, 1980, p. 115 f. Ian Birchall 1980 agrees, but for opposite reasons: lamenting the failure of *NLR* to constitute itself as a political party, Harman detects in this diversity *eclecticism*, the worst of leftist diseases.
7   Anderson 1980, p. 206.
8   Anderson 1980, p. 21.

itself a defining category for class structure.[9] The result of Thompson's book, the best example of his historian's craft, 'is to resolve the complex manifold of objective-subjective determinations whose totalization actually generated the English working class into a simple dialectic between suffering, and resistance whose whole movement is internal to the subjectivity of the class'.[10] Thompson's analysis lacks the kind of anchorage in determinate relations of production the likes of which set marxism apart from other explanations.[11] Put more bluntly, on Thompson's analysis we cannot speak of objective classes at all: when classes are silent they do not exist. In this understanding the whole of marxist science is worthless. And this is indeed Thompson's argument against the scientific legacy of marxism in the critique of political economy, ignoring for all purposes the distinction between essence and appearance which *calls forth* a critical marxism.[12]

Thompson's alternative to the theoretical rigour of *Capital* is to turn to the *German Ideology*.[13] Anderson's reply is that the marxist history is a science of history, the novelty of which resides in the concept mode of production.[14] Anderson pursues his case by indicating that not Althusser's fantasies but rather the works of those other advocates of the science of history, the *Annales* school, are responsible for notions of differential time.[15] There are, then, other ways to engage history than to seek immersion in it (Thompson) or to deny it altogether (the early Althusser, Hindess and Hirst). Anderson's appeal is for a specifically marxist history – not simply the history of the working-class movement, but not simply a logically deduced class structure either. If Althusser denies history, or makes it merely conceptual, Thompson makes marxism coextensive with history. We note parenthetically that Thompson's notice will surprise mainstream historians. Against it, Anderson's argument is that marxist

---

9   Anderson 1980, p. 33.

10 Anderson 1980, p. 39.

11 Anderson 1980, p. 42.

12 The classic formulation is in *Capital* vol. III: 'all science would be superfluous if the outward appearance and the essence of things directly coincided' (Mandel 1976b, p. 817). Apart from the question of agency and the subject vis-à-vis structure, this must be the central lesson of the Althusserian episode: the problem of reading and interpretation. Althusser extends the critical dimension latent in Marx and Freud because the world is not so simple as it seems. As Anderson notes elsewhere (1980, p. 172) Thompson's opposition of Reason and Desire itself replays current French fashion – whereas for marxism knowledge and desire are inseparable (Anderson, 1980, p. 167).

13 Anderson 1980, p. 61.

14 Anderson 1980, pp. 64, 60.

15 Anderson 1980, p. 73.

history can be characterised only by its combination of historical research and theoretically informed presentation.

As Johnson has it, *neither culturalism nor structuralism will do!*[16] It is a sad indicator of marxism's crisis that such a sensible argument as Anderson's has been met with a relative silence. We share Anderson's hopes for new arguments within, and also without, marxism.

---

16   We pass by many other issues raised by Anderson less germane to this paper. Two separate problems warrant mention, one positive, one negative. First, with a little care Anderson rescues Althusser from Thompson's characterisation of the Stalinist hack. Readers who found Thompson's damnation of Althusser convincing cannot fail to feel the guilt of the rush to judgment. Marxism should have no time for the 'where were you in 19–?' game: in its ultimate regress, we all become guilty at some stage. There are always times when others see better and act better; guilt itself is a source of self-destruction. The pivot in Althusser's intellectual biography is China; Thompson has no right to judge all by Hungary '56, for he too was on the wrong side earlier (Anderson, 1980, p. 118 n. 46). That the Althusserians failed to establish the relationship between Maoism and Stalinism – their political unity as theories of domination – is a separate problem. Thompson does himself no justice by conflating theory and politics, nor by equating effect and intention. The second, negative problem is Anderson's continuing flirtation with Trotsky. Time and again Anderson deals out unconvincing assurances that continuing problems have already been dispatched by Trotsky. With reference to the failure of classical marxism to elaborate an ethics, Anderson tells that the 'sole significant exception is Trotsky, whose *Their Morals and Ours* remains a defensive and occasional case' (1980, p. 98). Later *The Revolution Betrayed* is presented as the still unsurpassed framework for analysis of Soviet society (1980, p. 117). The most innovative work in this area would not agree (Rakovski, 1978; Konrád and Szelényi, 1979; See Fehér, Heller and Márkus, 1983). Anderson's enthusiasm for Bahro's *Alternative* is justified, but it is hardly just to present it as a 'major utopia' (Anderson 1980, p. 174 f.). More balanced here are the reviews of Bahro by Arato and Vajda and by Szelenyi in *New German Critique* Numbers 19 and 20 respectively. The problems of Stalinism and Trotskyism in Anderson are related in a peculiar way. Anderson explains well the biographical centrality of popular-frontism for Thompson (1980, p. 142 ff.) and of the Cultural Revolution for Althusser. His own continued Trotskyism is implicitly of the same nature: Trotskyism was a central biographical reference point for the second *New Left Review* generation (1980, p. 152 ff.). Anderson's running defence of Trotsky (extended on pp. 78 and 154, where Althusser and Thompson are reprimanded for failing to take up the *History of the Russian Revolution*, the classic of historical materialism) is biographical and in this specific sense pre-rational. We note parenthetically that if marxist historians can learn much from Trotsky, better the Trotsky of 1905 (Beilharz, 1981b).

2

Having witnessed such an advance and such a radical self-criticism,[17] having assessed both Thompson and Althusser and having seen virtues and limits in both arguments, we should not be surprised to find Anderson's radical turn incomplete. Its primary symptom, reverence for Trotsky aside, is an endorsement of the so-called theory of history sketched in Marx's 1859 *Preface*. The enthusiasm generated by Cohen's *Karl Marx's Theory of History* is shared by Anderson, as well as by some whose approval is more contentious.[18]

Like the response given it, Cohen's Deutscher prize-winning book is remarkable. Even such critique as has been levelled at it has been marked by distinct respect.[19] Yet Cohen's book has the remarkable claim of 'saving' Marx's 'theory' of history without much reference to theory or to history (his fidelity to Marx is of relatively little importance, except in that it signals a fascination with the Author). The old saying has it that too many marxists write books about other books: Cohen's study has an awkward privilege in that it is a book about a paragraph. An immense superstructure of material has arisen on the base of this paragraph: and rarely have so many hung so much on so little.[20]

In the period of Bolshevism's dominance people referred to Bolshevik argumentation as 'speaking Russian'. Cohen's argument is a Russian argument, recalling Plekhanov and to a lesser extent Bukharin: but it is spoken in the language of British analytic philosophy. Cohen is proud of analytic philosophy (see his Foreword); it will be seen that this is a misplaced pride. Cohen's 'defence' of Marx is a bold reinstatement of the rationalist view of progress associated with that paragraph in the 1859 *Preface*. He articulates its basic argument as the Primacy Thesis. Productive forces are given primary responsibility for produc-

---

17   Anderson, 1980, pp. 138 ff., 206 f.

18   A. Quinton, *Times Literary Supplement* 4/1/80, praises Cohen. Like Singer in his *Marx* (1980, esp. Ch. 7), Quinton is inclined to use Cohen not to prove but to disprove Marx. This is surely telling of the nature of Cohen's logic. (This judgement is not political but theoretical. The present writer presumes that marxism belongs to a long German-Italian tradition and not that of British analytic philosophy). Quinton endorses Cohen's idea that Althusserian thought is short of rigour. This argument is not impressive: the rigorously internal logic of Althusser resembles Cohen's all too closely.

19   Levine and Wright 1980.

20   The paragraph itself is too well-worn to bear repeating: Cohen quotes it in full (Marx and Engels 1961: Bd. 13, 8 f.; cf. Marx 1970, p. 20 f.). Similar arguments to Cohen's are put by W. Shaw, a student of Cohen, in *Marx's Theory of History* (1977) and J. McMurtry, *The Structure of Marx's World-View* (1978). Less given to determinism, if uninspiring, are M. Rader's *Marx's Interpretation of History* (1979) and D. Gandy, *Marx and History* (1979).

tion relations rather than vice-versa.[21] Cohen argues that it is not a question of simple correlation between forces and relations of production (an argument which few would contest) but a case of a determining relation. Productive forces both explain relations – analytically – and determine their development, historically. This is the traditional argument espoused by both orthodox marxists and their bourgeois enemies. Economy becomes the moving principle of socialist politics: ideology becomes once again mere epiphenomenon, mere superstructure. Cohen's first specification – productive forces *explain* relations – introduces an historiographical problem. It hamstrings historical research, for there is little need of it if we know the true path of history already. The second – productive forces break through relations – reinstates the classical automatic view of history. After the upsets and doubts of the sixties and seventies, it is comforting to discover that History is once again on our side.

If Cohen's conclusions are suspect, so are his premises. His argument has its ontological basis in the human nature theory common to bourgeois thinking across centuries, and not without expression in Marx. Men and women are understood as accumulating animals, not social or political animals, but calculating rational beings who seek to minimise the pain of scarcity and maximise technological pleasure.[22] *Needs* are understood here only as *material* needs: there is no place for a conception of socialism as less goodies better distributed.[23] Cohen's rationalist argument presumes that interest determines capacity, as Levine and Wright point out:[24] but avoiding as they do that dreaded theorist (Habermas) Cohen's reviewers fail to link up his rationalism with his predilection for analytic philosophy. Analytic philosophy is, after all, instrumental rationality, end-means rationality in theory: the syllogistic framework guarantees 'if A, B, then C' without enquiring as to the nature of A.[25] Cohen's argument is ultimately pre-critical: it fails to ask questions of the nature of technology and needs, instead reinstating a naively Victorian progress-theory. If we examine the end of Cohen's logic as well as its premises, the real inadequacy of the argument is exposed. Failing to radically question *Marx*, Cohen bypasses the most important and imbalanced message in the 1859 *Preface*. If the Marx of the *Preface* is a determinist, then so much the worse for Marx. *After* Cohen's favourite passage, Marx says that: 'mankind thus inevitably sets itself only such

---

21   Cohen, 1978, p. 134.

22   Cohen, 1978, p. 152.

23   See Heller 1976, 1972; Cooley 1980.

24   Cooley 1980, p. 59.

25   The worst case of this thinking in Cohen's book is at p. 172 f., where the reader is offered twelve variations on the theme 'if p then q'.

tasks as it is able to solve'.[26] Today the converse formulation is better: humanity can solve only such problems as it sets itself. It is the *setting* of these tasks
which is problematical, not least of all in a conjuncture in which people in the
west must choose *less* development and opt for a destructuring of needs and
not their infinite material development. The problem is not only that Cohen's
theory of history as forces-breaking-through-relations does not work. It is also
to be said that even if it did work, we should be the opponents of its technological juggernaut if we understood socialism as radical collective reworking of
needs, techniques, human relationships and practices.

3

Anderson's endorsement[27] of Cohen's thesis undercuts his argument for a new
synthesis of theory and history. If forces break through relations of production as a general transhistorical proposition there would seem to be little need
for any new work. The theoretical positions of Comintern orthodoxy accepted, there is little political option but a return to the automatic marxisms of
the Second, Third and Fourth Internationals. The acceptance of the forces-
relations theorem as an historiographical principle presumably means that
history, having been explained already, leaves only the task of procuring raw
historical material and pouring it into the categories of a general theory of
modes of production.

Anderson's endorsement of Cohen denies the most provocative insight in
his own historical work (and it is an argument which Cohen also avoids):

> one of the most important conclusions yielded by an examination of the
> great crash of European feudalism is that – contrary to widely received
> beliefs among Marxists – the characteristic 'figure' of a crisis in a mode of
> production is not one in which vigorous (economic) forces of production
> burst triumphantly through retrograde (social) relations of production,
> and promptly establish a higher productivity and society on their ruins.
> On the contrary, the forces of production typically tend to stall and recede
> within the existent relations of production: these then must themselves
> first be radically changed and reordered before new forces of production
> can be created and combined for a globally new mode of production.

---

26   Marx and Engels 1961: Bd. 13, p. 9; Marx 1970, p. 21.
27   Anderson 1980, pp. 40, 65, 75 f.

In other words, the relations of production generally change *prior* to the forces of production in an epoch of transition, and not vice-versa.[28]

The radical import of Anderson's conclusion has the effect of turning the 1859 *Preface* upside-down. Not the least irony here is that Anderson's attack on the traditional wisdom of so-called historical materialism prompts a necessary re-consideration of Weber.[29] Weber's argument in *The Protestant Ethic and The Spirit of Capitalism* affects the spiritual or attitudinal dimension of social change, where beliefs are held to be crucial to the maintenance and changing of social orders and social relations. Weber cites the traditional society where accumulation is stalled because men do not wish to earn more (work harder) but rather to perpetuate their existing forms of life: the opportunity of working less is more attractive than that of earning more.[30] Claiming to leave the relation between economy and ideas (religion) open and reciprocal, Weber concludes that neither the one-sided materialist nor the one-sided idealist causal argument can be adequate: each 'accomplishes equally little in the interest of historical truth' if it functions as a prime-mover or hidden historical hand.[31] As an economic historian, Weber rejects innuendos of simplism: neither economy nor religion moves history in any simple primary sense.

Weber's own interpretation of the transition from feudalism in spirit complements Marx's elaboration in the *Grundrisse*. The old traditional labour-process is reorganised: accumulation is inserted as its motive: labour is intensified, specialised by the insertion of machinery, centralised geographically. The weavers are turned from peasants into labourers; the putters-out break their traditional forms of work organisation, developing a real interest in marketing and expansion, and with it price-cutting, capitalising on the increased productivity of cooperation. Hence emerges the spirit of capitalism.[32] Marx's discussion in the section of the *Grundrisse* entitled 'Precapitalist Economic Formations' focuses on the objective conditions of capitalist development. The worker is released from the soil as his/her natural workshop:[33] the relations

---

28 Anderson, 1974, p. 204.
29 We leave aside the question of specific transitions here, as Cohen's argument and Anderson's approval concern generalities. We leave aside also Weber's methodological 'innocence': his refusal to distinguish narrative and theoretical structure in *The Protestant Ethic* (E.g. Weber, 1958, p. 47) and his assumption that concepts *emerge* from the text rather than structuring it.
30 Weber, 1958, p. 59 f.
31 Weber, 1958, p. 183.
32 Weber, 1958, pp. 66–8.
33 Marx, 1973, p. 471.

of the worker to the earth, to the control of the instrument of production, to the raw materials of that process are all broken. The free worker emerges *as subject*: separated from the objective conditions of production, the worker now confronts alien conditions of production as purely subjective labour capacity.[34] Merchant capital inserts itself into these new but now already-existing relations as historic middleman.[35] Capital as a power *'does nothing but bring together the mass of hands and instruments which it finds on hand'.*[36] The merchant's drawing together of peasants who weave and spin proletarianises them by concentrating the labour-process.[37]

Clearly Marx's understanding of capital is not the same as Weber's. Capital is for Marx a relation which becomes dominant only where generalised commodity production dominates a social formation (with labour-power functioning as a commodity and with the extraction of relative surplus-value). But the point of arrival – from feudalism, the transition to capitalist production and bourgeois society – depends on the reproduction of capitalist values and the destruction of surviving feudal values. Marx would agree with Weber that the traditionalist attitude – work less, earn the same – must be smashed by the ideological premises of capital, the desirability of accumulation for the bourgeoisie and of work for the proletariat. Expansion is written into the practice of the capitalists and into the concept of capital.[38] Work in bourgeois society becomes not only the norm but the primary source of identity. Work defines our being, or non-being, if we work at home or do not 'work' at all; the question 'what do you do?' is taken to be identical to the question 'who are you?' Bourgeois society as we know it is impossible without this ideological basis.

The transition to and the reproduction of capitalist production is dependent on its internalisation in its bearers. Marx's peasants, like Weber's, accept the Protestant ethic when the future becomes clear to them.[39] For Marx the transition to capitalism signals the emergence of the subject and of ideology as we know it. What Weber takes to be the main thesis, Marx presumes (when, for example, he suggests that 'Protestantism, by changing almost all the traditional holidays into workdays, plays an important part in the genesis of capital').[40] Though the self-constituting subject emerges as characteristic of developing

34   Marx, 1973, p. 497 f.
35   Marx, 1973, p. 505.
36   Marx, 1973, p. 508.
37   Marx, 1973, p. 510.
38   Marx, 1965, p. 558, 1978, p. 543, 1973, p. 408.
39   Marx, 1973, p. 284 f.
40   Marx, 1965, p. 262, 1978, p. 240 n. 124.

capitalism its importance has rarely been recognised in the marxist tradition. For if being determines consciousness at the level of production, consciousness itself is a determining factor in consumption and reproduction.[41] Humans combine the functions of architect and bee: it is no solution to seek the closure of the problem in a simple acceptance of either a 'production paradigm' (Marx) or a 'communication paradigm' (Habermas). Historicity is the ground where communication and production, ideology and economy are united. Whether the objective conditions or their ideological acceptance are causally prior is unimportant unless we are obsessed with fundamentalist zeal. Ideas, after all, are part of reality. The reproduction of social formations is dependent on the reproduction of the lived ideas of those social formations. At least as regards a possible transition to socialism, the transformation of lived ideas as they are crystalized in everyday practices constitutes a necessary priority in the struggle for socialism. Without a conception of possible alternatives as well as critical perspectives masses of people cannot be expected to struggle for socialism.

4

What does this leave of historical materialism or marxist history? This is a difficult question, for if we deny the 1859 *Preface's* determinism and criticise the relatively pre-critical nature of the *German Ideology*, the basis of historical materialism in Marx's work is not clear. Perhaps marxist wisdom on history is less unique than is typically thought, even if we do prefer its conceptual rigour over alternative explanations. As regards the argument for the principle of historical specificity it seems that marxists have no monopoly on the case. So, what's left? Anderson's reply is that marxism's distinct theoretical apparatus is that delineated by the concept mode of production.[42] Since the uptake of *Reading Capital* it has been customary for marxists to explain a mode of production, in abstraction, as a combination of labourer, non-labourer and means of production.[43] The concept *mode of production* was not established with reference to specific modes, however, perhaps because of the difficulties which the question of transition presented for Althusserian theory, with its notions of conjunctural coincidence ('levels') the 'last instance' and the primacy of production relations never articulated in their interrelation. The theory of mode of production implied or at least *facilitated* a universality – all modes could

---

41   See the interesting prospectus by Gerry Gill (1979).
42   Anderson 1980, p. 64.
43   Althusser and Balibar, 1975, Part 3, esp. 212 ff.

be characterised with the combination labourer/non-labourer/means of production, suggesting a general theory of modes in which as a matter of course forces break through relations as content might break through form, technique through society, base through super-structure, matter through ideality.

The forces/ relations theorem in Cohen's rendition is, at any rate, universal. Indeed, the theorem is only possible as a general theory of modes of production: if it were merely specific to one transition (e.g. from feudalism to capitalism) then it would only be a specific historical explanation. (The argument would still be problematical if it were held to be true only for the transition to socialism after a transition to capitalism, for the political parallel is vacuous). And more: the rigid stages-theory of history is strictly Western-Europocentric. It avoids not only the wider problems of world-systems but also the particular problems of the 'Asiatic' and *Eastern* European societies. It avoids cases like the Italian, where combined feudal and capitalist modes are frozen into a functional but parasitic couple. Coming itself out of Britain, Cohen's argument avoids its *decaying* capitalist mode: hardly a model of technological dynamism. And in Cohen's scheme the Eastern European societies cannot be conceived as *new* societies: since they must be *either* capitalist or socialist, a technological assessment presumably deciding the question. Here Cohen not only backs around real past history, but around the present as history and the past in the present: around *uneven development*. Surely utility should not be the only criterion for assessing a marxist argument, but this kind of refusal of reality is difficult to justify.

On the logical level the Asiatic mode of production – the 'non-dynamic' mode – raises more difficulties for Cohen's argument. His failure to confront the AMP goes with his acceptance of forever developing technology, where the concept of socialism is that of material abundance or massive surplus rather than the reconstruction of our already bloated systems of needs. There are, of course, those who see marxism as irredeemably bound up with the imperatives of technological domination. Though we dispute this with them, we certainly grant their long-established rejection of general theories of modes of production. (Those who have no taste for such iconoclasts as Castoriadis and Baudrillard would do just as well to consult Labriola or Gramsci). Castoriadis's argument against the tradition of historical materialism is entirely applicable to Cohen: Cohen's rendition of Marx's theory of history is neither historical nor materialist. It avoids contact with the real stuff of history, and its thesis is idealist, mirroring Hegel's *Philosophy of History* where the onward march is clear and socialism is the end-product of an ideal myth become materially incarnate. Only its prejudices are as British as Hegel's were German.

5

The rejection of general theories of modes of production does not necessitate the rejection of the *concept* of mode of production (unless that concept is cast so rigorously in advance as to make its ditching inevitable, as is the case with Hindess and Hirst).[44] The real problem at this point is the status of the concept mode of production. The dominant theoretical arguments have presumed mode to be an *economic* concept, as it is in the 1859 *Preface*. Rarely has it been considered that a mode might be rather a less rigid, anthropological concept involving culture as well as technique. When we think of it, there is nothing strikingly rigid about the word mode, nothing suggesting a thing or a composite object consisting necessarily of invariable components, labourer/non-labourer/means of production. The concept mode of production – *Produktionsweise* – suggests only a way, manner, form of production. Certainly this is the manner of its use in the *German Ideology*, where mode of production means mode of life,[45] involving an active life-process.[46] But Marx here explains only where analysis *begins* – with real, active sensuous people existing in the world that they make. Marx's return after the *German Ideology* to critical economy left his historical considerations barely developed. The hostility to 'abstraction' evident in the 1845 manuscript dissolves later, when Marx decides that 'praxis' is not so simple, that creative and wilful humans exist within practical and ideological structures which limit their actions and necessitate a critical (and therefore 'abstract') approach. So the problems of analytical beginnings were only compounded, not solved, by Marx.

If history is not an onward march through inexorable laws to the technological utopia, then neither is it mere contingency or subject matter for necessary stories of the real suffering of the dominated. History *is* existence: but the critical nature of marxism indicates the impossibility of understanding existence only *immediately* as experience. The positive lessons of Althusser, not registered by Thompson in his attack on theory, include the recognition of the deeper dimensions of existence. Even if in a distorted way, Althusser with Marx and Freud understood that the world was not a simple place which wore the truth on its sleeve, but a complex labyrinth where meanings, intentions, structures and actions were all mixed up, often masquerading as their other.

It may well be that historical materialism has no objective existence at all – that marxist history exists only as a practice, the uniqueness of which vis-à-vis

---

44   Hindess and Hirst 1975, c.f. 1977.
45   Marx and Engels 2004, Vol. 5, 31.
46   Marx and Engels 2004, Vol. 5, 37.

other historical practices is in its critical edge, its conceptual sophistication and its politically radical orientation. Like the other practices which together constitute the marxist project, a marxist history can have no positive guarantees for its political efficacy. An historical consciousness can help to avoid the all-too-vicious replays of history but cannot assure practical gains. History teaches but has no students; radicals must more and more become both the educators and the educated.

Negation and Ambivalence: Marx, Simmel and Bolshevism on Money (1996)

Money, like the city, presents itself as both the expression and the vital symbol of modernity. Simultaneously abstract and powerfully concrete, money nevertheless remains an underworked concept in sociology and in social theory. My purpose in this paper is to marshal three arguments in order to clarify how it could be that money is simultaneously central and yet marginal to our lives, theoretical and yet practical. There are, then, three major characters in this paper, two concrete, Marx and Simmel, one collective, in the form of Bolshevism. These figures turn a three-step – Marx, of course, leading; Simmel more light-footed; some representative Bolsheviks in progressive formation, somewhere between three-step and goose-step. To put it in different terms, my task is to make sense of two impossible books, Marx's *Capital* and Simmel's *Philosophy of Money*, and one impossible tradition, early, or high, Bolshevism.

Let me anticipate the line of argument. Marx's theory of money, such as it is, is one-sided; negation, negation, this is Moses and the Prophets. What Marx has to say about money is fascinating, but it is subordinated to the primary concept of commodification, and Marx proceeds as though money is not only conceptually marginal but also practically dispensable. Simmel does better, to begin, because he focuses upon money as such, because his analysis of money is more measured and ambivalent, and ambivalence is a key motif of modernity (that which, by the way, makes the work of Simmel and now of Bauman so important today). The heavy-handedness of Bolshevism, by comparison, may be circumstantial or conjunctural in part but it also results from Marx's too simple rejection of money, as though we knew (or could construct) another way of working in the world, beyond money. What this might suggest, for those still interested in changing the world, is something like a Simmelian socialism. Perhaps that juxtaposition is too anachronistic; a better way to begin to address some of these kinds of problems of money and city might be under another category, something like *Postmodern Socialism*.[1]

---

1 Beilharz 1994.

Marx's *Capital*

To the first step: Marx, and *Capital*. What is the theory of money in *Capital*? On first glance, it seems elusive, hard to find. Money, for Marx, is emblematic rather than central; it represents or stands for the problem, which lies elsewhere. Commodity stands behind money, just as production stands behind commodity. Money is a symptom of commodity, not the other way around. Marx's methodology is that based on senses of levels, or layers, essence behind appearance.

Capital is a theory or critique of capitalist production that commences from its phenomenal expression or appearance in the commodity-form. *Capital* is a theory of commodities and behind that, a theory of production, a theory of labour. Money is at best a symptom of this mysterious world of levels of activity and abstraction. Precisely because money is a symptom of capitalist production, Marx does not develop a sophisticated theory of money. The procedure Marx insists upon, from appearance to essence, from surface to depth, is pedagogical as well as logical; this is the explanatory procedure that Marx spent 20 years straining his brain over, in search of the best possible way to *explain* capitalism as such. The logic of Marx's architectonic is procedural in structure. The single commodity leads to the image of many commodities and then to the value-form. The elementary or accidental form of value leads to the total or expanded form of value. Those tables of equivalents in the first volume of *Capital* become more dense until Marx introduces the general form of value and then, in Section D of Chapter One, he introduces the money-form as the universal equivalent. A sack of flour might contain the same embodied labour-power as a coat, and they could in principle be exchanged for one another, but it is the money-form through which exchange more generally occurs, and in an ongoing rather than incidental way. Money, for Marx, is the logical result, the universal equivalent that signals (both historically and logically) the transition from barter to commodity exchange. There is nothing more universal than money when it comes to exchange; and if modernity is based on capitalism, the generalised production of commodities with labour-power functioning as a commodity, then money will be as ubiquitous as commodification is, only because of it. For Marx, of course, it is not money but commodity fetishism that is the source of the simulacra we inhabit. In his way of thinking it is not money that is the great leveller, but commodification.[2] In *Capital* Chapter Three, the chapter on money, money again is constructed by Marx as phenomenal, as inessential.

---

2   Marx, 1965, p. 89.

Here Marx says that money is a leveller, which does away with all distinctions, 'But money itself is a commodity',[3] and here, as in the *Paris Manuscripts* and in the *Grundrisse,* he significantly cites Shakespeare as a key voice against the power of money.

The logic of Marx's project is both plain and powerful. *Das Kapital* is a critique of capital, not of money. Money and commodities precede capitalism, but only capital is self-valorising, and its necessary processes of self-expansion have less to do with distribution or with markets than with the hidden abode of production. By comparison to Simmel, then, Marx has no thick theory of money, though in a different sense it could also be observed that both thinkers have a primary curiosity about social forms. Simmel's work, indeed, might be described as a theory of social forms; Marx, in contrast, views forms as vital but chimerical, illusory, distracting us from the real causes of the problems that we confront but which elude, because they enchant us, whether in the ghost-processes of alienation or in the fantasies of commodity fetishism. Marx's procedure in his master work, in any case, is to use forms as a way into the secrets of his intellectual laboratory. With Chapter Four of *Capital* the prolegomenon is virtually complete. Commodity operates conceptually in Marx's great work as semiology, or as staging. With Chapter Seven we encounter the descent into Dante's *Inferno,* the step down into the labour process that holds up all the magical worlds of commodities from K-Mart to Tiffany's. The argument is continuous with that of his whole life's work, after Hegel and Feuerbach, the slaves who move the world made invisible by the results of their labours, the massive powers we project onto gods now set upon commodities, as though they precede us. After a great deal of further argument there then arrives the grand finale. In *Capital* Chapter Thirty-Two we experience (on paper) the negation of the negation. The subterranean actors break through the artificial world that has been constructed by them, on top of them, over their dead bodies. The old mole of history surfaces at last, victorious. This negation of the negation can only mean the negation of false appearance, of the commodity-form and therefore of money.

Marx's logic is ruptural and apocalyptic. Where there was commodity, there will stand the free producer. There is simply no place in this way of thinking for money; it is a symptom, and must therefore pass together with its causes. Marx offers no clear indication of how the regime of associated producers might carry on in the absence of money. Obviously they must continue to exchange with each other, but it remains unclear how; through the general

---

3 Marx, 1965, p. 132.

store, or stock of goods, imaginably, from each according to their abilities to each according to their needs, neither a Commissar nor a Stakhanovite in sight. Logically, Marx's argument is all of a piece. If capitalism is defined as the generalized accumulation of commodities with labour-power as a commodity and money as a universal equivalent, then the negation of this bourgeois order of things indicates the necessity of a society without commodities, money, or the state.

Marx's argument has a compelling textual logic; many, indeed, have been persuaded by it. Such things are great books, that they provide us with blindness as well as with insight. If we take a momentary step back from the text, it can be observed that one dominant socialist argument concerning money through the nineteenth century indicated the necessity or desirability of replacing money with time-chits or labour vouchers. The obvious question that arises, even if it seems a pedantic one, is whether time-chits are not still money by another name. Time-chits may not be an independent universal exchange for us, but Marx and Simmel agree, nevertheless, that they are still money.[4] Thus Marx argues, for example in the *Grundrisse*, that in order to abolish money it is necessary to abolish exchange value and the dominant social form.[5] At the same time, it is important to note that the sensibility manifest in the *Grundrisse* is more appropriately exploratory; here Marx comes to grips, remarkably, with the power of technology, for example, so that it is certainly not beyond the bounds of imagination that he may have been capable of making a final truce with money, too. After all, the image of the individual as many-sided, as rich in needs, suggests a division of labour and therefore reliance upon exchange. In any case, time-chits seem to provide a final, illicit fallback position for Marxists, as well. But this pragmatic accommodation of money in fact does not register theoretically; it does not encourage the Marxist tradition to revise its negative or hostile view of money as such. Thus Marx pistol-whips poor Proudhon (and John Gray) in the 1859 *A Contribution to the Critique of Political Economy*, setting a nasty precedent for the war communists later to follow.[6] Not that Marx was alone in negating money; neither Morris's *News from Nowhere* nor Bellamy's *Looking Backward* allows for the existence of money, either.

---

4   Simmel 1978, pp. 426–7; Marx 1973, p. 136.
5   Marx, 1973, p. 145.
6   Marx 1970, pp. 83, 86.

Simmel's Philosophy of Money

This brings us to the second step, to Simmel, and his theory of money. Simmel calls his great work *Philosophy of Money*; we read it today more as sociology, if as a sociology of forms. If there is a philosophy here implied, it is a philosophy or an attitude of ambivalence. Together with Simmel we are given the sense that we could do better than money will allow us, but we could also do worse. Is Simmel's work then a response to, or a dialogue with, the ghost of Karl Marx? Simmel's *Philosophy of Money* contains two references each to Karl Marx and to Adam Smith. But the book is, despite *appearances*, a dialogue with Marx and a critique of Marx's *Capital*. Simmel suggests that his own labour is an attempt to construct a new storey *beneath* the work of Karl Marx.[7] Beneath? The pun refers, presumably, to those clichéd images of base or basis and superstructure; perhaps it is more a matter of constructing a new storey, and a new story. For Simmel's *Philosophy of Money* is a culturalist critique of Marx's structuralism, even if that kind of language seems more pertinent to our own times than to theirs. For Marx, money is a sign, a symptom, the expression of a problem rooted below, elsewhere.

For Simmel, in contrast, money is central, a core problem, it is 'the incarnation and purest expression of the concept of economic value'.[8] Marx and Simmel might seem at first glance to be saying the same thing, but I do not think so. For Marx money is expressive and negative. For Simmel it is also our incarnation, and ambivalent in its effects. So Simmel appraises money as ambivalent or mixed, whereas for Marx it is all negation, nothing added; for Marx money is a *loss* warranting its own negation. Why is this so, and what difference does this represent between Simmel and Marx? If for Marx, money is loss, for Simmel *exchange* is a form of life; perhaps it is *the* form of life. Anthropologically speaking, for Simmel, human beings are animals who exchange. In other words, exchange works as a general metaphor for society in Simmel's work. Social life is a flow. As Simmel puts it, 'every day of our lives comprises a process of gain and loss, of accretion and diminution of life's content'.[9] To put it differently, Simmel thinks economy in an anthropological or symbolic rather than strictly modern, economic or productive sense. For Simmel our humanity is constituted in exchange, of things, but also of symbols, ideas, emotions, energies. Thus where for Marx and the critique of political economy, economy

---

7 Simmel 1978, p. 56.
8 Simmel, 1978, p. 101.
9 Simmel, 1978, p. 82.

becomes the largest category, for Simmel 'economy' is a 'special case' of the general form of exchange.

The implication of Simmel's case against Marxism is devastating. The logic of Simmel's view is that Marxism has to be a kind of theoretical fundamentalism or absolutism, for it chooses to privilege labour as the *substance* of value, whereas modernity and its consciousness is relativistic. The distinction between Marx and Simmel is also evident in the difference between the style of *Philosophy of Money* and Marx's architectonic in *Capital*. These two big books might both be impossible, but in varying ways, for their difficulty takes on radically distinct forms. *Capital* is probably as close to the proper object of Lyotard's poke at metanarratives as you will find; *Philosophy of Money* meanders, essay-like, helping to explain why it might be that post-moderns could feel especially attracted to Simmel as a kindred spirit of sorts. Simmel's great work reads as a conversation of sorts; Marx's as a lesson, even if it is a brilliant one, or as an exposé, an unmasking of bourgeois society in sociological form. The kinds of knowledge claims we find embedded in these two works, then, strike up quite distinct epistemological profiles. Thus where Marx labours logic and cell-form, essence and appearance, Simmel inquires, as does Clifford Geertz in the parable of the globe and the tortoises, what fundament or ground strong knowledge-claims are based upon, and he answers, 'Dogmatism may be the base of certainty upon some criterion as upon a rock – but what supports the rock?'.[10] For Simmel, then, money is neither phenomenal nor essential, so much as it is paradigmatic. It is not something that counts as the universal equivalent of Marx, but rather it is the highest form of capitalism, the most abstract symbol of modernity. Money is, as Gianfranco Poggi nicely puts it, an epiphany, a vital third term.[11] So Simmel suggests, like Levinas and in sympathy with the heuristic of Marx, that money is a concept without content, is therefore a vital clue to the abstraction of modern culture.[12] Yet it is also more than that. Money in Simmel, like contract in Durkheim, rests on trust and not only in power. Money for Simmel is a social bond and not only a relation expressing bondage between those who possess it and those who do not. Compared to relations based on patronage, money facilitates freedom even if at the same time it cultivates the anonymity of the metropolis, the blasé attitude of the stranger, the disinterest of social distance. In contrast to Marx's *Capital*, the image of history in Simmel's *Philosophy of Money* remains this side of redemption, in perpetual and

---

10   Simmel, 1978, p. 116.
11   Poggi 1993.
12   Simmel 1978, p. 497.

restless tension, the future as master and slave never ending rather than the deceptively harmonistic image of communism in Marx.[13]

None of which is to say that they have nothing in common, Marx in one corner and Simmel in the other. Marx and Simmel can be read together as critics of modernity as abstraction. The difference is that Marx imagines a way through and beyond opacity. Further, there are some similarities in the absences across *Capital* and *Philosophy of Money*, as well as in their critical presences. Neither Marx nor Simmel sufficiently address politics, the state, the licensing of money, or credit. Neither could reasonably have anticipated plastic money or EFTPOS, phenomena that threaten to transform the nature of money as such, to supplant it as a 'final' modern form with the invisibility of finance as credit.[14] But the stronger point of distinction between the two thinkers and their great books remains the relative sense of balance or difference in Simmel. As Simmel's narrative unfolds in *Philosophy of Money* it becomes progressively more critical of money's negative effects, its collusion in the culture of labelling, cynicism, the often bizarre detachment cultivated by the blasé attitude.[15] Simmel then proceeds to posit a minimalist definition of freedom in terms of argument suggestive of vitalism – freedom involves release and relaxation, or the change of obligations.[16] Together with this pragmatic and processual sensibility concerning freedom, and in clear contrast to the residual romanticism in Marx's worldview, Simmel proceeds to indicate what might be called an incipient theory of separation.[17] For Marx, bourgeois exchange is unequal exchange; to put it more explicitly, in Marx's thinking exchange stands for loss. As John Roemer put it more recently, freedom in bourgeois society amounts to the freedom to lose, not to choose. Obviously weaker individuals and proletarians in general lose out in markets characterised by asymmetrical relations of power, by the dialectics of master and slave. Yet Marx's ontology seems also to suggest that loss occurs in more general, anthropological terms, for it rests upon some symbolic or utopian sense of self-sufficiency, independence whether collective or individually proletarian, and this helps to remind us that Marx was *also* an individualist. His image of communism never manages quite to cast off the romantic sense of creative, individual, typically masculine and productive wholeness. Simmel is different. Simmel thinks that exchange is good for you.[18]

---

13 Simmel 1978; Beilharz 1994.
14 Ritzer 1995.
15 Simmel 1978, p. 255.
16 Simmel 1978, p. 282.
17 Simmel 1978, p. 350.
18 Simmel 1978, p. 291.

Marx never quite transcends the Renaissance conception of man. Simmel, in contrast, is a modernist; his worldview is more fully modern, and for that reason more ambivalent than negative about money, anthropology, the state or the commodity-form. The point of my argument is not that Marx is an individualist and Simmel is not, but rather that Simmel works with something closer to a modern conception of individual subjectivity. For Simmel, modernity rests upon complexity, difference and dependence, therefore on interdependence and intersubjectivity. For Marx, the society of the future is suggestive rather of simplicity and independence as well as sociability. It would be going too far to say that Marx's utopia is based on the German sense of unity as oneness or *Einheit* that resurfaces elsewhere – left, right and centre in political rhetoric and political theory – but it is difficult all the same not to sense its presence in some aspects of Marx's harmonism.[19]

Simmel, then, makes it explicit that he approves of exchange and separation.[20] From the vantage points of the theory in *Philosophy of Money*, Marx begins to look a little like a medievalist, and this not only because he identifies labour as the *substance* of the commodity. Marx is also, as I have argued in *Labour's Utopias*, an avant-garde guild socialist, drawn at least in part to the conceptual harmonics of a closed communitarianism.[21] This is a matter of an interpretative tendency, not an iron law, in Marx's theory; again, it can be observed that an exception or contraindication to this tendency can be found in the *Grundrisse*, where work is read as necessity and freedom is rendered in ways that seem more appropriately projectual and modern. But the Bolsheviks did not read the *Grundrisse*.

The power of Simmel's text, then, lies in the ambivalence of its modernism. Simmel understands that, in Tönnies's terms, different socialist traditions and claims flow both back and forward, to *Gemeinschaft* and to *Gesellschaft*.[22] That is why money also cuts both ways. Money is expressive of modernity in that it encapsulates the ambivalence of modernity itself. Thus money at the same time facilitates freedom from patronage, only primarily as negative freedom.[23] So just as Weber discerns an affinity but not an identity between capitalism and democracy, Simmel claims a parallel between money and liberalism yet also notes the coincidence between money and tyranny.[24] In the end, figurat-

---

19   Beilharz 1992a.
20   Simmel 1978, p. 456.
21   Simmel 1978, p. 343; Beilharz, 1992a.
22   Simmel 1978, p. 346.
23   Simmel 1978, p. 400.
24   Simmel 1978, p. 495.

ively speaking, money is a sign of the tragedy of modern culture, a symbol of calculation and the reign of utility. Modernity, for Simmel, is dominated by law, intellectualism and money. Our lives as moderns are governed by number and by writing. This is evidently a path of thinking that runs somewhere between those of Marx and Weber, even as it arcs across them.

Bolshevism and Money

Now to the third step: Bolshevism. To introduce the idea or tradition of Bolshevism at this point of the argument is evidently to change register, from the criticism of individual projects in the case of Marx and Simmel to politically driven radical traditions which, in this case, followed Marx and whose purpose was less clear-thinking than the seizure of state power. To simplify the procedure I shall focus on several representative thinkers, Lenin, and Bukharin and Preobrazhensky, and on the experience of war communism as a frame. And it is that remarkable experience that throws the whole question of marxism and money into relief. Evidently social collapse goes together with apocalyptic thinking. But what might it mean, then, actually to envisage the end of money?

In the face of war communism we have to feel astonished, for this was more like primitive communism in a state of absolute scarcity than anything Marx associated with socialism. Marx's fantasy concerning the abolition of money may have a medieval or Renaissance flavour, but the claims of his theoretical thinking identify abundance as the necessary prerequisite in a setting that is at least industrial if not postindustrial. That Russians should have become marxists is one thing; that they could seriously have entertained the idea of the end of money after 1917 is another. Certainly the radical collapse of currency in situations of social crisis will jeopardise the status of money and inflate informal and criminal economic activity; only the conventional response is not to destroy money but to refloat and relegitimate it and the public life it helps to animate as well as constrain. Doubtless, then, relations of barter emerged to replace the collapse of money relations in the newly founded Soviet Union, and there are some understandable coincidences between the collapse of currency and arguments for the end of money. Yet more generally, it should be added that the literature of the period manifests a kind of scholasticism that is frightening, whether it be viewed as medieval and fundamentalist or modern and excessively cerebral. The leading Bolsheviks in this connection, Lenin, Bukharin and Preobrazhensky, knew their marxist texts by heart. The sense given by their own texts, today, is often like that provoked by mainstream economics, a preference for abstraction and modelling at the expense of all else, all other ways of knowing or spheres of existence.

Consider Lenin's great libertarian text, 'State and Revolution' (1917). Lenin uses Marx's critique of Lassalle in *Critique of the Gotha Programme* in order to ridicule the idea that workers could ever recover the full product of their labour-time under socialism. There has to be a reserve fund, which might in a different discourse or in a less charged situation be referred to as social capital. But then Lenin, who usually has at least one foot on the planet he stands astride with a broom, shifts into discussion of the transition to socialism. Lenin is emphatic that there is to be no money under communism, though he offers the dispensation that exceptions may be made under socialism, the preparatory phase or the transition to the transition. After nationalisation, in the first phase of socialism, every member of society performs part of the socially necessary labour, and each receives a time certificate from society (no state here) to the effect that he has done a certain amount of publically valorised work. With this certificate he receives from the public store of consumer goods a corresponding quantity of products. After a deduction is made for the public fund, to pay for Lassalle's pension, every worker therefore receives from society as much as he has given it.[25] No exploitation occurs, and no money (strictly speaking) changes hands. The whole of society becomes a single office and a single factory.[26] The proposals of Lenin evidently hang together; many took them very seriously, especially radicals in the capitalist west. Yet even in this immodest if uninspiring picture of Utopia money would be necessary. For time certificates, Marx and Simmel agree, are money by another name, socialist money at the least.

The Bolsheviks did not read Marx's *Grundrisse*, but they did read (or their followers read) Lenin's 'State and Revolution' (in any case, the Bolsheviks themselves had more urgent tasks to attend to). 'State and Revolution' was (if I recollect) one of Lenin's first texts to arrive in the antipodes. Its syndicalist impulses were resonant, it is worth remembering, with the influential views of the Industrial Workers of the World, who among other things were engaged at this point in time in the practice of counterfeiting in order to discredit the power of the bourgeoisie (Stalin had plainer views; he simply took the money and ran). In Australia and elsewhere those whose lives were turned by the October Revolution also read Bukharin and Preobrazhensky's primer, *The A B C of Communism* (1919), a title waiting for Orwell if ever there was one. There we read the following:

---

25   Lenin, 1977b, p. 470.
26   Lenin, 1977b, p. 479.

Communist society will know nothing of money. Every worker will produce goods for the general welfare. He will not receive any certificate to
the effect that he has delivered the product to society; he will receive no
money, that is to say. In like manner, he will pay no money to society when
he receives whatever he requires from the common store.[27]

Already by the Russian Revolution the analytical distinction had hardened,
between the first and the second stage of socialism or communism. Under
'socialism', the first stage of the transition, it is assumed that money will still
exist. Peasants, those quintessential representatives of backwardness, will still
use money, and of course money remains practically useful because it facilitates taxation.[28] However, in characteristic Bolshevik logic it is assumed that
there *is* a transition underway. 'Socialism ... is communism in the course of construction; it is incomplete communism ... from the very outset of the socialist
revolution money begins to lose its significance'.[29] Money will become worthless; there will be no black economy; such are the strident assurances we receive
from these commissars of theory. However, it may also be the case, we are told,
that money will not completely disappear until small-scale industry itself disappears.[30] This is Kautsky's revenge, the class bipolarisation theory of Marx
turned into guarantee; there will be no peasants, or small industry; where there
was bourgeoisie, there shall be proletariat, workers all, not a Bolshevik in sight,
politics an absent presence.

   The 'further reading' section that is appended to each chapter of *The ABC
of Communism* in this case laments that 'there is very little literature dealing with this subject'. Yet the confidence of the Bolsheviks is disarming. The
work of Marx here, incomplete though reformed as catechism, is taken as sufficient proof that money is something we can do without. And remember, this
advice is offered as good in the very period of war communism when the state
nationalised virtually all industry, outlawed private trade, forcibly prevented
the peasants from marketing their own products and sought to requisition
surpluses, when money lost virtually all value, industrial production declined
dramatically and towns starved to the extent that there was not only a revival of
cannibalism but also the development of markets in human meat. The tragedy
of the human condition here is only compounded by the tragic irrelevance
of Bolshevism to its conjuncture, at least until the introduction of the New

---

27   Bukharin and Preobrazhensky, 1967, p. 333.
28   Bukharin and Preobrazhensky, 1967, p. 334.
29   Bukharin and Preobrazhensky, 1967, p. 335.
30   Bukharin and Preobrazhensky, 1967, p. 336.

Economic Policy in 1921. How could Bolshevism have been so astral in its imaginary industrialism when the heavily agrarian economy was in tatters? One is
reminded here of Castoriadis's maxim, that we ought first of all to read Marx's
Capital in the light of Russian history and not Russian history in the light of *Capital*. A more pragmatic observation might be that just as socialists until Gramsci
seemed unable to discern that chaos led to barbarism rather than to socialism,
so were socialists throughout the west incredibly slow to realise how dangerous a social phenomenon inflation was, not only for Weimar in the 1920s but
also for Australians living on fixed incomes after the 1970s. This may well be
to digress, although one wonders about the surrealism of a great deal of radical
argument since Marx. The more central issue, in this context, concerns the conceptual inflation of money and abstraction in modern culture. Alongside the
overwhelming ghosts of alienation and reification are the ghosts we ourselves
generate, of scholasticism, of surplus abstraction, too much time spent with
books or, rather, failing to place and distance texts in the worlds we actually also
inhabit. It seems too simple to put it in this way, but we need to learn to live with
books, rather than through them, to learn as Castoriadis intimates from what
Bolshevism became, not what it promised us and generations before us who
took the tradition at its word.

Some final observations by way of conclusion. My concern here has been to
work around a series of propositions regarding money via the ideas of Marx,
Simmel and Bolshevism. Perhaps I should confess to an interest in this, at
least inasmuch as for some years in my youth I was convinced by Marx's case.
More and more it now seems to me that Marx's politics are hopeless precisely
because they are too full of hope, because they rest on a minimal or negative
sociology and far too readily become redemptive. More recently, in *Labour's
Utopias – Bolshevism, Fabianism, Social Democracy* (1992) I have defended German Social Democrats like Kautsky against the dominant reading, partly on
the grounds that their project might be characterised beyond its early or naive
sociology as one of Weberian marxism, which suggests a politics of critical
affirmation. Simmel's project, similarly, seems to me to be suggestive of this
kind of project, where for example money has its place – if only it would keep
to it.

There are other positions that are within marxism but outside of Bolshevism that may also be useful here, including for example Hilferding's *Finance
Capital* (1910), a major work suggesting (in effect) that finance capital may not
be the final stage of capitalism but the first form of organised capitalism (and
organised capitalism, of course, is also always disorganised; these terms should
not, *pace* Lash and Urry, be taken to represent societal types). More generally, as
others such as Ritzer have insisted, to puzzle over money today is necessarily to

puzzle over credit, the simulacrum that holds life in the west together. There is a different, and in a sense more fundamental, challenge, as well, to rethink and to place informal economy as a major sphere of modernity; and here my argument would simply be that the dominance of excessively formal conceptions of public economy has marginalised illegal or subterranean activity, which also holds the contemporary world-system up.

Finally, when it comes to money in particular, and more generally, Marx's own sociology points in at least two different directions. Marx's utopian projections fairly uniformly indicate the possibility of increasing the simplicity of social forms and relations. Other marxian tropes, like those of the sorcerer's apprentice in the *Communist Manifesto*, the ghosts of the past in the *Eighteenth Brumaire* or the commodity fetish in *Capital*, indicate rather that humans increasingly develop the propensity to encourage social relations and forms of thickened opacity. The latter, I think, is a far more fecund if frustrating line of thought. Marx agrees with Simmel that modernity rests upon commodification and on increasing abstraction. Since the close of their own fin-de-siècle and the opening of ours, senses of social opacity have expanded beyond imagination. Information technology is part of that process, but so is the multiplication of individual identities, the escalation of geographical mobility and social speed, and the dislocation of sense of place that earlier suggested coincidence between actors, forms of association and interests. We do not now know of any apparent ways to break this magic spell. The challenge then becomes more appropriately modest. As Richard Tawney put it, in the vernacular of his own English location between the great wars, money is like muck, or shit. The point is not to destroy it, but to make it useful by spreading it around. A modest aim, by comparison to Marx's; yet at the end of the twentieth century, it is perhaps not too great a concession to admit that those who ask for everything risk getting nothing. The fate of our lives is to live with ambivalence, and to begin to sort out what this might mean.

CHAPTER 4

Marx, Modernity and Motion (2011)

It all started with Marx.

Did it all start with Marx?

Maybe not, but Marx is a good place to start. Marx, that son of the loco-motive, Marx, who spoke of revolution as the locomotive of history, of mod-ernity as revolution, an idea thoroughly anticipated by Thomas Carlyle.[1] Steam power and trains figure centrally in all this. The cultural revolution of modern-ity arrived with the train. There it is, in Dickens, in *Dombey and Son*, in Gaskell's Cranford novellas. There it is, disruptor and pollutant, in Turner's *Rain, Steam and Speed* (1844), jostling with the Roman aqueduct, threatening to crowd out the scene and soil the neighbourhood, or the image of pristine, auratic nature. The image of the locomotive prostrate was traumatic for the young Weber, still during Marx's lifetime, and miles away from the English locus of the Industrial Revolution. Dickens also encountered the experience of train trauma. Trains brought distress.

So it didn't all start with Marx.

No, but Marx is a good place to start. Because it started around Marx.

That famous image from *The Communist Manifesto* is a good place to start. Marshall Berman made a career out of it: 'All that is solid melts into air'. The irony is that this is a licentious translation, which owes more to *The Tempest* than to Marx's text (Engels drafted a prior version, 'Principles of Commun-ism', a catechism that bears little relation to the final text). Shakespeare's words appear as: 'Our revels now are ended. These our actors,/As I foretold you, were all spirits, and/Are melted into air, into thin air' (4.1.147).

Marx's German is conceptually much tighter, his thinking smaller than this; he is not making an ontological claim about humanity, or modernity, but an ambit claim about the capitalist revolution that arrives with steam, whether in locomotion or in factory production. Yet his world, like Shakespeare's and Goethe's, is populated by ghosts, spectres, masking and magic. And if the spirit of capitalism was naked, the magic of the commodity-form introduced capital's own special system of enchantment.

The original is less fully evocative than the title of Berman's book indic-ates. Marx says in German, *'Alles Stehende und Standische verdampft'*. All that

---

1 Hogan 1995.

is standing and estate like, of the old feudal world, turns into steam, into vapour. Steam is the driver of the two most significant early modern technologies: of steam-powered machine production, and of the train. Both the early satanic mills and those monstrous contraptions portrayed by Turner were steam-powered. Samuel Moore's enthusiastic overtranslation of Marx nevertheless has wings. It is a powerful image, suggestive of the power of capital as creative destruction long before Werner Sombart or Joseph Schumpeter put a specific name to this idea of capitalist revolution.

So it all started with steam, historically. Theoretically, it all started somewhere else.

It all started with Newton.

Did it all start with Newton? Maybe.

Before locomotion, it all started with motion.

In the 1970s, the Left critique of Marx identified the enthusiasm for 'lawfulness' as a weakness, a sign of the positivist or scientistic times.[2] What was less apparent, when some worried over 'laws' or 'laws of tendency' of capitalist development, 'relative autonomy' and all the rest, was that Marx in *Capital* chooses to establish the laws of motion of capital. The idea of motion, likely, is more productive than that of laws, of lawfulness. What is capital? It moves. It depends on the process of self-valorisation, or else it falls over.

Newton commences from the possibility that there are distinct kinds of motion, linear and circular; and this is already apparent in the development of the idea of revolution, which can be constellational or linear, given to repetition or to progressive development or even to rupture. Certainly Marx retains a sense that history might be governed by repetition, as tragedy, farce and so on, wearing the masks of the past as it stumbles into the future. Marx does not have an image of history as eloquent as that of Benjamin's Angel, but then his moment was different. What becomes infectious in Marx is the idea of capitalism as permanent revolution, *perpetuum mobile*, the self-driven driver, the force of perpetual motion, a force right out of Newton's universe. Although Marx does not employ the words, the image and potential of creative destruction is clearly implicit in the dramaturgy of *The Communist Manifesto*. Capitalism is a self-driven force: like the vampire, it depends for its lifeblood on labour, but it also cannot stand still. Capital is defined by its need for expansion, for self-valorisation; once set in motion, it can no longer be controlled. The capitalist revolution is irreversible, like a runaway train, even though the young Marx still thought that it might be possible to go back, to greener days.

---

2   Thompson 1978b.

The imagery of revolution here could be further unpacked. Newton maps the laws of physical motion in the *Principia*; Marx extends this imagery to the laws of economic movement in *Capital*. But for Newton, to use a later language, what these laws suggest is systemic reproduction. Marx also describes system reproduction, but against his will, for what he really wants to demonstrate is the collapse of capitalism. The scientist in Marx gets the better of the revolutionary. Both these mechanisms, in Newton and Marx, revolve around a centre or origin. Marx explains the revolution of capital better as recurrence than as the rupture of his political desire. Marx wants two new revolutions – the revolution of capital and the revolution against capital that results in socialism. Marx wants a new kind of revolution, but what he explains is the old, circular kind. He fails to resolve this fundamental tension between revolution and repetition.[3] Unable to renounce his dream, he then finally reinserts the revolutionary politics of *The Communist Manifesto* into the penultimate chapter of *Capital*, where revolution as rupture arrives unannounced. But Marx is closer to Newton than he thinks.

Marx's revolution in permanence becomes capital's permanent revolution. The swirl of modernity takes all in its path. While Berman squeezed a book, *All That is Solid Melts into Air*, out of the phrase 'all that is solid', the other, more resonant image in Marx, in the *Manifesto*, remains that of the sorcerer's apprentice. Marx's literary source (or that of his translator) here is not Shakespeare's *Tempest* but Goethe's *Faust*, where the bourgeoisie remodels the world in its own image: nothing is sacred. Its overpowering image, and that of *The Communist Manifesto*, is that of a socially or politically licensed choice which inevitably runs out of control, and becomes irreversible. The imagery crosses over Goethe and Shakespeare. Marx refers to Faust the developer, but his sorcerer is not a magician. The word he uses is not Zauberer, it is Hexenmeister, a master of witches.

> A similar movement is going on before our own eyes. Modern bourgeois society with its relations of production, of exchange and property, a society that has conjured up such gigantic means of production and of exchange, is like the sorcerer, who is no longer able to control the powers of the nether world which he has called up by his spells.[4]

---

3   Mehlman, 1977; Beilharz, 2005b, 2005c.
4   Marx and Engels 1848, p. 38.

From Goethe, to Marx, to Frankenstein, to Fritz Lang's *Metropolis*, finally to Mickey Mouse in Disney's *Fantasia*, to contemporary sociology in the work of a figure like Zygmunt Bauman we cannot escape from the image of a society (or an economic regime) out of control. We no longer await for the sorcerer to return, to undo the damage done by the apprentice. We no longer know who started it; it all seems beyond authorship, although we still suspect that it all came from that moment, when it was in the beginning that there was the deed.

Did it all then start with Goethe?

It all started with locomotion.

It all started with locomotion, then it accelerated with automotion. As Wolfgang Schivelbusch puts it in his remarkable work, *The Railway Journey: The Industrialization of Time and Space in the Nineteenth Century*, it all began with the mechanisation of motive power. As Schivelbusch[5] observes, this was a revolution. In the economic life of the pre-industrial era, as he puts it, wood was the prime material, universally used in construction and combustion. Wood was organic; steam was manufactured, and manufacturing. Trains were described as projectiles. Patterns of stimuli morphed. But more, as Schivelbusch explains, steam brought a cultural revolution with it, or else humans organised a cultural revolution around it. Traffic on the waterways was still governed by organic time, although steam power had its accelerating effect there, too, as the revolution in the canal system anticipated that on land by rail. Steam power seemed in contrast to be independent of nature.

Time could be more closely regulated, and this in turn necessitated the revolutionisation of time through a standard system of time calculation. The locomotive gives you Greenwich time. More, as writers such as de Quincey began to anticipate, steam opened a new sublime, which was much later popularised by technology historian David Nye as the industrial sublime.[6] Trains transformed landscapes, as Turner had anticipated, through levelling, cuttings and embankments. Railroad travel annihilated time and space, even as it constructed them. It coincided with the architectural revolution that opened, symbolically, with the Crystal Palace in 1851, then gave us those early cathedrals of capitalism and modernity, the great railway stations.

Everyday life was transformed as a result. As Schivelbusch narrates the process, Hachette began to produce books that could be read on trains. It was not only reading that was transformed. Patterns of social intimacy and social

---

5   Schivelbusch 1979, p. 1.

6   Nye 1994.

intercourse were opened up (and some closed) by the compulsory proximity afforded by train compartments. Travellers could pick up not only little books to read or to pretend to read or to be distracted by, they could also pick up friends or lovers. Train compartments might even be democratic spaces, even, exactly, as they were segregated by class and sometimes by race and gender. They would introduce new patterns of the evasion of sociability as well as conversation; people would learn to hide behind newspapers, just as they now hide behind their earpieces. Trains became places of crime, disguised by noise and motion. The American open carriage addressed some of these problems by introducing serried ranks rather than compartments, and what we would now call airline seating to maximise privacy.

In the USA the railroads were the carrier of industrialisation, rather than the consequence of it. But the maladies of train travel were more frequently worried over in Europe than in America. Americans, as commentators from Alexis de Tocqueville on observed, were more than happy to move, to escape, to change, to go West or elsewhere. Anxieties spread about fatigue and excessive stimulation. Accidents! Noise! Trauma! Railway spine! As Schivelbusch observes, there are some uncanny resonances of these narratives again, here, in the work of Marx. As he puts it, in *Das Kapital* Marx provides a definition of economic crisis that reads like a translation of the technological accident back into the economic sphere. In the nineteenth-century perception, the cause of technological accidents was the sudden disturbance of the uncertain equilibrium of the machine, or the relationship between curbed energy and the means of curbing it. Marx defined the economic crisis as the disruption of the uncertain balance between buying and selling in the circulation of goods.[7] The model of society, or certainly that of the economy, has by this stage become mechanical. If society, or economy, stops in this way of thinking or is interrupted, it will fall over. More, as Schivelbusch indicates (although he hints at this as a possible research project, and barely enters into the matter), the possible connection between Marx and Freud opens at this point. Accident and crisis point to neurosis.

Freud's was an anticipation of another modernity, a modernity whose psychodynamics were to precede Marx's. Like Max Weber's world, Freud connects us into the twentieth century. Here automation, rather than locomotion, would become the carrier and motive force of modernity.

If the Crystal Palace was one symbolic harbinger of what would be the locomotive age, the 1893 Chicago World's Columbian Exposition would sit at the

---

7   Schivelbusch 1979, p. 132.

opening of the automotive era, even if that was motored out of Detroit rather than Chicago. The best parallel work to Schivelbusch here is by Marco D'Eramo, *The Pig and the Skyscraper. Chicago: A History of Our Future*.[8]

The American transition from railroad to highway was itself little short of revolutionary. As D'Eramo observes, Chicago in the nineteenth century was originally a 'railroad republic'. As he puts it, 'railroad' in this moment might stand for the kind of communism that aims to impose a programme for the national economy as rigorous and inflexible as was a national railway timetable, the very prototype of centralised planning.

For Marx, it all started in Manchester. For D'Eramo, it all started in Chicago, or at least Chicago is as good a carrier as you can find for the story of early modernity. Commissar Trotsky led the Russian Revolution, or at best the civil war, from his locomotives: two of them, one at the head, one at the tail of his carriages. This was a different kind of railroad communism. Railroad capitalism was highly regulated, high density, coordinated time and timetabling, big factories and offices. As D'Eramo[9] reminds us, this is the image bank of Chaplin's *Modern Times*.

'Car capitalism' produces a radical decentring and derailment. With cars and trucks low-density points can easily be connected. Suburban networks replace urban nodes. This is the American, or what we think of as the Californian, pattern of settlement. 'Capitalism on wheels' gives you suburbia, malls, strip shopping, sprawl. In Chicago or Detroit Grand Central Station falls into ruins; it is replaced by the modern maze of the Los Angeles freeway and in turn by the shine and postmodern muzak of O'Hare Airport.

Chicago pioneers Fordism, but with the Fordism of food production. Chicago pioneers both the pig and the skyscraper. This is a field that has found its best critic in Eric Schlosser, in *Fast Food Nation*.[10] The conveyor belt can be traced well back beyond Ford and Taylor, but one of its signal moments arrives with the abattoir. As D'Eramo has it, the disassembly line precedes the assembly line. At peak, 126 men would work on the Chicago disassembly line to butcher a single pig.[11]

But if Chicago pioneered pig, skyscraper and even futures trading, the industrial image we have of modernity emerges from Detroit. If the nineteenth century was the century of the locomotive, the twentieth was the century of the automobile. Taylor was its early analyst and advocate. Ford was its champion,

8   D'Eramo 2001.
9   D'Eramo 2001.
10   D'Eramo 2001.
11   D'Eramo, 2001, pp. 28, 33.

in Highland Park and River Rouge. Albert Kahn was its architect and Charles Sheeler its artist.

Yet Ford was also on the cusp of the modern. Greg Grandin shows this especially well in *Fordlandia*,[12] his analysis of Ford's Brazilian utopia in the 1930s. Henry Ford never stopped being a small-town boy, with small-town prejudices, even as the mode of production he became identified with dragged American localism and parochialism into the new age. Lured into the Amazon Basin by megalo narcissism, Ford wanted to control all the materials supply lines that went into the Model A Ford. The resulting mega capitalist organisation was also, as D'Eramo has it of the railroad system before it, a kind of communism that sought to impose a national and even imperial grid and model onto the topography and culture of Detroit and the world. It resulted in massive administrative overreach as well as hubris. And its reach took it well into the depths of the Soviet Union, as in the planning and construction of Magnitogorsk; Albert Kahn again, as in Detroit, as in Brazil. There was a Fordist imagination that came together with the project, and its ambition was universal.

Detroit became famous as Motor City. Ford built an infrastructure around it that made it clear: his project was the New Man, and this is why Gramsci[13] identified this pattern of modernity as Fordism, in particular. Its result was proverbially that of the sorcerer's apprentice. For Ford's desire for 'small-town' was ruthlessly squashed under the wheels of the automotive juggernaut. The automotive revolution matched the locomotive revolution, and outpaced it, reconfiguring urban and suburban structure and everyday life, leaving cities like downtown Detroit looking like the backblocks of the tornado tunnel.

In Detroit Ford was known as the 'sociologist manufacturer', but 'Fordism' was a proletarian swear word, and not only a Gramscian or German (or Soviet) category. Then General Motors outmanoeuvred Ford, and eventually the whole automobile industry came to its knees faced by Honda and BMW. But not before the face of the United States had been transformed and the automobile had become the creeping projectile representative of a civilisation choking on its emissions. The images of speed and beauty slowed up facing mothballs. Those postwar cars built in the image of the space race and aerodynamics stalled on the freeways of Disneyland, or were dug into the earth by artists who wanted to bury them.

So, did it all start with Marx?

---

12   Grandin 2009.
13   (1971)

Maybe. Perhaps with Leo Marx. In 1964 Leo Marx published a landmark book called *The Machine in the Garden: Technology and the Pastoral Ideal in America*. This Marx's optic opens with Nathaniel Hawthorne's sleepy hollow in Concord, Massachusetts, and its invasion by the figure of the locomotive. As Leo Marx observes, this is a common plot device in this period: 1844, the year the other Marx boy writes his Paris Manuscripts. The pastoral idyll is shattered by the arrival of the Iron Horse. It represents Noise, Industry, Machinery ... modernity. It speaks of the invasion of Eden; and it recalls Blake and Wordsworth.[14]

It also emerges from an older tradition, linked back to Virgil. But it is a specific story about modernity, too. The first American railroad began operations in 1829. Like Carlyle, like Karl Marx, Hawthorne's real interest is psychic, cultural more than symbolic or political.[15] The question of the locomotive is what does it do to us, or our forebears? Does it change our nature, transform our very personalities? Leo Marx's personal expedition takes us back to *The Tempest* and its American and New World connections. This is not strictly Virgil.

Nor is all period American writing strictly pastoral. The message of *The Machine in the Garden* is not about the rejection of industrial modernity and its turbulence. It concerns rather the extraordinary capacity of American culture to hold these two images of modernity and tradition together. Something had to change to make this possible. Jefferson, the early Mill and the early Karl Marx imagined the good society as based upon self-sufficiency, not growth. But like Ford, later, Jefferson's policies had the consequence of creating precisely the kind of society he did not want.[16] As Leo Marx says, it did not occur to Jefferson that the factory system was a necessary condition of technological progress. In 1786, the year after the first edition of *Notes on Virginia*, with its plea that workshops remain in Europe, Jefferson was in England. 'This was a moment, as Boulton put it in a letter to his collaborator, James Watt, when the population seemed to have gone "steam-mill mad"'.[17] Jefferson was also taken by the Newtonian moment. This was the moment of the orrery, the clock-work universe where everything moves in complete harmony.

The European intellectual response was less enthusiastic, or at least that part of it represented by thinkers like Schiller and Carlyle. Schiller bemoaned the culture of mechanical fragmentation in his *Letters on the Aesthetic Education of Man* (1795), itself a significant influence on Karl Marx. Carlyle developed one of the most powerful critiques of the mechanical *Signs of the Times*. By the 1840s

---

14   L. Marx 1964, p. 18.
15   L. Marx 1964, p. 28.
16   L. Marx 1964, p. 140.
17   L. Marx, 1964, p. 146.

the enthusiasm for the Machine, and the Locomotive, was also mounting. As Leo Marx[18] observes, the locomotive came to be the perfect symbol because its meaning need not be attached to it by a poet; it is inherent in its physical attributes, at least in the cultural context in which it emerges.

Marinetti modernised the image in 1909: 'deep-chested locomotives whose wheels paw the tracks like the hooves of enormous steel horses bridled by tubing; and the sleek flight of planes whose propellers chatter in the wind like banners and seem to cheer like an enthusiastic crowd', but more emphatically, in images at least as animate as mechanical:

> We say that the world's magnificence has been enriched by a new beauty; the beauty of speed. A racing car whose hood is adorned with great pipes, like serpents of explosive breath – a roaring car that seems to ride on grapeshot – is more beautiful than the Victory of Samothrace ... We want to hymn the man at the wheel, who hurls the lance of his spirit across the Earth, along its line of orbit.[19]

It was Alexander Pope, before Karl Marx, who wrote of the annihilation of time and space; and it was Leo Marx[20] who called the larger phenomenon the technological sublime. American culture first combined the locomotive and the pastoral. It was now represented by the giganticist expanse of Ford's River Rouge Plant, no more the Sleepy Hollow. It was no longer the prime mover, the figure of the locomotive or the automobile, that centred the canvas. The industrial universe instead spread, and human figures disappeared from it. Detroit collapsed, and industrialism went south, or east, where there would always be bodies pliant.

Did it all start with Marx? Who knows? Where will it end?

---

18   L. Marx 1964, p. 192.
19   Marinetti 1909.
20   L. Marx 1964 pp. 194–5.

CHAPTER 5

The Marxist Legacy (2011)

What is the fate of marxism, a hundred and fifty years after its original inception at the hands of Marx and Engels? The results of this story are mixed, and contradictory. On the one hand, marxism seems completely exhausted, expired, perhaps returned to the mainstream as the renewed common sense that capitalism is the central world power and protean agent of creative destruction. We are all Marxists now, perhaps again especially after the Global Meltdown. On the other hand, the status of marxism is newly marginal, at least in the hands of transatlantic university radicals, for whom marxism remains the truth. For marxism became the *de facto* consciousness of a good part of the global radical or university left in the 1960s, and its residual influence is still apparent but often unworldly.

At the beginning of the twentieth century, it was apparent that marxism had some significant influence in civil society, at least in countries such as Germany, where the Social Democratic Party claimed to enshrine Marxist values. But the SPD was, infamously, a society within a society, and socialism has long acted historically as the counterculture of modernity. At the end of the twentieth century the picture was unrecognisably different. After the Russian Revolution, which no one had expected in 1900, marxism became the ideology of Soviet state power. After 1989, the world power that was Soviet communism had disintegrated, and marxism was presented in the media as a museum piece. But then there was globalisation, and marxism again became a presence, as the mistranslated image of *The Communist Manifesto*, 'all that is solid melts into air', was rediscovered as the *urtext* of the creative destruction process itself. For the other side, meantime, for the opponents of marxism, Marx could be portrayed as the evil genius who somehow was vitally responsible for the Soviet disaster itself.

How do we find a way through all these trails and clues, to begin to make sense of the Marxist legacy today? This chapter makes five moves in this direction. The first, on Marx, addresses the moment of theoretical establishment. All discussion here must still begin from the question of the nature of Marx's project. The second section addresses the theoretical mainstreaming of marxism after Marx. Often referred to as the period of classical marxism, this centres on the experience of the German Social Democrats and the challenges they faced in seeking to reconcile reformist practice with (often) revolutionary rhetoric. But this moment was lost to vision, in effect, when the Bolsheviks seized

Russian state power in the name of Marx, and marxism henceforth was identified with Soviet state power, a political and historic elision from which the
emancipatory project of Marx would never recover. The third phrase discussed
here involves the revival of the marxian legacy, often via the heritage of critical theory, into the 1960s. Humanist marxism reemerged in this period, only
to be suppressed again in a fourth phase, here referred to as the Return of the
Hard Left. Under the influence of Louis Althusser and his followers, marxism
took a scientific and renewed Bolshevik, first pro-Soviet, then pro-Chinese turn.
Fifth, and finally for our purposes there, there is the intriguing and divided phenomenon of postmarxism, itself formed in the wake of the postmodern. The
postmarxist moment bifurcates into two streams, one of which is fundamentalist and revivalist, the other of which wears its marxism as a light cloak.

Marx's Project

Did Marx have a project, or is this a category we impose on his work, like that
of others, after the fact? There are many ways to read Marx, or various Marxes
available to us. If we begin from the necessary sense that Marx is the starting
point, then we also need to accept that we are all after Marx, and in this sense
we are all postmarxists, literally after Marx and after marxism, the latter understood as the world-historic project of transforming the world announced by
Marx in his 'Theses on Feuerbach'.

Marx can be read as poet, follower of world literature, journalist, revolutionary, historian, or philosophical anthropologist. These days we often classify him
as a sociologist, though that thought would never have occurred to him. One
way to identify the unity of his thought is to read it as the critique of political economy. This is one arc that holds together the major instalments of his
work, from the *Economic and Philosophical Manuscripts*[1] to the *Grundrisse*,[2] the
Contribution to the Critique of Political Economy[3] through to its culmination in
Capital.[4]

If economics was to become the dominant discipline into the twentieth century, political economy was already making this claim to hegemony a century
earlier. Of course its ambit was broader than that of economics. Political economy was a moral philosophy, that discourse which enquired into the origin

---

1 Marx 1975 [1844].
2 Marx 1973 [1857–8].
3 Marx 1970 [1859].
4 Marx 1965 [1867].

of new wealth and its social consequences. Marx's original critique of political economy was based on its failure to historicise. Rather than explaining capital as private property, political economy universalised it. Rather than viewing capital as a process, it viewed capital as the effective cause of labour, whereas in fact, Marx claimed, it was the other way around: labour produced capital, capital was only dead or stored-up labour. As he was later to suggest, capital was like the vampire or the werewolf that consumed labour without mercy. And this was to become a significant part of Marx's style, or dramaturgy, where images of magic, enchantment, and the supernatural all jostled together, where capitalism was a phenomenon like the world of the sorcerer's apprentice. The spells that had let loose these demonic forces could no longer easily be controlled or reversed. This, in turn, becomes a significant tension throughout Marx's work, where humans both have agency to change the world, and are simultaneously entrapped within processes beyond their ken and influence. But can we be both, at the same time, or only one or other?

Marx's early critique of political economy asserted the centrality of alienated labour to capitalism. The object of socialism, then, would be the pursuit of the autonomous or creative capacity to labour, to make the world through expression. This is what pitted Marx against 'primitive communism'. Socialism, for Marx, could only be imagined as the freely achieved results of the collective labourer. In this, while Marx is often pictured as the man of Enlightenment, he is also the best son of Romanticism.[5] For like Schiller, and differently, Rousseau, Marx dreams of a human wholeness, of a world before the division of labour and its cult of fragmentation. Marx's original utopia, concealed behind his and Engels's public disdain for writing recipes for the cook shops of the future, is plainly rural and romantic.[6] Marx's utopia only becomes grey, rather than green, as he himself adjusts to the sense of industrialism's permanency, its non-reversibility. While the younger Marx identifies freedom or autonomy with this sense of return to control over the labour process, the later Marx concedes that perhaps freedom may be found only outside labour, in the creative space made available by the free time afforded by automation. This is part of the fascination of Marx's work, that it changes colour irreversibly across the opening phase of the cultural revolution of modernity.

Marx and Engels confuse this situation by insisting that their position is that of communism, not socialism. This is proleptic, for as Durkheim showed in his Bordeaux lectures on socialism, the commune is passed; socialism, understood rather as the response to scale, complexity, and the need for regulation

---

5   Beilharz 1994.
6   Beilharz 1992a.

is modern, whereas the idea of communism historically rendered is indeed premodern. Marx and Engels sought what we would now call product differentiation, or at least distinction for their views. They wanted to insist not only that their view was distinct from that of the crackpot dreamers (seas of lemonade, etc.) of utopia, but also that their socialism was in some sense or other necessary or scientific, evolutionary, the necessary consequence of feudal and capitalist development and its crowning glory. Marx thus built his project on an unresolved tension between the need for action, revolutionary or other, and the dull compulsions of material life, where the working class had no alternative but to sell their labour in order to survive. His hopes for revolution were pinned on various possibilities, some voluntary, some structural. He believed that the association of labourers on the factory floor itself would encourage socialism; that it was necessary actively to change the world, not just to interpret it; that capitalism would collapse under the weight of its own contradictions, such as the tendency of the profit rate to fall; and that socialism would be the next, best evolutionary form for capitalist dynamism to take. He believed all these things at once, or at different moments of his life, or more precisely he left a series of hints as to possible sources of change without ever developing a coherent theory of revolution.[7]

Marx projected revolutionary capacity onto the proletariat itself. Socialism became the world-historic vocation of the proletariat. But the wage-slaves remained tied to the wheel, and then later, after the postwar boom, their political and labour representatives became the best lieutenants of capitalist expansion.[8] One thing, however, that Marx did not do, in all this, was develop a theory of the vanguard party. The essential revolutionary sympathy of Marx is with the idea of working-class self-activity or capitalist collapse leading to socialism. Very few Marxists, Russians included, believed in the combat communist party, the object of which was to seize state power, before 1917. Even Trotsky was still sympathetic to menshevism, or the reforming stream in Russian marxism. The idea of the combat or conspirational party, 'one wise man worth a hundred fools', arrived only with Lenin in *What Is To Be Done?*[9] And even Lenin adhered to the principles of classical marxism in his greater achievement, *The Development of Capitalism in Russia*.[10]

---

7   Draper 1977.
8   Bauman 1972.
9   Lenin 1902.
10   Lenin 1899.

Marxism after Marx

Marx died in 1883. It was only after his death that marxism became identified with a party, or movement: the German Social Democratic Party. Karl Marx called himself a communist, but he was no Bolshevik. He would have called himself a revolutionary, but he was no putschist.

Engels died in 1895. By that stage, Engels had conceded the possibility of an electoral or parliamentary road to socialism. Indeed, if the proletariat made up the vast majority of the population, why should they not simply vote socialism in, once the popular franchise had been sufficiently expanded? This was the context for the formation of classical marxism.

The SPD combined any number of political tendencies, but it is conventional to differentiate between three. One was represented by Rosa Luxemburg, a spontaneist revolutionary in the spirit of Marx, an opponent of what she called 'barracks socialism' but a revolutionary all the same. By the dawn of the new century, the status quo in the SPD was predictable but embarrassing. It was a party of reform, but with revolutionary credentials. It worked through the networks of civil society, generating a thick, alternative culture of clubs, societies, mutual aid facilities, and so on. But it never put away the Sunday china which called for Revolution. This is where the standard jokes about pragmatic socialists come from: parlour pinks, or else like radishes, red on the outside, white on the inside. Luxemburg's revolutionary response was to demand that the SPD's politics be brought into line with its rhetoric. If it claimed to be revolutionary, then the SPD should be prepared to behave in a revolutionary way. The best representative of the second view, the reformist, or right-wing alternative, was Eduard Bernstein. Bernstein called not only for reform, for the adjustment of rhetoric towards the reformist practice of the SPD, but also for revision, for the rejection of Marx's axioms about class bipolarisation and the alleged decline of the middle class. As far as Bernstein could see, the middle class was expanding. And marxism, or social democracy, would need to factor this vital change into its worldview and practice if it was to have a significant effect on the world locally, in Germany.

The third dominant position in the SPD, which in a sense was hegemonic, was associated with the views of the 'Pope of Marxism', Karl Kautsky. Kautsky was happy to sit on the contradiction, to argue for the necessity of maintaining revolutionary rhetoric and reformist practice. Comrades could live with contradiction. 'We are a revolutionary, but not a revolution-making party'. Kautsky held onto the automatic theme in Marx, where in the fullness of time socialism would emerge, later. Always later. As August Bebel, another Social Democratic father put it, socialism would drop into our laps like a ripe fruit. And this, indeed, was widespread Marxist commonsense until the political arrival, later in Italy, of Antonio Gramsci. Gramsci's great realisation was that, left to itself, the way the world worked was that the other guys won; or to put it more precisely, whoever mobilised hegemony successfully would win. Gramsci returned marxism, in a sense, to its 1840s inflexion in Marx's project. Here, will was everything; necessity was a theological category, and the idea that socialism would necessarily arrive by itself was a political disaster, an invitation to reaction or at least to the reactionaries at the door.

The achievement of German Social Democracy was thus an extraordinary combination of institution- and culture-building in this world, held together with the redemptive or religious belief in the coming of the new world. This German culture in turn dominated that of the Second International. The Second International collapsed in August 1914, after German SPD parliamentary representatives voted for war credits, and the hope of internationalism foundered on that great emergent reality of the twentieth century, nationalism. But the dominance of the SPD in the world socialist movement was really punctured only in October 1917, when the Russian Bolsheviks took state power.

Enthusiasm for the Russian Revolution was initially widespread. After all, the Bolsheviks had done something, whereas the grand old men of social democracy only ever talked about it. While Gramsci was not a hard Leninist, he too enthused for the radical and voluntarist nature of the breach they had entered into. Gramsci indicated this in an essay entitled 'The Revolution Against Capital'.[11] His argument was twofold. The Russian Revolution was a revolution against capital, but it was also a revolution against the complacency that had followed *Das Kapital*. Waiting for the revolution had finally been shown as the sham it was; the Bolsheviks had shown the will to act, to lead.

Gramsci's own enthusiasm got the better of him. The Russian Revolution was not a Revolution Against Capital, but a revolution against a decadent feudalism with some major nodes of capitalist development forming within it. This was precisely Gramsci's later insight, that while it was courageous, the Bolshevik Revolution really just pushed over a rotting Tsarist edifice. This meant that the enormity and ultimate impossibility of the task that the Bolsheviks had set themselves only slowly became apparent. After Lenin's death in 1924 and Trotsky's exile in 1927, Stalin set out to build the primary accumulation of capital in the Soviet Union by coercion and terror of a kind that made the Enclosure Acts pale into insignificance in their own levels of violence and destruction. Gram-

11   Gramsci 1975 [1918].

sci's insight shifted into the sense that, again contra Marx, the presenting issue for Marxists now was not the anatomy of political economy but the power and persuasion of civil society.

The banner and beacon of revolutionary marxism, meanwhile, was taken on by the lonely figure of Leon Trotsky. Originally in sympathy with the spontaneism and anti-Jacobinism of Rosa Luxemburg, Trotsky in power became the best of Bolsheviks.[12] Marginalised, expelled, and finally murdered by Stalin in Mexico City in 1940, Trotsky became the leader of the loyal opposition, and a major intellectual influence on the postwar left.[13] Always full of revolutionary optimism, Trotsky remained convinced that the conditions for world revolution were ripe, that all that was lacking was the appropriate kind of Trotskyist leadership. His advocacy of the idea and slogan of Permanent Revolution also indicated a doubling. One aspect of Permanent Revolution was the claimed inevitability of socialist revolution; whatever form a revolution initially now took, it would consequently grow over into socialist revolution. But second, all revolutions would spread globally; revolution could no longer be contained at national borders, except by the treachery of Stalin's 'socialism in one country'. Many of the finest left wing minds came to follow this position of Trotsky's, from Isaac Deutscher to Ernest Mandel, C.L.R. James, Raya Dunayevskaya, Perry Anderson, and *New Left Review* more generally. The sticking point, for this tradition, was to be found in the question of the nature of the Soviet Union, and whether the traditional categories of Marxist thinking could explain it. Was the Soviet Union, by the 1930s, still recognisably socialist? Should it rather be called capitalist, or state capitalist? Only the more innovative of thinkers, from Bruno Rizzi and James Burnham to Heller, Fehér, and Markus could step outside of the conventional Marxist categories in order to argue that Soviet societies were a new kind of modernity *sui generis*.[14] Whether analytically or politically, the Soviet Union had become a kind of fatal attraction for Marxists the world about. Yet some, from Kautsky on, had always refused the possibility that socialism could be built in the USSR. They were right, and Marx would have agreed with them. Socialism would come after capitalism, or it would not come at all.

---

12   Beilharz 1981b.
13   Beilharz 1987.
14   Fehér, Heller and Márkus, 1983.

The Marxian Legacy

If we understand Marx's project as the critique of political economy, a social-philosophical critical theory with an emancipatory intention, then its ethical distance from Bolshevism, let alone Stalinism, will be apparent. Yet the elision of these differences, and the careless identification of Marx and Bolshevism, remains. Marx is widely, and quite mistakenly viewed as a totalitarian. But even viewed simply as an historical trend, totalitarianism is twentieth century, Marx nineteenth, and while culture is fundamental, ideas do not themselves have this kind of causal effect. Marx wanted to change the world, or that we should ourselves change it, but what he bequeathed us intellectually was a critical theory with an emancipatory intent.

The idea of critical theory, in the context of the history of marxism, is usually associated with the Frankfurt School for Social Research. In terms of its reception, critical theory is often reduced to the cultural pessimism associated with works such as Horkheimer's and Adorno's *Dialectic of Enlightenment*[15] and Marcuse's *One-Dimensional Man*.[16] The Frankfurt School achieved much else beside,[17] but its main theses did indeed include this idea of modernity as entrapment, Marx plus Weber, as it were in the early period spirit of Kafka's *Metamorphosis*. Critical theory can indeed be viewed as Marx plus Weber, commodification plus rationalisation. Two earlier intellectual links helped to make this bond, well before *Dialectic of Enlightenment*, and long before critical theory became a kind of household word for radicals.

The first significant link in this process was provided by Georg Lukács, in his 1923 essay 'Reification and the Consciousness of the Proletariat'.[18] Lukács was a Hungarian marxist taken in by Weber to his Sunday circle. His essay was a brilliant synthesis of Marx's and Weber's themes of commodification and rationalisation, the more remarkable as it anticipated the motifs of Marx's Paris writings, unavailable in any language until 1932. Lukács' work anticipated the work of Karl Löwith, who in that year[19] pinned Weber and Marx together in his brilliant essay *Max Weber and Karl Marx*. Löwith viewed Marx and Weber not as combatants, as in the infamous image of Weber as 'the bourgeois Marx', but as social philosophers with a primary interest in the human condition in modernity. The difference between them, according to Löwith, was that they

15   Adorno and Horkheimer 1973 [1944].
16   Marcuse 1964.
17   Wiggershaus 1994.
18   Lukács 1971.
19   Löwith 1982 [1932].

characterised this condition differently – Marx through the image of alienation (the Paris writings now having become available), Weber through the
master-image of rationalisation.[20] Obviously there remained significant differences between Marx and Weber, not least those of disposition, over the ethics of
responsibility versus the ethics of ultimate ends, the respective weight given to
material and ideal factors in history and so on. Yet Marx's revolutionary rhetoric
became hollow when read against the fatalistic logic of the argument concerning commodity fetishism. The problem, for Marxists, seemed now to be that
we were stuck with capitalism, and that things only got worse when hothead
Bolsheviks tried to shortcircuit history by barging into 'socialism' now.

For the critical theorists the scenario was different. The German working-
class movement had failed to rise to the moment into the later 1920s. Even
without the disastrous experience of fascism, capitalism had shown enormous
resilience and integrative capacity. This argument was revived into the 1960s,
when Marx's early work became available in English, and student radicalism
peaked. Its best exemplification was in Marcuse's *One-Dimensional Man* (1964).
By this stage, the idea of totalitarianism, further popularised by Orwell's *1984*
(1948), had spread to the west. The inmates of modernity, or at least their radical
representatives, began to fear that totalitarianism was not specific to Stalinism
or Nazism, but was endemic to capitalism, even to modernity itself. The iron
cage was everywhere; conformism was abundant. The United States was bomb-
ing the daylights out of Vietnam, and governments such as that in Australia had
reintroduced military conscription. It may not have been totalitarian, but on
some days it seemed hard to tell.

Critical theory was sometimes teased for its aristocratic components, its
disinclination to praise popular culture, jazz or Americanism, its sometimes
overwhelming sense of cultural pessimism, and all these sentiments echo the
larger and older traditions of aristocratic radicalism, for which the old world,
in general, was better than the brashness and shock of the new. The European
critique of modernity was born as a critique of the mass, mass society, mass
production, mass migration, the mass man, the image of life based on the factory, on its regimentation and yesmen, the conformism of following orders. This
was also Marcuse's anxiety into the 1960s – that the ludic or erotic components
of being had been submerged into dull regimes of compliance, consumption,
and getting on. Perhaps this was the moment when sociology began to shift
its focus from the realm of production to that of consumption. Gramsci had
already anticipated the cultural turn in marxism thirty years earlier.

---

20   Ibid.

Marcuse was not the only high-profile critical theorist, though the fact that he remained in the USA after Horkheimer and Adorno returned to Germany placed him strategically to be more significantly influential into the 1960s. More, he wrote in jeremiad form, unlike the laconic and dense Adorno, anticipating, in this sense, the later popularity of Zygmunt Bauman, another critical Cassandra figure. The second generation of critical theory became associated especially with the work and figure of Jürgen Habermas, who turned back to the inspiration of Kantian universalism. Where Marcuse saw systemic closure and frustration, Habermas saw possibilities for change, reform, and democratisation. His early work drew together marxian and weberian themes and filaments, again seeking a critical theory with a practical or emancipatory intention in the manner of Marx.

Critical theory simultaneously began to pluralise in the East European regimes which had been established as extensions of the Soviet empire after World War Two. Into the 1960s dissident forms of humanist marxism were emerging in Yugoslavia, Czechoslovakia, Hungary, and Poland. In Hungary the students of Lukács formed the Budapest School, who like others held the radical principles of Marx against the state which claimed to rule in the name of Marx. Its leading figures – Agnes Heller, Ferenc Fehér, Ivan Szelenyi, George and Maria Markus – left to seek exile in Australia, where they made significant contributions to the critique of Soviet-type societies, among other things. Leading dissidents in Poland, including Zygmunt Bauman, Leszek Kołakowski and Wlodzimierz Brus, were 'allowed to leave' in 1969. The Yugoslav movement gave birth to *Praxis* and then to *Praxis International*. Of all these, Bauman perhaps became the most significant follower of the critical theory of modernity. His most influential mid-career book, *Modernity and the Holocaust*, both builds on and extends the classical Frankfurt tradition of *Dialectic of Enlightenment*.[21] Here modernity also turns back and feeds upon itself.[22]

These kinds of developments were more influential in the United States than in Britain. British marxism, powerfully influenced by *New Left Review*, began with some sympathy for radical humanism but soon cashed this in for the harder edge and stiffer scientific claims of Althusserian marxism. Journals like *Telos*, whose earlier sympathies were for phenomenological marxism, gave critical theory a better reception across the Atlantic, while purpose-built or dedicated journals like *New German Critique* also promoted critical theory and its co-currents and trends. *Telos* also further promoted the work of Gram-

---

21   Bauman 1989.
22   Beilharz 2000.

sci, which was kick-started in Australia by Alastair Davidson in 1968, three years before *Selections from the Prison Notebooks* became available.[23] Finally, *Telos* and then *Thesis Eleven* helped to profile the work of Cornelius Castoriadis, where the marxian project was reformed as the project of autonomy. As Dick Howard showed in his *Marxian Legacy*,[24] there was a libertarian line that ran from the young Marx through to Rosa Luxemburg, then later to Castoriadis. Raya Dunayevskaya had anticipated this lineage earlier, in significant period works such as *Marxism and Freedom*.[25] For these thinkers, socialism would be democratic or it would not be at all. Only this urging failed sufficiently to contemplate its own outcome: that it would not be at all.

The Hard Left

Humanism was a sitting duck for those with harder heads. What did it mean, to say that because we (or our forebears) had made this world, we could remake it, make it anew? Were there not harder structures or systems which would bounce back, fail to respond to hippie enthusiasms and the wash of good intentions? The hard left was not given to endorsing Marcuse, but they often seemed to share his sense that the beast of modernity (or rather, capitalism) would not respond to suggestion, or to the ballot box. Something more forceful, more revolutionary, would be required. The work of Louis Althusser offered the necessary toolkit. Althusser wanted marxism to be a science, and its politics to be revolutionary, the latter at least until the French events of May 1968, when revolution was made by Althusser to look more like a good idea than a practical project. Althusser intervened powerfully into a dispute which now likely looks arcane, but kept marxologists in work for a long time. This was the dispute over the Young versus the Mature Marx.

Into the 1960s the new Marx, the newly discovered Marx, was the Marx of the Paris Manuscripts. These are, as Marx once wrote to Engels in their later years, green, in contrast to the later grey of theory and the dull industrial culture of factory civilization which it sought to explain. Reading the young Marx was fun, more or less; reading *Capital*, in contrast, was hard work. Althusser sternly took on the duty of reading *Capital*, writing a very serious book called *Reading Capital*, and insisting that we should all read *Capital* seriously, in its multiple

---

23   Davidson, 1968; Gramsci, 1971.
24   Howard 1977.
25   Dunayevskaya 1982 [1958].

volumes, preferably in the original.[26] The early Marx was Marx before he was Marx, foreplay rather than the real action. *Capital* was taken to represent a new form of knowledge, building upon a significant epistemological break or rupture. We all became epistemologists. Nobody seemed to notice that this was a step away from practice, rather than towards it. But these were times of great seriosity, and high illusions, as well as very serious scholarship.

Yet there was something important in this mission. Marx's early writings give us the perspective of his laboratory. We can watch him thinking, and it can be an exhilarating experience. But his life's work was *Capital*, and the architectonic of that work repays serious close reading. Rightly or wrongly, Marx had become convinced that the mode of presentation of this work was crucial; that there was a best way to explain capital, and that he had sorted it out. He was also convinced that capital was the privileged category, to be accessed via the logic of the commodity form. It did seem something of an irony that none, or few, of the Marxists had read Marx, because it was too hard. And this was part and parcel of the story of the fate of marxism. Engels, Kautsky (the pope of Marxism), then Lenin, and finally Stalin had reduced Marx's theory to a series of axioms or platitudes about surplus value, historical and finally dialectical materialism. Marxists got by reciting these axioms in their daily denunciations of capitalism. Marxism had become its own caricature.

Althusser blew the whistle on this state of affairs. After Althusser, it was inadmissible for Marxists to cut corners. They were now compelled to deal with their own theoretical heritage. A few clichés concerning the ubiquity of alienation and the need for revolution would no longer do.

Some followed Althusser slavishly, replacing old clichés with new. Others such as Nicos Poulantzas took more interesting paths. Poulantzas picked upon some of the staples of Marxist sociology, such as class and the state, and history, with reference to the problems of fascism and dictatorship. But all of this ended badly. Poulantzas committed suicide, leaving a fine book, *State, Power, Socialism*,[27] which also responded to the legacy of Rosa Luxemburg. Althusser murdered his wife, and himself died a sad and lonely death.[28] Althusser flirted with Maoism; Poulantzas with the then significant European trend called Eurocommunism.

Across the Channel, Althusserianism had the peculiar echo-effect apparent in the work of Hindess and Hirst. They took on the period interest of Marxist historians and anthropologists in modes of production. Their initial pur-

---

26   Althusser and Balibar 1975.
27   Poulantzas 1978.
28   Althusser 1993.

pose was to generate a non-historical theory of history. As their collaboration eased, Hindess turned via Foucault to matters of political philosophy, Hirst to broad problems of radical English ideas, Thatcherism, and the critique of globalisation-talk.

One of the ironies of the Althusserian experiment was that while it was dismissive of history, in contrast to theory, historians drank here as well. Marxist history had been steered hitherto by humanists such as E.P. Thompson, who bombed Althusser in *The Poverty of Theory*.[29] Marxist historiography nevertheless became more sophisticated in dialogue with Althusser, as is evident in the work of the *Radical History Review* or *History Workshop Journal*. Stronger Marxist views like those of Immanuel Wallerstein, mediated by the work of the Annales School and Fernand Braudel, became highly influential as world-systems analysis via the Braudel Centre's *Review*. Althusserian marxism remains influential still today in journals such as *Rethinking Marxism*.

Alternative positions had been sketched out by culturally sensitive thinkers such as Henri Lefebvre in Paris and Stuart Hall in London. Marxism's influence spread out through the cultural turn, into cultural studies and later into geography and urban studies. The work of Castells helped to carry it through into work on networks, globalisation and the information society. The stiff edge of structural marxism shifted into the school called analytical marxism, where analytical logic was taken to be the vital supplement which would fill Marx's deficit or add the newly necessary ingredient. This is indeed one way to view the history of academic marxism, especially with its institutionalisation in western universities after World War Two. Marxists often respond to their predicament in an additive or supplementary manner. Some add phenomenology, some add structuralism. Some add epistemology, some add analytic logic or psychoanalysis or mathematics. Some seek to add culture, following Gramsci. The difference between this way of thinking, often fashion-prone and sometimes smelling of desperation, and the tradition of Critical Theory is that when Weber meets Marx the result is transformative, a synthesis of both theoretical perspectives. For critical theory, the contribution of Weber is not regional, but fundamental. It is not catalytic, but is itself transformed in the process. This might be one reason explaining its persistence.

---

29   Thompson 1978b.

Post-marxism

After Marx, there are the Marxists. Karl Marx famously denied that he was a Marxist. Then, after the Marxists, there are now the post-marxists. All this is historically necessary. We are all, now, after Marx, and in a different sense we are also after marxism, in its classical form. As a theoretical legacy, classical marxism in the manner of Kautsky persists. But in an historical sense, the classical marxism of the German Social Democrats is eclipsed by the victory of the Bolsheviks, who successfully appropriated the name of marxism for themselves. Into a bipolar, and then Cold War world, it suits both protagonists, American and Soviet alike, to identify marxism and Stalinism. Marxists, of course, persist, not least as the bearers of the Trotskyist illusion, that they are the true inheritors of Lenin and the loyal opposition. Castoriadis, himself momentarily a Trotskyist in the 1940s, later called Trotskyists 'the Stalinist bureaucracy in exile'. But while the remnants of marxism in this form still persist, there are also further developments, often characterised as post-marxism.

Postmarxism makes sense; if we are after Marx, we are also after marxism. The phenomenon bifurcates, however, and in this it follows the post-modern, whose semantics it extends from the realm of modernism and modernity into that of marxism.

Debates about the post-modern often split over the relative weight given to each term.[30] As Bernard Smith put it, post-modern enthusiasts often mistook the tail for the kite.[31] The modern was the kite, the post-modern its tail, rather than the other way around. In some arguments, the post was valued above the modern, which was now presented as archaic. In others, the post was merely the appendage, representing cultural forms in aesthetics and architecture which emerged after the collapse of the Long Boom. Similar differences in possibility emerge with the idea of the post-marxist.

All this takes on a different light, in addition, after the fall of the Berlin Wall in 1989 and the subsequent collapse of communism. A post-Soviet world is also, in a particular sense, a post-marxist world, though the subsequent triumph of capitalism also called out the revival of a kind of generalised marxism in the anti-WTO movement. Globalisation, ironically, revived the analytical fortunes of Marxists, as did the GFC and the return of the Spectre of Depression. In a perverse, historical sense Marx's triumph was best exemplified by the Chinese experience, where a residual kind of institutional marxism in the form of the

---

30   Beilharz 1994, 2010b.
31   Beilharz 1997, p. 159.

Chinese Communist Party went together with the victory of Chinese quasi-capitalist productive forces.

To be post-marxist, then, is in a sense now unavoidable. Some of the best Marxists have been historians, such as Bernard Smith and Eric Hobsbawm, or sociologists such as Stuart Hall, as well as geographers such as David Harvey or critical theorists such as Fred Jameson who have worn their categories lightly, combined interests in the critique of culture and power, taken technology as seriously as cultural development. Different radical journals, from *New Left Review* to *Thesis Eleven*, have worked the field after marxism in distinct ways. Other bodies of work, such as those associated with Laclau and Mouffe, have followed versions of the additive approach indicated above: add psychoanalysis, add Wittgenstein, add Schmitt. The exemplary, or foundational, text here was *Hegemony and Socialist Strategy* of Laclau and Mouffe,[32] where marxism and other intellectual currents are juxtaposed, perhaps, rather than integrated. But the predominant influence in post-marxism globally has been more stridently Marxist, less post- than Marxist.

The two most influential post-marxist contributions come from Žižek, and Negri and Hardt respectively. Both have developed cult-followings, and block-buster sales, and in the case of Žižek, cults of personality (try Youtube). Žižek's approach has also been additive (add Lacan, in particular) but also comedic (add Hitchcock, and jokes about Lenin). Žižek's approach is also contrarian, essentially provocative. Sometimes this style is defended as a kind of agonism; often it is simply offensive, as in Žižek's claim that Lenin (now without humour) was basically a nice guy who strayed into politics.[33] This is reminiscent of the Woody Allen joke in which Albert Speer is surprised to discover that Hitler was a Nazi.

Žižek's marxism is a kind of post-bolshevism rather than post-marxism, where the semantic weight falls on the Bolshevik rather than the post. In some circles he has been called a Bolshevik clown, though here the weight is on the adjective more than the noun.[34] Where Lenin in 1917 calls for socialism as electrification plus Soviets, Žižek today calls for socialism as free internet access plus Soviets. Neither seems especially likely.

Negri and Hardt offer a different kind of postmarxism, which perhaps is really best defined as neo-marxism, for its purpose is to renew and refresh the old, stale revolutionary project. Negri connects back to the Italian ultra-left tradition of the *autonomista*, where, in contrast to Castoriadis's more open

---

32   Laclau & Mouffe 1985.

33   Žižek 2002.

34   Žižek 2002; Beilharz 2005a.

and ontological use of the idea, it is workers' autonomy or autogestion that matters.[35] Negri also connects back to the notion of Engels, adopted by the Trotskyists C.L.R. James and Dunayevskaya into the 1950s, of 'the invading socialist society', for which the most powerful trend towards socialism apart from autonomous proletarian struggle is the internal evolution towards socialism within the heart of capitalism itself. Where others, earlier, viewed capitalism as doing socialism's work via the internal socialisation of capital, Negri and Hardt project this capacity onto globalisation. In contrast to the dominant, reactive mood of most radical critique of globalisation, their book *Empire*[36] returns to the axioms of automatic marxism, only Empire now itself lays the ground for socialism. Socialism, once again, is imagined as the egg or embryo of socialism within late capitalist developments. Immaterial labour, exemplified in the new communications technology, represents the promise of socialism in nuce. Little wonder that *Empire*, with or without the later added enthusiasm for the idea of the Multitude, should have been such a hit with a needy residual left. For it works like a kind of mosaical or magical marxism, reinstalling both spontaneism and revolutionary guarantees at the same time, bringing the millennium closer in ways that echo Cecil B. DeMille more than Karl Marx. The problem with this kind of automatic marxism is precisely that it is too Marxist, too orthodox in its millennial hope and desire to inscribe the future of socialism within the path of capitalist development. Yet again, it results in a combination of public militancy with a long-term strategy of waiting for the revolution.

Conclusion

What then, finally, was Marx's legacy? The specificity of the question is important. Marx's legacy: not Lenin's, or that of Bolshevism, or Marxism–Leninism. What is the marxian legacy?

Marx is the proverbial son of the Enlightenment, but also of romanticism. As Berman shows, his project is deeply imbued with the modernist spirit, of embracing the whirlwind of creative destruction.[37] Yet Marx also longs for a gentler, slower Renaissance world. The moment of his intellectual formation, in the Roman-French town of Trier, connected him to these European legacies and also meant that he could imagine modernity as reversible (a prospect we

---

35   Wright 2002.
36   Negri 2000.
37   Berman 1984.

have now well and truly lost). Marx elaborates on Schiller's critique of fragmentation in developing his youthful theory of alienation. He develops a critical theory with an emancipatory intention. He learns to historicise, to think
and explain the new world in terms of drama, dramaturgy, ghosts and spirits,
fetishes, mythologies, masking, in images as powerful as that of the sorcerer's
apprentice. He proceeds via the critique of political economy to theorise power
and culture, to centre on technology as a culture.

The power of Marx's diagnosis of modern times is not equalled by his prognosis. Marx shows a fundamental weakness in his attraction to populism, the
image of two fundamental working classes, especially early. He installs the proletariat as the motor of history, an imputation which the proletariat never quite
understands correctly. His sense of the permanent revolution of capital spills
over into the telos of guaranteed socialism, which it never is. He was a powerful
critic of capitalism as modernity, who understood the centrality of capital as a
relation and as a self-naturalising illusion. He was a dreamer. His intellectual
origins were before modernity, but the scope of his vision was beyond it. His
legacy is best imagined as what Ernst Bloch called the warm stream of marxism.

Was he an original? Yes, and no. The power of Marx's work lies in the brilliant synthesis that he generated from the work of others, working within on
the critical horizons of both the streams we conventionally separate as Enlightenment and Romanticism. Perhaps, in our own times, the fate of his thought
is to return to the cultures from which it was initially created, as avant-garde
returns, finally, to the mainstream.

Second Circle

∵

CHAPTER 6

Socialism: Modern Hopes, Postmodern Shadows (2001)

Socialism, today, may seem to be part of the past; perhaps this is necessarily so. To begin to consider the arguments involved across various socialisms as social theory already means to begin to break up these firm, if imaginary distinctions between past, present and future. For if the socialist traditions often think back, they also necessarily reach forward. Socialism is one central trend in the critique of modernity, for socialism rests on the image of modernity as it is and as it might be. Its main strength has been its capacity to call out the critique of the present by comparing it with senses of pasts and distinct possible futures, or else by comparing innovative experiences in some times and places with more routine achievements elsewhere. Socialism thus functions as critique, via utopia; and at the end of the twentieth century we might conclude that it works better in this critical register than as a politics aimed at the possession of state power. Socialism is, as Zygmunt Bauman puts it, the counterculture of modernity.[1] Into the millennium, the presence of socialism may be more discernible as a culture than as a politics. In this broader sense, socialist argument replays various claims and counterclaims associated with modernity and critique via Romanticism and Enlightenment. Both rural and urban, modern and anti-modern, socialist theory remains the alter ego of capitalism.[2] Thus, socialism runs parallel arguments to many of capitalism's claims, including its obsession with economy and, into the middle of the twentieth century, with the state. Similarly, socialism runs a dialogue of its own with America and Americanism as the putative model and future of modernity.

To begin, it is important to register two historical facts. First, socialism has a history, a plurality of traditions across place and time. Second, the fact that Marxism comes to dominate socialism does not mean that the two are identical. Socialism has a history; of which Marxism is a part. Socialism precedes, and postdates Marxism.[3] These facts raise other issues, such as the extraordinary power of local cultures, to the extent that, for example, some

---

1 Bauman, 1976, 1982.
2 Beilharz, 1994.
3 See generally Sassoon 1996.

communist traditions remain far more deeply marked by local stories than by the grand narratives of Soviet Marxism.[4]

Socialism as a social theory coincides not only with the radical aspirations of the French Revolution but also with the earliest reactions against the Industrial Revolution. Arguably there are two streams of development. Socialist argument has a local, practical current which emerges into the 1830s and emphasises cooperation, contrasting socialism to individualism and hoping for a maintenance of the older orders and habits against modernization.[5] It also has an intellectual, or middle-class stream which incorporates these local insights often into more ambitious schemes or hopes for the future. Robert Owen and Charles Fourier were earlier representatives of this intellectual stream, which really comes into its own with Marx, where for the first time the socialist project becomes a property dispute between warring intellectuals. Marxism in a sense abducts socialism, but especially after 1917, when the Bolsheviks pin the Marxist flag to their own attempt to seize power and construct the socialist order in the Soviet Union. Socialism consequently is identified with Marxism and with the Soviet and subsequent claimed socialist roads from China to Cuba and elsewhere into the Third World. Marxism thus becomes an ideology itself, and sacrifices its capacity to criticise the present.

Does this mean, however, that socialism can only ever be a negative or oppositional trend? The point for any consideration of socialism as social theory is that politics and critique do not get on well together, at least when it comes to state power. But this obsession with the state came late, discernibly into the inter-war period of the twentieth century. Socialism is often identified with statism, but this is misleading. The earliest socialists like Owen and Fourier favoured the local level of analysis and viewed cooperation or self-management as crucial, and Marx follows them in this; even Marx's greatest work, *Capital* itself, presents its theoretical object at the level of the capitalist factory, and the socialist regime of associated producers as its alternative. Early socialists worked more at the level of the exemplary politics of the commune than at the level of large-scale organisation, and again Marx follows them in this, for he fails to bridge intellectually the gap between the individual factory and the globalised world-system. Local socialism thus historically coincides with the idea that small is beautiful, and thus reveals the power of its own romanticism or anti-modernism. For it is only with the work of Weber, Simmel and Durkheim in different ways that sociologists centre upon scale and complexity as irrevers-

---

4   Davidson 1982; Tiersky 1983; Touraine, Wieviorka and Dubet 1987; Beilharz 1993b.
5   Bauman 1982; Wright 1986.

ible features of modern social organisation. Marx's social theory is still guided by the spirit of Rousseau, in that problems of scale and complexity are largely withered away. This is exactly what motivates later turns to market socialism in Eastern Europe, and marketism, say, with the later work of Alec Nove: the recognition that markets deal better with scale than bureaucracies do.[6]

Socialists from the beginning, then, are active in dispute as to whether socialism involves more progress or modernity or less. Some, like Saint-Simon, anticipate Durkheim in presuming that socialism will be modern or it will not be at all, presuming therefore in this that socialism is a state of affairs to be achieved rather than an ethic or an attitude. Marx's own work indicates the shift from romanticism to modernism. Others dug in on different positions. Thus Ferdinand Tönnies' incredibly influential defence of community, *Gemeinschaft*, versus association, or *Gesellschaft* (1887), was a leading example of the romantic socialist case, where socialism was the opposite of everything that capitalism indicated – size, mobility, speed, rootlessness, restlessness, dirt, promiscuous sex, legalism, money and contract, and urban frenzy.[7] Tönnies' views in turn called out Durkheim's modernist socialism in *The Division of Labour in Society* (1893) and in his Bordeaux lectures on socialism (1894–5), where Durkheim sends Rousseau and Tönnies back to the eighteenth century and insists instead that the idea of the whole Romantic personality be replaced by the expanded solidarity afforded by industrialism.

Today we forget that Durkheim and Tönnies were both socialists, and this is one reason why we fail sufficiently to think of socialism as a social theory. Perhaps the more explicitly recognised period dispute here was that between William Morris and Edward Bellamy, whose competing images of the socialist future clearly indicate corresponding critiques of the present and social theories appropriate to their understanding. Bellamy published his sleeper wakes novel, *Looking Backward*, in 1888. Constructed against the image of capitalist waste and disorganisation, Bellamy posited the image of socialism as highly organised, without friction, and in effect militarised, nationalised, well-fed, fit and, to our eyes, grey.[8] William Morris hit the roof at this philistine good news, and wrote in return 'News from Nowhere' (1890), an explicitly rural, Thames Valley utopia where modernity was not celebrated but pushed away, small was beautiful and beauty was central to the quality of living, as Ruskin before him had insisted.[9]

---

6 See, for example, Nove 1980.
7 Tönnies 1974.
8 Bellamy 1989.
9 Morris 1962a.

The history of socialisms since has worked this contradiction, among others, between the sense that the idea of socialism involved more modernity, or less. The significance of Marx's work here emerges most fully, for it covers both aspects, a fact which his followers generally avoided. Marx offers at least five images of utopia. To track them is to witness Marx's own embrace of modernity as industrialism, or his transition from green to grey. The Marx known to us in the English language from the 1960s was different to the Marx of the Soviets. The extraordinary efflorescence of Marxism into the 1970s involved a humanist phase, manoeuvred by the *1844 Manuscripts*, followed by a structuralist moment led by Louis Althusser. But in the 1960s the Marx for today was deeply romantic in spirit, more in tune with Schiller's lament for human fragmentation than Levi-Strauss' science of the human mind. The great Marx of the period was the Marx set against alienation, implying a wholeness and authenticity which capitalism had destroyed, making it necessary to destroy the Destroyer in turn. The utopia implicit in Marx's *1844 Manuscripts* was one of guild labour, where the medieval connotations denied the very idea of the division of labour. Marx put a Fourier spin on this in the famous passage in *The German Ideology* (1845), where the good society, playfully pictured, would involve hunting, herding, fishing and criticism – a horticultural life, not a smokestack in sight.[10] All this changes across the period that Marx leaves the green of the Rhine for the dirt of Dean Street and the British Museum. His subsequent images of utopia evoke automation, and the trade-off between boredom and free time in the *Grundrisse* (1857–8), and the self-managed factory in the third volume of *Capital*. A fifth possible utopia is glimpsed in Marx's correspondence with his Russian admirers into the 1870s, where Marx allows the dispensation that communal socialism might still be feasible in Russia.[11]

Marx, of course, denied utopia, but dealt in it every day of his life, again, necessarily so. For his purpose was to show, at first, that capitalism was a blot on the natural landscape, and then, later, that it was not the only possible way to organise modernity or industrialism. Marx's social theory remains central not only because of its critical power and influence, but because of its capacity to contain this contradiction as it coincides with the progressive entrenchment of industrialism. The young Marx, like Owen and Fourier, can still imagine that industrialism is reversible. By *Capital* (1867), the realisation has changed; already in *The Communist Manifesto* (1848) this other modernist stream is apparent, that the real challenge is to harness the forces of production to popu-

---

10   Beilharz 1992a, pp. 7–8.
11   Beilharz 1992a, p. 11.

lar need. But there are other transformations across Marx's work as well. One is powerfully apparent in the 1859 Preface to *A Contribution to the Critique of Political Economy*, where Marx makes plain his substitution of political economy for the earlier, Hegelian curiosity about civil society. This is a landmark in the history of Marxism, for it indicates plainly that henceforth Marxism's concern is within political economy itself. Marx and subsequent Marxists became the wizards of economic analysis, predicting capitalist breakdown, falling profit rates and inevitable proletarian revolution. This logical turn away from politics or culture within Marxism was not to be remedied until the later appearance of Antonio Gramsci. Culture and politics became epiphenomenal, within Marxism, the result of economics rather than realms in their own right. Socialism became a result of capitalism, as classes had their interests inscribed into them by the structural relationship of exploitation between bourgeoisie and proletariat. Marxists spent their lives trying to work out why the proletariat failed to live up to these projections, rather than wondering about the logic or interests of the projectors themselves. As later critics such as Castoriadis and Baudrillard would put it, Marxists were neither historical nor materialist and were not revolutionary but messianic; they had succumbed to their own mirrors of production.[12]

Marxisms proliferated after Marx, not least with the political success of the Bolsheviks. The diversity of Marxisms did not generally acknowledge the diversity in Marx's own work, partly because it was unknown, and remained so until the Marx renaissance of the 1960s. Marx's influence touched his contemporaries, but Marxism did not take off as a political force until its institutionalisation by the German Social Democrats closer to the turn of the century. Certainly, Marx influenced those with whom he came into creative contact, such as William Morris, though the content of Morris' socialism, sometimes referred to as his Marxism, was also thoroughly local. Romantic and technologically sensitive by turns, Morris was made to look like Marx because both insisted on the necessity of revolution. But revolution was not the property of Marxism, even if gradualism or enthusiasm for reform was the more common attitude among English socialists.

Marxism emerged as the ideology and theory of the first mass political party, the German Social Democrats (SPD). The SPD became widely known as a kind of counter-society or state within the Prussian state. Its greatest strength also proved to be its greatest weakness; its ghetto-nature made it vulnerable to the Nazis on their road to power after 1933, and its own messianism fed into the

---

12   Baudrillard 1975; Castoriadis 1987.

fatalistic slogan of the German Communists, 'first Hitler, then us'. Marx's legacy had left unresolved the exact question of how socialism would emerge. Would it automatically follow the collapse of socialism? Would it, instead, be the conscious result of self-organised activity? Or would it, as the 1859 *Preface* implied, involve some combination of these, where the correct economic conjuncture would call out the appropriate political intervention? Marx's inattention to the theory of politics left the question of the party unresolved, or absent. Marx's party, like Rosa Luxemburg's, looked like the whole working class. Only classes did not act, as such, so that political representation became necessary. Modernity caught Marx napping, together with Rousseau. The Bolsheviks closed this political hiatus by inserting themselves into it as the combat, vanguard party. The German Social Democrats set out practically to make another culture, working in general on the sense of maturational reformism – sooner or later, socialism would come, whether out of crisis or a gradual growing over, whether by electoral means or collapse.

The larger political legacy of Marxism left a dual possibility, reform or revolution. In *The Communist Manifesto* Marx and Engels had sketched out a ten-point, minimum programme of reforms; yet their tougher stance, outlined by Marx in the penultimate chapter of *Capital*, clearly indicated that socialism would arrive through revolutionary apocalypse. The German Social Democrats grew apart on the basis of this split. Some, like Eduard Bernstein, came to view socialism as a project of citizenship to be achieved by civilising capitalism. Others, like Karl Kautsky, were happy to combine revolutionary rhetoric with reformist activity, while others again, such as Rosa Luxemburg, wanted to adjust reformist reality to fit revolutionary theory.[13]

The SPD turned Marxism into catechism so that its rank-and-file members would have the revolutionary science at its fingertips. Marxist dogma insisted that the two basic classes, bourgeoisie and proletariat, would dichotomise until the vast majority of the working masses would bump off the capitalists. The 'Bernstein Controversy' over reform versus revolution involved two distinct issues; one, whether reformism was to be preferred, and two, whether Marxism must be revised in order to register this political recognition theoretically.[14] Was Marxism a set of axioms, beyond challenge, or was it a method of analysis open to necessary revision? The process by which Marxism became an ideology also involved its consolidation into scholastics. This is one of the clearest of historical cases in which a social theory intended to help explain and even change

---

13   Beilharz 1992a, Ch. 4.
14   Beilharz 1992a; Bernstein 1996; Steger 1997.

the world becomes an impediment to these processes. Marxism became, especially in the hands of Kautsky, a general theory of social evolution where each mode of production emerged triumphantly out of its precedent. Kautsky set these formulae out in *The Class Struggle* (1895), an unrepentantly modernist text, where all that is missing from capitalism's industrial achievement is the crown of socialisation. Kautsky therefore set out to prove that all would become proletarians, peasants included, before the bourgeoisie could simply be shown the door. At the same time, it was Kautsky who insisted that left to their own resources, the workers would never achieve more than trade union or economistic consciousness, so they would always need good theoretical leaders like himself. Lenin agreed, and built an ideology on this view in *What is to Be Done?* (1902). Kautsky eventually came to the opposite conclusion after 1917, like Bernstein, arguing that history could not be forced.

In effect Bernstein and Kautsky formed a long-term intellectual alliance, as Bernstein continued the Marxian impulse of reforms in the ten-point programme while Kautsky carried on the revolutionary rhetoric of *Capital*. Bernstein's position was closer to the ethics of Kantianism or new liberalism, while Kautsky's sociology shifted in the direction of a Weberian Marxism in his 1930 magnum opus, *The Materialist Conception of History*.

Max Weber had taken sides with Bernstein, however, in preferring revision as the normal attitude for social science and theory. Kautsky, for his part, agreed with Weber that specialisation was our fate, and therefore that modernity would overdetermine socialism rather than the other way around. Lenin's utopia, best formally revealed in *State and Revolution* (1917), still sought a new world characterised by simplicity rather than adjusting to complexity, something of a contradiction given the driving modernism which otherwise characterises his work. When it comes to Bolshevism and the massive shadow which it casts over the twentieth century, it is Lenin who is dominant as actor but Trotsky who is the imposing theorist. What was Bolshevism, as a social theory? Like other streams of socialism, Bolshevism is plural and its paths were many, though Lenin and Trotsky still stand out, together with Bukharin, to Lenin's right and Preobrazhensky, to Trotsky's left. Lenin's theoretical writing is more occasional, and less systematic than Trotsky's. Lenin in a sense combines Luxemburg's desire to radicalise practice with a kind of pragmatism which values political expediency above all else. Unlike Luxemburg, Lenin was always a Jacobin, for whom one wise man was worth a hundred fools. His ultra-utopia in *State and Revolution* combines the putative libertarianism of 'all cooks can govern' with the grim insistence that the practical model for socialism would be the post office. This futuristic or modernising scenario stands in contrast to Lenin's other views of the prospect of socialism, which tend to be populist and rural or at least based upon the idea that Soviet socialism will remain agrarian and not only industrial. Lenin dreamed of extending direct democracy into Soviet experience, but the challenges of modernisation without democracy became overwhelming.[15] While his final utopia looked more distinctly Maoist, accommodating Russian agrarian realities rather than forcing them, Lenin's high Bolshevik utopia was something more like the image of German capitalism, symbolised by Americanism ascendant. Like Trotsky, Lenin's belief that the success of the Russian Revolution depended on the German Revolution was not merely strategic, or even economic; Lenin viewed the 'organised capitalism' analysed by Hilferding to be the basic model for Soviet modernisation.[16] Lenin's model of socialism as modernity was something like capitalism without democracy, or with the lure of an impossible, direct democracy held over it by the Bolsheviks. Its political logic remains populist, in that it pits the people against their exploiters and renders the alternative exploiters – the Bolsheviks – invisible in the process.

Lenin's response to various failures and setbacks was to introduce the New Economic Policy, which in 1921 recognised the status quo as the framework for future Soviet efforts. Trotsky, in contrast, accepted NEP with hesitance, for his model of socialism had always been industrialist and modernising. Trotsky's was a Faustian Bolshevism, one prepared even to risk life and limb for the thrill, the prospect of even glimpsing what men and technology could do. Trotsky hoped not merely to follow the Germans and Americans, but to outdo them, not least through developing enthusiasms for the principles of Taylorism and scientific management. Americanised Bolshevism – that was the way forward.[17] Anything is possible – this is the motivation; the rational mastery of nature, and thereby of humanity itself, this is the canvas. Trotsky's impulse is a kind of developmental romanticism, where the frenzy of creation reaches out into the sublime.

The image of socialism in the Bolshevik tradition thus disperses across a spectrum, even if we consider Lenin and Trotsky alone, from a modest hope of feeding people on the one extreme to the project of endlessly reconstructing the world, on the other. The futurism of Trotsky embodies something of the productivism, or obsession with technology, which becomes characteristic of Marxism into the twentieth century. Socialism becomes a matter of harnessing the best of capitalist technology to what are claimed to be more benign ends. The line back to Marx is plain: if abundance is the practical precondition of

15   Beilharz 1992a Ch. 2; Arnason 1993.
16   Beilharz 1992a, p. 24.
17   Beilharz 1992a, p. 30.

socialism, then socialism becomes another way of doing capitalism, or at least another form of organising capitalist technology. The producer, or more specifically the proletarian, becomes not only the subject of history but also the citizen; and his incapacity to rule as well as to produce at the same time quietly keeps the Bolsheviks in the business of 'politics'.

Russian radicals had long been divided into localists and westernisers; the distinction was by no means peculiar to Russia. British socialism, too, divided between those who sought more wilfully to return to or to extend the past, and those who sought to modernise it. The conflict between traditionalists and modernisers was acted out in various British sites, not least of them Fabianism. The Fabians became known into the 1930s as progressivists, reformers and statists, sometime apologists for authoritarian regimes or at least for the principles of social engineering which underpinned them. Fabianism began as an alternative life movement, caught up as various European socialisms were in the 1880s with vegetarianism, alternative dress and bicycling.[18] Its substantive theoretical impulse came not only from John Stuart Mill and Owen but from Cobbett, Carlyle, Ruskin and indirectly Morris, for whom the old image of England's green and pleasant land looked more interesting than the prospect of Coketown or the Satanic Mills. The opposition to modernity or civilisation became major themes of social criticism across socialisms and kindred positions such as Distributism and Catholic ruralism. More recently, these kinds of issues have been pursued with regard to broader questions of British industrial culture and the residual presence of Romanticism even among the captains of industry.[19] British socialisms have long been more heavily influenced by medieval than modernising claims and motifs, at least until Wilson and then Blair.

The strongest English variant of medievalism was Guild, or Gild socialism, associated with various theorists such as Sam Hobson and Orage and Penty and *The New Age*, but defended most ably by G.D.H. Cole, who took its legacy into Fabianism, where it was lost as statism triumphed with the Beveridge Report into the 1940s. The guild socialists viewed utopia as a coalescence of local unions modelled on the medieval guilds, autonomous and capable of holding together the moments of conception and execution or head and hand. The image of society involved would be based on direct democracy, only the producer would remain privileged; after all, Adam Smith's jibe against trade unions was more accurately addressed to guilds, that they were conspiracies against the public, closed and traditionalistic in the absolute sense. Cole's early

---

18   Britain 1982.
19   Wiener 1985.

hope was for the federation of these self-governing units, a veritable example of small is beautiful.[20] Different local English lineages also claimed that the way back opened the way forward; the ethical or Christian socialism based on the idea of fellowship among men and stewardship of nature led by R.H. Tawney was a major contributor to the labourism associated with the British Labour Party into the 1930s.[21]

While Tawney worried about compassion and mutual responsibility, and Cole echoed the early Marx's enthusiasm for the autonomy of labour, others like the Webbs puzzled over waste and inefficiency. Beatrice and Sidney Webb began from positions closer to liberalism or cooperation, with the added sense of evolutionism associated with the work of Beatrice's childhood tutor, Herbert Spencer. The idea of evolution alone – progress from lower forms to higher – plainly locates the Webbs on different terrain to that inhabited by the guildists. This point of their mentality was closer to Marx's, that the development of society made progress possible. Only the Webbs' image of utopia lacked the monomaniacal developmentalism of Trotsky; their hope was rather to service such a minimum of provision as might enable all to flourish in their interdependence.[22] Revolutionaries have enjoyed the prospect of casting Fabianism as mere 'gas and water socialism'; the problems of provision, of health, education and housing nevertheless remain fundamental. Socialism for the Webbs, then, consisted largely in practical terms of reorganising the wealth that society already possessed. Social problems could be measured, their existence publicised and appropriate reforms enacted to see to their resolution. Social solidarity could be developed upon the emerging patterns of social evolution, so that, as in Durkheim's view, each would depend on all the rest. All citizens, in this view, would have a place in the division of labour; the middle classes, tempted by their location and tradition to social parasitism, would also need to find their social vocation.

The opposition to social parasitism motivated various different kinds of socialism. Some, like Marx, viewed the bourgeoisie as implicitly parasitic, or without social function. Others, like Lenin, viewed aristocrats, fat capitalists or coupon-clippers as parasites; for the Webbs, it was middle-class folks lacking in social conscience who were parasites, at least until they took up the cause of reform. For others, like Lenin and Trotsky, again the *kulaks* or rich peasants became the enemy. And for socialists and radicals of anti-semitic bent, from

---

20   Wright 1979.
21   Wright 1987.
22   Beilharz 1992a Ch. 3.

Hilaire Belloc to Werner Sombart, it was finance-capital which was parasitic.[23] Socialists had their distinct enemies, then, as well as their heroes, proletarian or mock-proletarian for the Bolsheviks, factory-inspectors for the Webbs, savants for Kautsky, scientists for Wells or Trotsky. But for Fabians the citizen would not be conceived as the proletarian, as in Bolshevism. Indeed, as the Webbs went on to suggest in their *Constitution for the Socialist Commonwealth of Great Britain* (1920), vocational electorates should be developed alongside geographical forms of representation in order fully to register the significance of work in political life.[24] The evident weakness in this, as in much else of socialist theory, is the failure to take seriously the private sphere and the gender consequences thereof. 'Work', in this discourse as in most others, refers to paid public work, rather than to the labours of the home. Not that socialists failed to address domestic labour, which they did from Bebel through to Wells; only they continued to presume its gendered nature, themselves reflecting the traditionalism of patriarchy which itself violates the ethics of modernity and yet holds it up.

Fabianism in effect dissolved into the state, victim, like British liberalism, of its own success with the 1945–51 Labour Government. Fabianism had better articulated the common sense of the labour movement referred to historically as labourism, where the politics of socialism was constructed in terms of the defence and protection of workers and their families. Fabianism built upon labourism an infrastructure of research, organisation and agitation, pushing an ethic which sought to tie together the gradual modernisation of society and the solidarity imputed to its traditional forms. All this became fundamental to the post-war regimes of reconstruction, until they were washed away by the processes of crisis and globalisation which ran through the 1970s to the 1990s.

The idea of the Russian Revolution was exhausted by the 1940s, being replaced in romantic Western imaginations by images of Chairman Mao or Che Guevara. Yet the image of October excited many earlier, including Shaw and in Italy the young Antonio Gramsci. The younger Gramsci was a council communist, taking up a position for the new proletarian, self-organised order, espousing a kind of social democratic syndicalism not unlike the view of G.D.H. Cole. Gramsci embraced the October Revolution as 'The Revolution Against Capital', by which he referred both to the power of capital and to the fatalistic influence of Marx's *Capital*. His view was that the Marxism of Kautsky and his Russian equivalent, Plekhanov, had become a deadweight on Marxists, who passively accepted Kautsky's maxim that their job was to wait for the revolution. Gram-

---

23   Belloc 1913; Sombart 1951.
24   Beilharz 1992a, p. 62.

sci insisted on extending the voluntaristic and democratic element in Marx, that which indicated that socialism was only possible as a result of the action of self-organised masses of men and women. Gramsci insisted that Marxism was a politics, and not just a political economy: a statement of will, and not only a recognition of constraint, and he was stubborn in this insistence until he was personally constrained within Mussolini's prison walls, where he wrote the famous (if thematically scattered) *Prison Notebooks*. Gramsci's *Prison Notebooks* reinstate the Marxian formula of the 1859 *Preface*, that people make history but not just as they choose. The *Notebooks* also reconfigure Marxist politics by placing Machiavelli at the fore, and conceptualising the Italian Communist Party as the New Prince. More significantly, the *Notebooks* foreground culture, ideology and common sense as the practical field within which bourgeois societies ensure their self-reproduction. Hegemony, and not only force, ensures social coherence; socialism, conceived as the practical project of a new class alliance, or new historic bloc, therefore depends on the possibility of counter-hegemony.[25]

Gramsci was a revolutionary communist, who was subsequently reinvented as a culturalist predecessor of the Birmingham School of Cultural Studies. He was not only Italian, but more specifically Sardinian, a peripheral Marxist who understood uneven development without falling for the hypermodern cosmopolitanism of a Trotsky. Vital to his legacy is not only *The Prison Notebooks* (1971), but also *The Southern Question* (1926), where Gramsci opened the case that modernity would always ever be traditionalistic as well as progressive. Gramsci's contemporary, often grouped with him and the German philosopher Karl Korsch in the retrospective category of 'Western Marxism', was Georg Lukács. The Hungarian Marxist Lukács not only founded the later Budapest School after 1956, but also was a central voice in the formation of the Frankfurt School into the 1920s, for Lukács was the pioneer of a kind of Weberian Marxism, refracting together (as differently did Simmel) the themes of commodification (Marx) and instrumental reason (Weber) to develop the theme of reification.[26] The so-called Western Marxists therefore developed the political and cultural spheres of analysis which had been neglected since Marx's call that vision lay in the analysis of political economy rather than civil society. In the case of Lukács's analysis, culture emerged only to show, by other means, the impossibility of socialism except at the hands of a magically endowed intellectual proletariat. The legacies of Gramsci and Lukács were either institutional-

25   Gramsci 1971; Davidson 1977.
26   Lukács 1971.

ised or ignored by their respective communist parties. Korsch wrote one of the best books on Marx, *Karl Marx*, in 1936 before taking up American exile, where his influence was negligible except for the impact upon marginal local council communists such as Paul Mattick.

The critical theorists of the Frankfurt School, most notably Theodor Adorno, Max Horkheimer and Herbert Marcuse, migrated to America to escape Nazism. There they cultivated the anti-modern or at least anti-American thread of the German tradition, viewing American culture as either candy floss or televisual totalitarianism.[27] The Frankfurt School, in common with Lukács, pursued a kind of aristocratic radicalism quite at odds with Gramsci's curiosity about popular culture and folk wisdom. The trajectory of Critical Theory, in contrast, was influenced not only by the failure of socialist revolution in the West, but also by the outcome of Nazism in the Holocaust. 'Western Marxism', so-called because of its guiding sense that Western cultures offered different challenges to those facing others like the Bolsheviks seeking socialism in the 'East', was also deflated by those developments in the West, where the prospects of socialism gave way to the power of barbarism.

In the meantime, German Social Democracy became historically institutionalised as a form of social management into the 1960s, as did labourism in Britain. The extraordinary extent of the post-war boom and the arrival of mass consumerism through the 1950s combined with the effects of the Cold War saw socialism lose impetus again until the 1960s, when critical theory and Western Marxism were revived or reconstructed especially by student radicals from Berkeley to the London School of Economics (the latter founded by the Webbs). Radicalism rode the wave, perhaps especially in the United States. American socialisms are long of lineage and rich in variety, though they have often been marginalised within scholarship by academics with short memories. The famous question put by Sombart in 1906 was, *Why is There no Socialism in the United States?*,[28] presuming that socialism was something necessarily to be measured by its presence or absence at the level of central state power, rather than within civil society or as a counter-current to modernity. Yet far from being a mere absence, socialism has a rich American history, from nineteenth-century utopian experiment, through Bellamy and the Bellamy Clubs, to the Industrial Workers of the World and various intellectual permutations from Lewis Mumford to the pragmatism of Max Eastman and Richard Rorty. If the answer to Sombart's question, rephrased as why was there not *more* socialism in the

27   Jay 1973; Wiggershaus 1994.
28   Sombart 1976.

United States, was material abundance, then the real tease was yet to come, as more of that material abundance into the 1960s brought out the New Left with a vengeance. With Marcuse, Habermas, Gorz and Mallet, traffic increased both into English-speaking cultures and back to the centres as radicals struggled for equal rights and dreamed, still, of the end of alienation.

The Marx of the 1960s conjured up themes going back to alienation as well as commodification. Indeed, whether via Marcuse in *One Dimensional Man* (1964) or the newly translated Marx of the *1844 Manuscripts*, the essential message provided by radical social theory often seemed singular: the world needed to be changed all at once, which in effect, given the power of capital and its culture, meant not at all. Other socialisms were eclipsed by Marxism, and Marxist humanism was scorned by the rising star of structuralism, which also established an image of structure or history as unshiftable.[29] Reformisms could easily be made to look feeble by armchair revolutionaries who claimed a radical distance from the Soviet experience but whose vocabularies were basically Bolshevik.[30]

Marxism revived as a critical theory, perhaps for the last time before expiring, as State Theory.[31] State Theory was often caught up with the idea that a theory of politics could be derived from the analysis of capital. Thus, again, was Gramsci rediscovered as a political theorist.[32] Thus, for example, Laclau and Mouffe sought to use Gramsci as a way out of the impasse in *Hegemony and Socialist Strategy* (1985). The sticking point in Gramsci remained that of Bolshevism, or Jacobinism; was the party still the key agent of social transformation, or was it merely a collective noun for the various related social movements which held it up?

The collapse of Marxism as the key presence within socialist social theory at this point came in at least two different forms. The first involved the rediscovery of methodological pluralism, in principle available in Weber but politically accessible through the work of Foucault. Foucault widely replaced Althusser, who had replaced Marx. Power was discovered to exist throughout modernity, and not only in economy. The second point of erosion involved the rediscovery or renegotiation of democracy, via liberalism as political theory in the re-emergence of social movements and the reappraisal of civil society.[33] On both these accounts, Marxism now appeared to be a regional theory rather than a

---

29   Dosse 1997.
30   Beilharz 1987.
31   Jessop, 1982; Frankel 1983.
32   Sassoon 1988.
33   Cohen and Arato 1992.

general theory. The fact that liberalism could be seen as radical again gave a second chance to various non-Marxian socialist alternatives.

The general problem, inasmuch as it could be named, was now reidentified as the problem not of capitalism but of modernity. Working out of the Budapest School tradition of Weberian Marxism, Agnes Heller and Ferenc Fehér identified the field of modernity as at least threefold, characterised by the differing logics or dynamics of capitalism, industrialism and democracy.[34] This was, in effect, to return to one of the earliest socialist sensibilities, that socialism was less a state of affairs to be achieved upon the negation of private property than it was a restatement of the priority of the social against individualism. The striking locational difference was that, by the end of this century, socialism lived in the academy perhaps more than anywhere else, as its claims to being taken seriously as a culture of social theory had outgrown its street credentials as a practical politics. After all that has occurred in its name, socialism remains the kind of critique and utopia which it began as, diminished in its certainty just as its existence is warranted by what surrounds it, part of the past and thereby of our present. Formally speaking, socialism might be said to have returned to the civil societies and social movements which originally called it forth. For as socialists have declared that the core of their utopia is democracy, and not only equality, so have their ambitions returned to the horizons of social democracy and the radical liberal heritage which often informs it. If socialism began as the claim to pursue the ideals of the French Revolution, supporting the expansion of democracy against power or capitalism, then its Marxian claims to absolute difference may have been illusory. Socialism remains part of the critique of modernity; neither term seems possible without the other.

---

34   Fehér and Heller 1987a.

CHAPTER 7

Social Democracy: Kautsky and Bernstein (1992)

While the image of Bolshevism has been more or less shattered by the collapse of communism in Eastern Europe, and while Fabianism looks vague – promising, or hopeless, depending on one's position – as ever, the status of German Social Democracy is at first sight difficult to determine. On the one hand, and practically, German Social Democracy has been multiply ruptured – by the Great War, through Weimar, then to be delivered into the hands of Hitler, resurrected and transformed into Social Administration by Brandt and Schmidt. On the other hand, the theoretical legacy of Social Democracy remains potent. Social democracy as a project has never yet been fulfilled, but of the traditions analysed here its legacy is the most potentially positive.

As with Bolshevism and Fabianism, there are predictably stylised views of the nature of Social Democracy. The easiest, from left or right, is simply to declare it moribund because of the visible impasse of parliamentary socialism in Western Europe today. It is equally easy, subsequently, to view the leading thinkers of the movement – Eduard Bernstein and Karl Kautsky – as neo-Victorian idiots, relics, fossils or fools. Only more recently has there been an attempt to reassess both Bernstein and Kautsky, to actually read their works, and to discover the nuances and insights contained in them. For the experience of the Social Democratic movement, and the theoretical labours of its leaders were in fact monumental cultural institutions, which provide all kinds of insights into the tradition called socialism. The experience of the SPD, indeed, could be said to contain its own practical utopia – the 'state within the state', more accurately viewed as a society within a society which provided relations of identity, support, and sustenance for very many middle- and working-class German citizens up to and after the turn of the century. Theirs was, in fact, as Vernon Lidtke has shown, an alternative culture, and not just an island of socialist utopia drowning in a dominant sea of Junker capitalism.[1] In this sense, then, the practical utopia of Social Democracy can be seen in its voluntary associations, singing and bicycling clubs, clubs for smokers and for anti-smokers, just as the practical utopia of Bolshevism might be seen in the workings of the early Soviets and that of Fabianism in its municipal enthusiasms and summer schools.

---

1   Cf. Roth 1963; Lidtke 1985.

Marx, of course, had viewed his socialism as other than utopian – in the fundamentally expressive catchphrase of Engels, there was an essential divide between socialisms utopian and scientific. Science arrived together with Marxism, in the account of the founders. Yet, as we have seen, Marx's own work was resplendent in its utopic dimensions, from the *Economic and Philosophical Manuscripts* through to the last writings. Kautsky and Bernstein, Marx's leading legatees, took on Marx's disdain for public blueprinting. As often as not, their public stance was to ridicule utopianism while presenting their own utopias as emergent states of affairs. This is true even though Kautsky was to adhere more closely to the utopia of the associated producers, with lives governed by the cleft between freedom and necessity, while Bernstein developed an image of the future more akin to that of civilised capitalism in its social liberal form.

Dietzgen and Bebel

But before Kautsky and Bernstein there were other figures. One vital early figure who has long since slipped into the mire of obscurity is Joseph Dietzgen. Dietzgen was literally a home-grown Utopian, a tanner by trade, without formal education. Marx actually liked his work, which is enough to warrant curiosity itself.[2] Dietzgen's work was enormously influential in Britain, where there was indeed a Dietzgen cult. It was published alongside that of Labriola by Charles H. Kerr of Chicago.[3] The significance of Dietzgen here is that his popularity arguably had a great deal to do with something which would likely have upset Marx. For Dietzgen developed a Religion of Social Democracy, and delivered it in sermons between 1870 and 1875. Dietzgen believed that socialism was a new form of knowledge, a new epistemology, but this new dialectics begot a religion, which was a science in its premises yet acted as the new philosophy or cosmos of belief. *Work* was the name of this new Redeemer. Socialism truly concerned itself with the salvation of mankind.[4] Redemption could now be sought through socialism, through the conscious, systematic organisation of social labour.[5] The logic of Dietzgen's position was that religion was a kind of human need – in order actually to dethrone a fantastic and religious system of life, it was necessary to put a new, rational system in its place.[6]

---

2 Marx to Engels, 7. 11. 1868 (Marx and Engels 1975, pp. 203–4).
3 MacIntyre 1980, pp. 129–40; Rée 1984, pp. 3–7; Buick 1975.
4 Dietzgen 1906, pp. 94–5.
5 Dietzgen 1906, p. 101.
6 Dietzgen 1906, p. 139.

Throughout Europe socialism had developed as a kind of secular religion, as Stephen Yeo has demonstrated in his essay on 'The Religion of Socialism'.[7] Socialist churches and Sunday schools were merely the practical manifestation of this need. While Dietzgen was adjusting the horizon upwards, August Bebel was at the same time addressing more systematically the material dimension of the future. His 1879 tract, *Woman Under Socialism*, was according to Steinberg the most influential single SPD publication (Social Democratic readers in Germany as elsewhere disappointed their superiors by otherwise reading in natural science or romance).[8]

Bebel's is a work of major significance, not least of all in that it registers the arrival of the other sex in the socialist utopia, indeed, even privileges it. Bebel's utopia, like that of Bernstein two decades later, was not a proletarian society but a *new* society. It is a society to be based on large-scale production, but also on decentralisation.[9] In accordance with the Gotha Programme of 1875, Bebel decrees that all will be obliged to work, but on condition that they will be free to choose their work. Following the images of freedom and necessity in Marx, Bebel's utopia is one where work, necessity, can be reduced to two-and-a-half hours a day.[10] Bebel's future rests on the integration of mental and manual labour and the combination of industrial and agricultural activity.[11]

Bebel thus recognises differentiation, but does not tie individuals to their ascribed functions. As I have observed, his is no masculinist utopia – at the very least, and unlike Lenin's compulsory post office model of socialism, women do indeed inhabit this world, and unlike Wells's, they are not portrayed as either madonnas or breeding machines. Bebel proposes, in fact, that women might spread their day's energies across trade, education, art and administration – almost an urban equivalent of Marx's rural idyll in *The German Ideology*.[12] He addresses the question of domestic labour, but argues, like Morris, as though it must remain the prerogative of women alone. Men do not participate in reproductive labour, here; and mechanisation is advanced as the solution to domestic labour, by means of central laundries, socialist kitchens and communal provision. Bebel waxes lyrical over the virtues of shoeshiners and vacuum cleaners; clearly he shared the overly optimistic hopes for technology

---

7   Yeo 1977.
8   Steinberg 1976.
9   Bebel 1971. Quoted from Bebel 1976.
10   Bebel 1976, pp. 25, 29.
11   Bebel 1976, pp. 48, 91.
12   Bebel 1976, p. 129.

which were part of the milieu of early modernism and essential to arguments such as those of Wells and to local Marxists like Lily Braun.[13]

Likely Bebel saw his task in *Woman Under Socialism* as being to explain and to popularise Marx's views for a significant section of the membership of Social Democracy, actual and potential. Thus he follows Marx in ascribing a centrality to work, and yet moderates the early Marx's anthropology by arguing that while there can be no enjoyment without work, there ought to be no work without enjoyment. Bebel also confirms Marx's sense that the object of socialism is not to universalise the role of the proletarian, but to abolish the proletarian way of life,[14] and this latter theme spans an interesting debate, characteristic of all the traditions surveyed here, whether socialist culture is bourgeois culture or proletarian culture universalised, or whether it is something altogether new. Yet all this seems simultaneously to sound like a programme of modernisation, which undoubtedly it was, appealing to a better life for all in all possible ways, and legitimating the SPD rather than seeking to develop Marx's fragmentary utopic elements into a systematic theoretical view. At the same time, the achievements of Bebel's book are considerable: without flights of fancy, without abolishing marriage and women, *Woman Under Socialism* presents a sweetly reasonable image of socialism, moderate and modernist, balanced and differentiated. A significant shift emerges when we turn to the work of the Red Pope, Karl Kautsky. The general orientation of his utopia is proletarian, based on universal labour for men and women alike, yet its impulse is also ultimately democratic.

Karl Kautsky: The Red Hope

At least since the leading work of Massimo Salvadori it has been acknowledged that Kautsky was more than the 'Red Pope'.[15] As Salvadori argues, Kautsky has a history which both precedes and postdates his office in the papacy of the Second International. For our purposes, it needs to be recognised that Kautsky not only developed a systematic and nuanced version of Marxism but also that he returned again and again to the image of socialism as a future. And yet by the time of Kautsky, and notwithstanding the obvious jokes about Marxism as a religion, Marxism had also become more secular. Where Dietzgen, like the early Marx, following Feuerbach saw socialism as spirituality recovered, and

---

13   Bebel 1976, pp. 126–8.
14   Bebel 1976, p. 25.
15   Salvadori 1979, 1989.

while other traditions like the Fabians viewed theirs as the religion of humanity, Kautsky's hopes were optimistic without being eschatological. With Kautsky and Bernstein, in fact, social democracy enters an epoch of sobriety which justifies its description as Weberian Marxism.

Kautsky discussed utopianism as early as 1896, when he wrote on William Morris for the SPD's humorous periodical, *Der Wahre Jacob*.[16] While he rightly viewed Morris as a romantic, he also took his distance from Edward Bellamy, whose *Looking Backward* he reviewed in *Die Neue Zeit* for 1889. Here his stance on utopianism resembled his position on religion – science stood supreme in the realm of knowledge, but this did not mean that religion or utopianism did not have their place. Utopianism as Kautsky understood it belonged not to the sphere of science, but to that of art. He wrote:

> It is no surprise that one finds today a widespread craving to see what the future will be like, and this superficial optimism is harmless and by no means to be undermined, as long as it doesn't presume to have an effect on reality, on the political and economic struggles of the working class, as long as it asks nothing more than to be a branch of Socialist poetry. We even believe that utopianism could give rise to a significant work of art if there existed an artist who, full of enthusiasm and imagination, and possessing a profound knowledge of the human soul, as well as knowledge of the current development of society would envision the future. *Poeta vates* – The poet has a right to want to be a prophet.[17]

Kautsky knew the literature of utopia, and was prepared to take it seriously – to a point. In the same period, he wrote his major work on Thomas More. Kautsky possessed a strong sense that socialism could be legitimated by establishing its precedents or forerunners, even if at the same time stressing their differences from contemporary socialism after Marx. According to Kautsky, two great figures stood on the threshold of socialism: Münzer and More.[18] Kautsky thus acknowledges from the outset that More is a premodern thinker, yet one with astonishing insight. In particular, for Kautsky, the idea that each individual ought to be attached to a particular handicraft is simply reactionary. The factory system had placed socialism on a different basis. Mechanisation meant that, once the proletariat directed society, the individual worker could shift from job to job, bringing into play a number of muscles and nerves whose harmonious

---

16   Kautsky 1896.
17   Kautsky 1889.
18   Kautsky 1927.

activity would impart vitality just as unproductive gymnastics did in Kautsky's Germany.[19] Evidently Kautsky preferred dialectics to gymnastics.

Further, More seeks to restrict the needs of the citizens of the future: but here technology steps in to save the day, for it is in increased production, rather than restricted consumption, that the path to free time lies.[20] In all this Kautsky is prepared to view More with a degree of charity which he bestows on no other 'forerunner'. Indeed, he proposes that 'More's communism is modern in most of its tendencies, and unmodern in most of its expedients'.[21] So while Morris and others are good critics, More is the only Utopian who for Kautsky offers an extendable legacy. It is difficult not to draw the conclusion that this preference was a personal one, however, for on balance Kautsky agreed with Durkheim that modern socialism rested upon a qualitatively different sociology to the premodern.

Alongside Kautsky's specific discussion of the Utopian genre we find a series of utopic images in his substantive works: *The Class Struggle* (1892), *The Agrarian Question* (1899), *The Day After the Revolution* (1902), *The Road to Power* (1906), *Ethics and the Materialist Conception of History* (1906), *The Labour Revolution* (1925) and *The Materialist Conception of History* (1927). It is here, rather than in Kautsky's response to the field which he constructs as utopian, that we discover the architectonic of his own socialist future.

In *The Class Struggle* Kautsky offers the rudimentary contours of his own picture of socialism. What is striking about this image is its unrepentant modernism. For Kautsky the future was bound to that of the city. It was free of ancient relics such as handicraft – small production was simply doomed to disappear. Factory labour would be universalised – 'woman will cease to be a worker in the individual household, and will take her place as a worker in the large industries'.[22] The proletariat in control would thus, for Kautsky, make its pact with machinery – and this does indeed suggest a difference of opinion between him and Morris. For in Kautsky's view, socialism would be characterised by freedom in leisure, beyond work. The hope was not the freedom of labour, but *freedom from* labour, which itself would allow freedom of life, freedom for artistic and intellectual activity, freedom for the noblest enjoyment.[23]

19   Kautsky 1927, pp. 206–7.
20   Kautsky 1927, p. 209.
21   Kautsky 1927, p. 214.
22   Kautsky 1971, pp. 133, 17, 127.
23   Kautsky 1971, p. 157.

Kautsky wrote *The Agrarian Question*[24] in order to test, or prove, Marx's essential proposition that along with the centralisation of capital, capitalism produced the concentration of the mass into the proletariat. Socialism, as the process which would crown this prehistory, would necessarily extend its forms – if capitalism was characterised by massive scale and an intensive division of labour, so then socialism would be – and this would be a process which would mark not only industry, but also agriculture. Two features of the book warrant its inclusion here. First, Kautsky finds himself unable to argue, finally, that the process of capitalist concentration is in fact characteristic of agriculture: he is a better sociologist than Marxist, so to speak, and this aligns his work with that of the early Fabians rather than the Bolsheviks. Second, Kautsky provides here more hints by way of his image of the future.

In discussing agriculture under feudalism, to begin, Kautsky shows that his interest in history is not just contextual. Indeed, he quotes Heinrich Müller, the Swabian writer who in 1550 painted a picture of medieval abundance, tables groaning with food, wine drunk like water, 'and you could eat, and take away, anything you wanted – there was growth and plenty'. While Kautsky does not take this opportunity to launch into medieval sylvans, his discussion is suggestive of a modernism less than complete in its hopes. More predictable is Kautsky's general proposition, that small farming is simply wasteful – fifty peasant plots require fifty ploughs, fifty harrows, fifty carts, whereas a larger holding might work with a tenth of this number.[25] As in industry, the larger enterprise can develop the division of labour and thus facilitate the development of skill. Kautsky does not here seem to regard the mobility of individuals in agriculture as a virtue in the way he does in industry.[26] In economic terms, scale confers advantage in terms of credit, commerce, and transportation.[27] The argument is not unlike that which we find in Marx, or in Webb – rural idiocy prevents access to culture, which is a right for all.[28] But co-operatives have their limits; they are best given to medium-size enterprise.[29] The small enterprise is doomed, but less impendingly so than the classical premises of the Erfurt Programme would have led the Social Democrats to believe. The general developmental process can in fact encourage an increase in small enterprises, according to Kautsky.[30]

---

24   Kautsky 1988a, p. 30.
25   Kautsky 1988a, p. 97.
26   Kautsky 1988a, p. 101.
27   Kautsky 1988a, p. 104f.
28   Kautsky 1988a, p. 116.
29   Kautsky 1988a, p. 125.
30   Kautsky 1988a, p. 141.

Thus, as Alavi and Shanin comment, while Kautsky sets out to prove the theses of Marx's *Capital* for agriculture, he ends up explaining the opposite, i.e. the permanence of the peasantry.[31] Next 'the possibility that the peasants might survive is conceded, explained and then politically and economically disregarded insofar as the dynamics of change are concerned'.[32]

Partly Kautsky's predicament resulted from his philosophical commitment to a general theory of societal evolution. Alavi and Shanin go so far as to suggest that Kautsky here privileges social development or progress over proletariat, party, even socialism.[33] Certainly Kautsky argued explicitly within the pages of this text that

> Human society is an organism, not animal or vegetable in character but of its own specific type although no less an organism. It is not merely an aggregation of individuals. And as an organism, it must be organised in a uniform manner. It would be absurd to imagine that one part of society can develop in one direction, and another part, of equal importance, in the opposite direction. Development can only go in one direction.[34]

Kautsky's bind is evident: he confronts uneven development, he needs to acknowledge empirical deviations from the capitalist/socialist telos, yet he also needs to restate 'the axiom that the development of modern industry necessarily leads to socialism'.[35] Yet social development, evolution, progress, take precedence over the interests of the proletariat.[36] At the same time, however, Kautsky fumbles with this concept of evolution, qualifying his earlier statement of unilinear evolution with the proviso that society is not an organism whose parts all develop at the same speed.[37]

Yet the overall logic of *The Agrarian Question*, and of Kautsky's work as such, is that big is beautiful. Co-operation undoes itself as it develops in size, now resembling other large capitalist enterprises, and the idea of 'village communism', Marx's so-called 'Russian road', is simply rejected.[38] The city is the site of utopia. Kautsky thus reenters the worlds of his chosen Utopians – here, Bellers,

31 Alavi and Shanin 1988, p. xiii.
32 Alavi and Shanin 1988, p. xvii.
33 Alavi and Shanin 1988, p. xvi.
34 Kautsky 1988a, p. 303.
35 Kautsky 1988a, p. 303.
36 Kautsky 1988a, p. 325.
37 Kautsky 1988a, p. 329.
38 Kautsky 1988a, p. 339.

Fourier, Owen – in order to discuss (and defend) child labour, not in its capitalist form but in its anthropological underpinning.[39] To exclude youth from productive labour is hardly better than licensing their exploitation by capitalism – for humans do need to engage in work. Schooling must also remain a vital part of the process of formation, though Kautsky also places considerable weight on experience and on the significance of popular culture.[40] In this context he briefly discusses the role of the state under socialism. He inveighs against the libertarian proposition that the state or public administration ought to be abolished. Kautsky's proletarian state is not Lenin's:

> Such matters are currently far too complex, diverse and extensive to be carried out as a secondary occupation, as a dilettante after-hours activity. They require trained specialists, paid officials, for whom such matters are their sole concern. The idea of government of the people by the people, meaning that public affairs should be attended to by representatives of the people, unpaid, in their free time instead of by paid officials is a utopia, and a reactionary, undemocratic utopia at that.[41]

The hand may be that of classical social democracy, but the voice is the voice of Weber. For, somewhat like the Webbs, Karl Kautsky shared the characteristic ambivalence of Victorian and Wilhelmine sociology – an overemphatic enthusiasm about the principle of social organism and social evolution coupled with a clear vision of the necessity of differentiation and social division of labour. And this, again, is what drives a wedge between his views and those, say, of Morris. For while Kautsky in closing refers more positively to a possible (limited) revival of handicraft, as the demand for cheap articles will fall under socialism, his general scenario of the future remains as generally modernist as is that of the Webbs.[42] Certainly Kautsky succeeds, however, in imparting to his reader the sense that central, large-scale industrial forms will dominate the socialist horizon, regardless of local peculiarities in its silhouette.

Kautsky becomes less coy about such details in his 1902 essay, *The Day After the Revolution*, where he turns directly to problems of the future. In the pretext to *The Day After the Revolution* Kautsky offers one of his characteristic moderations of view. Having already decided for the freedom/necessity, leisure/labour couplet he nevertheless offers the coda that even factory work can

---

39   Kautsky 1988a, pp. 359–60.
40   Kautsky 1988a, pp. 362–3.
41   Kautsky 1988a, p. 425.
42   Kautsky 1988a, p. 443.

be improved, all the same: the factory can be turned from 'a place of monotony, repulsive forced labour into an attractive spot for the joyful activity of happy human beings'.[43] Once again, we see that Kautsky was not entirely dismissive of the romantic current. Yet the general picture remains hypermodernist. In *The Day After the Revolution* Kautsky sketches a utopia not unlike that of the Webbs' *Constitution*, with the difference that it is staffed entirely by proletarians. Kautsky explains, Webb-like, that socialism will be characterised by a plurality of different property forms – nationalised, municipal, co-operative and private.[44] Now he openly rejects Morris's utopia: the 'machine will remain the ruler of the production process'.[45] Against Bebel, he also rejects the Renaissance conception of the individual, offering in its place an industrialised caricature where a seamstress, for example, can work in a nationalised factory, at another time make dresses for private customers at home, or establish a co-operative with her comrades.[46] Leonardo here is modernised, turned not into a scientist (Wells) but into a flexible labourer for whom diversity exists merely across a single industrial sector. The suggestion is less diverse than that of the Webbs, because there is missing here any sense, say, of social service, even though the latter theme can be said to exist in Kautsky's commitment to ongoing public administration. Again Kautsky's conceptual orthodoxy gets the better of his analysis. Following Marx's argument about the centralisation of capital and its accompanying tendency to proletarianisation, Kautsky fails to differentiate between proletarian and citizen. The only human identity we see here is the function of the proletarian. Kautsky's ethics are circumscribed by Marxist sociology – his commitment to the two-class theory with its axiomatic bipolarisation means that class subsumes to itself function and, more generally, action. Where in Bebel we get a diversity of practices, in Kautsky we are offered a diversity of property forms as some kind of insurance that there will be diversity in the conduct of everyday life. Only this sleight of hand allows Kautsky to assure the reader that his utopia will facilitate the greatest diversity and possibility of change, and then to close with some grandiose gestures towards the fraternal, pre-Trotskyist collective superman of socialism.[47]

To turn to *The Road to Power* is to return to the triumphalism of Kautsky's *Class Struggle*. Here, in 1906, Kautsky continues to defend what others stigmatise as 'prophecy', now as the materialist reading of the direction of social

---

43   Kautsky 1910, p. 20.
44   Kautsky 1910, p. 127.
45   Kautsky 1910, p. 165.
46   Kautsky 1910, p. 166.
47   Kautsky 1910, pp. 166, 189.

evolution. Again Kautsky denies that his view is teleological, yet assures readers of the inevitability of socialism, and offers his classic expression of automatism: that Social Democracy is a revolutionary party, but not a revolution-making party.[48] The truisms of orthodoxy are equally characteristic of his *Ethics and the Materialist Conception of History*, which was probably one of Kautsky's most widely distributed works in English, published like Dietzgen and Lafargue by Kerr of Chicago. This text helps better to explain the circumscription of Kautsky's ethics by the Marxism in his sociology. Kautsky, unlike Bernstein, rejects Kantian ethics as though it were glue for the bourgeois morality of reconciliation. Darwin's stress on struggle makes him, and not Kant, an ally of socialism. The end of evolution, or its proper beginning, is socialism. Social freedom has to do with the greatest possible shortening of the period of necessary labour.[49] Socialism's freedom is different from that espoused by the French Revolution, primarily because of the difference between attitudes to property.[50] But finally, Kautsky claims, the ethics of socialism differ because Marxism alone has a scientific basis. Moral indignation might come in handy in the struggle for socialism, but socialism is freestanding, as its proper concern is with the scientific examination of the laws of the development and movement of the social organism, for the purpose of knowing the necessary tendencies and aims of proletarian class struggle.[51] Science precedes ethics – here we find a similar flaw to that in the work of the Webbs, where sociology practically precedes ethics, where the question of how efficiently to organise the social organism typically precedes the questions, what ought I do?, how ought I live?

Kautsky penned *The Labour Revolution* after the Bolsheviks came to power. It was only now that Kautsky was to become an open and vital defender of parliamentary forms, to more publicly view socialism as the fulfilment of bourgeois civilisation and not just as the crowning of capitalist economy, and, in the process, to link up arms again with his old friend Eduard Bernstein, who had defended these views all along (and suffered for it, especially at the combined hand of Bolshevism). Unlike Bernstein, Kautsky still at this stage remained ambivalent about democracy, viewing it as the precondition of socialism and as a barometer of working-class strength, and yet also seeing it as a positive institution in itself. Democracy in *The Labour Revolution* is never merely a means, but not yet fully quite an end either.[52] But now Kautsky enters more

---

48   Kautsky 1909, pp. 22, 49, 50.
49   Kautsky 1907, p. 197.
50   Kautsky 1907, p. 196.
51   Kautsky 1907, p. 202.
52   Kautsky 1925, p. 28.

fully the kind of debate conducted between the Webbs and Cole over guilds and other organisational forms proper or improper to socialism, the rights of consumers versus those of producers, and so on. Such debates had been brought to a head by practical matters of socialisation following the German revolutions. As we would expect, Kautsky's case is closer to the Webbs. The Webbs had, indeed, sent Kautsky a copy of their *Constitution*, though it appears from their correspondence that it never arrived.[53] Certainly Kautsky shared the Webbs' reservations about guilds – he was unimpressed by the propos- ition that parliamentary forms should be welded to economic or functional interests.[54] At the same time, Kautsky simply rejects the suggestion that con- sumption leads production; to accept this, as did the Webbs, would be to deny the priority of class struggle.[55] Others, like Lenin, who also claim to march under the banner of the class struggle are still, however, befogged by syndic- alist fantasy. Kautsky specifically reprimands Lenin here for his naivety in *State and Revolution*. What Lenin hopes for – the whole of society organised as one office and one factory – 'that is a prison, not a factory', says Kautsky. The only virtue of the fabulous ignorance of the Bolsheviks, according to Kautsky, is that it made them bold. 'For Russia and for Communism the luck was not so obvious'.[56] Unlike the Webbs, Kautsky was always to maintain his wits about him regarding the Russian experiment – his 1918 *Dictatorship of the Prolet- ariat* was merely one instalment in a long and principled critique of the Soviet path.

The Labour Revolution rests on the now familiar argument about utopia and evolution – 'thanks to Marx', in the German tradition at least, 'we are now familiar with the idea of social evolution. We no longer seek the per- fect society, which would render any further development impossible, but only a solution of the specific problems which capitalism presents to us'.[57] Kaut- sky's was thus a limited utopia, dependent on variable property forms, with the necessary bureaucracy subordinated to the practice of politics. Against Lenin, it need be acknowledged that a 'democracy which tried to dispense with bureaucratic assistance would only be capable of solving simple problems' – whereas complex social forms would likely continue to produce complex prob- lems.[58] Kautsky also rejects the distributive principle 'to each according to their

---

53   S. Webb to Kautsky, 5.1.1923, Amsterdam, Kautsky Papers, IISH, DXXIII, 70.
54   Kautsky 1925, p. 99.
55   Kautsky 1925, p. 102.
56   Kautsky 1925, p. 128.
57   Kautsky 1925, p. 143.
58   Kautsky 1925, p. 156.

needs': productivity ought to determine remuneration, not the formal principle of equality.[59] At this stage Kautsky returns to the critique of guild socialism.

Even a critic as distant from English experience as Kautsky understood that the English labour movement had undergone a sea change in terms of its attitude to the state. For the mid-nineteenth century movement the state had been bureaucratic anathema. By the twentieth century, under the influence among other things of Fabianism itself, the state had come to be seen as the legitimate instrument of legislation. Guild socialism, Kautsky argued, represented the synthesis of these theoretical strategies: it unified state and syndicalism, allowing the latter to remain the dominant motif.[60] Like the Webbs, he rejected syndicalism as too complicit in the utopia of *State and Revolution*, and argued that it was simply too backward-looking, linked as it was in Germany and England alike to the building trade, with handicraft rather than with mechanical production.[61] Against Cole, and specifically in criticism of *Self Government in Industry*, Kautsky now advanced the case against guilds in detail. The essential problem about guild socialism, as with syndicalism, was that workers' democracy was too particularistic.[62] Yet as we have seen, Kautsky's utopia is for all this constructed in the image of a generic *homo faber*. Evidently Kautsky is, however, empirically sensitive to the existence of *homo consumer*, so that he offers the sound observation that rather than arbitrate later, social mechanisms involving consumers in decision-making concerning production may dissolve potential problems in advance. Here Kautsky enters again the Austro-German socialisation debate, defending Bauer's *Der Weg zum Sozialismus* and endorsing the principle of joint control between production, consumption and science (which would seem to mean the state).[63] He remains unconvinced of the need to destroy either money or the state.[64] For Kautsky the so-called 'second phase' of socialism is infinitely removed from the present; it may in fact be similar to 'the Millennial Kingdom'. Socialism, in any case, very clearly stands on the shoulders of capitalism – it develops its forms of life in order that it may bring to the 'whole of humanity not merely bread and security of existence, but also civilisation and freedom'.[65]

---

59   Kautsky 1925, p. 169.
60   Kautsky 1925, pp. 195–6.
61   Kautsky 1925, pp. 196–7.
62   Kautsky 1925, p. 201.
63   Kautsky 1925, p. 203.
64   Kautsky 1925, pp. 259, 224.
65   Kautsky 1925, pp. 262, 283.

On the one hand ... on the other – this seems to be the way in which Kautsky's Marxism proceeds, and it is this ambivalence which drove Trotsky and Lenin to view Kautsky as a renegade. Kautsky had rejected Bolshevism, and yet argued for a proletarian utopia, proletarian class struggle, proletarian democracy, only to baulk at the outcome when Lenin presented him with the baby of the Soviet utopia for his approval. When pressed, or thus distressed, however, Kautsky spoke against 'proletarian aristocracy'.[66] Kautsky sought after a class conscious and intellectually developed proletariat, even if he secretly hoped that its con-sciousness would resemble his own. Yet he was absolutely no Bolshevik in Lenin's sense of the professional revolutionary, the Jacobin who made a pact with Social Democracy, and he made this clear enough in his argument in *The Materialist Conception of History*, that belief was no precondition of socialism, that one did not need to be a Marxist in order to be a social democrat.[67] As I have suggested, however, the tension in Kautsky's thought was not merely that between philosophical generality and historical specificity, though this was indeed a central feature of his thinking. There is also a tension here between a liberal, or universalistic political current and a proletarian sociological cur-rent. Class analysis too often got the better of Kautsky, so just as he tended to be dismissive of the peasantry he also tended to blot out the middle class or the intellectuals, acknowledging them – just as he did the peasants – only to deny them, and to return to the general postulates of Marxism concerning the almost universal and burgeoning working class standing against the ever-diminishing ranks of capitalist magnates.[68] Lenin, as we have seen, was a dif-ferent puzzle – theoretically dogmatic to the point of despair, he also became progressively more empirically pragmatic, taking seriously third classes to the extent of finally ditching the syndicalist scenario of *State and Revolution* in favour of a multi-class utopia.

One substantial issue on which Lenin and Kautsky actually disagreed – his-toriographical commonsense notwithstanding – was exactly this issue of class analysis. Kautsky took the intelligentsia seriously – he did not deny his own existence – but he was also given to a general sociology in which intellectuals were *Kopfarbeiter*, those who worked with their heads while others toiled with their hands. Yet, as we have seen, Kautsky fetishised science and consequently was obliged to argue that real Marxists were those who were possessed of such Science. This view he defended publicly in *Die Neue Zeit* in 1901–2.[69] Lenin then

---

66   Kautsky 1920, p. 214.
67   Kautsky 1988b preface.
68   See e.g. Heimann and Meyer 1978, pp. 128–35.
69   Kautsky 1901.

seized upon these arguments for his own purposes in his 1902 tract *What Is To Be Done?* Lenin's view was that the professional revolutionaries alone could provide the leaven of correct theory for the well-intentioned but ultimately aimless spontaneous activity of the working masses. Kautsky had argued that the vehicle of science was not the proletariat but the bourgeois intelligentsia; this historically accurate observation was turned by Lenin into the theoretical guarantee for his own claims to power.[70] Kautsky's theory, once again, was contradictory. On the one hand he praised proletarian culture and self-education, as we have seen, for example, in *The Agrarian Question*, where formal education is appreciated but not idolised; on the other hand, he viewed Marxism as a qualitatively superior form of knowledge which did not originate in experience. The tension is one that is evident in Marx's own work: on the one hand, the logic of experience (or the logic of history) drives the masses into action, on the other hand they really must read *Capital* in order to understand themselves and their world. Kautsky viewed intellectuals as both necessary, for theoretical development, and at the same time superfluous, because history itself was looking after these things. Lenin, by comparison, viewed theory as openly and plainly as any political operator – as a means and will to power. The status of theory is different, for Kautsky, and partly because of his primordial Darwinism. For Kautsky not only espoused the utopianism of progress, but also on every other day enthused for the utopia of absolute knowledge. This hope for a unified science sets Kautsky's project well apart from the pragmatic approach to knowledge characteristic of Lenin's practice, if not always his theory.

Kautsky returned again to these kinds of issues in his magnum opus, *The Materialist Conception of History*, though he had also examined them earlier in an essay which Lenin avoided, 'The Intelligentsia and Social Democracy'. Here Kautsky had defended the idea of an alliance between science and labour, and he imagined a reciprocal alliance at that.[71] He did not use the language, but he seems to have been thinking of something like Gramsci's organic intellectuals, not Lenin's professional revolutionaries. The point of comparison with Gramsci is one which recurs in *The Materialist Conception*, but there are many other resonances here as well. Kautsky viewed the book as his most important, but it was allowed to disappear, under communist polemic (Korsch) as much as behind the proverbial veil of silence. The general message which the book imparts is not unlike that suggested by the analysis of the Webbs' work, above: caricatured as philistines, these were actually sensitive and fascinating

---

70   Lenin 1977c, pp. 383–4.
71   Kautsky 1895.

thinkers, whose legacy remains far more potentially productive than that of Bolshevism once the pyrotechnics have died down. Partly this is so because of the milieu within which these *fin-de-siécle* socialists laboured. Kautsky, for his part, formed this milieu as much as he was formed by it – its real monument remains the journal he founded and edited through the period, *Die Neue Zeit*, which itself remains the best measure of German socialist culture in the period. Everything was to be discussed; everything was problematical, everything was interesting. Little wonder that Lenin turned Kautsky into a renegade. Kautsky opened his study with the proviso that subscription to the materialist conception of history was no prerequisite for adherence to the SPD. The reason for this pluralism becomes more clear as Kautsky proceeds to introduce the materialist conception itself. For as Kautsky confesses, what he has in mind is not a one-sided explanation of history to counter Weber, but a 'developmental history of mankind'.[72] This puzzle rests on another tension, that between Kautsky's commitment to encyclopedic knowledge and his sense of the tentative and fragile nature of knowing and being. Thus, for example, Kautsky here (as elsewhere) discusses everything under the sun, has apparently read everything, has views on everything (yet without the manic sense of overload characteristic of Shaw) and at the same time wants to establish limits to knowledge and to politics. Against Trotsky's open-ended scenario in *Literature and Revolution*, then, Kautsky posits a limited goal:

> Even after the general realization of Socialism, human freedom will of course remain limited, just like our knowledge of the world on which this freedom is founded. We shall never completely fathom all problems posed by nature, and we will hardly be able ever to foresee all consequences even of our own social activity ... instead of speaking of a leap from the realm of necessity into the realm of freedom, one would probably do better to speak only of an extension of the province of freedom within the realm of causal necessity, the boundaries of which are unassailable.[73]

The argument is stated more succinctly later on:

> The final goal of the proletariat is not a final goal for the development of humanity ... like the process of acquiring knowledge, that of social development is also unending ... An enduringly perfect society is as little

---

72   Kautsky 1988b, p. 6.
73   Kautsky 1988b, p. 28.

possible as an absolute truth. And both the one and the other would mean nothing other than social stagnation and death.[74]

Kautsky in this sense, and like the Webbs, was more thoroughly evolutionist a thinker even than Marx – no millennium could put an end to this process of change, no last instance could ever come – not even theoretically.

In stark contrast to the Prometheanism of Trotsky, Kautsky instead volunteered the proposition that human beings were naturally conservative. The mind itself was conservative, governed by habit and tradition rather than by the Faustian passion for change upon change.[75] Like Durkheim, he argued that morality, state and society transcend the individual sociologically.[76] Evolution was a complicated story, not simply the onward, upward arc toward socialism but a fragmented and halting process. Again like Durkheim he argued that morality rested less on class bases than on what societies *considered* to be good or evil. Morality is not freely chosen, but is autonomous.[77] Now Kautsky rejects the suggestion that society be viewed as an organism – Spencer and Schäffle are mistaken to do so, because unlike the animal organism the organisation of society is composed of individuals, each of whom possesses individual consciousness.[78] A new culture can only arise under socialism out of the abolition of the proletariat, not its universalisation; and yet the process must perforce remain indeterminate, for 'Nothing is more erroneous than to believe that the search for what is new ... is inborn in the human spirit'.[79]

Anticipating Trotsky, Kautsky argues in his analysis of early civilisation that the small family farm is a necessarily barbarous institution, for it is all necessity and no freedom. If the proletarian movement takes hold of the whole mass of the people, the resultant process of mental diversification may actually enable the whole of civilisation further to be uplifted, and this not for single individuals but for the whole of humanity. 'The result could seem to be a race of supermen. But they would be supermen only in comparison with humanity as it has been hitherto'.[80] For in the meantime there would still remain a division of labour and co-operation within it. Here Kautsky argues against the growing interdependence theory of division of labour associated with Spencer

---

74   Kautsky 1988b, p. 464.
75   Kautsky 1988b, pp. 34–8.
76   Kautsky 1988b, p. 43.
77   Kautsky 1988b, p. 69.
78   Kautsky 1988b, p. 70.
79   Kautsky 1988b, pp. 101, 103.
80   Kautsky 1988b, p. 133.

and Durkheim and influential on the Webbs. Formal altruism, for Kautsky, cannot be overpowered by actual antagonism.[81] Yet property relations reflect the conservative character and the mind – when a certain technology and its associated system of property have existed for some duration of time, the *power of tradition* also comes into play.[82]

Kautsky's sense of continuity, of the weight of history and the place of tradition lead him to confirm a utopic vision that of all in Marx's work is closest to that in the third volume of *Capital*. This is already clear from the works discussed hitherto, but is further clarified in *The Materialist Conception*. Writing just after the publication of Marx's *German Ideology*, Kautsky takes time to argue against its utopia, huntsman-fisherman-shepherd-critical critic, at least inasmuch as he interprets this utopia as indicating a non-industrial future. But actually, for Kautsky, the Marxian message is different: it concerns not the flight from the division of labour, but its transformation. The rural examples which Marx draws on are redundant, but the idea of spreading activities over the day lives on. The socialist goal for Kautsky must involve both the reduction of the extent of the working day and the pursuit of different activities within its extent – four hours, say of eight, in the mine or factory, the remaining four in agriculture, or building, or driving, or in art or science.[83] For Kautsky this new, flexible socialist division of labour would have different results from those hoped for by Durkheim: rather than producing professional or vocational solidarity, this less fixed identity will serve to minimise the role hitherto played by interest in politics.[84]

Kautsky thus rejects not only Trotsky's Prometheanism, but also Marx's. At the same time, however, he refuses Durkheim's – and the Webbs' – sense, that identity can be given and social solidarity best achieved by a fixed and limited place in the social machine. This, and other dimensions of his thought, arguably place him closer to Weber. Indeed, Kautsky repeatedly and systematically returns to Weber in *The Materialist Conception*, both methodologically, with reference to the place of mind or ideas in history, and later, politically. Kautsky discusses, and praises *The Protestant Ethic*.[85] None of this is surprising, except for the fact that Marxists hardly ever take Weber seriously, except as a stalking horse. Certainly it ought to be unsurprising given the sobriety and balance of Kautsky's own views, on mind, say, and given the somewhat

---

81   Kautsky 1988b, p. 189.
82   Kautsky 1988b, pp. 209, 212.
83   Kautsky 1988b, pp. 260–1.
84   Kautsky 1988b, p. 262.
85   Kautsky 1988b, pp. 356–60, 368.

arbitrary nature of his self-description as materialist. This then issues in specific discussion of 'Politics as a Vocation'. Kautsky agrees with Weber, as we have seen earlier, regarding the necessity of differentiation, organisation and bureaucracy: the two thinkers stand shoulder to shoulder against Lenin. And here it is difficult not to conclude that Kautsky simply rejected, to all intents and purposes, his own earlier claims to Marxist science, and drew rather upon the different major streams which made up *fin-de-siécle* German social theory.[86] Unlike Weber, Kautsky never, however, felt the calling to politics; he was happy to be an intellectual. The sociology of intellectuals was another theme to which he now returned. Here he proposed, as Mannheim did later in *Ideology and Utopia*, that intellectuals were not a class but could take up the cause of another class.[87] Now, into the new century, a new kind of intellectual was brought closer to the proletariat by new working conditions. This process of development made it necessary, further, to renounce the old definition of intellectuals. Intellectuals today included not only the academically trained, but all those who in a democracy found themselves placed in democratic vocations, as writers, as party or union officials, as parliamentary representatives.[88] The intelligentsia thus took on a new historic significance, though (on the other hand ...) the major class divide, bourgeois versus proletarian, was still the fundamental class cleavage.[89]

Back, then, to the proletariat, Kautsky's fundamental class. The proletarian, for Kautsky, is a more universal figure than the bourgeois. And more, miraculously, the theses of *The Class Struggle* – of *The Communist Manifesto* – still hold true. But now, Kautsky argues, economistic struggle expands into struggle for the transformation of state and of society. The key to this process is democracy. The democratisation of the state is one task; other, new and special organisational forms will still yet have to be created.[90] Not crisis, but only the strength of the proletariat can see the instauration of socialism; this involves the growing political power of the working class over the shrinking economic claims of the bourgeoisie.[91] Within this framework nestle both a minimum and a maximum programme for the proletariat. At the least, the proletariat will grow in health and in strength.[92] On a broader horizon, individuals will outpace Rousseau and

---

86   See generally Liebersohn, 1988.
87   Kautsky 1988b, p. 397.
88   Kautsky 1988b, p. 399.
89   Kautsky 1988b, pp. 399–400.
90   Kautsky 1988b, pp. 410–11.
91   Kautsky 1988b, pp. 426, 435.
92   Kautsky 1988b, p. 513.

even Bentham, for they will encounter qualitatively new kinds of happiness.[93] Kautsky agrees with Marx that all those would-be Raphaels shall be so under socialism. 'The general availability of education will facilitate the full development by everyone of all his [sic] potentialities, the promotion of which is in the interest of society'. The increase in free time will allow the individual further to develop potentialities should the nature of work limit these – leisure time will allow productive labour, work in science or art, or play or sport. 'In this regard, socialism will offer a hitherto unheard of possibility of the free development of the individual personality', but for Kautsky this could at most be a modernised and socialised Faust with collective sensibility overriding the will to be all.[94]

What emerges from any reading of Kautsky's work, as opposed to its Bolshevik resumé, is a sense of difference, distinction, and ambivalence. Kautsky is nowhere near as consistently given to the defence of democracy as Bernstein, indeed his primary values seem rather to be progress and proletariat. In this regard Kautsky does bear some responsibility for Lenin's views, as we have seen. Kautsky's early utopic visions generally lack any detailed sense of political forms, and it is of course the earlier Kautsky who is the vital figure in Bolshevism's intellectual formation. By *The Labour Revolution* and *The Materialist Conception* Kautsky makes his democratic credentials far more plain; they are there in the earlier work, but the citizen is still shrouded as the proletarian. Peter Murphy's critique of social democracy as a belated convert to democracy itself is thus well-aimed – at Kautsky, but not at Bernstein.[95]

Bernstein: A Good Man Fallen among Liberals

Eduard Bernstein has been even more extensively caricatured than Kautsky, for his period of Marxist orthodoxy was relatively short-lived, though he persisted long in viewing himself a Marxist. The stock response to his alleged 'decline' has, once again, been to blame the Fabians. Thus just as *Soviet Communism* has been uncharitably viewed as the declining view of two octogenarians, so Bernstein's refusal of orthodoxy has been viewed as a disease acquired while off the Continent, in England. Bernstein was obliged to leave Germany by the threat of imprisonment under Bismarck's anti-socialist laws. He was, indeed, something of an Anglophile, following as he did Marx's sense that England was

---

93   Kautsky 1988b, p. 517.
94   Kautsky 1988b, p. 524.
95   Murphy 1990.

further down the road of capitalist development and, especially, of the process of development towards democracy. Over a century an entire literature has been generated about the question whether in fact Bernstein was a Fabian.[96] The short answer to the question is no, but this has not served to prevent much ink being spilled over the issue. (Karl Korsch did in fact join the Fabians while on his own English sojourn; hopefully a fresh century of debate will be avoided in this case.)

Did Bernstein then have any substantive affinities with Fabianism? The answer to this question is also in the negative, but this time with qualification. Cosmetic similarities are apparent – Bernstein shared with the Fabians a generally evolutionary conception of socialism, but then, as we have seen, this was a general motif present in all labour movements in the nineteenth century. Certainly the company of the Fabians was conducive to heresy – and Bernstein actually came to realise that he was living a lie while addressing the Fabians on 'What Marx Really Taught' in 1897. He had set out to defend Marx, and came to realise that he could not persuade his audience because he could no longer persuade himself.[97] Subsequently Bernstein became not only the great (or miserable) reformist, but also the leading revisionist.

Bernstein was always something of a conservative among Marxists: he took tradition seriously, and viewed history as a process somewhat less than given to rupture. Unlike some others, such as Belfort Bax, he also shared with Marx and with Weber the sense that modernity was a mixed blessing. Bax, in debate with Bernstein, had identified modernity with capitalism and offered a completely negative appraisal of both. In this regard at least Bax was a less nuanced thinker than his co-author William Morris, for despite Morris's own medieval aura, he did not want simply to turn back. Bax attacked Bernstein as a rotten Fabian, an apologist for the culture which produced 'shoddy'.[98] Bax's own utopia, more or less explicit, seems suggestive of primitivism, Rousseau and the noble savage – for the savages, at least; this was a logic later to produce the moral approval of Bolshevism for the Russians but not for the British. 'Unlike Bernstein', said Bax, 'we regard modern civilization as, *per se*, a curse and an evil. (This, I suppose, is what Bernstein calls Romanticism)'.[99] Capitalism, or modern civilisation, and socialism were absolutely antithetical for Bax – Bernstein had 'unconsciously ceased to be a Social Democrat' in order to deny this.[100]

---

96   Hirsch 1977; Bax 1988, pp. 61–5.
97   See Rogers 1983.
98   Bax 1988, p. 61.
99   Bax 1988, p. 62.
100   Bax 1988, p. 64.

Like all revolutionaries, Bax simply refuses to accept that to ask for everything is to demand nothing, to which the powers that be will only too happily oblige. Bernstein, by comparison, actually wanted the world to change but, like Kautsky and others, suspected that there were substantial obstacles – like tradition, habit and memory – to the scope of this change. Bernstein was not a postmodernist, or for that matter an antimodernist. He believed that progress was a value worth defending, that slavery was worse than wage-slavery, and so on.[101] Characteristically, he uses *Capital* to make his point. He then proceeds, in a series of articles in *Die Neue Zeit*, to discuss utopia more formally. He agrees with Marx and with Webb that utopianism in the old sense, 'the recipe for the cook-shops of the future', is obsolete. But there is a new kind of bad utopianism for which capitalism and socialism are worlds apart, for which socialism is a negative and apocalyptic view rather than one which affirms the world and then sets to work on it.[102] The Weberian resonances are unmistakable: in order to change the world, we must be of the world. But this does not, for Bernstein, add up to a disaggregated Fabianism, a patchwork of administrative policies for the reform of the respective compartments of social and administrative life. In individual investigations and as pragmatic socialists, the Fabians have achieved much that is excellent, according to Bernstein – but they have deprived the socialist movement of the compass which keeps it from just fumbling about in the dark.[103]

Like all other socialists, then, Bernstein makes rhetorical attacks upon utopianism while still, necessarily, working with an image of the future. And like Kautsky, he knows the literature of utopia and praises it as both inspirational and pragmatic. He praises Owen and Fourier for the detail of their thinking – for they were practical dreamers, so to speak, who viewed their proposals as feasible, discussed scale and architecture, needs and passions – they were reformers, offering defensible precedents for Social Democracy.[104] Bernstein appraises the desirability of local organisation, yet admits the impulse of modernity toward scale and differentiation. This raises practical, but also moral difficulties, and here Bernstein argues, like Weber, that the effects of welfarism upon the personality must be taken into consideration. Citizens must take on duties as well as rights in order to aspire to active citizenship.[105] Individuals, consequently, ought still to be responsible for their own welfare under social-

101   Bernstein 1988a, pp. 66–7.
102   Bernstein 1988c, p. 74.
103   Bernstein 1988c, p. 77.
104   Bernstein 1988c, p. 83.
105   Bernstein 1988c, p. 91; and see Weber, 1988, p. 415.

ism – responsibility is the reverse but coupled value of autonomy. The alternatives are tyranny or chaos.[106] Socialism thus involves the pursuit of social
self-help, and like the Webbs, Cole and Kautsky, Bernstein here advocates intermediate institutions in order to facilitate the process. Most of the functions at
present carried out by the state must be taken over by self-governing democratic bodies.[107]

Regarding work, Bernstein like Kautsky views it as a responsibility for socialist citizens: this is already implicit in his conception of individual responsibility.
Again he turns here to Owen and Fourier, both of whom argued in defence of
child labour on the basis of the anthropology *homo faber*. The point seems
arcane, given the reconstruction of the image of the western child into the
twentieth century, but the claim is consistent with the sense that humans need
both to work and to play (Bellers).[108] It is also consistent with the claim that
capitalism is the historical prerequisite of modern civilisation, but that this
civilisation is by no means limited to the capitalist economy – child labour, like
adult labour in its capitalist form is to be transformed but not abolished.[109] But
now Bernstein was to let the cat out of the bag, and set it amongst the pigeons.
For in 1898 he began to question the so-called 'final goal' of socialism. The 'final
goal' of socialism Bernstein viewed as the utopia of windbags. The movement,
the process of socialism was more important. The message of Bernstein's now
clichéd phrase – the movement everything, the goal nothing – is in fact both
sensible and defensible, only it produced so much purple outrage that his sundry enemies, Parvus, Luxemburg and the rest, were unable to concede the point
(Parvus was sufficiently wild, and stubborn, to write no less than seventeen articles against Bernstein; Luxemburg wisely saved her energy and wrote instead
one brilliant polemic, *Reform or Revolution?*).

The controversy preceded the publication of Bernstein's central work, *Vor-
aussetzungen des Sozialismus*, characteristically mistitled in English on Ramsay
MacDonald's mischievous advice as *Evolutionary Socialism*. The German title
was significant, for Bernstein viewed socialism as a premise from which we
depart, not a goal at which we arrive. Thus the *goal* is nothing, because socialism is not a goal but a principle. In response to criticism, Bernstein summons
up the language which he used in the criticism of Fabianism: 'A movement
without a goal would drift chaotically, for it would be a movement without direction. No goal, no direction. The movement needs a compass, but this goal is

---

106   Bernstein 1988c, p. 94.
107   Bernstein 1988c, pp. 95, 97.
108   Bernstein 1988c, p. 105.
109   Bernstein 1988e, p. 151.

not the realisation of a social plan so much as the implementation of a social *principle*.[110] Thus the so-called goal, or *principle* of socialism was intact; and the *movement* Bernstein defended as a gesture both theoretical and strategic. Bernstein defended the labour movement both as an institution and as a process, a moving towards socialism. And as Weber had pointed out, there was in any case nothing self-evidently reformist about this stand – the idea that the movement was 'everything' could just as well be the view of syndicalism.[111] Bernstein, for his part, argued (against Parvus) that not syndicalism, but state enterprise, municipal enterprise, co-operative enterprise led the way forward.[112] But more than this, Bernstein actually feared revolution, as he feared chaos. Certainly he was more hard-headed about state power than Parvus – for he simply argued that socialists could not spurn capitalism the day after the revolution unless they wanted economic life to come to a complete standstill, and thus set the stage for reaction. The theory of collapse was hopeless – like Gramsci, like Kautsky, Bernstein viewed socialism as a new order itself the product of order, not chaos.

Indeed, Bernstein proposed, if revolutions call forth all the slumbering potentials of humanity they also call out the idiots, and the world is still such a place that the idiots have a good chance. More generally, he suggested, socialists would do well to remember the power of memory and tradition – the world was not such a simple place, not even when old régimes crumbled.[113] In sad anticipation of later years he now wrote that when 'all trade has come to a standstill and all commerce has ceased, people do not ask whether something is socialist but whether it will help them get work and food'.[114] Bernstein was thus prepossessed both with ordinary human questions about suffering, and with postulates of social theory concerning the power of the imaginary. Like Weber, he argued against the dichotomy materialism and idealism, rather in defence of the category *interest*.[115] Like Durkheim, he proposes that moral concepts are more durable than economic developments, and that precisely because they are more conservative, they are to some extent independent of such developments. And thus he criticises Marxism's deafening silence on matters of ethics.[116]

---

110   Bernstein 1988d, pp. 193, 215.
111   Weber to Michels, 4. 8. 1908, quoted by Scaff 1987, p. 744.
112   Bernstein 1988b, p. 218.
113   Bernstein 1988b, pp. 220–1.
114   Bernstein 1988b, p. 222.
115   Bernstein 1988c, p. 233.
116   Bernstein 1988c, pp. 238–43.

Bernstein's own proposals become more clear when we turn to the book entitled *Evolutionary Socialism*. Reformism was not really the centre of controversy here; Vollmar and others had been counselling that for years.[117] But reformists and radicals had for too long been content to live with the combination of reformist practice and revolutionary rhetoric, since it had even been enshrined in the Erfurt Programme of 1892.[118] Bernstein simply hoped to bring theory into line with practice; Rosa Luxemburg, by contrast hoped to bring practice into line with theory, while Kautsky, meantime, was happy to live with the contradiction. What generated the most hostility to Bernstein's case was, in retrospect, the least controversial of his claims. Bernstein had the tenacity to question the holy grail of classical Marxism – the proposition that capital would become more concentrated just as the proletariat would expand. Bernstein rejected the theory of capitalist collapse and the theory of class bipolarisation. According to his biographer, Peter Gay, Bernstein sketched all this out not in a treatise but on an envelope:

> Peasants do not sink; middle class does not disappear; crises do not grow even larger; misery and serfdom do not increase. There is increase in insecurity, dependence, social distance, social character of production, functional superfluity of property owners.[119]

Bernstein argued that society was positively not becoming simplified but rather graduated and differentiated in its structure. The middle classes were a normal feature of this story and not an aberration.[120]

Crisis was not the motor of socialism; capitalist collapse was not inevitable. Socialism was better understood as the movement towards an order based on the principle of association. Consumer association was to be preferred to producer co-operation; co-operation itself could facilitate the process of the formation of social capital.[121] Unions were the democratic element in industry, but they were one actor alongside others, and were not representative of the proletarian state *in nuce*.[122] Politics was not primarily a matter of classes but of citizens. 'The idea of democracy includes, in the conception of the present day, a notion of justice – an equality of rights for all members of the community' –

---

117 Vollmar 1891.
118 The Erfurt Programme is reprinted in Steenson (1981, pp. 247–50).
119 Gay 1962, p. 250.
120 Bernstein 1965, pp. 60–6.
121 Bernstein 1965, pp. 96, 118, 124.
122 Bernstein 1965, pp. 139, 141.

democracy actually meant the suppression of class government, not its extension into the proletarian state.[123] Thus social democracy 'does not wish to break up this society and make all its members proletarians together; it labours rather incessantly at raising the worker from the social position of a proletarian to that of a citizen, and thus to make citizenship universal'. The aim of social democracy, for Bernstein, was not to set up a proletarian society, but rather a socialist one.[124] Socialism was best viewed as the heir of liberalism; the security of civil freedom was always a higher goal for social democracy than the fulfilment of some economic programme.[125]

Bernstein thus realises that the weight of both the Marxist and the German political traditions predispose social democracy to take both politics and democracy insufficiently seriously. While social democracy has been captivated by the figure of the proletarian, German political discourse has been constrained by the fact that even its language offers no special word for 'citizen' – there is only *Bürger*. Bernstein however is ultimately unfussed by this awkwardness – he already argued, against Lassalle, that 'we are *all* citizens (*Bürger*)', and against Luxemburg, he interpreted *bürgerliche Gesellschaft* not as bourgeois society but as civil society.[126] His opponents here suggested, as had Bax in a different setting, that bourgeois civilisation was entirely rotten: the challenge for Bernstein was rather to sort out what was defensible in bourgeois civilisation and what was not, for as he wrote elsewhere, socialism by definition cannot be completely new – history does not work this way, and never has since there were states, for no social principle alone is ever completely pervasive.[127] Luxemburg, by contrast, adhered to the theory of capitalist collapse,[128] while Kautsky at this stage sat on his hands, the two of them avoiding like the plague the ethical question why people ought to struggle for socialism at all.

Bernstein had let the cat out of the bag by claiming that socialism and liberalism were actually somehow related, and not just historically. Of course, this meant that socialism could never be a cultural, ruptural event; it also suggested, however, that socialists ought to follow liberals in turning their eyes to action, to behaviour, to conduct, to ethics and to politics. Like Marx, then, but also like John Stuart Mill, Bernstein proposed that the 'aim of all social measures ... is the development and the securing of a free personality'. Autonomy is the precon-

---

123   Bernstein 1965, p. 143.
124   Bernstein 1965, pp. 147–8.
125   Bernstein 1965, p. 149.
126   Bernstein 1965, p. 148; Tudor and Tudor, 1988, p. 23.
127   E. Bernstein, 'Möglichkeiten Sozialismus', Bernstein Papers, IISH, E123, p. 14.
128   Luxemburg to Jogiches, 2. 7. 1898, in Tudor and Tudor (1988, p. 225).

dition of social emancipation; democratic organisation from below leads the way to the realisation of socialism. The conquest of democracy, the formation of political and social organs of democracy is the indispensable precondition to the construction of the new order. More explicitly, Bernstein simply asserts that it is democracy which is the prerequisite of socialism (and not the other way around).[129] Democracy is not an instrument, but rather is the substance of socialism.[130]

Much of this argument represents a clear advance over classical Marxism's disinclination to take politics seriously. In some ways it is hard to believe that Lenin could have written *State and Revolution* almost two decades after Bernstein penned these principled yet pragmatic guidelines for socialism. Likely the outbreak of war explains this refusal of Bernstein's strategy: for Bernstein's case was indeed naively gradualist, resembling here the worst of new liberalism and not only its best. Thus advanced Rosa Luxemburg, polemical scalpel at the ready. Bernstein was certainly guilty of the central charge levelled by Luxemburg – he did indeed believe in the gradual accumulation of reforms, thus indicating altogether too teleological a concept of history as progress resting at the basis of his work. While Luxemburg's work and image still exert a great deal of influence within socialism, her own arguments here remain less than convincing; in a certain sense Luxemburg won the debate because the left was too readily inclined to kill the bearer of gradualist tidings, Bernstein himself.

Luxemburg's own utopia is difficult to glimpse. Plainly her axiom was the self-activity of the working class. This meant, however, that the question of reform or revolution reduced, in her eyes, to the class question whether the movement was to be petty-bourgeois or proletarian in character.[131] This qualm had been expressed earlier by Hans Müller, in his missile against the party elders, *Der Klassenkampf in der deutschen Sozialdemokratie* (1892). Müller had advanced the thesis that Bismarck's antisocialist laws had effectively changed the class composition of the SPD, as its proletarian leaders, black-banned by old employers, were obliged literally to become petty-bourgeois in order to make a living. The consequence was that the identity of the party had been transformed.[132] While the account may be historically accurate, the implication – common to the views of Müller and Luxemburg alike – is puzzling, for socialism after all has never been a purely proletarian theory or practice, and indeed the idea that socialism should be proletarian has in fact been a major obstacle to

---

129   Bernstein 1965, pp. 149, 160, 164 f.
130   Bernstein 1965, p. 166.
131   Luxemburg, 1971b, p. 54.
132   Müller 1892; and see Carchedi 1987.

its realisation. As Marx had suggested, socialism could be intellectual or exper-
iential in its derivation; there is in principle no necessary (or historical) incompatibility between the middle class and socialism at all. Socialism has never
been a movement composed solely of Dietzgens, real or imaginary. Socialism
can be the sigh of the oppressed creature or the political choice of an intellectual; biography is plainly significant in the history of socialism, but it ought not
to be viewed as a kind of magical explanatory 'last instance'. Rosa Luxemburg,
for example, was hardly ever proletarian in her existence, which in some ways
was reminiscent of Beatrice Webb's; only she was unable adequately to address
the question, while Bernstein could simply respond that in the society of the
future the individual would appear not as proletarian but as citizen.

For Luxemburg, the proletarian hammer blow alone would introduce the
new régime amidst the context of crises and collapse.[133] The physiognomy of
the new régime itself, however, remains unclear, for while Luxemburg lambasts
Bernstein together with 'Mrs. Potter-Webb' they did, at least, give some sense
of their imagined future, whereas Luxemburg keeps us guessing.[134] Like other
revolutionaries, Rosa Luxemburg interpreted the historical exhaustion of German liberalism as indicating its intellectual end, into the bargain. The result
is that while, like Trotsky, Luxemburg looks like the hero for today (or at least
for the sixties), Bernstein, (like T.H. Marshall in the fifties or Agnes Heller in
the nineties), actually explores questions to do with citizenship, democracy,
and action because he transcends the economistic or systemic definition and
reduction of civic life. Bernstein's utopia is like that of the Webbs (or Marshall
... or Heller) in that it can be caricatured as a capitalist, or middle-class utopia. But virtually all save the most sublunar Utopias can be thus criticised. The
problem in the context of this discussion, however, is not only what constitutes a sufficiently radical utopia, but also what seems to be suggestive of a
way forward. In this light Bernstein's socialism is interesting because, like Kautsky's, it bears some distinctly Weberian sensibilities, but also, and significantly,
it posits socialism as one of the warring gods between whom we must choose.
Bernstein was world-affirming where Luxemburg was world-denying. But more
than Weber, Bernstein also saw a line which could run between these two sharp
extremes, to affirm democracy and citizenship while denying the features of
bourgeois civilisation which worked against them.

---

133   Luxemburg 1988, p. 269.
134   Luxemburg 1971b, p. 103.

Social Democracy on the Cusp of Modernity

The fate of the Social Democrats in Germany was closer to that of Weber's blackest fear, the iron cage, than that of seizing a future and acting on it. Certainly the SPD was never cured of its teleological habit, and while Bernstein's strategy was briefly enshrined in the Görlitz Programme of 1921, it was only again to be replaced by the triumphant Kautskyism of the 1925 Heidelberg Programme. Bolshevism in the meantime had become the source of inspiration, as Shaw and later the Webbs were to show. Bernstein, like Kautsky – like Weber – understood how badly the Bolshevik victory would set back their cause. As Bernstein wrote in a fragment:

> The socialistic theory of the bolchewists [sic] is, as much as it does not off-handishly recede behind Karl Marx, a marxism made coarse, its political doctrine is an overvaluation of the creative power of brute violence and its political ethics are not a criticism but a coarse misunderstanding of the liberal ideas that in the great French revolution of the eighteenth century have found their classical expression. But just as by the unbending language of facts they have already seen themselves compelled to subject their economic policy to a thorough revision the time will not stay away when in the face of the rebellion/revolt of the ineradicable striving of the peoples to freedom and right they will also have to fundamentally revise their policy and their ethics.[135]

While it is unlikely that there will be a Bernstein revival in Eastern Europe, the legacy of Social Democracy will in all likelihood be drawn on there as frequently as in Western Europe, by radicals arguing in defence of citizenship and the principle of civil society. This has a great deal to do with the fact that Bernstein and Kautsky effectively modernised Marxism's utopia, yet they did so in a way in which, unlike the Webbs, did not risk turning it into an administered society. They did not view administration as a substitute for politics.

This is one factor which sets Social Democracy apart from Fabianism, though as I have suggested, Fabianism's faults were not necessarily those poked at by its jocular critics, nor is Fabianism without its instructive features. Yet Social Democracy arguably comes much closer to the so-called citizenship school, or to the tradition of ethical socialism, than Fabianism ever did. The problem

---

135   E. Bernstein, 'The socialistic theory of the Bolsheviks', fragment, n.d., Bernstein Papers A123.

with English ethical socialism is that, somewhat like the guild socialist tradition with which it has some affinities, the temptation is to gaze too solidly backward rather than forward, the implication being that if medieval ethics are superior to those of utilitarianism (which they undoubtedly are) then somehow medieval social theory will also be adequate to the tasks set us by modernity.[136] The same central issue thus arises again: how can socialism 'transcend' bourgeois civilisation while retaining its defensible practices and beliefs?

As has been suggested throughout this study, one binding feature common to socialist utopias since Marx is the claim that socialism is no longer a state to be postulated and realised, but rather an incipient and emerging state of affairs of one kind or another. Whether revolutionary or reformist, whether given to proletarian or multi-class organisation, however given to recognising or succumbing to social differentiation, labour's utopias view themselves as immanent rather than millennarian in character. Labour's utopias, at least those surveyed here, thus largely break with the image of Cokaigne, the idyll of earlier utopias, rivers of wine, garlicked fowls begging to be eaten and so on. Social Democracy takes this process of rupture the furthest, and consequently is the most modern or potentially 'postmodern' of labour's utopias. In this regard it is absolutely no accident that Kautsky takes on from the industrial pact, freedom beyond work, work as necessity, which Marx sketches in the third volume of *Capital*. Nor is it any accident that Kautsky and Bernstein have little patience for the Fourieresque idyll of *The German Ideology*. For in modernity the problem is not that I am free to be hunter, critic, shepherd, and so on, but that my necessary identity is that of parent, teacher, writer, administrator, editor, domestic labourer, son, lover and so on. After Weber we all of us bear many identities pertinent to our respective spheres of activity: the problem is less in trying to expand them, than in striving to live up to each of them and to the respective expectations which participants in each of these spheres of existence then place upon us. Doubtless in this setting Cokaigne still looms attractive, but likely the closest any of us get to this passed past is in leisure, in company or communing with nature as we know it.

What is striking about Bernstein and Kautsky's utopias in this regard is exactly the extent of the advance. We can see this by returning to two other leading works in German thought, and that of its labour movement in particular: Ferdinand Tönnies's *Community and Association* and Paul Lafargue's *The Right to be Lazy*. Tönnies is usually read as a leading sociologist, as though he were not also an influential social democrat. Lafargue, on the other hand, is

---

136   Dennis and Halsey 1988; See Beilharz 1990.

usually viewed as a socialist demagogue and not also as an interesting, if profoundly misleading sociologist.

Tönnies published *Community and Association* in 1887. The book was a vital prompt for Durkheim's *Division of Labour in Society*, for it viewed modernity largely as loss rather than as gain – it was a deeply romantic work, notwithstanding Tönnies's claims not to be taking sides. For as the title suggests, modernity for Tönnies introduces a rupture, a great divide between *Gemeinschaft* and *Gesellschaft*.[137] This was his essential proposal, wickedly reversed by Durkheim – that organic social bonds were dissolved, to be replaced by mechanical systemic relations. Though it was much more, the study also emerged in its reception as a positive reappraisal of medievalism – something which Bebel, Kautsky and Bernstein rejected, because they saw Wilhelmine Germany as still too much governed by a living feudal legacy.[138] The logic of Tönnies's argument, however, was directly to the contrary – the acid of modernity stood to dissolve the edifice of tradition. Household and economy would be further formally separated, town subordinated to city, obligation would decline, individualism become rampant, and all this would serve to produce a new and dismal cosmos and imagination. Plainly Tönnies's argument was influenced by Marx, for certainly it was his view that all that was solid would thus melt into air. It is equally plain that Tönnies's affinity with Marx was with the early Marx, with romantic hope of redemption rather than the modernist pact with the present.

Tönnies's view was also inward-looking, in a certain sense. The community could be self-sufficient; the individual in modernity cannot. Men may be obliged to suffer the market, but women can make peace in the home.[139] This is not Kant's world, the world of the cosmopolitan, nor Montesquieu's, nor Marx's – though it may be reminiscent of Rousseau. Tönnies too felt this impulse, for like Cole he came by 1922 to argue for something like guild socialism as a means to salvage part of the past.[140] The claim need not be made here that Tönnies was extraordinarily influential in terms of labour's utopia – it could just as well be the case that the theses of *Community and Association* reflected these views as formed them. It is certainly true that men and women in the German labour movement shared, for example, the noble, or simply practical but patriarchal view that women ought to be protected from modernity, or at least from its pernicious effects on the factory floor.[141] Yet what a

137   Tönnies 1974.
138   See e.g. Bebel 1988, p. 302.
139   Tönnies 1974, pp. 186–7.
140   Tönnies 1974, pp. 227–8.
141   See e.g. Frevert 1987.

contrast this is to the utopia of Bebel, or of Kautsky. For these moderns there was no necessity at all that the public sphere be a masculine realm, certainly not so far as paid work was concerned. Following Marx's positive anthropology, their premise was that human beings need to work, creatively to labour, regardless of their sex.

This is an appropriate note upon which to introduce Lafargue, for he too looked back for socialism, and rejected Marx's positive anthropology in the process. Lafargue drew broad respect in the Second International, not least of all as a philosopher. Lenin called him 'one of the most gifted and profound disseminators of the ideas of Marxism',[142] which says as much about Lenin as it does about Lafargue. Lafargue's work is a veritable mélange, combining true mediocrity with real insight.[143] In general his insights occur only occasionally in his ethnological considerations where there can be found some interesting anticipations of recent French structuralism.[144] Such insights are buried under an avid eclecticism and an unsuccessful mimicry of the grand heroic style of writing. Some central characteristics of Lafargue's thought can nevertheless be indicated. Lafargue combines a romantic critique of capitalist technology with an unbridled enthusiasm for the noble savage.[145] This combination produces what might be called an inverse Hegelian philosophy of history, where Europe represents the terminal senility of civilisation as we know it.[146] The anthropology at work in Lafargue is familiar: there is a strong emphasis on the healthy natural instincts of the savage, which are beaten out of him by so-called civilization.[147] Lafargue admires Hobbes as the father of modern materialism, and presents arguments resembling those in Rousseau's *Emile*.[148] Religion and the work ethic are seen as the major fetters on essentially revolutionary forces.[149]

These arguments are stated more clearly in Lafargue's most famous work, *The Right to be Lazy*. Lafargue's treatise, a refutation of the earlier socialist maxim, 'the right to work', characterises that position as base and slavish.[150] He takes as his motif Lessing: 'Let us be lazy in everything, except in loving and drinking, except in being lazy'.[151] In an argument with distinct Nietzschean

142　Lenin 1977a, p. 304.
143　Kolakowski 1978, chap. 6, dismisses Lafargue on the grounds of his mediocrity alone.
144　Lafargue 1975, pp. 154, 155, 119.
145　Lafargue 1975, pp. 99, 119, 91, 4 f., 145, 167.
146　Lafargue 1975, pp. 9, 208 f.
147　Lafargue 1975, pp. 114, 147, 204, 207, 161, 177.
148　Lafargue 1975, pp. 18, 141, 177, 1907, p. 67.
149　Lafargue 1975, p. 135 and Chapter 1.
150　Lafargue 1907, p. 16.
151　Lafargue 1907, p. 9.

resonances as well as echoes in Wilde, Carpenter and Morris, Lafargue explains work as the product of a herd mentality which has permeated the labour movement: 'In capitalist society work is the cause of all intellectual degeneracy, of all organic deformity'.[152] The proletariat is *manly* but corrupted by Christian enthusiasm for labour; the noble savage is far superior to the mechanical slave of bourgeois society. The image of Athens haunts the background.[153] An extensive and absurd argument follows as proof of the corruption of work: the witless proletariat causes crises of overproduction by working too hard, while they should only take what they need from stock; their insistence on work and more work forces the bourgeoisie into a condition of unhappy laziness.[154] Here Lafargue reveals a class ambivalence towards hedonism, which is taken to be enervating for the bourgeoisie and yet at the same time a basic component of the socialist future.[155] Laziness, facilitated by automation, is understood as an instinctual return to a state of nature;[156] Lafargue shows no understanding of the need for work, so that his argument accords with the view of Adam Smith rather than with those of his unfortunate father-in-law.[157]

The glimpses of utopia in Lafargue's work recall Trotsky's *Literature and Revolution*. Parallels exist in the Olympian imagery, in the Nietzschean undercurrent, in the presumption of abundance with its actual concomitant – that some, the 'speaking tools', must continue to labour so that others might create or contemplate. The image of paradise portrayed in the essays presented together with *The Right to be Lazy*, 'Socialism and Intellectuals' and 'The Bankruptcy of Capitalism', confirms this Utopian scenario. Like Trotsky's utopia it is dependent on mechanised production, Lafargue's radical criticism of technology notwithstanding.[158] Yet it is also, and essentially, the presocialist utopia of Cokaigne.

Looking back on Lafargue's work, the most surprising thing is that he was not laughed out of town (or city). Lafargue was indeed a respected figure, but it is difficult, on this intellectual basis rather than on that of his family affiliations, to see why this should be so. Like Wells, he seems basically to offer a personal program as a utopia. Doubtless the proletarian response to the process of capitalist industrialisation involved nostalgia for a past, real and imagined, as well

152   Lafargue 1907, p. 10.
153   Lafargue 1907, pp. 16, 56, 12, 57 ff.
154   Lafargue 1907, pp. 24–42, 38.
155   Lafargue 1907, p. 34 ff.
156   Lafargue 1907, p. 44.
157   An illuminating source for background and character is F. Engels, Paul and Laura Lafargue, (See Engels, 1959).
158   Lafargue 1907, pp. 103, 109.

as futurism or modernist desire to break with the past and embrace the future. Yet the proposition that the future will consist of inactivity rather than activity of a measured sort, and in hedonism rather than in contemplation sounds like little more than a preferred wish-desire, a fantasy in the bad sense rather than a utopia in the good sense.

While romanticism and nostalgia were certainly in the air for the German labour movement, so too was the sense of relative sobriety which we have come to associate with Max Weber. Indeed, it can be argued that Bernstein and Kautsky came to profess something like a Weberian Marxism, with the emphasis spread equally across these constitutive terms. Weber, like Tönnies, was also part of a certain liberal, social democratic milieu in Germany, and of course here as with Tönnies it can be argued that the milieu was as significant as the thinker. Weber was in correspondence with Bernstein, and the paths of such figures crossed in other ways as well.[159] As Harry Liebersohn has shown, the entire German intellectual scene between 1870 and 1923 was fruitful and fecund, to the extent that authorship of particular ideas is even more difficult than usual to explain. Kautsky, as we have seen, was thoroughly well read in Weber, but more so, these were people who each read what the others read as well as wrote and responded to what the others also encountered in German politics and culture. This meant that Nietzsche was in the air even for socialists, as Hinton Thomas has shown, and that the travails and ecstasies presented by modernity were encountered as shared concerns by several generations of German thinkers.[160]

Conclusions

Bolshevism, as we have seen, consisted especially in the figures of Lenin and Trotsky of an amalgam of eighteenth-century views, often seizing on the mechanistic rather than the emancipatory moments of the Enlightenment. Fabianism was deeply scored by its origin in nineteenth-century British culture. The primary distinction between Fabianism and Social Democracy is the centrality to Fabianism of utilitarianism, however rendered or refined. Where Bolshevism was uniformly hostile to liberalism of all stripes, Fabianism was always deeply implicated in utilitarianism in particular. Social Democracy, by comparison, rejected utilitarianism but affirmed liberalism, especially in the case

---

159   See for example Weber to Bernstein, 1904, Bernstein Papers, D817, and see the chapters on
      Weber, Bernstein and Kautsky by D. Geary and J. Breuilly in Mommsen and Osterhammel
      (1989); Mommsen (1984); and see generally Weber (1988).
160   H.R. Thomas 1983; Liebersohn 1988.

of Bernstein. Social Democracy took on from Marx the vital element of romanticism which Cole later suppressed and about which Beatrice Webb remained ambivalent. Social Democracy thus remains a more clearly ethical tradition, for it is more easily able to address the Kantian question: What can I know? What ought I do? What may I hope? Bolshevism, by comparison, departed from a putatively proletarian morality, or viewed cynically, from the question, how might I seize state power? while Fabianism set out from a collective question, how might society best/most effectively be organised? Even Cole, for example, wrote in a fragment:

> I know of no better political principle than Jeremy Bentham's famous Utilitarian principle of 'the greatest happiness of the greatest number' ... It does indeed (however) require interpretation in the light of the second principle – that each man [sic] must be broadly accepted as the best judge of his own happiness.[161]

Happiness was not usually seen as the primary value for the Social Democrats, indeed we might say, with Bernstein, that happiness was an end, not a premise. Resting on the cusp of modernity and of modern social theory, Social Democracy viewed the scenario in terms closer to Weber. The choices are constrained, but choices they are. Unlike Weber, they viewed socialism as one of these choices, the warring god to whom we could turn when it finally became clear that neither the Promethean Marx nor the Sisyphean Weber could adequately guide us into the new century.

Significantly, however, the Social Democrats eschewed any interest in simply rejecting Marx. In fact they seem to have been rather slow to grasp the idea that there were socialists – such as the Fabians – who were not in some way Marxists. It is equally likely that the Fabians took all socialists to be potential sympathisers. The Fabians did understand, however, better than the Social Democrats and conventional wisdom that there were real differences between their worldview and that of the Germans. For if there was to be any suggestion that Bernstein was a Fabian, there could be no such implication that Sidney Webb might be a Marxist. Webb wrote to Bernstein that the problem was not one of indifference to Marx, or of ignorance of his work, so much as that he was actually unconvinced. Bernstein had suggested that perhaps Marx was beyond Webb's ken; Sidney replied that

---

161   G.D.H. Cole, untitled ms, 'I know of no better political principle', Nuffield, Cole Papers, B3/3/F Box 8, folder 5, p. 1.

all I can say is that I am a worse heretic than you suppose. You are charit-
able enough to imagine that I err only through ignorance – alas, it is more
than that. Incredible as it may seem I have long since read the books you
suggest, and yet stick to my opinion regarding the law of rent.[162]

Nearly forty years later Webb wrote to Kautsky, again in terms suggestive of the
difference in their socialisms,

> Our work, as you will remember, has always been in the nature of analysis
> of the actual structure and function of social institutions ... what we are
> concerned with is describing the institutions as they now exist without
> considering any theoretical origin and still more without predicting any
> actual result in the future.[163]

Clearly there were fundamental differences between Webb and the Social
Democrats concerning both the nature of capitalism and that of socialism.
The distance between Kautsky and the Webbs on Soviet communism itself is
massive, because the Social Democrats did still envisage a new society where
progress was made in terms of individual development. This much of Marx's
legacy they did still embrace.

Viewed in this light, it becomes evident that the weakness of Fabianism lies
in its ethical foundations. Bolshevism is a different kind of problem, for it has no
ethics at all, save perhaps a party ethic. Fabianism, by comparison, maintains
an ambivalent relationship to an ethic which is fundamentally flawed. Utilitarian ethics is completely hopeless. Any position which claims as its foundation
the premise that *pleasure* ought be *maximised* is doubly decadent; because
'pleasure', like 'happiness', is an end rather than a premise, a term for a passing
condition rather than a deep human aspiration, and because the quantifica-
tion principle only makes this worse, introducing the calculus of mathematics
where it has no place. Now the Webbs were never simply utilitarian, nor were
the Fabians uniformly so, as Alan McBriar has shown.[164] Sidney Webb remains
utilitarian, but focuses on the minimisation of suffering more than the maxim-
isation of pleasure. Beatrice evidently empathises with John Stuart Mill's belief
that Socrates dissatisfied is better than the animal satisfied. Neither can accurately be described as a hedonist, and yet both still work within the wake of

---

162   S. Webb to Bernstein, 15.10.1895, Bernstein Papers, D816.
163   S. Webb to Kautsky, 17.10.1933, Amsterdam, Kautsky Papers, IISH, DXXIII, 75.
164   McBriar 1962, pp. 149–55.

utilitarianism. It may not be the utilitarianism of Bentham so much as that of John Stuart Mill which constrains their socialism, but the limits are still there.

Social democracy is ethically superior to both these other traditions because it reaches back through Marx to Aristotle, and while it is now widely accepted that Marx has no politics, or practical theory of changing the world, his thought does indeed contain the elements of an ethical basis which connect directly into arguments about the human condition. All of labour's Utopias look both forward and back; the followers of Marx, sobered by Weber's time, alone here manage to look back, in ethics, and forward, with hope but circumspection, for they are firmly located in the present but understand something of its historicity.

CHAPTER 8

Edward Bellamy: Looking Back at American Socialism in the Nineteenth Century (2003)

Who was Edward Bellamy? Obvious: the most influential utopian writer of the nineteenth century was also the greatest philistine, if not fascist. The power of this image reflects that of the aura of its initial protagonist, William Morris. Morris pounced on Bellamy's *Looking Backward* in his review in *Commonweal* the year after its initial publication in 1888. Morris spat that Bellamy's utopia in *Looking Backward* was cheap and nasty, a cockney paradise. What an interesting sign of our times, then and now, that the aristocratic logic of the critic should look so much more persuasively obvious than the denigration of its putative victims. Morris' initial volley was followed by a more influential counter attack, in *News from Nowhere*, which set the frame more clearly as one of urban philistines (Bellamy) versus advocates of the rural idyll (Morris). The appeal and moral authority were impeccable, and remain extraordinary, even if the character of Morris' utopia remained more substantially aesthetic, and medieval, than Bellamy's. Who was Bellamy?

Obvious, philistine if not fascist. A mere technician of socialism.

Locating Bellamy

Scholarly intuition is enough to tell us there has to be more going on than this; that reception blurs, as much as it clarifies, and that the will-to-classification inevitably does violence to its subject matter. Read in context, Bellamy begins to look more like a smalltown New Englander, a fantasist, and a utopian in the Spartan tradition. The reception of Bellamy, and his credentials as a sociologist or social theorist, is constrained by the absence of a leading critical intellectual biography. As we might come to expect, Bellamy's ideas are appropriated or pilloried for other reasons. Interpretations of Bellamy are less about him, or them, than about us, today.

There are three major works pertinent here, Arthur Lipow's *Authoritarian Socialism in America: Edward Bellamy and the Nationalist Movement*,[1] John

---

1 Lipow 1982.

Thomas's *Alternative America*,[2] and the more recent essays of Franklin Rosemont.[3] The title of Lipow's book makes clear its preference – Bellamy appears
as the bearer of authoritarian socialism in America. Lipow reads the history
of socialism through the particular optic of Hal Draper's 'two souls of socialism'. These two souls are noble and ignoble, libertarian and authoritarian, from
below and from above. Lipow's study is based on considerable scholarship
and insight, yet its materials are only allowed to breathe through this grid.
The moral dualism involved allows Bellamy only a momentary presence as an
incipient democrat, with the publication of *Equality* in 1897. The limit of this
argument is in its rationalism. As though there are only two views, for democracy and against, which means that Bellamy is a Fabian and the Fabians are
Stalinists. More, it is to make of Bellamy a political theorist (or a theorist of
antipolitics) rather than a mystical fantasy writer who stumbled into politics.
Certainly Bellamy was allergic to politics, but so then was the utopian aspect of
Marx. There is no politics in *The German Ideology*, only criticism in the evening.

Lipow's case is that Bellamy is a radical anti-individualist; as I shall suggest
later, this seems to me to misread Bellamy, whose theoretical thinking is weak
not at the level of the individual but at the intermediate or mediating level. The
logic of Lipow's scheme is that there are only good and bad socialists, us and
them, libertarians emphasising individual, collectivists emphasising state. Bellamy manages however to emphasise both, or rather to identify them through
a particular communitarian cosmology.

It would only be a slight exaggeration to say of Lipow's case that its great
discovery is that Bellamy is not Marx; so that, for example, others can here be
criticised for what are also in fact limits in Marx. In one place, for example,
Lipow mocks Gronlund who, he says, is caught in the contradiction of trying
to reconcile a fatalistic social theory with the idea that actors make their own
history.[4] This is, of course, a contradiction quite central to Marx's own work.
The strongest aspect of Lipow's work is that it connects Bellamy to Nationalism, though at the cost of subsuming the thinker to the movement. In addition, Lipow foregrounds the pertinence of the middle class or new class to
reforming socialism, which again is significant, though insufficient to explain
the emergence of technocratic politics into the twentieth century. The critique is so devastating as to make us wonder why Bellamy attracted at all,
except as a magnet for middle-class melancholics on the make. In limiting
the history of ideas to two logics, or 'souls', Lipow reduces Bellamy to the

---

2 Thomas 1983.
3 Rosemont 1988, 1990.
4 Lipow 1982, p. 81.

analogue of a foreshortened Fabianism and to the precursor of totalitarian collectivism.[5] Viewed as intellectual history, this approach is open to the criticism that it is both procrustean and proleptic. This is, so to say, 1888 viewed from 1968, Chicopee viewed from Berkeley.

Chicopee matters; New England matters. Bellamy never left Chicopee Falls (later Chicopee) more than momentarily. The location is crucial to his work and sensibilities, as various commentators have noted, as it was transition itself in Bellamy's moment. The ambivalence of Chicopee Falls was exactly that it was mixed modern, becoming modern before Bellamy's eyes. Chicopee Falls, the Falls themselves, were both the natural sublime, and the source of industrialisation. Yet the ethical and ecological impulse of Bellamy's work by *Looking Backward* was to be seen as dull and materialist, when its actuality was closer to Morris's utopia than he might have dreamed.

But the image of the city, Boston, and the industrial army remains central to *Looking Backward*, which is plainly no blueprint for mass democracy in the spirit of Rosa Luxemburg. This begs the question, however, whether *Looking Backward* should be read as a political manifesto, any more than the infamous horticultural-critical utopia in *The German Ideology*. If Lipow's prosecutorial approach to Bellamy limits his capacity to allow for nuance, John Thomas's approach in *Alternative Americas* opens the vista up, though comparatively, as his subtitle indicates, via *Henry George, Edward Bellamy, Henry Demarest Lloyd and the Adversary Tradition*. Thomas's 1983 book is likely the best available analysis of Bellamy, though its cluster approach and partial eclipse by the Lipow study, published in 1982, seem to have afforded it less influence. Thomas begins by locating Bellamy and his others immediately, with reference to the aftermath of the Civil War (ergo the image of industrial army) the ghost of Rome and the Money Power of the Gilded Age. Thomas focuses on Bellamy's early, unpublished 1874 text 'The Religion of Solidarity', as does Lipow if to different purpose. Lipow views this extraordinary text as a founding document of atomistic collectivism. Thomas takes the 'Religion of Solidarity' rather as a leitmotif of Bellamy's belief which, together with his fantasy writing and fiction, as in the novel *The Duke of Stockbridge*, on Shays's Rebellion, aligns the early Bellamy with William Dean Howells rather than Henry George or Demarest Lloyd. The informing premise of 'The Religion of Solidarity' is the human instinct for perfect communication with the infinite, the drive to break through the barriers of time and circumstance that prevent the individual from joining the cosmic.[6]

5   Lipow 1982, p. 200.
6   J.L. Thomas 1983, p. 86.

Thomas deals frontally with aspects of Bellamy's views which evoke post-modern complaint. Bellamy's period prejudices included the kind of proletarian primitivism which saw the working class as a 'dark people', though his period feminist credentials were strong, which opened the way to alliance with Charlotte Perkins Stetson. The image of the proletarian dark people could also lead in differing directions. In Bellamy's case, the dyad of elevation and subordination, exemplified in the image of progress, opened onto a 'two nations' theme for which socialism, or Nationalism, was the solution. *Looking Backward* was less a political manifesto than a religious fable, an account of the triumph of the sacred over the secular forces of evil.[7] The aspects of fantasy and romance are not merely formal; after all, Bellamy had been writing fiction as well as journalism for years now. At the same time, the new fantasy in *Looking Backward* involved a project of industrial reform.

This indicates not only a social fantasy, but also a concern with the possibility that individuals, such as Julian West, can break from the past, leave behind the old self and begin anew. There is a psychological level here which has barely surfaced in Bellamy analysis before. Religious conversion saves Julian West, as it saved Bellamy himself, from Puritanism and into transcendentalism. The latter echoes are palpable, as when Bellamy like William James evokes the call to 'the moral equivalent of war' as the key to the stoic virtues necessary to recast society in the image of Sparta.[8] The implication of Thomas's argument, however, is that Bellamy is the predecessor of technocracy rather than totalitarianism. To foul the metaphor, this would indicate at least three possible souls of socialism (why stop at three?) – revolutionary, reformist, totalitarian. Here Bellamy would anticipate F.W. Taylor, not Stalin, and the difference remains significant. The most significant test case in Marxism here would be Gramsci, advocate of Taylorism and Americanism. Meanwhile, the revolutionary critique of Taylorism, as in Braverman, never comes up with a feasible alternative to factory civilization – Bellamy, in contrast, fails to come up with an alternative to fixed paternalistic structures of governance.

As Thomas makes clear, the locale of Bellamy's utopia was less the East End of London than the garden city. The new Boston is the figment of a pastoral and preindustrial imagination, a cross between Chicopee Falls before the mills and Olmsted's Central Park. In summary, *Looking Backward* is vision more than theory in the systematic sense, and Bellamy is prophet rather than engineer. Bellamy becomes a reluctant politician, or publicist, after 1888, another conver-

---

7   J.L. Thomas 1983, p. 237.
8   J.L. Thomas 1983, p. 245.

sion. He is unable to return to fiction, or fantasy, partly because of the urgency of the times, partly because, as he puts it elsewhere, the experience of parenthood makes it impossible to turn away from the social problems that his children will inherit. He is obliged to be social, and socialist. The Nationalist Clubs are organised independently of him; he is sceptical as to their feasibility. The Clubs take off, and he responds, but he puts his energies mainly into the sequel, *Equality*, where the magic of *Looking Backward* disappears into programmatic detail, Nationalism becomes Public Capitalism, democratic institutions finally arrive, and militarism gives way to organicism. A minimum programme of specific reforms is added. The post office replaces the image of the militia as model – an uncanny anticipation of Lenin's Germanising *State and Revolution* twenty years later – and civil service stands in for military service. The theme of service persists.

Looking Backward was an American utopia, a particular kind of New England utopia, which Bellamy nationalised. In Americanising it across the Midwest, Bellamy also began the process of its dissolution back into the political culture from whence it came. The strongest supporters of Nationalism were not middle-class social engineers aspirant but farmers. They did not aspire to the life of Manhattan any more than Bellamy did. Contrary to the later imagined divide between Bellamy, in the East End, and Morris on the banks of the upper Thames, Bellamy views life as happening in the regions in between cities, closer in emphasis to Ebenezer Howard, Geddes and Mumford than to *Sex in the City*. As H.P. Segal argues, elsewhere, Bellamy seeks among other things to resolve the tension in the American imagination later identified by Leo Marx between the machine and the garden. Bellamy modernises the garden, which is to say that his is a mixed modernism, the very condition which William Morris denied him.[9]

The most surprising recent rendition of Bellamy is that by Franklin Rosemont. This version is the opposite of Lipow's, for here Bellamy is not only libertarian but libertine. Rosemont foregrounds the most utopian aspects of Bellamy's *Looking Backward*, where for example Bellamy is antiwork – no one works after 45. More, Bellamy is surrealist in sympathy, against the tyranny of memory and repression, eros-affirming. For Rosemont, this 'unknown Bellamy' anticipates the Marcuse of *Eros and Civilization*. The case is overdrawn, but it has its bases in Bellamy's work, not least in the fiction that precedes *The Duke of Stockbridge*, in *Dr. Heidenhoff's Process* and the essays that surround it, where memory and guilt are viewed as primary obstacles to human development.

---

9   Segal 1988.

Rosemont's logic, however, practically inverts Lipow's, making of Bellamy some kind of revolutionary, which fits neither the temperament of Bellamy nor the detail of his writing. At the very least, however, Rosemont's point sticks – there is a fantastic, magical and psychologically radical dimension to Bellamy's early work which has systematically been excluded from its politicised reception. The depth and difference in Bellamy's thinking has been politically flattened in its reception. The appropriate echo may less be Marcuse here than Fourier. This may not of itself make Bellamy's work a resource for rethinking socialism, but it suggests a quality and purpose of mind worthy of recognition, not least in terms of the traditions of American social theory.

Looking for Clues

Bellamy's papers are gathered in the Houghton Library, Harvard, together with a wealth of materials donated by his first published biographer, Arthur Morgan. There are no secrets in these papers, though there are various items of interest, and the collection in total conveys a clear sense that however negative the later intellectual response to Bellamy may have been, there is a countertrend peaking with Morgan into the 1940s which understood his legacy with altogether more nuance.

The Bellamy papers include manuscripts, typescripts and letters. Correspondence, for example from W.D. Bliss, editor of the *Encyclopedia of Social Reform* and editor of the shortlived *American Fabian* (1896–1902), makes clear Bellamy's location in a typically mixed milieu, which at some point involved Christian ethics, theosophy, transcendentalism, Emerson, and Carlyle. To take it in its own terms, rather than in those of external axioms concerning 'two souls', this is a milieu of Christian rather than labour socialism.

The key document which suggests the depth of this thinking is 'The Religion of Solidarity'. Bellamy's is a passionate, magical pantheism of sublime emotions. He asserts a kind of cosmological solidarity, for which we are at the same time merely individual and yet universal. As he puts it, the human soul seeks a more perfect realisation of its solidarity with the universe.[10] The prospect of solidarity offers the hope of self-abnegation in the social. 'In losing our personal identity, we should become conscious of our other, our universal identity, the identity of a universal solidarity'.[11] Solidarity involves self-sacrifice; this is

---

10   Bellamy, no date b, p. 12.
11   Bellamy, no date b, p. 18.

the motivating force for the later invention of the industrial army in *Looking Backward*, not compulsion but service. Individuality, alone, here, is partiality, segregation, partition, confinement, 'a prison'. Universal solidarity, in contrast, is not only an imperative but an instinct. The instinct of solidarity in the moral universe correlates with the attraction of gravitation in the material world. The instinct of solidarity, according to Bellamy, is the centripetal force to which individuality, which particularises, is the centrifugal force: the two are mutually balancing.[12]

The immediate question is less whether we, here, now, find this persuasive, than what it means for Bellamy's utopia. This kind of organicism, or mechanism may imply collectivism, but this is a collectivism of individuals. The ethic here is closer to service than to self-sacrifice. As Bellamy writes,

> We should hold our lives loosely, and not with the compulsive grip of one who counts the personal life his all. The workman does not sacrifice himself to his tools, so should we not seek to serve the individual, which is the serf of the universal, by any sacrifice of those universal instincts, whereof the chief is unselfishness, which constitute true morality.[13]

The question of how well Bellamy got the balance right needs to be set within the contextual question, what it was that Bellamy was opposing. Like the generation of founding socialists in England, he set socialism (Nationalism) against individualism, the emergingly dominant ideology of his time. This adversarial approach does not remove the individual from the social model, so much as it bends the stick back the other way. This is why Howells called his own utopia Altruria. It was a strong local sentiment.

Howells understood Bellamy as a kindred spirit, even if their relationship was sparsely exercised. As Howells wrote in his introduction to Bellamy's *The Blindman's World*, Bellamy's location of his fiction is the American village setting was 'distinctively American', for theirs were village people more than folks of country or city. *Looking Backward* and its material dimensions, as Howells understood, were pitched neither at city dwellers, who already knew them, nor at country dwellers, who scarcely knew them at all, but to the immense average of town-dwellers. As Howells put it, you need to 'start heaven from home', which is what in his eyes Bellamy achieved.[14] Even better, then, to discover with

---

12   Bellamy, no date b, p. 13.
13   Bellamy no date b, p. 19.
14   Bellamy 1898, pp. ix–xi.

Arthur Morgan that Bellamy originally set *Looking Backward* not in Boston, but in Asheville, North Carolina, with the USA as nothing more than an administrative province of the great world nation.[15] The example of an imaginary Boston in the year 2000 spoke more globally than small-town. But if Boston was not New York City it was not Washington D.C. either. Bellamy viewed big cities as pagan, and contemporary politics as filth.

The absence of politics from *Looking Backward* has more to do, conceptually speaking, with the absence of mediation here. 'The Religion of Solidarity' is less a sociological than a metaphysical statement, where there is only Universal and Individual. If the presence of the category solidarity here immediately alerts the sociological mind to the presence of Durkheim, the connection is absent. There are no intermediary groups or associations, as in Durkheim, no civil society or particularity as in Hegel. Individuals in *Looking Backward* have families, but their lives seem practically solitary. The logic of singularity and universality catches up with Bellamy, as in the argument that the business of the country ought be turned over to one massive single firm, or trust. Here the one is the many, and the echo is not with Durkheim's mediating associations in the Second Preface to *The Division of Labour in Society* but with his more troubling speculation on the state as social brain in *Professional Ethics and Civic Morals*. There are other echoes of Hegel, as well. Hegel envisaged the middle class, or at least the civil service, as the universal class in *The Philosophy of Right*, though it is plainly to our eyes particularistic. Marx, of course, could see right through this, but only to solve the problem by offering an alternative universal class, and blocking out civil society by seeking its anatomy elsewhere, in political economy.

The more immediate connection may be with our friends the Fabians, who also worked about the particularism of labour politics and imagined the civil service to be above interest. The autobiographical parallel with the path of Beatrice Webb is apparent, where conversion to socialism resolves the period religious crisis of belief, and sociologists become the secular clergy. Otherwise, the imputation of Fabianism to Bellamy is about as useful as the discovery that Bernstein was a Fabian too (so was Korsch). The actual points of contact between Bellamy and the Fabians are no more than passing. The short lifespan of the *American Fabian* itself serves to make the point that Fabianism had no organic presence in the USA; it is an imperial and colonial phenomenon. Fabianism failed to take off in America because of all the other things already in motion – the final issue of *American Fabian*, sympathetic-

---

15   Morgan 1944.

ally, is dedicated to Edward Bellamy. What is more surprising, perhaps, is that Sidney Webb enjoyed Bellamy's fantasy more than *Looking Backward*; in the Webb letters Sidney expresses considerable admiration for *Dr. Heidenhoff's Process*.[16]

Alongside 'The Religion of Solidarity', *Dr. Heidenhoff's Process* may be one of the most interesting texts with which to locate Bellamy. Its plot concerns the use of galvanic therapy to cure the guilt-ridden, a theme better conveyed in its German title, *Dr. Heidenhoff's Wunderkur*. The story thus resembles the plot of *Looking Backward* eight years earlier, at least inasmuch as it rests on redemption or conversion, here called thought-extirpation. This is the Bellamy who calls out to Franklin Rosemont. Bellamy has Dr. Heidenhoff announce that 'Memory is the principle of moral degeneration. Remembered sin is the most utterly diabolical influence in the universe'. More:

> ... there is no such thing as moral responsibility for past acts, no such thing as real justice in punishing them, for the reason that human beings are not stationary existences, but changing, growing, incessantly progressive organisms which in no two moments are the same.[17]

A kind of vitalistic psychology underpins Bellamy's writing. The theme is also pursued in an unpublished paper entitled 'How Many Men Make a Man?' which is not, as we might perhaps expect, an argument for the social construction of identity so much as a scheme of multiple individual identities across the life path. Bellamy suggests that there are seven stages of life, for boys:
- puling infancy
- boisterous childhood
- sighing adolescence
- ambitious manhood
- staid maturity
- slippered old age, and
- second childhood.

In this context, human or masculine identity for Bellamy involved the sense that an individual has of the present moment and the relation of his attitudes together with the memory of previous states.[18] Childhood and adulthood are, at the very least, worlds apart.

---

16   Webb and Webb 1978, pp. 86–7, 93, 209.
17   Bellamy 1880, pp. 120–21.
18   Bellamy no date a, p. 2.

... the idea of personal identity does not conflict with the theory of nonidentical personalities, for personal identity does not imply even the memory of past personalities, much less identity of consciousness with them.[19]

More emphatically, for Bellamy, 'our personalities are in constant flux',[20] and the very idea of personal identity as sameness is a misnomer. Identity is not identical; our changing selves die daily.[21]

How does all this then rest with the apparent stasis of utopia, or the infinity of the universal? If Bellamy's utopia is indeed mixed, rather than unmixed modern, he might perhaps be forgiven along with his various inmates for failing to deal with the sociological imperative of change. No positive utopian tract offers sufficient sense of anticipation as to exit, Marx's least of all. Bellamy's utopia is normally contradictory, but it is a utopia, and is therefore open to Durkheim's charge in *Socialism and Saint-Simon* that it reaches back, to communism, to Plato, rather than fully forward.

There is indeed, on closer inspection, a French utopian connection here, but it is neither Saint-Simon nor Fourier. The most suggestive biography of Bellamy, by his follower Mason Green, though widely used by early Bellamy scholarship, was never published. The typescript is in the Houghton Library. Morgan hits the tripwire in his biography, identifying Fénelon's *Telemachus* as an influence on Bellamy.[22] He quotes Green:

When asked by the writer whether any one book had influenced him in planning *Looking Backward*, he replied: 'Telemachus', possibly.[23]

Morgan adds, dismissively, that its 'similarity to *Looking Backward* is less than that of numerous other Utopias'. No one else makes the connection, says Morgan, who therefore chooses not to pursue it. Mason Green, however, picks up on the Fénelon connection, and takes it seriously. For Green, to the contrary,

It is easy to understand how Fénelon's masterpiece should have had charms for him, its dominant concem for the welfare of all peoples,

19   Bellamy no date a, p. 6.
20   Bellamy no date a, p. 8.
21   Bellamy no date a, pp. 8, 10.
22   Morgan 1944, Ch. 12, p. 13.
23   Morgan 1944, Ch. 22, p. 13.

its penchant for romance dealing in scenes most absorbing when most unusual or unreal.

More, for Mason, Fénelon's utopia is written from the standpoint of the people. Economic peace leads to contentment.[24] The connections between Bellamy and Fénelon are more diverse and suggestive yet, as perusal of *Telemachus* indicates. Telemachus, the young son of Ulysses, travels the Mediterranean world and learns patience, courage, modesty and simplicity. Fénelon insisted that one must 'go out of oneself', even 'hate oneself'. The highest stage of the love of God is from a pure charity, and without the slightest mixture of self-interested motivation.[25] Fénelon argued for a republican monarchy, in which the key notions are simplicity, labour, the virtues of agriculture, the absence of luxury and splendour, and the elevation of peace over war and aggrandisement. His was a proto-Rousseauean, demilitarised Spartanism.[26] Fénelon writes in 'On Pure Love' that

> His glory and perfection consist in going out of himself, *sortir de soir* in forgetting himself, in losing himself, in being swallowed up in the simple love of infinite beauty.[27]

This disinterested love, or pure charity leading to loss of self in Beyond or God is remarkably similar to Bellamy's desire in 'The Religion of Solidarity'. Renunciation of self into God, into the social is where Bellamy begins and ends.

Why did Morgan, and all that followed miss this clue? The connection with Fénelon is interesting, rather than definitive. Morgan, for his part, had an agenda of his own, one equally connected back into Bellamy's transformative logic, even as it bridged the gap into Morgan's world and the TVA. For Bellamy's first published biographer was also a hydraulic engineer and first Director of the TVA. Morgan deserves a critical biography of his own, for his achievement was extraordinary. The central catalogue in Harvard Library lists no less than 75 publications by Morgan, mainly on the TVA. As Thomas observes in *Alternative Americas*, the enthusiasm for the TVA in the early thirties called up all kinds of resonances with the work and ideas of his trio, George, Lloyd and Bellamy.[28] Morgan's model was producerist, decentralised, and cooperative,

---

24   Bellamy and Green no date, p. 64.
25   Riley 1994, p. xiv.
26   Riley 1994, p. xvii.
27   Riley 1994, p. xxii.
28   J.L. Thomas 1983, p. 363.

a world perhaps more evocative of Kropotkin than Marx, though it is always worth remembering that Marxist giganticism arrives only with the Bolsheviks. Marx's utopias were small. This utopia in Morgan may be engineered, but it is not technocratic, at least not in the urban sense of the new class aspirant. It is local and regional rather than totalitarian, federally planned and underwritten, locally enacted.

Is Bellamy then ever technocratic in the sense that Lipow argues? The logic of developmentalism is certainly apparent in his work. His is not the kind of absolute naturalism for which nature is always best left alone. The Spartan Aspects of *Looking Backward* are located in Boston, not in Asheville or Chicopee. The good society is not naturally occurring, but has to be constructed. In one place Morgan quotes from Bellamy's notebooks, in a passage which sounds at first reminiscent of Trotsky's Faustian developmentalism in *Literature and Revolution*:

> Men and women will be broader and less intense correspondingly in their relations to one another, while a thousandfold more than now occupied with nature and the next steps of the race, i.e., that which is at present called the superhuman. The heart of man will … be set less and less on the perishable, and more and more on the spiritual and the infinite toward which man now tends. So shall passions … be directed to the general elevation of the human type

– just as the impulse drives away from particular to universal.[29] Where Trotsky envisages a population of eggheads, however, Bellamy's vision is consistent with the foundational idea of the religion of solidarity. Likely we should, all the same, resist the temptation to turn Bellamy into a strong social theorist. The point, rather, is that the apparently idiosyncratic amalgam of ideas and forms both past and present that go to make up his work is typical. Bellamy's thinking cannot fully express his moment any more than the rest of us, yet read as part of that culture it speaks to us still, in all its power and frailty. Everything seemed possible, in the face of decline. A century later, we retain the sense of decline alone. Perhaps our modernity is less mixed. Socialism now is less, even, than fantasy. We no longer seek, as Howells said of Bellamy, to start to heaven from home: heaven is at home. Change remains beyond us.

---

29   Morgan, no date, p. 102.

CHAPTER 9

The Other Trotsky (1982)

Forty years after his murder Leon Trotsky remains both influential and enigmatic. His continuing influence can be ascribed to his status as revolutionary oppositionist: if one rejects Stalinism the ready option is Trotskyism. A legitimate halfway-house to radicalism, Trotskyism becomes for many a permanent refuge instead. The enigmatic character of Trotsky's work is another matter altogether. Wide-ranging in scope and varying substantially in tenor before and after October, the nature of Trotsky's *oeuvre* is confused rather than clarified by much of English-Language secondary literature. Having been previously portrayed as Antichrist,[1] Trotsky has more recently been cast a Renaissance Man.[2] Less ludicrous if little more enlightening, the recent studies by Mandel[3] and Hallas[4] do more to clarify their own relations to Trotsky than to clarify Trotsky's own positions. Indeed, the Bolshevik image of Trotsky as the Man of October is still hegemonic. This image allows room for manoeuvre for the less dogmatic of his followers who nevertheless generally endorse Trotsky's self-image as the best Bolshevik after Lenin. Few attempts have been made to 'save' Trotsky from Bolshevism, or at least to clarify his earlier anti-Leninist positions.[5] The thesis I want to present is unambiguous. It has two arguments – one, that there *is* indeed another Trotsky, and two, that this other Trotsky is not such as to provide a viable alternative to his dominant Bolshevik face.[6] His deficits have much in common with those of early western Marxism.

The existence of the other Trotsky has long been acknowledged in continental discourse. The crucial absence in the English literature is of course the untranslated 1904 *Nos tâches politiques*,[7] *Our Political Tasks*.[8] It goes without

---

1 See Carmichael 1975; Payne 1977.
2 Segal 1979; Heller 1978.
3 Mandel 1979d.
4 Mandel 1979.
5 Important here are Carlo 1977; Geras 1981.
6 The Bolshevik Trotsky has been well enough criticised elsewhere. See *inter alia* Beilharz 1979b. A much expanded and revised critique, drawn on here, is in my PhD in progress, *Genesis and Transition in Trotskyism: A Critique*, chs. 1–3. A useful recent addition to the published materials is Ramsay, Corrigan and Sayer 1978, especially Ch. 3.
7 Trotsky 1970a, 1970c.
8 Among the contributions to the discussion are Brossat (1974) and Projekt Klassenanalyse (1971). NLB announced an English edition of *Our Political Tasks* some time ago, without result.

saying that there is no consensus in Europe over the meaning of the other Trotsky, or his relation to the Bolshevik Trotsky: but these issues have been discussed for at least a decade.[9] Though the English speaking audience was given a glimpse of the other Trotsky in Deutscher's *The Prophet Armed*,[10] the heretical image was no sooner shown than spirited away.[11] Deutscher's form of presentation mirrored Trotsky's own self-denial; generations of leftists took on the repression of Trotsky youthful anti-Leninism.

1

Who was the other Trotsky? His distinguishing characteristics can be summarised briefly.[12] Symptomatic of the early Trotsky's location between Bolshevism

---

Pirate editions have existed and Geras (1981) uses the unpublished NLB translation by Brian Pearce. A valuable precis in contained in Knei-Paz (1978, pp. 185–206). It is difficult not to agree with Knei-Paz (p. 193) that the general Trotskyist silence on these issues is politically symptomatic. (Also unavailable in English is the contemporaneous *Rapport de la delegation Siberiane* 1970b).

9   The early discussion originates, of course, in arenas like *Socialisme ou Barbarie*. In the more recent literature, Avenas and Brossat (1971, Ch. 4) for example acknowledge the existence of another Trotsky who cannot however be turned on the Bolshevik Trotsky, but is better forgotten. Indeed, to defend the young Trotsky is by definition to defend the Menshevik problematic (Avenas and Brossat, 1971, p. 100 n. 3). Brossat's judgement is better balanced, when he says that Trotsky's politics before October are profoundly contradictory (1974, pp. 11, 127 f.).

10 Deutscher 1954, p. 88 ff.

11 Eastman set things off on a bad foot: 'If I have told the reader anything in this book, I have told him (sic) that Trotsky is a Bolshevik' (1925, p. 171).

12 We leave aside here the question of whether another Trotsky again will emerge from the recently opened second section of his Harvard Archives. The index to the Archive, *Exile Papers of Lev Trotskii 1929–40* (Harvard, Cambridge 1975) indicates that the contents consist primarily of correspondence to and from Trotsky, Sedova, Sedov, and the secretaries, some papers (including household papers, contracts etc.) and the Dewey Commission exhibits. The correspondence above will certainly necessitate a new intellectual biography of Trotsky, already overdue, and will facilitate more adequate inner-party histories and further work on the oppositional networks of the thirties. There are few manuscripts in the new archive – one by Trotsky, 'What I Think of Stalin' (1940), others by Burnham, Rizzi, Shachtman. Overall the contents hardly seem sufficient to sustain the enthusiasm of some Trotskyists. See e.g. the notice of *Cahiers Leon Trotsky* (1979), some barely disguised glee at the alleged prospects of great discoveries on the behalf of Pierre Broué and his co-workers (See *Cahiers Leon Trotsky* 1980; Robrieux and Broué 1980). (In addition, it should be noted that Day (1973, Ch. 8) implies the existence of yet another Trotsky – this time, as market socialist into the later twenties).

and Menshevism, *Our Political Tasks* is as Knei-Paz indicates more an attack on the former than a defence of the latter.[13] While vitriolic in the extreme, its attack on Leninism is theoretical as well as personal. The well-known quote on 'substitutionism' is but the tip of the iceberg. Against the argument for the vanguard party Trotsky endorses the notion of the party evident in Marx and also in sections of the German revolutionary left: the vanguard party should reflect and educate the mass movement, whose active participation is a crucial factor in the struggle for socialism.[14] Trotsky's emphasis on the self-activity of the working-class correlates with the form of critique now known as prefigurative: that is, the organisational forms applied in struggle are seen to overdetermine the political outcome of such struggle. Socialism by nature cannot be introduced by centralist, autocratic or bourgeois means. The other Trotsky is resolutely opposed to Jacobinism and to the professionalisation of socialist politics.[15] In short, his positions both critical and postulative are based on the premise of the First International, that the emancipation of the working class could only be achieved by that class itself. Not the least irony here is that Trotsky's critique of Lenin's practice would apply even more strongly to his own after 1917.

A dimension of the other Trotsky even less discussed is his historiography. *1905* has been sadly overshadowed by *The History of the Russian Revolution*, obscuring its real achievements. Two main points should be made here. First, like *Results and Prospects*, *1905* indicates an extreme sensitivity to historical specificity combined with a rare theoretical rigour.[16] Both dimensions provide a sharp contrast to the abstract internationalism of *The Permanent Revolution* or *The Transitional Program*. The quality of Trotsky's analysis of the peculiarities of Russian development in *1905* brings to mind even contemporary debates like those in world-systems analysis or the *Science and Society* debate.[17] Russia is understood as a paradigm of uneven development.[18] In contrast, say, to the British case, Russian capital is theorised as first of all imported and state dependent. The absence of organically developed capital signals the absence of an assertive bourgeoisie, the analysis as a whole therefore providing the basis for the theory of Permanent Revolution. Trotsky's theorisation of

---

13   Knei-Paz 1978, p. 186.
14   Knei-Paz 1978, p. 190.
15   Trotsky 1970a, Ch. 4; Knei-Paz 1978, p. 199 ff.
16   For specific methodological statements see Trotsky 1973a, pp. 67, 354, chs. 23, 24 *passim*, also 1974a, p. 64.
17   See e.g. Hilton 1976.
18   Trotsky 1973a, p. 53; useful here is Sawer 1977.

Permanent Revolution concentrates at this stage on the distinct nature of the Russian experience: against the universally applicable theorem later developed, the analysis in *1905* relates specifically to Russia.[19]

Second, the political arguments in *1905* are also noteworthy. In contrast to the post-October focus on the Party, the interest here is in the Soviet. The Soviet itself – the proletariat organised – is seen as the embryonic workers' government.[20] The, Soviet, and not the Party, takes the leading role. The Soviet functions as counterstate: the general strike disorganises the old state power, and it is the Soviet which fills its organisational vacuum.[21] The Party functions here merely as the enlightened section of the proletariat, which comes to its head not in terms of domination but in terms of influence: parties in the Soviet have only the right to debate, not to vote, voting being the prerogative of the workers' representatives. Instead they were merely political experts serving as consultants.[22]

Trotsky in *1905* in fact rejects the military approach to insurrection characteristic of Bolshevism in power, asserting rather the priority of the enlightenment of the people as to the impending conflict and what was at stake in it.[23] The primary role of the barricade for the other Trotsky is not mechanical but moral.[24] It lies in its ability to bring workers and soldiers face-to-face, inducing the shock of recognition in both and thereby effectively demobilising the repressive apparatus of the Tsarist state. Revolution here is understood as the process of the 'moral regeneration of the people': it is cast in images of rebirth and enlightenment.[25] In contrast to the later authoritarianism of *Terrorism and Communism*, *1905* is marked by a passionate humanism on behalf of the oppressed and their perpetual struggles against the existing powers and the Black Hundreds.[26] Clearly the young Trotsky is an impressive marxist. Reflecting his own self-denial, his neglect for the image of the

---

19   The universally applicable theorem is manifested in the later Trotsky in the compulsory option of socialism (the Russian way) or barbarism (the Italian Way). See Beilharz 1979b, pp. 143–6.

20   Trotsky 1973a, p. 266.

21   Trotsky 1973a, pp. 267 f., 272 f.

22   Trotsky 1973a, p. 388 f.

23   Trotsky 1973a, p. 410.

24   Trotsky 1973a, p. 411.

25   Trotsky 1973a, pp. 194, 412.

26   It should be mentioned that Trotsky's humanism resurfaces in the years of exile: see e.g. his 'Testament' (1974b, pp. 162–4). Similarly, Trotsky's sense of specificity revives in his analyses of conjunctures in crisis, viz. his analyses of German fascism and of the Spanish Revolution.

Man of October is symptomatic of the hegemony of Bolshevik politics in the revolutionary left still today.

2

The positions of the other Trotsky have a number of parallels in western Marxism. These parallels are instructive, for the 'rediscovery' of another Trotsky should not be taken to indicate a simple preference for him in the manner of young/mature Marx debates. Indeed, the marxism of the other Trotsky is still quite problematical.

The other Trotsky has much in common with other prefigurative tendencies in western Marxism, with Luxemburg, Gramsci, council communism. Trotsky's prefigurative argument in *Our Political Tasks* resembles other prefigurative arguments in that, while 'correct', it is too easy.[27] Its negative premonitions tell us only what is *not* to be done. This might not be a problem were the gradual enlightenment of the working class assured. However, we know all too well that it is not. More explicitly, the argument as it has been reformulated: 'socialism will be democratic or it will not be at all': seems to give insufficient attention to the far more likely case that it will not be at all. The scenario now shifts from the option between bourgeois democracy and democratic socialism to your choice of barbarisms. In other words, the prefigurative argument rests on a fundamental optimism, which in political form re-emerges as spontaneism. Relying on a fictitious self-motivating subject *a la* Lukács, the problem is simply that spontaneism doesn't work – the masses do not adequately organise themselves. Needless to say, we are not advocating here the traditional alternative: to organise them for their own good from above in forms which militate against self-organisation. But the proposed alternative of the other Trotsky is no solution either: not for Tsarist Russia, nor for the West today, where time is becoming ever shorter.

Further parallels with Rosa and Gramsci are multiple. Trotsky's affinity with Rosa is evident: their arguments for democratic organisation from below, the opposition to Jacobinism, the featured phenomena of general strike and enlightenment express a rare and lost trend in Marxism.[28] Less well observed are Trotsky's parallels with Gramsci. Trotsky shares Gramsci's idealism, in the

---

27   Though not itself immune from these problems, a good survey is C. Boggs 1977.
28   See especially the essays by Geras and Carlo, and Geras (1976). Cf. my review of Geras (Beilharz 1980).

positive sense that ideas are seen as fusing agents in the actual process of radicalisation. Like Gramsci in occupied Turin, Trotsky in Soviet St. Petersburg is
a voluntarist, an enemy of Jacobinism, an advocate of grassroots activity in
workers' councils, a theorist of working-class initiative in the face of a politically bankrupt bourgeoisie. In Gramsci as in Trotsky these positions are located
within the scheme of uneven development.[29] But the young Trotsky was never
to be known adequately by Gramsci, who understood the later Trotsky rather
as a left intransigent like Bordiga.

Like Trotsky, Gramsci also became a Leninist: but of a peculiar kind, as the
extent of the debate on his Marxism shows.[30] Gramsci's later understanding of
the limits of the idea of the factory council as the proletarian state in embryo
led to the subsequent theorisation of the party as the new prince.[31] The limits of
this conclusion, together with the unresolved contradictions in Gramsci, have
been well indicated in Laclau and Mouffe's important essay.[32] To take up only
the positive dimension of Gramsci, the potential working up of democratic
forms of struggle is certainly absent from the late Trotsky, who lapses instead
into a fetish of leadership.[33] Where Gramsci turns his attention to the problem
of popular consent to bourgeois society, Trotsky turns to the development of a
new cadre and a new International. Consent is never really a problem for Trotsky who, whether young or old, shares with Lukács the notion that because
inherently revolutionary, the working class can and will act out its objective,
historic interest. Here is at least one element of continuity between the young
and later Trotsky.[34] It produces a crucial absence in Trotskyism: the ability to

---

29   Gramsci 1972.
30   The materials here are voluminous. Important recent contributions include Mouffe 1977,
      Buci-Glucksmann 1980, and Sassoon 1980a. Important recent review articles include Sas-
      soon 1980b, and Nield and Seed 1981. Bibliographical surveys include Mouffe and Sassoon
      1977 and Beilharz 1979a.
31   Gramsci 1971, pp. 123–205; Cf. Sassoon 1980a, pp. 224, 226, 230.
32   Laclau and Mouffe 1981.
33   That is to say, Trotsky's *Transitional Programme* is not accurately transitional at all. The
      Transitional Programme is in fact contradictory: it can sustain both interpretations, that
      its demands are transitional and that they are not transitional but rather reformist. Little
      in Trotsky's programme – sliding scales of wages and hours, the disclosure of business
      secrets, extension of public works, workers' control and selective nationalisation etc. –
      appears much more radical than Mitterand's proposals for France. See further: League for
      the Revolutionary Party (1979). This argument is detailed in chapter 3 of my Ph.D.
34   Another element of continuity in Trotsky's marxism is the use of personification and gen-
      erative metaphor as analysis. Whether personifying the strike in *1905* (106 f.; see also 409)
      or applying gynaecological or medical metaphor in *The History of the Russian Revolution* or
      In Defense of Marxism, Trotsky continually resorts to images which indicate the evolution-

face the fact that bourgeois society reproduces itself because its bearers actively consent to its reproduction.

Hegemony and consent were not problems for Trotsky because neither Tsarism nor liberalism were hegemonic in Russia; neither could mobilise perpetual popular consent. Beyond the orthodoxy of the Second International, the Bolsheviks understood that socialism was an act of conscious will and not just the burp after History had swallowed capitalism. But the forms which they proposed and practised were not adequate to the tasks set. Trotsky's ambivalence toward democracy and his fluctuation between voluntarism and determinism seem to correlate with the shift from the earlier conjuncture to that of Stalinism. In order to transcend such ambiguities, it would instead have been necessary to ask, what strategy should be followed to *popularise* socialism in the bad conjunctures, in the low points of history? As the twentieth century continues its decline and the dustbin of history becomes progressively more crowded, that question still has to be faced – and answered.

---

ary necessity of socialism. (On generative metaphor, which generates its own conclusions or solutions, see Schön (1979). Thanks to Margaret Rose for this reference).

CHAPTER 10

The Young Trotsky (1991)

Who was Trotsky? or rather, what was Trotsky? The images pervade. In what his French admirers appropriately call the *iconographie* there is Trotsky, in his youthful mugshots, defiant in his cell before the trial of the 1905 Soviet, aboard his military train in the civil war; airbrushed out of the frames of October, fishing, in exile, on the Sea of Marmara, feeding his rabbits in Coyoacan, reading his proofs; lying dying, his brain shattered by Stalin's assassin.[1] For each phase there is a persona – dressed in smocking, now besuited with pince-nez, in military garb, now in leather, now in white; alternatively the oppositionist, 'The Pen', 'Antid Oto', man of the people, professional revolutionary, soldier, commissar, finally exile on the planet without a visa, homeless hero and martyr of the Revolution.

Who then was Trotsky? There are so many images that some might simply deduce that there are too many Trotskys to make sense of. Yet the elements of continuity are also there – an obsession with Revolution, an identification of Revolution with History or modernity. They explain Trotsky's resistance to the vanguard party, which was to dissolve only in 1917 when the Bolsheviks finally became the missing link in the process in which his life was submerged. Trotsky forged his Faustian pact with the Party and with state power in October, when it became clear that the Russian Revolution could not make itself. The outsider became transformed into the armed Prince, Rousseau into Machiavelli, and then into the Prophet Unarmed when History took its wrong turn, elevating Stalin over Trotsky, leaving Trotsky, in Deutscher's memorable phrase, as the last remaining revolutionary from the lost Atlantis of the October Revolution.[2]

In the annals of intellectual Trotskyism, it is the heroic image which pervades. Trotsky is presented, for example, by Perry Anderson as the premier historian of marxism, while Norman Geras prides Trotsky as the creator of a literature of revolution.[3] Followers such as Ernest Mandel celebrate Trotsky as the foremost critic of fascism, while critics such as George Markus draw attention to his status as the primary founding analyst of the Soviet Union in *The Revolution Betrayed*.[4] While Markus' purpose is to advance upon the level of

---

1 Wyndham 1972.
2 Deutscher 1970b, p. 480.
3 Anderson 1976, p. 97, 1980, p. 154; Geras, 1986, pp. 3–41.
4 See Mandel's Introduction in Trotsky 1971 and; Fehér, Heller and Márkus 1983, p. 9.

understanding of Trotsky, however, these other writers come in praise, as do his more recent biographers, Cliff and Broué, still endeavouring, unsuccessfully, to supplant the work of Deutscher.[5]

Viewed in a different light, Trotsky's intellectual achievement lies elsewhere. Three submerged moments in Trotsky's thought are suggestive of this. One is the brilliant, if deeply flawed scenario of hypermodernism sketched out in *Literature and Revolution*, where Trotsky dares to dream and to expect a radical and perpetual transformation of all that is social or human.[6] Another is the ruminations in the recently published philosophical *Notebooks* of 1933–35, where Trotsky's evolutionary thinking takes on more subtlety when it is explained as bearing a catastrophic architectonic, as contrasted to the systemic orientation of, say, Bukharin. The *Notebooks* certainly make fascinating reading, alongside the 1935 *Diary*, though it is tempting to align them on the whole with Lenin's *Philosophical Notebooks* rather than with Gramsci's *Prison Notebooks*.[7]

The other source of insight is that of Trotsky's early work, before Bolshevism, before absolutism, before the Revolution. The purpose of this paper is to establish and further examine the content of Trotsky's early work, which is barely recognised as an intellectual and political achievement alongside that of the *History of The Russian Revolution* or *The Revolution Betrayed*, and this essentially because of its essential anti-Bolshevism.[8]

Rebel without a Cause

The young Trotsky could not have anticipated all these problems of interpretation, for though he lived for Revolution he did not yet live only for October. Trotsky was born Bronstein, on the day which was to become that of the October Revolution, 26 October 1879. His rural boyhood became as distant to him as was feudalism itself from his Americanist conception of modernity. The rupture opened when the boy, aged nine, went to live in Odessa. Here lay the founding elements of his cosmopolitanism, the theatre, the opera, the smell of printers' ink, the petty injustices of school life which so impressed that he was in consequence frequently to call on images of the classroom in the writ-

---

5 See Broué (1988) and Cliff (1989) to indicate the continuing hegemony of Deutscher's work is not to endorse (cf. Beilharz 1986, 1987).
6 This dimension is discussed in Beilharz (1992a), Chapter 2.
7 cf. Trotsky 1986.
8 See earlier Beilharz (1981b). One indicator of the marginal status of early Trotsky's work is that it is thinly theorised even in the wide ranging collection of essays in Gori (1982).

ings of his later life. For the young Trotsky the classroom, like the country, was grey to the green of life and the vibrance of the city. Odessa struck him so profoundly that he first encountered Paris as a larger Odessa, and preferred Odessa. Here he met the work of Dickens, of Goethe and Shakespeare; he read more of Tolstoy and of Pushkin and started a magazine, upsetting the authorities and alienating his family. But he was, so far, a rebel without a cause.[9]

Trotsky was not always a marxist. Marxism was not yet part of his world, and Trotsky's first encounters with it were unequivocally negative. His sense of social injustice led rather to that idiosyncratic posture of rebellion characteristic of adolescence. Marxism was for him an intellectual prison. He did not want to be bound by a worldview which, as he declaimed, sought only to bring dryness and hardness into all the relations of life. He read rather Mill and Bentham, and Chernyshevsky. Trotsky now left the cultural warmth of his lodgings in order to live a spartan communal existence with other young rebels and the radical gardener, Shvigovsky. Together, like later generations, they ran an informal university where Trotsky's brief was to lecture in sociology and to write plays, authoring their own propaganda. Such apparently harmless activity was not so innocent in the eyes of the Tsarist authorities. The young Trotsky thus began a long relationship with the Tsar's prisons. Eventually he served time in almost twenty such institutions where, again like generations, he acquired a political education. Finally he met the work of Marx, and Lenin, and Labriola. And soon he was to take a fake passport with a new name and what was to become an historic aura – Trotsky.[10]

The marxism which beckoned Trotsky was that of the Second International, exemplified in the culture of the German Social Democratic Party. In prison, he began to embrace the marxist worldview. In *My Life*, Trotsky relates that even as a schoolboy he had been attracted to the general over the particular, law over fact, theory over personal experience, the romance of Odessa over the dull tedium of the Ukrainian steppes. In prison he grappled further with these issues. Where did ideas come from? Was history a process characterised by the combination of differing logics, or was there some factor which was privileged? Did not economic life govern the direction of history? Confronted by these quandaries, Trotsky embraced historical materialism. Uncertainty repelled him; he would later describe it as the consequence of petty-bourgeois vacillation and nervelessness. Trotsky thus read Labriola's *Essays on the Materialist Conception of History*, a treatise defending contingency against inevitab-

---

9   Trotsky 1975, chaps 3, 4.
10   Trotsky 1975, chap. 8.

ility, as a verification of his own view that material forces, primarily those in economic life, provided the masterkey to explaining and making universal history. During the same period of confinement, however, Trotsky also began to address the problem of contradiction or uneven development in history. In prison he began a major study of freemasonry, discovering among other things the differences between its national forms. Sometimes masonry was reactionary, sometimes progressive, even revolutionary. Particular experiences did in fact undermine the generalities to which Trotsky was attracted. Further, the upshot of his study of masonry was that the past would dominate the present; ideology and culture did possess a formative power after all. But if this was so, ruptural social change could never achieve the social transparency to which revolutionaries aspired: the implication was closer to Freud than to Marx, suggesting as it did that consciousness could not consciously be changed. Trotsky's prison notebooks were lost, but the tension established in them was to remain a major motif in Trotsky's understanding of history. The particular continued to struggle with the general, fact with law, experience with theory, history with historical materialism.[11]

The Cause

Plainly marxism fulfilled a need for the young Trotsky. He resisted it only so long as he could, for he needed an instrument to turn against Russian populism and upon anarchism. The sharp knife of marxism offered defence against Russian capitalism and offence upon its looser opponents. Trotsky encountered marxism further via Lenin's *Development of Capitalism in Russia* and in the first volume of Marx's *Capital*. He shared Lenin's sense that the process of capitalist development was well underway in Russia, and yet that it directly affected only a minority of the people. He read the Bernstein-Kautsky debate over reform and revolution and can only have been obliged to support Kautsky: for Bernstein proposed not only to eschew revolutionary politics but also to plug the marxist canon. In other debates his views were less orthodox; like many (Lenin aside) he read and admired the 'God-builder' and relativist Bogdanov, who only later was to be cast as a *marxisant* eccentric. Having escaped exile to Western Europe, he imbibed there its extraordinary political and intellectual culture. Henceforth his lifelong cause was to be that of Marxism.[12]

---

11   Trotsky 1975, pp. 123–7.
12   Trotsky 1975, pp. 147–8.

Yet Trotsky was no Bolshevik, indeed, he was Lenin's most vehement critic. Notwithstanding his later political identification with Bolshevism or his personal obsession with Lenin, Trotsky entered the twentieth century arms linked with social democrats like Axelrod and Martov, mind attuned with socialist revolutionaries such as Gramsci and Luxemburg. His cause was that of marxism, but his vocation was not that of the professional revolutionary. His belief was that the masses themselves carried the impulse to socialism. He had nothing but scorn for the notion shared by Kautsky and Lenin that, left to itself, the working class could only ever generate the trade-union consciousness of economic grievances.[13] His intuitive sense of the nature of history was closer to that of syndicalism; he agreed with Parvus that the general strike itself was sufficient to place the democratic workers' government in power.[14] His contempt for Lenin and Jacobinism was sufficient to warrant the major early work *Our Political Tasks* (1904) which, significantly, was repressed in English for eighty years. Here Trotsky launched an attack on Bolshevism rather like that later to be turned on him by democratic socialists. Together with his reflections on the 1905 Revolution and his early formulations of the theory of Permanent Revolution, *Our Political Tasks* provides leading clues to the nature of Trotsky's early marxism.

For if Trotsky was not always a marxist, neither was he a lifelong Bolshevik. Once when Lenin had chastised Luxemburg for not 'speaking Russian' with sufficient fluency, Trotsky had retorted in her defence that she did speak an excellent marxian. Such was his own inflexion in *Our Political Tasks*. Dedicated to the Menshevik Axelrod, Trotsky employed his missal not only against Lenin but also to defend his newfound cause – the self-emancipation of the working class. Trotsky's case was authentically marxian, and was thus both rhetorical rather than logically persuasive in tenor, and morally naive rather than Jacobin in its ethical orientation. Like Marx the young Trotsky believed socialist revolution to be built into the order of things. Both believed the working class to be revolutionary by disposition; both consequently viewed the party as of secondary rather than primary significance in the revolutionary process. The difference which was to emerge historically between Marx and the later Trotsky was that Trotsky's pact with History led him finally to accept the idea of socialism at any cost. Marx, by comparison, put his hopes in history alone, and never ceased to believe that socialism could only be the task of the workers to whom he imputed this responsibility. The philosophy of history in *Our Political Tasks*

---

13   cf. Kautsky 1901, pp. 79–80; Lenin 1977c, pp. 383–4.
14   See generally Trotsky 1974a.

thus vitally anticipates Trotsky's conversion to Bolshevism in 1917. Rather than providing an enigmatic reversal or adding just another image to the panoply of Trotskys, Trotsky's Bolshevism grows out of this context in which revolution is the ghost in History's infernal machine.[15]

Trotsky's Early Tasks

Marx ascribed a revolutionary vocation to the proletariat already in his early writings. *Capital* then took over from the *Communist Manifesto* the presupposition of a revolutionary working class compelled to burst bourgeois social relations asunder.[16] This proletarian mythology was to become the theoretical commonsense of *fin de siècle* socialism. Kautsky, the Pope of German socialism, described the Social Democrats as revolutionary, but not revolution-making.[17] Revolutions made themselves. Only the revisionist Bernstein was sufficiently candid to recognise in this belief what he was to call 'Calvinism without God'.[18] For Trotsky, in this period, God was the masses, not the Party. Trotsky shared with Marx the view which Sorel explained as a political mythology of catastrophic revolution. Lenin, by comparison, was the broker of the Revolution. Trotsky's biography was among other things the transition from one to the other.

In *Our Political Tasks* Trotsky pilloried Lenin for his mechanistic view of politics. In *One Step Forward, Two Steps Back* Lenin had rendered politics as organisation. Socialism for Trotsky was an irreversible molecular process which ran deep through the current of modern history, an elemental, nature-like force which made organisational politics an unwitting farce conducted over it. The ant-like activity of organisational work would in Trotsky's eyes be washed away by the spring torrents of history. The historic inevitability of socialism was simultaneously a process of political self-determination of the proletariat. For the young, unlike the later Trotsky the present task was not party building or the conversion of the intelligentsia to marxism, but rather the tapping and cultivation of this already existing and developing process of proletarian hegemony. Not the vanguard party, but the mass party, the class as party was to be the centre of socialist argument and agitation. Theory here was strictly secondary, rather than primary. Sectarian body battles among the intelligentsia missed the

---

15   Trotsky 1970a.
16   Marx 1965, chap. 32.
17   Kautsky 1909.
18   Bernstein 1965, p. 7.

point that a theory of political development would not replace a politically developing proletariat itself. The politics of Lenin's paper, *Iskra*, were wasted precisely because they elevated conversion of the intelligents over other practices, then necessarily endorsing the empirical consciousness of the proletariat in paternalistic manner. *Iskra* was obsessed with the press and the programme rather than with proletarian self-activity. Its politics were formalistic rather than substantive, incidental more than fundamental.[19]

Against this position Trotsky held that of his 'dear teacher', Axelrod. Unlike Lenin, Axelrod was no empty windbag or self-seeking aspirant to the role of Robespierre. Axelrod was a genuine proletarian ideologue, in the sense that were only to be found in Germany. He did not speak with the intelligentsia, only about them; for him the intelligentsia was not the audience, the object of persuasion, but one political force among others. For the young Trotsky intellectuals were the auxiliary to the working class and to History. The Party was merely the consciousness and will of the organised class. As Marx and Engels had put it in the *Manifesto*, the party was no more than the most enlightened section of the class; it saw further, but it was of the class, not superior to it. As in the young Gramsci, so in the young Trotsky was the party an educator, not an administrator. The party based itself on the given level of consciousness of the proletariat and sought simply to raise it. The proletariat was to be the subject of policy, and not only its object; it was not only to be a political audience, but also a 'collective actor'. As in Luxemburg, the centre of politics was the development of the conscious and autonomous activity of the proletariat. The failure to encourage and to enlighten this activity led, meanwhile, to substitutionism on the part of Lenin. 'Substitutionism, always substitutionism' – this was the motif of frenzied party-building conducted in isolation from such cultivation. The Bolsheviks viewed themselves as the brain of the slumbering proletarian giant which, for Trotsky, had motivating powers of its own and needed rather to be wakened than to be led.[20]

Trotsky acknowledged in *Our Political Tasks* that his politics would likely be seen as syndicalist, for the logic of his case was workers' autonomy. The prospect did not seem much to bother him. Bolshevism, after all, was hopeless. So was liberalism, for the Russian bourgeoisie was insufficiently muscular to take its place on the stage. Class politics, and not the abstract rights of man and citizen, was in any case the watchword. Here again Trotsky revealed his substantial affinity with Marx. Citizenship was, unfortunately, a value which received short

---

19   Trotsky 1979, pp. 25–40.
20   Trotsky 1979, p. 51.

shift in their hands. Against Lenin, but with Marx, he poured scorn on the idea that the division of labour was a central principle of socialist politics. The problem was to make society anew, not to replicate its already existing and limiting forms. He effectively argued against the reduction of *praxis* to *techne* which critical marxists later proclaimed a hallmark of Bolshevism (see for example Habermas[21] and Lubasz).[22] Politics was not technique; it was not administration. It was education. The division of labour so deeply admired by Lenin perpetuated all these problems inherited from bourgeois society. Bolshevism was a philosophy of disastrous consequences for party life, as it cultivated only empty specialisation.

The craftsman, the whole person, and not the dissected modern detail worker was rather the model appropriate for the party member and proletarian. Lenin wanted the party to be a machine, Trotsky wrote, its individual members cogs. Trotsky summoned against Lenin Marx's blistering criticism in *Capital* of the capitalist division of labour which reduced individuals to exactly such cogs. In parallel to the strategy of capital, he argued, the Bolshevik project separated mental from manual labour, expropriating conception and leaving only execution. Labour was left a helpless, brainless hulk; the Bolshevik Party, like capital, itself sucked up the human attributes of labour. Conscious activity was separated from executive activity, social democratic thinking from the technical means of its application ... socialism from revolution. Without an adequate educational project, the Party would at best reproduce the division between leaders and led, rather than begin to overcome it. The party could not be allowed to go this way. It could not be a 'huge factory' or a barracks, as Lenin desired. Everyday life educated the proletariat, not the discipline of the factory or the self-appointed führer of socialism; the real aim of socialism was to transcend these.[23]

With Lenin the organising head, the professional party itself set about removing lesser, merely empirical heads. Lenin had now implicitly and explicitly embraced Jacobinism. The barrister Bolshevik decreed that those who would rebel against him were bad; but his own rebellion was good. His enthusiasm for Jacobinism showed Lenin again to be a bourgeois thinker. Just as he shared with capital a factory-enthused view of the world, so he espoused the politics of bourgeois self-emancipation which corresponded with the apogee of the French Revolution: in theory, the appeal to the rights of abstract man and citizen; in practice, the guillotine. Trotsky unfortunately imagined the relation

---

21   Habermas 1973.
22   Lubasz 1976.
23   Trotsky 1979, pp. 84–90, 102–4.

between the theory and practice to be necessary; the real problem was that the guillotine was presumed to be the appropriate means of pursuing abstract 'virtue'. For Lenin, as for Robespierre, all the crevices of society were then to yield intriguers, hypocrites, aristocrats and worst of all moderates. In this humanity divided itself into two parties: the good and the bad citizens. Suspicion became the means of establishing the difference. Jacobinism, for Trotsky, thus became manifest as a profoundly negative form of politics, whereas social democracy was by comparison the most optimistic of parties, because it alone heard and responded to the riddle of history. The Jacobins, by contrast, endeavoured to behead the class movement. Liquidation stood in for education; and Marx's leonine head would have been the first to roll under Maximilien Lenin's rule.[24]

Trotsky's pamphlet was for all his disdain addressed to the intelligentsia rather than to the masses. Its turgid prose and lambast had little evident effect. *Our Political Tasks* was later to become a bludgeon with which the Soviet prosecutor Vyshinsky would ruthlessly beat Trotsky in the thirties, in the Moscow Show Trials.[25] For Trotsky was eventually to become so obsessively identified with Lenin in his own mind that these juvenile barbs were to reemerge as an embarrassment, and they have been treated as such ever since by followers who, on his own advice, identify Trotsky and Lenin both as men of October. Yet as historians since Deutscher have observed, the young Trotsky showed acute sensitivity in his critique of nascent Stalinism.[26] More than Deutscher and other sympathisers would allow, Trotsky also laid here the basis of the radical critique of Bolshevism as a necessarily authoritarian, compulsory and compulsive aberration from socialism's libertarian impulse. In this sense *Our Political Tasks* anticipated Trotsky's own biographical path into the politics of Jacobinism. In 1904, the young Trotsky, the oppositionist, the 'syndicalist', had already unwittingly anticipated the path of the Russian Revolution. The difference was that, in its decisive act, he would stand not apart from Lenin but together with him, in pride and defiance, Saint-Just to his Robespierre.

Dress Rehearsal

Between 1904 and 1917 stood 1905. Trotsky was later to baptise the 1905 Soviet the dress rehearsal, the major prologue to the October Revolution which followed it. He read history backwards; for the substance of 1905 was far more

24   Trotsky 1979, p. 124.
25   Dewey 1972, pp. 329–33.
26   Deutscher 1954, pp. 88–97.

consonant with the democratic, or at least libertarian temper of Trotsky's politics in *Our Political Tasks*. His own analysis of the events, published as *1905*,
also announced his talents as historian, more particularly historical sociologist and political historian. In *1905* Trotsky argued, in anticipation of much
more recent attempts to explain the Russian enigma, that the history of Russia was an unbroken chain of heroic efforts to provide the military organisation with continuity.[27] He now developed his case for Russia as the paradigm
case of uneven development. Trotsky's Russia was simultaneously the acme of
highly concentrated capitalist development and the accretion of centuries of
backward misery, the forced combination of American technology and Tsarist forms, primeval barbarism welded to urban modernism. Russia's own cities
had commercial and administrative, and not manufacturing or productive histories; liberalism had failed to prosper in the absence of the guild structure
of Europe. As a result, the bourgeois intelligentsia was retarded, civil society
weighed down under feudal tradition, a hothouse culture for economic development coexisting uneasily with archaic local political forms and customs.
Here lay the genesis of Trotsky's theory of Permanent Revolution, already fore-
shadowed in *Our Political Tasks*. Revolution was on the agenda, but not at the
behest of a spineless bourgeoisie; consequently the proletariat would take its
place at the helm of history, and by the logic of perpetual motion be obliged to
open a revolutionary process which would conclude only in the establishment
of world socialism.[28]

The ghost of Marx haunts these pages, too. Trotsky did not write literary
political history in the manner of Marx's *Eighteenth Brumaire*; his prose is more
sober and constrained. But like Marx, Trotsky views revolution as enchantment, and he employs some of the metaphorical modes of presentation so well
deployed by Marx in his historical writings.[29] Trotsky's view of the historical
process in *1905* is, in a sense, the *Manifesto*'s thesis telescoped and universalised.
As European capital beats down customs barriers and Chinese walls, so does
it plant there the basis of revolutionary development which can no longer be
bourgeois in form. Industrialisation on a world-scale is a necessary process, but
it can no longer be initiated, or at least controlled by capitalists. Capitalists were
truly the sorcerer's apprentices. For Trotsky the first to industrialise would be
the last to achieve socialism, as the last would be first. The mole of history was
bound to surface, blinking but alive and enthusiastic, in the east rather than
in the west. Trotsky's historical sociology thus sets the stage upon which the

---

27   Trotsky 1973a, p. 23.
28   Trotsky 1974a; Beilharz 1979b.
29   Beilharz 1987; Rundell 1989.

play of political history unfolds. Actors are hypnotised, somnambulists; they represent the mountainous forces of classes but they bear the individual attributes of Gapon, of Witte, of Yanovsky. In keeping with the elemental teleology established in *Our Political Tasks*, individuals are less themselves than the forces which they personify.[30]

The problem of the role of the individual in history perpetually plagued Trotsky's historiography. The tension between particular and general now reappears. Marx had taught, in *Capital*, that individuals were bearers of their class character-masks, obliged to follow the structural imperatives of capital or labour. In his historical writings Marx had portrayed great individuals such as Bonaparte as mediators between historic classes. The consensus in the Second International was elaborated by Plekhanov, for whom individuals could only represent classes, or epochs. The message was clear – if socialism was inevitable, individuals could only be its historic agents or enemies; they could not be its active initiators, for such initiation was without purpose or reason. Trotsky himself rarely took such an absolutely determinist view; but given his predilection to see elemental forces in history as themselves moving events, the role of individuals in his construction of history was somewhat compromised. This problem remained, for Trotsky, because unlike Plekhanov or Kautsky, or imaginably Marx, he did not accept that the failure of socialism to emerge autogenetically was the end of the story. Trotsky's view, like Lenin's, ultimately refused this outcome; if history did not move itself, it could be pushed, as it plainly was in October 1917 – and pushed hard, if not far.

In *1905*, however, it was the Soviet and not the party which was the major actor; in the young Trotsky's writing the Party is almost invisible. As the proletariat acted collectively, for the young Trotsky, so did the Soviet. The workers' council of self-management was a qualitatively new, non-party organisation working through the production process, but not restricted to it. The general strike was pervasive. The socialist movement was given its cue. The Russian journalists of socialism who had for years lived like moles now knew something of open skies, fresh air, the free word. Their weapon was the word, and the revolutionary word was in the open. The Pen was in his element – he was a leader without being a Jacobin. The 1905 Revolution was, as Trotsky so passionately hoped, a learning experience for the Russian workers. The tedium of everyday life ruptured, the horizons of possibility lifted. A tremendous, mysterious process took place; and amidst this chaos there arose the need for a new order. Again, Trotsky's history is reminiscent of Gramsci's view of the

---

30   Trotsky 1973a, pp. 92–3.

bienno rosso in Italy, as it is evocative of Orwell's sense of the new, nascent Spanish order in *Homage to Catalonia*. Here were workers, seeking dignity in chaos, seeking control of lives previously enshadowed, baking the city's bread, printing their own views and not those of others, behaving not as cogs in any machine but as more complete individual personalities, representing the dawn of a new collective era for mankind.[31]

Trotsky portrayed the Soviet as phantasmagorical because, in part, it was. He tells, for example, of a blind and illiterate war veteran who, covered with crosses and decorations, complained of dire poverty and begged the Soviet to 'put a bit of pressure on Number One' the Tsar. While the Soviet was conspicuously less than all powerful, the point was that it had acted as a counter-power – it was really a workers' government in embryo. The Soviet had taken on practical responsibility for matters of state, so that the blind war veteran was simply addressing his needs to what seemed to him to be the real alternative seat of power. As Trotsky understood, the general strike strategy rendered the existing state power obsolete; this meant that the strike, or the Soviet, was obliged to assume state functions. It ran the railways and the postal and telegraphic services. It intervened authoritatively in economic disputes. Above all, it formalised direct democracy through new organs of power, the councils themselves. Although private property and the state bureaucracy remained intact, the actual running of the national means of production and commerce lay in the hands of the Soviet. Through the use of the political strike the proletarian masses not only stated their opposition to the status quo, but also their positive claims to autonomy. This was exactly, in Trotsky's eyes, the educative process of socialist revolution *in nuce*. For every such strike gave rise to a whole series of new facts, both material and moral, which set in train open-ended processes of confirmation and radical enlightenment. The formal defeat of the Soviet amounted to little, for a great deal had been learned about the fragility of Tsarism, the tenuousness of capitalist relations, and about the power of proletarian self-activity. The mass here was really everything, the party the mere crest on its massive tidal movement.[32]

In all this Trotsky ran a line between revolutionary politics and reformism, between Bolshevism and Menshevism. Bolshevism he had already despatched in *Our Political Tasks*; Menshevism now revealed itself to be even more hapless, wedded to mechanical recipes, 'first the bourgeoisie, then us', searching in vain with magnifying glass in hand for the nonexistent sans-culottes to get

---

31   See Clark 1977; Spriano 1975; Gramsci 1977; Trotsky 1973a, pp. 123, 161, 212–13, 244.
32   Trotsky 1973a, pp. 410–11.

the business into conformity with the pattern set in France after 1789. While the Bolsheviks sought to be the head to the corpus of the workers' movement, the Mensheviks instead took to their beds; they would not budge until history was properly repeated. Neither could accept that the next phase was to be dominated by the proletariat; Trotsky and Parvus alone saw this as necessary, and Trotsky alone viewed this as an active transitional rather than parliamentary interim regime. More, the Russian Revolution would be the prologue to world socialist revolution. Trotsky here ventured more of the theory of Permanent Revolution with which his name was to become so closely identified: henceforth the proletariat would be unable to contain itself, within bourgeois political forms or bourgeois nation states. Socialist revolution would grow over uncontrollably from bourgeois to proletarian tasks, and from individual nations across the entire world system. What was less clear, to the young Trotsky, was whether this envisaged process was actually necessary or simply possible. His youthful historiography was informed by a nice sense of specificity and contingency; yet the process under analysis was also granted a causal inevitability and a determining power. Revolution, Trotsky wrote, was the natural element of the marxist politician such as himself; it came and went, crawled or leapt, and yet its movement was also, clearly, inexorable. Trotsky simultaneously believed history to be an enormous machine working in the service of his ideals, moving slowly, barbarously, but moving, swallowing up his own life's blood as fuel, and still not devouring fast enough.[33]

History did, of course, finally swallow up Trotsky's last drop of blood, but not in the figurative sense which he now entertained. The young Trotsky evidently believed that history was a teleological source, which chose its instruments at will and drove its mission home. He was, however, equally committed to will, organisation, education, enlightenment and moral development as the human motivations of socialism. Trotsky was the apparently impossible, humanist and determinist at the same time. Contrary to his Bolshevik disciples, however, it should never be denied that Trotsky's humanism was there. Indeed, it was the major stream in the social and political thought of the young Trotsky.

Revolution in Permanence

By 1905 Trotsky had staked a claim to revolutionary authority in his own right. Perched between Bolshevism and Menshevism, a major actor in the events

---

33   Trotsky 1973a, p. 365.

of the Soviet, he was no longer Axelrod's quibbling if correct student but was now an historic personality himself. In 1906 he penned a retrospective on these shifts and developments. It was entitled *Results and Prospects*. In it he explained more of his developing theory of Permanent Revolution, which was subsequently to receive its final explication in *The Permanent Revolution* of 1930. *Results and Prospects* commences from the premise that the Russian Revolution, now an actual fact, was the inevitable result of the contradiction between capitalist development and the forces of ossified absolutism. No bourgeoisie stepped forward to bear this cause, thankfully, for Trotsky, because the very idea of resorting to analogy with 1789 or 1848 was anathema. Trotsky agreed with Parvus, that the essential difference between these revolutions was that there was in Russia no craft or guild class to become hegemonic and thrust itself into power. Capitalism in Russia did not in fact result from the developments of the handicraft system. Absolutism had rather assisted in fettering the country with the shackles of capitalism which it could not, itself, restrain. The Russian way was new.[34]

Trotsky again resisted the proposal that Jacobinism ought to provide the model for socialist politics in Russia, but this time his criticism was muted. Jacobinism was not our way, but it had to be defended against the calumnies and stupid vituperations of anaemic, phlegmatic liberalism. Plainly Trotsky's vitriol was to be directed outward in future. Heroic Jacobinism he now viewed as something of an inspiration; the shadow of the guillotine had somehow receded. Not that Jacobinism became a model, for it never did, in Trotsky's self-understanding. Lenin was the only Bolshevik proudly to proclaim it his lineage. For Trotsky, socialism did not rest on compulsion, on forcing individuals or history; socialism remained the *élan vital*, the evolutionary motor of everyday life and paradoxically of capitalist development itself. The growth of industry, the growth of large entrepreneurs, the growth of towns, the growth of the proletariat in general and the industrial proletariat in particular, all prepared the way not only for struggle but also for victory.[35]

The Russian Revolution could only initiate this process. Without direct State support of the European proletariat the working class could not remain in power and convert its temporary domination into a lasting socialist dictatorship – this much was already clear to Trotsky in 1906. The historical scenario seemed still to alternate in his mind – necessity; possibility ... the proletariat obliged to behave thus and thus, revolution to be necessarily socialist and inter-

---

34   Trotsky 1974a, pp. 100–6.
35   Trotsky 1974a, chap. 7.

national, but only possibly … now Trotsky was agreeing with Kautsky, that inevitability dissolved into possibility, now slipping into the language of probability, and finally inevitability. As he had asserted in his autobiography, necessity always captured contingency in his mental processes.

By 1906 the transition from possibility to inevitability seemed almost complete. The revolution in the east would now infect the western proletariat with a revolutionary idealism and rouse in it a desire to speak to their enemies 'in Russian'. Mass parties like the German Social Democrats would likely become obstacles to socialist revolution. The German revolutionaries were philistines, schoolmasters, prognosticators. Trotsky had yet to make his pact with Bolshevism against these timid, ridiculous timewasters. Another decade, opening the Great War, was to pass before Trotsky embraced Lenin. But the basis for their later partnership had been laid. When the Party eventually knocked at the door, Kautsky may have been in his slippers but Trotsky was dressed and waiting. He had always resisted the temptation to burst through open doors. When History beckoned, Trotsky was finally to concede that proletarian self-activity was not enough. Unlike Kautsky, Martov or Plekhanov, Trotsky had been awaiting the revolution in the hope that it would really come.

Conclusions

Trotsky had always dreamed of being a writer. State power had not been his lifelong hope or vocation, but when the moment came Trotsky happily left behind the pacific realm of his prisons, his study in Vienna, and enthusiastically entered the laboratory of Soviet socialism and Soviet Man. There would now be no time for thinking, as he himself recognised – the word had given way to the deed. Everything now seemed possible; in the rush to practice, Trotsky left judgment behind. Now having awaited, and then run with History, he could only blame it when things turned bad, initiating the later hackneyed claims that it was adverse historical circumstances alone which were responsible for the strangling of proletarian democracy.[36] The teleology of History here overpowers Trotsky's early hopes for social democracy. But there is no point in waiting for democracy: it has to be worked upon, particular towards the general. Politics may involve more than education, but in both there remains a great deal of learning.

---

36   Trotsky 1937.

Isaac Deutscher – History and Necessity (1986)

Despite the now extensive analyses of Trotsky's Marxism, little work has examined the way in which Trotskyism functions as a political discourse. Trotskyism establishes its political conclusions in advance in and through its use of metaphor which presumes the transition to socialism to be already underway, or even guaranteed. This tendency is evident in Trotsky but is perhaps best exemplified in the work of Isaac Deutscher. Deutscher is one of the few great figures in Marxist historiography. Lionised by those within the revolutionary tradition, Deutscher has simultaneously been castigated by liberals and social democrats as an apologist for Stalinism.[1] Both these views seize on only one dimension of Deutscher's thought. His fascination has to do rather with the contradiction internal to his thought. Deutscher is a contradictory thinker because he is a Jacobin, simultaneously revolutionary *and* fellow traveller, and this is so by necessity of his own logic rather than mere circumstance. His is a kind of Khruschevist Trotskyism, for Deutscher views the mess of Stalinism as the prerequisite of Soviet socialism, the latter to be parcelled out from above by those who know the universal good.[2] Yet there is much more to Deutscher than to Khruschev, not least because of the elaborate cultural context within which Deutscher constructs his view of Soviet history. Deutscher was a writer of extraordinary literary quality, but this is the source of the problem as well as of his achievement. The argument of this paper is that these issues and this contradiction in Deutscher can best be explained through the examination of his historiography. We attempt to problematise Deutscher's Trotskyism by investigating, in outline, its correlates in arguments related to Greek tragedy, to Carlyle's philosophy of history, to Goethe, Shakespeare and Hegel, establishing thereby the extent to which history functions in Deutscher as God, *deus ex machina*, or as Director of its universal drama. If history functions as theatre for Trotsky and Deutscher alike, then it is also appropriate to discuss the course of Soviet history and the subsequent development of Trotskyism in this light.

---

1 See, for example, Anderson 1976; Tarbuck 1977; Ali 1978; Mandel 1979d.
2 On Khruschev see Miller and Fehér 1984.

Deutscher and Trotsky: History as Theatre

Like Trotsky, Deutscher relies on generative metaphor in order to ground his philosophy of history. As Donald Schon[3] explains, generative metaphor is that which *generates* its conclusions already in its premises. Trotsky and Deutscher alike depend on the sense of movement or inevitability associated with geological development and gynaecology. Critics like Hannah Arendt[4] and Susan Sontag[5] have explained this striking dependence of Bolshevik argument on the imagery of gangrene, decay and the surgeon with reference to the linguistic legacy of the French Revolution. The imagery of the theatre is equally fundamental to Trotskyism, and it is this imagery which is of special interest to us here, for while Trotskyist thinking clearly rests on notions like generation/degeneration, the image of the theatre is more revealing of the Trotskyist historiography. For the semiological baggage of Trotskyism is never declared – the plot of History unfolds, good deeds are done by men good or evil, the audience undergoes catharsis, the moral is clear for all to see as the moral play called History closes. Trotskyism as a discourse thus seduces its audience by explaining Soviet history through these accepted, if tokenised, cultural symbols.

Deutscher's *magnum opus*, the Trotsky trilogy on which we focus here, resembles in many ways Trotsky's own great work, his *History of the Russian Revolution*. The tragic mode sets the very tenor of Deutscher's work, expanding as the story/tragedy develops. Deutscher informs us, for example, in the Preface to *The Prophet Armed* that Trotsky's life is to be understood as a classical tragedy in secular form.[6] The extent to which it can be called secular is open to some doubt. In closing the same volume Deutscher concludes that 'at the very pinnacle of power Trotsky, like the protagonist of a classical tragedy, stumbled'.[7] Trotsky had been doomed, in Deutscher's understanding, to act out practices which he had earlier damned as 'substitutionism'. Deutscher's philosophy of history can be epigrammatically glimpsed at this stage in chapter titles of the trilogy. The first chapter of the first volume is entitled 'Defeat in Victory'. In the final chapter of the third volume the signs are reversed: the outcome of Trotsky's tragedy, for Deutscher, is rather 'Victory in Defeat'. In his overall assessment of the period, 'Stalin's victory over Trotsky concealed a heavy ele-

---

3   Schon 1979.
4   Arendt 1973.
5   Sontag 1978.
6   Deutscher 1954, p. vii.
7   Deutscher 1954, p. 486.

ment of defeat while Trotsky's defeat was pregnant with victory'.[8] The itinerant Trotsky then appears in the trilogy in sundry guises – as Oedipus,[9] as Sisyphus,[10] as Cassandra,[11] Lear,[12] Hamlet,[13] as the last citizen of Atlantis, as well as in numerous Titanic and Homeric guises.[14] History here is no longer represented as tragedy; it is Tragedy.

Deutscher's reliance on the unfolding and duplicity of classical tragedy is also evident in his use of the imagery of masking and clothing. Here Deutscher's arguments display some similarity with those of Carlyle. Deutscher has Stalin steal Trotsky's clothes, for example, in *The Prophet Unarmed*,[15] and in *The Prophet Outcast* puts the argument that those who steal the Left Opposition's clothes fulfil their programme in so doing.[16] But where Carlyle has men find adequate clothes, in Deutscher the clothes themselves seem to play the part.[17] Perhaps this is in accordance with Carlyle's observation that men pay reverence to the clothes rather than their bearers.[18] What emerges from the Trotsky trilogy, however, is a sense that history has its reason, yet is hopelessly enigmatic. As Kenneth Burke puts it, this is an order of discourse in which men function as spirits, but clothing envelops their deeds in mystery.[19] Deutscher's historiography conceals as much as it clarifies.

The historical-cultural themes associated with Goethe and Shakespeare in western civilisation are also apparent in Deutscher's historiography. The themes of Greek tragedy, and in Carlyle, already raise questions about the role of fate in Deutscher's historiography. Deutscher draws explicitly and implicitly on Goethe's image of the duality of souls in order to explain the contradictory combination of the apparently incompatible. As Goethe has Faust plead that he possesses two souls,[20] so does Deutscher claim that major figures and problems in contemporary communism are Janus-faced, like Jekyll and Hyde.[21]

---

8   Deutscher 1970b, p. 515.
9   Deutscher 1954, p. vii, 1977, p. 31.
10   Deutscher 1970b, pp. 477, 510–11.
11   Deutscher 1966, p. 179; Deutscher in Trotsky, 1973b, p. 13.
12   Deutscher 1970b, p. 435.
13   Deutscher 1966, p. 29.
14   Deutscher 1970b, pp. 480, 512.
15   Deutscher 1970c, p. 454.
16   Deutscher 1970b, p. 63.
17   Carlyle 1896, pp. 189–190.
18   Carlyle no date; and see generally Burke, 1969, pp. 118–19.
19   Burke 1969, pp. 118–119.
20   Goethe no date, pp. 1112–13.
21   See, for example, Deutscher, 1966, p. 87.

CHAPTER 11

Deutscher presents Stalinism as a combination of Bolshevism and Byzantium[22] and explains the fate of Eastern Europe after the war as a combination of conquest and revolution, retrogression and progression.[23] His reliance on this imagery confirms the way in which his thinking is structured by Diamat. Things can never be allowed to be what they are, or what they appear to be; Diamat casts off the husk, reveals their substantial and subterranean nature. Stalin understood as Robespierre *and* Bonaparte, Trotsky as Danton blended with Babeuf, Russia presented as a combination of Oriental and European components or of market and plan,[24] all these Deutscherian couplets demonstrate the principle of unity of opposites, where one element must eventually come to dominate the other. Dualism in Deutscher is therefore a historiographical expression of the traditional Marxist logic which makes a motor of contradiction. Socialism retraces its roots to Heraclitus.

Perhaps more predictably, the Faustian nexus is also present in Deutscher's view of revolutionary politics as the business of doing deals with the devil.[25] Certainly his writing is deeply imbued with the sense that human action inevitably sunders intention from its acts. Even the glimpse of such arguments provided here gives the sense that for Deutscher, as for Shakespeare, 'Our wills and fates do so contrary run that our devices still are overthrown; our thoughts are ours, their ends none of our own'.[26] Indeed, Deutscher says of Trotsky that 'If he was an actor, then he was one to whom ... theatre and life were one',[27] conjuring up the imagery of *As You Like It*: 'All the world's a stage, And all the men and women merely players ...'[28] Understood thus as theatre, history allots the parts, hands out the glory and disrepute; it acts as *Geist* in authoring the drama and in allocating vice and virtue. Tamara Deutscher relates that Bradley's *Shakespearean Tragedy* was Isaac's bedside book, along with Collingwood's *The Idea of History*,[29] and this comes as little surprise for the trilogy conforms fully to Bradley's characterisation of the substance of Shakepearean tragedy.[30] History, then, is here subsumed to Tragedy: to repeat, it *is* Tragedy.

The deepest affinity of all in Deutscher's historiography is with Hegel, for it is here that Deutscher's necessitarian philosophy of history emerges most

---

22   Deutscher 1970a, p. 271.

23   Deutscher 1970a, p. 480.

24   Deutscher 1969b, pp. 76, 66, 162 ff.

25   Deutscher 1954, p. 329.

26   Shakespeare no date b, pp. III, iii.

27   Deutscher 1970c, p. 27.

28   Shakespeare no date a, p. II. vii.

29   Deutscher 1971, p. 80.

30   See generally Bradley, 1929, and see 1955b.

fully. With Hegel, Deutscher consolidates the argument that History has its own cunning. Deutscher argues for inevitability in history,[31] formally refusing the Great Man argument because it undermines the case for inevitability. He argues that history seeks out its agents, not only in the Red October but also later in China and Yugoslavia, where, in telling language, 'the revolutionary trend found or created its organ in such human material as was available'.[32] Objective reality determines subjective reality for Deutscher, calling forth such forces as will do History's bidding. Great Men step forward only as the personification of historic, i.e. class, forces.[33] The argument has a precedent in Trotsky, who also juggled clumsily the concepts of 'will' and 'necessity', living out the first under pretence that he embodied the second.[34] Deutscher and Trotsky alike claim a 'materialist' status for their work, in the conventional sense, and both consequently fudge the question of will. Despite Trotsky's own voluntarism in 1917, Deutscher is bound to argue that history sets itself only such problems as it can solve, using whatever human material comes to hand. Marx's maxim in *The Eighteenth Brumaire* is henceforth reversed: after Deutscher, history makes itself through and over men, just as it pleases. Similarly, Collingwood is overturned, as history becomes a process of gains through losses.

The Hegelian ruse of history is introduced in order to explain this paradox of modern revolutionary history. In Soviet history, Deutscher argues,

> the Hegelian List der Geschichte, the sly irony of history, comes into its own. Circumstances force men to move in the most unforeseen directions and give their doctrines the most unexpected contents and significance. Men and doctrines thus serve purposes sometimes diametrically opposed to those they had envisaged.[35]

The Hegelian ruse functions in Deutscher as a theory of progress through barbarism. Deutscher cites Hegel to the effect that (Soviet) 'History is not the realm of happiness' but rather that of achievement.[36] As in Hegel's *Philosophy of History*, so in Deutscher's theory does history evolve from east to west. As in Hegel, so in Deutscher do great men act out the world spirit unknowingly, finding

31   See, for example, Deutscher 1970a, pp. 13–14.
32   Deutscher 1970b, pp. 245–346.
33   Deutscher 1953, p. 13.
34   See, for example, Trotsky 1974b, p. 46, 1978, p. 429.
35   Deutscher 1966, p. 236.
36   Deutscher 1977, p. 97.

themselves doomed to unhappiness.[37] As in Hegel, but unconsciously so in Deutscher, is the unfolding of the *Weltgeist* a theological perspective.[38] The barbarism of Stalinism remains for Deutscher the prelude to the fulfilment of world history in socialism. Deutscher of course denies the inherent logic of his argument, which seems to suggest rather the permanence of barbarism and the impossibility of socialism, understood in its emancipatory sense as the willed product of mass human activity. He simply presumes the necessity of the ongoing transition to socialism in history. Even his own authorities, Faust, Hamlet, Sisyphus and Cassandra suggest rather a future of desolation and futility. All that is sacred is consequently profaned, for, as Marshall Berman puts it in his analysis of Faust, if good can be created through evil then the maxim ought to be reversed: 'The road to heaven is paved with bad intentions'.[39]

Deutscher and the Course of the Soviet Union

History, for Deutscher, consists then in its ironies; it scripts the play, or enacts it, allotting parts so that its will be done, whosoever is given the task. Stalin was chosen by History to do its bidding: 'The trend of the time found in Stalin its "organ". If it hadn't been Stalin it would have been another'.[40] The logic involved explains why Trotsky's was a happy fate, despite all: in power, his lot should have been to act out Stalin's part. There is Victory in Defeat, then, for the Russian Revolution as well as for its expressive (read animating) spirit. By historic proxy, this ironic victory is also extended to the Soviet Union's progeny in Eastern Europe. Deutscher accepts Trotsky's thesis in *The Revolution Betrayed*, that there is a contradiction or dualism in the Soviet regime between its socialist forms of property and its bourgeois forms of distribution.[41] Like Trotsky he accepts the priority of these property forms over distribution and consequently advocates the defence of the USSR.[42] The Russian Revolution has for Deutscher achieved the material prerequisites of socialism *ex post facto*, opening now the possibility/necessity of post-Stalin reform.[43] Forced industrialisation therefore produces the basis for the real establishment of Soviet socialism, finally,

---

37   See generally Hegel 1956; see also Lowith, 1957; White, 1973 Ch. 2; A. Heller, 1982.
38   See Hegel 1956, 1980.
39   Berman 1984, p. 48.
40   Deutscher 1953, p. 41.
41   Deutscher 1970c, pp. 303–4.
42   See, for example, Deutscher 1980.
43   Deutscher 1970c, p. 462.

in the Khruschev era. Industrialisation brings about modernity and therefore establishes the precondition for Soviet democracy. Deutscher's argument is a classical expression of economic determinism. Stalinist modernisation for Deutscher cuts the political ground of ignorance from under the regime's feet: as he himself explains, 'I maintain that urbanisation and modernisation are "curing"[!] the Soviet Union from Stalinism'.[44] Stalinism was inevitable for Deutscher, but so, now, is destalinisation.

Deutscher's view of the course of Soviet history was widely influential within and without the Trotskyist movement. His explanation of the decay of the Russian Revolution was more widely accepted in the movement than his prognosis of its future after Stalin. Michel Pablo put a similar prognosis within the movement: the Fourth International split over his views. Deutscher was widely regarded as the *de facto* theorist of Pabloism in the Fourth International. Pablo, like Deutscher, had argued that the most important impetus to reform would come from within the Soviet bureaucracy itself. Pablo's conclusion, that the bureaucracy would install socialism, or at least its basis, through a process of war/revolution encompassing centuries, emerged from the same kind of objectivist logic.[45] For Pablo as for Deutscher, destalinisation meant that world revolution was on the agenda again. In Deutscher's understanding Trotsky's theory of Permanent Revolution proves itself through its unconscious representatives, Mao and Khrushchev.[46] For Deutscher the installation of 'socialism' in Eastern Europe 'on the point of the bayonet' was equally inevitable. Deutscher proclaims the world-historic vocation of Stalinism to the extent that he attacks the Hungarian rebels of 1956, who in his mind strove, again tragically, heroically but foolishly, to 'wind back the clock' which had been set forward by communism.[47] Those who refuse the gifts of history or the Party receive their just deserts.

Deutscher's 'apologism' for the Soviet experience therefore needs to be seen as the direct outcome of his necessitarian philosophy of history. His stance is not accidental or arbitrary, but issues rather from his philosophy of history. To say this is not to suggest that the affiliations of other apologists like the Webbs were merely idiosyncratic and not theoretically explicable. The point is rather that Deutscher's view of history as the unfolding of the theatre of necessity, coupled with his political Jacobinism, allows no other conclusion. Deutscher's historiography is effectively a *historiosophy*, where all that occurs must ulti-

---

44   Deutscher 1969a, p. 196.
45   See generally Marie 1980 Ch. 8.
46   Deutscher 1970b, pp. 311–312; Deutscher, Introduction in Trotsky, 1973b, p. 36.
47   Carlyle no date, p. 156; Deutscher 1966, pp. 45–6; 1970b, p. 517; Fehér and Heller 1983.

mately be for the good of mankind, even if men and women do not realise this. Modern Marxist historiography, then, like that of its founder, remains deeply structured by the French Revolutions.[48]

But there are of course special features in Deutscher's historiography. If, in Deutscher's view, all that occurs is certain, then Great Men represent only Great Forces. Yet Deutscher's rejection of the Great Man sits uneasily with his fascination with great men. It is surely significant that while a historian like E.H. Carr wrote a history of the USSR, Deutscher wrote *biographies* of its leaders. To the extent that Deutscher follows Carlyle, in the practice of hero-worship, he ends in producing an *aristocratic* mode of tragic presentation. The tragedy is stylised, throws light on the greats only, minimises or excludes the common people. The scope of Deutscher's playwriting is to limit the focus to great men, restricting participation to heroes, to the contest of the base and the sublime. Deutscher turns a truly popular tragedy into aristocratic tragedy; his writing lacks the elements of the popular and the grotesque, the crowd and the fool. The mass suffering which is the fabric of the Soviet experience is not the centre of his focus; rather, his interest is in the fate of the heroic individual. Deutscher's use of aristocratic personification is therefore simultaneously historically inaccurate and politically insulting to the Soviet people who endured forced industrialisation and collectivisation and purge trials, who perished in the war against fascism and who then, as now, bear the burden of Soviet history. Deutscher's historiography cannot adequately register this, for its focus is on the forces which 'produce' the process and on the results which he claims emerge from contemporary revolutionary history. In this regard, Deutscher's Jacobinism is best revealed in his argument that revolutions can be engaged from above, for it is the *results* and not the processes which matter. It is this language of Deutscherism which remains widely influential within the Fourth International today, framing, for example, Ernest Mandel's defence of Pol Pot's Kampuchea as a 'workers' state'.[49] Method there is in this madness.

Trotskyism: From Revolution to Reconciliation

Trotsky's own record on the question of revolution from above was ambivalent; the early and vehement critic of Jacobinism became, in power, its best proponent.[50] This ambivalence also structured Trotsky's views on the possib-

---

48   Mathiez 1955; Law 1982; Feher 1984.

49   Goodwin 1979; Mandel 1979a.

50   See Beilharz 1981b, 1987; Trotsky 1970a.

ility of installing socialism from above in Eastern Europe.[51] Trotsky was politically compromised by the existence of a Soviet Union to which he felt honour bound, whatever reservations he felt about its potential post-war incur-
sions. Trotsky at least could legitimately refer the problem back to October, to
the regime's popular origins, and somewhat less impressively to the property
forms thus established.[52] But Trotskyism after Trotsky developed the necessitarian rather than the liberatory moment in Trotsky's own work. The logic
of the arguments of Deutscherism and Pabloism became ironical indeed; if
the onward march of the twentieth century showed that history chose agencies other than the Fourth International, be they Stalinist Communist Parties,
guerillas or 'petty-bourgeois nationalist' leaderships like Castro's, then history
might equally likely allocate the new International a reactionary part.[53] For if
the conscious enemies of Trotskyism can thus become its unconscious agents,
so then can the Trotskyists themselves become obstacles in History's way. Trotskyists who associate with the course of history have no option here. If history
chooses an agent other than the Bolshevik Party to fulfil its will, then this agent
must ultimately represent the best interests of the theory of Permanent Revolution itself. Trotskyists are then theoretically bound to accept and even celebrate
the judgment of History, even if it be, 'apparently', against them. It is this logic
which leads to the indecent spectacle in which Trotskyists have become the
best defenders of their own murderers. Necessitarian premises produce necessitarian outcomes. If the process of Permanent Revolution acts in strange ways,
then those who espouse it are compelled to authorise its acts and its chosen
agents, the cost or reward being their own martyrdom.

Trotskyist thinking typically operates on the basis of a series of associations.
Most fundamentally, Trotskyists associate the concept 'socialism' with the fact
of nationalisation and the principle of central planning, associating all this
with the experience of communist history after October. Trotskyist historiography, best exemplified in the work of Isaac Deutscher, rests on an inner
affinity with the Hegelian philosophy of history. Trotskyists accept the principle
that *Weltgeschichte ist Weltgericht*, that the history of the world is the world's
court of judgment,[54] only they read its verdict of socialist defeat as though it
meant victory. The interpretation of history dominant within the movement
today paraphrases, and parodies, Hegel:

---

51   Trotsky 1973c, pp. 9, 18–19.
52   See Beilharz 1987.
53   See, for example, Pablo 1974, p. 146.
54   Hegel 1976, p. 216.

All actions, including world-historical actions, culminate with individuals as subjects giving actuality to the substantial. They are the living instruments of what is in substance the deed of the world mind and they are therefore directly at one with that deed though it is concealed from them and is not their aim and object.[55]

Postwar developments vindicate Trotskyism at the cost of subordinating the Fourth International to the status quo of 'actually existing socialism'. Revolutions 'on the point of the bayonet' and Third World revolutions alike necessarily become socialist, despite the intentions of their leaders the 'real' becomes the 'rational'. But where Hegel saw history as the fulfilment of consciousness and freedom,[56] Trotskyism sees in it the fulfilment of necessity. The language of necessity in Trotskyism, substantiated by Deutscher, turns the theory of Permanent Revolution into a language of reconciliation.[57] In contemporary Trotskyism the rhetoric of revolution in the west co-exists with the language of reconciliation in the east. Trotsky's own priorities are here reversed; history dictates that this be so, for its 'victories' have occurred elsewhere than in the west. After Deutscher, Trotskyism's revolutionary soul is eclipsed by the reality of Soviet power. This may be an irony, but *pace* Deutscher it is no 'irony of history'. The final issue of Trotskyism in a language of reconciliation must be seen to emerge, rather, from its own contradictions as a Jacobin historiography.

---

55   Hegel 1976, p. 218.
56   Hegel 1956, pp. 19–20, 23.
57   On which see Bradley 1955a, pp. 72, 83.

CHAPTER 12

Political Economy and Transition: Ernest Mandel (1987)

Ernest Mandel is probably the best known of all contemporary Trotskyists, and one of the most influential of modern marxist economists. Few figures on the left today create such controversy, attract such adoration and vilification. Mandel is the theoretical and political leader of the United Secretariat of the Fourth International. His arguments remain among the most hegemonic in the revolutionary left today. Born in 1923, Mandel became a revolutionary in 1939, joining the Trotskyist movement in his native Belgium in 1940. He was active in the resistance throughout the occupation. In 1946, under the pseudonym 'Ernest Germain', he was elected to the leadership of the Fourth International, where he was affiliated with Michel Pablo. Throughout the fifties and sixties he was active in the Belgian trade union movement and in the Belgian Socialist Party, within which the Trotskyists then operated. He edited *La Gauche*, organ of the Socialist Party left, before the Trotskyists were expelled from the Party in 1965. An astute dialectician within the Fourth International, Mandel became known as one who changed his positions with ease, rarely pausing to reconcile such shifts with his earlier positions. Mandel is also the author of works of considerable scholarly achievement, most notably *Marxist Economic Theory* and *Late Capitalism*. His works have been published in 30 languages, and range from journalism and programmatic materials to economic treatises and criticism, from sophisticated scholarly interventions to crude Trotskyist polemics. It is this combination of scholarly and political practices which sets Mandel apart from his peers, and which often produces strange effects in 'revolutionary journalism' and 'revolutionary scholarship'.

For there is a strong tendency in Mandel to append rhetorical conclusions to substantially empirical and non-revolutionary works. Similarly, earnest theoretical writings like *Late Capitalism* traverse all manner of economic terrains only to issue, unexpectedly, in scenarios of socialist revolution which have no recognisable relationship to the preceding analysis. The tension between science and revolution is by no means evident to Mandel, whose Trotskyist traits include a fundamentalism in which science is held to 'prove' the positions of orthodox marxism, whether basic or modified. For Mandel science itself is a revolutionary weapon, and nowhere is this more clear than in his attempts to apply Marx's 1859 Preface – a scheme which, on historical judgement, explains social stability rather than change – in order to prove the 'inevitability' of social-ist revolution. Integrated into his theory of long waves of capitalist develop-ment, Mandel's particular variation of the forces-relations formula provides an illustrative case of innovation within the parameters of orthodox marx-ism.

Mandel's Relation to Trotsky

Mandel idolises Trotsky. His *Trotsky – A Study in the Dynamic of His Thought* is little more than hagiography. Trotsky is viewed as the source of the basic truths of modern revolutionary marxism. He is credited with a power of proph-esy; he takes on an aura of infallibility.[1] Such problems as are acknowledged in Trotsky's marxism are reduced to questions of mistaken timing or miscal-culated prediction.[2] Mandel's admiration is more fulsome for the Bolshevik Trotsky: his attitude towards the young Trotsky is a compromised, vehement yet ambivalent rejection, as Mandel is attracted to the early Trotsky's spon-taneism yet repulsed by his anti-Leninism.[3] On balance, Mandel prefers the image of the Bolshevik Trotsky, where spontaneous working-class energy is viewed in Trotskyist manner as a steam which is dissipated in the absence of a Party-piston.[4] Mandel's substantive affinities with Trotsky are many and varied, but are nowhere more apparent than in basic principles. Mandel's anthropolo-gical perspectives shift variously with the nature of the subject matter at hand and with the scope of projection. When speaking specifically of people as they are and might be, Mandel espouses a labour ontology, viewing the capacity to perform creative work as a basic characteristic of human nature. This labour ontology produces a basic humanism, manifested in the naïve argument that what people make they can also unmake.[5] Such sentiments are combined with many others. In one place Mandel suggests a dualistic anthropology based on class – the bourgeoisie are by nature competitive, while proletarians are natur-ally co-operative.[6] In another place Mandel reduces the argument for socialism to a statement of 'faith in the positive anthropology'.[7] In discussing problems

---

1 Also see Mandel 1978a, where quotations from Trotsky suffice to both dispatch the opponent and close the case (pp. 33, 47).
2 Mandel 1979d, p. 128.
3 Mandel 1979d, p. 53, 1973a, p. 15, 1977a, p. 93 f.
4 Mandel 1977a, p. 98.
5 Mandel 1977a, p. 98.
6 Mandel 1981, p. 77.
7 Mandel 1974c, p. 28.

of transition, however, Mandel introduces the negative anthropology, arguing that people will strive for better things only under a regime which offers material rewards.[8]

These contradictory positions find their explanation in the Trotskyist determinism which understands egoism as the product of scarcity, and altruism as the result of abundance.[9] Mandel thus views history as the history of the struggle for surplus, as surplus is the condition of existence for class society and, subsequently, for socialism. Mandel's choice of the revolutionary subject capable of achieving such a society is strongly influenced by the Jacobin dimension of Trotskyism. As Mandel himself puts it in one place, the proletariat must emancipate itself; yet only the Party can achieve liberation.[10] This additional level of association is characteristically Trotskyist. Mandel's general debt to Trotsky is evident in his basic working categories, which are those of Dialectical and Historical Materialism. Under the pressure of the renewed criticism of the marxist renaissance, Mandel has been obliged to articulate these positions with more clarity than Trotsky ever did. Significantly, however, the result is little improvement on Trotsky's own positions. For Mandel, Dialectical Materialism's basic premiss is that everything changes and is in perpetual motion; this premiss is taken to be a universal truth. 'Motion, universal motion, governs all existence'. This universal motion involves the dialectics of nature as well as those of history and, in addition, the dialectics of knowledge.[11] Dialectical Materialism is the only exception to this rule. It never changes. Mandel outlines the categories of Dialectical logic: the unity and contradiction of opposites, quantitative and qualitative change, negation and surpassing.[12] Contradiction is explained as internal in character, as is content to form; here Mandel offers the significant illustration of the contradiction between forces and relations of production. As will be seen below, the principle of internal contradiction is a binding thread of Mandel's marxism, one which concludes in his theory of endogenous technological revolutions. For it follows from Mandel's first principle, concerning motion, that all 'motion is a function of the internal contradictions of the phenomenon or set of phenomena under consideration'.[13] The epistemological basis of 'automatic marxism' and the theory of Permanent Revolution is here already set in motion.

---

8   Mandel 1973a, p. 10.
9   Mandel 1974a, p. 668.
10   Mandel 1973a, p. 11.
11   Mandel 1979b, p. 157 f.
12   Mandel 1979b, p. 163 f.
13   Mandel 1979b, p. 164 f.

Dialectical Materialism functions in Mandel's work as the basis of a science which aspires ultimately to an empirical status. The status of marxism itself is viewed as ultimately empirical, though Mandel's own marxism shifts steadily between fact and fancy. Mandel views social science as the empiricist practice of fact-gathering. Social science is understood here as a parallel practice to natural science. Arguing against Korsch, Mandel claims to accept Hilferding's division of marxism into science and revolution. He argues that marxism is meaningless if understood as anything other than science (and science of a most particular kind).[14] Symptomatically, he echoes Engels's claim that empirical proof is the final tribune of epistemology.[15] Mandel makes clear his belief in marxism as a predictive science, implying a literal image of crisis where, in accordance with traditional medical meaning, the specialist diagnoses and awaits the further decline of the patient, world capital.[16] The sequence of Mandel's logic is clear; science can only be revolutionary if it tells the truth; revolution is written into the order of things, therefore an accurate science cannot but be revolutionary.

Mandel's first principles are further clarified in his explanation of the canons of historical materialism. Marxism is explained as a socio-economic determinism 'in the last instance'. 'Historical Materialism is a determinist doctrine', Mandel explains. 'Its fundamental thesis affirms that it is social existence which determines social consciousness'.[17] History for Mandel unfolds through a dialectic of forces and relations of production: each mode of production grows like a human being through phases of vigour and sterility.[18] The scope of Mandel's work indicates that marxism is viewed as a universal theory, and as a theory of universal history, within which the analysis of bourgeois society is merely an application of the 'general' methodology. Nowhere is this universalistic pretension so apparent as in the scope of *Marxist Economic Theory*, where (to name a few), Mandel indiscriminately strings together examples across centuries, from New Guinea to Siberia, from Mesopotamia to Morocco, Cyprus to Ceylon, Samoa to Byzantium – all in order to discover the nature of something called the marxist theory of society.[19]

Leaving aside till later sections Mandel's central affinities with Trotsky in the theory of organisation and transition, two striking similarities should be

---

14   Mandel 1976b, p. 13 ff.
15   Mandel 1975a, p. 140.
16   See e.g. Mandel 1978c, pp. 9, 13, 62, 84.
17   Mandel 1979b, pp. 175, 183.
18   Mandel 1979b, p. 180.
19   Mandel 1974a, chaps 1–4.

observed before proceeding to the analysis of Mandel's relation to Marx. First, Mandel's writing is structured by contrived metaphor. As will be seen, his theory depends on metaphor, particularly in his arguments for long waves of capitalist development and for the hybrid, neither capitalist nor socialist, nature of the USSR. More generally speaking, the entire range of Trotskyist metaphor burdens Mandel's texts: instinct, eruption, molecular movement, images of disease and gynaecology introducing the medical experts of the Fourth International and so on.[20] Rarely is Mandel's use of metaphor convincing, and seldom is it conducive to literary persuasion. Mandel is an able rhetor, yet his general style of argument is never so persuasive as Trotsky's. A debater rather than an orator, Mandel is particularly heavy-handed with opponents in argument, and this is a second striking similarity with Trotsky, even though with Mandel it is lifted to new heights. That Mandel should espouse the orthodox bifurcation of knowledge into categories of 'proletarian' and 'bourgeois' science, is perhaps little cause for surprise.[21] But Mandel's criteria for discourse are more stringent yet. In one place, for example, Mandel disallows as 'eclectic' the form of argument which proceeds 'on the one hand [class] – on the other'.[22] Following Trotsky, such uncertainty must, for Mandel, be understood as petty-bourgeois vacillation or outright betrayal. In another significant case, the discursive morals of Stalinism are summoned by Mandel in order to dismiss the arguments of the class traitors, Djilas and Burnham. 'These people have in effect crossed the class lines and joined the bourgeoisie ... Nothing more needs to be said about this [new class] thesis'.[23] Dubious though he was of Bruno Rizzi's analogous argument, Trotsky at least took it sufficiently seriously to warrant reply, however inadequate that reply may have been. Indeed, it could be said that Trotsky was obliged to take such arguments seriously, as they represented legitimate extrapolations of tendencies in his own thought. With Mandel, in comparison, the polemical sabre has lost whatever critical edge it had in Trotsky's hand. Relieved of the contradiction appropriate to a differentiated world and hardened through constant repetition through changing times, Mandel's 'discursive' style marks the further consolidation of Trotskyism as an orthodoxy in its own right. This said, certain absences and presences might be expected in Mandel's relation to Marx's work.

---

20   See, for example: Mandel 1979d, pp. 56, 75; 1978a, pp. 194, 199; 1974a, p. 501; 1977a, pp. 108, 121, 1975a; pp. 469, 486, 571; 1978c, p. 35; Mandel and Novack, 1974, p. 35.
21   Mandel's *Introduction to Marxism* presents materialist dialectics as the proletariat's epistemology (1979b, pp. 160, 169).
22   Mandel 1975a, p. 516.
23   Mandel 1973a, p. 34.

Mandel's Relation to Marx's Work

Mandel takes Marx and marxism to be intact, uncorrupted by internal contradiction and untouched by the twentieth century's tragedy of errors. For Mandel, the present proclamation on the Western left of the 'crisis of marxism' lacks substantial roots and should be seen as a bourgeois conspiracy rather than as a practical representation of radical malaise.[24] Mandel sees himself alone as the true interpreter of Marx, to the extent that he denies that his own work constitutes one interpretation of Marx among others. He refuses outright the hermeneutic principle that the task of constructing truth or adequacy in understanding lies with the interpreter rather than the text.[25] Mandel himself clearly constructs his own Marx.

There are three texts which allow the critical examination of the relationship between Mandel and Marx: his study of Marx's own theoretical genesis, and his two major economic treatises, *Marxist Economic Theory* and *Late Capitalism*. Mandel's registration of the importance of recent debates is witnessed in the first work in his intervention in one of the earlier disputes over the question of the relationship between the work of the young and the later Marx. In *The Formation of the Economic Thought of Karl Marx. 1843 to 'Capital'*, Mandel argues a middle road. According to Mandel, the young Marx sheds his philosophical chrysalis in order to emerge an *economist*.[26] In this understanding there could be no other course for Marx than fully to embrace the *data* which Mandel takes to be the stuff of real marxist science. Mandel reduces Marx's contribution to the discovery of the real meaning of the theory of surplus value.[27] Worse yet, Mandel never comes to his subject matter – the formation of Marx's thought from '1843 to *Capital*'. His analysis halts ten years short of *Capital*, as though the contribution and theoretical system of *Capital* were somehow established in its 'research' (for Mandel, 'data'). *Capital*, for Mandel, existed in Marx's brain already with the (early) solution of the problem of the Ricardian-Malthusian population laws: 'Once this [preparatory] work was accomplished, *Capital* was ready: all that remained was to write it'.[28] Its writing nevertheless took another ten years, a fact which Mandel cannot grasp, as he presumes *Capital* to step fully grown from the earlier drafts in the *Grundrisse*. Theory, too, is telescoped by Permanent Revolution.

---

24   Mandel 1980c, p. 42.
25   Mandel 1969c, p. 4.
26   Mandel 1971c, pp. 23, 33, 44, 89, 209.
27   Mandel 1971c, pp. 83, 166.
28   Mandel 1971c, pp. 153, 210.

Mandel's own major economic works can be seen as attempts at rewriting *Capital* with the 'dialectical scaffolding' removed, substituting his own empirical understanding of science for Marx's Hegelian project. In *Marxist Economic Theory* Mandel fails to constitute the object of his analysis, instead discussing everything under the sun. In the absence of a clearly defined theoretical object Mandel is obliged to discuss universal history. He traces the historical development of universal equivalence and the emergence of commodity production rather than unfolding their modern conceptual dimensions or determinants. Having arrived historically at capitalist production, Mandel offers the classical orthodox arguments in order to characterise it. For Mandel capitalism distinguishes itself by: the existence of the tendency of the profit rate to fall (realised in a cyclical manner); by the contradiction between the effective socialisation of production and the private form of appropriation (the play on words – the implicit elision of the difference between 'socialisation' and 'socialism' – goes undeclared); by the anarchic planlessness of capitalist production; and by the presumed revolutionary proletarian telos which transforms class struggle from the economic level onto the political.[29] This definition provides the framework into which there is accommodated a mass of empirical material which is taken as proof of the validity of the positions of orthodox marxism.

Mandel recognises some of the limits of *Marxist Economic Theory* in the Preface to the German edition of *Late Capitalism*, speaking particularly against its excessively descriptive and insufficiently theoretical nature.[30] Having recognised the problem, however, Mandel does not go far in rectifying it. The structure of *Late Capitalism* resembles in general the structure of the 1857 plan for *Capital* rather than that eventually applied in *Capital* itself, with the exception that, in ending, *Late Capitalism* mirrors the penultimate, apocalyptic chapter of *Capital*. This latter dimension is perhaps *Late Capitalism's* only strong similarity to *Capital* vol. I – it mimics the latter's worst thesis, the allegedly inevitable 'double negation' of proletarian revolution. Following carefully executed considerations on analytical problems like the world market, the armaments industry, the service sector and so on, socialist revolution steps unexpectedly from the text: 'The final abolition of capitalist relations of production will be the central objective of the mass revolutionary movement of the international working-class that is now approaching'.[31] Mandel's variation on the marxian

---

29 Mandel 1974a, chap. 5.
30 Mandel 1972, p. 7.
31 Mandel 1975a, p. 589.

double negation can itself be negated on no less than four grounds: the movement of which he speaks is not a mass movement, is not revolutionary, not
international, and its impending victory is not imminent; this can be said at
least in the absence of a substantial argument to the contrary.

The means by which Mandel claims to construct the argument which supports this structure and its revolutionary issue does not differ radically from the
method applied in *Marxist Economic Theory*. In *Marxist Economic Theory*, the
structure of *Capital* vol. I is viewed as historical-logical in form. In *Late Capitalism*, Mandel reduces method to research, ascribing to Marx his own positivist
method of research, 'to-ing' and 'fro-ing' between empirical material (which is
taken to be the starting point) and its lawful expression. Mandel proposes a 'six-
fold articulation of Marx's dialectical method'. The six stages follow from fact
gathering and analysis to the production of laws of motion, the establishment
of the relationship between the whole and the parts, with empirical verification
of the foregoing stages and, finally, renewed empirical and perhaps theoretical
considerations concluding the process.[32]

Much of the controversy surrounding Mandel's work has arisen from this
association of the practices of empirical science and marxist theory. Mandel
claims, for example, to prove theoretically the argument for the tendency of the
profit rate to fall due to the rise in the organic composition of capital (that is,
due ultimately to the increase of the proportion of constant capital or technology to that of labour in the production process). As Bob Rowthorn has pointed
out, however, in criticism of Mandel, profit rates have fallen in recent years due
to 'empirical' rather than 'theoretical' factors – the so-called 'profit squeeze' has
limited the share of surplus value going to industrial capital.[33] Mandel, that is to
say, attempts to establish an empirical argument by theoretical means; like the
state capitalists, he collapses different levels of abstraction appropriate to each
form of argument. Another critic of Mandel, Athar Hussain, has argued that
Mandel's is a self-verifying and self-congratulatory framework: anything that
moves is taken by Mandel to prove his case.[34] Further, the way in which Mandel
conducts his empirical analysis undermines his justification for using marxian
categories. Mandel simply presumes that statistics 'translate' directly into a
marxian discourse, but in the process of, for example, treating price as equivalent to value, he collapses the basic marxian distinction between essence and
appearance, thereby jeopardising his own orthodoxy. Mandel makes marxian
theory practically obsolete as an analytical device by working on the empirical

---

32   Mandel 1975a, p. 16 f.
33   Rowthorn 1976, p. 67.
34   Hussain 1977, p. 443.

level, then claiming to prove the dogmas of orthodoxy, his articles of faith beyond discussion, with empirical material which belongs to another discourse altogether. As Mattick explains, however, data is simply not readily convertible into marxian discourse, for Marx's is an abstract theory which, by nature, is ill-disposed purely to empirical verification.[35] Marxists are always right, especially in political economy.

The form of Mandel's argument undermines its *raison d'être* as economics with a marxian intention. It is not enough, for Mandel, to be a competent and original economist: he must also be seen to be a revolutionary economist, on the basis that science is the fount of revolution. Here is the logic of Kautsky and Hilferding: socialism is not only desirable, but necessary. But the projection of modern economic science – with a marxist twist – as revolutionary in effect, and of socialism as necessity, is self-delusion. Science is only what it is: it can 'tell the truth' as best it can, but the most it can possibly achieve is competing representations of the world. The practice of politics, understood as the realm of social change, is another thing altogether. Even prior to a formal consideration of Mandel's treatment of the question of transition a basic misconstruction can be anticipated. Transition cannot be seriously theorised if it is not taken as a political problem in its own right. The economically sophisticated Trotskyism of Ernest Mandel succeeds only in offering more elaborate reasons for its refusal to face this situation.

Transition: Mandel's Analysis of Soviet-Type Societies

Mandel's marxism in general, and his thinking about transition in particular is, like Trotsky's, bound up with the experience of the Russian Revolution. Mandel's treatment of transition in the East will be dealt with first here as a preliminary to the criticism of his proposals for transition to socialism in the West. First, however, some methodological observations are in order. Mandel's writings on the problem of transition are marred by the application of an inappropriate level of generality. Transition in Mandel's usage usually refers to the transition between modes of production in universal history. The proper object of specific transition – in this instance, the transition to a new form of social organisation in the USSR – is deflected from the beginning onto a broader plane via the medium of the general theory of modes of production which Mandel espouses. 'Transition' functions in Mandel's work as an economic category

---

35   Mattick 1981.

residing 'between' modes of production. 'In transition' comes to function in Mandel's usage as an equivalent to 'in limbo', a fact which militates against the construction of a precise definition of the nature of the USSR.

Mandel constantly avoids analysis of the USSR as a specific case, deflecting discussion onto a quasi-typological plane concerning transitional societies 'in general' in accordance with the transhistorical scheme of 'historical material-ism'.[36] Mandel's rhetorical advice that transitions take a long time, or that the USSR is neither here (capitalism) nor there (socialism), can be of little intel-lectual consolation.[37] For as he himself admits, there can be little parallel in the experiences of the transition from slave, to serf, to free labour and the transition to socialism – in which case, the transhistorical discussion about transition is either obfuscation, or else further proof of Mandel's universalistic pretences. For when pressed to explain the specifics of Soviet transition, Man-del falls back onto common sense – 'transitions take a long time'.[38] But Mandel is not uniformly evasive about the precise nature of the USSR. His general the-ory of history, taken from Trotsky, after all indicates that an either/or verdict must be delivered: capitalism *or* socialism, this is the only choice for industrial societies. Mandel is welded, as is Trotsky, to the institutional legacy of the Red October. He is bound to present the course of Soviet history as an artificially prolonged aberration from its original socialist reality and intention. Mandel's earlier diagnosis of the condition of the Soviet state comes directly from the pages of *The Revolution Betrayed*: the Soviet economy is seen as being marked by the contradictory combination of a non-capitalist mode of production and a basically bourgeois mode of distribution, therefore it is transitional between capitalism and socialism, this condition explaining its residual use of capital-ist economic categories. For Mandel, as for Trotsky, the contradiction between the Soviet mode of production and its mode of distribution is to be explained by the continued existence of scarcity, that is, by insufficient productivity.[39] Mandel ignores the development of Soviet productivity (or productive forces) which has occurred over 60 years, and this latter without substantially trans-forming either production relations or distribution. Nothing has changed since the thirties for Mandel: like Trotsky, he follows Preobrazhensky in arguing, still decades later, that the transitional society is marked by the antagonistic coex-istence of market and plan.[40]

---

36   Mandel 1978b.
37   Mandel 1979d, p. 87.
38   Mandel 1979c, p. 116 ff.
39   Mandel 1974a, pp. 565, 572.
40   Mandel 1974a, p. 573.

Mandel's definition therefore suggests that the USSR is a combination of capitalist and socialist elements. When pressed, however, Mandel denies the existence of 'socialist elements' in the USSR.[41] What might its nature then be? In more recent writings, Mandel introduces a new metaphor into the Trotskyist tradition: the argument that the USSR is a hybrid form of society. The modification is as follows:

> The production relations specific to the transitional society are thus a hybrid combination of essentially non-capitalist economic planning and the elements of commodity production (with their drive towards private appropriation and private enrichment) which arise from the basically still bourgeois distribution relations.[42]

Elsewhere Mandel compounds metaphors, now adding an astronomical image in order to deal with the problem of how the regime reproduces itself: 'Once launched into orbit, the structure remains in this orbit and can be directed from it only by social revolutions or counterrevolutions, by explosions ... [or] perturbations'.[43] The continual and increasing contestation of the Trotskyist definition of the USSR since Trotsky's death is evident in Mandel's attempts to discredit alternative theories while attempting to sustain Trotsky's with the 'hybrid' qualification. According to Mandel, the rejection of existing explanations – that the USSR is either capitalist or socialist or else is the regime of a new class – would necessitate the admission that 'we are dealing with the specific, hybrid relations of production of a specific country (or group of countries)'.[44] Yet, again, the fact that Mandel writes in a period of lively marxist debate has had little effect on his basic premisses. Nor do his conclusions differ from Trotsky's, notions of the 'hybrid' society notwithstanding. Mandel follows Trotsky's political line – for Mandel, also, the USSR remains a workers' state which, like the corrupt trade union, nevertheless warrants defence – and adheres to Trotsky's strategic response, agreeing that a political revolution will provide the necessary corrective.[45]

In the analysis of other East European societies Mandel follows through the necessitarian logic developed by Trotsky: socialism could now be produced not only from above, but also across national boundaries. He develops a new

---

41   Mandel 1980b, p. 117, 1977b, p. 6f.
42   Mandel 1974b, p. 10.
43   Mandel 1978b, p. 28.
44   Mandel 1978b, p. 30.
45   Mandel 1974b, p. 15.

metaphor to cover the discrepancy between the Soviet state and its progeny –
where the USSR has become a degenerated workers' state, the satellites are
deformed. Though mutant, they maintained real socialist potential because
of their paternal pedigree: nationalised forms of property had been endowed
upon them by the Soviet Union.[46] Socialism here could not logically be regener-
ated, nor could the *raison d'être* of the Fourth International any longer easily be
defended; the old mole kept breaking through the surface in the wrong places,
nowhere near the Trotskyist headquarters. What could Trotskyist leaders like
Mandel do but applaud it?

Like Trotsky, Mandel understands socialism as essentially a matter of planning or nationalisation. Mandel views economic problems as the major problems of the transition to socialism. In *Marxist Economic Theory*, the key problem of the transition period is determining the optimum growth rate; the hardest problems to be solved during the period of transition from capitalism to
socialism are those of agriculture and distribution.[47] Since politics follows economics, economics must be given first priority. Mandel's attachment to socialism seems to spring from an interest in efficiency.[48] In keeping with his methodology, his arguments lead logically to priorities which are quantitative rather
than qualitative in nature, inclined to the logic of redistribution rather than to
that of the restructuring of social relations, and this holds true for East and
West alike. Mandel argues as though alienation results from scarcity rather
than relations of domination, in Eastern Europe at least, and identifies bureau-
cratisation with the continued existence of market and money relations rather
than with the concentration of power in the Party-state.[49]

What overall judgement can be made of Mandel's position on transition in
the East? His earlier formulation, duplicating Trotsky's, is entirely vulnerable
to the foregoing criticism of Trotsky's own theory with the qualification that
whatever credibility Trotsky's analysis has in 1937, Mandel's repetition lacks
decades later. Trotsky's own belief that the USSR was still 'in transition' during his lifetime may be theoretically dubious, but it is not lacking in personal
justification or immediate plausibility. That Mandel can simply repeat Trotsky's
analysis years later is altogether different. Mandel's justification for this repetition is the combined presupposition that nothing essential has changed, and
that the USSR must by definition be transitional in the first place. He refuses
the possibility that the USSR might be a permanent social order rather than a

---

46   Mandel 1970b.
47   Mandel 1974a, p. 621.
48   Mandel 1969b, pp. 12, 293, 298.
49   Mandel 1971c, p. 194, 1969b, p. 280.

society 'in transition'.[50] Mandel does not substantiate his case with adequate empirical or logical evidence. All manner of arguments to the contrary are ignored; only those like state capitalism are engaged, because they can be theoretically pulverised. Mandel insists that the USSR, like all things in a dialectical world, must still be 'going' somewhere. It must be going somewhere, else doubt is cast on the scheme of the general theory of modes of production ending by fiat in capitalism, then socialism. And it must be going towards socialism, as it is a regime allegedly marked by the signs of socialism in the fact of its attachment to the principle of planning.

Mandel's introduction of the notion of the 'hybrid' society must be seen as an ill-chosen revision, intended to close the debate over the question of the nature of the USSR by coopting elements of the alternative explanations into his own. The result, the notion of the hybrid society, is a contradictory and potentially explosive one. Mandel's choice of metaphor is particularly inept. That society which is hybrid cannot be heading toward socialism; arbitrary crossbreeding cannot simply be 'undone' by specialists at a later date. The logic of the notion of the hybrid society suggests exactly that which Mandel rejects: that the USSR is a new being, a new society. The derivation of Mandel's metaphor is unclear. If it is vegetable, then the problem arises that the hybrid specimen is not easily propagated. If animal, it may refer to the mule – inelegant but practical, a beast capable of carrying the burden of History. Mandel's hybrid society in any case cannot be undone, so it cannot possess the transitional telos which he ascribes to it. A transitional society is going somewhere; a hybrid society is here to stay, though it may well succeed in propagating itself in Eastern Europe, on the point of a bayonet. Mandel's most recent qualification seems to suggest that the USSR is not so much a hybrid as a mutation.[51] Even more than the hybrid notion does this argument suggest that Soviet-type societies stand alone, *sui generis*. But this is exactly the argument which Trotskyism is constituted against, and precisely the logic which Trotskyism has so long resisted, for it violates the Trotskyist philosophy of history. As Hillel Ticktin has argued, Mandel here is trapped within the definition and tradition of Trotskyism. Mandel is prevented from thinking his theoretical position through to its logical conclusion by the structural constraints imposed by the concepts of the Trotskyist tradition.[52]

---

50   Mandel 1969b, p. 275 f., 1978b, pp. 30, 34.
51   Mandel 1980b, p. 117.
52   Ticktin 1980, pp. 128, 135.

Transition in the West: Mandel's Theory of Socialist Revolution

Mandel views world revolution as an objective process which has dominated the recent history of the modern world. It is a process which has detoured through the Third World: the epicentre of world revolution passed, from 1948 to 1968, from Western Europe to the East, implicitly returning to Western Europe with the May events in France and later activity in Italy. Revolution remains on the European agenda for Mandel, but has been re-routed. In the West, the situation is quite simply that the revolution has been betrayed, delayed by bad leadership. Yet in China, and in Yugoslavia, revolution triumphed despite bad (Stalinist) leaderships. The anomaly in such a judgement indicates the continuing tension in Trotskyism between objective and subjective views of the necessary conditions for socialist revolution, for Trotskyism simultaneously accepts the Leninist contention, that socialism is the product of an organised vanguard at the head of a 'mass' movement, *and* endorses the older marxist idea of the Second International, that socialism is written into the order of things and will out. This tension in Trotskyist thinking becomes particularly clear in Mandel's work, enabling him simultaneously to argue vanguardist and spontaneist strategies. For example, the Cuban Revolution, conducted in the absence of a Leninist Party, is nevertheless deemed socialist, at least to the extent that the standard recipe for deformed workers' states – political revolution – does not apply.[53] Such inconsistencies do not bother Mandel, who changes feet as circumstance dictates.

The situation in the West may be less immediately clear than it is in Cuba, but is nevertheless favourable for Mandel, even in the extreme. The events of 1968 demonstrated that new 'detonators' like the student movement can set off broader social explosions, but they can of course have real effectivity only if integrated into the workers' movement or at least into its aspiring leadership.[54] In the West, the subject of revolutionary change remains the working class, and its Party, the Fourth International, the piston in search of some steam. 'Spontaneous' revolutions, following the examples of Yugoslavia, China and Cuba, do not seem to be on the agenda in the West. Mandel relieves Trotsky of his task of awaiting the American Labour Party; he maintains a naïve faith in the revolutionary capacity of the American working class, for the most powerful and numerically largest proletariat in the world cannot fail to perform eventually.[55] Only then, finally, will the theory of world revolution

---

53   Mandel 1979c, p. 104.
54   Mandel 1969d, p. 51 f., and see 1969e, 1971b.
55   Mandel 1979c, p. 200 ff., 1979b, p. 82, 1970b, p. 15 f.

be vindicated and the historic vocation of the Fourth International fulfilled, piston and mole united.

Mandel's political thinking is derived directly from Trotsky's. Both maintain that the situation for revolution is rotten-ripe. Some examples offered by Mandel as proof of this historic trend are even more fantastic than Trotsky's own projections. According to Mandel, conditions were being created in 1954 for a Trotskyist upsurge in the Soviet Union.[56] Similarly, the demonstrations on the attempted assassination of Togliatti after the war provided for Mandel an instinctive posing of the question of power.[57] More recently, Mandel has confessed that he and his friends seriously anticipated a German revolution as the outcome of the Second World War.[58] Such errors, which can presumably like Trotsky's be put down to bad timing, are extreme manifestations of Mandel's general perspective. It is his belief that all countries will follow the same road to socialism; it is his general prognosis that 'it is most unlikely that capitalism will survive another half century'.[59] The revolutionary telos is seeking a place to set itself: until it comes home, to the West, the epicentre of world revolution will shift as Reason dictates.

How is Mandel's faith in this revolutionary telos sustained? Its primary condition of existence is the conflation of economic and political forms of class struggle. The direct association of these forms of struggle produces the proletarian telos which breaks out sporadically until it finds its home in a situation characterised by a decayed regime and a growing Trotskyist (or Stalinist?) Party. For Mandel, economic struggles *grow* into political struggles. The strength of his belief is indicated in his endorsement of the Prussian Minister von Puttkammer's enunciation that 'every strike contains the hydra of the revolution'. Like Trotsky, but again with less justification decades later, Mandel cannot differentiate between industrial relations and socialist politics.[60] For Mandel, the trigger of socialist consciousness is the collapse of capitalism: social revolution is the outcome of world economic crisis. Mandel belongs to the tradition in marxism which takes the proletariat to be the historic bearers of socialism, though stand-ins may be accepted. The proletariat only needs its immediate consciousness shattered by capitalist crisis to break out of its present mould. The proletariat absorbs bourgeois ideology in its everyday existence, but is really revolutionary by disposition. Its real nature as the chosen class is beyond

---

56   Mandel 1970b, p. 15 f.
57   Mandel 1979c, p. 12.
58   Mandel 1979c, p. 117.
59   Mandel 1978c, p. 194, 1976b, p. 86.
60   Mandel 1973b, p. 1.

dispute: its 'revolutionary mission' is inscribed in its 'objective roots'. Capitalist society bipolarises into miniscule bourgeoisie and homogeneous, overwhelming proletariat.[61] Mandel adheres to the Trotskyist tradition in determining the status of the proletariat without, or even despite, reference to its actual consciousness. 'Late Capitalism' is held to provide an excellent school for the proletariat, says Master Mandel, for though it integrates the class into its structures, it also breeds working-class militancy.[62]

For Mandel the spontaneous strivings of the proletariat emerge fully in a situation of crisis. Normal situations produce reformist consciousness, crises produce revolutionary consciousness. These understandings in Mandel result from the combination of two maxims: that being determines consciousness, and that revolution is written into the order of things. Capitalist collapse, the objective determinant, forms subjective political will, rupturing the normal relationship between being and consciousness.[63] Social change occurs for Mandel first 'objectively', in society rather than in individuals; socialism is achieved in 'reality' before it is in consciousness, as though socialism, the social order premised on the development of consciousness, could arrive unheralded 'behind the backs' of its subjects.[64] Within so implausible an argument there is a familiar logic. In arguing that individuals can improve only after they have experienced abundance at the hands of a benevolent society, Mandel reveals the logic of Jacobinism basic to his thought. If politics in the new society does not consist of the practice of the sum of its willing participants confronting social problems, then it must be the domain of benevolent despots who act on their behalf. Mandel's image of social revolution continues the tradition of Bolshevism, where the Party leads the masses to overthrow the bourgeois state in order to inaugurate the 'new' society for the good of the people.

Mandel's theory of socialist revolution is an articulated variant of Marx's 1859 Preface, where the forces/relations formula functions as objective component, the source and determinant of social change, and the Leninist Party functions as subjective component. The maturity of objective conditions is seen as prior to the subjective moment. The latter is nevertheless held to be indispensable. The subject, the proletariat, is reduced to the Party: 'The Leninist theory of organisation ... constitutes the *marxist science of the subjective factor*'. The 1859 Preface provides the objective basis of the subjective possibility of

---

61   Mandel 1974c, p. 18, 1983a, p. 200 ff.
62   Mandel 1975a, pp. 183, 498, 585.
63   Mandel 1970a, p. 34.
64   Mandel 1974a, p. 655.

socialism.[65] The 'incompletion' of Marx's 1859 Preface warrants the introduction of an external factor, the Leninist Party, which crowns the work of the endogenous factor, the productive forces. Yet it is only endogenous necessity which makes this intervention possible. This is true to the extent that Mandel allows for cases in which socialism is the product of such forces alone, even in the absence of a healthy Bolshevik Party. Yet Mandel simultaneously holds that the absence of revolutionary victories (in the West) is the result of the crisis in the 'subjective factor', that is, in proletarian leadership. Mandel's theory of revolution is therefore not only a revision of the 1859 Preface, but is also a reworking of the *Transitional Programme*, where objective conditions are understood to be ripe, but explained more systematically with reference to economic cycles and crises, and where the 'subjective factor' (and the Fourth International) still lags behind.[66]

As in Trotsky, so in Mandel does this argument pertain less directly to specific individual nation-states than to a world process of socialist revolution which is held to be unfolding, subject to uneven development and delays brought about by treacherous leadership. Mandel is nothing if not an internationalist. His international commitment to socialist revolution and to the Fourth International are constructed at a high level of abstraction, again eschewing specificity. The slogans of Mandel's political agitation are abstract and rhetorical; according to him, the only legitimate orientation for socialist politics today is – towards the Socialist United States of Europe![67] The sequence of logic is clear: international revolution – the necessary response to the internationalisation of capital – necessitates international organisation. Mandel defends the principle (and the practice) of a 'single centre' of world revolution. His argument, that the world concentration of revolutionary initiative is necessary in order to deal with centralised capital, recalls the arguments of the early Comintern. He argues like Trotsky after 1933, that such problems as emerge in the International are circumstantial, rather than immanent to the idea of a centralised International. Significantly, Trotsky and Mandel alike see the construction of the International as the solution to the problems faced by socialists. Their common premiss is that organisational responses can solve cultural problems, that an organised International can negate the cultural absorption of the popular masses into bourgeois society.[68] In keeping with his notion that the world system is more than the sum of its parts, Mandel invests the Interna-

---

65   Mandel 1976a, p. 278, 1977a, p. 81.
66   Mandel 1979b, p. 127.
67   Mandel 1978a, p. 36, 1975a, p. 341.
68   Mandel 1978a, p. 41.

tional with a mystique, suggesting that it is somehow more than the sum of its parts, the national Trotskyist parties. His loyalty to the Fourth International is therefore to be understood as loyalty to the idea of an International.[69] This abstract organisational loyalty corresponds with his refusal of the priority of national specificities, serving further to elide even his own principles and commitments.

This level of misplaced abstraction, so common to Mandel, is also evident in his more directly political thinking, which is always 'utopian' to some degree in that it typically presumes the achievement or establishment of the state of affairs under discussion. Mandel usually argues as though he has already arrived at some transitional point, thence moving the focus onto the consolidation and extension of gains which are presumed to have been made. In one place, for example, Mandel slips from a tactical argument about revolution into the presumption of the actual existence of dual power, moving on to considerations of the extension of this non-existent dual power situation into socialism. He proceeds to explain not how socialism arises, but how it can be protected, avoiding always the problems of its beginnings.[70] A more spectacular example of Mandel's ethereal politics can be found in his proposed solution to the contradictory problem, how to increase both accumulation and consumption in the transition period. Mandel proposes, as solution, that arms expenditure be transferred to socially useful needs – an eminently sensible suggestion, but one which is totally impracticable, in the absence of a separate demonstration as to how the world might arrive at a situation which would allow such a project of social engineering.[71] Even Mandel's more immediate proposals posit the existence of that which is yet to be achieved: he issues assurances that the workers' state *will* wither, *will* be more democratic than the bourgeois state, *will* eliminate careerism; and even guarantees that Soviet democracy *will* be exercised by workers and poor peasants.[72] Regardless of chronology in projection, Mandel's claims are based on nothing more than assurance, yet are presented as necessity.

Two levels or types of utopia can be discerned in Mandel's work: a more immediate variant approximating the 'Government of Soviets', and a more abstract variant reminiscent of Trotsky's image in *Literature and Revolution*.[73] Mandel's immediate 'utopia' is, in a specific sense, no less utopian than his

69   Slaughter 1974, pp. 29, 41, 43.
70   Mandel 1979c, p. 17 ff.
71   Mandel 1974a, p. 613 f.
72   Mandel 1979b, pp. 101, 120.
73   Trotsky 1925.

advanced variant, for its precondition is a regime of direct democracy. Mandel refuses absolutely the legitimacy of representative government, to the extent that he reduces the question of the status of parliamentary forms in the transition to socialism to the level of tactics rather than theory. According to Mandel, the citizen in a regime of representative democracy 'is neither a protagonist nor even an actor in the political drama. He can only have a walk-on part, as a spear carrier'.[74] The theatrical image is eye-catching, but misses the point: everyday politics is not an epic in bourgeois society. Mandel's image of the new society is one dear to the Trotskyist tradition, and best expressed in works like those of C.L.R. James: it is a composite of Athens and the early days of the Russian Revolution, the regime of associated producers where cooks govern, using recipes from Mandel's cookshop.

Beyond the realm of direct democracy lies another image of the future, which immediately brings to mind Trotsky's rationalist fantasies in *Literature and Revolution*. The resemblances are almost complete: Mandel anticipates in socialism the achievement of a situation of social transparency in which all men master all social relations and all develop scientific aptitudes, as 'nothing now stands in the way of progressively transforming all men into scientists and scholars'.[75] (Presumably all women will still be doing the washing up.) Unlike Lafargue's socialist hedonists, the citizens of Mandel's utopia need leisure to work, to pursue science and politics. For mankind's first task is not in responding to local or national needs, but in working out a Faustian agenda, a plan of economic development encompassing the irrigation of the Sahara and the transformation of the Amazonian jungle.[76] 'Humanity will master its geographical surroundings, the configuration of the globe, the climate and the distribution of great water reserves, at the same time preserving or restoring ecological equilibrium. It will overturn everything down to its own biological foundations'.[77] The scenario is Trotsky's, or Goethe's, with an added twinge of ecological conscience. Mandel's spear-carriers, the ordinary citizens of East and West, would very likely have difficulty raising enthusiasm for such a project.

There is also a more practical dimension to Mandel's political proposals. Practical politics does enter into Mandel's proposals concerning the *Transitional Programme*. If neither of Mandel's 'utopian' proposals have much bearing on reality, then what are the effects of his transitional proposals? Much of

---

74   Mandel 1978a, p. 164f.
75   Mandel 1971c, p. 115.
76   Mandel 1974a, p. 614.
77   Mandel 1979b, p. 187.

Mandel's earlier notoriety on the revolutionary left springs from his interpretation of the *Transitional Programme*, with its proposals for 'structural reforms'. In the early formulation spear-carriers can become titans through the pursuit of such reforms. The main purpose of the strategy of structural reforms is to effect an integration between the immediate aims of the masses and the objectives of the struggle which effectively challenge the very existence of the capitalist system itself.[78] Understood as an alternative to the mere juxtaposition of minimum and maximum programmes, 'structural reforms' are thrown up which objectively challenge the operation of capital; in function, therefore, 'structural reforms' seem to be identical to the programme of transition drawn up by Trotsky. In a more recent argument, however, Mandel presents the demands of the *Transitional Programme* – the shorter working week, sliding scale of wages and so on – as defensive in character, and therefore preliminary to the transition to socialism proper. According to Mandel this defensive programme must be integrated into the overall anticapitalist struggle of 'transitional demands', including nationalisation, workers' control, popular committees and a people's militia.[79] In this later definition, Mandel seems to be calling Trotsky's *Transitional Programme* nothing more than a defensive strategy, reserving the label 'transition proper' for the elementary phases of the revolutionary process (the overthrow of the state). No explanation is given as to how defensive trade union struggles might grow into anticapitalist transitional struggles; no such explanatory obligation falls on Mandel's shoulders, for he believes political class struggles to be the natural outgrowth of economic class struggle. To explain, here, is nothing: to assert, is everything.

Mandel probably introduces these later qualifications into the argument in order to rectify a situation which allowed his proposals for transition to be cast as 'reformist'. Indeed his earlier calls for structural reforms bear a close resemblance to the arguments of his besworn enemies, the Eurocommunists: the fundamental goal of structural reforms is to take away the levers of command in the economy from the financial groups, trusts and monopolies and place them in the hands of the nation, to expand the public sector and workers' control.[80] Here Mandel is caught in a polemical trap. Burdened by unrealisable utopias, he must specify a practical political programme. But his economic catastrophism and rationalism militate against the consideration of practical political programmes. Mandel argues that to work in and against bourgeois society is impossible without integration. What policies might then be pursued

78   Mandel 1969a, p. 7.
79   Mandel 1978c, p. 206 f.
80   Mandel 1971a, p. 78.

by revolutionaries living in bourgeois societies? Mandel concedes that 'revolutionary vocational practice', organised radical work by teachers, doctors and others, can be of some positive effect – provided, of course, that such activity is subsumed organisationally to the Fourth International.[81] Mandel refuses the argument that socialism, if at all possible, could only be the work of consciously organised alliances and movements. He rejects social movements. The basis of his position is a kind of political ontology of labour: he argues that social movements can only fill vacuums which are created by the default of the labour movement to fulfil its historic tasks.[82] He cannot therefore allow detailed attention to the politics of contestation: revolutionary posturing, and theoretical guarantees prevent Mandel from taking new political forms into earnest consideration. These forms, and their theoretical implications, simply do not register on the grid of the orthodox.

Leaving behind his earlier arguments for structural reforms, refusing other attempts to bridge the present and future, Mandel's politics seem therefore to cleave precisely into the bifurcation of minimum and maximum programmes, the only 'bridge' being provided by a revolutionary class telos. Mandel's politics therefore reflect those of the heritage which he seeks to renounce. That such a bifurcation should be the outcome of Mandel's theory comes as no surprise; it is already visible in the revolutionary stand of Trotskyism. The revolution will continue to be delayed, but it can still be nurtured; in the meantime, such empirical or defensive struggles as are thrown up and deemed sound must be guarded. Mandel's Trotskyism is, as Sartre put it years ago, after all 'a waiting art'.[83] Mandel is obliged by the tradition within which he works to limit the potential in contestatory struggles or issue-movements as they relate to both state and economy. His strategic response to the state is no more sensitive than his one-dimensional view of economic struggles. If the state is nothing but the tool of the ruling class, it can belong either to the bourgeoisie or to the proletariat. If it belongs to the bourgeoisie, it can only be seized or overthrown all at once, in one decisive act: as it is monolithic and lacking contradiction, it cannot be the site of contesting groups and interests but only the exclusive spoils of the ruling class.[84] In economy it is also a case of 'all or nothing'. Mandel allows that the demand for workers' control has a place in the programme of structural reforms, but no more: self-management can come only after the revolution, after the seizure of power. The state must be overthrown

---

81   Mandel 1975a, p. 266f.
82   Mandel 1983b, pp. 159–62.
83   Sartre 1969, p. 99.
84   Mandel 1978a, p. 178.

before self-management can be contemplated. Everything must be changed all at once, or it will not be changed at all ... unless it is changed by Stalinists or petty-bourgeois adventurers, when the criteria are modified.

These arguments place Mandel squarely in the Bolshevik tradition, and in the Bolshevik lineage of Trotskyism, marking him off clearly from the later Pablo and other 'radical Trotskyists' who stress that practical change, however humble, is possible now. However qualified Mandel's position may be in relation to both his own heritage and his own earlier positions, the overall logic of his marxism is traditional rather than radical in nature, and imaginary rather than practical in disposition. His fundamental commitment to the inevitability of revolution and the guarantees of world history serve to prevent Mandel from undertaking a serious contemplation of transition or practical politics, for such a consideration must begin taking issues and people as they are and not as they ought to be. Mandel fails therefore not only to address problems of transition, but also avoids facing the present conjuncture. As Hussain points out with specific reference to the British case, Mandel's proposal of a transitional recipe combining soviets and nationalisation could not be less appropriate, given that parliamentary forms remain hegemonic and nationalisation discredited in England.[85] But if it is the conceptual structure and limits of his tradition which establish Mandel's politics and prevent his advance onto the terrain of contemporary struggles, his can hardly be viewed as a case of simple Bolshevism. Mandel's revolutionary telos is of a special and original kind, being theorised to a high degree of sophistication in his own technological variant of the 1859 Preface. Mandel's theory of technological revolutions and long waves is the culmination of his intellectual project, and provides the structure which ultimately encompasses and supports his revolutionary politics. It is here that this criticism of Mandel must conclude.

Mandel's Theory of Technological Revolution and Long Waves

Mandel first fully articulated his argument about technological revolutions and long waves in *Late Capitalism*, revising his position in certain respects in *Long Waves of Capitalist Development: The Marxist Interpretation*. Mandel's images, if provocative, are also problematical. The combined metaphor of waves and revolutions simultaneously suggests movement of repetition and breakthrough: the synthesis of the two images might be taken to imply a repet-

---

85   Hussain 1980, p. 358.

itive but spiral motion in economy, or else to suggest that revolutions occur as waves, cyclically and automatically. Two main difficulties emerge here. First, the precise relationship between the schema of waves and that of revolutions is unclear. If waves predominate, then a repetitionist and anti-revolutionary philosophy of history is suggested, boom followed by crash *ad nauseum*. If, on the other hand, revolution or rupture is dominant, what then becomes of the cyclical trends of the economy? Second, it should be observed that the nomenclature in both its metaphorical derivations contradicts the Trotskyist programme, denying the scheme of prolonged decay outlined in the *Transitional Programme*. At the root of the metaphorical confusion lies the tension in Mandel's work between science and revolution. Mandel's argument is compromised by the contradiction between accurate economic analysis and his desire to see the revolutionary telos vindicated. Either economic cycles reproduce capitalism, or they do not. For Mandel, the revolutionary scientist, they must do both.

Mandel details his scheme of long waves in *Late Capitalism*. His argument is that in the history of international capitalism, cyclical movements of seven or ten years' duration exist within longer spans of approximately 50 years, of which there have so far been four, characterised respectively by handicraft made or manufacture made steam engines, machine-made steam engines, electric and combustion engines, and by electronic apparatuses and the gradual introduction of nuclear energy. Ours is the long wave of the third technological revolution.[86] According to Mandel each long wave can be divided into two parts: an initial phase of application and subsequent accelerated accumulation, followed by a phase of generalisation, bringing with it a tendency to gradually decelerating accumulation as technology is cheapened and loses its 'revolutionary' effect. According to the general contours of the scheme, 'we should today have entered into the second phase of the 'long wave' which began with the Second World War, characterised by decelerated capital accumulation'.[87] The rapid succession of recessions in the central imperialist countries is taken to confirm this hypothesis. Mandel's scheme of periodisation is the basis for his choice of the term 'late capitalism' to describe the present epoch. As the title of its French edition – *Le troisième âge du Capitalisme* – suggests, late capitalism is the third and final age of capitalism: it followed classical capitalism, analysed by Marx, and imperialism, analysed by Lenin, and it is also the third stage of the technological revolution, the stage of capitalism corresponding with automation, its highest preterminal development.

---

86   Mandel 1975a, p. 120 f.
87   Mandel 1975a, p. 121 f.

It is Mandel's argument about the decelerated phase of accumulation characteristic of the present epoch which is significant here, as it raises the question of revolution and the revolutionary status of the factor of technology. Both as regards the general theory itself and as regards the nature of the present epoch, critical attention must be focused on the character of the motor force which drives technological revolutions forward.[88] The central question can be posed as follows: are technological revolutions and their accompanying long waves endogenous or exogenous in origin? This question immediately raises another, that of the status of Mandel's forced combination of the views of Trotsky and Kondratiev. Against both logical and historical arguments, Mandel insists that the theory of long waves is marxist in parentage.[89] He combines the incompatible in order to form the basis of his theory. Trotsky's theory was constructed against Kondratiev's primarily because Kondratiev took change to be endogenous in origin. More than this, Trotsky denied even the idea of the comparison of short, ten or seven year cycles with 'long' cycles. Kondratiev's theory had, for Trotsky, to be seen for what it was – not a theory of change, but one of equilibrium. As Richard Day has it, Mandel agrees with both Kondratiev and Trotsky at the same time, 'something which is logically impossible'.[90] Mandel's procedure – contrasting the views of Kondratiev and Trotsky, only to retain the logic of the former in tandem with claims of political fidelity to the latter – is completely unconvincing. Despite claims to pluralist explanation, Mandel privileges the explanatory and historical power of waves driven by technology.[91] But if technology is the motor of history, what then becomes of human agency, or in marxist terminology, what becomes of the class struggle?

Having 'forgotten the class struggle' in *Late Capitalism*, Mandel later introduces the notion of long waves of class struggle which correspond to long waves in economic growth. He fails completely to specify the basis of construction for this more political cycle in statistical, historical or theoretical terms. The long wave of class struggle seems to be nothing more than assurance presented in diagrammatic form. The wave of class struggle functions as an effect of the long wave of development itself, as is indicated in Mandel's claim that class struggle 'intensifies' with the depressive period of the long wave.[92] There is, however, a

---

88   We leave aside here other grounds of criticism. It has been argued by one critic, for
       example, that Mandel's theory cannot be sustained theoretically or empirically. See
       A. Kleinknecht 1981.
89   Mandel 1980a, p. 1.
90   Day 1976, p. 82.
91   Mandel 1975a, p. 126 ff.
92   Mandel 1980a, p. 48.

considerable shift in the arguments involved. Mandel attempts to throw focus back onto the political within the confines of the 1859 Preface scheme, suggesting that social development is not automatic but contingent on the class struggle. He wishes to argue that the cause of the downturn is endogenous, whereas upturn, being contingent, is not endogenous.[93] Mandel's determinism is accentuated by each attempt at its public denial. His recent arguments about 'relative autonomy' do little to improve his case, as the 'relativity' given with one hand is constantly retrieved, dialectically, by the other. The overall logic of Mandel's theory remains unaltered, if qualified and more closely specified: technology remains the prime mover of social change, and automation remains the great force for socialism. There are no substantial differences between the scheme in *Late Capitalism* and that in *Long Waves*: technical change in the later version is still endogenous but exogenously triggered, externally detonated.[94] The argument of *Late Capitalism* is likewise based on the principle of endogenous development with external triggering mechanisms. The argument that the internal causation of long waves by technology is externally triggered by wars and revolutions functions as a theoretical 'last instance' of determination, while practically politics and history are reduced to economic and technological after-effects, or fuses.

Mandel's afterthought six years after the first publication of *Late Capitalism*, that class struggle rather than technology determines the course of history, is too little, too late. It serves only to shift emphasis within his modified 1859 scheme: either politics or economics is determinant, as circumstances require. This is exactly the ambiguity which is the hallmark of orthodox marxism: orthodox marxism is always correct because it cannot be proven wrong. Either the economic or political factor can always be blamed for the non-event of social revolution. Whatever the situation, whatever the outcome, all defeats and 'victories' can be explained within the existing paradigm. By this means, Trotskyism maintains its claim always to be correct, no matter how frequently it is refuted by history or by criticism.

Conclusions: Mandel and the Technological Road to Socialism

Ernest Mandel's economic interest and background serve to add a novel dimension to contemporary Trotskyism. Retaining from Trotsky basic philosophical

---

93   Mandel 1980a, pp. 49, 55.
94   Mandel 1980a, p. 21.

principles as well as notions of impending collapse and organisation, Mandel's view of socialist transition is qualified by an intense faith in technology and automation. In this regard, and more emphatically than Trotsky, he is a 'Department I' marxist, awaiting the results of the self-development of the productive forces. Mandel modifies Lenin, defining socialism as soviets plus automation and television (the latter to be used as an instrument of direct democracy rather than privatised 'leisure').[95] Automation takes on a central role in Mandel's marxism, and one which is all the more perplexing given his stated opinion on technology. Against Mandel's dedication to technology as the prime mover of history can be placed his professed position:

> *Belief in the omnipotence of technology is the specific form of bourgeois ideology in late capitalism ...* All bourgeois and many self-styled Marxist theorists of the omnipotence of technology elevate it into a mechanism completely independent of all human objectives and decisions, which proceeds independently of class structure and class rule in the automatic manner of a natural law.[96]

Into which category would Mandel fall were we to apply his own terms of criticism to the theory of long waves and technological revolutions? Mandel accepts the proposition that automation and capitalism must reach a point of incompatibility, thus implying that the complete fulfilment of the third technological revolution is identical with the advent of socialism.[97] The alternative – socialism or barbarism – resolves itself, for those who operate with this technological vista, into a choice between socialist automation and capitalist decay. In its most emphatic formulation, it is Mandel's position that 'All the historical conditions of capitalism are concentrated in the twofold character of automation'.[98] Automation presents simultaneously the threat of destruction and the possibility of emancipation. Within his own variation of the 1859 Preface, socialism presents itself as the fulfilment of history, understood as the progress of technique.

With specific reference to the nature of capitalist society, Mandel's arguments reflect the least satisfactory dimension of the *Grundrisse* – its tendency to discuss socialism both as end and as process in a determinist manner. Certainly Mandel endorses the *Grundrisse's* technological utopia, if in combina-

---

95   Mandel 1975b, p. 6.
96   Mandel 1975a, pp. 501, 503.
97   Mandel 1975a, p. 206 f.
98   Mandel 1975a, p. 216.

tion with elements of the image of the regime of associated producers in the third volume of *Capital*. More fundamentally, he is committed to the notion in the *Grundrisse* that capital is immanently self-expansive, that it is an ambiguous power which, in striving for both self-emancipation and self-preservation, inevitably brings itself to the point of self-destruction. The logic at work here is analogous to that in Mandel's theory as such: despite class struggle, whether in its cyclical or immediate form, the implication is that capital somehow revolutionises itself. In his limited analyses of capitalism, and in his more extended interest in history as the unfolding of technological progress through successive modes of production, Mandel's marxism advances an 'automatic' view of history, which forecloses the discussion of problems of social change.

It has been argued in this chapter that following and modifying Trotsky, Mandel's theory of history forecloses even on the possibility of a close scrutiny of the specific political or cultural situations or formations which arise in the twentieth century. This foreclosure is no mere deficit or absence, and is more emphatically true of Mandel than of Trotsky, for Mandel produces even stronger arguments than Trotsky for the certainty of socialism, and this in an age where its likelihood seems even more remote. Indeed, it may even be the case that Mandel's arguments herald not progress but reaction. Mandel fails to understand the complications thrown up for transition by the technological theory of history. The short-term replacement of labour by machines serves not to introduce socialism, but rather to prolong the crisis, increasing unemployment and extending low-paid work. Automation here is the harbinger not of socialism, but of increased capitalist wealth and extended working-class poverty. Mandel's 'scientific' analyses and his 'revolutionary' predictions do not mesh. For all his 'revolutionary' professions, Mandel's 'scientific' theory has more in common with the theory of capitalist equilibrium than it has with Trotsky and the 'revolutionary' tradition.

Hussain's charge that Mandel's 'science' is an exercise in astrology, stands perhaps in need of modification: it can also be usefully viewed as an exercise in astronomy. Those who deal with the circular movements of bodies, whether celestial or terrestrial, can after all only observe and not influence their movements. The notions of fate and prediction remain central to Mandel's cosmological constellation.[99] Mandel's attempts to combine science and revolution are bound to fail, for capitalism cannot simultaneously reproduce itself in theory and transform itself into socialism in rhetoric. The work of Mandel, this most innovative of Trotskyists, founders on the rocks of its claims to

---

99   Hussain 1980, p. 348.

be simultaneously 'scientific' (in Mandel's specific sense) and 'revolutionary' (in accordance with the Trotskyist tradition). The rhetorical revolutionism of Mandel's science serves to undermine both its scientific and its political cred- ibility. Striving after the identity of revolution and science, it ends in denying both; presuming social transition to be already under way, it serves only to work against its possibility.

CHAPTER 13

Daniel Bell – American Menshevik (2013)

Daniel Bell was a *Mensch*. More, he was an American Menshevik. He was cosmopolitan, internationalist, emerging from the left at City College New York, an often Trotskyist milieu, though Bell was not. He joined the Young People's Socialist League aged 13. His was a culture of labour, debate, journalism, dispute, position and counter-position.[1] I got to know him while I was working at Harvard over the turn of the century, 1999–2000. Given the incredible industry of the ivy league, I found that with two or three exceptions – Peter Marsden, Patrice Higonnet, Orlando Patterson – the academics of my age were too busy to spend time with me. My friendships otherwise were either with the elders – Bell, Nathan Glazer, Bernard Bailyn – who had time to look back, or with the graduate students beavering away on coursework or dissertations, whose intellectual lives were just opening up.

Danny Bell was curious about the world; he knew where Australia was, and that interesting things occasionally happened there. Australia was on his world map. He would always serve single malt, Highland Park (a strange echo of Fordism), and Australian wine, Barossa shiraz and Hunter Semillon. He would often tease me about *Thesis Eleven*, with bad repetitive jokes about getting on with *Thesis Twelve*, and so on. As with Irving Horowitz, whom I also got to know in this setting, he was fluent in the language of Marxism even though he didn't believe in it. His conceptual grasp of the language and logic of Marxism was acute. He joked about Marxism with the particular affection of a lapsed insider – an old Menshevik – one who knew and even perhaps still loved some aspects of a place that he had come from, earlier, in a previous yet continuous life. He enjoyed teasing me – 'you were wrong!' – and himself, reminding me that, for example, all that mattered for a book's success was its title, *The End of Ideology* for example. We enjoyed corresponding as well as talking.

16 February 2000: we had survived Y2K together:

Dear Peter Beilharz:
As I may have told you, I come to William James [the Harvard Sociology building, I.M. Pei] only infrequently, since I usually work at home and sometimes at the Academy [the American Academy of Arts and Sciences,

---

1 See more generally Brick 1986; Waters 2002.

up the road in Irving Street]. It was only today that I came to William James and found the cornucopia of books and magazines from you.

Thank you very much. I appreciate your kindness. As you'll understand, I am now trying to complete some long-overdue commitments, and it will take me some time to begin to look through and read your books and essays, and the one of Zygmunt Bauman that you kindly included. I will put my finger on the book and turn the pages, for I found out a long time ago that there is a kind of osmosis which takes place and much knowledge flows through such channels.

20 July 2004:

> ... I would be very pleased to tape a talk with you [later published in Thesis Eleven] ... either on my work or my projected book, *The Rebirth of Utopia*, which I have under contract for Harvard. I have begun with a title, which is 90 per cent of the game: now I have to find some substance. To the extent that here is one, the scarlet thread running through it is the malfeasance of messianism. The sub-theme, of course, is: the philosophers have interpreted Marx; the time has come to change him.
>
>   as ever
>   Dan

Daniel Bell was known for many things, perhaps best for *The End of Ideology* and among scholars of modernity for *The Cultural Contradictions of Capitalism*. He referred famously to himself as a liberal in politics, a conservative in culture and a socialist in economics. This, for once, was no joke. As I have suggested, while he spoke largely in the language of Weber, his connection to Marxism was umbilical. This is nowhere more evident than in his astonishing study *Marxian Socialism in the United States*, which will be the major focus of my discussion here, though I shall conclude with some remarks on *The End of Ideology*, for it is indeed a book whose title has obscured the quality and nature of its contents.

Marxian Socialism in the United States[2] was published in 1952. He was no longer the young socialist, or YPSIL, at 13; now he was 30. This remains one of the best works in its field, for two reasons: he knew a lot about American socialism, and he knew how to organise it intellectually. His starting point, unsurprisingly, is the absolute locus classicus in the field, Sombart's *Why Is There*

---

2   Bell 1996.

No Socialism in the United States? (1906). This was a prime example of Bell's joke about a book known only, really, by its cover. The clichéd version of Sombart's thesis was that the prospects of American socialism had been scuttled by abundance, by 'reefs of roast beef and apple pie'. Of course, there was a longer version of the story, multivariate in nature, and pointing in the same direction as Bell's second stimulant, Perlman's 1928 theorem of the 'free gift'. The logic of Sombart's case was to point to American exceptionalism: the most developed form of capitalist experience, embodied in the American case, was different to the European path.[3] Perlman's cue was to point rather to democracy as the 'free gift'; what would later be called path dependency indicated that, unlike the Europeans, the Americans (like the Australians) did not really have to struggle for democracy; and once in it, who needed socialism?

What is striking about Bell's argument is that it is, from the first, cultural and political rather than more conventionally historical or structural. Even more fundamentally, Bell wants to claim that the failure of American socialism is the crippling effect of its own worldview.[4] Bell manipulates the Weberian motif of *other-worldliness*, the ethic of ultimate ends or redemption, rather than the ethic of responsibility. American socialism is in, but not of, its world. To use the kind of language associated with *Thesis Eleven* or the critical theory tradition articulated earlier by the Budapest School in the period of its Australian exile, American socialism was lost in the excessive romanticism and redemptive politics of the twentieth century. In different terms, American socialism was too often elsewhere, in Europe, in the USSR, then later in China, Cuba, or else in its own archives, its past, not in its present, or in its own world. Socialism failed to deal sufficiently with Americanism. Not entirely, but largely. And this becomes a major motif right through to recent work, like that of Seymour Martin Lipset and Gary Marks, *It Didn't Happen Here*.[5] So the shadow here hangs heavy, and it remains controversial, especially for those of us who live outside of the United States (and think that maybe exceptionalism is a broader trend): it is the spectre of American exceptionalism. The oddity about the American discussion of American exceptionalism is that it actually serves to posit the American (US) path as the norm, rather than the exception. The USA becomes the special case by which others are to be measured, at least until Robin Archer turns this upside down in his fascinating counterfactual study, *Why Is There No Labor Party in the United States?*[6]

---

3   Bell 1996; Sombart 1976 [1906]; Beilharz 2009.
4   Kazin, in Bell 1996, p. x.
5   Lipset and Marks 2001; echoes of the early Mothers of Invention?
6   Archer 2007.

The conversation about exceptionalism remains interesting, though it may ultimately be less productive than that on Americanism. A comparative perspective would look rather to stories of socialism in the new world, in the antipodes or settler capitalism. In any case, Americanism or Fordism was identified by Gramsci among others as the major civilisational trend of the time, something understood also by Lenin and Trotsky and certainly by Stalin. Even the CPUSA understood this, at least superficially: its 1938 slogan was 'Communism is Twentieth Century Americanism'.[7] Yet even at a semantic level, the connection or identification is deceptive. Why, in the USA, would you need communism (Americanism) if you already had Americanism? Or was this some kind of boosterist convergence theory, or Frankenstein desire to bolt the two ideologies together?

None of this means that Bell fails to take American socialism seriously. He does; and by any measured account, including his own, socialism in the USA is a significant current or at least counter-current from about 1890 to 1950. Where there is cultural traffic from Europe, there will then be socialism – in Chicago, in New York, where he found himself, in Milwaukee, in California, Ohio, Colorado, Texas ... and so on.

Yet Bell's thesis is also controversial. Does it really make sense, finally, to say that socialism was European, and not American? America was also a mixed modernity, substantially European not least in its heartlands, New York, Chicago, Detroit. Then there was the significant force of Midwest Canadian/American agrarian socialism, as tracked by Marty Lipset,[8] and a long tradition of radical activity south of the border, both in and against the state, not least in Mexico. Socialism was a significant current in American radical and labour history. In a broader, cultural sense, Americanism was also in some senses German, at least inasmuch as German-American cultural traffic spread from jazz to telecommunications, Josephine Baker to AEG. German and American modernism danced tightly until fascism.[9]

But for Bell, the American Socialist Party, the best candidate for American socialism in the twentieth century, was simply too Marxist, romantic, redemptive. The CPUSA, like the ASP which it follows, generates a society within a society, a radical ghetto; and the effect was to cut these societies off from the labour movement, which itself was very clearly located both in and of that world. The choice facing us is stark, and cheerless: it is that between either redemptive

---

7   Kazin, in Bell 1996, p. xxxii.
8   Lipset 1971.
9   Nolan 1994.

or institutional politics – in Australian terms, it is the choice between empty revolutionism and soulless labourism. The implicit connection and contrast between American and Australian experience here is quite clear. For Bell identifies the cultural dominant in the USA as *labourism* in all but name.[10] In the USA, as in Australia, there is no third way: no Menshevism, no classical social democracy. In the USA it is De Leon or Gompers. This, for Bell and for us, is the tragedy of twentieth-century socialism.

Bell's view is that revolutionary politics takes no responsibility, a view directly inspired by Weber. Not that Bell is unsympathetic to Marx. He works, in particular, with the idea of ghosting, a sympathy which he shares, at a distance, with Bernard Smith in the antipodes.[11] Bell, like Smith, draws on the spirit of tragedy and repetition in Marx's *Eighteenth Brumaire*, and displays a sophisticated understanding of the Marxian dynamics of class.[12]

Nevertheless, for Bell, socialism was never sufficiently popular, or populist. It chose to eschew the mainstream. Not that there weren't significant exceptions, however flawed. Edward Bellamy's *Looking Backward* was the second biggest selling novel in nineteenth-century America, after *Uncle Tom's Cabin* – the spirit of reform was in the air. By 1891 there were 162 Nationalist or Bellamy Clubs spread across the United States from Boston to Los Angeles. Then there was the project of American Fabianism, where Bellamy crossed over with Charlotte Perkins Gilman and the astonishing presence of the Reverend W.D.P. Bliss, author of the massive *Encyclopedia of Social Reform*.[13] This was the context in which New England muckraker and liberal Henry Demarest Lloyd campaigned not only for co-operation and social justice but also for what he called 'the New Zealandisation of the World'.[14]

But labourism, in our usage and in Bell's,[15] was also a deeply compromised project, viewed from any more radical perspective. It was less a communist Americanism than a capitalism for the proletariat. The point to which labourism became worldly was, and still is, its greatest limit; even today, if we look at the Labor Party in Australia, entirely accommodated to brave new worlds as they each arrive, indeed, happy to bring them on. Ratbags to the left of us, opportunists to the right. So the worm turns. As Bell writes:

---

10   Bell 1996.
11   Beilharz 2013.
12   Bell 1996, pp. 10–11.
13   Bliss 1970 [1897].
14   Lloyd 1900a 1900b; Coleman 1987.
15   Beilharz 1993b; Bell 1996.

If, as Max Scheler says, moral indignation is a disguised form of envy, underneath the proletarian veneer was a hot desire for riches … one can find regularly in the pages of *International Socialist Review* – which labelled itself 'the fighting magazine of the working class', and of which William D. Haywood was an editor – a large amount of advertisements which promised quick returns through land speculation. In the June 1912 issue, a full page advertisement proclaimed: 'Doubling or Tripling Your Money Though Clean Honest Investment'.[16]

This was Americanism writ large – continuous with its Puritan legacy, no work here, but clean and honest, getting in ahead of the railroad and so on. Perhaps, from this perspective, the problem with American socialism was precisely its Americanism.

Bell stacks up the examples. The cover of the January 1916 issue of *ISR* is a visual of a hungry man in the snow, the inside half page has an ad stating that a salesman could make $300 per month selling a cream separator.[17] Split consciousness? Maybe not. For Bell's point is not, I think, cynical – 'look at the clay feet of our erstwhile proletarian heroes'. The point, like that explained for the Australian case by Humphrey McQueen in *A New Britannia*,[18] is that labour also, whatever else, has a petty bourgeois utopia at its heart. The utopia of labour, historically, is often to escape from the labour market.[19]

This was the spirit of Americanism which eroded the spirit of American socialism both from within and from without. Then there was the Great War, where for Bell the left discredited itself by opposition; and then there was 1917. By 1919 there were two communist parties in the USA; by 1920, in the antipodes, there were two communist parties of Australia. Socialism's impulse, as Bell puts it, was too often elsewhere. The Soviet example couldn't have been further away from Americanism, notwithstanding their subsequent flirtations and connections, from culture to industry.[20] Once again, the radical telos was pointing elsewhere, away from suburbia and the heartlands of the consolidating American Dream, this even up to the powerful comedy of Khrushchev debating Nixon in 1958 over the respective merits of Soviet and American kitchen technology and design.

---

16   Bell 1996, p. 86.
17   Bell 1996, p. 87.
18   McQueen 1970.
19   McQueen 1970; Beilharz 2012.
20   Ball 2003.

Communists, for Bell, were another family, beyond his ken, as were Trotsky-ists. Communists, for Bell, were neither in nor of the American world. Com-munists from Trotsky to Browder understood the power of Americanism, the mirror of their dreams of production, Detroit on the Volga, Magnitogorsk. But somehow their fantasies, Faustian in the case of Trotsky, always got in the way. Soviet communism, for Trotsky, was Bolshevism shod with American nails. For Daniel Bell, Bolshevism was already well over by the suppression of the Kron-stadt Rising in 1921. Socialism in America, for Bell, was essentially over by 1950.

Yet socialism remains, for Bell, an ideal independent of a theory of history. He refused to let go of utopia entirely. Contrary to common reception, he argues in *The End of Ideology* that the end of ideology is not the end of utopia. In this, these resonances in *The End of Ideology* anticipate the related themes of Zygmunt Bauman in his 1976 classic, *Socialism: The Active Utopia*.[21] Bell refers already in 1960 to the rise of the new left as a force and queries its novelty, or at least its sense of distance from the old left.

The standard criticism of Bell is that he failed to anticipate the '60s alto-gether. This is unfair. Bell anticipates the critique of *The End of Ideology* in the afterword to his book on American socialism. Referring again to Sombart's *Why Is There No Socialism in the United States?*, he writes that, like many other dis-quieting works, Sombart's book was known only by its title. History, or radical politics, repeats itself.

While it is well past time to rescue *Marxian Socialism in the United States* from the massive condescension of prosperity, *The End of Ideology* also deserves revaluation. In its defence or recovery, a first observation is that the book in fact has 'no thesis'. It is a collection of essays whose diversity beggars easy charac-terisation, let alone dismissal. Bell was no fool, nor was he any advocate of the end of history. There is, again, some sophisticated Marxian philosophy here, for example in the essay 'Two Roads from Marx: The Themes of Alienation and Exploitation and Workers' Control in Socialist Thought'. One essay in *The End of Ideology*, Chapter 12, actually comes from the book on the history of socialism in the USA. There are other essays on crime, class, anxiety, status, the post-war regime, Keynes, Schumpeter and Galbraith, the left, the right, the unions, even one (by way of a conclusion) on the end of ideology – about which Danny Bell was wrong, in the sense that global history took another path, but right, in a different sense, that instead of the dull global hegemony of technocratic cap-italism we end up with the 'There Is No Alternative' of neoliberalism. On one subliminal point Bell was clearly correct: there was to be no significant polit-

---

21   Bauman 1976.

ical sphere, dissensus or agonism in either of those two scenarios, neither in technocratic capitalism nor in neoliberalism.

Bell still shines, in *The End of Ideology*, as an essayist. Its peak achievement, in my view, is the essay entitled 'Work and its Discontents'; some things stay the same. Bell begins, as a young lower east side socialist would, with Virgil, and Montaigne. He was a journalist and a cosmopolitan as well as a sociologist, a liberal, a conservative and a socialist; he knew about traditions, that these were always precedents, that we always arrived long after the conversation had started. For there are some universals here, as well as particulars, but his core concern is with the concept of 'efficiency'. Bell opens with the issue of time, here with a fellow called Jeremy Bentham, and his smarter brother, Samuel, and their idea, the Panoption.[22] This is 1960 – somewhat ahead of the coming French Revolution. The point, however, for Bell is that the factory is combined with the prison. Jeremy Bentham wanted to combine the two, as functional equivalents. Then, with Bell, the personnel step up: F.W. Taylor, Frank Gilbreth. He connects scientific modernism to aesthetic modernism, Frank Lloyd Wright, Bauhaus, Klee, Kandinsky, Duchamp. Then Mayo, 'Born in Australia in 1880' ... the Hawthorne Project; Colin Clark, another significant Australian actor on the world stage, Bellamy's *Looking Backward* but also Samuel Butler's antipodean utopia *Erewhon*. The cast is Shakespearean – they tramp on and off Bell's stage, each with something meaningful to say.

Bell's own conclusion to this brilliant essay is that changes to the mode of production will diminish the proletariat, increase automation, and expand the salariat – all of which is played out, true, but in our time globally rather than locally or nationally, and under the overwhelming power of the process of casualisation. Work represents the worst of things, as Bell understands, but also the best. So what might the future hold for us?

Bell's essay on efficiency is a critique of mechanical civilisation and its discontents, but its inspiration is Dewey rather than Ruskin. Bell answered these questions differently to us, likely, then and there; and we would also have our differences over them now. But he was a cultured intellectual, asking significant, big questions and answering them in ways at the same time substantial and provocative. His life experience spread across the twentieth century; he dealt with the effects of modernity and modernism, two world wars, communism, capitalism, culture. Bell was not the creature of the new mass university system, itself Fordist and more, but a citizen of the world who had little time for academic ritual or gatekeeping. Will we see his likes again?

---

22   Bell 1960, Ch. 12.

Third Circle

∴

CHAPTER 14

Nicos Poulantzas and Marxist Theory (1980)

For Athol – who dialogues with me still – Peter Beilharz

⁚

Nicos Poulantzas died on 3 October 1979 in Paris, aged 43. He was the author of six books, theoretical works which most people could not afford, let alone understand. Socialists should not feel obliged to mourn the dead simply because the world – or Parisian fashion – tells us they were Great. So why mourn Poulantzas? Other recent deaths, such as that of Marcuse, have not been unexpected. The entire generation of socialists which has survived two wars is now disappearing: we can expect many more theoretical obituaries in the next decade. Though older than some of us, Poulantzas was of our generation. He spoke to those of us now in our twenties and thirties. And as Paul Patton pointed out in his obituary (*Tribune*, 7 November) Poulantzas served as a point of introduction to the classics of marxism, or at least to a particular view of them.

What was it that Poulantzas had to say to us? Why was it important? What was his effect on the Australian left? We can proceed to these questions through the necessary historical context. The young Poulantzas left Athens for Paris where he examined law as a follower of Lukács. By 1965 Paris, renowned for its vulnerability to theoretical fashion, was swept by the new trend in marxism initiated by Louis Althusser. Poulantzas followed in the wake of this wave without conspicuously joining the Althusserian entourage.

Unlike the others (e.g. Balibar). he did not co-write or co-publish with Althusser, but nevertheless came to be thought of as one of them. Poulantzas' distance from Althusser was an important one because those directly associated with Althusser later found it difficult to modify their positions. Poulantzas did not publicly proclaim himself to be an Althusserian, and thus was more readily able to cast off the Althusserian shell when it became uncomfortably restricting.

Most English-speaking marxists came upon Poulantzas in the early 1970s. Poulantzas had written a moderately scathing review of Ralph Miliband's book *The State in Capitalist Society* in *New Left Review*. New Left Books then translated Poulantzas's own book on the state, *Political Power and Social Classes*. Other translations followed, notably *Fascism and Dictatorship* and *Classes in Contemporary Capitalism*. These works witnessed a certain gradual development in which Poulantzas became progressively less structuralist. The main limitation of his study of fascism was that the living histories of the Italian and German wonting classes were forced into inadequate structuralist schemes. The most notorious of these schemes was the so-called 'new petty bourgeoisie'. NPB in structuralist jargon. The 'NPB' was a strawman category which soaked up problem cases which could not be incorporated elsewhere in the set of structures. But Poulantzas was nevertheless able to distance himself from Althusser, and particularly from Althusser's mechanical position on the state (again constructed in terms of RSA's, ISA's, CMP's and other kinds of BS).

Poulantzas's study of class and his analysis of dictatorships in crisis saw further developments in the historicisation of marxist politics. In his last years this growing realism meant that Poulantzas rejected his structuralist standoffishness and became a left euro-communist. His final book, *State, Power, Socialism* contains many indicators of substantial developments yet to come. Poulantzas came to the conclusion that the Leninist theory of revolution was not only obsolete but was also inadequately thought out in the first place. He came to reject the structuralist notion of the state as a monolithic bloc free of contradictions, arguing instead that it was an ensemble of relations between people and other people, and between people and things. The ritualistic references to class struggle in his earlier work became more concrete.

If the state was not a 'thing' and could not therefore be 'smashed' some alternative response to everyday politics must be arrived at. In standard marxist terms Poulantzas was arguing for 'revolution from within', not precluding the possibility of violence but avoiding the old argument that a vanguard would seize state power on behalf of a passive majority who would of course remain passive under the new regime. But this last book was not free from elements of despair either. Poulantzas was casting off the security which structuralist-marxism had to offer and therefore had to admit that after all the prospects for socialism were not good. No doubt such elements of political despair participated in Poulantzas's eventual decision to take his life.

Marxists have always had a soft spot for science, for certainty. We can sleep better if we believe that history is on our side. This is an important factor in explaining the great popularity of Althusser in the English-speaking world. It is comforting to feel that we have all the answers, and anyone knows that Althusserians have all the answers. Like strangers overseas they find all solved in a phrase-book which closely resembles the Glossary to *Reading Capital*. It is still something of a heresy to suggest that Althusserian marxism has had a negative effect on the Australian left. The new Australian left was taken to the cleaners by Althusser but nevertheless took out franchise for the exclusive sale of his wares. Anyone looking up back numbers of *Australian Left Review* or *Intervention* will see clear evidence of this. It remains a real and living problem, for a reformed Althusserian has about as much credibility as a humanist stalinist.

Structuralist-marxists rarely paused to consider the real nature of their project. Structuralism began in France in the study of linguistics. People like Saussure argued that language was like a game of chess, there were rules to its system and basic units in its composition. Saussure, however, did not believe that these understandings could be transferred to the study of history or of economics. The originator of structuralism, it seems, was one of the few who understood that the study of society could not be reduced to the study of its structures. In contact with the Prague school another Frenchman, Levi-Strauss, denied Saussure and applied structural linguistics to the study of anthropology. Levi-Strauss claimed that his system had 'practically unlimited capacity for extension'; Levi-Strauss's own work was, however, quite productive; his studies were still relatively 'innocent' in terms of what was to follow. Other Parisians such as Barthes also showed that structuralism could do much to enlighten us as to the meaning of social signs.

But people like Althusser could not enlighten us much, for they wanted to universalise structure into what they understood as Science, i.e. Historical Materialism. A long, long way from Saussure, Althusser sought to explain the world as a set of structures which speak through humans. Althusser's project was based on the death or denial of the subject and the theorisation of the world as an immovable object. After the failure of May 1968 such a theory had an obvious appeal to disillusioned marxists. Structuralist marxism had a peculiar appeal to the English-speaking left because of its fundamental positivism. Like any other theory with a claim to strict scientificity, structuralist-marxism rested on a belief in absolute scientific truth. History could be known, and known objectively, known without reference to us as particular participating subjects. Such claims to objectivity unite the entire history of bourgeois thought. If the world of objects is in permanent control of the world of subjects, the project of changing the world is impossible.

How can it be that the Australian left was taken for such a ride? Perhaps it can be explained this way. Structuralist marxism was never much more than a sophisticated variation on the Comintern base-superstructure schema. We should know the tune well enough: rub any Althusserian up the wrong way and you hear it with the order and precision of a juke-box. A social formation is a combination of three levels (?), the economic, the political and the ideological. The economy is the primary determinant (?) i.e. the last instance (?) and the other levels are relatively autonomous (?) and capable of overdetermining (?)

the other levels. On the economic level forces of production break through relations of production and the Great Day arrives. If it arrives, it has been explained; if it fails to arrive then we can blame relative autonomy. The alternative outcomes of the scheme are either the reduction of everything to the economy, in which case the last instance comes all the time and revolution is automatic; or the severance and absolute autonomy of levels. Nothing has been explained except that society exists of three building blocks which might lie directly one on the other or which might be cushioned by layers of relative autonomy.

What kind of marxism is this? What can be the place of class struggle here? What is the place of the subject (i.e. people) in its series of architectural structures? This is politics made easy: but not so if marxism is a politics which seeks to actively change the world so that people can become more autonomous or free from domination. If the capitalist social formation is built of bricks, it is held together by the living mortar of hegemony. The politics of bourgeois consensus then moves into focus. Poulantzas was able to work his way out of the Althusserian Scheme because he chose to focus on the 'level' of politics.

Notions that the world reduces to sets of immovable or self-moving structures cannot theorise the transition from one social formation (capitalism) to another (socialism). Thus Althusser's appeal for sociologists: structuralist marxism explains not how we can overcome capital but on the contrary how it is eternal. In the structuralist scheme capital quietly reproduces itself unless a non-correspondence between forces and relations of production occurs. Need the futility of this kind of automatic marxism still be pointed out? How long will it take for us to accept that socialism only makes sense in terms of the conscious struggles which we and other progressive forces take up?

Poulantzas's work was a long process of dialogue from within the Althusserian framework with Gramsci and Lukács. It is this dialogue which enabled Poulantzas to work his way out of the structuralist labyrinth. Gramsci is important for Poulantzas because he was the first marxist to give serious reflection to politics as the decisive realm. For Gramsci the problem was one of facilitating the unity and autonomy which might allow people to take hold of their futures. Any rallying point which emerged in spontaneous struggles should be the contact point for marxists; the world could be responded to only in its own terms, 'common sense' could be transformed into 'good sense'. The working class could come to understand how it had made the world of capital which in turn made it. People could come to understand the world in the process of changing it.

Lukács has a different importance for marxism. For Lukács, as for Gramsci, the world is a world in motion. There can be no point in inquiring into its origin, into what comes first chicken-and-egg style. Men and women have never known the world in itself, they have only known it as they have constituted it.

As Marx first understood in the *Theses on Feuerbach*, politics begins with the world as it is. Both materialism and idealism in the old sense are transcended, because neither material forces nor ideas can be elevated to the status of prime mover if we are to maintain this focus on the combination of object and subject.

Marxism's point of departure then is not the sham objectivity of Althusser but the practices of real subjects in the world. For marxism there is but one order of reality which can be understood in different ways. There is no room in marxism for nonsense about the 'real world' and the 'thought world'. The world can be understood in its subjective or everyday manifestations, or it can be understood critically or objectively. This means not that there are two worlds but that there are two ways of understanding one world, understanding it gut-wise or intellectually. Marxist politics is about the everyday world and the problems involved in changing it; marxist critique is concerned with decoding the chaos of everyday so that it can be systematically understood. Taken as a whole marxism is the project in which changing the world and understanding it can be combined. The development of marxist politics has been delayed for so long because people like Althusser have blurred this distinction. They have acted as though it were enough for marxist intellectuals to understand the world; but we know well that our object must be to understand and change it.

Lukács also made mistakes; in particular he read the unity of subject and object as an identity. He thought that the subject, the working class, could come to understand and overcome its object, capital, simply by coming into contact with it in the labour-process. This was a different kind of automatic marxism, one based on the misconstruction of the correct principle of combination of subject and object. Structuralist-marxism in comparison only ever attempted to explain the objective world of structures, assuming that its subjective aspects were either silenced or alternatively were the mere consequences of structures. The subject here could only be reduced to victim or to Pavlovian outcome. In exaggerating the strength of the objective world the Althusserians reproduced the logic of the fetish of commodities, allowing the reproduction of a world view in which objects or structures are treated as the insuperable commanders of their producers, who must toil on endlessly beneath them.

Poulantzas began within this framework but was able to work his way out of it by focusing on politics and on the subjective moment. He was thus able to achieve something of a balance, a theoretical perspective in which we, the subjects of bourgeois society, can become conscious of its objective structures and be able to respond to these structures with a view to transforming them. Poulantzas's transition was slow and painful. Its most grating symptom was Poulantzas's difficulty in explaining class. Poulantzas began explaining class with the structuralist categories of structure and bearer. He misused the productive-unproductive labour debate to determine the working class as that class which produces material commodities. Only later did he see that whatever the situation in terms of objective class structure, class exists politically only in class struggle, when people take up positions regardless of whether they produce commodities as things or services. Poulantzas only realized late that class is therefore crucially subjective for marxist politics. In returning to these political/subjective interests he again ran the risk of becoming one-sided, of arguing as though the world were a world of subjects without objective structural limits and characterisations. He made the mistake of theorising class separately from capital, of abstracting from the objective moment, mode of production and labour-process.

His work on the state likewise avoided the accumulation process and the state's role in it. But what developments we witness here in comparison to the drone of the Althusserians! Poulantzas came to reject the classical reform-revolution dichotomy precisely because of the one-sidedness of these positions, which presume that revolution is either a concrete objective seizure of power or that socialism is the gradual internal accumulation of improvements.

Needless to say, not only Gramsci and Lukács but also the 'Italian Road' lurks behind these developments. Poulantzas came to argue that the autonomous movements were central to the struggle for socialism, that agitation and participation was necessary in all aspects of contemporary political life. In this context the Historical Compromise must be seen as a compromise with established powers at the expense of autonomous struggles. Whatever the case with the PCI, Poulantzas was moving beyond the traditional dualism of party communism and council communism, beginning to visualise the struggle for socialism as a systematic exercise in prefigurative pluralism, a struggle in which only the particular victims of an oppression could respond to it by articulating their interest.

Poulantzas indeed introduced us to the classics of marxism. But this in itself does not set Poulantzas apart as a man who dared to think. People like Mandel, for example, introduce many to Trotsky, but do little more as neither the originator nor the contemporary have much to say to us. Poulantzas's great merit was to reintroduce the present generation not only to the classics of marxism-leninism but also to the innovative theorists of marxism's political tradition, Gramsci and Lukács, and in the process of this introduction to contribute many new insights himself. Poulantzas' own uneven development was the development from structure to subject. His last writings suggest that he was beginning to combine them in a way which marxism has always pursued. Like many great forerunners Poulantzas has passed us the baton. If we believe that we must both understand and criticise and respond to and change the world, then the real struggle still remains before us. Poulantzas's place in the history of marxist theory was that of a rare educator who understood that in these senses the majority of marxists still need educating.

CHAPTER 15

Louis Althusser (1992)

Louis Althusser was born in 1918 in Algeria and died in Paris in 1990. He was, as one obituary put it, the last Marxist philosopher (*Le Monde* 31 October 1990). His work was extraordinarily influential in France, England and Australia throughout the 1970s and 1980s. Yet those who come to Althusser afresh, into the 1990s, would be justified in wondering what all the fuss was about. Titles like *For Marx* and *Reading Capital* are hardly likely to be as alluring to postmodern eyes as good narratives like Foucault's *Discipline and Punish* or his *History of Sexuality*. Yet Althusser and Foucault were very much part of the same milieu. Althusser, for his part, brought together two of the dominant streams in postwar social theory – Marxism and structuralism. More than Sartre, he was a Marxist, a lifelong member of the French Communist Party, the leading defender of the work of the 'mature' Marx, *Capital*.

Althusser was the leading theoretical antihumanist in Marxism, playing an equivalent role, in effect, to Levi-Strauss, but explicitly within Marxism and as a philosopher. His interest was in structure, not in action or praxis, and yet he remained committed to the possibility of socialism. Like the later Marx, and like Durkheim, however, he was also concerned to explain the problem of order: how capitalist societies could reproduce themselves even against (or with) the will of those who sought to transform them. This concern took Althusser, finally, into the realms of social theory charted by Gramsci: ideology and consciousness.

Althusser was thus a vital transitional figure in postwar social theory. His contribution was to raise some good questions (less uniformly often did he provide good answers, but such is the task of social thinking). His work made it possible for him, and for others after him, to ask further questions about, among other things, economy and society, ideology, philosophy of science, and interpretation.

Economy and Society

Marx identified his own central contribution to social theory as the recognition that economy was the most influential or determinant instance of society. Ideology, belief, culture, law, language and religion each made sense only with reference to economy (1859 *Preface*). Subsequent Marxists were given to puzzle over the exact relation between economy and society. Could cultural forms be deduced from or read off the economy? Was economy the basis of society and all else mere superstructure? If so, then how could the residual existence of traditional elements in modernity (such as the church) be explained?

Althusser made two advances here. First, he insisted that all societies or social formations combined different modes of production. Capitalist societies such as France always contained residual elements of feudalism; France could simultaneously be a highly technocratic and thoroughly traditional society, combining nuclear physicists on the one hand and peasants on the other. Russia could simultaneously carry elements of bourgeois and socialist revolution.[1] The observation itself was not new: Gramsci had made it in *The Southern Question*, Trotsky in *1905*. There was no such thing as a pure capitalist society; rather, all existing societies were characterised by uneven development. Althusser's insistence was that this be registered theoretically, something which Marx had failed to do in the general theory of capitalist production which he offered in *Capital*.

Second, this meant that while economy was determinant, it would not always be dominant: residual or 'secondary' elements could in fact dominate societies. Economy, politics and ideology were thus necessarily related to each other, but sometimes in such a way that the dominant economic class (the bourgeoisie) would not be the leading political class (as, for example, the petite-bourgeoisie might be, under fascism). While Althusser was not a world system theorist, this ideal of mixed modes of production and implicitly interrelated social formations reintroduced into theory the problem of imperialism or the structures of global capitalism. For while, say, Russia at the turn of the century did not have its own entrepreneurial bourgeoisie, it did have a small but strong capitalist sector in which the proletarians were local, and the bourgeoisie French, English or American in origin.

These elements of Althusser's work were influential both upon anthropology[2] and on political economy.[3] What Althusser avoided here was the question of how the transition from capitalism to socialism might occur. His interest in the systemic or synchronic dimension sometimes resulted in the charge that his theory simply bolted Marxism onto structural functionalism in order to explain how the world could not be changed at all.[4]

---

1   See Althusser 1969, pp. 94–116.
2   See, for example Godelier 1972; Terray 1972; Seddon 1978.
3   See Taylor 1979; and see generally *Journal of Australian Political Economy*.
4   See for example Clarke 1980.

Ideology

Althusser's proposal that economy was ultimately, but not practically, determinant of social life opened the theoretical possibility that societies were held together not by economy but by ideology or consent – the insight most usually attributed to Gramsci. Althusser's work, even though itself distant from Gramsci's, actually helped to produce the Gramsci boom of the 1970s. Moreover, while Althusser gave all the external appearances of being a good and reliable communist, he also helped to legitimate the importance of Freud and Lacan for social theory. Both psychoanalysts were structuralists, in the sense that they viewed surface signs as symptoms of other, deeper orders or disorders. This approach resembled Marx's distinction in *Capital* between appearance and essence as levels of reality.

The crucial concept here is that of overdetermination, that something incidental or contingent can actually cause or at least represent something apparently more fundamental; the Freudian slip is not a slip but represents something meaningful.[5] Overdetermination thus introduces into Marxism the possibility of a far more nuanced conception of causality than the orthodox would allow. The truth of a society will no longer be where Marxists claim to find it – in economy – but can be displaced elsewhere, and needs therefore to be read symptomatically. This was to open the possibility of a radical escape hatch from Althusserianism, for if ideology was the overdetermining factor, then the determinant nature of the economy was a kind of bluff, a slumbering last instance never to be called on. Althusser's attempt to modify the base-superstructure theorem, to moderate the economism within Marxism, led to the explosion of orthodoxy in other hands, and to the transformation of communism into the reconstruction of the project of radical democracy.[6]

Althusser's interest in social reproduction thus became focused on the institutions which seek to naturalise the status quo: the school, the political party, the trade union, media, the church. His was not a stress on what Marx had called the dull compulsions of everyday life – get up, work, eat, sex, sleep – but on the ideologies and belief systems of capitalism and their agencies. Althusser addressed these concerns in the influential essay 'Ideology and Ideological State Apparatuses',[7] which again betrays the influence of the Gramsci whom Althusser textually marginalised. Althusser's approach confuses the issue by arguing as though society is the state; this is one other point of contact with

---

5 Freud 1939; Althusser 1969, pp. 101–16; Laplanche and Pontalis 1973, p. 292 f.
6 Laclau and Mouffe 1985.
7 Althusser 1971.

Foucault's temptation to argue that capitalist democracies are in fact totalitarian. The Gramscian component was developed by Poulantzas – especially in his last work, *State, Power, Socialism*[8] – by Laclau and Mouffe, and by Stuart Hall and others within cultural studies. Similarly, Althusser's enthusiasm for Lacan played a part in the opening of Marxism to psychoanalysis, sexuality and feminism. Like Foucault, Althusser was no feminist, but this has not prevented his work from serving as a path in the development of French-English-Australian feminism in the 1970s and 1980s.[9]

Philosophy of Science

In a less significant register, arguably, than in economy or ideology, Althusser also enabled further questioning about the philosophy of science, or the conditions of the creation of knowledge. His defence of the work of the later Marx was posited on the premise that Marx initiated, around 1845, an epistemological break, or scientific rupture. Marx was not always a Marxist: he came to produce Marxism as a new science only later in his life, as he created a new vocabulary and theory.[10] In some places, for example in the General Philosophy Department at the University of Sydney, Althusser's affinities with Kuhn were recognised, for Kuhn's idea of a process of scientific revolution or paradigm shift in knowledge was in some respects analogous to Althusser's epistemological break or theoretical-scientific rupture.[11] This particular dimension of Althusser's work – his relation to Bachelard, Canguilhem and others – was relatively underdiscussed, with the exception of Sydney journals like *Working Papers in Sex, Science and Culture*.

While the idea of rupture seems now, in retrospect, significantly to overstate the possibility of breaking with traditional languages and ways of knowing and the novelty of Marxist concepts, Althusser did here usefully raise the question of shifts in the creation of knowledges. Notable examples are the discussion of Engels's use of Lavoisier's 'discovery' of phlogiston and of Montesquieu's discovery of the continent of history.[12] What these signify, perhaps more than Althusser ever understood, is the theme of Marx's *Eighteenth Brumaire* or the message of Freud, that we always confound our pursuit of the new by con-

---

8   Poulantzas 1978.
9   Barrett 1980; Grosz 1989.
10 Althusser and Balibar 1975.
11 Kuhn 1962; Althusser 1969, pp. 31–9; Lecourt 1975.
12 Althusser 1972; Althusser and Balibar 1975, pp. 150–8.

structing it in terms already known to us, re-enacting the past while we fancy ourselves trailblazing into the future.

Interpretation

Perhaps Althusser's greatest, if unwitting, contribution was his partial and halting exposure of the necessity of interpretation. In the politically overcharged atmosphere of the 1960s – after the death of Stalin, Khruschev's secret confession of Stalin's crimes, the invasion of Hungary and the Sino-Soviet split, as well as the discovery of the young Marx – Althusser declared that the question was clear: the challenge was how to read or construct Marx. His own version was single-minded – the question for Althusser was how to read *Capital*, and how to read it in a certain authorised manner, repressing or ignoring its Hegelian dimension (in chapter 1, volume I). Althusser did not exhort his readers to read the *Grundrisse, The German Ideology* or the *Paris Manuscripts*, but the logic of his argument was to shift interpretation away from the text and toward the reader. His demand that we 'return to Marx' was unintentionally hermeneutic, for if we read symptomatically, then the question of interpretation is thrown open: there are logically as many possible readings of Marx as there are readers of Marx, as many Marxes as there are interpretations of Marx.

In Althusser's own terminology, overdetermination warranted overinterpretation: the notion of the talking cure introduced the theme of knowledge as conversation or dialogue between reader and author (and potentially between readers). Althusser was thus unwittingly subversive of Marxism, for he invited readers to open the Pandora's box of interpretation. He thus helped to set the scene for the more favourable reception of both hermeneutics and deconstruction. And even if in dogmatic inflexion, he did require of us that we *read Marx* – and his students began to read not only *Capital* but the young Marx, and Hegel, Hyppolite and Kojève, Gramsci, Weber and Nietzsche ... to *read*, to think theoretically, to seek out the problematic or constellation of concepts within theories and how they worked.

There is, of course, a great deal more than this to Althusser, and to the retrospectively bizarre yet ultimately fruitful phenomenon of the Althusserian moment. Althusserianism was a cult and is, in this sense, reminiscent of the 1960s as such. Here I have emphasised the positive dimensions. The negative are equally striking: we need think only of Althusser's peculiar demand that we treat Lenin as a philosopher, his posturing Maoism, the internality of his logic or the pompous jargon of his lexicon, the extraordinarily hermetic conception of theory outside of history, and the resultant intellectual gangsterism practised by his English and Australian enthusiasts.

The extremity of his theory invited the intellectual execution of Althusser by Edward Thompson in the work of his own excess, *The Poverty of Theory*; more balanced assessment was offered by Richard Johnson[13] and by Perry Anderson.[14] Althusser had already pre-empted much of this response in his own *Essays in Self-Criticism* and had come closer again to Gramsci in his last writings.[15] The story ended in sadness. The manic depressive finally strangled his wife, and disappeared into an institution. Poulantzas, his most brilliant follower, committed suicide in 1979. Althusserianism disappeared as a formal force, like a message in a bottle into the depths of the channel. It would be hard to imagine Althusser's theory as a central influence into the twenty-first century, but equally difficult to deny its centrality to our own time.

---

13   Johnson 1982, Chapter 5.
14   Anderson 1980.
15   See, for example, Althusser 1978.

CHAPTER 16

Prehistoric Modes of Textual Production, or, Books Begat by Other Books: Hindess and Hirst (2011)

A very serious book arrived in Melbourne in 1975, or thereabouts. I bought *Precapitalist Modes of Production* at the International Bookshop, upstairs at 17 Elizabeth St., for $24.80. It was a long time ago. It was a lot of money; I signed it 'Pete', a hangover from high school; my Box Hill phone number has six digits. This was prehistory.

How did we know the book was important? I cannot remember. We did not know the authors; they had no prehistory for us, even though they had published widely, independently of one another. But there were rumours about a journal called *Theoretical Practice*, a very impressive title. I later secured a complete back-set from Grant Evans when he closed his La Trobe office, heading off to Hong Kong. Some were complete photocopies. Obviously, *Theoretical Practice* sold out.

We had, of course, all been reading Louis Althusser, more or less unsuccessfully. For myself, I tried several times to read *For Marx* in 1972, my first year out of high school. My first year Politics teacher Alan Rice told me I should read it, if I called myself a Marxist. Reading *Reading Capital* was easier, actually. And then, by that stage, there were reading groups, though they were mainly for reading *Capital*, not for reading *Reading Capital*. Althusser was right: we all read *Capital*. And contra Althusser, this also meant that we read *Capital* historically, and that we read it looking for history, not least in Chapters 10, 15, Parts 7 and 8, including Marx's visit to Mr. Peel at the Swan River in Chapter 33. So we knew that capital and capitalism had a history (Hindess and Hirst must have liked this passage, Mr. Peel and the Swan River, which they quote in extenso not once but twice. Perhaps they knew that Paul would come to visit Perth, or that Barry would become an antipodean exile, already then). And we believed that capitalism had a prehistory. We were likely to be well disposed to the idea that modes of production had a history too; that capitalism was a pimple on the arse of a long series of stories in world history. So we were ready, in a sense, when *Precapitalist Modes of Production* arrived, even if we were less than well-prepared for the idea of a non-historical encounter with the idea of history.

Revisiting the book today is an interesting exercise, familiar and alien by turns. It means encountering your own past, and our small collective past, in my case, around the left of the Communist Party and the Monash University Politics Department in the middle 1970s. It is, of course, a lost world, and yet its memories are easily refreshed. *Precapitalist Modes of Production* exudes the theoretical confidence of Marxism of its period, even in its opening sentence, stentorian in tenor: 'This book is a work of Marxist theory'.[1] It sought out controversy, not least in the claim that there could be no Asiatic mode of production, that feudalism did not depend on serfdom, that transition needed to be understood in a non-evolutionary manner, and so on. For these were still years in which, while some of us were reading *Capital*, most Marxists read the world through the prism of the 1859 *Preface*, and the idea of successive and evolutionary modes of production leading finally and triumphantly though capitalism to socialism still ruled. Contrary to Balibar's insistence, *Precapitalist Modes of Production* (PCMP) itself insisted that there could be no general theory of modes of production. In any case, as Hindess and Hirst indicated, it was not altogether obvious where to start when it came to Marx, who had bequeathed us the concept of one mode of production, capitalism, and a few hints about all the other possible modes of production.[2] So Hindess and Hirst proceeded to discuss each in turn: primitive communism, the ancient mode, slavery, the Asiatic Mode of Production (AMP), the feudal mode of production, and the transition from feudalism to capitalism. There were even some hints toward communism, understood as beyond modes of production, where there would be no non-labourers, no surplus production, no mode of production, and therefore no social formation (!), no classes, no state, and no politics[3] – not much at all, in fact.

This was a work of theory, as its authors informed us in no uncertain terms. History does insinuate itself in the text, as example, inevitably; even if the concept dog does not bark, the discourse of the concept of history cannot be completely non-historical. Thus, in the discussion of the slave mode of production, for example, Hindess and Hirst pause to concede that the southern states in America did suffer from serious soil erosion.[4] The controversy over the AMP is more loaded, as it is politically overdetermined as well. Hindess and Hirst genuflect to the necessity of concrete analysis; as in the early work of Melbourne journal *Intervention*, Lenin's *Development of Capitalism in Russia* seems to be almost a sacred text here. But their question is less whether there were, or are actual historical approximations to the AMP, than whether

---

1   Hindess and Hirst 1975, p. 1.
2   Balibar 1975, p. 6.
3   Balibar 1975, p. 27.
4   Balibar 1975, p. 168.

the AMP is conceptually possible. The prose is symptomatic of their entire project and moment.

> Any such concept is general and abstract. It is the product of theoretical work: the work of application of the concepts of a problematic to a definite problem posed within it. Concepts are not produced by generalising from the description of any set of 'given', 'real' conditions – concepts are not derived from or confined to any particular set of observables. The concept AMP can only be constructed if there is a space for it in the theory of modes of production, if it is a possible mode of production according to the concepts of that problematic.[5]

Concepts Can No More Be 'Asiatic Than They can Be Green or Feline'

Hindess and Hirst set themselves against the kind of marxology which reads tea leaves rather than reading *Capital*.[6] Lichtheim and Wittfogel, for example, are ridiculed for turning away from the core text to the journalism of Marx looking for clues concerning the AMP. This is a clearly Althusserian strategy: some texts are privileged over others, and theory is privileged over textual fact grubbing. But even a theoretical argument of this calibre occasionally looks like it might implode. Thus, Hindess and Hirst concede, in their later discussion of the transition from feudalism to capitalism, that the very semantics of mode of production in Marx are weak. They write: 'Let us note that the word mode is frequently used by Marx in the sense of manner or fashion ... mode of production ... refers to the manner of producing, that is, to the technical organisation of the labour process'.[7]

The same issue presented itself to me in an essay I published on 'Marxism and History' in *Thesis Eleven* 2, 1981. There I wrote, in serious prose, that

> The real problem at this point is the status of the concept mode of production. The dominant theoretical arguments have presumed mode to be an economic concept, as it is in the 1859 Preface. Rarely has it been considered that mode might be rather a less rigid, anthropological concept involving culture as well as technique. When we think of it, there is nothing strikingly rigid about the word mode, nothing suggesting a

---

5 Hindess and Hirst 1975, p. 179.
6 Hindess and Hirst 1975, p. 180.
7 Hindess and Hirst 1975, p. 268.

thing or composite object consisting necessarily of invariable components, labourer/non-labourer/means of production. The concept mode of
production – *Produktionsweise* – suggests only a way, manner, form of production. Certainly this is the case in the *German Ideology*, where mode of
production means mode of life, involving an active life-process.[8]

But this is to turn away from *Capital* or *Reading Capital* in its specificity, toward
the unholy family. Our authors, in any case, are almost done at this point, for
the time being at least. Their conclusion states even more boldly their indifference to history, or perhaps especially to historians, and this is moot. The
culture of British communism was dominated by historians, after all, and this
was one of the book's saving graces, that it placed the practice of history and
historians under question. Ergo their fury, especially when it came to the author
of *The Poverty of Theory*, and the gloves were off, bricks and chains out, the
Muggletonian Marxist himself ready rather for mugging than musing. Among
other things, Hindess and Hirst had understood that history was a problem for
Marxists, where history quickly became the philosophy of history, and Marx's
view of successive modes, actual or imputed, came too readily to resemble
Hegel's east-west side story in *The Philosophy of History*.[9] In the meantime,
there was work to be done – the work of self-criticism.

Where did the idea of self-criticism come from? It had an unsavoury political past, going back at least to the Great Purges, but the new 1970s fashion for
self-criticism was voluntary, not externally enforced or imposed. Nevertheless,
its logic was somehow disturbing, suggestive of closure, and the need to behave
as though it were possible to choreograph the reception of one's own ideas. I
remember the day the next, this time little, pink book arrived from the International Bookshop in my mailbox. This time it cost less, $6.95, and was petite,
75 pages in contrast to the earlier pink book's 323. Perhaps it was a postscript
rather than a book, but there it was: *Mode of Production and Social Formation. An Auto-Critique of Precapitalist Modes of Production*, 1977 in response to
1975. Again, its opening line was poignant: 'This text is the product of another',
as though texts author themselves, or beget others. The lineage, of course, is
longer, for there is another, only partly visible autogenetic text here: *Mode of
Production and Social Formation* is begat by *Precapitalist Modes of Production*
which is begat by *Reading Capital* (which is begat by *Capital*); it all really begins
with *Capital*, which is the ruptural moment with all things Marxian that go

---

8 Beilharz 1981a, p. 16.
9 Hindess and Hirst 1975, pp. 312–13.

before. More, the second text of Hindess and Hirst seems perhaps to transpose the epistemological break from Althusser onto this project, only the shift has accelerated from 'early' to 'late', as befits the times.

So what was the ground of the autocritique? The new child rejected the pertinence of the concept mode of production. Why? because mode of production could not escape from economism, where class relations were bound to appear in a narrow way. *PCMP* points to the class struggle but does not finally arrive there.[10] The compass belongs to Lenin, or perhaps Mao, via Althusser, for the dictum is clear: there is no longer to be any privileging of the economy. Concepts of relations of production and conditions of existence must henceforth replace those of modes of production.[11] More, the autocritique rejects epistemology, which might not actually be a bad idea.[12]

What then was the logic of this self-criticism? It remained formal and scholastic, regardless of its inherent interest. In discussing Etienne Balibar's own self-criticism, Hindess and Hirst wrote that 'Despite a brilliant and penetrating critique of his own work, Balibar had produced no basis for theoretical advance beyond the positions criticized'.[13] The same seems to be true of their autocritique, which really begins to progress only when the text begat by texts begets another text, or two, this time in the form of the two volumes of *Marx's Capital and Capitalism Today*, where both the field of Marxism and of capitalism begins to expand if not quite fully to historicise. For the conclusion to the autocritique plainly points out of the Marxian labyrinth, where Marxist debates signal the failure of Marxist theory to analyse modern western capitalism beyond the text.[14]

What, then, was the effect of these books that we all then read or pretended to read? Published two years after the founding text, the autocritique refers only to two other views of *PCMP*, those of Maurice Dobb and John Taylor. Dobb had helped to pioneer earlier historical debates on the transition from feudalism to capitalism first in his own 1946 book *Studies in the Development of Capitalism*, then in the so-called *Science and Society* debate of the 1950s.[15] This was followed later by Jack Cohen's translation and Hobsbawm's discussion of Marx's fragment from the *Grundrisse, Precapitalist Economic Formations*.[16] Dobb's review

---

10   Hindess and Hirst 1975, p. 4.
11   Hindess and Hirst 1975, p. 6.
12   Hindess and Hirst 1975, p. 21.
13   1975 p. 35.
14   Hindess and Hirst 1975, p. 74.
15   Hilton 1976.
16   K. Marx 1964.

was both short and polite. He was impressed by the skill, ingenuity, and insight of the book but completely unconvinced by its claims or argument.[17]

Taylor's review was incredibly long, at 41 pages, and fully in earnest – it even came in two parts, so that perhaps reviews now were also begetting other reviews. There were other very long reviews, like Asad and Wolpe's in *Economy and Society*,[18] which claimed that our writers were still mired in empiricism. And there were other books again, as Taylor took PCMP further again in his major study *From Modernization to Modes of Production*,[19] where his author details also reminded us that he too was connected, had been an editor of *Theoretical Practice*. It was a sign of those theoretical times that Taylor took PCMP very seriously indeed. PCMP, after all, was a serious work: it centred Marx's discourse on *Capital*, and it smelled of rigour. PCMP worked from *Capital* out, rather than through the trivia-heaps established by working anthropologists and historians as they dug and deposited detritus alongside the objects of their labours. This was Taylor's first point of orientation. Second, PCMP built on the work of Althusser and Balibar, and this too indicated its gravamen. Third, the text was important through its negative example.[20] The book demonstrates the limits of formalism. Taylor's approach is to grant Hindess and Hirst the legitimacy of their object, rather than simply to dismiss it, to take seriously the task they have set themselves. His major objection, however, is substantive. The AMP comes out of a significant problem, and the concept cannot or should not be disallowed on conceptual grounds alone. For Taylor, Hindess, and Hirst misconstruct the idea of the AMP only to reject it, whereas the AMP is best understood rather as a non-developmental mode of production. He adds theoretical objections, with especial reference to transition. At the same time, PCMP is important because it recognises that the issues at hand have to be addressed with reference to Marx's shifting problematics, understood as instalments in the project of developing historical materialism.[21]

Perhaps Hindess and Hirst should have waited for more reviews than the two they engage with in *Mode of Production and Social Formation*, or perhaps they read other reviews and discounted them. There were others, though not many, and to the best of my knowledge, there were none in Australia, at least not in the obvious journals, say, *Intervention* or *Arena* (*Thesis Eleven* was hardly, yet, a glimmer in the youthful editorial eye). Rod Aya blew the skimpy British

---

17   Dobb 1976.
18   Dobb 1976.
19   Dobb 1979.
20   Taylor 1975, p. 127.
21   Taylor 1976, p. 69.

vessel out of the water in a review in *Theory and Society* in 1976. Formalistic and scholastic, Aya charged, Hindess and Hirst were, to anticipate another blistering critique, merely rearranging words on the page. 'What the authors do, basically, is waste an entire book toying with concepts that are admittedly inapplicable to the real world ... spurious, misdirected, or plain silly'.[22] Take that! Naked textual emperors!

Two bigger bombs arrived in 1978. The first, hard but more temperate, was built by Philip Corrigan and Derek Sayer. It appeared, with deferential front page thanks to Edward Thompson, in *The Socialist Register* for 1978. Its claims were apparent. Hindess and Hirst had introduced a Trojan horse into the hitherto placid play yard of the British Marxist historians. Their sins were also apparent: circularity, theoreticism, more interestingly, intellectualism. Hindess and Hirst were, in fact, bourgeois.[23] Bourgeois! The novel point here, even if it characteristically for period Marxism engages criticism via precedent, was to place the charge of intellectualism in the context of the 1902 argument that Lenin took from Kautsky, into *What is to be Done?* – that knowledge came from intellectuals, not from the factory struggles of the proletariat who, left to themselves, could only be expected successfully to generate trade union consciousness. Corrigan and Sayer's is a fascinating text. Prosecutorial in voice, it reads like an internal document or dossier, 'please explain'. Corrigan and Sayer's report card read like something that you would get carpeted within Communist headquarters in King Street or Dixon Street, for failing to toe the Party Line. Their own work left some considerable grounds for explaining. Their collective 1978 work with Harvie Ramsay, *Socialist Construction and Marxist Theory*, for example, still basked in the glow of Mao Tse Tung Thought; nobody, then, had clean hands here.

Meanwhile, Edward Thompson was preparing a bigger bucket. Written in 1978, *The Poverty of Theory* arrived in 1979, Hindess and Hirst its bearers, or *Träger*, or local incarnations of the wicked Althusser, himself Proudhon reborn. This remains an extraordinary document, because it is also something like an internal document, a fierce polemic sustained over 200 pages by more spleen than Baudelaire could ever have summoned over so many Paris nights. So, even though he writes that 'life is too short to follow (for example) Hindess and Hirst to every one of their theoreticist lairs',[24] Thompson plays with his victims, like the family cat whose spirit he evokes and who shares the back cover

---

22   Aya 1976, p. 624.
23   Corrigan and Sayer 1978, p. 210.
24   Thompson 1978b, p. 196.

photo with him; Hindess and Hirst, Hindessian-Hirstian.[25] Indeed, Thompson has altogether too much fun, even glee with his game.

> The intermission is now over. Philosophers and sociologists are requested to cease chatting in the aisles, and to resume their places in the empty seats around me. The auditorium is darkening. A hush falls in the theatre. And Althusser resumes the stage.
>
> The great impresario has returned refreshed, and in an uncustomary mood of geniality. He announces that the heavy epistemological drama will be suspended: we have done with history and tragedy for the time. Instead, he will present a burlesque sketch of his own composition, a little influenced by Sade. A superannuated clown with pretensions to epistemological respectability, will be brought in (the audience must please keep straight faces at first), quizzed, exposed, mocked, tormented, and finally booted and hooted off the stage. From the wings he drags on, gouty, dim-eyed, a fool's cap upon his head, that poor old duffer, Frederick Engels.[26]

All this is amusing enough, though it is also a shame, as its enthusiasm risks backgrounding some more important themes, such as the issue of the status of structuralism as a major intellectual revolution of the twentieth century. Thompson's enthusiasm begins to look like a general hunting party against theory as such.[27] The argument against Althusser, in particular, becomes more visceral when it shifts specifically to politics. Here, caustically, Thompson refers to Althusserianism as a general police action within ideology, as Stalinism at the level of theory.[28] Like Corrigan and Sayer, Thompson wants to insist that Althusser is both bourgeois and Stalinist at the same time – quite an achievement for any Marxist. Althusser, according to anecdote, was far too internally or locally prepossessed to be affected by any of this, asking when told of Thompson's diatribe, '... who is he?' Little wonder Edward was furious.

If Althusser was a bourgeois stalinist, so then, by extension must his followers, Hindess and Hirst, have been. The encounter with Thompson feels primal, traumatic, and oedipal. But in the meantime, the bad boys of British Marxism had found new friends, Tony Cutler and Athar Hussain, and there were another two books, two volumes of *Marx's Capital and Capitalism Today*.[29] These are

---

25   Thompson 1978b, p. 335.
26   Thompson 1978b, pp. 242–3.
27   Thompson 1978b, p. 300.
28   Thompson 1978b, p. 323.
29   Hindess and Hirst 1978.

also important works, where we can begin to see a reversal or at least a modification of the textual involution characteristic of the earlier work. *Marx's Capital
and Capitalism Today* commences from the fact of the centrality of change.
After Marx, after Hilferding's *Finance Capital*, there would need to be new work.
Value theory was cast into doubt; in contrast to orthodoxy, the idea of 'laws of
motion' of capital were brought into question; and economic agents began to
emerge in institutional or organisational form, in contrast to the traditional
kind of class analysis which simply imputed interests to so-called class actors.
Nevertheless, the new texts struck close to the classics, Marx, Hilferding, and
Rubin. They veered occasionally into the actual sphere of production, as in the
discussion of British and Japanese motorcycle production, but even if British
Marxism also leaked, here the Japanese were not much better at it. Perhaps the
cover visuals of these books were still the most symptomatic – Dürer, a Marx-
like Christ Cleaning the Temple. For both Hindess and Hirst, the best was yet
to come.

This is an obvious question for further discussion and analysis. How did this
work lead to what followed? How did it differ from the prior independent work
of Hindess and Hirst? Are these matters of shifting problematics, or might they
best be explained by other means?

This was, I think, an extraordinary moment in the history of recent Marxism,
now lost, gone. It pointed out of the Althusserian field, even if unintentionally.
It showed the irreducible importance of the precapitalist world, of world history, of the non-West, and it opened wide the discourse about the status (and
attraction) of the fields of history and anthropology. These were the years when
we all read Meillasoux, Terray, and Sahlins, then turned back to Lewis Henry
Morgan, later to Marx's *Ethnological Notebooks*, and new worlds indeed opened
to us, beyond capitalism and modernity, to Asia, to antiquity. More, the work
of Hindess and Hirst showed the power of Marxist theory, of thinking through
the problematic, of the importance of transition and the most elusive transition of all, that from capitalism to socialism. Anthropology and history in this
light would appear not only as open horizons but also as problematical fields
and practices with particular problems and specific limitations of their own.

For Hindess and Hirst, this represented an extraordinary project in the context of a remarkable collaboration, which in turn then separated and followed
distinct but related paths. The intensity of the moment of its intellectual production is still palpable. If some aspects of its achievement now look like a
deterrent, then the spirit of its enthusiasm remains inspirational. Would we
repeat it? Maybe not. Should we celebrate it? I think so, even if in retrospect
it indicates a kind of progress more incremental, accidental, and hesitant than
we might have hoped for, when we were younger.

CHAPTER 17

The Decline of Western Marxism: Trotsky, Gramsci, Althusser (2003)

Western Marxism has long been in decline. Today, even its referent is less than evident. Western Marxism, typically associated with Gramsci, Lukács and Korsch, arose at that moment that Bolshevism abducted the Marxian legacy. Marxism, in period language, went east, where the structures of civil society were gelatinous and the state primordial. These days we speak rather of North and South; and there is indeed a good case to make that Gramsci was a Southern Marxist. The eastern frame of reference should still matter, not least as the original orienting device and home of the most interesting thinkers of critical theory, such as Bauman and Heller. Trotsky in contrast was a northerner, even though his influence often went south, as did Althusser's, to Latin America. In the last two cases, however, this was a Jacobin appropriation of Bolshevism. Trotsky and Althusser travelled as Marxist-Leninists. Gramsci alone added something more substantial, in his essay on the Southern Question. He started in the south, and stayed there, even in Turin.

Marxism today more generally is in decline, globally, north and south.

The best symptom of this is the bizarre reception of that bizarre book, Hardt and Negri's *Empire*.[1] It is one thing that *Empire* solves the crisis of Marxism by turning it into magic again, the magic and fantasy of socialism, communism ever working away within the heart of capitalist globalisation. Various thinkers, rather following Weber, have called for the reenchantment of the world. Here we have the reenchantment of Marxism via Disney. The sorcerer's apprentice indeed turns out, in this depiction, to be Mickey Mouse. It is another thing, however, to see middle-class radicals lapping all this up, from the comfort of their armchairs, where they can readily empathise with these Cecil B. de Mille images of the multitude stirring against, or within the heart of Capital. All this is enough to make the old western Marxism look respectable. Thinkers like Trotsky and Althusser had their illusions, or delusions, whether of grandeur or defeat. Gramsci, whose thinking travels best of these three across time and place, has nevertheless suffered more, perhaps for being dressed as the man for all seasons.

---

1   Hardt and Negri 2000.

These three books revisit these Marxist masters of our time, or of the time that has just now passed. Trotsky and Gramsci of course inhabit lost worlds, but their appropriation in the English language accelerated into the 70s. This was also the moment of Louis Althusser, though Althusser's presence is more peculiar, heightened to the extent of absolute dominance in England and Australia and then gone, *disparu*, like the flame that expands dramatically just as it is about to disappear. Trotsky, in the meantime, is also gone, though his spirit lives on in the antechambers of journals like *New Left Review*. And Gramsci still hangs around, as an Englishman, though the closure of the Birmingham School should make this presence more spectral. Gramsci's thinking is plainly still in use, in some version or another; Trotsky has all but disappeared together with the eclipse of his object, the Soviet Union; and Althusser remains an absent presence, apparent in some of the more arcane versions of postmarxism, otherwise, like structuralism, treated as Atlantis. Probably Althusser, of all these, most deserves a thorough rethinking and reassessment; perhaps the time for this is ripe. We shall have to wait.

Ian Thatcher's *Trotsky is* the most conventional of these studies. It appears in the Routledge Historical Biographies Series, and is the most conspicuously trade-oriented of these books. The studies of Gramsci and Althusser are also presented as introductions, but of different kinds. Thatcher's pitch is straightforwardly historical; Crehan's Gramsci is explicitly aimed at anthropologists, who have hitherto taken their Gramsci half-baked, from the pages of Raymond Williams' *Marxism and Literature*,[2] while Montag's Althusser has become a literary theorist too.

Thatcher's *Trotsky* is a good and useful book, though it tries to have it both ways, being presented both as a way in for newcomers and as a replacement for Knei-Paz's magisterial 1978 text, *The Social and Political Thought of Leon Trotsky*. Frankly, I do not think that the Knei-Paz book will ever be replaced, whatever its limits. The Knei-Paz book is frontal, theoretical and sophisticated. Thatcher's approach is more directly historical, contextual and introductory. Thatcher wants to revisit Trotsky, without passion, which is undoubtedly what Trotsky generally generates. At the end of it all, one wonders: Trotsky without passion?

Thatcher's approach utilises his language skills in Russian. Early Western views of Trotsky, for example, are set against the early Russian and Soviet reception. Among the English-language works, Thatcher offers applause for Max Eastman, and indicates the usual cautionary note about the incredibly influen-

---

2   Williams 1977.

tial work of Isaac Deutscher. Knei-Paz's work is criticized in terms more implicit, and methodological or disciplinary, rather than explicit, 'Knei-Paz made
several errors of judgment in how he conceived his study'.[3] Is it possible that
Knei-Paz simply had a different approach? Thatcher's implicit appeal is to the
common-sense historicism of English-speaking culture: in order to understand
something, you need to know where it came from. At the end of the day, this
common sense may also result in good sense, but this sensibility should not
be allowed to preclude the possibility of other ways of seeing, or thinking. The
ultimate question is, what does the new book add?

Thatcher's narrative is clear and insightful, if compromised by its dual purposes of introduction and innovation. Do we need to be told that Trotsky in 1905
wrote 'from a Marxist perspective', or that the 'people' means ordinary workers and peasants?[4] Thatcher's story is nevertheless well told, and what a saga
it is – from libertarian anti-Jacobin in 1904, to dictatorial War Communism by
1920. The libertarian common-sense was that the revolution was betrayed not
by Stalin in 1936 but by Lenin and Trotsky in 1921. Trotsky whistles while Stalin
organises; Trotsky is expelled, then finally murdered in 1940, leaving abundant material for Hollywood movies and considerable grounds to suggest that,
were he to have lived, he may have shifted out of Bolshevism altogether. By the
moment of those last debates and the writing of *The USSR in War*, Trotsky had
opened the in-principle possibility that the USSR might be a new form of totalitarian regime. This was a significant shift of emphasis from the analysis in *The
Revolution Betrayed* of 1936, a book which remains both deeply flawed and yet
an astonishing contribution to the sociology of Soviet-type societies. Thatcher
informs us that the 'system described by *The Revolution Betrayed* was clearly
not socialist', but transitional, opening a line of argument subsequently occupied by thinkers like Ernest Mandel for decades. Yet the political logic of this
position was also defencist – the USSR was a workers' state, however deformed
or degenerated. Practically, the USSR had to be socialist, because of its origin.

Thatcher's assessment of Trotsky seems to me, finally, to miss something of
the nature of this project. He criticises Trotsky for failing to provide any guarantees that the USSR would have been richer or more democratic under his
own guidance. Guarantees, of any kind, seem less than pertinent here. If Trotsky had maintained his early democratic credentials he, too, would have been
swept aside by Bolshevism, only twenty years earlier. Then, in Thatcher's final
judgement, 'it is doubtful whether Trotsky made any lasting contribution to

---

3   Thatcher 2003, p. 18.
4   Thatcher 2003, pp. 34–5.

Marxist thought'.[5] My own early study of Trotsky, *Trotsky, Trotskyism and the Transition to Socialism* (1987) was criticised inter alia for its unremittingly negative and critical response to these phenomena. But at this point even I have to come to Comrade Trotsky's defence. In retrospect, there are at least four aspects of Trotsky's Marxism that count as major contributions. Two are early – the emancipatory critique of Bolshevism as Jacobinism in *Our Political Tasks* (1904) and the work of historical sociology gathered in the essays on 1905. One spans the distinction between Trotsky before and after his Bolshevik turn – the theory of Permanent Revolution, which, however flawed, looks original enough to me. The last aspect includes *The Revolution Betrayed*, a pioneering if ultimately mistaken work, compromised by Trotsky's own personal investment in the object of his analysis. Other contributions could also be identified, as in the work of R.B. Day on Trotsky's political economy or more generally, in the signal importance of the ideas of uneven development. Trotsky's legacy emerges from Thatcher's study as negligible, even though it is historically central to the path of the twentieth century. The limit of this view seems, to me, to reflect its disinterest in what followed, not least in the radical Trotskyist stream of the French movement that led to *Socialisme ou Barbarie*. If it is a considerable source of strength that Thatcher draws on in his deployment of Russian-language materials, what is striking here is the absence of the French reception. The single most significant bibliographical absence here concerns not Castoriadis or Lefort, but the dedicated journal *Cahiers Leon Trotsky*, now more than twenty years old.

Enter Gramsci. Kate Crehan's book is one of the best recently published in its field. Its purpose is also dual, to essay Gramsci and to address anthropologists as specific users of Gramsci. The connecting term, obviously, is culture. This is a volume in a new series, 'Reading Gramsci', edited by Joseph Buttigieg, who is the editor of the Columbia translation of the Gerratana edition of *The Prison Notebooks*, the project which will eventually replace the 1971 Hoare and Nowell-Smith standard one-volume edition of *Selections from the Prison Notebooks*. Both Buttigieg and Crehan deserve congratulations for all their labours, even if Buttigieg in the series introduction repeats the standard view of English-language *Gramsci Studies* which screens the antipodean version out. Louis Marks and Gwyn Williams started Gramsci Studies moving in 1957 and 1960; Alastair Davidson translated Gramsci in Australia in 1968, in *Antonio Gramsci: The Man, His Ideas*, three years before Hoare and Nowell-Smith generated their more comprehensive version. Even within the prison of the English language, we in the antipodes were reading Gramsci into the late sixties, before the

---

Gramsci boom. This is of some importance to us, who started *Thesis Eleven* in 1980, because Davidson was our teacher. His contribution has never fully been recognised, not even with the publication of his major work, *Antonio Gramsci: Towards An Intellectual Biography*.[6]

Buttigieg's series introduction indicates that Crehan's is to be one of many studies, each to take up an aspect or tangent of the Sardinian's work. This is a wonderful prospect. Crehan's book bodes well for what is to follow. The opening cue, however, is unnecessarily positional, what Australians have been known to call pissing on the gatepost (as in the canine marking turf). '... as Michel Foucault noted in a 1984 letter to the Gramsci scholar Joseph Buttigieg, Gramsci remains an author who is cited more often than he is genuinely known'.[7] So? What else is new? Genuflection to Paris performed, the argument begins. Crehan uses a kind of compensatory, documentary approach, strong on both argument and on quotation for those who are new to Gramsci, or who drop his name without opening his texts. Like Thatcher, she begins with biography but then goes elsewhere. Gramsci, of course, was an historicist. It was for this reason that he wrote that the experience on which Marxism was based could not be schematised: it is history in all its infinite variety and multiplicity. His work was like that of the early Trotsky, but where Trotsky succumbs to teleology and the logic of necessity (and this is what makes Deutscher his most significant follower) Gramsci stays with the idea of contingency. It is this sense of contingency, incidentally, which explains Gramsci's sense that he should in prison write something for eternity, *für ewig*. Crehan worries over this idea; it seems to me that if Gramsci understood one thing while he was in prison, it was his own contingency. This was precisely the right time to write *für ewig*.

Crehan is correct, however, to worry over the status of Gramsci's writings. All too often enthusiasts treat the *Prison Notebooks* as though they are a theory. This is why the Gerratana/Buttigieg project is so important; you have to see the Notebooks as Notebooks, *in extenso*. Crehan uses a simple semantic device to push this sense – instead of quoting Gramsci and then referring to this 'theory' or even this 'passage' she says 'in this Note'. The point is not only that the Notes are disaggregated, but also that the situation parallels Marx's – the most important texts, Gramsci's Notes and Letters (as in *The Paris Manuscripts*, *The German Ideology* and the *Grundrisse*) were never intended for publication.

Gramsci names problems, like hegemony; he does not resolve them. One result is that enthusiasts identify hegemony and ideology. The even bigger prob-

---

6 Davidson 1977.
7 Crehan 2002, p. 1.

lem, for Crehan, is culture. Anthropologists work with three common assumptions regarding culture. First, cultures are systems. Second, cultures are discrete and bounded. Third, the societies which come under study are conceptualised in terms of a hard dichotomy between tradition and modernity. Crehan argues that the common anthropological practice is to project these meanings onto Gramsci. A useful discussion on culture, civilisation, romanticism and nationalism follows.

None of these anthropological assumptions are shared by Gramsci. Cultures are mobile, contested; internally fissured not least between oppressors and oppressed, and mix modernity and tradition. Gramsci is less interested in the anthropological disciplinary complex, than in relations, and how these create shifting social forms. Crehan rejects the standard image, of culture as mosaic, and keeps the image of hybridity at a distance. I find all this persuasive – as Nicholas Thomas put it, hybridity is almost a good idea, but not quite. What works better, because it is more positively mobile and yet can register asymmetries of power without taking on the unhappy biologistic connotations of the hybrid, is the idea of cultural traffic.

So next Crehan turns to Gramsci's views, to establish and clarify the difference. Crehan does not make the connection to Castoriadis or to Heller here, but the implication of her reading of Gramsci is that culture facilitates autonomy. Culture involves, for Gramsci, the exercise of thought, the acquisition of general ideas, like cause and effect; it is Socratic, it means thinking well, whatever one thinks, and therefore acting well, whatever one does. Culture is organisation, self-discipline, coming to terms with one's own personality, rights and obligations. One can imagine Gramsci saying that culture is history. History is contingency. Yet Gramsci was also an orthodox Marxist, at least inasmuch as he saw classes as the primary actors, even when classes are refracted through images like subalternality. Crehan finds this attractive; maybe class analysis these days is of more potential use in anthropology than in sociology, given the blurring effect that consumerism has on class relations in the West, or North? But Gramsci also talks of social groups, and it is not obvious that he views classes as empirical actors. Classes have empirical representatives, but they are precisely organisations, institutions, and not classes themselves. Classes only 'act' indirectly, if at all, via unions, parties, papers ... movements. If we read Gramsci as a movement theorist, rather than a class analyst, then the problems of Bolshevism, Jacobinism and the New Prince begin to free up. For there must surely be parts of Gramsci's legacy that we do not want, no matter how superior the logic of his claims might appear over and against those of anthropology.

The striking absence from Crehan's text here (unless I have missed it) is Gramsci's idea of the *historic bloc*. Crehan observes, for example that hegemony belongs to a class, or an alliance of classes. My recollection, not least in connection with the period debate over Thatcherism in *New Left Review*, is that the more powerful case is that hegemony is constructed via the historic bloc of interests that held together Thatcherism then, or Blairism now. If classes do act, they certainly do not act singly, only in concert, via the political forms available to them. Crehan's concern is that the key relationship is between dominators and dominated, not between the traditional and the modern. But again, when it comes to hegemony as mediated via the historic bloc, any firm distinction between tradition and modernity will fail to capture the invention of tradition, as Crehan later argues.

The notion of subalternality of course evokes the influence of the Subaltern Studies Group. As Crehan argues, however, Gramsci here was a kind of portal to Foucault. The associated problem arises, that Gramsci's Notes on the Italian peasantry are universalised by their users, only to be found wanting. Finally, Crehan brings anthropology and Gramsci more fully together, here via the work of Raymond Williams. One big problem here is the specificity of the distinct culture wars across the Atlantic. Williams, after all, had a different context, purpose and field, and different enemies. Crehan worries, in particular, that Gramsci is appropriated thinly by American anthropologists, who seem to have missed out on, or are indifferent towards cultural materialism. Here again, the point is that it is history, rather than culture which is at issue. This is the point to the old trick question: is a market an economy, or a culture? Obviously, it is both; and it is only the work of historical specificity that will clarify what is involved. Categories are can openers, which young academics will nevertheless dedicate their lives to. And this is why all categories, including class, which matters so much to Crehan, need to be used as questions, rather than answers.

In the lonely moment of the last instance, finally, there arrives Warren Montag, together with Louis Althusser. *Louis Althusser* is a clever if elusive book. Indeed, when I flicked through my review copy, I wondered for a moment if it had been dissembled, for there are very long passages on ... *Heart of Darkness*, and *Robinson Crusoe*. Montag's book is the most innovative of the three books under review, though it almost certainly risks losing its introductory readers promptly. It is more of a personal collage, reaching sideways to Macherey, Conrad and Defoe rather than working centrally through Althusser. Perhaps this is the license of literary theory. It is no longer the case that we all read Althusser, if we ever did. To even evoke the name is to return, for example, to the moment when *Thesis Eleven* was in formation: we *were* reading Althusser, E.P. Thompson, Poulantzas, less enthusiastically G.A. Cohen; and we were reading Marx's *Capital*, which by comparison was time well spent.

Certainly Althusser cast his spell, or at least his publicists did. The shortcut to *Reading Capital* was through Ben Brewster's Glossary. And the spell was there, as Montag reminds us. The care given to the idea of reading by Althusser was enough to capture any young Marxist seeking legitimation for all those hours spent in silent, late nights and early morning reading.

But if the anthropologists, according to Crehan, take in their Gramsci from literary theory, here, with Althusser, the literary theory came via political economy. Marx, of course, read *Robinson Crusoe*, so the circuit is intact. Whether the sidetrip with Kurtz is essential, or rather just interesting, may well be another matter.

Althusser sought a scientific approach to knowledge, to history, even to literature, though in this last instance it was Pierre Macherey who did the running in *A Theory of Literary Production*.[8] These were the days when production was a master trope. This was the logic of economism rampant, so that even aesthetics needed to be viewed as a production, no room for ideas like creation here. *Reading Capital* faithfully followed Marx's logic, that capitalist production, once understood, would yield the understanding of everything else by extrapolation. For all its profundity, as Montag reminds us, we should begin from the fact that *Reading Capital* was a seminar. The essays in *For Marx* were more variegated. The idea of overdetermination, borrowed from psychoanalysis (we all read Laplanche and Pontalis) was widely, in comparison, identified as a way out of economism (I remember, in that period twenty years ago, discovering in separate conversations with Stuart Hall, Ernesto Laclau and my teacher, Alastair Davidson, that 'Contradiction and Overdetermination' was all their favourite Althusser text). The emblematic sense, corresponding to this in the context of Marx's work, was that Marx was better viewed as the author of the *Eighteenth Brumaire* than of *Capital*. This logic seems to be quite at odds with that of *Reading Capital*, a text which in places could be so fascinating as to make you wonder whether you were being taken in. The most influential text, however, was very likely 'Ideology and Ideological State Apparatuses', with its famous inclusion of the idea of interpellation. And then there were the later writings, including *The Future Lasts a Long Time*,[9] which some seem to have read with pathos and others with bewilderment.

If there are many Marxs, at least two Trotskys and Gramscis – early and late – there are many Althussers. Balibar captured one distinction with the image that there were two kinds of Althusserians, Althusserians of the Conjuncture and

---

8   Macherey 1966.
9   Althusser 1993.

Althusserians of the Structure. Or, we could say differently, there were those who put Althusser's insights to work, and those who recited the axioms. Perhaps the problem here is that the more intellectually sophisticated Althusserianism became, the less useful it was. Where the younger Trotsky and Gramsci acted out humanism, or historicism, Althusser discovered that humanism was psychologically untenable. History gave way to Structure; action might at most be construed as production. In the interim, Althusser's work could do nothing positive with Gramsci; Marxism, we were instructed, was Not a Historicism. Freud, and Lacan, and now it seems especially Spinoza were the real treasures in this Trojan-horse construction.

As Montag puts it, for Althusser the function of art was not so much (qua socialist realism) to make reality visible as to make visible the myths that govern us. Fetishism was a tolerable trope, but not alienation. Montag takes us through Brecht and Beckett to contemplate this (the outsider might be forgiven for wondering how Beckett, the absurd, escapes what is served up here by Althusser for existentialism). Then Macherey, Foucault, Freud, Spinoza. For Macherey, the artist has no more prospect of autonomy than the proletarian – both produce. Notwithstanding the scientific distance taken here from romanticism, Louis Althusser seems to emerge from this text, or from under his own as tragic hero, 'left to sail on darkened waters, reflected stars scattering around his fragile craft like so many resplendent splinters of shattered glass',[10] 'the whole nothing more than a still-motion photograph of innumerable splinters of shattered glass as they descend in divergent arcs, never to reach the ground'.[11]

It is collage, not detritus or shard that follows. Montag intelligently manoevres bits of text and interpretation. He is, after all, Reading Althusser. Then *Heart of Darkness* arrives. This seems to me to be a peculiar gesture, not least in a book of this kind but also because it risks rerunning the kind of interpretation it sets out to reverse. Montag quotes Hochschild, in *King Leopold's Ghost*, to say that we should beware universalising Kurtz, which is always what happens. Kurtz is a metaphor for everything; *Heart of Darkness* is read as a parable for all times and places, not as a book about one time and place.[12] Yet if Marxism is not an historicism, what has this to do with Althusser? Montag's strategy seems to be to do what you could do with Althusser, but which Althusser failed to do. Montag's reading of Conrad is persuasive, except that he plays hard on the internationalism of the international workers' movement, which was also quite gifted at nationalism-in-the-making. The German Social Democrats, for

---

10   Montag 2003, p. 68.
11   Montag 2003, p. 131.
12   Montag 2003, p. 86.

example, had read Locke and not only Marx, and some of them thought imperialism was a good idea. Then, after seventeen pages of Kurtz-analysis, Robinson Crusoe arrives in the company of Friday; and here, it seems, Althusser has found his Monday. Sixteen pages later, Althusser returns, leaving a single footprint on the sand, leaving this metaphor awaiting Foucault, who hoped rather to be washed away.

Montag's exit goes back to *The Future Lasts a Long Time*, and to the question of Althusser's self-deprecating confession. This is powerful prose, not least as it reminds one of Althusser's modesty in self-mockery. Here was a man who could claim, in the presence of philosophers, that he knew nothing of philosophy, only a little Marx and Lenin. This was a Marxist who could seek out the problem of the concept of time, and at the same time argue that contingency was another word for the unknown. There is so much that we will never know.

CHAPTER 18

Review of Cornelius Castoriadis, *Political and Social Writings* (1989)

Those who have come more recently to social theory might be forgiven for experiencing it as a battle between warring titans on the Paris Frankfurt axis. There is Habermas, or Derrida (or Lyotard, or Baudrillard) ... this is the choice, these are the alternatives. Or so it seems, for such is the staging of modern/postmodern social theory in the 1980s. Yet Habermas is somehow unsatisfying to the soul; and French theory, well ... it reminds us of the mouse that roared, provocative but superficial, and far too noisy to be especially meaningful.

In the wings of such a staging stand others: Agnes Heller, Ferenc Fehér, Alain Touraine and in this company, with it, and yet stridently independent in their own ways, there are also figures such as Claude Lefort and Cornelius Castoriadis. Like these other thinkers, more substantial than the present palaver, Castoriadis has a history. Castoriadis's reputation as a theorist probably dates from the publication of *The Imaginary Institution of Society* in 1975. Yet as readers of those old Solidarity pamphlets, or followers of the long defunct journal *Telos*, or *Thesis Eleven* will know, Castoriadis's political writings go back to the mid-1940s. The publication of these two volumes of *Political and Social Writings*,[1] and the anticipated publication of a third volume,[2] finally fill a massive gap in the records for English speakers who might otherwise be deceived by the false options of Paris-Frankfurt marketing strategies. What then are these writings?

David Curtis has translated largely from Castoriadis's 10/18 series of collected writings. Some of these appeared in and have become the classics of that magical journal, *Socialisme ou Barbarie*. The first volume, 1945–55, bears the subtitle, 'From the Critique of Bureaucracy to the Positive Content of Socialism'. Here we find classic *Socialisme ou Barbarie* texts such as *The Relations of Production in Russia*. Most of the essays in this first volume relate to the Soviet experience; some of them emerge directly from the Trotskyist and post-Trotskyist milieu which Castoriadis then inhabited. Curtis opens the volume with a series introduction. Curtis's introduction is such a good piece that it is

---

1 Castoriadis 1988a, 1988b.
2 Castoriadis 1992.

difficult not to plagiarise it. He emulates Castoriadis's strength of position and insight, but also his wit, and wit, I shall propose here, is actually a defining characteristic of Castoriadis's work, for it is expressive of his attitude to the world as such.

Curtis himself has evidently swum via the pass between the Scylla and Charybdis of the Paris-Frankfurt axis. Plainly he is attracted to Castoriadis's sense of the significant, independent path in politics and theory. As Curtis tells us, *Socialisme ou Barbarie* has now belatedly had the perverse pleasure of discovering that everyone agreed with it earlier, but somehow did not own up to it. As an article in *Liberation* for 28–9 June 1986 put it, 'Many are the intellectuals who, in the 1970s, have, how should one put it, "boasted" to having signed an article "in *S. ou B.*" or "at least to having belonged to the same political territory as the review": to which Castoriadis responded in jest, "If all these people had really been with us at the time, we would have taken power in France somewhere around 1957"'. The humour is significant; for Castoriadis rightly mocks this pathetic attempt to rewrite history, by no means the sole prerogative of Stalinist wishful thinkers, but he also reminds us that he was indeed a revolutionary Marxist, a Marxist militant. The pertinence of biography, itself always significant, is even more heightened in the case of Castoriadis, for he was not an armchair Marxist, but a political actor from the Greek Civil War through to his Paris exile. He and his friends did indeed contemplate seriously, and not fantastically, the logic of state power and its seizure.

And this is merely the opening of an odyssey through which Castoriadis listens – especially to voices of the working class – but also speaks and judges. It is a road, apparently convoluted, which leads from Trotsky to Marx to Freud, to Aristotle and back. Castoriadis's path out of Trotskyism into radicalism is an intriguing story. Where his colleagues, C.L.R. James and Raya Dunayevskaya, stayed within the house of Hegel, abetting Old Man Trotsky, Castoriadis was prepared to view Trotskyism as the halfway house to radicalism which it potentially was. But this also meant that Castoriadis's path was more of a puzzle. So while James and Dunayevskaya developed their sense of a following, Castoriadis's voice has been more lonely, but also more persistent and more fully challenging.

The texts in the first volume spring, in the first instance, from this radical Trotskyist milieu. Castoriadis shares with James and Dunayevskaya the fundamental commitment to workers' autonomy. Self-management – later transposed into the category autonomy – is the essential value informing Castoriadis's lifework. For Castoriadis the true content of socialism was neither economic growth nor the expansion of free (empty) time as such, but the instauration, for the first time in history, of people's domination over their lives and therefore especially of their work. Castoriadis's image of socialism was both egalitarian and stateless, and here there were some similarities between his views and those of Hegelian Trotskyists like James and Dunayevskaya. One essential difference between them, however, was that Castoriadis rejected the Hegelian fix; his hope of socialism was not that it should somehow 'prove' theory, but that it should reconstitute theory, and reconstruct life. Hegel, for Castoriadis, was the thinker not of spirit, or system, or subject, but rather the worldly soul who decided that *Weltgeschichte ist Weltgericht*: world history is the world's court of judgement.

The theme of history is a central one for Castoriadis. It was the path of history into the twentieth century which eventually, for Castoriadis, decided against Marxism. Marxism, as he once characteristically put it, was moribund because 'historical materialism' was neither historical nor materialist. It postulated and preached rather than listened, watched and responded to the movements of the old mole of working-class self-activity. It nailed up the catatonic laws of *Capital*, rather than the pragmatic *Theses on Feuerbach*. But if there are, in a sense, two Marxes for Castoriadis, they are not the usual two, those of 1844 or 1867, *Economic and Philosophical Manuscripts* or *Capital*. The choice is rather that between the *Communist Manifesto* and *Capital*. Marx's putative critique of political economy becomes transfixed by bourgeois thinking – this theme, likely better associated with Baudrillard in English, was actually first put by Castoriadis. Similarly, as Cohn-Bendit freely acknowledged, the theses of *Obsolete Communism* were plagiarised from Castoriadis. For like Touraine, in this regard, and unlike all structuralisms and posts, Castoriadis starts from the premise that the world moves. People are always making history, even within and against the interstices of totalitarianism, History is a project, a making/doing; theory merely the elucidation of these things. Postrevolutionary society henceforth will not simply be a self-managed society: it will be a society that self-institutes itself explicitly, not once and for all, but continuously. The problem, now, was not simply to transcend capitalism, but to uproot the several-thousand-year-old forms of social life which contain us.

The way from Athens to Paris, and from Paris to Athens, will present a major interpretative task for Castoriadis's intellectual biographer. Certainly, those who know the more recent writings, *The Imaginary Institution of Society*, or *Crossroads in the Labyrinth*, or *Devant la Guerre* or *Domaines de l'homme* will puzzle over this early Castoriadis if they do not already know him. For although the *Imaginary Institution* in fact begins with the 1964/1965 text 'Marxism and Revolutionary Theory', that text already represents Castoriadis after Marxism, whereas these two volumes of political and social writings represent the Marxist phase. Elements of continuity, however, are equally evident. As early as 1946 Castoriadis anticipated the *sui generis* theory of Soviet-type societies, for example, in arguing that Soviet economies bore no resemblance to capitalist economies, even though there was a symmetry between their power relations, class relations where directors governed workers.

As I have suggested, this sense of domination and proletarian response is characteristic of Castoriadis's political writings, but is not merely a response. Castoriadis's views become clear in his own New Communist Manifesto, 'Socialism or Barbarism'. Here Castoriadis reasserts the centrality of class struggle: class struggle against capital, but also against the Gestapo and the Gulag. He privileges class struggle, not production; action, not system. He views the working class as the actor which takes on modernity's challenge of autonomy. And so he traces its outbreaks, from Poland to Hungary 1956, and, in the second volume, subtitled 'From the Workers' Struggle Against Bureaucracy to Revolution in the Age of Modern Capitalism' (1955–60) from wildcat strikes in Detroit to the shop stewards in Britain in the fifties. Along the way, Castoriadis analyses class power in the Soviet Union and the question of agrarian relations in the USSR, the issues of relative weight of the kulaks and the bureaucracy, the nature of the Yugoslavian bureaucracy and the colonial relations between the Soviet centre and satellites. He discusses the question of Stalinism, French Stalinism, and puts Sartre back in his place in joining the argument over *The Communists and Peace*, alongside Lefort, Merleau-Ponty and the very Ernest Mandel. His tongue is sharp; he will not bear fools gladly, an attitude which seems all the more admirable now, in our times, when so much paltry rubbish still passes for understanding. Sartre's apologies for Stalinism, Castoriadis pungently argues, show him for what he is: the prototype of the Modern Intellectual in the process of constructing, with the Materials of Reason, the Bridge of Opportunity across the Flood of History. This is not mere show of hurt, or pride. The issue, for Castoriadis, is that Sartre too happily views us as victims, and must therefore be obliged to sacrifice the kingdom of freedom for a Party (and a Stalinist party at that).

Now Castoriadis returns to the Marxism of the *Communist Manifesto*. The constant upheaval of modernity, for Castoriadis, is no absolute human tragedy, tragic though it may well be. The sorcerer's apprentice has a double apprenticeship to pass on to the proletariat: the working class is threatened and challenged by modernity. Regardless of what stance we today might take on this notion of working-class self-activity, the moral superiority of Castoriadis's argument is clear. His courage is equally clear in 'The Bureaucracy After the Death of Stalin'. While Western communists exhorted their Soviet heroes to sit on their bloodied hands, prognosticating endlessly over whether the *New*

York Times Khrushchev speech was a 'forgery' or not, Castoriadis was already three years earlier denouncing Stalinism for what it was. Yet the balance was always there, for Castoriadis has long refused the dualistic and simplistic morality of fellow-travelling. Thus we also find here texts such as the 1954 'Situation of Imperialism and Proletarian Perspectives', where Kautsky and Lenin are examined alongside the question of the Russo-American pursuit of world domination.

From the overall perspective of Castoriadis's work, however, the central text here is probably 'On the Content of Socialism', a three-part essay which stretches across these two volumes. As the world is unable to stop moving, so Castoriadis – unlike the Hegelian Trotskyists – is unable to stop thinking. 'On the Content of Socialism' charts this process, then later summarised and advanced on in 'Marxism and Revolutionary Theory'. The first to go, here, is Trotsky: the entire edifice of his thought is mythological. Once rid of the Trotskyist outlook, we see that Soviet society is in fact a class society, divided between bureaucracy and proletariat: a class society, but neither capitalist nor socialist. The content of what is not socialism elucidated, the problem then becomes postulative. Again, the idea of socialism for Castoriadis seems to spring from the *Communist Manifesto*, or rather from the historical movement which Marx and Engels there charted.

Along with the *Manifesto*'s motifs of movement, creation, threat and challenge, there is the maxim of the Workingmen's International: the working class can free itself only by achieving power for itself. Socialism, the self-institution of society, is then further explained in the second instalment, taking up these claims from 1955, two years later. Here Castoriadis argues that socialism aims at giving *meaning* to people's life and work, at enabling their freedom, creativity and personality. Viewed on the scale of everyday life, the ultimate problem of history becomes an everyday problem. Socialism is autonomy, people's conscious direction of their own lives. Capitalism, private or bureaucratic, is the ultimate negation of this autonomy, and its crisis stems from the fact that the system necessarily creates this drive toward autonomy, while simultaneously being compelled to suppress it. People ordinarily experience their own lives as something alien to them; but with these sentiments even Sartre would agree. The difference, for Castoriadis, is this: the creative faculties that people are not allowed to exercise on behalf of a social order which spurns them (and which they, in turn, spurn) are now utilised against that social order.

This excess, denied creativity for Castoriadis erupts in incidents which seek to instaurate socialism: Russia in 1917–18, Spain in 1936 Hungary in 1956. Castoriadis's vision, in 1957, was what today would be called 'workerist': as he observes, his views have some similarity with those of the Dutch council communist

Anton Pannekoek. He actually refers here to the 1950 Melbourne edition of Pannekoek's *Workers' Councils*. But is the vision that of council communism? Here lies the difference. For council communism, like syndicalism, is a labour utopia based on the ur-image of production. Castoriadis's image of the future, by contrast, is based on the value of autonomy, as it is realised and denied in the process of creation called history. If we think as Castoriadis does, the point then becomes that the workers council is an expression of the process; it is process with which he really identifies. Thus he argues, even here in 1957, that it is necessary to condemn any fetishism of the council form: 'The council is not a miraculous institution', as he puts it. Yet Castoriadis does, here, argue for the simplification of social organisation and for something like social transparency, in short he does seem to have in mind something like Pannekoek's imagined future, and absolutely not a Bolshevik barracks regime. In this connection, as I have mentioned, he privileges the place of work as an organisational site: but not only because it is the unit of production, rather because it has become the primary unit of social life for so many people. Collectivities based on common work, Castoriadis proposes, offer fertile soil for direct democracy – his own clear preference – just as the ancient city, or the democratic communities of free farmers in the United States of the nineteenth century, did in their time.

It would be interesting to know how Castoriadis would couch his views on these matters today. Given the rich and allusive nature of his writing and the breadth of his sense of traditions, Castoriadis consistently gives the sense of thinking more than he is able to say, especially in the practical context of the deadlines and production schedules of the life of a small journal. Thus he alludes, on one occasion, to the vanity of socialist constitution-making, and may well be thinking of the Webbs' oddity, *The Constitution for the Socialist Commonwealth of Great Britain*. But beyond such arcane fantasies as those of the Webbs, what of law? and what of constitution-*making* as one act of instauration? Or again, on at least one occasion, Castoriadis discusses the idea of a federation of workers' councils and the institution of a central assembly of councils and a government of councils: what would he say, now, of the tentative revival of the guild socialist idea in Britain? of the new enthusiasms for G.D.H. Cole, and for pluralism?

One issue that does become clear from Castoriadis's project is his own romanticism, and with it, his hostility to administrative reductions of politics. As he puts it in 'Modern Capitalism and Revolution' the objectivistic view of the economy and history can only lead to bureaucratic politics, whether reformist or Stalinist. Rejecting the analysis of *Capital* Volume I as objectivistic and denying the principle of class struggle which Marx had earlier espoused,

Castoriadis equally rejects the circumscription of freedom by necessity in *Capital* Volume III. The first task of socialism ought, in this view, be to tackle the so-called 'realm of necessity' itself, to transform the very nature of work. The problem, according to Castoriadis, is to put poetry into work, for strictly speaking, poetry means creation. 'Production' is not something negative that has to be limited as much as possible for mankind to fulfil itself in its leisure. The point is not to attach a leisure backyard to the prison house of industry. The instauration of autonomy, for Castoriadis, must also, and primarily, be the instauration of autonomy in work.

Clearly Castoriadis's romanticism looks simultaneously forward and back; it is as though Castoriadis views Athens through the prism of creation in the *Communist Manifesto*. Castoriadis simultaneously seems to long for a lost, and desirable past, and for a future which is possible, yet elusive. His romanticism is thus neither simply that of, say, John Ruskin or William Morris, but nor is it that of futurism, or of his old teacher, Leon Trotsky. Here I would take issue with the interpretation of Lefort and Castoriadis offered by Peter Murphy, reviewing Lefort's *Political Forms of Modern Society* in the previous issue of *Thesis Eleven*. Murphy's brilliant essay rightly reminds us of the connection, canvassed here too, between Trotsky and Castoriadis, and on the whole I would certainly agree that there is no such thing as a post-Trotskyist, there are only Trotskyists, whatever they these days choose to call themselves. But Castoriadis, as I have argued, is something of a special case, to put it mildly. I do not mean by this to suggest that the relationship between Trotsky and Castoriadis is insignificant. The vital connection, however, in my view is that between Castoriadis and Marx. Whatever Castoriadis owes to Trotsky, he does not take on the Faustian futurism of *Literature and Revolution*.

Castoriadis's politics are not those of Permanent Revolution in life, they are those of the imagination, witnessed in recurring references to Marx's passage in *Capital* Volume I on architects and bees. Castoriadis's philosophical anthropology is not that of *homo faber*, but that of *l'homme imaginaire*. In this context, the striving to autonomy can as well be conceived as a radicalised Kantian imperative as it can a Faustian urge to change for its own sake.

Does Castoriadis in fact commit himself to a politics of endless change, change on change, in an onslaught against order, stability, tradition? I think not, because tradition, too, matters for Castoriadis. Here I think of an image used by Castoriadis in his 1974 'Reflections on "Rationality" and "Development"' published earlier in this journal. In this text Castoriadis remembers that, in the country of his birth, the generation of his grandparents had heard nothing of long-term planning, of 'externalities' of the continental drift or the expansion of the Universe and yet, even into their old age, they continued to plant olive trees and cypresses, without considering costs or returns. For they knew that they would die, and that they should leave the earth in good order for those who would come after them, perhaps simply for the earth itself. They knew that whatever 'power' they had at their disposal would only produce beneficial results if they obeyed the seasons, paid heed to the winds and respected the unpredictable Mediterranean, if they pruned the trees at the right moment and allowed the year's vintage sufficient time to mature.

Clearly this story suggests something about Castoriadis, too, and his own biography. Castoriadis, too, sits and ponders, listens and argues, lives in order but laments the repressive effects of the existing social order, and its imaginary order. Unlike Faust, or Trotsky, he does not exhort us to remould the planet; he is aghast by those who would, and do. Yet the sense of the potential in humanity, not in 'genius', but in individuals, remains.

And this is why, finally, Castoriadis is also necessarily witty. His humour is no mere embellishment: his sarcasm rests on this sense of hope, and its fragile expression in everyday life, where things can be counted on to go wrong, where idiots will always be in charge. Here again there is some distance between him and the rationalist Trotsky, who was never exactly a barrel of laughs. But Castoriadis is no clown. He is rather more the jester, who sits on the edge of the stage ridiculing the unfolding events, mediating between world history and us, in the audience, showing us how *Weltgeschichte ist Weltgericht*, and edifying us in the process, elucidating the events and the process we watch, throwing up his hands at it all and yet knowing, also, when to be silent: when not to laugh, but to cry, and to understand. So it is fitting that Castoriadis offers no solution, no Book, and in his understanding no Theory. People make their own history, even if they do not make it very 'well'. As he concludes in 'Modern Capitalism and Revolution', the 1960/61 text which closes the second volume of these writings, entire populations are now caught up in a vast movement of privatisation; everyone takes care of their own problems, and thus the affairs of society as a whole elude us. To put it in other terms, there is too much Freud in Castoriadis for hlm to be anything like Faust the Developer.

For Castoriadis, the pre-rational – not the irrational – is the category related to rationality. As he remarked in 'Marx Today', an interview published in these pages in 1984, people need certainties, need psychological and intellectual security; they consequently tend to abdicate the task of thinking for themselves and to entrust it to others. More, we could add today, the age of insecurity seems to generate a need for depressive and hopeless sociology, whether it be that of Althusser or Foucault. So long as we continue to bemoan our pathetic status as universal victims, we shall be so and too often we will be comfortable victims, at that. As Castoriadis says, he offers no Good News concerning the Promised

Land glimmering on the horizon, no Book to exempt us from having to seek the truth for ourselves. What Castoriadis does offer is a worldly hope, and a project, no Book but these books, these texts and others by way of a challenge, that we ourselves should seek out our own autonomy.

CHAPTER 19

Budapest Central: Agnes Heller's *Theory of Modernity* (2003)

Agnes Heller's work has long been caught up with the idea of History and history, histories, the big world pictures and also the small personal stories which run alongside and under their hypostatised versions in the politics of state or in popular culture and its mythologies. Modernity, or the modern, is the other big theme in Heller's work, this again with the matching emphasis on the experience of modernity and its core value of contingency. Together with this enthusiasm for the value of contingency, Heller insists on the necessity of pluralism. Having learned her Marxism from Lukács, as Weberian-Marxism, Heller's theory has always had Marx as its guide, even as her personal project becomes detached from Marx after *The Theory of Need in Marx*.[1] The angel of history who persistently shadows her work into the more recent period, however, is that of Weber. Weber's spirit is closer to that of our own times, and his perspectivism and methodological pluralism better reflect postmodern sensibilities, a life after high modernism, after Fordism, after the big dreams and nightmares of totalitarianism.

The best statement of this methodological pluralism in Heller's work in its sociological form came in 1983, with the publication of the programmatic Fehér-Heller statement 'Class, Democracy, Modernity', in *Eastern Left, Western Left*. Marx's temptation is to reduce modernity to capitalism, to sidestep civil society and to leave the state in the background, as epiphenomena. Fehér and Heller, in the 1983 text, begin rather with the Weberian-Marxism ambit, that modernity is the period and the region in which capitalism, industrialisation and democracy appear simultaneously, reacting to, reinforcing, complementing and checking each other.[2] This formulation was a theoretical anticipation of the projects now collectively assembled, twenty years later, under the categories which refer to alternative or multiple modernities. America is not the only modernity (or capitalism, or empire) on this thinking. The very same year[3] Fehér and Heller together with György Markus published their remarkable analysis of Soviet-type modernity in *Dictatorship Over Needs*. Over

---

1   Heller 1976.
2   Fehér and Heller 1987a, p. 201.
3   Fehér and Heller 1983.

the following years, Zygmunt Bauman[4] published *Modernity and the Holocaust* and Jeffrey Herf[5] published *Reactionary Modernism*, and the species of German totalitarian modernity were on the map alongside the Soviet experience. In this period of their Australian sojourn, the Hungarians also came to know something of this lazy or accidental modernity. Having begun in a small country, in Hungary, and travelled via another, in the antipodes, Fehér and Heller's next step was to America, to New York, to the centre of the web, to the aura left by Hannah Arendt at the New School. The books continued, personal instalments in a personal theory. Their reception was never spectacular; there was no choreographed spectacle, no A-list book launches of glitterati; there was always more work to do, commuting between New York and Budapest.

A Theory of Modernity came in under the radar.[6] Heller's reception in the centres has always been marginal. Fifteen years spent teaching in Manhattan has not shifted this – perhaps because she changes her mind? Or perhaps because she happily goes her own way. She does not seek a school, or to establish a constituency. As Heller puts it in opening *A Theory of Modernity*, it is entirely possible that the self-same author will devise more than one theory of modernity in a lifetime. The pretexts exist, as in the 1983 essay 'Class, Modernity, Democracy', as do the post-texts, like *The Three Logics of Modernity*.[7] As Heller observes, *A Theory of Modernity* can also be read as the closing frame of a trilogy, which began with *A Theory of History*[8] and had *A Philosophy of History in Fragments*[9] as its interval. The formal difference between the first two volumes is striking, not least in voice. *A Theory of History*, ironically, is closer to traditional philosophy of history, while the *Fragments* book shifts away from the more authoritative tone of historiography towards the fictive which ends in *An Ethics of Personality* with imaginary letters between imaginary relatives.[10] At a different level, the two earlier books could be incorporated conceptually, as universal and particular, the fragment.

One point of consistency across Heller's theory, however, lies in its attention to the everyday. Heller's is not merely a sociology of modernity, or, if it is, it includes a sociology of modernity as everyday life. Modernity has its

---

4   Bauman 1989.
5   Herf 1986.
6   Heller, 1999
7   Heller 2001.
8   Á. Heller 1982a.
9   Heller 1993.
10   Heller 1996.

dynamics, at higher levels of abstraction, from rationalisation to commodification and differentiation, but it is mediated by the level of experience. Heller's
own encounter with modernity, or modernities has been extraordinary, and yet
common – from Budapest to Auschwitz, to the Hungarian version of communism, through to exile in Australia, hope in America, and the entirely unexpected
return to Budapest after the fall of Communism. Through all this, the quality of insight in Heller's work depends on intuition, and experience counts as
much as insight or intellect. Agnes Heller therefore sets out, not to survey other
peoples' theories of modernity, but to generate a personal theory that will nevertheless have some universalistic claims. Even the biggest theoretical claims,
here, are personal, for the presence of Marx persists, as does the ghost of Weber
via Lukács, where it all began, in Budapest all those years ago. Marx recedes;
Weber persists because of the breadth of his frame of reference, and because
attitudinally he was the first swallow of the postmodern, identified more conventionally into the 80s with the figure of Nietzsche, even more fashionably
with Heidegger.

In my recollection of the time we spent together in Melbourne over the years
from 1978–86, it was Ferenc Fehér who prompted the heightened sense of
being-after. Here the postmodern was not a project, but a condition, or a sensibility. Or to use the language Heller uses in *A Theory of Modernity*, it is a matter
of perspective. Heller presents this book as a theory of modernity from a postmodern perspective. Much of what passes for postmodern, in comparison, is
actually closer to the perspective we call modernist, as in the mantra 'all that is
solid'. Postmodernity is not the stage that comes after modernity. It is modern.
Modernism is also part of the postmodern, even though modernist modernity
cannot regain its absolute self-confidence. Modernist modernity was locomotive; its image of transience, such as it was, was the railway station. The residual
traditionalism of this earlier modernism lay in its hesitance to embrace motion
fully, and in its use of the future as a horizon or destination beyond rather than
a present of *Jetztzeit*. Some of these future horizons were awful. The locomotive breath pushed its victims to Auschwitz and to the Gulag. Our postmoderns,
in comparison, accept life on the railway station, this perhaps especially in
Europe; in America, in comparison, the poor stick with Greyhound, the tourists in the airport terminals. Whatever the form of propulsion, today, the future
is closer, ever unknown with Heller. We now live on Budapest Central. Yet the
moral implication of living in this transience is not bad; it implies responsibility for the present, rather than the abstract and always potentially dangerous
commitment to the distant future of utopia or dystopia. This is an ethics of
responsibility, or care, rather than of ultimate ends.

Marx was the locomotive of classical theory, Trotsky his great historic inheritor. Weber was too melancholic for this, seeking respite rather in Ascona, while Hegel stays settled in the old Weimar. Marx lived up to his own expectations in at least one sense – he was the most revolutionary of theorists, ultimately the advocate of both technology and redemption. Modernity, here defined as capitalism, is dynamic and future oriented. Marx cannot finally disentangle the goal of human autonomy from the drive to rational mastery. If Romanticism and Enlightenment are the two faces of modernity, then it is Marx who manages most powerfully to wear both of these masks. This is why Marx is so central for us, as Castoriadis showed, and why he remains so inseparably bound to the Promethean spirit, too close to the gods for us as mere mortals.

Now we are a world after Marx. Modernity is autopoetic, and functional – this much of Luhmann is retained by Heller. We move, we choose or are forced to move, to fulfil or to fail in our destinies, not to follow the prescriptions of our birth. We retain this sense of romantic action even as we suffer under the weight of the forces we call structures. This is precisely what we call contingency, and it is central to Heller's thinking, which is at least as much a philosophy of experience as it is a sociology of action. We make ourselves; in this sense we choose ourselves, however successfully. The world moves, and we also move it.

Yet this theory of action occurs within the theory of modernity and its logics or dynamics. Heller's is not a naïve argument; but it refuses that kind of victim thinking which runs through from Rousseau, where we can only ever be creatures of our circumstances. Heller now suggests that there are three logics of modernity: the logic of technology, the logic of the functional allocation of social positions, and the logic of political power. Modernity is best seen not as a homogenised or totalised whole, but as a fragmented world of some open, but not unlimited, possibilities. These logics are plural, and pluralising. Ours is neither the world of the iron cage, nor of hopeless globalisation. These three logics of modernity can work together, or in tension; they need carriers, or agents.

It is not technology, but mentality or imagination that enframes. Yet if the first logic of modernity is typically indicated by the word technology, the second logic refers to markets, labour markets, and money, all the ingredients of *Gesellschaft*. This is the point at which romantics come out in a rash, for they compare not the old world and the new, but the new and an (old) ideal, that of *Gemeinschaft*. Merit and meritocracy may not work, but it is a better (more modern) guide than the value of mindless tradition here. Monetisation frees people from personal dependency. Monetisation may not be very dignified, but it does expand the realm of freedom. Heller's shadow thinker as sociologist here, then, is neither Marx nor Tönnies, but Simmel. Her philosophical *döppelganger* is Kierkegaard. Nor does this sensibility then mean that societies like ours can be equal, or satisfied, or dispense with alienation, neither the reality nor the concept. The rich do not sleep on Budapest Central. But we still have to hold modernity to its promise, of democracy and freedom. For, to repeat Heller's is not a naïve sociology, even if its concern is to identify room to manoeuvre. Nor is it a sociology of action, waiting for the next social movement. Its optimism is more immediate and anthropological. The world moves, the big world moves, but so do the smaller worlds we inhabit. Contingency depends here, less on technological necessity than on historical imagination, positive or negative. Liberal democratic modernity offers more room to move than the alternative modernities of fascism or communism, because of the tension built into its first two terms. The main value of liberation is freedom; for democracy, equality is the highest value. Power and democracy are in constant tension.

The mood in which Heller's theory of modernity is offered is positive, and open. Its frame, the logics of modernity and its institutional relations, foreground the immediacy of personal lifeworlds, home, place, things. She closes *A Theory of Modernity* with an opening, for it is, in this way of thinking, easier to answer questions than to leave them open. The last lines read as follows: 'Postscript: perhaps I have answered too many questions – more than I should have. If this is so, please re-translate my answers into so many new questions'.[11] Heller's is a theory of modernity based on democratic personality.

Which might return us, finally, to the question of the relative marginality of her work. Perhaps the problem with most mainstream critical theory is that it appeals because it combines the appearance of an immediately democratic or mimetic attraction ('here, you can deconstruct yourself') with the romantic gloom characteristic of our time ('nothing will change, it can only get worse', for the others at least). The challenge of Heller's work, in contrast, is after all closer to the spirit of Enlightenment and the real strength of its call, not only to think for yourself but to be, to act as yourself. This is a big ask. The call to autonomy is not easily heard in the Babel of noisier theorists.

Tucked away in a footnote, Heller's *Theory of Modernity* also casts out a line to its own solitude:

> It is not contingent which authors and works become 'famous', or prescribed reading, or themes for conferences, and quoted many times; many authors are neither worse nor less interesting than those who have 'made

---

11   Heller 1999, p. 235.

it', and yet they remain entirely unknown, and rarely published. It becomes important, for example, where one happens to be born. A man or woman who is born in Paris has a thousand times greater opportunity to become prescribed reading than a person born in Australia. Whom one knows, who is quoting someone, and who meets whom (by accident) are also important factors of selection.[12]

Budapest Central has more than one centre, just as does the railway system of Melbourne or New York. Heller's message is like the song of the metro busker, the chance encounter with the troubadour that makes you see the world differently, even if just for a moment, as a new line of vision opens up. Everyday life has its own epiphanies. If you're in the wrong centre, you'll risk missing it, or hearing its echoes at a distance. You can walk on; you might pause, read the book, imbibe the spirit of this most grateful commuter of modernities. There are crossroads in the underground, and not only in the labyrinth; there are exits and arrivals, even after Auschwitz. There is the present. There is the gift.

---

12   (Heller, 1999, p. 283 n. 19)

CHAPTER 20

Agnes Heller's Theory of Modernity (2009)

For Agnes, with affection

∵

Over the last twenty years there has been a sea-change for radicals, and a radical semantic shift with it. These days everybody talks about modernity. Modernity includes capitalism, but is not exhausted by it. Sometimes we call our moment postmodern, though no longer with much enthusiasm, more as a statement of fact or an attitude. But then, twenty years ago, the key signifier was capitalism. This indicated the residual power of Marxism, however radical. For period Marxism, into the eighties, all social problems were structural symptoms of the crisis of capitalism.

These days, we are back or forward with Weber, who understood full well that modernity was our fate and that capitalism was its most fateful force. This Weber, via Lukács, was brought back to us by thinkers like Agnes Heller. Heller's contribution to rethinking modernity as modernity has not been alone, but it has been vitally influential without gaining much formal recognition for its influence. The fact that we now routinely speak of being modern or culturally postmodern owes a great deal to her work.

But let us begin by stepping back, or to the side. For there were obviously others involved, and one other in particular: Heller's life-partner, Ferenc Fehér. Agnes Heller's vast project includes fascinating work on the emotional division of labor between the sexes. The relationship between her perspective and Fehér's is bound to be complex, but it is tempting to say as a first characterisation that Heller focuses on the bright side of modernity and Fehér on the dark side. Certainly a strong motif in Heller's work is that we 'choose ourselves', whereas Fehér's temper is more fateful, as in his extraordinary essay 'In the Bestiarium'.[1]

Fehér and Heller wrote together and separately. One of the key essays to be discussed here, 'Class, Modernity, Democracy',[2] was collaborative. Another

---

1 Fehér, 1987.
2 Fehér and Heller 1987a [1983].

key work in the critique of modernity, *Dictatorship Over Needs*,[3] was published together, as well as with György Márkus, though with separate and distinct contributions. Yet the methodological message of *Dictatorship Over Needs* is loud and clear: Soviet-type societies, neither capitalist nor socialist but *sui generis*, also offer a distinct path in modernity which is politically rather than economically constituted in its derivation. This is one theme upon which each of these thinkers emphatically agreed. Their contributions are written by each independently of the other, though sometimes the hand is hard to tell.

To set the mood, consider the essay by Fehér entitled 'The Status of Postmodernity'. Heller views the sociological character of the diagnosis of modernity as uncontroversial, an emblem of even the most ordinary empirical sociology. Fehér suggests that the postmodern, in contrast, is neither a historical period nor a trend with well-defined characteristics. Postmodernity, he says, is the private, collective time and space, within the wider time and space of modernity, delineated by those who have problems with or queries addressed to modernity and artistic modernism; by those who want to take it to task, and by those who want to make an inventory of modernity's achievements as well as its unresolved dilemmas.[4] The postmodern pluralises spaces and temporalities; it evokes the sense of 'being after'.

Twenty-five years after the postmodern controversy, Heller's response is historical or at least situational. Postmodernism is a kind of *cause célèbre* into the eighties; its progressive style and avant-garde self-consciousness are entirely reminiscent of early modernism's self-importance.[5] Nevertheless, the remaining issue, after all the fuss has died down, is that the postmodern interpretation of modernity has replaced the modernist interpretation of modernity; that is, we now see ourselves differently than we did before. Perhaps we simply expect less, these days, than we did in the sixties.

Postmodern is also, therefore, post-Marx. Yet Marx remains central, as Heller acknowledges in 'Marx and Modernity',[6] though here Marx also acquires a fascinating intellectual travel companion: Niklas Luhmann. In this context, Heller volunteers seven theses on Marx (not eleven). Again, she takes modernity as an obvious challenge, the problem *par excellence* of contemporary social theory, which Marx manages remarkably to anticipate, though simultaneously to misconstrue. Modernity is dynamic and future-oriented; economic expansion and industrialisation comprise its main features, though it is also rationalised

---

3 Fehér and Heller and Markus 1983.
4 Fehér 1991.
5 Heller 2007.
6 Heller 1984a.

and functionalist in character. Science, rather than religion, becomes the basis of the accumulation of knowledge. Traditional customs and habits are dismantled, uncloaked, and traditional virtues are lost. Certain values become universalised, while canons of creation and interpretation dissolve and, finally, the concepts of 'right' and 'true' become pluralized.[7]

Heller weaves her theses around these claims. Marx was indeed a modernist; this not least because he did not entirely identify industrial capitalism and the modern, for to equate these would be to leave out socialism. Industrialisation, in this Marx-contra-Marx view, is therefore logically a larger concept than capitalism; this is why, and how, capitalism self-revolutionises itself into communism in Marx's later worldview. At the same time, however, Marx's logic points backward as well as forward, for the image of the utopian society of direct producers precedes his diagnosis of capitalism as modernity.

Rationalisation, in contrast, we associate historically with Weber, though as Heller proposes, Marx anticipated this as well, which explains Lukács's magical synthesis of the two streams in *History and Class Consciousness*.[8] In Marx's case, the prime carrier of the process of rationalisation is factory labour. Functionalism enters as the principle of economic organisation shifts from status to function performed, which is also to say that capitalist classes are mutually constitutive; this is why *Das Kapital*, despite its author's best intentions explains not revolution but reproduction. Revolution in *Das Kapital* is a conceptual trick, which covers over the later realisation (as in Hannah Arendt) that Marx's essential failure was to develop a theory of politics at all.

Luhmann plays the role of the joker in this story, for he is anti-Marxist rather than Marxist, yet through him, Marx also becomes a systems-theorist. The joke is on Marx, for Luhmann. Not only class or economy but all of culture is functionalised. Marx unwittingly substitutes a modern social theory for a premodern, transitory one; but this science then remains, all revolutionary claims to the contrary notwithstanding.[9]

The text which lies behind these claims is the most apparently systematic essay ever published by Fehér and Heller, 'Class, Modernity, Democracy', the style of which even reads like a scientific manifesto. This is the place where Fehér and Heller open up the idea that modernity is best understood as a period and region characterised by three interlocking logics, those of capitalism, industrialisation and democracy.[10] Capitalism might expand throughout

---

7   Heller 1984a, pp. 44–5.
8   Lukács 1971 [1923].
9   Heller 1984a, p. 45.
10   Fehér and Heller 1987a, p. 201.

modernity, but this historical expansion could never be conceptually rendered as primary or all-explanatory. Capitalism struggles with democracy, and the logic of industrial expansion does not always coincide with the private prerogatives of capital. The result is that

> In our view, modernity is a dynamic (in other words, unstable) coexistence of these different trends, in proportions varying from one society to the other, rarely in harmony, rather in more or less constant collision. Any radical position which embarks on explaining the vast period called modernity has to account for all three factors and their interrelations. A monocausal explanation of any kind is either a self-delusion or an ideology.[11]

Like capitalism, Marx is therefore placed within modernity, not the other way around. Moreover, viewed in terms of historical sociology, the theorem anticipates the more recent project of alternative or multiple modernities; for again, the experience of the Soviet Union has to be placed within this conceptual constellation, as does the disaster of Nazi modernity – democracy, in both cases, being submerged by particular logics of industrialisation, politics by anti-politics.

Fifteen years later Heller returns to these themes, though of course they are also constant for her. Having written various instalments of theory, *A Theory of Instincts*, *A Theory of Feelings*, and *A Theory of History*, she then publishes *A Theory of Modernity* in 1999.[12] The mood has changed since the pioneering 1983 essay; the addressee has changed, and the voice has become more fully postmodern, this signalled nowhere better than in the lines which close the book: 'Postscript: perhaps I have answered too many questions – more than I should have. If this is so, please re-translate my answers into so many new questions'.[13]

Heller presents her book as a personal theory, one theory of modernity among others. It is a generous, rather than demanding book, though all Heller's writing also makes its demands on us as readers (for postmoderns in a hurry, a condensed essay version of its core theses appears in *Thesis Eleven* 75, 2003). The approach is autobiographical as well as philosophical, but it is also intuitive. The experience of totalitarianism is central to it. Heller chooses three primary interlocutors: Hegel, Marx and Weber. Weber appears here as the first

---

11   Fehér and Heller 1987a, p. 202.
12   Beilharz 2003.
13   Heller 1999, p. 235.

swallow of the postmodern trend, this even though he is also more fully modern than either Hegel or Marx. In her self-understanding, this book can also be seen as the last instalment of a trilogy, the earlier volumes of which were *A Theory of History* and *A Philosophy of History in Fragments*. Yet this trilogy only appears so after the fact. As she explains here, the destiny of modernity became the major shared theoretical concern in her collaboration with Fehér. Fehér's early death put an end to other plans, which were only to be revived in the middle nineties due to the enthusiasm of others for it, in Caracas, in Pisa, and in New York. So there emerged a need for the settling of accounts. Heller's voice here is firm, well-considered, but also paradoxical. Consider this:

> Postmodernity is not a stage that comes after modernity, it is not the retrieval of modernity – it is modern. More precisely, the postmodern perspective could perhaps best be described as the self-reflective consciousness of modernity itself. It is a kind of modernity that knows itself in a Socratic way. For it (also) knows that it knows very little, if anything at all.[14]

Marx's utopia, now, is simply too far away. For high modernism legitimated modernity with the future, not the future of the present but of a distant future allegedly incipient in modernity itself from its gestation onwards. The result of this pursuit of Heaven, however, was the achievement of Hell.[15] So here, the spirit of Kierkegaard hovers, not the Owl of Minerva – if modern thinking is paradoxical, then postmodern thinking more so.

Yet the path of the narrative is also historical, with Hegel as the spirit of the eighteenth century, Marx as the dream of the nineteenth, and Weber as the sober anticipation of the twentieth century. Now Heller revisits the subject matter of her earlier essay on Marx and modernity. 'I will sum up Marx's modernist concept of modernity (chiefly capitalism) in eight theses ...'.[16] The same motifs follow: modernity is dynamic and future-oriented, rationalised, functionalist, scientised, detraditionalised, canons of creation and interpretation erode, concepts of right and true are pluralised. Thesis 8 is new: 'The modern world is inscrutable, and human existence is contingent'.[17] Commodity fetishism, here, exemplifies the modern experience of disorientation; the newly disenchanted world is simultaneously re-enchanted. Marx is a systems-

---

14   Heller 1999, p. 4.
15   Heller 1999, p. 81.
16   Heller 1999, p. 31.
17   Heller 1999, p. 33.

theorist after all. Weber, in comparison, pluralises worldviews and fates – we are fated to choose our own gods, history does nothing for us. The competing logics of modernity, like the Weberian value spheres, cannot be reduced to one another. Postmodern or contemporary creatures understand themselves as visitors in a place and time of which they know little and where they can only do small things.[18] Of course, this is confessional, too; this is where Agnes Heller stands, and we with her.

A Theory of Modernity proceeds to detail not only the sensibility of modernity but also its sense. Heller now distinguishes between the *dynamics of modernity* and the *modern social arrangement*.[19] The dynamics of modernity precede the epoch; they reach back to Athens. They are reframed by Enlightenment and romanticism, each of which also needs its other. Marx's infamous 'all that is solid melts into air' signals the impossible dream of Enlightenment, present or perhaps future alone, without past. For romanticism, in contrast, not all that is solid melts. Life is not a technological problem to be solved: it needs to be lived.[20] The dynamics of modernity are both destructive and self-destructive at the same time.

The dominant modern social arrangement, in this context, is the everchanging status quo. The modern social arrangement includes the distribution of social positions, the social division of labour, and so on. This is Luhmann's distinction, though not only his, between stratified and functionalist social models. Stratified societies are governed by prescriptive status models – I am my father's son, my mother's daughter, bound by the time and place of my birth. The modern social arrangement, in contrast, is performative; presidents are not, normally, begot by presidents. Modernities, consequently, are mixed; some will have the formal institutions of modernity without the dynamics; but at the same time, there will never be any 'perfect modernity'.[21]

Heller distinguishes between three logics of modernity: the logic of technology, the logic of the functional allocation of social positions, and the logic of political power. This is Heller's personal perspective: modernity is not to be seen as a homogenised or totalised whole, but as a fragmented world of some open but not unlimited possibilities. Further, these logics do not operate like natural forces. They develop because they are developed by historical actors or agents.[22] Thus, for example, the essence of technology is not technological. It

---

18   Heller 1999, p. 39.
19   Heller 1999, Ch. 3.
20   Heller 1999, pp. 44–5.
21   Heller 1999, p. 52.
22   Heller 1999, p. 67.

does not reside in the machine, in the thing. It resides in the way people think and operate.[23] But unlike Heidegger, Heller will not totalise this view.

For Heller, the one single dominant imaginary institution of world explanation in modernity is not technology but science. Technology elevates science to its position of dominance, not the other way around. But there is also more than one imaginary institution in the modern world.[24] Technological imagination, for example, coincides in modernity with historical imagination.

Heller's second developmental logic of modernity encompasses the logic of the division of social position, functions and wealth. It could also be called the logic of civil society. It includes the idea of modernity; however, this idea is never attained. Moreover, it depends on the contestation of justice. At this point, Heller takes a sideways glance at Soviet-type modernities. Soviet-type modernity functionalises social arrangements, yet it outlaws the contestation of justice. As a result, the three logics of modernity present in Soviet-type societies behave not just differently, but differ essentially from the three logics under liberal democracies.[25] Liberal democracies have a greater capacity for survival because they couple the market with private law and human rights. Market, here, indicates in the first instance the labour market. The labour market means that it is in the market that men and women allocate themselves by choosing or finding a place in the hierarchically structured institution.[26]

With Simmel, now against Marx, Heller proposes that monetarisation has contributed essentially to the destruction of the pre-modern, prescriptive social arrangement. Modernisation rests on monetarisation. This is one key difference setting apart European and American models of modernity. Europe's stronger residual pre-capitalist traditions explain both the welfarism of its state institutions and the persistence of some leftovers of socialist language. Romantics, of course, abhor this development to monetarisation. The limit of their perspective is in its holiness – in its presumption that the point of comparison is not past and present, but present and imaginary future, or utopia,[27] The upside of the situation is equally apparent. Monetarisation frees men and women from personal dependency. Monetarisation is no guarantee of dignity, but it does offer increased freedom.[28]

---

23   Heller 1999, p. 69.
24   Heller 1999, p. 70.
25   Heller 1999, p. 83.
26   Heller 1999, p. 84.
27   Heller 1999, p. 86.
28   Heller 1999, p. 87.

Yet some threads of the argument connect us to the past, and so Heller persists in arguing that at the same time monetarisation is accompanied by the homogenisation of needs structured into 'alienated' needs. She writes:

> I use the Marxian expression of 'alienated' needs because I find it fitting. Needs are alienated if they are superimposed on men and women who then become obsessive, working as a kind of compulsion. Systems of needs sold by the media and forms of life are also superimposed on the single person; they become effective through imitation.[29]

More free than before, but never yet quite free, we are bound to remain dissatisfied. The members of the underclasses are not the only citizens who carry the weight of social domination and oppression, but they are the most significant.[30] Modernity never reaches perfection or an equilibrium of social inclusion.

Enter the third logic of modernity: political power, or domination. The state forms of modernity include totalitarianism, liberalism, and modern democracy. Bolshevism does not exhaust totalitarianism, but pioneers it. The secret of the totalitarian state is the totalitarian party, in turn pioneered by Lenin.[31] Totalitarianism is based on the prohibition of pluralism; this is its organising principle. The modernity of totalitarianism is evident in this, but also in its basis in modern technology. German fascism, and to a lesser practical extent Soviet communism, are clearly entwined by the technological capacity and will-to-power of modernity.

> Yet, it is not the factual employment of technological devices but the mobilisation of technological imagination that essentially matters. Gas chambers are not employed because they are available just like guns, but because their employment appears as a case of problem solving.[32]

Nazism specialises in the rational pursuit of efficiency in murder. 'The question is the productivity of mass murder, the per capita expenditure (in money and effort) of the task of murder'.[33] This technological problem which the Nazis set themselves first had to be set, and this task was not set by the technological

---

29   Heller 1999, p. 90.
30   Heller 1999, p. 93.
31   Heller 1999, p. 104.
32   Heller 1999, p. 106.
33   Heller 1999, p. 106.

imagination. The problem here becomes a technological problem as the result of translation through an ideological system, in this case that of Nazi ideology.

Modern democracy seeks to limit, or actually succeeds in limiting totalitarian possibilities because it combines majority rule and representation, even if all states contain totalitarian capacities at the very same time. The main value of liberalism is freedom; the main value of democracy, in contrast, is equality.[34] Modern liberal democracies, as the juxtaposition implies, rest on a struggle or tension between the two principles. There is simultaneously an ongoing war between the legal and illegal use of violence. In this context, Heller turns to the discussion of culture and civilisation.

Agnes Heller's contribution across a life's work probably deserves to be called philosophy rather than sociology, though its sociological dimension and sensibility is inescapable. This is perhaps one point of contrast between her work and that of Zygmunt Bauman, best known for his part in critical sociology. The connections between the two are apparent, though they are not entirely synchronised. The above-mentioned discussion of Nazism in *A Theory of Modernity* crosses over with and amplifies Bauman's *Modernity and the Holocaust*.[35] At this point of her text, Heller's path parallels that of Bauman's earlier *Culture and Praxis*.[36] Like Bauman, Heller identifies three concepts of culture: high culture, cultural discourse, and, following Markus, the anthropological concept of culture.[37] Modernity differs from other cultures or cultural formations in that it is omnivorous. Here Bauman is momentarily her interlocutor, especially with the ghostly image of the shift from gamekeeper to gardener and industrial farmer.[38] Yet for all the abundant legislators, there must also be interpreters. For all the omnivorous modernism, there must still be nostalgia, utopia, the sense that the future could indeed be different from the past.

The concept of civilisation also divides, this time into technological and moral dimensions; only here the system of reference is everyday life rather than abstraction. Here there is what Heller calls a 'pendular movement' between conformism and chaos. This pendular movement is also evident in historical judgment and historiographical controversy. Heller's example, unsurprisingly, is in the contested interpretations of Nazism or Bolshevism (though the former prevails). Two decades ago, according to Heller, technological imagination was identified as the major issue, this trend exemplified by Bauman's work. Now, in

---

34   Heller 1999, p. 109.
35   Bauman 1989.
36   Bauman 1973.
37   Heller 1999, Ch. 8.
38   Heller 1999, p. 143.

reverse trend, the 'historical imagination' explanation gathers influence once more. But alongside this, a new trend emerges, which emphasises the total contingency of the emergence of totalitarian states and their survival.[39]

Now Heller's book opens like a flower, to discuss time, space, place and home, justice, happiness, perfection, authenticity. So *A Theory of Modernity* closes with an ethics of personality. Happiness is elusive for moderns not least because it is subjective, yet remains ineffable. The elusive nature of happiness comes to be felt as a deficit. But the modern condition is, as Heller puts it, still the human condition.[40] With Kierkegaard, we have to choose ourselves, lest others choose on our behalf.

Perhaps this *is* a sociology, too, and not only a philosophy, and this not only because it evokes David Riesman's Weberian distinction between the inner-directed and outer-directed personalities who together make up *The Lonely Crowd*. Agnes Heller's is a philosophy, or sociology, of contingency, but it is not only that. Contingency occurs in time and place, and it is framed by traditional residues as well as by technological and historical imagination. Tucked away in a footnote at the end of the text we find the following thoughts, no doubt also framed by place, time, and circumstance, from Budapest to Melbourne to New York, and back to Budapest again.

> It is not contingent which authors and works become 'famous', or prescribed reading, or themes for conferences, and quoted many times; but it is entirely contingent which do not. There are at least ten times as many authors who are neither worse nor less interesting than those who have 'made it', and yet they remain entirely unknown, and rarely published. It becomes important, for example, where one happens to be born. A man or woman who is born in Paris has a thousand times greater opportunity to become prescribed reading than a person born in Australia. Whom one knows, who is quoting someone, and who meets whom (by accident) are also important factors of selection. And, in addition, it is often the case that the world famous too, are dancing, symbolically, just for one summer.[41]

Agnes Heller has danced for so many summers, in so many places and worlds, never to be idolised, never perhaps sufficiently fashionable for publishers and impresarios, too stubbornly independent, speaking in her own voice as well

---

39   Heller 1999, p. 161.
40   Heller 1999, p. 226.
41   Heller 1999, p. 283 n. 19.

as through those of her chosen interlocutors, Kierkegaard, Hegel, Marx, Weber, and the others, with Ferenc Fehér, and after him. She has always been marginal, in one sense or another; always self or inner-directed, yet so willing to share and with such a wealth of wisdom to convey. The dancer is the dance. Play on.

CHAPTER 21

Ferenc Fehér and Political Theory – Notes for a Biographer (1995)

Ferenc Fehér was a leading presence and a major thinker in the intellectual life of three continents. He was also, in particular, I would suggest, a pre-eminently political thinker. But how are we to make sense of his work and his legacy when it comes to politics? Let me begin with three assertions. First, Fehér deserves an intellectual biography, but this task will present a major challenge – for his was a life as dissident and pariah. He never became a star, and perhaps this was also dispositional; he disliked adulation and despised the cult of intellectuals which now so deeply saturates academic culture across the West. The second assertion follows on from the first. Agnes Heller deserves an intellectual biography. Or in other words, there are two different projects here and these two projects are separate but inseparable. Who writes the biography of Heller must also write that of Fehér and vice-versa. The most fruitful endeavour in biography in this case would likely be a collective biography, as in that of Leonard and Virginia Woolf.[1] The third assertion is related, but shifts, and returns to a reservation made earlier. Fehér's political life crosses over three vital and distinct moments: Budapest, Melbourne, New York and back, to where he began and where he died.

In this memorandum I want to sketch around these markers in order to suggest some of the central features and themes of Fehér's political theory. These are, then, little more than notes for the biographer whom Fehér deserves. By that virtue, these notes are also demands on any interested party. For my interpretative premise is that these connections are vital to placing Fehér's work. There is no understanding Fehér without thinking about Heller, and vice-versa; no real chance to understand Fehér's politics without placing it within those geographical shifts across cultures and boundaries and the cultural horizons that went with them.

---

1 See e.g. Alexander 1992.

1

The relation between Fehér's project and Heller's is not obvious. One way of opening this particular hermeneutical horizon would be as follows. Fehér and Heller together are philosophers or, if you prefer, theorists and critics of the human condition in modernity.[2] But whereas Heller's work (in English) consists in a Marxian phase followed by the development of a personal theory (of needs, everyday life, feelings, instincts, history and ethics), Fehér's work is essayistic, critical, sceptical, nagging, responsive. If we could view Heller's work as essentially an analysis (and sometimes a celebration) of the bright side of modernity, then Fehér's project might alternatively be seen as an attempt to plumb some of the depths of its dark side. And here one detects, also, differences of emphasis in the anthropological premises at work. Heller emphasises that, against all barriers, we choose ourselves. Although Fehér finds Freud and the traditions of psychoanalysis unattractive, his own work is nevertheless shadowed by the sense that we are also creatures who do evil, who betray each other, who are frail and who cannot help it. To evoke a different image, Heller somewhere summons up the themes of the famous Gauguin triptych, 'What are we? Where have we come from? Where are we going?', questions which I think Fehér would answer with perhaps more caution or circumspection or sense of reservation, for there is a sense of burden here, of Sisyphus perhaps more than Prometheus, or a preference for both over the figure of Faust. But there is also a bright side to this sensibility in Fehér, for he shares with Heller a sense that anthropology is ordinary, pedestrian and material as well as elevated and spiritual; a good deal of human activity goes into just putting food on the table, and this is nothing to be sneered at. Just holding life together, indeed, is a major commitment and accomplishment. In fact, this sense of modesty, and dignity, is a fundamental sub-stream in Fehér's thought, which leads him finally to a more positive assessment of post-communism than is found elsewhere on the Left because in his eyes at least now the scenario is more open: ordinary people will henceforth be allowed to make their own mistakes, in this sense at last to make their own history.

The device of bright side/dark side of modernity as a way of thinking Heller and Fehér is thus an opening, but no more. For Heller's thinking is also, as I have suggested, critical and sober, and Fehér does not fit the role of Adorno, say, as cultural pessimist. He is not a dark theorist, but a thinker who demands that we give warrant to the dark side. The biographer of Fehér (and Heller) will

---

2   Heller and Fehér 1988; Murphy 1988.

therefore need, I think, to address Heller's writings on the idea of an emotional division of labour, and he or she will need to puzzle over the dynamics of this particular collaboration or intellectual division of labour.[3] My advice to this biographer, then, would be to the effect that when it comes to *politics*, it is the presence of Heller which needs to be reckoned with in Fehér's work rather than, say, that of the looming figure of Lukács so evident in Fehér's work on aesthetics. To say this is also to summon up the figure of Marx, and here the echo is obvious.

Agnes Heller's work first became known in the English language as a theory of *needs*. As always, in the process of reception, the context was lost – *Theory of Need in Marx*.[4] As you look back through Fehér's political writings – back across the pages of *Thesis Eleven* into those brilliant essays which appeared in *Telos* – the presence of Karl Marx is striking, even, in retrospect, surprising. Budapest, we need to remind ourselves, was the moment of Marx-Renaissance, holding the regime against the claims of Marx: 'this is what you tell us is *socialism*?' The presence of Marx in Fehér's work is a constant, another important puzzle for our biographer to contemplate, for Marx, of course, was no specialist in politics (or in aesthetics, for that matter). But Marx was good at history, adept at irony, and skilled in the defence of freedom, all of which are leading motifs in Fehér's work. To put it more bluntly, Marx was no Jacobin; and, as I will suggest, it is indeed Jacobinism which becomes an important negative symbol for Fehér, whose primary enemy became those would-be redeemers of East and West, those who do not let ordinary people make their own mistakes, and deal with them.

Needs are a primary concern for Fehér. Needs-talk refers us inevitably to the priorities of the early Marx; to propositions concerning the primacy of suffering and the vitality of sensuous human activity. But the young Marx was also the most redemptive of all. More deeply immersed, perhaps, than Heller in the political lexicon and legacies and doublespeak of socialist traditions, Fehér's major contribution in this regard was to twist this Moebius strip over into the Soviet context. Now there emerged the idea of *Dictatorship over Needs*. The transposition seems obvious only in retrospect – dictatorship of/over the proletariat, dictatorship of ideas, dictatorship over needs. Fehér's first formulations on the subject appeared in *Telos* in 1978. 'The Dictatorship over Needs' is a characteristic Fehér intervention – short, dense, sparky, compressed. It is a quality of essay that stands alone, or with those parallel lightning attacks of Castoriadis.

3	Á. Heller 1982b.
4	Heller 1976.

Its themes are multiple, but several stand out. First, Fehér is evidently engaged in a process of deep puzzling over the sociology of intellectuals and political power. What Fehér increasingly came to identify as the problem of Jacobinism was an intellectual phenomenon. Without self-flagellation, Fehér raised here all those concerns which so many now identify with the French: worries about the logic of political representation, fears about those who claim to know the needs or interests of others, anxieties regarding the redemptive paranoia of those best identified not as enlighteners but as *rationalists*. Already the distinctions apparent in the workers' movement at the turn of the century generated concern: for while the empirical masses actually fought for formal democracy, the radical intellectuals already felt a secret contempt for that sham 'freedom'. Thus, Fehér's political concerns worked through the field associated with the names of Marx and Michels, Sorel and Bernstein, Kautsky and Trotsky, Lukács and Weber.

This was a proposition with a sociological result and anthropological premise. The sociological conclusion was with Marx, against Marx, *after* Marx: societies that came about as a result of anti-capitalist revolutions and in the wake of their military and political expansion are *political societies* – societies where politics dominates economics, at least up until crises in the manner of 1989. Fehér thus flipped over the analytical basis of all hitherto existing social-ist critique of Soviet-type societies, for which interpretation must follow the critique of capitalism – you read the polity off from the economy, not the other way around. What Fehér suggests here is a sense of political determin-ation which also has effects for Western liberal democracies. At least since Karl Polanyi's *The Great Transformation* (1945) it has been recognised that bourgeois states have also politically licensed distinct economic forms and practices, just as today they license processes of globalisation which are presented as neces-sity. To recognise the centrality of politics here, however, is also to indicate the presence in Fehér's thinking of that hermeneutical model of conversation which was his own. He wrote essays because he liked to talk, to respond, where necessary to disagree, and vocally. So that the point about reading a social form politically is also a dialogical one, one which acknowledges that understand-ings are perspectival, that it is less important to argue about where we begin to understand and more significant where, for the moment, we end up, how the horizons of world and text and experience are negotiated together.

The anthropological connection now also becomes more apparent. The problem with the politics of redemptive radicalism is that it rests upon the contempt of intellectuals for everyday life. The problem which Fehér locates in Jacobinism, but not in Marxian radicalism, lies in the arrogance of its ration-alism. Here, Fehér argues, we are confronted with the age-old dream of hyper-rationalistic social theory: the image of certainty, in politics, of the guaranteed society. The image is not only impossible, and outright dangerous, it is also patronising, for it avoids the frailty, the fallibility of humans *tout court*. Guaranteed society, in which dysfunctions resulting from people's 'empirical frailty' are ruled out, is based on a voluntaristic conception of freedom and a deep anthropological pessimism. This combination Fehér takes to be a defining characteristic of Jacobinism.

Fehér proceeded to elaborate these themes in the Fehér-Heller-Markus volume *Dictatorship over Needs* published in 1983. This book, I think, can deservedly be called the best *sui generis* of Soviet-type societies ever produced, even if it was a case subsequently thrown out of the world court of history. Neither simply capitalist nor meaningfully socialist, Soviet-type societies were an experience without precedent. The Budapest School is often, often unfairly, associated in the eyes of its enemies with that throwaway line of Lukács, that if the facts controvert my claims, 'so much the worse for the facts'. I remember one public exchange into the 1990s when a well-sharpened superior wit asked Fehér what now was the status of his analysis of the Soviet-type societies, which had ceased to exist. Fehér smiled, and announced that on this particular issue he was indeed very happy to have been wrong. These societies could not reproduce themselves; what was surprising was how long they actually got away with it. But it was also Fehér's belief, and hope, in spirit with Max Weber's advice to the young Lukács, that the passing of the Soviet phantom might again make it possible to argue for the politics of socialism in the West.

There were other, more general messages in *Dictatorship over Needs*. In rejecting the idea that Soviet experience was premodern, a throwback, the Hungarians now further pursued the question of the precise constitution of modernity itself. Obviously the historical phenomenon of modernity relied on and manipulated traditions. As in Freud, the past is always with us, as a shadow, only now collectively. This sensibility about history had two different correlatives. First, Fehér and Heller simultaneously published their brilliant prospectus, 'Class, Modernity, Democracy'.[5] The debate about the postmodern had exploded, and Fehér initially took it on in these two different registers, to do with the nature of modernity in the sociological sense and to do with aesthetic modernism. Second, Fehér's sense now of being culturally transplanted into the West increasingly meant that the audience was different than it had been in Budapest. Between 1978 and 1986 Fehér and Heller were working in Melbourne and in Canberra. Part of this experience produced an unappetising

---

5 Fehér and Heller 1987a.

rediscovery of that Jacobinism which was still alive and well in the West. In Budapest Fehér had sought to hold that regime against the claims of Marx, a discrepancy sufficient to induce laughter or mockery if not tears and anger. Now he confronted Western leftists who claimed radical credentials but often also sought, with however much sophistication, to defend those oppressive regimes. In this context – after Budapest, now in Australia – Fehér replaced the more specific concept of dictatorship over needs with the more general, the problem he called Jacobinism. For here, in the West, the redemptive radicals resurfaced, more Rousseau than Marx, ambitious for the prospects of human-kind but contemptuous of plebeian lives out in suburbia, with takeaways and television.

The lines of argument in Fehér's thinking clearly ran back to the concerns about needs and the first obsession with the image of equality, the levelling spirit already translated way back by Marx as 'primitive communism'. These orientations connected directly into those of *Dictatorship over Needs*: a book with an explicitly Western leftist addressee, and those of *Eastern Left, Western Left*.[6] Lenin, in other words, was not only a Russian. There were little Lenins all around, alongside aspirant Stalins and eloquent would-be heroic Bronsteins. Remember, Fehér was worried about anthropology, about the apparent rup-ture between good people and bad ends, about the hovering presence of evil and the magnetic lure of power, about the shadow of violence and terror which we pretend to be under control. Only a category as broad as Jacobinism could begin to capture the ubiquity of this modern phenomenon, indeed itself a flaw inscribed in the very heart of the modern project. To thus connect, again, the stories of the Russian Revolution to those of the French Revolution was also to link up politics and antipolitics and East and West. The cusp of political modernity, in this way, could be aligned through the figures or symbols of Robe-spierre and Lenin, Saint-Just and Trotsky.[7] Not for nothing did Fehér return so often to that infamous anthropological confession of Trotsky, lampooning poor Kautsky: that 'man' is a lazy animal, that violence is therefore the tool of pro-gress and civilisation and socialism, that all men can be as gods, but later, after the hyper-revolution.

Yet this was a socialist plea on Fehér's part, that humans could not be forced to be free, to be virtuous, but that they could nevertheless do better. The soci-ological supplement to this profoundly ethical sensibility was spelled out in the essay on 'Class, Democracy, Modernity'. There the core theorem was that

---

6   Fehér and Heller 1981, 1987b.
7   Fehér 1988.

the field called modernity consisted of at least three combined logics – those of capitalism, industrialisation and democracy. The experience of Soviet-type societies indicated the presence of the middle logic, that of industrialisation, along with some remnants or residuals of markets and the usual transparent claims to one-party democracy. Before the moral collapse of Western leftism, and prior to or coincidental with the radical enthusiasm of Western leftists for social movements as a substitute actor for the inert and consumptive proletariat, Fehér and Heller here also blew the whistle for democracy, perhaps the sole value with which socialists are now left. Heller had anticipated the slogan of radical democracy already in *A Radical Philosophy*.[8] Fehér's mood was apparently more cautious, more oriented to *realpolitik* than to philosophy, but the axiom was held in common – the idea of radical democracy was defensible not because it was realisable, rather because it was desirable, a choice of values in the world.

2

Somewhere around this point there occurs the shift to America, and to New York. If this was not exactly a reluctant move, neither was it excessively enthusiastic. The image of America was, as I recollect, quintessentially mixed for the Hungarians; the best and the worst of modernity, as some razor-sharp mind put it. Manhattan in some ways might be viewed as the condensation of that symbol; the New School and the Guggenheim, Columbia and the Metropolitan Museum along with the bombsites, real and metaphorical, the mole people and corpses on the street. Yet America is also, like Europe, an idea or better, a series of competing ideas, and it contains the three competing logics which Fehér and Heller had defined as fixative of modernity – capitalism, industrialism and democracy. The problem, of course, is that the last is in perpetual tension with the others, constricted and contained by the former. America is the land of democracy and money and democracy speaks in a different voice. Plainly its democratic claims were different to the norms and values which the Hungarians associated with the idea of a radical democracy. At the same time, this was the moment when Marx somehow became a more distant presence, and not for them alone by any means. Of course Marx had less resonance in America, where the dominant alternative voices were social democratic, liberal or communitarian and the American version of French theory was increasingly

---

8   Fehér and Heller 1984b.

replacing any lingering commitments to the leftover legacies of the Frankfurt School. And then the Berlin Wall came down, and the old Soviet Empire collapsed.

As elsewhere, then, in radical culture the dominant dates are symbolic – 1936, the Hungarian Revolution, 1968 – here, more for Prague than Paris; 1989. For Fehér and Heller, this transition also involved a renewed engagement with thinkers like Hannah Arendt and Alexis de Tocqueville, on the promises of locality, the stain of politics or the will-to-politics, and the ongoing tension between democracy and material culture. But 1989 meant first and foremost the promise of a return – a homecoming to Budapest, and a new moment of creation, symbolised best of all in the making of new constitutions.

Earlier I suggested that, as an orienting device, the sensitivities of Ferenc Fehér could be aligned to the negative, the critical, to the dark side of modernity and of the human condition. That this is only an orienting idea becomes increasingly apparent when we consider his views on and reactions to the collapse of communism. This was not just a matter of negative celebration, that the incubus at last was gone. Indeed, by Fehér's criteria, the problem of 'communism' or Jacobinism could not be gone, only shifted from its locus in state power and societal domination. There are always little Lenins, even after the fall of communism. For Fehér, the symbol of 1989 was like that of 1956, a moment of renewed self-discovery, a new field within which people could learn, act in rectitude and in error, make mistakes and continue on. So this became the dominant tenor of his writing on Eastern Europe after 1989: that superior Western analysts might perhaps for once quell the intensity of their desire to give advice, and instead listen. Whether criticising the minimalist politics of Richard Rorty or the elevated communication theory of Jürgen Habermas, Fehér's sense was of wonder, that after the apparent freeze the world was still capable of moving.

Viewed in a more specifically historical way, Fehér's sense was also that the positive aspects of socialist culture could not simply evaporate. Eastern fascinations with monetarism were overstated, and anyway relatively specific or short-lived. Questions of social solidarity, or of what used a century ago to be called the 'social question', continue to return, eternally, in Australia or America as in Eastern Europe. Neither Fehér nor Heller have ever accepted that extreme position espoused by Hannah Arendt, with her contempt for the so-called intrusion of the social question into politics. In the case of Fehér, here under discussion, I would hazard the guess that this may be (among other things) because the spirit of Fehér's concerns is not Greek, or tied to the world-images of the classics. Fehér's worldview lacks that nostalgic element which is characteristic of so much of the work of the Frankfurt School and of romantic anti-capitalism as such. Fehér's political project was modern, if not modernist, governed by the frame of anthropological universals from birth to dying, but without a strong sense that the new world was always worse than the old one. In other words, the crux of Fehér's project was something like a postmodern humanism. His were a politics characterised by a culture of tolerance and diversity combined with a morality of personal responsibility, an image of argument governed by a Kantian imperative to speak coupled with an equally important readiness to listen, to judge and to take a stand.

Fehér's political theory is in quite a distinct way a Weberian kind of Marxism. For the brilliant pyrotechnics of *History and Class Consciousness* did not touch him in the way they inclined, say, the Frankfurt School to the God's-eye-view of everyday life from above and beyond. The Lukács we sense the presence of in Fehér's political writing is not the Lukács who uses the idea of reification as a keyhole into processes of cultural independence from the lives of mortals. The Lukács you feel in Fehér's work is the younger man attending Max Weber's Sunday circle, listening to the Weber who viewed politics as a slow business, a little less redemptive than tedious, less like the sublime, more like the habits of putting bread on the table.

In this way Fehér's political purpose was not to import the canons of intellectual debate into the public sphere, so much as the other way around. This may be one factor which helps to explain the relative limits to recognition which Fehér received. His purpose was not to moralise, to lecture, to tell other people how to live, to offer the intellectual's correct views on absolutely everything as some kind of stone tablets which must be publicly valorised. His manner was not to kick against the world as too stupid, too uncultured, too thick to understand. The logic of his argument was exactly the opposite – that recognising differences in capacities and tastes, we should work rather from an image of public argument about things that matter, using that process to decide in due course what those things were. The motivating impulse for this kind of practical political theory was plainly out of that early Marxian thinking which was still engaged with the work of Ludwig Feuerbach. Once we could learn not to project our own capacities onto gods who could not help us, the next challenge was to transcend that humanist version of this thinking, for which, as in Trotsky, men would be as gods. What Fehér himself called the pursuit of a post-Machiavellian politics might more precisely be described as the project of a post-Faustian politics.[9] Machiavellian politics it seems now we are stuck with. But a politics after heroes, that is still a prospect which can be imagined. To speak thus of Fehér's politics as a postmodern humanism is then to begin

---

9   Fehér 1979.

to give adequate recognition to the sense that humanism as the twentieth century knew it was still a premodern humanism, a humanism less of humans in all their frailty than of humans, or some individuals, cast as gods or heroes. Fehér's message, to the contrary, was that we need to get used to the fact that we are mortals, that the sublime has no place in politics, that the road to hell is paved *inter alia* with good romantic intentions. If Fehér's message is still yet properly to be heard, this may well reflect the fact that moderns and postmoderns alike still cannot live without heroes, even if now those heroes are writers and celebrities rather than professional revolutionaries. The political legacy of the work of Ferenc Fehér was different, to remind us that we are existentially alone, and that this represents a challenge as well as a threat.

This will be the biggest challenge, finally, to the biographer of Ferenc Fehér. For the biographies that pour out of the publishers, on Sartre and Foucault and de Beauvoir and Wittgenstein and Baudelaire and Keynes and on and on, typically work the line of that genre between casting their subjects as heroes or as villains. Fehér's response to the discovery that our heroes are also villains of one sort or another would have been merely to shrug his shoulders and raise his eyebrows. We should be surprised by the fact that our heroes have feet of clay? Let us take this for granted, rather, and get on with our work.

CHAPTER 22

Critical Theory – Jürgen Habermas (1995)

Critical Theory and Jürgen Habermas – the tradition identified with the Frankfurt School, and its leading contemporary advocate. Simply to state these two names is to suggest some of the complexities and issues involved in making sense of the Critical Theory tradition. Let us take each term in turn. Critical Theory, today, is understood by transatlantic intellectuals to refer to the concerns of both philosophy and literary theory. For criticism, of course, is a widely shared practice, neither peculiar to Germany nor a monopoly of the left. After Jacques Derrida and deconstruction, after Jean Baudrillard and cultural studies, 'critical theory' is widely practised in its lower-case form, and associated generically with the interdisciplinary conduct of critique. Why then *critique*? To speak of 'critical' theory is to make it plain that other kinds of theory are less than fully or properly critical. And this was, indeed, Max Horkheimer's intention in distinguishing between 'traditional' and 'critical' theory. The founding Director of the Frankfurt School, Horkheimer was committed to the principle of Marxism, championed in our own time by Jürgen Habermas, that theory ought to have a practical intention. Both thinkers also set out from the premise that, contrary to the Marxism of Karl Marx or Georg Lukács, the proletariat had now lost its historic moment; to change the world was an interesting demand, but a less than straightforward proposition. By the 1930s the working class looked more like part of the problem than its solution. The working class, in this view, had been integrated.

Whatever 'critical theory' is taken to refer to today, the connotations of German Critical Theory here are evident. In this particular context, Critical Theory refers to the project of the Frankfurt School, so-called for its place of origin in the Institute for Social Research in 1923. Yet the signifier 'Frankfurt' itself is only partly suggestive of what Critical Theory was to become after some of its Jewish leaders (such as Theodor Adorno and Horkheimer) fled Nazism to take refuge in (of all places) California, home of the Hollywood Dream. Not that these thinkers – Adorno, Horkheimer, and variously Herbert Marcuse, Erich Fromm, Leo Lowenthal, Otto Kirchheimer, Franz Neumann and Friedrich Pollock – all shared the same purpose. They had different capacities and interests, enthusiasms and limits. In this founding generation Adorno was to remain the towering presence. Only Marcuse in the radical years of the 1960s achieved a similar degree of influence, close perhaps to that in recent times of Michel Foucault.

Critical Theory, in this context, might be briefly defined therefore as the German School (or better, circle) of cultural critique identified with Frankfurt neo-Marxism. Enter Habermas, our second constituent term, and the subject of this chapter. Habermas is the leading intellectual representative of second-generation Critical Theory. Born in 1929, he was among other things Adorno's assistant during the period when the School returned to Germany after World War II. The relationship between the two generations is a complicated matter, for to skim through work by, say, Adorno and Habermas is to wonder what connection there might be at all. Adorno was a philosopher and the author of an argument often aligned with cultural pessimism, the logic of which is that the twentieth century and even modernity itself are long arcs of irrevocable decline. This was a philosophy of history – most powerfully evident in *Dialectic of Enlightenment*, written during the war but published in 1947[1] – cast in the shadow of the Holocaust. It inverted Marx's and Lukács's sense of a triumphal onward march wherein the proletariat would establish socialism upon the pre-existing cultural achievements of the bourgeoisie. After Auschwitz, the direction of history was downward, the dream of enlightenment could no longer be sustained.

While Habermas's work does not return to a Lukácsian optimism, a sense of qualified historical progress nevertheless marks his work. This sense finds its culmination in the argument that modernity is an unfulfilled project, less a tangent of irreversible decline than a moment of perpetual stalling within a field of greater possibilities.[2] But this is only part of the difference between first-generation and second-generation Critical Theory. Readers of Adorno and Habermas who scan more widely cannot help but be struck also by the differing extent of their claims. Adorno's philosophical mode, elevated into an art form, cultivates the aphorism.[3] What is both striking and difficult about Habermas's work is that, rather than being cryptic or evocative, it becomes expansive and systematic to the point almost of being encyclopaedic. In this regard, the project of Habermas is more like that of the syncretic Cambridge sociologist Anthony Giddens. For Habermas's work is characterised by an ever-expanding optic, culminating in the most comprehensive of his works, the two-volume *Theory of Communicative Action*. While the meaning of Critical Theory is transformed across the generations, the extent of Habermas's own work also changes dramatically. Its early scope may be defined as the reconstruction of Marxism as a critical theory, and more specifically as a critical

---

1 Horkheimer and Adorno 1973.
2 Habermas 1981.
3 Adorno 1974.

sociology. This is a significant peculiarity in Habermas's reworking of Marxism or critical theory, for sociology in Germany had in the meantime been
effectively destroyed by Nazism. To reconstruct sociology after the war meant
also at least partly to Americanise it. Thus Habermas's key thinkers shift from
Marx and Freud to Talcott Parsons, Jean Piaget, Lawrence Kohlberg, and so
on.

All this hints at the problem of reception. For Habermas's work shifts historically, sometimes engaged more with the arguments of the first generation,
and at other times less so. But it is also received by different readers in different ways. Several issues immediately suggest themselves here. The first is
that since the 1980s Habermas has been received or presented especially as the
advocate of modernity against postmodernism. The dominant image of Habermas into the 1980s is the Voice of Reason, a Teutonic opponent of Foucault
and Lyotard. This indicates the immediate problem, namely that his work is
frequently read out of context. And this is a major issue, for Habermas's own
method of reading and interpretation presumes that there is a larger logic or
trajectory at work in any thinker, a whole of which the fragments are parts. The
second issue is that the English-language presentation of Habermas focuses
on his big theoretical books, and has hardly engaged with his more directly
political interventions against, for instance, revisionist attempts to rewrite or
to erase the history of the Holocaust, or against racism in the new, reunited
Germany.[4] Habermas has a political and oppositional stature that rarely breaks
through in English, except perhaps when the few desperate remaining revolutionary Marxists appropriated his work after 1989, or when theologians turn
to it for inspiration – for Habermas remains a philosopher of hope, however
residually.[5] The third issue which complicates the reception process of Habermas's work is that some of his major early writings have only just been translated. It would be an overstatement to say that English-speakers have received
his books in a reverse sequence to that in which they were actually written.
But it is true that because the serial appearance of Habermas's work has been
uneven and occasionally reversed in English, this has had some significant
effects.

We need, therefore, to begin at this beginning, with a sketch of the content of
Habermas's books as they have appeared in English, in order to establish some
ground for the controversies which have occurred in response to his views. The
second section of this essay accordingly provides a summary of Habermas's

---

4   E.g. Habermas 1989a.
5   Peukert 1986; Callinicos 1989; Holub 1991; Dews 1992.

works. The third sketches some of the controversies more directly, adding a more critical perspective to the reconstructive. The fourth section offers some comments by way of a conclusion.

Habermas in Translation

Habermas's major works as they have appeared in English are as follows:
- *Toward a Rational Society*, German 1968–9, English 1970
- *Knowledge and Human Interests*, German 1968, English 1971
- *Theory and Practice*, German 1968, English 1973
- *Legitimation Crisis*, German 1973, English 1975
- *Communication and the Evolution of Society*, German 1976, English 1979
- *Theory of Communicative Action*, volume one 1981, English 1984, volume two 1981, English 1987
- *The Philosophical Discourse of Modernity*, German 1985, English 1987
- *On the Logic of the Social Sciences*, German 1967, English 1988
- *The Structural Transformation of the Public Sphere*, German 1962, English 1989
- *Moral Consciousness and Communicative Action*, German 1983, English 1990.

This is by no means the whole of his work, which extends further into various volumes of essays, uncollected essays in journals, interventions in newspapers, interviews, and so on. But it does suggest some sense of the scope of the project. Let us enter the labyrinth.

Habermas's intellectual project stretches back into the 1950s. His earlier work included critical essays on Marx, the Marx-industry, freelance journalism, and work on the rationalisation of industry and of human relationships.[6] With the 1960s came the radicalisation of the universities, in Germany as elsewhere. The volatility of this period has frequently been observed. It reminded many of the Weimar Republic, when radicalisation took students off to the political extremities of both right and left, and it sometimes became difficult to distinguish between the two. Socialists, in the interwar years, had after all on occasion become national socialists or national Bolsheviks, and fascists agreed in some respects with Bolsheviks; both sought alternatives to bourgeois culture, and often to parliamentary democracy. Marxism then travelled east, became the state ideology of the Soviet Union, and transmuted into communism, not least of all for Germans across the Berlin Wall. Into the 1960s enthu-

---

6 Dews 1992, p. 187.

siasms spread for the renewal of a libertarian Marxism, a Marxism that would turn against industrialism as well as upon capitalism. Herbert Marcuse became the major prophet of this trend, arguing (as had Adorno and Horkheimer) that modern society was irredeemably flat, one-dimensional, and itself totalitarian.[7] Although Habermas's intellectual formation was also dominated by the shadow of Nazism, his response was less pessimistic. Fascism was to him a political turn rather than part of an irreversible historical trend to global decadence. 'Never again!' This is the maxim that frames Habermas's project, and leaves it with the residual optimism that holds up modernity as a project yet to be fulfilled.

Toward a Rational Society[8] anticipated many themes which would later become motifs of his work. Students could be politically active in ways that the workers' movement could not so readily be; this anticipated the later enthusiasm for social movements. But this recommendation also pinpointed a difficulty anticipated by Max Weber, namely that the politicisation of the universities could also be dangerous. These problems ran along with larger trends, such as the scientisation of politics and of public opinion. Modernity cut both ways; it expanded the space for freedom and democracy, and at the same time took it away. Habermas thus picked up on Adorno's fear that the greatest achievement of modernity would be its rational domination of nature, but added that human action also formed technology.[9] The rationality of domination called for analysis of symbolic interaction. Labour, in other words, was like technology, and never more than part of the human story; there was also praxis, and practical philosophy. Culture needed now to be theorised alongside power, and in its own terms. Marxism, traditionally, had worked upon the premise that the key to explaining bourgeois society lay in the critique of political economy.[10] But where Adorno had constructed an image of the culture industry as unilaterally determining, and closing off social options, Habermas coupled this argument with a sense of contingency. If the working class was now locked into welfare capitalism, it could not be argued that the social system would merely reproduce the status quo indefinitely. For human beings also have the capacity to learn.

Habermas still insists to this day that he is a Marxist. This is an interesting badge. Partly it can be understood as political, in the everyday sense; partly there is a substantive sense in which Habermas remains committed to sections

---

7   Marcuse 1964.
8   Habermas 1970.
9   Habermas 1971, p. 88.
10   Habermas 1971, p. 101.

of the Marxian oeuvre, to its reconstruction and critical intent. In different ways, however, Habermas had by the 1970s evacuated Marx's theory, treating class and class struggle as no longer central, cancelling out the labour theory of value, and introducing instead his own linguistic turn. These developments became more fully evident in *Knowledge and Human Interests* (1971). Here Habermas develops the sense that language, or rather communicative action, is the vital defining attribute of the animals who call themselves humans. The resonances in the argument run back to Aristotle's notion that human beings are best defined as citizens, city-dwellers. It also evokes Immanuel Kant's answer to the question of what is enlightenment: namely the capacity to be autonomous, which depends on the capacity to speak for oneself. Human beings, for Habermas, are deliberative and democratic animals who are able to modify their practical, social and political arrangements by virtue of their very contingency. Critical theory, in this earlier Habermasian formulation, has the capacity to enlighten societies in the same way that psychoanalysis can be revealing of the self. Emancipation remains the interest which guides the critically oriented sciences.[11]

If Kant and the Greeks are at work in the shadows here, the project at this point also looks at least from one perspective like an attempt to rethink and possibly to synthesise Marx and Freud, or at least to rethink and expand Marxism as a social theory which is capable of dealing with work, language and power.[12] This perception may have been strengthened by the translation of Habermas's next book, *Theory and Practice*, the constituent essays of which precede *Knowledge and Human Interests* by some years. *Theory and Practice*[13] opens with a reflective introduction on 'some difficulties in the attempt to link theory and praxis', and one of its key essays seeks to situate Marx's as a critique between philosophy and science. Habermas defines discourse as increasingly central, in connection with a consensus theory of truth. The idea of consensus, in turn, rests upon the utopia of an ideal speech situation.[14] Knowledge always serves interests; the point, however, is politically to define and articulate those interests. 'Critique' now begins to turn on another pivot, that of 'crisis', and here Habermas begins to anticipate the arguments developed later in *Legitimation Crisis*.[15] At this stage, however, Habermas's terms of reference remain closer to those of Adorno than to the language of systems-theories, and anticipate the

11   Habermas 1971, p. 308.
12   Habermas, 1971, p. 313.
13   Habermas 1973.
14   Habermas, 1973, p. 19.
15   Habermas 1975.

possible division of humanity into two newer classes – social engineers, and the inmates of closed institutions.[16]

By the middle 1970s, the left and the student movement in Australia and across the Atlantic had revived interest in Marx's political economy, and added to it a newer enthusiasm for the critique of the state. It was in this setting that Habermas's *Legitimation Crisis* appeared, a firmer title than the literal translation of the German original (*Problems of Legitimation in Late Capitalism*). This is arguably Habermas's most programmatic book, for it is more concerned to sketch out a research programme than to convey the results of sociological research. Further, the method echoes not only Marx but also Parsons, for it claims to indicate general attributes of a model of late capitalism which, like the political economy in Marx's *Capital*, would be applicable to all like cases. This argument was in turn to anticipate a broader interest in theories of societal evolution. Increasingly Habermas was working on the frame of general theory.

Legitimation Crisis begins from that formal distinction between system and life-world that was hinted at in Habermas's early work, and which later was to become central to the general diagnosis in his magnum opus, *Theory of Communicative Action*.[17] The use of the language of crisis is significant. Habermas seeks not only to remind us of the contingency of social forms, but also to multiply Marxist sensibilities concerning crisis. In the old Marxian theorem of capitalist collapse, economic crisis in the base of society leads to collapse in its superstructure. In sympathy now with the idea of the autonomy of social spheres, Habermas begins to propose a multiformity of crises. Crises could occur in political processes in the form of a legitimation crisis, or in everyday life as a motivational crisis. Crisis could even afflict the dominant rationality of a social system. Crisis, in addition, has a necessarily subjective component – it depends on the degree of awareness of social crisis in the life-world.[18] The logical implication of the systems-argument is evident: crises could fuse, spill over from some sub-systems into others (such as health care, say, into politics), but by the same token crises could be screened off from other social sub-systems. Late capitalism was thus simultaneously more stable and yet more fragile than the social formations which preceded it.

More than any other of his books, *Legitimation Crisis* probably increased Habermas's standing with Marxists. It is simultaneously Marxistic, in that it takes political economy seriously, and effectively Weberian, in that it draws attention to problems of organisational principles, politics and ethics. At the

---

16   Habermas, 1973, p. 282.
17   Habermas 1984, 1987b.
18   Habermas 1975.

same time, it gestures both back to Habermas's earlier concern with developmental psychology, and forward to his enthusiasm for theories of societal evolution. The logic which clips these two interests together is to be found in the sense that there is some kind of homology between the development of individuals and of societies. Habermas here retains a sense of the impending possibility that Adorno's nightmare could still be realised: democracy, today, still contains something latently totalitarian, as it facilitates prosperity without freedom.[19] This is only ever half the story, however, because individuals and societies still possess the capacity to learn from the experience of fascism, to develop spheres of autonomy, and to mature personally as well as socially. These concerns became more fully evident in *Communication and the Evolution of Society*.[20] This volume opens with further analysis of language and the speech act, which is significant because, as Habermas seems to ascribe some kind of telos or end to individual and social development, so apparently language itself in this view manifests the potential for democratic development. Such claims were later to elicit controversy in works by Jean-François Lyotard and Carol Gilligan, which are discussed in the next section.

The first generation of the Frankfurt School had always taken psychology, and more particularly psychoanalysis, seriously. The centrality of socialisation or internalisation followed directly from the task of seeking to explain the experience of German fascism, which after all was a popular regime, reproduced not only by coercion but also by consent. Moreover, if contradictions in the economic base did not themselves assure the collapse of capitalism or the arrival of socialism, then questions of popular belief, authoritarian populism, narcissism and paternalism all emerged in clearer forms as central to social reproduction. Habermas presumes, following Kant, that there is a path of psychological development which progressively takes individuals from dependence to the maturity of speaking and acting for themselves. As Axel Honneth has suggested, the theoretical problem here may be that Habermas fails to distance himself sufficiently from the categories of Adorno's philosophy, which sets society, always incipiently totalitarian, against alienated individuals. Having evacuated classes and social groups from his theory, Habermas downplays the extent to which social order is arrived at through social struggle.[21] Communicative action, in other words, remains relatively abstract; the more Habermas relies upon more global categories of social systems, the less apparent their historically contingent and contested character becomes.

---

19   Habermas 1975, p. 123.
20   Habermas 1979.
21   Honneth 1991, p. 303.

Habermas's concern with problems of moral development conspicuously derives from this concern with autonomy and authoritarianism. 'Never again!' After the trial of the notorious Holocaust supervisor Adolf Eichmann, Habermas's question was obvious. Why do people follow evil? How is authority internalised? The analytical problem, I think, is that Habermas transposes Jean Piaget's categories of psychological development into politics via the work of Lawrence Kohlberg. Piaget's concern was to establish hypothetical arguments concerning stages of child development which would suggest the difference between competencies, say, in number, or sense of space or time. All those who watch the children around them know there is something in this, and that the thirsty or greedy child will take the tall glass filled high on the assumption that it contains more liquid than a tumbler filled low. But can this kind of thinking-in-stages then be transferred straightforwardly into arguments concerning right, wrong and the motivation behind behaviour? Plainly the trigger of authoritarianism remains vital here, for it could easily be argued that those who supported Hitler were immature, rule-governed, and too much concerned to be good. But imaginably this can never be more than part of the story, and it may well be the case that Freud rather than Piaget remains more useful here; for supporters of Hitler were also, among other things, self-interested, terrified of socialists, racist, and even perhaps on occasion high-minded nationalists. To follow such a line of inquiry, however, would be to retain a sense that humans are also ever irrational, or else that they practice a multiplicity of rationalities. As I shall suggest later, this is perhaps the major flaw in Habermas's project: its implication that everything can be explained, and that the purpose of sociology is to annex social theory into systems theory alongside theories of language, method, epistemology and action, so that eventually everything can be covered. For the project is, finally, encyclopaedic, and this is an age increasingly sceptical of the possibility of a grand theory of everything.

Communication and the Evolution of Society marked a further expansion of Habermas's project by introducing the idea of reconstructing historical materialism. This lateral shift is like the one in *Legitimation Crisis*, which is simultaneously for and against or beyond Marx. Viewed as a logical possibility, as a potential research programme, the idea of reconstructing historical materialism makes a great deal of sense. Marx's project could be seen as the critique of capitalism, as the mirror of production, but it can also be read as an anthropological theory of history or of successive social formations. If modernity is best explained in terms of its configurations of power, language and culture, then surely these categories can also be read back, historically, in order to enquire into what has made world history both unitary and different. Again, the problem seems to be a certain elasticity in the concepts, categories or ways of thinking involved. Just as cognitive skills do not directly map out phases of moral development, so too patterns of individual development fail to do more than suggest possible paths of anthropological development. We need to ask why Habermas presumes development as a norm, and also to wonder about the apparent slip between an anthropology of individual development to maturity (Kant) and an anthropology of successive social formations (Marx). All the same, it is difficult not to admire the extent of Habermas's scholarship and the breadth of his curiosity. For here, within the covers of one book, specific contemporary analyses of modern world democracy and the welfare state coexist with longer-term diagnoses of pre-capitalist societies. If Habermas's project is foundationalist, committed to the defence of reason and system, and therefore in this sense modernist, it does not make the basic error (fundamental to much sociology) of imagining modernity to be a complete rupture with tradition.

Within this expanded frame of reference there now appeared Habermas's magnum opus, *Theory of Communicative Action*. This major elaboration of his thinking can be understood among other things as a fresh engagement with the thought of Max Weber. Weber was always a presence in Frankfurt theory; implicitly or explicitly, much of the Critical Theory tradition can be understood as an attempt to rethink the first textual encounter with Weber in Lukács's *History and Class Consciousness*[22] and their alignment as kindred philosophical spirits by Karl Löwith in *Max Weber and Karl Marx*.[23] Weber had feared, as had Adorno, the domination of modernity by instrumental or calculative reason; the echo in Marx's theory is striking, for he had built *Capital* (1867) upon the sense that commodification is a problem because it violates quality or difference as it quantifies the incommensurable. In either perspective, the horror of modernity is that it is governed by the power of number. For Weber, however, rationality has to be pluralised conceptually; there are always competing rationalities, and this sense of cultural thickness and complexity immediately places Weber and Habermas in a relationship of affinity. Marx and Weber, according to Habermas, share the sense that modernisation is not only about rationalisation but that it is also characterised by differentiation.[24]

Yet, as Weber indicates when writing under the influence of Friedrich Nietzsche in *The Protestant Ethic and the Spirit of Capitalism* (1904/05), what is rational from one perspective is irrational from another. Rationality can nevertheless be categorised in different ways, and here Habermas follows the Kantian distinction in Weber's work between different rationalities appropriate to

---

22   Lukács 1971.
23   Löwith 1982.
24   Habermas 1984, p. 158.

the spheres of science, aesthetics and practical life.[25] This means that while Weber floats the possibility of a future 'iron cage' or polar night of icy darkness, he also indicates the counter trend, which leads to systemic differentiation.[26] Weber is taken up here less as a negative philosopher of history (in the manner of Adorno) than in terms of the theory of action. Action can be instrumental, and oriented either to the technical fulfilment of goals already indicated, or towards articulation of goals that people agree to be desirable. This then returns us to discourse, speech, speech acts, and to the rules and games of language and communication. The possibility of communicative action knocks out even the theoretical possibility of either the totally administered society (Adorno) or the carceral society (Foucault). Habermas turns at this point away from Critical Theory and toward alternative sources in social theory – to G H Mead and Emile Durkheim and Parsons – before closing his work by returning to Marx via Weber. This is to reclaim the realm of symbolic interaction, before turning to the deeper distinction between system and life-world. Now Habermas's early concern with the technologisation of society is reinterpreted. The risk today is that the system, economy, administration, threaten to colonise the life-world; in a different language, the argument might be that public colonises private. In other words, a process is going on around us that consistently works against the idea of the integrity of different spheres of existence, each with its appropriate modes of conduct or ways of thinking. Systemic rationalisation – modernisation, in a word – flattens out difference by working against the communicative rationality of the life-world.

Habermas sociologises the still essentially philosophical concept of the impending totalitarian or administrative society feared by the first generation of Frankfurt theorists. The life-world, that realm where sociability and personal politics prevail, always risks invasion by the administrative mentality which these days stands in for politics. There is, of course, nothing wrong with administration or accounting, but they need to be kept in their place. When it comes to the life-world, the argument should be moral and ethical, not simply concerned with output or efficiency. To use a different language, Habermas is deeply apprehensive about the increasing domination of the modern world by number. In this sense he remains a classicist, dedicated to the idea of harmony in proportion.

This critical inflection is carried within, and perhaps obscured by, a richly open and inclusive discussion of various texts in social theory and observa-

---

25   Habermas 1984, p. 240.
26   Habermas 1984, p. 248.

tions in anthropological works. The extent of Habermas's immersion in the classics of sociology is indicated by his insistence that 'no theory of society can be taken seriously today if it does not at least situate itself with respect to Parsons'.[27] Here he echoes the maxim credited to Max Weber that the minimum entrance requirement for discussing the modern condition consists in taking up some attitude to Marx and to Nietzsche. The twist in the Weber aphorism is sharper, however, for anybody who reads Marx may well dismiss Nietzsche, while those who take on Nietzsche will inevitably dismiss Marx. What seems at first sight like an arrogance in Habermas, however, may find its justification in the claimed difference between orders of discourse, for this is a matter of social science, and not politics. Only then would we still have to deal with Marx's plea that there ought not be two sets of rules, one for science and one for life. In the academy, we should certainly expect that all voices or texts have a right to be heard, but the politicisation of the liberal arts, for better or worse, seems to suggest that the culture of tolerance is becoming less likely these days. Appropriately enough, this is the scenario to which Habermas returns in closing – the question whether the colonisation of the life-world by the system does not face us, after all, as the fixed fate of an iron cage. System-rationality may not yet have submerged the rationality of action, but it certainly threatens to do so.[28] Social movements now emerge as potential counterbalances. Habermas seems here to underwrite the early-to-mid 1980s enthusiasm for that 'new politics' which looked, indeed, like a potential extension of the student radicalism of the 1960s.

But as Honneth indicates, this is not the best-developed dimension of the Habermas project. The unfolding of Habermas's work from the 1960s to the 1980s seems to indicate some process of increasing textual complexity and abstraction.[29] In his theoretical work, Habermas gives progressively more attention to systems-models and to textual argument; he continues his political writing in journalism and public work, leaving the theoretical elaboration to proceed as formal and social scientific treatises. English speakers have received far more of the latter.

One biographical peculiarity of this story is the way in which Habermas, who is in effect not only the leading but also the lone Frankfurter of the second generation, sketches out a research programme sufficiently ambitious to occupy an institute. Unfortunately, however, there is no institute, and what remains is a series of hints and insistences as to what might need to be done in order to reconstruct social theory or sociology. Habermas successfully twists Critical

27   Habermas 1987b, p. 199.
28   Habermas 1987b, p. 333.
29   Honneth 1991.

Theory away from philosophy and turns it towards sociology, but the closer analysis of social texture and contestation suggested simultaneously by history or politics seems to escape from his work.

Single-handedly, as it were, Habermas now takes on postmodernism, defending the project of modernity against its detractors. *The Philosophical Discourse of Modernity*[30] was initially a set of lectures. This has probably become Habermas's most widely read and most caricatured book. The problem, however, is not entirely the jaundiced reception it has elicited from academics who identify social theory with French deconstruction or postmodernism. There are two essential aspects to Habermas's critical project. One is to establish a critical distance from postmodernism in order to distinguish between modernity and modernism, to defend modernity as a field of possibility, and to set postmodernism against the background of its predecessors in Romanticism or antimodernism. Habermas's sense of tradition, however, gets in the way. For the second component of his attack on postmodernism involves the reduction of its various arguments to their alleged precedents. Derrida, Foucault, and (implicitly) the absent Lyotard all become 'new conservatives', a category which conceals at least as much as it reveals.

If we glance back momentarily to Weber's aphorism concerning Marx and Nietzsche, some of the issues involved here begin to fall into relief. Habermas does indeed stand in Marx's shadow, in the way that Nietzsche shades the figure of Michel Foucault. Interesting as it might be to read these opposed thinkers against one another, they nevertheless face in different directions. Marx thinks totality, Nietzsche the fragment; Marx looks to the Rousseau who sees the light, Nietzsche to the Freud who tells of the wolf in men. Marx is effectively a humanist, Nietzsche a nihilist. What is unfortunate in the stand-off between the warring theoretical titans of Paris and Frankfurt is that these tensions or contradictions are also those which others, like Weber, struggled to shape into half-truths.

In a sense, Habermas attacks the French with such vehemence because they are repeating what Adorno said from his position of paternal privilege, namely that the world is beyond improvement if not understanding, that democracy is a bad joke, that the entire Kantian hope of human and social improvement had been buried with Hitler if not before, and that we should stay home and lock the doors. The limit of this debate is that it becomes too readily stylised and distorted, for in effect each side tells only half of the story. For Habermas, the French case rests so heavily on negation and denial that it misses the obvious:

---

30   Habermas 1987a.

we can be outraged by barbarism only because we live in an Enlightenment culture. Whereas the French think that modernity, like socialism, has had its chance and failed, for Habermas it is the failure which represents the challenge. We are not, on his account, postmoderns; if we are, then postmodernity is only the name for a modernity grown conscious of itself. Habermas's purpose is to reintroduce the tension, the vital sense that modernity involves gains and losses. In this sense, Habermas aspires to follow Walter Benjamin's acute sensibility in his *Theses on the Philosophy of History*, that there is no document of civilisation which is not at the same time a document of barbarism.[31] Where the French (from their position of privilege) deny modernity's achievement, Habermas affirms it; he does so too heartily, whether for rhetorical or for other reasons. Modernity, of course, creates more spaces and opportunities for some people than others; democracy is always constrained by asymmetrical relations of power. Needless to say, although Habermas knows all this, it does not figure centrally in his argument, which remains old European. Indeed, while his social theory remains framed by the Holocaust, it lacks a stronger informing sense that there is always an underground, that suffering always accompanies the achievement of modernity, and that different actors experience these phenomena in a more thoroughly positive or negative way.[32]

Habermas's stance, then, is to oppose the opposition, be they postmodernists or post-structuralists. This reflects his own sense of politics and political engagement. For while Habermas calls himself a Marxist, he also describes his position as social democratic, or 'solidaristic', and the ambiguity is less apparent in Germany where the two have been historically intertwined. What this means is that Habermas sees us and himself as inhabiting and defending a culture or a mainstream, rather than being outside it. While he may be too jaundiced towards nay-saying intellectuals, who after all are not outsiders but also privy to the best spoils of civilisation, he may also give too scant regard to the underworld they claim to inhabit or to represent. This is where Nietzsche stands in the door, for he is the greatest of nay-sayers, the original philosopher-Antichrist and antihumanist. With Nietzsche, Habermas places Heidegger, whose work he considers distracting but whose commitment to Nazism he finds impossibly objectionable. His critique of Heidegger is telling. What is irritating is the unwillingness and the inability of this philosopher, after the end of the Nazi regime, to admit his error with as much as one sentence – an error fraught with political consequences.[33] Habermas's response is striking

---

31   Benjamin 1969, p. 256.
32   Beilharz 1994.
33   Habermas 1987a, p. 155.

because it is constructed so plainly in the language of moralism and rationalism. What Habermas refers to as Heidegger's fascist 'error' seems to indicate that for Habermas, Heidegger's politics could easily have been different. But they were not, as they were not for very many Germans who were anti-Semitic or happy to see strong leaders or high levels of employment. For a leftist or a democrat there is no argument about Nazism. But modernity is also inhabited by various others, who will never share these critical premises or conclusions.

Perhaps it is less than surprising that the French philosopher who fares best in this attack is Foucault. Certainly, in his later years, Foucault drifted back towards the Kant of 'What is Enlightenment?'. As Habermas indicates, this mix is also evident in Foucault's work on psychiatry, where a 'double movement of liberation and enslavement' is described which Foucault later traces along a broad front in various reforms of the penal system, the educational system, the health establishment, social welfare and so forth.[34] Unfortunately Foucault then loses the sense of balance between the bright and dark sides of enlightenment, just as Horkheimer and Adorno did before him. Where Foucault attacks humanism as a mask for disciplinary power, Habermas defends humanism against power. But certainly a sense of Habermas's engagement with Foucault is discernible, whereas others (like Lyotard, about whom Habermas has stronger reservations) are all but absent from the text.

Habermas closes *The Philosophical Discourse of Modernity* by returning to the defence of his own position, namely communicative or intersubjective rationality. The contemporaneity of his argument with the French was then punctuated awkwardly, this time by the English translation of his much earlier contribution to the philosophy of social sciences. *On the Logic of the Social Sciences*[35] had first appeared in 1967; those trapped within the English language would only now trace back his apparently more arcane arguments with Karl Popper, Hans Albert, Carl Hempel and Ernest Nagel. More significantly, 1989 saw the final translation of Habermas's first and arguably his best book, *The Structural Transformation of the Public Sphere*.[36] Where the *Logic of the Social Sciences* filled a gap for those choosing to follow the trajectory of Habermas's work, *The Structural Transformation* met a more urgent need. Its publication was to coincide with renewed political and scholarly enthusiasm for the very idea of the public sphere. Its translation, of course, coincided with the collapse of communism. But through the 1980s socialism as a separate dynamic was also unwinding. People no longer spoke, as they did in the early 1980s, of a crisis of

---

34   Habermas 1987a, p. 246.
35   Habermas 1988.
36   Habermas 1989b.

Marxism. The idea of socialist politics itself had collapsed. Social movements were widely enthused about as potential social forces which might fill the void left by the further rationalisation of electoral politics and the workers' movement. There was revived talk of civil society, and a renewed desire to identify socialism as democracy.[37]

These were incomplete developments, and they were not always coherent. For after all, if socialism is really about democracy, then why not own up and call it that? And so too social movements lost the lustre which disappointed socialists had first put upon them. The really positive facet of the arrival of Habermas's book was different, for it signalled not only the rediscovery of politics but also what Habermas was pleading for so strongly in *The Philosophical Discourse of Modernity*, namely a rethinking of the negative claims in *Dialectic of Enlightenment*. *The Structural Transformation of the Public Sphere* had begun as Habermas's postdoctoral work. Adorno was disinclined to support it, and so eventually it was overseen by the labour historian, Wolfgang Abendroth. The logic of Habermas's thesis is exactly to put an unwelcome emancipatory twist on *Dialectic of Enlightenment*, by treating its image of modernity-as-closure as not the whole story. Not that the long-term consequence of Habermas's thesis violates Adorno's; rather its message is that the public sphere had flourished briefly in bourgeois form in the epoch of the great revolutions, only to be smothered through colonisation by instrumental reason, and especially by its modern media forms. This reading is structured within the frame of what today would be called historical sociology, for the text discusses the particular forms, strengths and weaknesses of the public sphere as they emerged historically in England and France. Now the work in *Legitimation Crisis* fell into different relief. For here was explained the very appearance of a public agenda which social actors could endeavour to influence; thus, Habermas delineates the long road from the French Revolution to the welfare state. Similarly, the often dense discussion of speech and language takes on a different kind of urgency, for the public sphere is where talk becomes transformed into politics. And in the meantime, there had been a dramatic expansion of discussion about public and private spheres, which made the arrival of the English text even more timely.

Moreover, the book on the public sphere upheld essentially the same claims for the recognition of modernity as did Habermas's attack on recent French philosophy. Enlightenment was to be understood as a project yet to be fulfilled; democracy had hung up its claims, but modernity had yet to deliver

---

37   Keane 1988; Cohen and Arato 1992.

adequately. Similarly with the public sphere. Facilitated yet compromised by its bourgeois actors, the public sphere nevertheless posited the value of open participation, even if it did not fulfil it. This is the core of Habermas's politics as a critical theorist working from within society against society's unfulfilled claims, and through critical affirmation rather than negation. As earlier Marxists would have put it, the situation is obvious: if the bourgeoisie offer you freedom, demand it! If they do not deliver, then continue to demand it! For alongside the progressive disappointment of modernity is the ongoing promise of freedom within it. The public sphere, in short, represented an opening, and could always become more open.

Habermas thus discusses here all manner of pertinent detail – family forms, the organisation of house-design, publication of journals and letters, public opinion. To identify the public sphere as bourgeois was also to suggest its inner contradiction. As Marx had understood, because bourgeois ideology still persisted in presenting a particular interest as the general will, there was another opening for political argument in the cleavage between claim and reality. If Marx was prepared filially to dismiss all this talk about citizenship, Habermas wants to pick up the baton and pass it on. Marx, like Foucault, was struck by the fraudulence of the offer; Habermas, more like the social democrats, seeks rather to insist that it be cashed in. Mass media and the culture industry then arrive, with different purposes; the world eventually fashioned by the mass media becomes a public sphere in appearance only. Critical debate and participatory democracy effectively evaporate as their promise is offered.

Habermas's thesis gestures in the direction of Marcuse's one-dimensionality, but its conception picks up on the aspect of arguing for democracy. This is made apparent, for example, in the massive volume of critical responses entitled *Habermas and the Public Sphere.*[38] This is a remarkable collection, not least because it opens up spaces within which feminist critics and historians set out to extend Habermas's work by establishing the relation between masculinity and the public sphere via (for example) discussion of the work of Joan Landes on the issue of maternal citizenship in the French Revolution.[39] Argument returns here to the realms of politics, contingency, action and social history. The generosity of Habermas's own response to these various arguments is one thing. The other, broader point of significance in this reception-in-reverse, where the first book shall be last, is that it suggests something of the fecundity of the project first anticipated in 1962.

38   Calhoun 1992.
39   Calhoun 1992, p. 199.

Habermas in Dispute

Habermas's response in debate is not always so tolerant as his response to Cal-houn and his writers suggests. In *The Philosophical Discourse of Modernity*, as I suggested above, Habermas seems to respond in kind, perhaps as the rules of rhetoric dictate, when it comes to critique of the one-dimensional construction or rejection of modernity. That is why his engagement with Foucault is more sympathetic. But if Habermas is a theorist with a project – to defend the idea of communicative action, and to construct around it various supporting sub-theories of language, social science, evolution and crisis – then his is also, as Robert Holub shows, a responsive position. His arguments about social science were formulated in controversy. He has participated in various other controversies: with Gadamer on hermeneutics, tradition and prejudice, with Luhmann on systems theory and the place of social action, and against the revisionist historians of fascism as well as against the French philosophers.[40] The most striking aspect of his public disputes with Gadamer and Luhmann is that they seem to obscure the way in which Habermas also accommodates substantial parts of their views in his theory. As regards hermeneutics, Habermas cultivates a method of reading which places tradition in a sympathetic light, and suggests a circular interpretation of the conceptual constellations which form the projects of others. The idea of a consensus theory of truth also suggests the significance of conversation as a model on which both theories rest. With reference to systems theory, Habermas may reject Luhmann's indifference towards, say, democracy, in the same way as he refuses Gadamer's defence of the idea of prejudging, but especially after *Legitimation Crisis* the image of system and sub-system is ubiquitous. As far back as his early work, and culminating in the *Theory of Communicative Action*, his theory is held together by the warring co-ordinates of system and life-world.

About other aspects of thinking incorporated into his theory, Habermas is more defensive. Earlier I referred to his extension of Piaget's schema of cognitive development via Kohlberg into a theory of moral development. This he defends internally, and not least of all against the significant criticism of Kohlberg by Carol Gilligan in her book *In a Different Voice*.[41] The implication of Gilligan's book, to simplify, is that Kohlberg's theory of development is a story for boys. The maturing subject reaching post-conventional, universal-rights morality may be a masculine construction, but this is not necessarily the pattern

---

40   Holub 1991.
41   Gilligan 1982.

followed by women. In other words, patterns of motivation, justification and action may be different for men and women. Kohlberg's logic, on this basis, conceptually backs women into 'immaturity'. While there has been a great deal of controversy and even methodological debate over these claims, the response of Habermas in his most recent English-language book, *Moral Consciousness and Communicative Action*,[42] is technically dismissive. Habermas acknowledges that there is some empirical or moral difficulty in the implication, following Kohlberg, that by strict definition more than half the American population is morally immature.[43] According to Habermas, Gilligan fails to recognise that the question of whether what I ought to do is the same as what I would do concerns only the motivational and not the cognitive problem of mediation.[44] Viewed from outside, this distinction hardly seems devastating. In general, Habermas here speaks as though those who take on Kohlberg do so in order to supplement the idea of moral stages. The final logic of Gilligan's book, however, is to place the whole idea of moral stages under question. One need not accept the implication that difference works dualistically and across gender lines in order to follow the point: The message may not be that men and women by definition think differently, but rather that different people do. Habermas simply rehearses Kohlberg's insistence that his proposed stages of moral development form an 'invariant, irreversible, and consecutive sequence of discrete structures'.[45] If one steps outside these strictures, which after all belong to a research programme and not to the sphere of everyday life, the power of the argument is somewhat diminished, as are its clichéd premises regarding the alleged capacities and competences of the adult and the child. If Habermas's argument is thus to be viewed as 'old European', then so be it. So much the worse for children, and other outsiders.

The invisibility of Lyotard in Habermas's *Philosophical Discourse* has already been remarked upon. All the more strange it seems, on reflection, for Lyotard (more so than, say, Foucault) is plainly Habermas's opponent in this debate. What is at risk between them? Lyotard strikes the first blow in *The Postmodern Condition*,[46] where he wickedly constructs Habermas as the professor, as though he himself were not one also. But the postmodern is often characterised as an attitude, and it is 'attitude' which sets French against German. The tension between them can easily be imagined in caricature or cartoon; each

---

42   Habermas 1990.
43   Habermas 1990, p. 175.
44   Habermas 1990, p. 179.
45   Habermas 1990, p. 127.
46   Lyotard 1984.

sub-system or addition which Habermas seeks to add to his theoretical edifice is for Lyotard, the joker, just another balloon ready to be pricked. Habermas, like Goethe before him, believes truth to be a norm, an orienting device, even if it can never be achieved. In this sense, Habermas's is a hermeneutic of suspicion; more like Foucault, here, Habermas seeks to unmask, whereas Lyotard hopes to deflate. Against the hermeneutics of Gadamer, however, Habermas wants to insist that there is some relation between truth and method; prejudice, authority and tradition must all be brought under rational scrutiny. Gadamer's refusal of this strategy reflects among other things his own romanticism.[47] Lyotard, similarly, shows up on Habermas's screen as romantic and relativistic: where Habermas's view of language is oriented to the utopia of consensus, Lyotard's argument begins and ends with dissension. Lyotard's is an agonistic theory of language; Habermas's is a progressive one.[48] Lyotard's postmodern world is filled by the languages of the Tower of Babel; Habermas's image is of conversation without intimidation. Needless to say, the logic of Lyotard's position already presumes difference and dispute, and therefore casts Habermas as the opponent if not the enemy. Lyotard's premise is to presume that arguments will always differ and remain beyond resolution. And here the shadow in the background is Freud's: man is a wolf to man.

The possibility that the disagreement between Lyotard and Habermas might be less severe is difficult to see. This is more emphatically the case because Lyotard seems to interpret Habermas's claims about the possibility of consensus as real rather than normative, which is in effect to accuse Habermas of ignoring the effects of power or violence on practices in culture or language.[49] As is the case with the use of Kohlberg's stages of moral development, Habermas's obvious riposte is that the utopia of undistorted communication does not describe any existing state of affairs, but is heuristic, part not of a political programme but of a thought-experiment. The equally obvious reply which one can imagine from Lyotard is that distinctions between the factual and the counterfactual are hard to preserve. By way of response, Habermas in turn would probably refer to the necessity of philosophical universals in thinking. We can recognise that we will never achieve democracy or freedom in anything other than a nominalistic sense, but we cannot live without these norms as social goals. They facilitate processes of discernment and judgement, and help us to decide and to act.

47   Gadamer 1975.
48   Holub 1991.
49   Holub 1991, p. 142.

Habermas in Conclusion

In comparison with this kind of romantic argument (if that is a reasonable description of Lyotard's position), Habermas's stance is rather classicist, or at least works within and out of tradition. Frankfurt theory was indeed that already, enmeshed as it was in German thinking, whether that of Marx, Weber or Nietzsche. However, after its initial development in a more conventionally sociological pattern of research, the idea of Critical Theory became identified with Adorno's cultural pessimism. Frankfurt took a philosophical turn, a turn towards negation. Habermas's difficult purpose, in this setting, was to seek tentatively to direct Frankfurt out of this impasse by reforming it as a sociology. In this way, his turn to Parsons is objectionable only in the sense that it duplicates Parsons' own slide from a leading concern with a theory of action to a residual focus upon structure or system.[50] The difference between Parsons and Habermas, however, remains conspicuous. It centres on the figure of Marx. Marx arguably was accepted into American sociology only in the later 1960s; Parsons was no exception in this. Habermas, by contrast, effectively starts with Marx and always returns to him, however sobered he may be by encounters with less fully redemptive thinkers. The commonsense of Marxist culture tells us that, even in his own lifetime, Karl Marx insisted that he was no Marxist. Habermas, instead, refuses to break with this claim to tradition. In the 1990s his interest may no longer be in what earlier were called 'theory' and 'practice', but he remains committed both to explaining and criticising the world, and to arguing for its humanisation or radical change.

How might Habermas and Critical Theory then be assessed? The logic of my argument is that Jürgen Habermas has been working both in and against the Frankfurt School. Horkheimer and Adorno knew this, which was one reason why there emerged some distance between them. The first generation of Frankfurters followed Marx and lived with the collapse of Marxist hope. In their lifetimes, Marxism became a state ideology of an eastern imperialism, while the German culture (which among other things claimed philosophy for itself) also incubated Nazism. Habermas's challenge was to register these ruptures, and to reform them in a philosophy where hope and reason might be recombined. Second-generation Critical Marxism, however, was to coincide with the emergence of mass tertiary education, which both encouraged the student radicalism of the 1960s and served to enmesh Marxism with the academy rather

---

50   Parsons 1937, 1951.

than with the organisations of the workers' movement. Marxism's insertion into this critical culture also stood for incorporation into the practice of social theory in a broader sense. But as a sociology, Marxism as critical theory became increasingly general and abstract.

As Helmut Dubiel argues, the perspective taken up by critical theory, focusing on domination in the first generation and emancipation in the second, also brings with it an attitude, the former more given to resignation, the latter to hope. In this sense, the two most significant texts of the longer Critical Theory tradition are *Dialectic of Enlightenment* and *Theory of Communicative Action*. The first generation of Critical Theory, oriented primarily toward a theory of domination, is mainly concerned with the mechanisms by which individuals reproduce their condition of submission. The second generation, in contrast, is largely interested in the idea of the emancipatory potentials of individuals and groups.[51] The earlier version of Critical Theory draws attention to conformism; the later version constructs domination as a human as well as social phenomenon.

Attention might now turn to the prospect of a third generation of Critical Theory, of which Axel Honneth is the most prominent member. Honneth's first major work, *Critique of Power*,[52] is among other things a settling of accounts with Critical Theory, which is engaged by way of a critique of Horkheimer, Adorno, Habermas and Foucault. In summary, Honneth's view is that Critical Theory originally involved an attempt to supplement the critique of political economy by adding psychoanalysis as the superstructure. Entering this edifice, Habermas effectively takes on the same task, replacing Freud with Piaget and Kohlberg and adding various other supports as sub-theories which are either logically foundational or supplementary. What recedes, or remains marginal in this process, is that struggle for resources and recognition which makes the social edifice possible.[53] Honneth's case thus runs in parallel to that of Alain Touraine's request for a 'return of the actor'.[54] The research implications of this critique point in two different directions at the same time. First of all, it is now necessary (so to speak) to add the dimension of 'internal' colonisation (within nation states) to that of colonisation of the life-world by system. Asymmetrical relations of power are ubiquitous, especially after Keynesian economics and globalisation; talk of autonomy and democracy needs now to proceed in this frame of recognition. Second, future outcomes of societal evolution

---

51   Dubiel 1992.
52   Honneth 1991.
53   Honneth 1991.
54   Touraine 1987.

ought now to be viewed in terms of that struggle for recognition which is primary to human existence.

Habermas's great contribution to Critical Theory is to turn it in this direction, even if his own theory then fails to ground it sufficiently in the way in which Honneth recommends. Habermas's theory is therefore paradigmatic of the development of ideas – able to recognise the problems it faces even if it cannot always solve them, and opening up new possibilities for those who would be so bold as to stand on the shoulders of giants. As far as Habermas is concerned, it can truly be said that no serious thinker or critic in the liberal arts today can avoid taking a position on his work. The challenge of a critical theory remains before us.

CHAPTER 23

Bernard Smith: The Quality of Marxism (2013)

Bernard Smith was one of Australia's most significant writers and intellectuals. He was born in Sydney in 1916 and died in Melbourne in 2011. His published work spanned 60 years. His most influential works include *Place, Taste and Tradition* (1945); *The Antipodean Manifesto* (1959); *The Myth of Isolation* (1961); *European Vision and the South Pacific* (1962); *Australian Painting* (1962, three further editions to follow); *The Death of the Artist as Hero* (1988); *The Critic as Advocate* (1989); *The Art of the First Fleet and The Art of Captain Cook's Voyages* (with Joppien, from 1985, multiple volumes); *The Spectre of Truganini* (1980); *The Boy Adeodatus* (1984); *Imagining The Pacific* (1992); *Noel Counihan – Artist and Revolutionary* (1993); *Modernism's History* (1998); *A Pavane for Another Time* (2002); *Two Centuries of Australian Painting* (2003), and his final book, *The Formalesque* (2007). The formal invitation to the launch of his last book bore the following text: 'Bernard published his first book, *Place, Taste and Tradition*, in 1945 and *The Formalesque* may be his last'. And so it was.

I got to know Bernard from 1993 after a chance encounter with our mutual friend, the Cambridge archaeologist Peter Gathercole, a student of Gordon Childe's. I published a floater on Bernard's work in *Thesis Eleven* in 1994, and we in turn published various papers by Bernard in the journal. My smaller curiosity expanded; the floater was insufficient, so I wrote a monograph, the first book-length study of his work, in *Imagining the Antipodes* (1997). I have continued to engage with his work subsequently. The textbook published by Trevor Hogan and I in 2006 followed in the tracks of *Place, Taste and Tradition*. It was entitled *Sociology: Place, Time and Division*.[1] Its successor is *Sociology – Antipodean Perspectives*.[2] Its frame is Smithian in that it seeks to open the optic by insisting that the antipodes matter, understood as a relationship more than a place, and that all this is held together, whether in dependence or in innovation, by processes of cultural traffic. As to Bernard Smith, we hardly know him yet. This essay seeks to contribute to interpreting and understanding better what it was that he came to say. Now that he is gone, we are confronted for the first time by the task of seriously following his own methodological strictures, *ex post facto*, truly to make sense of what he left us.

---

1   Beilharz and Hogan 2006.
2   Beilharz and Hogan 2012.

One of Bernard Smith's key sensibilities concerned the idea of distance: taking a distance, letting the dust settle, sitting with the owl of Minerva, at the sunset, seeking to make sense of the world after the fact. Now that he has gone, it is a good time to seek to take some distance on Bernard Smith's work. What did he come to say? What did he set out to achieve? Why, in this context, was he so insistent and persistent in his marxism?

Bernard Smith was a Marxist. Five words: what might they mean? In earlier encounters with Bernard's work, I have used different metaphors to suggest the nature of his relationship to marxism, to Marx in particular: that his marxism was like a string bag, formed by the objects or other ideas or facts that he chose to accommodate in it; that he wore his marxism not like the iron cage in Max Weber's *Protestant Ethic* but like a light cloak, as a badge or a kite rather than as a compass.[3] The parallels in the history of marxism might be scholars like Eric Hobsbawm or, outside it, Fernand Braudel. Other Marxist resonances might include Raymond Williams, he who famously asked what it was that a thinker or writer had come to say, and Jack Lindsay, of whom more anon.

Bernard Smith insisted upon his marxism, across the path of his life. But were his politics those of a Marxist? Yes, and no. Mainly no: he was an oppositionist. His object was less to change the world than to stop it getting worse. He was an anti-Nazi communist, initially, a '40s rather than a '30s or Depression communist. The dominant motif of his '40s politics was that of civil liberties. The triggers for his radicalisation were to be found, however, in the late '30s. Its triggers were Spain, the Spanish Civil War, and the rise of Hitler. Its symbolic icons were Guernica, the place and the painting; and Hitler's 1937 Degenerate Art Exhibition in Munich. He was not a primarily political, let alone redemptive, personality. As he wrote in third person, reflecting back at a distance on his life in the first volume of his autobiography, *The Boy Adeodatus*: 'Bernard was not interested in politics [at his one-teacher school in Murraguldrie, out back of Wagga]; but politics was becoming interested in him'.[4]

Later in life, his politics were still reactive: in the struggle against the overdevelopment of inner-city Sydney and Melbourne, against the forgetting of genocide against Australia's indigenous people in *The Spectre of Truganini*. His positive politics were cultural. They famously took the form of a manifesto, itself both a positive and negative text, in the 1959 *Antipodean Manifesto*; and they were crowned in the greatest monument to his life, the RAKA Awards. Sometimes the tenor of his politics was straightforwardly and period liberal demo-

---

3   Beilharz 1996a, 1996b, 1997.
4   Smith 1984, p. 236.

cratic, as in his 1986 urging in 'The Writer and the Bomb' that the best immediate step was to write to your Member of Parliament.[5] His brief encounter with
what passed for actually-existing socialism in the late '40s made his preferences
clear – given the hypothetical choice between living in Gottwald's East Germany and Menzies' conservative Australia, Australia ruled.[6]

He had attended the University of Sydney, BA incomplete: was he then an
Andersonian? Andersonian scepticism dominated the Sydney Left, along with
communism; Anderson, indeed, had at one stage occupied the position of Theoretical Advisor to the Communist Party of Australia.[7] Anderson's position
notoriously was described as a will not to reform, which was the role of the
servile state, but to oppose.[8] Unlike Anderson, Smith was not a contrarian; nor
was he ever a Trotskyist. He was an oppositionist, indeed, but never a revolutionary. Smith was never an enthusiast for Bolshevism – why? Precisely because
Bolshevism, like Jacobism, seeks to force history, or else to leap over it.[9]

The question remains: what kind of marxism was this? Let us step sideways,
and ask the obvious philological question: what did he read? By the 80s, when
some of his most sophisticated encounters with Marx were published, he had
read everything: the *1844 Manuscripts*, the *Grundrisse, Capital, Theories of Surplus Value*. As the 1986 essay 'Marx and Aesthetic Value', reprinted in *The Death
of the Artist as Hero*, shows, Bernard Smith's marxism worked at a significant
level of theoretical sophistication. But what did he read when he was young,
and how did he escape the dead hand of dialectical materialism, the standard
fare of his formative period in the 30s and 40s?

This question begs another: what was the available Marx in that formative
period, anyway? Marx's translation history is famously patchy, and in the English language, late. What did the young Bernard Smith have available to him
from Marx's project? The *1844 Manuscripts* were published in German in 1932,
and coincidentally in English and American translations by Bottomore and
Struik respectively in 1964. This meant that the message of Marxist humanism
was repressed through the history of Marxism-Leninism, but was available for
the rising generation of 1968. The *German Ideology* was published in German in
1932, and in English in 1938. *Capital* Volume I appeared in German in 1867 and in
English in 1887. Its more popular editions appeared with the Modern Library, in
New York in 1906 (the version used by Smith) and later in popular editions with

---

5   Smith 1988, p. 66.
6   Smith 2002, p. 459.
7   Beilharz 1993a.
8   Kennedy 1995.
9   Beilharz 1987.

Charles H. Kerr in Chicago and Dona Torr in London. The *Grundrisse* was first fully translated into English in 1973. The Introduction to the *Grundrisse*, notable for its fragment on the universality of Greek art, appeared earlier, in the 1904 Kerr edition of Marx's 1859 *Critique of Political Economy*, and was therefore in principle available to Smith, as were odd texts such as Francis Klingender's 1947 *Art and The Industrial Revolution*, appreciated by Smith but positioned by him as 'too narrow' in its orthodoxy.[10] He had read *The German Ideology* and *The Theses on Feuerbach*, Engels's *Origin of the Family, the State and Private Property*. Like others of his generation, however, Smith imbibed a theoretically sophisticated marxism from the work of others who understood philosophy and read German, such as Max Eastman and especially Sidney Hook, particularly Hook's *Hegel to Marx*, which focused on the young Marx and the young Hegelians, Ruge, Bauer and Feuerbach. He spent serious time with Spengler's *Decline of the West* and *Man and Technics*, and Toynbee's *A Study of History*, as well as the kindred civilization analysis of Sorokin.[11] Smith's thinking itself became civilisational, committed to the fundamental sense that western culture recycled motifs such as those of progressivism and romanticism.

Smith explains further in the essay 'History as Criticism' (1983). In writing his first great work on Australian painting, *Place, Taste and Tradition* (1945),

> I read everything I could then get hold of in English by Marx, Engels, Lenin and Stalin. [My interest was] Marxian rather than Marxist because although I wrote the book within the broad guidelines of historical materialism there were also considerable countervailing influences in the work, such as a voracious interest in Toynbee as each of his green volumes appeared, and a fascination with Heinrich Wölfflin's account of art in terms of style. Nor did I attempt to write the book within the terminology of marxism: proletariat and bourgeoisie, base and superstructure [etc.] ... I believe that my Marxian vantage point provided a better perspective on the development of Australian art than MacDonald and Lindsay's organic nationalism. It also provided more aesthetic space within which it was possible to revalue colonial and modern work.[12]

The alignment of concepts is characteristic of Smith's way of thinking: Marxian; colonial; modern, modernism, each term necessary to locate and make sense of the others.

---

10   Smith 1988, p. 35.
11   Beilharz 1997, pp. 9–10.
12   Smith 1988, p. 75.

In addition to Marx, Toynbee, Spengler, Hook, Sorokin, there was another proxy Marx figure here: Jack Lindsay. This filament connects Smith to Brisbane, where Smith later delivered the major text *Australian Painting Today* as the 1961 Macrossan Lectures, and links further back to the marxism of Vere Gordon Childe, an important source and anchor for the marxism of Jack Lindsay.[13] Smith was later to dedicate a major collection of essays to Jack Lindsay; earlier, his 1988 essays *The Death of the Artist as Hero* directly echoed Lindsay's *Death of the Hero* (1960). Smith's collected essays were dedicated to the memory of Norman and Lionel Lindsay 'in appeasement' and to Jack Lindsay 'in gratitude'.

Its preface identifies Lindsay's *Short History of Culture* (1939) as an important influence in Smith's own intellectual formation. The scope of Lindsay's *Short History of Culture* was prehistorical, or historical in a prehistorical sense – and thereby hangs a tale. For one serious bond between Lindsay and Smith was the idea that history was not present, but past: you needed some distance on history in order to make sense of the world.

Lindsay's reputation was always somewhat obscure: an Anglophile Marxist from Brisbane, with early Nietzschean leanings or longings, he became a scribbler. He wrote too much, at least 153 books up to the age of 83, almost three a year, more than many people are capable of reading. In the period of his English exile he took up solidarity with the Historians' Group of the CPGB. The CPGB Historians Group anticipated the view from below which became so popular into the 60s and 70s. It also followed interests in material history, the history of technology and of things, and Lindsay also wrote in these fields. He remained a humanist and a vitalist, and he defended a kind of open marxism, more easily recognisable to us today as a cultural marxism. His sympathies connected to Ernst Bloch and to Gramsci. The affinities between Smith, Lindsay and the GPGB Historians are apparent: their Marx was the Marx of *The Eighteenth Brumaire*.

The sense of distance or detachment also echoes in Marx, even in his most active and politically committed phases. As his most recent biographer, Mary Gabriel, writes in *Love and Capital*, Marx was always notoriously late for significant historic events. The *Communist Manifesto* was published too late to impact upon the 1848 revolutions. *The Civil War in France*, planned to coincide with the Paris Commune, appeared after its fall. Most famous of all was Marx's 1851 prediction that *Capital* would be ready for the Crystal Palace; it took another 16 years.[14] Politics, and history, always got in the way.

---

13   Beilharz 1991b.
14   Gabriel 2011, p. 514.

Bernard Smith chose to be late, as well as committed. For the early Smith, the Smith of *Place, Taste and Tradition* (1945), politics mattered because they were unavoidable: poets and painters were dying in Spain. His early politics were anti-nationalist, anti-nativist. He was intuitively indisposed to take seriously the kind of Herder-wisdom for which culture is only ever particular, and springs as it were from the ground. This predilection became clearer in his masterwork *European Vision and the South Pacific* (1960), where culture appeared not from any originary place but rather emerged from the dialectics of cultural traffic as it extended across the world system. But *Place, Taste and Tradition* was also an emphatically positioned document: it lacked the cooler scholarly detachment of *European Vision*. A similar distance opened between the politics of anti-fascism in *Place, Taste and Tradition* and the absolute centrality of period style and periodisation in *Australian Painting* (1962). Periodisation, by definition, can only be applied *ex post facto*, when the owl has flown. Time matters, then, for Smith, and we cannot force it. But there is also, as he recognised, a division of labour that holds up intellectual activity. Historians, for example, were themselves artists and producers rather than actors on the world stage. Smith was not given to refer to Max Weber, though Kant was certainly within his frame; the idea of spheres of interest and competence was fundamental to his work.

Bernard Smith was a traditionalist. Marxism was his tradition; but traditions face the past. Like Weber, he believed that we chose our gods, our traditions, as we had to serve them. Art, as he was given to say, 'has a history'. Art history has a history. Unlike some other postwar Marxists like Paul Sweezy, then, Smith did not embrace the idea of the 'present as history'. His epistemology was not presentist, and certainly not predictive. He liked to sit with the owl of Minerva, but he did not endorse Hegel's enthusiasm for the idea of *philosophy* of history, where the author became the end of the story. In this particular sense, and against the current of Marxism-Leninism, he was not a Marxist. He was not a triumphalist; his mood was rather with the spirit of Gramsci for whom, left to itself, history would always work out well for the other side, not for those of us who stayed facing left. What this suggests, perhaps, is the presence in his work of a marxism of irony, if not a marxism of the tragic.

With the Marx of the *Eighteenth Brumaire*, where there are ghosts, and we are creatures given to repetition rather than to progress, Smith is also here with Freud. Freud's presence is probably most apparent in *The Spectre of Truganini*, where it is forgetting, rather than rationality or progress, which is the leitmotif. In this way, of course, it is Freud rather than Marx who is the really radical or even revolutionary thinker of modernity. If we can never be masters in our own house, then the entire fantasy of the project of the rational domination of the

world begins to crumble. We arrive too late, too late perhaps even to understand, let alone to exercise the project of rational mastery.

Smith's marxism is that of the *Eighteenth Brumaire*, not that of *Thesis Eleven*.
As he puts his view with simple eloquence in 'History and the Architect' (1982):
'As I speak my words flow into the past'.[15] This historicist sensibility also informs
the strong distinction he wanted to maintain between art history and art criticism. Criticism is of the present, and is often therefore ephemeral: in the
present, it is increasingly likely that we will get it wrong. This remains the
strongest single difference between his own project, for example, and that of
a critic like Robert Hughes. It also helps to explain his distance from, his literal
disinterest in, so much of what these days goes to make up contemporary art,
which for him we could like or dislike but could not get a distance on.

Is this not, then, a tragic view of history, and if so, how does it connect
to Marx, marxism, historical materialism? As I have tried to suggest here, the
echoes with Marx and with the idea of a project of historical materialism are
substantive. Perhaps the most obvious textual or aesthetic symbol which suggests itself here by way of connect is Walter Benjamin's Angel of History. Smith's
view is ironic, because those who think they have understood or even believe
that they control the world have surely deluded themselves. Wisdom, in this
way of thinking, will always, necessarily, be retrospective. Yet Smith also is
wont to insist on the empirical temper in his work. As he puts it, big thematic
questions – the sacred versus the secular, the competing needs of science and
tradition, the national versus the international – are *empirical* matters.[16] And
this, after all, is also the spirit of *European Vision*: where it is experiment, effort,
mistake and sometimes insight as well as blindness that drive us on, however
we stumble.

The tension between the ideographic and the nomothetic remains unresolved, necessarily, both in Smith's work and elsewhere. Likely it is just another
of these matters requiring empirical response. Whatever the case, the message
is clear. Historians do not change the world; they wait. But they might change
the way we think, and as we think, so we are. This is another key insight discovered, or argued, in *European Vision and the South Pacific*. We are involved,
and detached, all at the same time.

This image of detachment brings us closer to the theme of isolation, which
Bernard Smith sets out to disentangle in his 1961 Macrossan Lectures. Distance,
and isolation, have long been standard default themes in antipodean histori-

---

15   Smith 1988, p. 89.
16   Smith 1988, p. 88.

ography. In this, it may be useful to connect Smith to other Australian writings. Elsewhere I have observed that there are significant connections between Smith's work and that of Russel Ward in *The Australian Legend*. The two had been mates together at the fledging ANU, but there are also lines of thought which connect them, for example on romanticism. When it comes to distance and isolation, the more obvious connection is with Geoffrey Blainey, though to the best of my knowledge their paths did not cross in this way.

The significance of Blainey's contribution to Australian historiography has been blurred by political controversy over the question of immigration in the early 80s. Signal among his many works, and likely better known for its title than for its message, is *The Tyranny of Distance* (1966). This is an extraordinary work in its own right, not least because it manages to enliven what is in fact a transport history as a key optic on white Australian life. For the colonies and cities that went to make up Australia first had to be connected, by traffic literal as well as cultural. Modern Australian history was therefore also the history of its transport technologies, their uptake and transformation. The Blainey thesis is brilliant. It does not, contrary to popular sensibility, suggest that the 'essence' of Australia consists in its being far away from the centres. What it implies, rather, is that 'Australia' is constituted by the traffic in between the cities and regions and other maritime regions. In this its themes are directly aligned or at least sympathetic with those of Bernard Smith.

The Tyranny of Distance does associate the themes of isolation and distance, though they are not in fact the same. Both themes do, however, imply that culture happens through movement or cultural traffic, both by ground and especially via the maritimes. Isolation, for Blainey, is the original colonial condition. He dedicates a whole chapter to the condition. His conclusion is entitled 'Antipodes Adrift'. Smith's 'The Myth of Isolation' takes on the challenge. It is a major contribution to the discussion of the provincialism question.[17] The cliché is that Australia is indeed too far away, irrelevant and provincial. Yet there are signs of recognition, and they are warming; proceed with caution. 'For the quality of a culture is best judged, in the long run, by informed critics separated from it both in time and space'.[18] All the same, it may be best, Smith tells us, to let these matters settle in any case; a later generation will make better sense of this belated recognition of the place of Australian painting on the world stage. The irony is telling. While the English have discovered Australian painting, in the 1962 Whitechapel show, local critics are so completely habituated to bleating

---

17   Beilharz 2006.
18   Smith 1988, p. 217.

about our isolation as to find themselves now lost in the confusion. Smith does not use the phrase, but the issue is what A.A. Phillips in 1959 called The Cultural Cringe. Smith's claim is that we may, in Australia, indeed be distant, but not isolated. His sentiment echoes Gauguin's: we need to know where we came from, have some idea of where we are going, and not be haunted by the fear of isolation.[19]

Culture is constituted through movement, through traffic.[20] 'Our European-based culture came to us in small transportable things that could be carried in ships, such as minds and books'.[21] In contrast to Hughes's argument in the Whitechapel document, this raises the possibility that we might be isolated in space but not in time. Spain happened for Bernard Smith in the backblocks of Wagga, in Murraguldrie, a one-teacher school amidst *pinus radiata* and not much else. It happened via radio and by letter: there was mail three times a week, and frequent letters from Lindsay Gordon, from whom Smith tells us he learned so much.

Smith lists his reservations about the idea of isolation. First, it rankles because it suggests exceptionalism; and Smith is interested in particulars, but perhaps especially in patterns. Exceptionalism suggests exoticism, a trope which conceals at least as much as it reveals. Second, isolation suggests definition by absence, or lack. The motif of isolation misses the point of intelligence, interpretation or action. What at first sight seems to be isolation often turns out to be a process of selection and rejection.

> At the beginning ... this process of selection and rejection is not apparent to any extent. That is not surprising. Our colonial painters, despite the time and distance from Europe, were certainly not isolated from the European tradition, for most of them were English and identified themselves with their homeland all their lives ... Colonial artists were European artists in Australia. There was no essential isolation in the colonial situation, for, despite the distance, ideas and styles come through.[22]

As Smith explained, colonial painting in Australia was essentially a branch of English painting: which is not to say that it was merely derivative, but precisely to acknowledge the fact that it was colonial, i.e. here and there, peripheral and central at the very same time. Culture results from a concatenation

---

19   Smith 1988, p. 219.
20   Beilharz, 1997.
21   Smith 1988, p. 98.
22   Smith 1988, p. 223.

of forces, environment, different European aesthetic movements, politics and social forces. The links with Europe were never broken – there was a constant coming and going of personnel, ideas and techniques and tools. And none of this was empty mimicry.

> Acceptance without question is the essence of provincialism: the colonial painters accepted picturesque and romantic conventions without question. An indigenous tradition, on the other hand, not only assimilates, it also rejects. Indeed it must exercise choice if it is going to be more than a pale imitation of the metropolitan culture of which it is affiliated.[23]

The only sense of isolation worth worrying about, for Bernard Smith, was isolationist politics, the kind of exceptionalism which in culture calls for an Australian painting or music or letters as though it can come only out of the ground or environment. What made culture live, in contrast, was the extent to which it instead resulted from the blend of innovation and tradition.[24]

So why did metropolitan critics choose this moment to discover Australian art? Contrary to the argument of the Whitechapel document, the modern movement since 1900 was largely correlated to the Renaissance tradition, and was stimulated rather by exotic art from Catalonia or Africa, Japan or the South Sea. 'With the expansion of European culture over the globe it is the exotic frontier cultures which have to a large extent determined taste and much of the movement of style. The presenting issue, now, would likely less be isolation, or exceptionalism, than the iron grip of modern primitivism'.[25]

Only the first of Smith's two Macrossan Lectures was republished as 'The Myth of Isolation'. The first lecture was overwhelmingly more powerful, pertinent, and prescient: it has provided the substance for much of the foregoing analysis. The second lecture was entitled 'The Rebirth of Australian Painting'. It was a theoretical survey, and indeed periodisation of the art scenes in Melbourne and Sydney, with reference to time and place. The other peripheries of the peripheries – Brisbane, Perth, Adelaide and so on – remained invisible, as did New Zealand in Smith's work. Likely it is no mere coincidence that leading New Zealand intellectuals pondered very similar issues at the same time, as is made apparent in the coterminous publication edited by Keith Sinclair, *Distance Looks Our Way: The Effects of Remoteness on New Zealand*.[26] Perhaps

---

23   Smith 1988, p. 225.
24   Smith 1988, p. 228.
25   Smith 1988, p. 229.
26   Sinclair 1961.

they were gaps for others to fill in, or fill out; perhaps these were more serious oversights. But he was there first, and it seems unfair to have expected a great deal more of Bernard Smith, considering the extraordinary nature of his achievement.

His final diagnostic was telling, and it backed into and moderated the more strident tenor of the *Antipodean Manifesto*.

> But if Australia is to continue to produce an art of international standing it will be, I believe, an art that emerges from Australian experience and gives a critical edge to it; an art that both celebrates and scarifies our beliefs and traditions; diverse in its interests ... while allowing the adherents of no doctrine to posture as an elect called by history to create the only true art of their time; an art which combines tolerance with a lively clash of conflicting opinion, an art contemptuous neither of ideas nor of intuition in the creative process, an art which at its best can rise above the interests and limitations of the nation and the self.[27]

Bernard Smith was a Marxist. Five words which say a lot and yet leave a great deal yet to be resolved. I began this exercise, seeking to take some distance on Smith's work, with those five words. Let me close with six: 'He was an historian, after all'.[28] Or five: 'He was an historian, after ...'

Now that we are after Bernard Smith, it is truly time to sit with the owl of Minerva, looking back in order to look forward.

---

27   Smith 1962, p. 32.
28   Beilharz 1997, p. 28.

CHAPTER 24

Zygmunt Bauman (1925–)(2010)

Zygmunt Bauman has an intriguing presence in English-speaking social theory. His influence is ubiquitous, but at the same time it is marginal. Little surprise: neither has he set out to establish a system, a set of operational theoretical tools, nor has he established a school. Across the years his modus operandi has been solitary and idiosyncratic; and his object has moved, though his sensibilities have remained more constant. He still identifies with sociology, as a field, and with socialism, as a norm or utopia.

Now that his work is well known, it is worth remembering that Bauman is not a celebrity. He is not a public intellectual, or at least not a TV-intellectual. But he writes for a public, even if it is an imaginary one, and this is especially true of his work over the last decade. There is a prehistory to this most recent phase of public writing; and there is another prehistory before that. Bauman wrote fifteen books in Polish during his first career when he was living another life that, quite reasonably, he imagined might be his last. Having joined the Polish Army in the Soviet Union in 1941 he was sacked from his rank as Major in 1953. He opened a new door, that to sociology and philosophy at the University of Warsaw, and eventually became one of its leading lights. Then, again (history repeats) he was sacked for the most honourable possible professorial crime – 'misleading the youth' – in the anti-Semitic purge of 1968. Driven out, he finally settled in Yorkshire, where his fields were still socialism and sociology. This, the opening English-language phase of his long life, generated at least thirty books, published in at least thirty languages, and covering an extraordinary array of interests, from utopia to hermeneutics, culture to mortality, postmodernity, intellectuals, violence, stigma, love, death and eternity.[1]

How could we characterise this project? Probably the two most influential academic books across this span are *Legislators and Interpreters*[2] and *Modernity and the Holocaust*.[3] But these are clearly scholarly works, works directed primarily to his students and peers, not so explicitly to the public, real or imagined. Yet there is a clear break or change of strategy in his writing and publishing. It coincides with his retirement, in 1990. *Modernity and Ambivalence*[4]

---

1   See e.g. Beilharz 2002; Tester and Jacobsen 2005; Elliott 2013.
2   Bauman 1987.
3   Bauman 1989.
4   Bauman 1991.

is his last powerful monograph, though it is also a text entirely continuous with *Modernity and the Holocaust* – it literally reads like its second part or extension. Several volumes of essays followed – *Intimations of Modernity*,[5] *Life in Fragments*,[6] *Postmodernity and Its Discontents*[7] and others. The sea change came with *Globalization* and the works that followed it, especially *Community, Identity and Europe* – all little books, keyword studies in brief compass.[8] These were examples of what he called the *Buchlein*, the little book, the strap hanger for the train or bus, no footnotes, or few, rather a condensing image put to work as the pretext for a complaint about the injustices and asymmetries of the world we have constructed.

Along with these, not always in the same format but designed to be user-friendly, was the flurry of work exercising the theme of liquidity, from *Liquid Modernity* to *Liquid Love*, *Liquid Life* and *Liquid Times*.[9] By this stage, some of Bauman's critics thought that he was fished out, given merely to repetition. Bauman's strategy was to repeat his claims in different ways, using different symbols – globalisation, community, identity, Europe, whatever – to connect the present to the traditions of critical sociology which he inherited, and indeed to repeat himself. For he was no longer thinking of his reader as someone (like me) who would read his entire output serially, awaiting each instalment in a personal scholarly trajectory. His new imaginary reader was rather the strap hanger who might read one book, and next be reading Richard Sennett or Alain de Botton or *Who Weekly* or *The Guardian*. So, for example, we find Bauman's influence acknowledged in a novel like Monica Ali's *In the Kitchen*.[10] This shows that his strategy for the little books has had some success: they are books that might even be read in the kitchen.

So there are now two different audiences, or constituencies, for the work of Zygmunt Bauman. One is popular, curious, tertiary educated but occasional in its encounter with universities. The other (us) has some professional investment in theory, like it or not, will view matters from different perspectives, not always given to democracy or to sharing, looking for clues or pendants with which to legitimise our work and to make it seem different or distinct from that of our competitors. How, amidst all this, do we find a line into this labyrinth?

---

5   Bauman 1992.
6   Bauman 1995.
7   Bauman 1997.
8   Bauman 2001, 2004b, 2004a.
9   Bauman 2000, 2003, 2005, 2007.
10   Ali 2009.

There are many, already, suggested. Some, like Keith Tester, value the literary aspect of Bauman's work. Others, like Anthony Elliott, want to stress its contemporaneity. My own inclination has been to stress its continuity, for this is the aspect of his work that shouts the loudest at me. Bauman, for me, is still a traditional East European critical theorist. He carries traditions that he takes very seriously, from Simmel, Freud and Weber, as well as many others, including novelists and anthropologists.[11] But the longest lineage for Bauman starts in Trier and ends in the British Museum, not too far from the library of the London School of Economics where he also laboured.

Marx and Surplus Population

In 1867 Karl Marx published *Capital* Volume I. It was to have a major effect on the life and work of Zygmunt Bauman, who had become a communist in Poland during the Second World War. For it contained a world-view, and a critique of capitalist civilisation as well as of political economy; and its frame reflected Marx's exile in the homeland of capitalism, an exile which Bauman was to follow, a century later, when he took up his chair at the University of Leeds, not too far from Engels's Manchester.

The power of *Capital* Volume I can be found in the rigour of its internal logic, the cell-form of the commodity leading to the ghosts of commodity fetishism, in its descent into the purgatory of the labour process, like entering Dante's inferno, in its majestic survey of the struggle over the working day, in its apocalyptic climax in Chapter 32, where Marx's drama finally closes with the expropriation of the expropriators. But the passages which extend most clearly from Marx's project into Bauman's are different. They arrive in Parts Seven and Eight, the last two acts of *Capital*. Part Seven Section 4 addresses 'Different forms of the Relative Surplus Population'. Marx's initial field of concern here is unemployment, though the idea of 'surplus population' is broader and more expansive. It travels across time and space, right through to the present, to Bauman's concern with the lost postmodern souls he calls vagabonds.

Even in his moment Marx understands the importance of partial employment. Regardless of cyclical trends, he tells us, unemployment has three forms, floating, latent and stagnant, liquid metaphors of the human condition that again anticipate Bauman's critique of modernity a hundred years later. Floating unemployment appears mainly in connection with machinery, in great work-

---

11   Beilharz 2010a.

shops that prefer to employ boys rather than men. The youth whose fate it is to float often float overseas – they are compelled to emigrate, following that part of capital which emigrates. The mechanisation of agriculture likewise compels local and regional migration. This is what Marx calls latent surplus population. Finally, by stagnant relative surplus population Marx designates those workers who are subject to extremely irregular employment. The lowest category of relative surplus population dwells in the sphere of pauperism. 'Exclusive of vagabonds, criminals, prostitutes, in a word, the "dangerous" classes, this layer of society consists of three categories', he tells us: those able to work; orphans and pauper children; and the demoralised and ragged, the mutilated and sickly.[12] In sum total these categories go to make up the industrial reserve army of the unemployed. All this, of course, is the result of progress, development, the further application of capitalist technology.

Marx returns to these issues historically in Chapter 27, on the expropriation of the agricultural population from the land, a theme which still resonates through Southeast Asia and Latin America today. In Thomas More's nightmare, sheep ate men; you can modify the images as you will for the inhabitants of the rainforests in those other lands today. After all, it was the introduction of local laws preventing the 'theft' of wood from the commons which had originally drawn Marx into the field of radical journalism, before he became a marxist.

Capital closes, infamously, with the double ending of Chapters 32 and 33. (Bauman was to introduce his own double ending, modern and postmodern, in *Legislators and Interpreters*). Colonisation, as Marx and Engels had anticipated earlier in *The Communist Manifesto*, would sooner or later expand to cover the planet. There would be nothing outside the rule of capital. Primitive accumulation would extend across the entire globe. And as Bauman would conclude, in his own time, the planet would be full. The connection and affinity between Bauman and his teacher is clear. While Marx's revolutionary choreography culminates in proletarian victory in the penultimate chapter of *Capital*, Chapter 33 opens the door to the world to them, and to the apparent solution to the problem of surplus population proposed by Edward Wakefield, namely, systematic colonisation in Australia. The prospect of migration to the New World provides the safety valve for the Old World. But by our time, and Bauman's own, this idea has been totally exhausted. It was already impossible in Marx's time. The point of connection is an obvious one, which perhaps drops out of sight because it is obvious. The politics of capitalism and of nation states is a geopolitics, a politics of space. Surplus populations will become a major attribute of modern times.

---

12   Marx 1965, p. 659.

Labour and Modern Capitalism

Marx's work never transcends its labour ontology, or departs from its founding preface, that men and women are suffering, sensuous, creative beings. Bauman's sociology can be characterised in many different ways, as a critique of modernity, as an East European critical theory, as a critique of consumption, whatever. Yet one of its enduring motifs is to be found in the idea of surplus populations, sensuous, suffering, creative beings who are told or compelled to move on. Movement is central to modernity, to power and to culture. Forced movement is one of its central facts of life. This theme can be traced through some of Bauman's most powerful works, from his English language beginning in the 1972 work *Between Class and Elite* to the 1982 classic *Memories of Class*, to the peak of his influence in *Modernity and the Holocaust, Postmodernity and its Discontents*; *Work, Consumerism and the New Poor*, and *Wasted Lives*.

So let us begin at Bauman's beginning. He had published fifteen books in his native Polish when he was himself driven into exile, like Marx, a political refugee, with all the irony of the great communist experiment: he was too marxist for a putatively marxist regime, so he and his family were harassed and then shown the door, the final exit of the one way visa out of Warsaw via Jerusalem. He had been out before, in moments of authorised scholarly pursuit, not least in the late fifties, when his curiosity took him to Manchester and to the London School of Economics and Bloomsbury, which has meant so much to so many, and Marx's drag as well, from Dean Street and Soho to the splendour of the British Museum. Marx was, as he himself said, a machine condemned to devour books, and also a machine condemned to produce more than his share of them, another characteristic that Bauman was to come to share with him. So it is clear. Zygmunt Bauman was attracted to England for the same reason as Marx was. They would leave you alone, even if they ignored you for a long time; they had the primeval experience of industrialisation, capitalism and modern class struggle; and, by Bauman's time, they had Marx, and they still tolerated marxists.

Its first results appeared in *Between Class and Elite*. It was based on Bauman's earlier work in Polish and was deeply connected to his earlier time and experience in Britain. Bauman is interested in a general theory of labour movements, understood as a prelude to a general theory of social movements. His interest is both in the movements themselves and in their representation. The latter matters, not least because the realities of class and suffering always strain against intellectual self-interest when it comes to the representation of some by others who do not suffer in the same way. Intellectuals always get in the way.

Bauman's curiosity invariably takes him onto the turf dominated by historians, not least of them E.P. Thompson. He contests some of the humanist confidence of Thompson's famous *Making of the English Working Class*,[13] both as regards labour's promethean origins and its present capacity. Bauman views class as a retrospective manner of naming a series of struggles against industrialism. 'Community' matters more than 'proletariat', in the beginning. Thompson, in others words, reads history backwards. The mass worker is a new, twentieth-century phenomenon; the pioneer workers of the industrial revolution still had their heads elsewhere, somewhere before fordism and modernity. But when labour organisation changes, and accommodates itself to capitalism, it does so with a vengeance. In the long run, labour provides the most able lieutenants for capital. Labour develops its own elites, with a thin relationship with those unskilled they actually claim to represent. The organisations of the labour movement became a career escalator.

The Industrial Revolution was a prime mover: it introduced the fact of motion or, as Marx put it, it normalised the possibility of geographical and social mobility. Population density and migration increased dramatically. Movement from the country to the cities became the Leitmotif of modernity that it still is. Capitalism's permanent revolution was one of movement. Surplus population constituted a kind of explosion within the old existing social relations and structures. Bauman gestures towards *Capital* as the authoritative source here, but also reminds us of Engels's major contribution in *The Condition of the Working Class in England*.[14] The general sentiment of his analysis, however, is that this was a matter of all that was solid melting. Industrialism normalised change or disintegration before the emergence of the new order was possible. The motif here is exactly the same as that later coined as 'liquid modernity' replacing 'solid modernity'. Estrangement ruled. The least advantaged were the pariahs, the 'navvies', the masterless men.

Having been there first, Edward Thompson pilloried Bauman and his book in *The Guardian* on 28 December 1972. It was bad enough that Bauman was a sociologist, but he also imagined he knew more about socialism than Thompson did. Bauman nevertheless persisted. He returned to Thompson's fields, in company with the unwelcome figure of Michel Foucault, in his major reprise, *Memories of Class: The Prehistory and Afterlife of Class*. Bauman was, in a sense, writing the marxian instalment missing from Foucault's project, where there was Discipline, Power, Hospital, Clinic, Prison – but no Factory.[15] For Marx, for

---

13   Bauman 1963.
14   Engels 1892.
15   See Foucault 1977.

Capital, of course, the factory was the characteristic institutional form and core of modernity. And Bauman follows this, until the 1970s, when consumption replaces work or production as the central activity of modernity, and the mall replaces the factory as its institutional embodiment. The factory is the Panopticon.

Here, again, the issue of representation is fundamental. For the new industrial class, the proletariat, there is another, new intellectual class, the helpers, from social workers to trades union leaders and politicians – no Panopticon without Bentham, no reform without its Fabians, no Russian Revolution without Bolsheviks. But it was the rapid erosion of protective institutions which was a major cause of discontent; and again, the obvious echo in Bauman's work is with the dismantling of the welfare state after the decline of the golden age of capitalism after World War Two. Alongside Foucault's *Discipline and Punish* and Thompson's *Making of the English Working Class*, the third pillar of Bauman's thinking is Barrington Moore's *Injustice*.[16] Socialism and the labour movement, on this way of thinking, represent reaction rather than progress, resistance to change rather than its enthusiastic pursuit. The results of industrialisation were unmistakable. The dissipation of locally based paternalistic institutions resulted in a massive production of paupers and beggars, vagrants and vagabonds.

Call it modern capitalism, call it the Industrial Revolution, the most powerful immediate effect of the great transformation was demographic. Now there was the beginning of material abundance. Together with surplus product and surplus value came surplus population. The historical novelty of the factory system, after its disastrous collapse in the Depression, was in its capacity to absorb labour. This was the exceptional moment of postwar fordism, when producers had been taught to produce and now were able also to consume, before they had to be taught that consumption, alone, was to be the primary source of identity. The factory, in any case, was at least as profoundly a cultural as an economic institution. Its purpose was to make new men, and women, and to bind them into the new order, not merely to generate profit or to extract surplus value.

Throughout the period of its consolidation into the twentieth century, capitalist culture worked through the politics of inclusion and, via inclusion, exploitation. Peasants became proletarians; pariahs eventually became factory fodder. But there remained problems of surplus population, of stigma, of others who did not belong or whose belonging was temporary or contingent. The proletarian was never quite unmarked in his universality; some were more completely included or assimilated than others. Not all were to be welcomed into

---

16   Bauman 1978.

the Panopticon, or into the Factory. There were other institutions yet to be fully designed and constructed, like those of the gas ovens, anticipated earlier in lightweight canvas form as the camps of the nineteenth century. The bodies of others had also been drilled through the slave trade and plantations, which as Bauman observes may in turn have influenced the formation of factory systems.

In the heartlands of the West, in the meantime, the proletariat had garlanded its chains with flowers. They had been lead actors, along with the bourgeoisie and the new class, in the construction of corporatism, which represented the inclusive moment of postwar capitalism. The outsiders now were those without hope, the postwar lumpenproletariat. The 'new victims' of this social arrangement would be those who truly missed out. For there was now, again, a discernable underclass in the cities of the West. And there were others. They might be marginals within these systems, or they might consist of the massed ranks of the dispossessed of the earth, the poor and excluded of the Third World.

Postmodernity and Intellectuals

Two turns follow, in the path of Bauman's work, in 1987 and 1989. The 1987 turn is to the postmodern, famously, in *Legislators and Interpreters: On Modernity, Post-Modernity and Intellectuals*. The hyphen gives it away – this was a pioneering work on the postmodern in sociology, before the connector became lost and the unitary term, 'postmodern', became naturalised. The title tells more, and less. First, the proper object of Bauman's enquiry is intellectuals; for the postmodern is first and foremost an intellectual preoccupation. Neither proletarian nor bourgeois would be much moved by it, except until the postmodern became a consumer good. But more, Bauman's enthusiasm for the idea of the postmodern was limited, analytical rather than celebratory. Something had changed, since corporatism or fordism or what he would later call solid modernity. And one aspect of this was that intellectuals, who hitherto were keen to step up not only to celebrity but also to power, might now step back, return to more modest claims to interpretation or translation between life-worlds. Second, and more surprisingly, we had met the enemy, and he (she) was us. For the problem in this book was intellectuals, Enlighteners, implicitly all of us would-be improvers, from Fabians to Bolsheviks to postwar social democrats, social engineers all.

While Bauman remained committed both to socialism and to sociology, and had long identified utopia as a norm rather than as a state-of-affairs to be achieved, this was nevertheless a step back or away from his own class. Another significant step came in *Modernity and the Holocaust*. Here, under the influence of Janina Bauman's childhood memoirs of life in and escape from the Warsaw Ghetto, *Winter in the Morning*,[17] Bauman chose to foreground the Holocaust as a way of seeing modernity. If the victims of the do-gooders in *Legislators and Interpreters* were the masses of ordinary people who were the victims of routine social engineering since the nineteenth century, then the victims of the Holocaust were also apparent. Outsiders, Romany, socialists, deviants, radical Christians, homosexuals, but above all, Jews. Jews, notoriously, had to be stigmatised, culturally alienated before they could be banished or destroyed. Vermin, weeds, dirt, matter out of place; all the most powerful stigmata were applied prior to the mass destruction of the Jews. But why? Because these people represented surplus population. 'Rootless', they could be charged with belonging nowhere, first to be driven to Madagascar, then east, into Poland, for the Final Solution. Nazism was also, fundamentally, a means of dealing with 'surplus population'.

Bauman could not fully articulate the case in this way, because of the pioneering nature of his work. And it is worth remembering that, while it now has been assimilated into social science common-sense, and despite its Amalfi-Prize-winning status, Bauman and his book were originally shunned.[18] Most of his initial reviewers did not welcome this messenger, but dismissed Bauman for blaming modernity, rather than the Germans, for this atrocity. Today, Bauman's message is rather accepted, even if as a necessary provocation, and students of Holocaust studies routinely approach their subject in terms of surplus population, viewing Nazism primarily as a massive project in demographic engineering.[19] The Holocaust, like the Enclosure Acts before it, was a topological project. Nazism was primarily a territorial politics, a project which necessarily included the deterritorialisation of others and the reterritorialisation of their spaces as German ground. Anti-Semitism was fundamental to this; but its territorial aspects plainly involved relocating and exterminating populations in order to establish the Third Reich in all its spatial grandeur. *Lebensraum* (the German and Nazi drive for more territory) was elemental.

Underneath all this there is a hostility on Bauman's part to the spectre of Faust, the legendary German figure who makes a pact with the devil in return for knowledge, and his children, those who want to set the social and natural world to rights. Faust is happy to cut up the world, as well as to sacrifice

---

17   Bauman 1986.
18   Beilharz 2002, vol. 2.
19   Blackbourn 2006.

others along the way. Hitler's project became a gardening state, seeking out the weeds and their eradication. So the Nazi kind of social engineering also had something to do with the Enlightenment impulse of setting-the-world to rights, even if and as the Nazis hated the Enlightenment. They used its technologies, and those of the industrialism it later licensed. They became Faustian gardeners with a vengeance, cultivators without a precedent. Gardening was a metaphor which Bauman had used in *Legislators and Interpreters*, where he contrasted the zeal of the do-gooders with the gentler ecology of the gamekeepers. Bauman's own temperament has long been apparent, in contrast. He has always been a gamekeeper.[20]

Liquidity

There remains an unavoidable tension in modernity. There are always others who need help. But is it better to help or not to help? Does the welfare state merely reproduce or even increase patterns of dependence? We all depend on others, almost every moment of our waking lives. To turn away is even worse. For there will always be outsiders, strangers in our midst. Bauman returns to these themes in his essay 'Parvenu and Pariah: The Heroes and Victims of Modernity' and its sequel 'Tourists and Vagabonds: The Heroes and Victims of Postmodernity'.[21] Here, before the idea of liquid modernity is coined, it is modernity itself which is restless: as Bauman puts it, 'modernity is the impossibility of staying put. To be modern means to be on the move'.[22] This is not a choice. We are driven to move by the disparity between the beauty of the vision and the ugliness of reality. This makes us all nomads, in this sense at least. Nomads are parvenus, arrivistes, in but not quite of. This is the tragedy of modern culture: we only feel at home in our homelessness and this is an ambivalence beyond cure. The same ambivalence holds true for tourists and vagabonds, even if the latter move by necessity as contrasted to the choice of the former. Tourists have credit cards; and the vagabonds serve them, or can do, carry their bags, hold their doors open, service them sexually. Neither tourists nor vagabonds can be fixed in place, though tourists get closer to fixity by choice (they can choose home) and vagabonds get closer to fixity by circumstance (there is simply nowhere else to go, until further notice). Tourists, as Bauman puts it,

---

20   Carroll 2007.
21   Bauman 1997.
22   Bauman 1997, p. 77.

in an early exercise of the notion, are the supreme masters of the art of melting the solids and unfixing the fixed. They do not belong, yet they can keep their distance. Tourists move, on this account; they do not arrive. Vagabonds, in contrast, are the waste of the world which has dedicated itself to servicing tourists. The background image of vagabonds is as Romany, and again Zygmunt Bauman is working here under the influence of the work of his wife, Janina. Tourists happily evacuate, leave their mess behind for the vagabonds to work over and deal with. Their worlds are attractive. Vagabonds move because they find the world unbearably inhospitable. Tourists travel because they want to, vagabonds because they have no other choice. Their momentary sense of tolerance or 'welcome' can be withdrawn at a moment's notice.

Bauman knows that these are metaphors, rather than concepts; he is not presenting this couplet, tourist/vagabond, as a replacement or updating of, for example, class relations. Nevertheless, he suggests that 'the opposition between the tourists and the vagabonds is the major, principal division of the postmodern society',[23] and it is a global divide, even as it is lived out locally in the metropolis as well. This is an extension of the older, Hegelian dialectic of master and slave. The poor, the dispossessed of the world, become the rubbish bins of the privileged. Vagabonds are trash cans for tourist filth.

Bauman pursues these themes further in *Work, Consumerism and the New Poor*.[24] Here, everything that is old is new again. For the worlds of division and exclusion that we face today still call out earlier images of pauperism and a literature which runs through Disraeli, 'The Two Nations', Carlyle, Gaskell, Ricardo and Mayhew, Bentham and Chadwick. What he here calls modernity phase two, consumer's modernity, however, summons up a different emphasis between production and consumption. For some years, by this point, Bauman had been travelling in company with the kindred spirit of Jeremy Seabrook. Here, in effect, their concerns merge, for there is also a fellow traveller to this 1998 book, which is the little book on *Globalization*, where the effects of displaced peoples is tracked globally, in a complementary dimension to that of the Keynesian welfare state which is the analytical object of *Work, Consumerism and the New Poor*. The point, after Marx, with Keynes, is that capital is not only the vampire which sucks living labour dry; it also expels labour, literally evacuates it from the core institutions of modernity. Capital prices labour out of work, so that there is now a global reserve army of the unemployed, while welfare provision remains local. The underclass, Marx's Lumpenproletariat, returns to haunt us. No longer

---

23   Bauman 1997, p. 93.
24   Bauman 2004d.

mere victims, they now become demons, moral rather than economic in their primary function, constantly reminding all of us of the horrible fates of outsiders, keeping our noses down and bums up. The figure of the poor person becomes a scarecrow, not only superfluous to economic needs but also scary.

The most powerful condensation of these concerns comes, finally, with *Wasted Lives – Modernity and Its Outcasts*. This is the point at which Bauman connects most powerfully back to the issue of humans as waste posited in *Modernity and the Holocaust*. 'Our planet is full'.[25] Not only full, but bloated, as parts of the planet are rendered unfit for habitation, and the world system of consumption has expanded to the point that there is nothing left outside it, even as its marginal members struggle to survive. The production of 'human waste', more correctly wasted humans, excess souls, surplus population, the redundant, is an inevitable outcome of modernisation. Colonialism no longer offers the outlet for surplus population that it once did. The vast masses of lost humans want in, want in to the cities, most evidently in the megacities of the developing world. We are awash in shit, in the detritus of an economy based on obsolescence of humans and materials alike. Bauman is too polite to use the word, but it is the image of shit, human waste, wasted humans, actual and metaphorical, which holds up this entire book. So Mary Douglas reappears in the text, along with the anthropology of dirt. More, as he puts it,

> Waste is simultaneously divine and satanic. It is the midwife of all creation – and its most formidable obstacle. Waste is sublime: a unique blend of attraction and repulsion arousing an equally unique mixture of awe and fear.[26]

This much across time, but so much inflamed by modernity and its recklessness. Modernity is excess. Surplus population is one of the great externalities of capitalist economy. Prisons become the most expressive of institutions for this dumping of human lives. Refugees become its most stigmatised object.

But in the meantime, at the turn of the millennium, Bauman has posited the idea and the telos of *Liquid Modernity*, and all that which follows – liquid love, liquid fear, liquid times. The primary sociological purpose of the idea of liquid modernity seems to be to clarify the periodisation of twentieth-century development outside of the language of postmodernity. Yet postmodernity routinely was used to describe the capitalist world after the 1970s, and liquid modern-

---

25   Bauman 2004c, p. 5.
26   Bauman 2004c, p. 22.

ity indicates the same kind of notional periodisation. Solid modernity is fordism. Liquid modernity is what comes after, fraught with uncertainty, fragility, precariousness. Liquidity, like the postmodern before it, might be an attitude rather than a fixed condition or a fact. If postmodernity was for Bauman a matter of experiencing modernity without illusions, then liquid modernity was a matter of taking on modernity without certainty, safety or security. Life, henceforth, would be even more precarious, especially for those who did not choose this but had it forced rather upon them. Certainly the rate of change seems to be accelerating, and the purpose of liquidity is to capture this mercurial quality of flux, inasmuch as it is open to capture at all. How will all this look later, after the fact, after the immediacy of our moment and its experience? As Bernard Smith is given to remind us, in the company of Hegel, it remains entirely possible that we only understand history after the fact.[27] What looks liquid to my generation, or Bauman's, might well look different to those who are just now entering this world, and experience it as normal. The fact of movement, and the problems of surplus population, will persist, and accelerate further.

The image of liquidity is an intellectual device, not a thing in the world. It is a way of seeing, and Bauman has always been fond of ways of seeing, of the metaphor of past social critique and new. Like its object, modernity, Bauman's critical theory keeps moving on, anchoring interpretation between past critique and new futures. Its fascination rests with this intricate sense of negotiation, where the interpreter represents the present in between. This much we owe to his example.

------

27   Smith 2007.

CHAPTER 25

Zygmunt Bauman (2011)

The Person

Over the past twenty years Zygmunt Bauman has become one of the most influential sociologists in the world. Partly this is because, from a solid earlier research base, he chose to go public, to write for an imaginary audience that commutes through the everyday life of our cities, rather than hiding in its libraries. Partly it is because of his capacity to identify central problems of concern and anxiety, and to mediate them with some of the central wisdoms of classical and modern sociology. The result might be called a postmodern sociology, though that was a category he resisted, preferring the idea of a sociology of the present, a sociology of the postmodern. This is what, more recently, might be called a sociology of liquid modernity. It moves, it slips and slides, it surprises us daily – and so do we.

Bauman is a solitary actor, founding no centre, no journal, no school. Though he is open to all, he is a private person; his most intimate companion over sixty-one years was Janina Bauman, whose work had a significant effect on his. He does not seek influence, he is not a TV celebrity, he eschews opportunities to court or to influence power, not least because it bites you, or threatens to swallow you up. Bauman is a private person, and we do not know a great deal about his life. The model for his work is conversational, and his conversation shifts rapidly across whatever associations appear. Ask him a question and chances are he will answer with a question back. For this is how he sees our vocation. Our job is to ask questions, more importantly than to offer answers. Intellectuals are important, in this way of thinking, but no more important than anyone else. And if social problems have putatively practical solutions, best we work on these together rather than expect the eggheads or scientists to come up with the perfect solution. Humanity muddles through, and sometimes the mess of its achievements is stacked high, and counted in lives, in bodies, hearts, and souls.

When pressed, Bauman sometimes says that he is (we should be) interested in birds, not in ornithologists. We should be concerned with the problems of the world, not with the attributes or frailties of its interpreters. We do, nevertheless, know something of this ornithologist.

The Context

Bauman was born in Poznan in 1925. His family fled into the Soviet Union with the invasion of Poland by the Nazis in 1939. Bauman studied in the Soviet Union, but joined the Polish Army in the Soviet Union in order to fight the Nazis and defend his homeland. Elevated to the rank of major, he was sacked in the anti-Semitic purge of 1953, and instead became a sociologist, working in the continental tradition with thinkers like Stanislaw Ossowski and Julian Hochfeld, for whom there was a significant connection between sociology, philosophy, and social criticism.

This story fits the pattern of a kind of East European Critical Theory, sometimes called a dissident or Renaissance Marxism, which came out of Hungary, Czechoslovakia, Yugoslavia, and Poland into the 1960s. It has strong sympathies with the humanist Marxist sympathies of those times. From the 1950s Bauman identifies strongly not only with socialism and Marx, but also with sociology. He has disdain for mainstream American sociology which he calls 'Durksonian' (i.e. Durkheim plus Parsons) but he loves Simmel, 'who started it all'.

Along with others like Leszek Kołakowski, Bauman was sacked again in the 1968 anti-Semitic purge, now charged with the most noble crime of all – 'corrupting the youth'. He and his family were 'allowed to leave' on a one-way exit visa, via Tel Aviv and Canberra, to Leeds, which became his other home. Earlier, he had studied in Manchester and at the London School of Economics. England he knew was a place that tolerated foreigners, even if it did not embrace them; and in this he followed in Marx's footsteps and shared Marx's connection to the home of industrialism and the strange combination of class struggle and communitarianism which it called out.

His is a sociology which solidarises with C. Wright Mills's vocation, the sociological imagination, and it is no accident that Mills was a visitor to Poland in the 1950s, a connection Bauman later followed up with mutual friend Ralph Miliband, who also came to Leeds. Bauman at no stage of his career hesitates to call himself a sociologist; only he also knows that sociologists, and intellectuals in general, are all too human, too tribal, too particularistic, too defensive, too much prone to repetition and self-reproduction, and too open to the charms of influence and power where they imagine they can set the world to rights.

Bauman's work is both reactive and programmatic. Across the path of his life, there are sixteen books in Polish and more than thirty in English. His production schedule increases with age, especially after his retirement from Leeds, and it accelerates together with his embrace of the popular format 'little books' which have become a staple for him in recent years. These are books you might find in the high street bookshop, and read on the bus or train. What this reflects is a highly variegated body of work, less a clear project or trajectory than might be discerned in the work of a more single-minded thinker. His work is reactive, but also innovative, and its diversity makes it difficult to categorise (a fact that he would delight in). Consider some of his topics: sex, death, love, consumption, production, labour, socialism, culture, modernity, ambivalence, hermeneutics, fragmentation, classes and elites, structuralism, the postmodern, freedom and dependence, the Holocaust, Poland and other Soviet-type societies, Stalin, ethics, globalisation, community, Europe, identity, flux, uncertainty, and so on. Some larger, world historic themes coordinate this life and work. Bauman was compelled to experience and to deal intellectually with fascism and communism. He then had to make sense of capitalism in its British heartland, in the wake of Marx, and with its transformation into a culture of consumption. Bauman's work is special because it connects the small detail of daily life to these world historic themes and shifts which made us, and the last century, the age of extremes, and what follows.

How to put order into this chaos which so dutifully reflects the mess of the world which we inhabit? Bauman's work can be organised around many themes or optics. The four used here are socialism and culture; the postmodern turn; modernity and the Holocaust; and the most recent, liquid turn.

Bauman's English-language work can be said to have two pivotal intellectual shifts or moments: one in 1987, when he takes on the postmodern; the second in 1989, when he takes on the Holocaust. These involve a significant shift of emphasis away from the ideas of capitalism and socialism, towards modernity. Accompanying these shifts, belatedly, there is the shift of addressee, from the well-documented academic monograph to the popular work, the 'little books' of the recent period. With the decline or closure of politics in the public sphere, Bauman turns his own energy towards expanding the sphere of public criticism upon which the prospect of a democratic politics depends.

The Work

Socialism and Culture

In the beginning, for Bauman, there was socialism, its British narrative, told by Marx, and its Polish hopes. Socialism, in this story, was many things. It was the manifestation of the real struggles of ordinary men and women, engaged both in hope and in fear, looking forward to the prospect of better worlds and longing for memories, nostalgic or real, of the lost worlds of lives calmer and steadier before the factory system arrived.

These issues are opened in what might be Bauman's most conventionally scholarly work in sociology, his first book in English, *Between Class and Elite* (1972). Like the later text *Thinking Sociologically* (1990) this book connects vitally to earlier Polish-language anticipations. Here it is labour, and the British labour movement which is to be the bearer of socialism. But in bearing socialism, it carries it, belatedly, into the state after the Second World War, with the result that labour and the Labour Party become completely institutionalised, transformed into creatures of the state and in this sense the best lieutenants of capital. In the beginning, of course, there was more. The labour movement was the exemplary social movement. And its nineteenth-century intellectuals were also exemplary of problems to come later, into the twentieth century. Messianic intellectuals could not help but project their own dreams onto others, typically more modest folk who dreamed of more bread and a safe roof rather than the utopias hatched for them by others.

Labour, then, has a culture, or cultures, both those of aspirations modest or immodest, and those of activity, of the *habitus* and experience of everyday life and its accumulated traditions. Labour had its own intelligence and *raison d'être*, as well as carrying its own dreams and those of others. Labour would always be looking back, as well as forward. Labour also had its own elite, and its medieval memories of guild and artisanal life. The mass worker and the image of mass society changed all this.

As it becomes legitimised and trade unions and labour parties become hesitantly accepted, the labour movement also becomes a career escalator. It generates new elites. These elites, in turn, have their own cultures.

Socialism, in all this, would remain beyond definition. Bauman quotes Hubert Bland: 'It seems that we are to work for socialism, fight for socialism, even die for it, but not, for God's sake, to define it!' Or at least this was the story once the Labour Party became a significant institutional actor. Bauman, for his part, had a clearer sense of what socialism was; and it was less a state of affairs actual or to be realised (as in Poland) than a utopia. This sense resulted in one of his most powerful early works, *Socialism: The Active Utopia* (1976). Here Bauman argued three of his most powerful pertinent claims: first, that we are all Utopians, like it or not; second, that the definition of socialism as utopia indicates that it is not a state of affairs but a horizon never to be reached; and third, that socialism becomes the counter current or counter movement of modernity.

Utopia, indeed, could be the singular image under which almost all of Bauman's work could be organised. For it contains our hopes and dreams, as moderns or post-moderns, and our fears and disillusion. It changes, for us as moderns, for we believe ourselves to be capable of realizing it, socially, for others, publically, or privately, at home, in our private lives. For utopia becomes dystopia, after the Russian Revolution and Nazism; and then what is left of utopia becomes privatised, channeled into the pursuit of love or intimacy or the consumer paradise.

Utopia matters for Bauman because it is ubiquitous; everyone has a utopia, larger or smaller, more or less systematic or implicit. The Utopian impulse is real; it makes us want more; it makes us want to do better, it refuses to accept (for socialists) that the poor must always be among us. Utopias relativise the present; they serve to remind us of our own historicity and contingency. Utopias are driven by hope, they are future-oriented but they also connect to the present. Yesterday's dreams (full employment, healthcare insurance, whatever) sometimes come true, across the path of the twentieth century. Utopias pluralise, or open possibilities regarding social alternatives, for there are always alternatives, even when we cannot see them. Utopias actually work, not globally but incrementally; little bits of them finally come to pass.

Yet the cold stream of socialism, that which leads to Bolshevism, becomes fundamentally implicated in the practice of social engineering. The proletariat (or whoever) needs to be led by those who know, and these wise men have a habit of sticking around after the revolution. This practical utopianism, where utopia is a design to be actually realised, is necessarily connected to order building. Engineering and technology become the solutions to all problems, in this way of thinking. Technocracy threatens to rule. The pursuit of certainty threatens to kill us all, or at least to imprison us with cages of iron and steel, bound together by piles of paperwork that lead to the heavens. Yet in its critical sense, associated with the warm stream of socialism, the utopia of socialism is as Romanticism is to the Enlightenment; its partner and necessary corrective. In one sense socialism is bound to be and to remain a utopia; for as Weber is rumoured to have said to Lukács, this experiment (the Russian Revolution) will set the cause of socialism back one hundred years. Read negatively, perhaps socialism will never recover from the experience of communism; read positively perhaps it is rather the case that socialism remains, simply, as one of the warring gods, always ahead of us of, inspiring in its very impossibility.

The argument of *Socialism: The Active Utopia* points in many directions, one towards the problem of sociology of intellectuals, those who claim to represent others and may well later represent a class or elite project of their own. That is not a new idea nor is it by any means only an idea with a right-wing lineage. Libertarians have always been suspicious of intellectuals and perhaps especially of the state and not only of capital; and there is clearly a libertarian impulse in Bauman's thinking, one that aligns his sympathies with those of Luxemburg rather than Lenin. For Bauman also insists on connecting the problems of socialism and intellectuals to culture, and by no means wants to limit culture to its high cultural or aesthetic dimension.

Why is culture so important for Bauman? Because it is to us humans what water is to fish. Everything that we do, including economic life, is mediated by culture; the idea that they can be separated is an example of the kind of analytical logic which Bauman views as so pernicious. Alongside these other early works of Bauman, another foundation work is *Culture as Praxis* (1973). Bauman begins from the recognition that culture is a hierarchical practice; it is based on discrimination, on claims regarding 'real' or high and other, or popular culture. Some have it, and others do not; even its semantics make it clear that culture needs cultivation, as in agriculture. But there is also a second, widely shared use of the idea of culture, which presumes in a less hierarchical manner that all peoples and all loci or situations have cultures. The labour movement, for example, has not only a culture but many cultures, or at least it used to. Culture indicates ways of being, which Bauman wants to address less as structures, in the manner of the then widely influential school of structuralism, than of practices, as in processes. Intuitively this aligns his thinking with that of Antonio Gramsci, and later Pierre Bourdieu. Structure, here, is less an outcome than an aspiration. Cultures seek to make chaos into order. Sometimes its ordering project can be lethal; for Nazis, and communists also had cultures, indeed the German and Soviet experiences depended entirely on their cultural ambitions. For it is not enough to carry the people with you passively; they have to believe in Big Brother.

Cultures also generate insiders and outsiders; they are exclusive as well as inclusive. Bauman turns in this early work to the figure of the stranger, or the outsider. So here he already anticipates later work like *Modernity and the Holocaust*, where the figure of the stranger is the Jew, and his work on the postmodern, where the outsider is the flawed consumer. But Bauman also wants to insist that there is a culture of critique, and this line of argument is developed further in *Towards a Critical Sociology* (1976). For sociology too readily becomes comfortable, aligned with the status quo and the insiders, even at the same time as sociology burns the fingers of those who claim too easily to represent the people, the poor or the outsiders.

A central category in *Towards a Critical Sociology* is the idea of second nature. Second nature, indeed, is a kind of synonym for culture, for the idea that we learn very easily to naturalise the worlds into which we are born, to universalise our own cultures, ways of thinking, being, doing, living, hoping. The tragedy of culture is that it ossifies; our greatest triumphs entrap us. And here another theme is posited which returns later: the problem of conformism, of playing along, of following the rules even when we are not subject to instruction or the threat of sanction. But more, playing along might be just that, understanding full well that obedience does not imply inner acceptance or conversion. Sociology, on this way of thinking, should be aligned with the dream of freedom, even as freedom itself should be aligned with the counter factual of dependence rather than imagined independently.

Arriving at the Postmodern

For Bauman's generation of East European Marxists, the most powerful conceptual dyad was capitalism/socialism. But if capitalism and socialism were conceived as cultures, even if (as in Castoriadis) actually existing socialism was viewed as a variation of capitalism, all these phenomena were nevertheless understood as cultural in their constitution. This was not a matter of comparing or contrasting two different economics or economic models. What was interesting and disturbing about these phenomena was their cultures, their ways of life and being, the personality types that they made available, encouraged, or prohibited.

It was only later, however, that this discourse became known as a discourse about modernity. The temptation for Marxists was to identify capitalism and modernity. These days, however, it is common for people to talk about modernity whether in the seminar room or in the daily news (e.g. does modernity have a future when it comes to ecology or sustainability). In retrospect, when it comes to critical or academic discourse, it seems reasonably clear that one of the reasons we speak more or less comfortably about modernity today is because twenty years ago there was a massive fuss about the idea of the postmodern. The controversy over the postmodern was multifaceted and multiform. It elided or combined at least two different concerns or anxieties. One concerned the idea that modernism as an aesthetic category was over; that abstract international style was no longer hegemonic, that pastiche now ruled whether in art or music or whatever else. The other concern involved the possibility that modernity as a social form was over; that we (whoever this we was) no longer wanted to live in the modular, American post-war model of growth, suburbia, cars, malls, and marriage. The meeting point, or vital seam which connected modernism and modernity, or postmodernism and postmodernity, was arguably most evident in the theory and practice of architecture. For here aesthetics and technology or economy combined. It was not just modernist aesthetics that rankled, here it was the chicken-coop idea of mass standardised housing and mass standardised human subjects, men, women, and children.

All this seems reasonably apparent in retrospect. It was less obvious what was at risk at the time, for many reasons. Postmodern enthusiasm appealed to many, back then, as it carried on the earlier modernist love of the new. Away with the post-war world! Away with cardboard people and one-dimensional lives! If Bauman was right, that culture ossified, then it would be reasonable to expect that the post-war world, which itself looked like utopia to those who had suffered wars and depression, would soon enough itself look like a concrete cage. Nothing stands still, not least culture and its horizons of expectations.

Several of these issues, then, called out to Zygmunt Bauman. And he was to share, however momentarily, in this enthusiasm for the sense that the postmodern might offer us a new hope out from under the incubus of modernism, that new creative forces might be released that would remind us that other ways of living were possible. Perhaps, as he later put it, the postmodern would offer us nothing more than modernity without illusions, or at least without the most disabling illusions of the twentieth century, fascism, communism, and the 'there is no alternative' (TINA) philosophy of economic liberalism. When Bauman responded to the idea of the postmodern, however, the particular theme to which he chose to connect was that of intellectuals and the sociology of intellectuals. The point of identification was powerful. The postmodern critique of modernity itself often took the form of the critique of Enlightenment. The Enlightenment was a project, a set of ideas and so on; but it was also necessarily identified with its carriers: the intellectuals, the saviors, the savants, Those Who Knew, the scientists, eventually the social scientists – us. This of course meant that we were invisible, the Elephant in the Room of Modernity. For social scientists learned very quickly how to represent those who could not readily represent themselves. Social science became a kind of social ventriloquism.

The key work in Bauman's project here was *Legislators and Interpreters* (1987). The postmodern only appeared as a subtitle, and so provisionally that it remained hyphenated: *On Modernity, Post-Modernity and Intellectuals*. Still at this earlier moment of postmodern debate optimistic as to its productive potential, Bauman's interest was to contrast the intellectual styles or personality types of moderns and postmoderns. Modern and postmodern were less historic phases of development or actual social states of affairs; rather they represented intellectual cultures and choices. Modern and postmodern represented different cultures, or worldviews, modern instrumental, rational and calculative, postmodern pragmatic, sceptical, suspicious. Modern was built on the pursuit of the idea of the rational mastery of the world; postmodern, on the sense of the impossibility and dangers of this stratagem. Modern played into the strategy of social engineering. Postmodern was gentler than this, more contemplative, but also more open to the risk of complacency.

Thus the two strong types of his title. Moderns fancy themselves as legislators, those who know how to put the world to rights, and view the negative consequences of social engineering merely as the next set of challenges. Interpreters want to move more slowly and cautiously, to act as mediators or messengers rather than as the Heroes of Modern Times. Interpreters are given less to absolutes and universalism. Yet as Bauman is wont to insist, these are not clear cut or simple distinctions. All of us appeal to universals at some point, as in claims regarding universal rights. And interpreters retain a significant kind of power.

Viewed from the perspective of *Modernity and the Holocaust* and its critique of fascism as social engineering, *Legislators and Interpreters* begins to look like a critique of Bolshevism, or of Marxism in power. Its critical message is also self-critical. For it is addressed to the engineering ambitions of the likes of Lenin, who believed in *What is to be Done?* that ten wise men (= us) were worth a hundred fools. Read further back, Bauman's work viewed as a critique of *les philosophes* is actually a critique of Jacobinism. Conceptually, the argument connects to that in *Culture as Praxis*, for Bauman's critical metaphor of choice is not, as in Foucault, the pastoral, but the idea of modernity as a gardening culture. Moderns, on this account, do not know to leave well alone. They cannot give countenance to gamekeeping, which is Bauman's own preferred ethic. Humanism too easily becomes twentieth-century paranoia evidenced in the anxious imperative that nothing can be left alone. The object of Bauman's critique is the Faustian impulse of modernity, to build and rebuild the world, to destroy and build it again, to fuse and weld creation and destruction as the central dynamic of modern times. Modern culture, for Bauman, may not always self-destroy, but it cannot leave behind the imaginary horizon within which all that is solid deserves constantly to be melted by us, as actors who cannot help ourselves. We are bound, after Marx, to be sorcerers' apprentices. We can no longer fool ourselves that we control this process, humanly created or unleashed, which now seems only and completely to control us.

Modernity and the Holocaust

Modernity turns back on itself; moderns turn into barbarians. This was also the theme of Max Horkheimer and Theodor Adorno, in *Dialectic of Enlightenment*. And it, in turn, becomes the leitmotif for Bauman's most widely influential work. *Modernity and the Holocaust* (1989). But for Bauman, the point was not that the loftiest of Europeans – the Germans – had turned into barbarians. It was more general. Any one of us could do this; any one of us could, or would, comply, serve, follow orders, stack up the corpses, pull the trigger, sign the forms authorising extermination. In itself this was shocking enough. For Bauman refused, in this, to follow the conventional morality which divides humanity into good souls and evil monsters. The point was not that there were no such monsters, but that modernity (which here meant the twentieth century's greatest achievement) made such behavior so much more possible. The development of the means of destruction developed apace with the development of the means of production. It became easier for modern humans to kill or to maim because they did not have to look into the face of other, simply flick a switch.

Bauman's intellectual formation was influenced by those continental sociologists, like Hochfeld and Ossowski, for whom there was no firm distinction between sociology and philosophy, or between social sciences, liberal arts, and humanities. Across the path of his life he was deeply influenced by thinkers like Marx, Simmel, and Gramsci. The path of his work is littered with references to those thinkers whose ideas spark for him, which associate or condense or enable him to mediate past classics and present predicaments. Alongside these many influences, one most profound on the thinking of Zygmunt Bauman was that of his wife and companion, Janina.

The Holocaust arrives as something of a surprise in his work. It is also something of a surprise for sociology, which hitherto left its study to disciplines like politics or history. The Holocaust serves as a modern light bulb or tragic Eureka for Bauman; and this is one source of the controversy and originally negative response to his work, which could easily be seen as disrespectful to its victims, given to using the Holocaust as a symptom rather than as the great modern tragedy itself.

Bauman tells us that his book, *Modernity and the Holocaust*, was prompted by Janina's *Winter in the Morning* (1986). Janina's book contains the memoirs of her childhood in the Warsaw Ghetto, and her subsequent escape and survival. It is a remarkable book, written entirely without self-pity, looking into the abyss of Jewish daily life in Nazi Warsaw without succumbing to it innerly. As Zygmunt Bauman puts it, the power of the experience of her own distance, writing daily, monthly, yearly, and its result, combining presence and humanity with all these horrors, all this made him think that he had misplaced the Holocaust intellectually. He had viewed it as though it were a painting on the wall. Now, after Janina's self-interpretation, he viewed the Holocaust as a window on the wall. Its optic was that of modernity itself. The Holocaust told a story about all of us, not only a tragedy of Germans and Jews.

For Bauman, the Holocaust was a rational and rationalised project of state-sponsored, ideologically motivated mass murder delivered by the best available

German technology. It was a kind of murderous Fordism, the logic of mass production in the manner of Detroit here applied to mass destruction factory style.
This is not, however, a technological determinism at work in Bauman's thinking. Nazism is or was a culture, a murderous variation on the idea of creative
destruction, where the creation of the Third Reich as a geopolitical project rested on the destruction of the Jews and others. Nazism was not only a politics
or an ideology or a technology combining freeways with cinema propaganda
and gas ovens; it was a population strategy whose purpose was to rebuild a
greater Aryan land for the world, or at least for its Aryan citizens. For Bauman,
then, the Holocaust involved a kind of modern chemistry where all the existing
ingredients – bureaucracy, anti-Semitism, and technologies – were combined
into a newly explosive result. This does not make modernity and the Holocaust
identical, or even co-extensive. But it does give us the optic of the eye in the
modern storm.

Nazism represented the apogee of the gardening state. It sought to eliminate
the Jews, the 'weeds', and to cultivate the superior stock. More, the Jews had to
be destroyed because they represented disorder. This involved the most systematic destruction of the state-identified *Other* in living memory. The result was
a particular kind of reactionary modernism. For modernity would, and would
ever be imagined as exclusively modern. All modernities were mixed, combining traditionalistic throwbacks and inventions with technological advance. The
Germany of the Black Forest was an invented tradition. Racism, as we know it,
is a modern phenomenon. Racism is a modern weapon used often to seek out
traditionalistic ends. Nazism exemplifies the social engineering project, now
applied to genetic business itself.

Bauman wants us to look into the mirror of Auschwitz, to contemplate the
possibility that we could have done this. This opens the possibility that his is
a sociology of conformism, a critique of conformism. Perhaps this is underwritten by the critique of technology, for there is a residual sense in which any
critique of Enlightenment rationality still draws on the legacy of Romanticism.
As Bauman says, the problem with technology is that we have no way of saying
no to it. We are too weak to say no individually to what is presented to us as
the onward march of progress, and we have no collective or social means by
which to discuss or to limit the growth of science and technology politically.
Thus Bauman's analysis of modernity and the Holocaust shifts into discussion
of the Milgram and Zimbardo experiments, not German, not Nazi, but American, Ivy League, democratic, liberal, and civilised. The point, again, is that all of
us potentially will follow orders, will inflict pain on instruction, just as the university students in those experiments did. Obedience becomes the substitute
for conscience. The image of the rational, self-legislating personality so central,

say, to Kant's view in 'What is Enlightenment?' is lost, absent. Moderns find it very difficult to escape from the horizons of heteronomy. Society, as Bauman puts it, becomes a factory for morality. And let there be no mistake, Nazi culture, too, had its morality, its own strong and clear conceptions of wrong and right, who were the real citizens and who were the parasites, who was visible and who was invisible, who had the right to the space to live and who had to go.

Bauman's 'German' book thus ends up in the United States, or stretching across the globe itself. The German question is pursued, meantime, in one of Bauman's most conceptually powerful books, *Modernity and Ambivalence*. Here Bauman shifts from the critique of modern action to the critique of modern thinking, or classificatory logic. Bauman seeks to value ambivalence, or at least to respect it. For it makes us human, this kind of uncertainty that makes us feel radical on Thursday, conservative on Friday; and it serves to remind us that our judgments are perspectival, or institutional. We need, then, to classify, to separate, or discriminate, but we also seem to need too readily to fix these sensibilities, so that A is not B when it may be both. Once classified, too much fixity or certainty ensues. We set out to distinguish, but end up essentialising. One can only be German or Jewish, bourgeois or proletarian, friend or foe, insider or outsider. Yet we all know what it means to cross over, even as we kid ourselves that we know the world because we have it classified and categorised.

The theme points back to Horkheimer and Adorno, to *Dialectic of Enlightenment*, to the critique of that European civilisation which strides (and stumbles) forward, turning the dream of progress into the mixed modernity of barbarism. And it also points back to Germany, and to the other Jews, the non-German Jews or *Ostjüden*. The East European Jews were even more liminal than the Jews of Germany, for they were cast as failed German Jews. After the worst of modernity's excess in the Holocaust, what is left is the thin gruel of assimilation, or inclusion on borrowed time, at the grace of the host culture and at their discretion. Assimilation is better than exclusion, but it always remains provisional, and it threatens the strangers with being accepted only at the cost of being denied, or swallowed up.

As Bauman puts it later, modernity seems to combine or to alternate between two differing strategies which Claude Lévi-Strauss claims characterise some other, earlier tribes. These are called *anthropoemia* and *anthropophagia*. The first involves assimilation in the literal sense, to include the other by swallowing him or her up, digesting them. The second indicates expulsion, vomiting out, rejecting the other in a visceral way. Bauman suggests that modern states constitute their populations through a combination of these strategies.

Turning Liquid?

Bauman retired from Leeds in 1990. His last seriously academic monograph, duly referenced and thoroughly argued, was *Modernity and Ambivalence*. His next step was to turn, or to return, to the essay form, though Bauman has always been an essayist even when writing at length. He follows Montaigne: the essay is an attempt at understanding, never final, and it invites response, further questioning and discussion. So the interval between the larger books and the little books is filled with collections of essays, including *Life in Fragments* (1995), *Postmodernity and its Discontents* (1997) and *Postmodern Ethics* (1993).

Then come the little books, themselves signalling a postmodern or liquid turn in terms of style, culture, or audience. If this is a publishing choice then it was a choice Bauman made consciously at the time, and not only a trend or pattern that is evident only in retrospect. The idea of a liquid turn, in contrast, only seems to make sense after the fact, when there is now a series of titles constituted with reference to this new icon: *Liquid Love* (2003), *Liquid Life* (2005), *Liquid Times: Living in an Age of Uncertainty* (2006). Whence this sense of liquidity? In some ways, the idea of liquid modernity represents a semantic or symbolic solution to the problem of the postmodern. In its earlier configurations, into the 1980s, the postmodern seemed to hold some prospect of emancipation from the stodgier constraints of modernism. Twenty years later the postmodern had well passed its 'use-by'. The controversy over the postmodern was exhausted, and a more nuanced sense of valuing modernity both positively and negatively was one result. Increasingly the postmodern was viewed as another modernist or *avant-garde* moment in the reaction against institutionalised or actually existing modernism.

At the same time, it remained the case that there was something going on, something changing in the West at an alarming rate. In the 1980s, the word often used to try to capture this sense of accelerating change was the postmodern. Then another, bigger word came along to claim the job: globalisation. Bauman also wrote a book about globalisation. But his new position was marked by the idea of liquidity. The intellectual reference, characteristically, was to Marx, to the famous winged phrase mistranslated in the English version of *The Communist Manifesto* as 'all that is solid melts into air'.

Bauman's reference was contemporary rather than poetic or lyrical. He was not referring to the apparent solidity of the capitalism of the 1840s or the traditional regime of the same time. The solid capitalism or modernity Bauman referred to was of his own time: it stood for the long post-war boom and the period of affluence, consumerism and the welfare state, full employment, nuclear family, Fordism, the American Dream and its British and other European sub-versions, antipodean, Latin American, and so on. This new post-war world achieved a kind of apparent solidity which made the postmodern turn itself look revolutionary, as the new uncertainty and anxiety of neoliberalism and globalisation took its place. Liquid modernity meant that the set repertoire of the post-war boom was gone: fixed, relatively clear gender roles, full male employment, a fixed working week and weekend for leisure, cold war clarities setting political parties well apart over a Keynesian consensus underneath, jobs for life – all gone. Liquidity replaced it with the manifold meanings of the German word *Unsicherheit* – uncertainty, unsafety, insecurity, a kind of existential loneliness in the face of endless change and the end of loyalty, whether personal, intimate, or institutional. Everybody and everything was now replaceable. An intimate relationship could be cast aside like a dead biro; for to embrace the liquid modern restlessness it was necessary always to be ready to move on, embrace change, and endlessly reshape the self, externally, physically, and physiognomically, and internally, viewing the subject or self as the material of endless transformation. The spirit of Faust had truly come home to haunt us.

Before the 'liquid turn' there is a political turn. This is signalled already in *In Search of Politics* (1999). Glossy globalisation, the good news for the well heeled and cashed up, works brilliantly for those Bauman calls tourists, but to the detriment of the landlocked outsiders he calls vagabonds. Globalisation is an attack on the nation state; by this virtue it is an attack on social democracy and the welfare state, for their practical parameters for reform have typically been national. Capitalism becomes even more globally footloose, while workers, peasants and vagabonds, especially the illiterate, unskilled, or non-English speakers are stuck. In this context, the singular presenting problem atop this global woe is the absence of political spheres, institutions, and mentalities that might begin to provide spheres in which we could address these problems. This is not only a problem at the global level, where we lack globally effective institutions or arrangements. Now it is also the case that local or state-based organisations have been politically emptied out. Not only is there no alternative, there is no one responsible. Nation states take advantage of globalisation by washing their hands of local responsibilities; everything now can be blamed on the whims or machinations of the world system. As a Brazilian acquaintance put it, 'the economy took my job away. Globalization took my job'. Poetically profound, this is nevertheless exactly the view that globalisation encourages.

Locally, or nationally, the problem is that there is no properly political sphere anymore. If we discuss the good life at all it is likely in our backyards, and in terms of the fleeting pleasures of hedonism. There are no open institutions in which we discuss how we should live. Actually existing institutional politics, in any case, has become the playground of media and celebrity. Perhaps the problem ultimately lies outside the political. For the underlying problem is the way we live, the culture we inhabit. This is a culture of speed, repetition, and gratification undergirded by a solid layer of anxiety that at any stage we might fall off, and end up with the vagabonds. Ours is a culture of restlessness, where the most dangerous and therefore impossible thing would be exactly to ask, how should we live? The prospect of a serious politics would depend on some sufficient space for contemplation, conversation, and debate. What we encounter instead is the televisualised circus of electoral politics, where the only significant issue is how many degrees of neoliberalism or regulation we are prepared to tolerate.

Contemplation of these issues took Bauman back to the realms he had visited earlier in *Between Class and Elite* and in *Memories of Class*. The result was a book called *Work, Consumerism and the New Poor* (1998). The poor, historically, are always with us; only now they become essential. Where they used to be surplus population, the queue outside in the cold looking in, they now have a function, in order for the rest of us to keep our noses to the grindstone. Now the poor are a scarecrow; their fate drives us on, and away from them, but they can never hope fully to be absolved or assimilated into society. To be a scarecrow, today, is to be what Bauman calls a 'flawed consumer', a latent rather than actual consumer; for while we are still judged by our status in work, our capacity to consume becomes vitally significant too. The Protestant Ethic is alive and well, at least in postmodern form; but this is a Brave New World we are entering, where uncertainty rules and loyalty is a liability. Bauman is backing into the idea of liquid modernity, itself to be formally announced in the book of that title two years later. At this point, he still refers to the present as 'modernity mark two', consumers' modernity.

Producers' modernity, modernity mark one, might on this account look back to the nineteenth century, when the 'people' look like the 'proletariat'. The stronger contrast, later made by Bauman into 'solid modernity', is with the post-war regime of the long boom, growth, security, and the Keynesian welfare state. Now the shopping mall replaces the factory as the symbolic center of everyday life. Under the influence of Claus Offe, Bauman now revisits the claim that the highpoint of the Keynesian welfare state offered a missed opportunity, one which still exists: the in-principle possibility of uncoupling work and income. But all that is scrambled by the arrival, in Britain, of Thatcherism, which begins to liquefy the solid achievements of the postwar bipartisan consensus.

Thatcher famously announced that there was no such thing as society, only individuals and their families. Her regime did not introduce but reinforced and legitimated the contemporary trend towards individualisation. And so Bauman's next book takes on *The Individualized Society* (2001). If *Work, Consumerism and the New Poor* connects to Offe, this book connects later to Ulrich Beck and, behind him, to the figure of C. Wright Mills, who observed much earlier that one of the standard pathologies of modern times was the imperative that we should somehow seek personal solutions to what are actually social problems. Only things now are more extreme; as the Paris graffiti was to put it, '1968: Changing the World; 1989: Renovating the Kitchen'.

The pendant to *The Individualized Society*, and to this political turn, is the collection of essays called *Society Under Siege* (2002). As politics has been sublimated into media, entertainment, or management by the suits, Bauman's interest now turns into culture, Big Brother, liquid modern pizza, and TV in lieu of the earlier bread and circuses. Prurience replaces politics. Privatisation replaces the idea of the public. We are consumed by our own consumption, like the snake eating its own tail.

Newism or Nowism

Now comes the liquid turn. It is formally announced in *Liquid Modernity* (2000). Liquids morph and move. This is Bauman's starting point – the metaphor of liquidity and its capacity to suggest contingency, transformation, chaos, movement, uncertainty. Fluids travel easily; they flow, spill, run out, pour over, leak, flood, spray, drip, seep, ooze; they are indeterminate, unlike solids, and unpredictable. These Bauman tells us, are reasons why notions like 'fluidity' or 'liquidity' speak to our times, or to our sense of these times. At the same time, the idea of liquidity suggests lightness of being. Liquid modernity not only corrodes solidity, it attacks time.

What has changed since Marx is that this new fluid world anticipated in *The Communist Manifesto* of 1848 itself solidified into the twentieth century and especially after the Second World War. The spirit of modernism melts, and then hardens into those new institutions of Fordism and the welfare state that we then take for granted, at least for a few decades. Modernity promised the prospect of a new solidity, of a kind even firmer than that offered by feudalism earlier. But it then began to disintegrate itself, at least in these post-war forms. The economy came to free itself even more than before from traditions, cultural, and political forms. More, power itself has become extraterritorial; we no longer know where it is, so that even if 'we' had the revolutionary will, we would not know where to find power in order to overthrow it, and we certainly would be in the dark as to what to do after that.

Solid modernity gave us the Fordist factory, bureaucracy, the Panopticon, Big Brother, and the concentration camp. Its class text was *1984*. It coincided with the logic of the Gardening State and it gave us the Iron Cage. But the process of creative destruction did not stop with that dystopia; and nothing, finally, stands still. Today, our lives are characterised by endless frenzy, and by heightened individualism. No one, and nothing, can be allowed to stand still. We end up shopping for life, to the point that we are no longer able to tell the difference. We cannot escape from newism, or nowism.

From *Liquid Modernity* there follows *Liquid Love* (2003). Its subject matter is the frailty of human bonds. All that is solid melts into air, not least when it comes to human relationships. This occurs not only in the workplace or in the public sphere, but also in the private and in the intimate sphere. We dispense of our relationships with the same ease as we throw out our old shoes. Connections become 'virtual relations'. We keep running, not least from commitment or from working at relationships that falter.

Love concerns care for the other, and this is a big ask in the age of super individualism. Love is brittle, until-further-notice, 'top pocket', so you take it out only when you need it, not as the other needs you. And children? They become objects of emotional consumption. We no longer know how to do intimacy, except when it comes to sexual contact and the exchange or exercising of bodily fluids. The only love left to us, in the common culture of our times, is literally liquid love.

And what happens locally also happens globally. Trust evaporates; cities become more divided and hostile; xenophobia multiplies. Modernity produces waste, and as Bauman proclaims in *Wasted Lives* (2004). Here the liquidity image is pushed to another logical extreme: the outcasts of modernity are as its excreta. Modernity expels its outcasts. Our planet is now imagined as full. Surplus populations represent waste, the redundant, the excess. The worries of Generation X, according to Bauman, are redundancy worries, anxieties about being classified as surplus to requirement, and missing out. There are too many people, too much waste, too much civilization, too much information, too many wasted lives. Refugees and prisoners become the most pathetic examples of this stigma.

Liquid Fear (2006) takes further Bauman's interest in uncertainty. The power of the imagery of liquidity peaks after the experience of Hurricane Katrina in New Orleans. Here, modernity literally (again) liquefies: it disappears, disintegrates, the city in effect disappears. The last piece in this string is entitled *Liquid Times – Living in an Age of Uncertainty* (2006). On Bauman's thinking, we (no longer?) cope because we now have abandoned the idea of dealing with consequences, or of planning. National governments license the abandon which they easily claim globalisation has forced upon them. Cities become dumping grounds for globally conceived and gestated problems. Urban politics become hopelessly overloaded.

These themes intersect with many others in Bauman's 'little books'. Several of the volumes are actually formatted as little books. These include *Globalization: The Human Consequences* (1998); *Community – Seeking Safety in an Insecure World* (2001); *Identity* (2004); and *Europe – An Unfinished Adventure* (2004). The first two of these titles, on globalisation and community, are works of provocation, Cassandra or Jeremiah warnings of dire straits ahead in the absence of decisive human action to divert further social disaster. Bauman's views on globalisation here are almost unremittingly negative. Almost, because Bauman is also skeptical of the G word. It is a phenomenon in its own right, like the postmodern. Even if it were completely fantastic, an utter fabrication, it would be of interest for what it says about us. For 'globalisation' has already become a vogue word; there is as much fuss about 'globalisation' as there is about globalisation. The more the word is stretched, the more experiences it seeks to make transparent, the more it rather actually renders the social world opaque. To the contrary, Bauman wants to argue, globalisation is a far less unified process than is often presumed. Yet it divides as much as it unites, and in this sense it is merely the contemporary extension of much older imperial processes of the world system. At the same time, its effects are diverse, too: what appears as globalisation for some means localisation for others. And localisation and globalisation are mutually constitutive, like master and slave, or freedom and domination, or tourist and vagabond. The much-acclaimed trend to 'liquidity' goes together with new and pernicious forms of tribalism. Meantime, new forms of 'absentee landlordship' develop, as the global rulers and elites are less and less tied to any significant sense of place or political responsibility. The globalised society is increasingly mobile, but asymmetrically so. Being 'on the move' means quite different things for generals and foot soldiers. The extension of criminalisation goes together with the expansion of the ranks of the vagabonds, those *sans papiers*.

Bauman makes it clear, however, that if he is here to tell us the bad news, it is because silence leads ultimately to complicity. He agrees with Cornelius Castoriadis that the trouble with contemporary civilisation is that it has lost the capacity to question itself. Bauman's adventures in globalisation then take us through the city, urban design and utopia, the desperate attempt of moderns to expunge the chaos which always returns immediately via the back door, and to the sterile landscapes of planned cities such as Brasilia. The result is uniformity, which breeds conformity, and conformity's other face is intolerance. Ours is a world in which no one seems now to be in control.

The problem with the idea of community, in contrast, is that it has been emptied of all content. Everybody likes the idea of community, which is proof enough that there must be something fundamentally wrong with it. It 'feels' good. Community is unavailable to us, which makes us lust after it all the more. It is a modern paradise lost. At least since Tönnies's *Gemeinschaft und Gesellschaft* (1887) – at least since Rousseau – modernity has generated premodern nostalgia for pasts real, or mostly, imagined. But the acid of the capitalist revolution melted these traditional solids. The prospect of community is destroyed by capitalism, not in recent times, as the prize for success is secession. The rich and powerful exit their relations and commitments; the rest of us, and those below us, are stuck, and stay put. 'Cosmopolitanism', in this context, belongs to the tourists, not to the vagabonds. Like Rorty, Bauman worries here that what is left of the 'cultural left' too often misses the point: it thinks more about stigma than about money, whereas two-thirds of the global population do not know the difference or at least the finer distinctions involved. Struggles over recognition replace those over redistribution, arguments for multiculturalism elide those to equality. In all this, we miss community because we miss security.

Communitarianism, then, is as much a response to globalisation as it is to neoliberalism. We rediscover the need for community at the very moment that its feasibility is least likely. Traditionalism of identity is a predictable reaction to modernisation; nationalism or parochialism is a predictable response to globalisation. And so it is that 'identity' becomes the new mantra.

There is too much fuss about identity, not least from comfortable middle-class intellectuals with overwhelming public neuroses. Bauman begins his book on identity by acknowledging the pertinence of his own identity – Polish, more than British, yet he had been denied his Polish identity by the regime that expelled him, or allowed him to leave; Jewish, as he discovered, even though his primary chosen identity was as a Polish communist and socialist. The implication, for Bauman, is clear. In these modern times identity is often itself equated with nationality; but nationality can be given and taken away. Being out of place is just as routine an experience as belonging, for many of us. And locality matters for many as much or more than nation or nationalism does. Identity is a relatively new obsession, coinciding with the wave of change that begins with decolonisation through to the contemporary process we call globalisation. For the need of identity is also bound up with the widespread sense of insecurity.

But if identity can be confused with, and by, nationalism, or as much by consumption as it used to be by production, then there are also other repertoires of identity available. One that Bauman identifies for himself, non-Jewish Jew, post-Pole, incomplete Briton, is larger. It is that of Europe itself. This is the subject of Bauman's little book *Europe – An Unfinished Adventure*. Ambivalence holds this together. For Bauman is also the ruthless critic of Europe and its remarkable capacity to achieve civilisation through and upon its own barbarism. Yet, Europe also remains an idea, or a project, and not only a place or an experience. Europe has been a great adventure, an aspirant world system, as well as a misadventure. Europe offered the nastiest state experiments, but also pioneered welfare or social state. The dream of universalism persists. Socialism, after all, was also a European project.

Interpretations of Bauman

This much on Bauman. But what is the Bauman Effect? What is striking about the secondary materials on Bauman, given the extent of his influence, is that they are relatively sparse and recent. In comparison, say, to the literature on Foucault or Habermas, work on Bauman is recent and thin. The first hallmark study was a *festschrift* edited by Richard Kilminster and Ian Varcoe, *Culture, Modernity and Revolution. Essays in Honour of Zygmunt Bauman* (1996). As its title and form suggests, these five essays centre around interests of Bauman's rather than analysing his work in detail, with the exception of the editorial contributions. The following year two special issues of journals appeared – one with *Theory, Culture and Society*, the other in *Thesis Eleven*. The first two monographs on Bauman were published in 2000. Dennis Smith's *Zygmunt Bauman. Prophet of Postmodernity* combines significant theoretical sophistication with a detective-like suspicion of Bauman's intellectual path and an enthusiasm to proclaim him a prophet of the postmodern, probably a role and certainly a phenomenon Bauman was later to reject. My own *Zygmunt Bauman: Dialectic of Modernity* focuses on themes of socialism and culture, modernity, utopia and intellectuals. In 2000 I published the edited *Bauman Reader*, which is mainly retrospective and historical in orientation. In 2002 I published the four-volume collection *Zygmunt Bauman: Critical Assessments*, drawing together all hitherto existing essays on Bauman's work, mainly in the English language.

Two more significant books were published in 2001. These were Keith Tester's in-depth *Conversations with Zygmunt Bauman*, and Junge and Kron's edited volume *Zygmunt Bauman – Sociology between Postmodernity and Ethics* (2007). In 2004 Keith Tester published the third monographic study of Bauman's work, entitled *The Social Thought of Zygmunt Bauman*. Tester, Bauman's student, shows with especial sensitivity the literary, filmic, and ethical dimensions of Bauman's project, fully cognisant of the centrality of Bauman's life path, communism, and fascism to his work. Tester and his colleagues also generated two extremely helpful edited collections, *Bauman before Postmodernity: Invitation, Conversations and Annotated Bibliography 1953–1989* with Michael Hviid Jacobsen; and *Bauman beyond Postmodernity: Critical Appraisals, Conversations and Annotated Bibliography 1989–2005* with Jacobsen and Sophia Marshman. These are extremely valuable in their attention to scholarly detail. As their titles imply, both volumes seek to save, or distance Bauman from, the postmodern, or at least to minimise the identification of his life's work with the postmodern. They seriously deepen the levels of analysis in Bauman scholarship.

A second wave of Bauman literature builds on this work. It begins with Tony Blackshaw's *Zygmunt Bauman* (2005). This is a work which tries to make Bauman easy, by adding an independent line of contemporary social criticism of the present. Does Bauman's work sufficiently cut into bite-size pieces? Readers can decide. The question begged is whether students are so immersed in liquid modernity as to necessarily need a quick fix.

A second major work of new analysis is to be found in Michael Hviid Jacobsen and Paul Poder's *Sociology of Zygmunt Bauman: Challenges and Critique* (2008). The purpose of this collection is to develop a reading of Bauman's work as a general sociology. Here the parallel is made between Bauman's project as a sociological hermeneutics and C. Wright Mills's sociological imagination, and themes such as metaphor, globalisation, genocide, consumerism, and freedom are privileged over the texts themselves. The work is conceptually clustered and connected out rather than in to Bauman's work. Whether this volume differs with the work of the first wave, or rather builds upon it, is less immediately apparent. What is beyond dispute, however, is the intellectual sophistication and depth of these essays.

A parallel text is Mark Davis's *Freedom and Consumerism – A Critique of Zygmunt Bauman's Sociology* (2008). Davis foregrounds the theme of freedom as the central coordinate of Bauman's work. Davis begins from the conviction that the first wave of Bauman interpretation is insufficiently critical. The first imperative is trying to work out what Bauman came to say. It is precisely because Bauman's work is hermeneutic, open-ended and necessarily unfinished that the idea of external critique and connection may be difficult. On the other hand, to foreground an issue like conservatism may throw light on Bauman's thinking but may also rather suggest that, quite reasonably, there is a point at which we should stop reading Bauman and simply turn to other currents again. No one thinker can do everything, not even one as catholic and as stimulating as Bauman.

Anthony Elliott's edited collection *The Contemporary Bauman* (2007) takes a different approach, combining the exegetical approach, extracting Bauman's own work with a more strikingly immediate emphasis on the contemporary – contemporary social life, and contemporary Bauman. Implicit here is one central debate: is the image of liquid modernity a metaphor, or a theory? Arguably it can be rendered as either, though viewed as a theory liquidity may overstretch its suggestive capacity. The idea of the postmodern, in contrast, was not primarily metaphorical, so much as putatively historical (modernity then, postmodern now) and negative (postmodern equals not modern). Liquidity is at the same time both a much larger and yet smaller category, image or device. The achievement of Elliott's collection, like this other second-wave literature, is to build on the establishment phase indicated by the first wave. Contrary to the assertion that literature on Bauman is now abundant, the field is really just opening. The challenge remains to think with Bauman as well as through his work; to take in his interlocutors as well as his own views; and, finally to move on.

Finally, a bridge between the two waves of work on Bauman has been published by Davis and Tester together in their edited volume 'Bauman's Challenge: Sociological Issues for the Twentieth Century' (2010). This collection connects interpretation and extension out. Bauman's ideas again are opened out to broader horizons from Abu Ghraib to the future of Europe.

Alongside this literature, and Bauman's own work, there nevertheless remains one especially privileged line of access to his project. This is to be found in the work of Janina Bauman, especially in *Winter in the Morning* (1986), republished in 2006 in a second edition as *Beyond These Walls*. Zygmunt Bauman's own work continues, meantime, and each new installment contains surprises as well as elements of continuity. For his project, like our lives, is characterised by both. Now read on.

Reader's Guide to Zygmunt Bauman

Is there a simple way into Bauman's work? Given its spread and diversity, the short answer is no. The early work is more demanding. *Socialism: The Active Utopia* (1976) might be the clearest early short work, followed by *Freedom* (1988). *Thinking Sociologically* (1990) is a wonderful introduction to Bauman's style of continental sociology. *Modernity and the Holocaust* (1989) remains a key work, followed by *Modernity and Ambivalence* (1991). Of the later, little books, *Work, Consumerism and the New Poor* (1998) and *Wasted Lives* (2004) remain among the most powerful. Any of the books on liquidity provide a fine point of entrance; as Bauman says, his is a house with many doors. But be patient, the little books are less easy than they might seem at first; every Bauman book is an invitation to a conversation, so there will always be demands placed on the reader, however brief the encounter.

Traditionally minded readers may find it useful to start with the first wave of Bauman interpretation, after his own texts, before attending to the newest work. But if there remains one privileged way in, it is via the work of Janina Bauman. Her autobiographical work, read in sequence, is a wonderful place to start for those who are not in too much of a hurry.

CHAPTER 26

Postmodern Socialism (1994)

Socialisms, Sublime and Sensible

If socialism is a modern project, then it would seem reasonable to expect to find at least traces of its presence in what is called post-modern. Furthermore, if socialism is also a creation of that field which encompasses Enlightenment and romanticism, then different kinds of socialism might be expected to combine these currents in different kinds of ways. Some socialisms of course, are more pedestrian or more poetic than others; some are more reformist than revolutionary; some are closely aligned with ideas of the sublime, and others are altogether detached from it.[1] How then might we organise these various socialisms intellectually?

One common and notional distinction described by Alvin Gouldner[2] is the divide between critical and scientific Marxisms. Various other binary alternatives suggest themselves: praxis Marxism versus structural Marxism, the cultural orientation as against the positivistic, and so on. Friedrich Engels[3] probably initiated this larger sense of bipolarisation when he insisted that there are only two kinds of socialism, utopian and scientific – theirs, and ours. This kind of thinking became a blight within Marxism, and not least because its obsession with truth or science – truth, or ideology – typically went together with another dyad, namely that since there are only two social classes (proletariat and bourgeoisie) there must be a necessary correlation also between class and truth. In this dangerous caricature, Marxism was proletarian science, and what the bourgeoisie called 'science' was really only ideology. Ideology – an Enlightenment term for referring generically to all ideas as systems of thought, or constellations of concepts – became appropriated by and associated with Marxism as a discourse which set itself against 'ideology' defined as other people's untruths.[4] From this it was but a short step to the Stalinist logic exemplified by the greatest opponent of Stalin, Leon Trotsky, when he claimed that there are only ever two moralities: theirs and ours, bourgeoisie and proletariat. The other – syncretised here as the bourgeoisie: all but us – was damned in advance; the proletariat,

---

1 Wright, 1986; Beilharz, 1992a.
2 Gouldner 1980.
3 Engels 1880.
4 Mannheim 1936.

meanwhile, was put in the awkward position of being told what its interests were by the self-appointed leaders of the revolution.

Now that the champion of world communism, the Soviet Union, has disintegrated (at least as an institutional force and imperial power) it is even more important to differentiate its streams, tendencies and traditions. 'Enlightenment' is used routinely in the polemics of postmodern discourse as a code word for 'terror'. Knowledge is power, vision is surveillance, reason is violence in this stance. In modernity, socialism has been pressed into similarly deadly equations, such as 'socialism equals marxism equals Communism'. Once again the clarification of terms is crucial but difficult, and always marks the beginning of a conversation rather than the end of one. Moreover, as I have suggested elsewhere, it is also helpful to differentiate between socialisms in terms of their relations to liberalism or to bourgeois society.[5] According to popular and scholarly common sense, reform and revolution are imagined by different socialists merely as different routes to the same utopia. By this argument, all socialists advocate negation of the actually existing rather than affirmation. Socialists are usually viewed as people who know what they dislike, not what they like, except in absurdly utopian terms. Part of the socialist tradition, however, emerges in tandem with liberalism, but separates from it when liberalism submerges democracy in claims to sovereign property rights. At such moments, the reformist or social democratic line insists not on the negation of property but on the fulfilment of the claims of the French Revolution. Socialisms, in short, differ radically and sometimes violently from each other.

Socialists and Communists

How are we to conceive of these socialisms? If we look back at Engels's attempt at classification, or Gouldner's, there are clearly moral dividers at work. Dualistic logic usually reflects the simple moralism of good and evil.[6] To recognise difference, before or after deconstruction, is to accept the uncertainty which accompanies diversity. If there are more than two positions, there are more than two discussants, and more than one set of claims to truth. Marx and Engels were unable to acknowledge this in *The Communist Manifesto* (1848), where they proposed a clear demarcation between authorised and obsolete socialisms, describing their own position as Communist mainly in order to set it apart

---

5   Beilharz 1992a.
6   Beilharz 1987.

from the others. For the founders of Marxism, their own position alone was sensible in comparison with that of the romantics.

The *Communist Manifesto* is a more significant text than many would allow, or than this much suggests. Its excessively schematic view of history as nothing but the story of class struggle opens up into much more evocative anticipations of a relentlessly expanding global system and a culture of irrevocable self-enchantment – a new world like that of the sorcerer's apprentice. This is the context in which Marx and Engels introduce their famous hyperbole: 'all fixed, fast-frozen relations, with their train of ancient and venerable prejudices and opinions, are swept away, all new-formed ones become antiquated before they can ossify. All that is solid melts into air, all that is holy is profaned ...'[7] It is difficult not to sense in these lines the presence of that delightful horror conjured up by the image of the sublime. Modernity presents itself to us as sublime – anything seems to be possible now. The power of humans is simultaneously awesome and horrible. Capitalism radicalises modernity, but it too can be radicalised. Marx is here at his modernist height; only the simultaneous presence of the image of a human fog of enchantment suggests something less elevating or crystalline in its line of vision. For Marx also plays consistently with images of enchantment and inversion. Sometimes he paints the world as a child would, with a layer of mystification like the sky on top – the pestilential breath of civilisation or opacity which critical theory or the proletariat alone can dispatch. Marx thinks of society as levelled, and as open to reconstruction or redemption.

Was Marx, then, merely a modernist? The text of *The Communist Manifesto* leaves us with a residual sense of loss, as well as of accelerating movement. Although Marx scorns the past, it creeps back in when (for example), he employs the notion of cash-nexus, borrowed from the medievalist romanticism of Thomas Carlyle.[8] What this suggests, as Marx[9] wrote elsewhere, is simply that critics of the present always summon up images of the past against it. Communism, as Marx and Engels understood it in 1848, was different because it was scientific – or at least, systematic – in its world view; but it was also modern, because theorists attached it to the modern working class. Communism sought to harness the economic and cultural dynamics of modernity in order to put them to a social purpose. To say that this line of argument was forward-looking, however, is not to deny that it also looked back. But in order to proclaim the power of their own position, Marx and Engels at the same time felt obliged

---

7   Marx and Engels 1848, p. 38.
8   Marx and Engels 1848, p. 38.
9   Marx 1852.

rhetorically to ridicule competing positions. A catalogue of fools and charlat-
ans ensued in the story of socialism as they charted it: feudal socialists, or
reactionary socialists, seeking to restore the old world; petty bourgeois socialists, chasing an impossible dream, the utopia of smallholding property; German socialists, weightless philosophers and literati; conservative, or bourgeois
socialists, socialists sans class struggle; and critical-utopian socialists, dreamers
like Fourier, who nevertheless roll out the red carpet for the new Communists
because they detect the nature of utopia, even if they fall short of establishing
its necessity.[10]

Plainly this part of the argument is built upon a double teleology, presuming progress to be built in and automatic. As capitalism broke through the old
bonds of feudalism, so communism arrived as its negative predicate. The old
socialisms were obsolete. Marxism, like postmodernism, nailed up its credentials on a coffin of its own manufacture, presumed its positions to be right
because the others were wrong. But Marxism and communism, as historical
ideologies, are presented as the end of the story, which they in turn then
rewrite in their own image. Socialisms, it needs to be said (despite the Marxists), precede Marxisms; the word 'socialism' first comes into use around the
time Marx was born in 1818. Significantly, socialisms have two different but
connected paths. Socialism as a practice emerges from both the new working class and the old artisanal movement.[11] At the same time it emerges as a
critical middle-class culture, via Henri Saint-Simon, Charles Fourier, Marx and
others from Karl Kautsky to Trotsky who take it on themselves to cross class
lines, to join the working class and articulate its views on its behalf. Socialisms then proliferate; and while socialism claims internationalism as its own,
it is also marked and formed by national and regional cultures. Thus the culture of French communism is very different from that of communism both
in Germany (where in turn there are marked differences between north and
south), and Spain, where the culture of Madrid differs from that of Barcelona.
It might be suggested in fact that this is a major explanation of the decline
of socialisms, for the globalisation of culture diminishes the significance of
those localities which socialism has emerged out of. Socialisms have always
been more local than international in origin and sustenance. Globalisation is a
double-ended process: it not only installs McDonald's in Moscow, but thereby
erodes the local or vernacular even while taking on its trappings or vocabulary.

---

10   Marx and Engels, 1848 Sec. 3.
11   Bauman 1982.

Marxism became dominant historically and politically around the turn of the last century for a complex of reasons. First, it was well organised. The German Social Democrats were the first mass political party; they then dominated the Second International organisationally. Marxists elbowed anarchists out of the First International, and successive waves of Bolsheviks stuck a pistol in the ribs of anybody who denied their control of the Third or Fourth Internationals. Second, Marxism was able to present itself as the most theoretically sophisticated form of socialism, which it probably was. The awkwardness here was that Marxists specialised in the critique of political economy. They were adept at juggling economic theorems, which they imagined could accurately establish the developmental path and impending collapse of capitalism; but they were ill-equipped when it came to explaining how or why people should struggle for socialism, and they were equally ill at ease when discussing how to organise it when it arrived. By the time of the Great War, Marxism had developed something of a scholastic air. This was one reason why the Bolsheviks took the mantle from the German Social Democrats in October 1917, for they dared to do what others merely spoke about – implement a revolution, seize power, proceed to construct the socialist order, and occupy the State instead of the cafes.

From its heavily Germanic origins, Marxism now became a largely Soviet phenomenon, at least until the success of the Chinese Revolution in 1949 and the Cuban Revolution a decade later. Communism now became an experience associated with the so-called Third World. The geographical shift, from western to eastern Marxism was also, more significantly, a political shift: for Marxism largely ceased to be a critique of political economy in capitalism, and became instead the ideology of authoritarian regimes which employed it as a theory of modernisation. By the 1950s, then, the short-circuit was complete: socialism had become Marxism which became Bolshevism and then Soviet communism. This series of fusions and elisions explains how easily so many spoke of the 'end' of socialism when the Berlin Wall came down in 1989. Perhaps, if the Germans had known of Pink Floyd's threat to reform for the occasion they might have thought better of the matter, for as in the earlier experience of Live Aid something significant was lost in the telecast. But that's globalisation.

Socialism and Romanticism

By the same process of elimination and homogenisation which aligns the Enlightenment rhetorically with fascism, socialism becomes identified with Stalinism. This is not to deny, however, that Stalinism is part of the story, for the history of socialism (like that of modernity) has its dark side. One major stream within socialism has always claimed to know the people's interests better than they themselves, or else has plotted the onward march of history. This results, in circumstances of social dislocation, in the construction of Jacobin and totalitarian regimes, and in the reign of empires like the old Soviet Union, based on dictatorship over needs.[12] For all that, it does not take an intimate acquaintance with Marx's own writings to sense the difference between this world and those of his own utopias. Marx was always closer to Schiller and Rousseau than to Stalin. Marx's own theoretical odyssey remains fascinating because eventually it comes to terms with industrial civilisation. The path of Marx's work, in effect, leads from nostalgic romanticism to ambivalent modernism. It changes over the years from green to grey. Whereas Weber, by the turn of the century, views industrialism as our unhappy fate (and Durkheim, at the same moment, treats this fate as largely positive), Marx's work from around 1840 to 1880 at first turns away from industry toward the romantic, and then belatedly embraces the modern more fully.

In fact, Marx's earlier utopias, before *The Communist Manifesto* and its imputation of Marxism or communism to the working-class movement, are strikingly reminiscent of the socialisms lampooned in the *Manifesto*'s own postulated catalogue of errors. The young Marx, it is worth remembering, had not really set eyes on industrialism. Consequently his early image of the working class was artisanal, and much closer to the shop, field and forge than to the conveyor belt and mass-production line pioneered by Henry Ford in the 1920s. The proletarian in Marx was a figure neither of Bolshevism nor Detroit. For Americanism as an economic culture set about expanding the division of labour, which Marx still abhorred as late as *Capital* (1867), declaring that to subdivide a person was to execute them.[13] But whereas the later Marx's spume could still fly at mention of factory civilisation, the early Marx (expelled from Prussia, scribbling in Paris) posited the unalleviated condition of wholeness as a social goal, even for us, as moderns. The young Marx's desire was essentially Schiller's. And in *The German Ideology*, every image of the good life in socialist society – hunting, herding, fishing – is pastoral: there is not a satanic mill in sight, or even a socialist workshop or Marxist printery. It is only later that Marx's utopia becomes accommodated to industrialism.

Marx's early work, then, is in sympathy with that long line of rural and romantic criticism of modernity as industrial. Engels drank deeply of Carlyle,

---

12   Fehér, Heller and Márkus 1983.

13   Marx 1965, p. 340.

as well as of his favourite Chateau Margaux (1848); Marx also based his negative view of the modern on what had been lost.[14] Neither Marx nor Engels
was discernibly influenced by Ruskin. More significant was William Morris,
who wove an English and romantic anti-capitalist tapestry out of themes from
Ruskin and Marx, not least because Ruskin spelled out the aesthetic and ethical critique of capitalism which Marx too often sneered at or merely presumed.[15]

The rural or pastoral element in Marx sets off at least two different lines of
speculation. First, it suggests that there is indeed a fundamentally romantic
or reactive element within socialism. As Touraine puts it, the workers' movement generates at least two major developments, one of which seeks to modify
or reconstruct modernity, and the other to transcend it.[16] The transcendent
mode often calls upon romanticism and utopianism to think through this project. In other words, labour's utopia is divided between those who seek freedom through labour and those who seek freedom beyond it. The fascination of
Marx's work is that it slides from the former to the latter, and eventually suggests (like Schiller) that freedom is to be found in play, beyond the realm of
necessity or work.[17] This divergence signifies the fact that different socialisms
will always disagree over the shape of the future. The vital point is that socialism is not only modernist. Indeed, its origins in the 1820s are reactive, since it is
against industrialism, against modernity, against the cash-nexus and the wages
system, against Manchester, against the factory system and urban poverty. In
effect, it is against the city.

Second, Marx's pastoralism also indicates just how important are the local
and non-Marxist contexts of different socialisms. To acknowledge the influence of Ruskin or Carlyle is to defer to a local (and in this case specifically
English) tradition which had little need of Marx. In the line that runs from
Ruskin to G.D.H. Cole, there are echoes of Rousseau and French syndicalism,
and also of William Cobbett and Carlyle; but there is hardly any Marx at all.
The idea of a socialism of guilds is powerfully suggestive of the elaborate local
manoeuvre involved in this juxtaposition of the present with a strongly fla-
voured past. Oxymoronic though it may seem, socialists are also conservative defenders of other traditions, and their own is deeply reactive against the
revolutionisation of time and space which modernity brings. Socialists are also
romantics.

---

14   Claeys 1987, 1989.
15   Ruskin 1901; Morris 1962b; Thompson, 1977; Meier, 1978.
16   Touraine, Wieviorka and Dubet 1987.
17   Beilharz, 1992a, chap. 1.

Finally, a recognition of this pastoral or rural inflexion in socialism is also important to the intellectual process of recontextualising socialist cultures. We can begin (as when explaining Enlightenment) by working at approximate definitions, and then expanding the optic to accommodate its nuances and specificity. If we thus recover some sense of the extraordinary diversities of national or regional socialisms, then it also becomes possible to think comparatively or typologically across the different experiences and examples. Socialisms are thus modernist, or anti-modern; and they are each of the things that the various national and regional socialisms are. But they also manifest some common characteristics, such as a lust after the pastoral, and it is useful to bear this in mind when we glance, however quickly, at Australian socialisms. For what seems to set Australian socialism apart – its bush myth – may be unique in content but is common in form to other socialisms. Certainly the case of Australian socialism is peculiar in the extent of its rural romanticism. This, it can be argued, reflects among other things the peculiarities of settler-capitalist development, that extraordinary process whereby British imperialism implanted in the antipodes a bourgeois culture-in-the-making, without establishing industry, or an entrepreneurial bourgeoisie to underpin it.

'Bourgeois' yet not bourgeois, 'modern' but not evidently industrial in the metropolitan sense, the Australian labour movement until the 1970s remained largely untouched by the modernising impulse. Labourists looked back, or at the beach; Marxists looked forward, but in the wrong direction.[18] 'Back to the land' was a common cry among socialists living different lives in many and varied settings. What is more remarkable, really, is the relative absence of modernists and boosters among the ranks of socialists in the latter parts of the nineteenth century. The power of romanticism among socialists was such that William Morris[19] vehemently attacked Edward Bellamy's industrialised socialist utopia, while the younger Cole[20] chastised the senior Fabians Beatrice and Sidney Webb for allegedly presenting socialism as nothing more than a decent business proposition. If intellectuals rejected modernity, however, it is less than clear that the masses were prepared to follow them.

---

18   Beilharz 1993b.
19   1984.
20   1918 p. 122.

Socialism and the Social Question

Is socialism about freedom, or equality, or emancipation, or material provision? Is it about freedom from work, or the right to work? Those who thumb through any anthology of socialist writings will find all the above. For example, Marx's son-in-law, Paul Lafargue, published a famous work called *The Right to be Lazy* (1907) in response to that slogan of the central European workers' movement, The Right to Work.[21] Oscar Wilde and Edward Carpenter envisaged socialism as a newly aesthetic culture; Alexandra Kollontai saw in it opportunities for new and free forms of sexuality; for Emma Goldmann it meant the right to dance, and for Lenin a new puritanism. Thus Morris turned on Bellamy, whose utopia he saw as a socialism of the stomach rather than of the soul; and while Trotsky dreamed of shifting mountains Lenin aimed more immediately at electrification, bread and soviets. Then there were disputes over means. Different socialists developed different utopias. Some expected them to arrive through the evolutionary trends of economic and social development, as though socialism were somehow built into capitalism or modernity itself, and would out. Others expected socialism to emerge either by the more or less unspecified human processes of propaganda, education and conversion, or by example; establishing forms of co-operation, living in communes, agitating, selling socialist newspapers, and meetings like Hyde Park, on the Domain or Yarra Bank in search of sympathic hearts and minds.

If socialism is the result of the French Revolution, and if its intellectual currents run along with those of romanticism and Enlightenment, then socialism is also one attempt to answer Rousseau's predicament. The French Revolution offered the prospect of liberty, equality and sociability, but its capacity to fulfil these hopes was limited. Socialism developed along with liberalism as an intellectual-political trend, as the project which would endeavour to hold the French Revolution to its claims. If modernity would not or could not deliver on democracy, then perhaps socialism could. On this point radical liberalism and social democracy were difficult to differentiate. Notions such as 'socialism' and 'liberalism', however, are like 'Enlightenment' and 'romanticism': *ex post facto* frames which simplify and separate things out unnecessarily. Many socialists, the younger Marx included, were liberals. Some became more wilfully self-defined as socialists in response to the consolidation of monopoly and suffering in the urban centres. Some, like John Stuart Mill, insisted that property could be redistributed, while others, like Marx, called for its abolition.

---

21   Lafargue 1907.

Questions of material life and the politics of provision became more significant because there was now a public sphere – a public space and agenda beyond the sovereign's court, in which public assemblies and parliaments, presses and parties, could all seek to influence government and legislation. Democracy and power could now engage more openly in conflict, though the power of property and the conservative nature of social institutions could also ensure that they ran in tandem. Yet the process of expanding suffrage, the arrival of various reform bills and the struggles of the Chartists and those involved in the women's suffrage movement nevertheless made it clear that increasing numbers of ordinary people might claim their voice. Little surprise, then, that conservatives would oppose the expansion of franchise, or the opening up of university entry requirements. For like too many radicals, they suspected that when the popular majority could vote they would vote for socialism, and that mass education would lead to increasing pressure for social change. Earlier, in Prussia, Bismarck had both banned the Social Democratic Party and proceeded to introduce rudimentary welfare legislation. In Britain, liberals agreed that 'we are all socialists now', because support for collective provision – what we would later call the welfare state – was widespread, and increasing.

Municipality rather than the central state was increasingly involved in the politics of provision, or what became known as 'gas-and-water' socialism. In Australia, a century later, Labor leader Gough Whitlam was to describe socialism as the suburban provision of sewerage. Thus the Fabian socialist Sidney Webb applauded the advance of municipal provision which, because it was ubiquitous, could no longer be denied. As Webb[22] observed, liberal individuals puffed themselves up as the great achievers and movers of progress and civilisation, whereas by the turn of the century they all relied on public and municipal provision. In this scenario the middle class would recognise its debt to society and agree to work for the common purpose, in hospitals, schools, and administration. It would bring the searchlight of research to bear on sordid living conditions, and discover ways to improve them. Collective ownership and administration were merely part of the process which necessarily led to the end of *laissez-faire*. These were not party-political positions, by any means; the Manchester liberal, Joseph Chamberlain (1885), simultaneously defended the same kinds of processes in *The Radical Program*. The poor should be housed, their children schooled, urban poverty whipped or at least the viciousness of its cycle broken. Social reform was both desirable and possible. But was this socialism?

---

22   Webb 1916.

The period between, say, 1880 and 1910 was a crucial phase in the history of socialism, for it was then that the socialist idea meshed more often with municipalism, and latently with the state, in the politics of provision. Socialism, the idea of 'making social', now became constructed increasingly as 'the Social Question'. Probably no pattern of thinking and prescription of policy captured this so clearly as the tradition called Fabianism. Fabianism's common-sense approach to social reconstruction was to suggest that social problems be identified and measured, so that support for their rectification could be agitated for, gained and then Legislated. Thus Fabians argued against the English Poor Laws and the stigmatised figure of the pauper, suggesting that to use poverty or destitution as a generic term unhelpfully constructs an internal alien in the population. The pauper, however, was not the problem, but rather ill health and the absence of education, food, work and housing. Socialism may have begun, more typically, in recoil from the city and the factory, sourced in the warm positive glow of a utopia or memory of life on the land. But by now socialism had become implicated in seeking better ways to organise and reform the city. This sense was based in part on an anthropological shift away from the utopia of a green and pleasant land, and towards civic pride in cities such as London, Melbourne or Berlin. But there was also the sense that socialism and radical liberalism are more usefully employed in urban reform than in revolution. Elsewhere, as in Russia, the revolutionaries also hoped however to achieve urban utopia, running water, and society organised along the lines of the post office.[23]

Gas and water, the grey images of the post office ... Is it any wonder that more elevated minds, seeking emancipation or self-development or the sublime, should have sneered at local socialism, or at the least looked down on it from the elevation which only arrogance affords? Its aims were modest and pedestrian; close, in fact, to the more strictly circumscribed hopes of our own times. Concerns about health, housing, clean air, food and water have not become any less significant in the 1990s. The difference is that we now believe provision (or survival) for all to be impossible. When Sidney Webb wrote in defence of gas-and-water socialism, therefore, he was also advocating a notion of the good society, a way of life yet to be widely achieved. Surely it is no accident in this connection that the pioneering work of empirical sociology in Britain was conducted by Fabian women, a group still largely unnoticed by feminists, socialists or sociologists.[24] Households matter, as do domestic labour and making ends meet; these kinds of problem were central for the politics of Fabian women.

---

23   Lenin 1977b.
24   Alexander 1988.

Critical theorists and revolutionary Marxists, meanwhile, could respond that all this was too sordid, too immediate, too localised, and too easily incorporated into the larger dynamics of the capitalist system or its weak ameliorative politics. Better to put a bomb under it, or at least a stinging pamphlet.

In this way, then, socialist reformers took on a greater sense of responsibility for the present, and pursued an ethics of responsibility rather than of absolute ends. Like other moderns, they sought to engineer utopia now, rather than to leave it on the architectural drawing boards of the Renaissance. Liberals and socialists alike became involved also in eugenics, for if city living was emasculating the race then the state should intervene in order to reverse the trend. Socialism became implicated in nation-building, and therefore in chauvinism. Its claims to citizenship included some subordinate nationals but excluded others. The Bolsheviks, in turn, took to state-building, using forced industrialisation and forced collectivisation as a means to construct a Soviet empire whose citizens were to reach that goal by the route of prison camps and internal colonisation. Whether by seizure or by permeation, socialists became modernisers, seeking to ensure the new material life through practical work, whether revolutionary or reformist. Socialisms in the more 'advanced' settings became less romantic and more sensible. But sensibility cuts both ways. For simultaneously, socialists became responsible for the state of affairs they had originally railed against. Had they any option? This was not simply a matter of incorporation into the system, but of seeking to make a difference. Fabianism shifted from the pursuit of a new spiritual life to managing everyday life; Marx left behind his youthful romanticism and accommodated his vision of socialism to the culture of industrialism. Ideas of safety, place and home became transposed into slogans of security and mechanisms for social security. The inability of Western socialists to think outside social security was to contribute to their increasing sense of irrelevance into the 1980s. The socialism of the stomach was now washed away by a new wave of individualism which left whole peoples starving.

The problem here is surely that socialism became subsumed into the Social Question, let go its critical character, and became too completely affirmative. Affirmative it should certainly be; for to reject everything is to fall too readily into redemptive ways which – after the Soviet and Chinese gulags and the Kampuchean massacres – we ought surely to be wary of by now. The road to hell is paved not only with good intentions but also with the skulls of those who got in the way. But socialism should always hold on to its critical orientation; to put it in different terms, radicals ought never to be or feel obliged to perform only such authorised and state-sponsored tasks as policy-making, state-design or legislation. Detachment as well as engagement is always called for. If socialism disappears into the state it will disappear forever. This is a good part of the story of how socialism evaporated in Australia.[25]

Was there any alternative to this development? If there was, then it is not easily discerned. Socialism is a voice or series of voices and ideas and arguments – sometimes arguments with its associated movements – which is part of modernity. How could it be insulated from developments in modernity without proclaiming its own irrelevance? From many perspectives, it was already irrelevant. Arguments can always be put for communitarian alternatives. Earlier socialists were good at community politics, and also at the politics of cultural transformation. They created cultures within broader cultures, as in the German or Italian cases, but such enclaves made socialist culture a ready victim of Nazi violence. In our own time, in Australia, the Left has not been shut down; instead, its institutions, presses, parties, shops and meeting places have simply dissolved. Radical culture is not therefore dead, but its presence is certainly less apparent than before.

After Socialism

The shocking irony of this is that the colossus of capitalism, against which socialism reacted and was first formed, now stands unchallenged astride the global system. Alternative arguments are hardest to find precisely when they are most needed. A global capitalism is triumphant, yet everywhere we are in chains, ranging from the actual servitude of low pay and daily violence to the symbolic chains of two-party politics and 'choice' between McDonald's and Hungry Jack's or Burger King. The Enlightenment stream of modernity hoped to organise life rationally; we know now that this cannot be done and that this image of a rational society is chimerical. Back, then, to revolution? Hardly, though the processes of social decay in Bogota, New York and New Zealand strikingly call out the old Marxists, as the 1990s has blown the whistle on these widespread 1960s fantasies of abundance for all. Redemptive politics is not something we have seen the end of yet; life will become nastier, and institutional and symbolic violence will continue to beget personal and political violence.

Back, then to reform? It is no accident that postmodern and post-structuralist politics often leads that way. After the libertarian blush of the 1960s, we are now stuck with local sites of struggle; even Foucault, with his rediscovery of

---

25   Beilharz 1993b.

government, is now put to reformist uses.[26] Postmodern radicals like Lyotard join hands with postmodern liberals like Richard Rorty against the violation of rights. This still included a politics, but a politics of the minimal, more like the 1930s in its opposition to fascism and to more barbarism than we already have. Self-cultivation again seems to be the theme of the day; and after all, working on and in the private sphere is not such a bad idea. The problem of modernity is whether this chasmic differentiation between market saturation and the private life is sufficient. Can there be no other spheres where humans interact than markets or households? In the wake of social-movement theory, enthusiasms revived for the idea of civil society, followed by revived arguments about community. Yet community, also, has been either too narrowly traditional and patriarchal or else colonised by the ever-expanding market. Shopping malls are no replacement for political clubs and salons, even if they seem to be less constrained than the grim silences of the law of the father, who unsmilingly dismembers the roast or beats the family.

What is left, then? Some think that both Enlightenment and romanticism and therefore socialism are all exhausted: everything is exhausted, us included. Here, at least, egalitarianism reigns. Enlightenment unleashed reason, which now controls us; the Enlightenment legacy has disappeared into the texture of existence, seeking to influence events but becoming lost in them. Romanticism, by comparison, could be viewed simply as irrelevant. Even the idea of nature is now perceived as a construction or a commodity: authenticity is a value hopelessly lost, and the smiling stranger standing in the doorway is nihilism. Nothing is left.

On a more pragmatic reading, and in comparison with this closed scenario, the reformist project of the Enlightenment could be constructed as something more tentative and ongoing. Modernity, after all, is always reforming itself, and the logic of the system is routinely violated or balanced out in its local regions or parts. Romanticism, meanwhile, continues to be a presence in our midst, both in its narcissistic forms and in its more positive manifestations as a sense of longing for the other, for meaning, for love, recognition, and freedom. Memory or *déjà vu* reminds us that in at least two senses we have passed this way before: in a general way, because modernity's hallmark is a sense of crisis, failure, dissatisfaction; and in a particular way, because this is the *fin de siècle*. Encountering the postwar boom in affluent societies, we imagined bizarrely that it would somehow last forever, mesmerised as we were by the

---

26   Minson 1985.

freeze-frame of full employment and the consumer revolution. But now social amnesia takes its revenge on us. Part of this experience is new; part of it, we have lived through before. If everyday life is governed by repetition, there may yet be room to move.

The Dualisation of the World

Modernity generates, or at least reproduces, an underworld, just as all hitherto existing societies have done, or at least those with written histories. Under and over, or side by side, modern societies reproduce the dualisation of the world into public forms and undergrounds, a trend which now accelerates with the process of globalisation. The human victims of this process are many. The conceptual victims include that old and static image of society as a manageable social system, and the planning principle of national sovereignty. This does not simply mean, as Marxists have complained for decades, that vital economic decisions are made elsewhere in the centres; nor is it essentially a problem of, say, the repatriation of profits by transnational companies. More to the point, the imaginary victim of this process is the Keynesian image of national societies in the West as all-inclusive organisational units, which give everyone a place and an income or an income substitute. Globalisation, then, is not simply a matter of relations of dependency between what used to be called First and Third World. For the moment at least, the so-called Second or socialist world has largely collapsed back into what until recently we have called the Third World. But the Third World also exists, or has been discovered, in the First: it is to be found not only in Rio or Bosnia but in Los Angeles and New York, each of which has its own underground. The converse, however, is also true: the Third World has its First World centres, say in Brazil, and its presence influences discussions about modernity and postmodernity.[27] For the modern, the so-called premodern and postmodern coexist (although not altogether easily) in urban formations all around the globe. The slums are still in the cities, but we have lost the liberal dream of their disappearance. Modern cities are still bounded by walls, only now they are concrete.

Keynesians, liberals and social democrats all imagined that this process would somehow be overcome. Inequality could be levelled, poverty exposed to the harsh light of publicity and information, middle-class publics could be shamed into reform, ghettos and enclaves and rookeries closed up, slums bull-

---

27   Rabinow 1992.

dozed, and cities reconstructed. Societies could function as inclusive organisms or unitary social systems, singular in their extent and sovereignty. Crime, the informal economy, could be cleaned up and made formal; everyone could become a citizen of their own particular nation-state. Simultaneously, global economic modernisation would promote this process of development internationally. Richer nations would help the poorer to develop economically, and offer them the fruits of Western civilisation into the bargain. These were some of the mainstream hopes and expectations propagated by reformers in the First World.

Needless to say, not everyone shared this scenario or shared its way of thinking. Many of those relegated by this theory into the category of the Third World would probably have laughed at it, or simply cried. Some Western critics also had their doubts. Marx, for example, both analysed the extraordinary dynamic capacity of capitalism and explained its persistent reliance on both wage-slavery and a reserve army of the unemployed; Spengler, for his part, stood stoically in the antechamber of modernism, fearful of imperialism but horrified by the prospect of what he saw as an empty, nomadic cosmopolitanism.

The idea of the sovereign nation-state continues to have a powerful presence in modern culture. Conspicuous in times of war or chauvinism, it has also had a less visible if powerful influence in public life, where claims to nation-building and citizenship have always coexisted. The politics of place may thus be a matter of region or community, but often it is also a matter of claims to national identity. People killed each other in the Great War not as Welsh or Bavarians but as British or Germans, and the story gets no happier on the road to what was called Yugoslavia. To argue about citizenship was also to claim a stake in national resources, rights and duties. In the positive register, social reformers have promoted mechanisms of inclusion based on arguments for social rights; more negatively, nations have endeavoured to reinvent themselves as the community, as the *Volk* which struggles against other nations and peoples, regardless of how these have been constructed and homogenised. Spengler's cultural communities have developed their own separate strategies for wars of expansion, branching out into policies of assimilation whenever the links between race and nation were palpably weakened.

Dualisation: Imperialism?

So what's new? Only a waking from the dream of reason, from the fantasy of a humanly engineered social system in which everyone has a place and life runs smoothly? If the dualisation of societies and their locations and life-chances represents the final violation of this liberal dream, then it is also linked to what earlier had been criticised as imperialism. Both liberals and Marxists were well aware of the problems of imperialism, if less so of colonialism, which they often defended as carrying on the process of civilisation. Liberals like J.A. Hobson[28] argued against imperialism precisely as a justification for developing the home market, thus anticipating by decades the later Keynesian utopia of a high-wage and high-demand national economy. This kind of argument reappeared later in the regionalism advocated by critics such as Mumford, for whom globalism not only concentrated economic and political power but also resulted in such anomalies as fish being caught at the seaside, processed in the city, and then returned snap-frozen for inedible local use. Local was beautiful, for these folks, and identities were local or at most national.

Marx's view was different. Although it would be an exaggeration to say that Marx had a theory of imperialism, there are certainly anticipations of it in his writing. His greatest work, *Capital*, rests however on an analysis of the factory system in national confines. Marx's own cosmopolitanism was European. His image of the global future could only have been modernist; the difference was probably that he imagined socialism rather than capitalism as the force which would knock out exploitation and close up the underworld. The image of that underworld is certainly a striking presence in his work. Engels, for his part, described and analysed the Manchester poor in his famous book *The Condition of the Working Class in England* (1844). Marx's early work was driven also by a sense of the anthropological centrality of suffering and by the experience of poverty, although as I have mentioned his reference point was not so much Britain (that pioneer of industrial misery at this stage) as the Rhineland, and specifically its loss of medieval land and wood-usage rights.[29]

But the underworld has a major place in the narrative of *Capital*, where Marx develops a fascinating rhetorical strategy. Together with the narrator, Karl Marx as Jules Verne, the traveller journeys from the world of appearance (or commodities) to the world of essence (or capitalistic production). At a crucial moment the shift from (so to speak) supermarket to factory floor is figured as a descent into hell. The life of the factory is Dante's Inferno. Marx claims that we need to enter this nether world either analytically or experientially in order to explain an apparently authorless world of commodities which confronts us as though it were reality.[30] The implications are frightening. The old Christian fear of the underworld is reinstated in the heart of modernity, as the core of

---

28   Hobson 1902.
29   Lubasz 1976.
30   Marx 1965; Prawer, 1978.

modern production and therefore consumption. Both factory and mine in this representation evoke an iconography of the male proletarian as hero, which British and Soviet historiography drew upon until well into the twentieth century. The implicit problem of what socialism (as a new social formation) would do about this is left unresolved. Although Marx's work suggests that the society of the mass worker is here to stay, he nevertheless posits as a political solution a self-managed and smaller-scale association of producers. This can only be taken to mean that Marx is tub-thumping, imagining work as hell as though it were peculiar to capitalistic production rather than characteristic of modernity or the human condition.

Marx's expectation that capitalist modernity would be globalised overlooks in two different ways the issue of the remaining power and presence of imperialism. First, there is a sense in which Marx identifies economy and society. On the one hand, Marx as historian argues as though there will never be a purely capitalist economy, and that because different modes of production are always combined, societies and forms of activity will always be mixed.[31] But on the other hand and at the same time, his image of the factory and of capitalism as a culture becomes absolutely hegemonic. Read in this way, Marx succumbs to the political economy he initially set out to criticise. His project becomes the mirror of production, a manifestation of that capitalist imaginary it seeks to negate.[32] To put it in different terms, Marx substitutes the proletarian for the citizen. Poverty and exclusion thus become signs of the proletarian condition: the victims of modernity are the proletarians. What this manoeuvre sidesteps is the fact that a worse fate than selling one's hide is the inability to do so. Marx explained capitalism as a system in which there is only one game, called property relations; you either own capital or you do not, in which case you sell your embodied capacity to labour. In this system, then, there are plainly winners and losers, respectively those who own capital and those who sell their labour. Excluded are those Marx first called the lumpenproletariat and subsequently the reserve army of the unemployed. Conservatives and liberals constructed these people as the dangerous or criminal classes. No longer the respectable poor, they became the social scum, the outsiders, immoral, shiftless, lazy and promiscuous.

The citizen who disappears from Marx's work reappears in a cloth cap as a worker and comes to dominate his portrayal of capitalism. A seductive and systemic logic in Marx's critical economy indicates that the new order comes

---

31   Althusser and Balibar 1975.
32   Baudrillard, 1975; Castoriadis 1987.

vampire-like to suck the life-blood of the workers; it is presumed that all of the male and non-capitalistic population will become proletarian. Poverty is constructed by Marx as the lot of the proletariat rather than of what has come to be known as the underclass.[33] The power of modern economy, as it loomed larger in the Victorian era, apparently convinced Marx as well as others that absorption into the system was the universal fate of the populace. It was a machine, as in *Metropolis*, which consumed all. The exaggeration is understandable; there had never been an economic force like this before. For Marx as for Carlyle, modernity was industrialism. This was precisely the problem, even if eventually Marx was to embrace it as the fate of the epoch.

One limitation of Marx's optic, therefore, is that the national focus presumes a rising and ever-expanding capitalist system which absorbs the population into the category of wage-labour, and secretly recasts the ordinary individual as proletarian. A second limitation is related to the idea of nation rather than of social system. By the time Marx finished *Capital*, 'society' had been foreshortened to 'economy' and represented emblematically as the factory, that site which explains exploitation as the necessary master-and-slave relation between capital and labour. Although Marx never lost this sense of the social underworld, he cast it systemically in national terms, implying the disappearance of a world-system characterised by exploitation and oppression. While certainly not oblivious to this angle on imperialism, Marx and Engels did not focus upon it. They discussed, however, the ironies of a situation in which a disaggregated Britain would enable the English working class to benefit from the exploitation of the Irish. Thus Marx and Engels stumbled upon the subsequently controversial idea of a labour aristocracy made up of those working-class people whose skills or expertise elevated them above unskilled or mass workers.

This suggestive if complicated idea was not developed until later, and by the Bolsheviks among others. The story of Marxism's migration from the centre to the periphery often then attracts the scorn of critics, who accurately identify the shift of socialism from West to East as part of a longer process, in which socialism becomes annexed not only to state power but also to tyrannical programmes of economic modernisation conducted from above. The process was more complicated than that, however, and also generated more developed insights, not least into the nature of imperialism itself.

---

33   Beilharz 1991a.

Imperialism as Uneven Development

That all knowledge is perspectival is widely agreed to nowadays; less frequently questioned is what this common understanding actually means. The image of 'perspective' is itself, of course, both visual and geographical, the latter being probably the more suggestive cue. Since Foucault, notions of the 'optic', and 'panoptic' have been disparaged too easily along the lines that the politics of the gaze is surveillance and control. What this misses is the romantic and aesthetic history of the optical, in which to see is to contemplate and absorb rather than to classify and dissect. The geographical metaphor, by comparison, evokes a sense of place and life, and therefore biography and experience. Thus modernity is 'viewed' differently from the periphery or 'outside', but not in easily predictable ways. Those who find themselves at the extremities of modernity may become its wilful advocates as easily as its sworn opponents. Some revolutionary traditions harbour both views at once: modernisation is bad when others control the project, but it will come good when morality and the Central Committee reigns, etc.

Lenin is often thought of as the premier theorist of imperialism. This is a mistake. He was essentially a practical politician who periodically engaged in theoretical debate for strategic purposes, principally to bludgeon his opponents and guarantee if possible that he would have the numbers. His own pamphlet *Imperialism, the Highest Stage of Capitalism* (1916) relied very heavily on other published work, Hobson's not least of all. The more significant Marxist theorists of imperialism were Trotsky and Antonio Gramsci. This fact is itself striking, for Trotsky and Gramsci were also modernists, and certainly more so than Lenin. Lenin's dreams of *State and Revolution* (1917) were plainly modernist, as was his enthusiasm for the principles of Taylorism, but his political sense led him to abandon these hopes in order to deal with those more limited and austere Russian realities which he and the Bolsheviks confronted.

By comparison with Marx, Trotsky and Gramsci were outsiders, one from Odessa and the other from Sardinia. As Marxists whose biographical formations were peripheral, they discovered and identified with centre and cities, but retained these earlier markings. Each thus worked with some sense of difference from an urban-rural axis, even if Trotsky noisily despised the country while Gramsci accommodated it more easily. Gramsci the hunchback was an outsider in body as well as in spirit. Trotsky came to champion the idea of combined and uneven development. As he explained in *1905*, the global system routinely mixed up modern and premodern. In Russian factories people with the cultural attributes of the peasantry worked with the latest in modern technology. Were the factory workers of Moscow therefore proletarians or peasants? Obviously both, even though the irritable Trotsky needed them to behave like what he thought of as proletarians.[34] Trotsky's work intersects various other period arguments such as Le Bon's on the crowd, although with the modifier that what terrified Le Bon titillated Leon Trotsky. Masses made revolutions. In his eyes, revolution could never have happened in the country, or at least if it did then its energy would have been lost or diffused without urban containment and the vanguard party to act (if only later, in 1917) as piston.

Trotsky also theorised the city, postulating the vital distinction between the city as market or bazaar and the city as administrative centre. But by the 1920s he was also to take on Marx's modernism and inflate it to the point of explosion. By 1924, in *Literature and Revolution*, Trotsky was to portray the socialist utopia as a place of radical genetic and social engineering. There would be no more wooden houses in the back streets of Moscow. Instead, in the new socialist Atlantis – a hyperdevelopmental and controlled world – literally no stone would be left unturned. Like Lenin's *State and Revolution*, Trotsky's book could be viewed as a flight of fancy, but it was not only that. It is also indicative of the worst and most dangerous trends in both romanticism and Enlightenment thinking. Here the idea of uneven development disappears. All that we have is developed or developing. Nothing is to be left in peace, for there is no virtue in tradition. Trotsky's mania for futurism goes beyond even Marinetti's. This is what people sometimes misidentify with the idea of a 'permanent' revolution, for Trotsky really believed (at least at this moment) that life is revolution, and that to stop is to fall into disarray.

Gramsci's thinking was finer than this. Unlike those northern modernists who dominated the Italian Socialist Party before the formation of the Communist Party, Gramsci was a southerner and an outsider, but unlike Trotsky did not want to forget it. The problem of socialism in Italy, as he put it, was therefore how to deal with the Southern Question.[35] Like all other nations such as France or Spain, 'Italy' was after all a recent fabrication, a result of war and violence, a fiction. In other words, what was called Italy was a microcosm of the world system. North and south were related as centre and periphery, and with consequences that politically could not be avoided. The people of Naples were poor because those in the north prospered, and this remained true even if the Turinese workers were also victims of the rules of the game. Gramsci knew too much to imagine that the north, untarnished, could ever be the image of socialism. His perspective was that of the periphery; but it was also that of the

---

34   Trotsky 1973a.
35   Gramsci 1972.

subaltern, of the informal as well as the formal economy, of realms outside the system as well as those it accommodated.

Whereas Trotsky became (at least in *Literature and Revolution*) a kind of socialist futurist, Gramsci became a modernist. Here the project of reconciliation with modernity is more like Marx's own than Trotsky's astral departure into the realms of social science fiction. Gramsci, like Trotsky, travelled to the centre and made it his home. Like Trotsky he too celebrated the syndicalist moment, that frenzy of enthusiasm for workers' control which Trotsky experienced in 1905 and Gramsci after the Great War. In a different and authoritarian moment, Trotsky had enthused about War Communism and the militarisation of labour. His own attitude to Taylorism was mixed, partly because unlike Lenin he rejected the idea that the Soviet Union could reasonably be described as state capitalist. Gramsci's attitude to Taylorism (or what he called Fordism) was much more enthusiastic in the 1930s. Incarcerated in Mussolini's prisons, Gramsci shifted from the localist or council communist perspective to a more vigorous defence of the idea of a new socialist party, which (recalling Machiavelli) he designated the New Prince. Focusing on the American experience of modernity, as did so many others, he now began to theorise Fordism not only as a means of organising production but also as a whole way of life which was city-based, puritanical by Italian standards, and accustomed to work, the nuclear family and consumerism. Henry Ford had viewed his own project as not merely a conveyor-belt strategy but a utopia – in fact, as a high-wage, high-demand economy with its own modular culture.[36] Gramsci was evidently taken by this image of a 'new man' more like Ford's dreams than Stalin's. This lapse into high modernism was not accompanied, however, by any political sense that such a project would in fact be widely achievable. Africa was still said to start at Naples.

Dualisation and Place

If imperialism is always with us, then the problem we keep returning to is whether dualisation represents anything new. To simplify, what changes is the location, geography or juxtaposition of the two worlds. We live in a post-Fordist or post-Keynesian world, not because we can think beyond their lexicons but because the idea of a modular economy or national society no longer seems imaginable. Dualisation is now visible in the heartlands; a new kind

---

36   Gramsci 1971.

of economic-cultural apartheid has appeared in cities, and not just globally between North and South or East and West. Of course it could be argued that this is not new either; what is relatively novel is that it is now recognised, described and analysed in its new and painful impermeability. This is truly part of what is called postmodern, the final sense that modernity is considerably less elastic than had been thought, and that the underground is always with us. But this, it could be replied, is not a new understanding either. Conservatives have believed this all along. And radical socialists, including ethical socialists such as Jeremy Seabrook,[37] argued consistently throughout the 1980s that the experiences called 'India' and 'Britain' make sense only in juxtaposition, that metropolitan unemployment in the 1970s needs to be read against the similarities and differences of the 1930s, and that what some call the leisure society others experience as the world of low pay and no choices.

The process called globalisation certainly extends these problems. Hence the endless hand-wringing about Disneylands and McDonald's, and so much so that one American scholar modifies Weber's image of the disenchantment of the world in order to describe what he now calls *The McDonaldization of the World*.[38] The point of this kind of argument is evident: accelerating modernity or the postmodern corrupts both ends of social and economic relationships, and lowers the quality of life for both consumers and producers. Yet beyond this world which most of us inhabit there remains another one, located in the enclave of privilege, high security, and privately policed mansions placed not (as they once were) well apart from the cities but inside them. This 'overworld' is thus visibly present rather than distant and shrouded by greenery, and still elusive yet no longer ashamed of its affluence. Thus we live now in a world which remains corrupt and knows itself to be so, but even celebrates the fact. Again, of course, there are those who would say, so what? What's new? Corruption, after all, is merely a traditional part of political and social life. The difference, perhaps, is that the return of scarcity in the West makes it harder now to identify corruption as the violation of a social norm. Corruption is a norm, even though the most powerful of interests still like to claim rhetorically that it is the outsiders who are corrupt. In this sense the underworld has grown, up, over, and out.

If the city has attracted too little scrutiny in the social sciences recently, having been parcelled out earlier to specialists in urban planning or development, the same is even more true of what might be called 'horizontal' place, namely

---

37   Seabrook 1985, 1988.
38   Ritzer 1993.

the underworld and overworld. Throughout the twentieth century, social stratificationists and theorists of class-mapping have understood and portrayed the relations of individual hierarchy, or sketched out bourgeoisie and proletariat in pyramidal form. Focusing often on an intrasystemic contradiction (like that posited between labour and capital), their only imagined underground has been the factory floor, the study of which in turn has been allocated to analysts working in industrial sociology or industrial relations. Informal economies have always been constructed as marginal to this big picture, having been viewed (like the petty bourgeoisie) as residual and transitional, and as remnants of the past rather than as part of the future of modernity.

As we enter the new *fin de siècle*, it may be appropriate to locate the underworld more centrally in ways of perceiving modernity. Already there are signs of a shift in focus. Rosalind Williams makes a major contribution to this process in her path breaking book called *Notes on the Underground: An Essay on Technology, Society and the Imagination*.[39] Williams argues powerfully that this subterranean, lateral and spatial way of seeing modernity is actually a strong undercurrent in its stock of cultural representations. Ever since Victor Hugo published *Les misérables* historians have been compelled to speak of the underside of modernity's space. Meanwhile the image of the outcast has become theatre – mere performance, with cocktails after. The same is true both of Marx's Dantesque inferno of capitalist production and Freud's imagery of depth, deep structure and subterranean reality. At the same time, Williams observes, excavating the site of modernity may be hazardous, because the apparent stability of bourgeois society may be undermined in the process.[40] For the subterranean is also demonic, satanic, whether we speak of Blake's dark satanic mills (a hell on earth), Chicago's Little Hell, Los Angeles or New York.[41] The resonances of this literature are overwhelming, as we reconsider, say, H.G. Wells's *The Time Machine* (1895) and think of the Los Angeles situation; for in Wells's book the oppressed labour in the bowels of the earth and surface periodically in order to eat their oppressors, or else in reality to lash out at other marginals who apparently suffer only slightly less than they themselves do. As Williams reminds us, quoting Leo Marx, the city in this context is a metaphor for displaced feelings. Anti-urbanism is an ontological response to modernity, which may help to explain why, with our heads elsewhere (on the beach, in the bush), we fail to comprehend the dualisation going on before us.[42]

---

39   1990.
40   Williams 1990, pp. 48, 54.
41   Williams 1990, p. 66.
42   Williams 1990, p. 145.

As John Kenneth Galbraith has suggested in a different register, the under-class plays the same functional role nowadays that Marx's reserve army of the unemployed did in a different explanation. Mainstream economic systems do not rely on the principle of functional inclusion, as Durkheim had hoped, but rather on functional exclusions. Galbraith's analytical conclusion is that hence-forth we need to develop a far more differentiated understanding of practices such as work, as well as a clear moral sense of where all this is heading. For the kind of work available (when it is available) to the underclass is different from middle-class work.[43] What this suggests in more generally theoretical terms is that the modern idea of a unified society has been shattered by the course of events. Without the Victorian civility (or servility) of upstairs-and-downstairs, dualisation can relocate the periphery in the centre. In a different sense, civil war also replaces international war as the major locus of violence in nation states. Violence turns inwards; we encounter a new kind of internal colonial-ism, because the idea of the cultural nation (nation-as-culture, in Spengler's sense) can no longer be sustained. If it is true to say that we do not all live in the same world, then it is also now the case that even as Australians we do not all belong to the same nation, except in a sense that is so formalistic as to be empty.

The Remnants of Discipline

Once the centre of Latin America is located in Miami, it broadens to include the informal or illegal economies which flourish in other metropolitan centres, including those of Latin America. Wherever formal policing fails by modern standards, informal policing by the Mafia intervenes. Yet the gaze of main-stream sociology has missed this point, at least since the Chicago School's interest in other forms of order was dismissed as hopelessly liberal and obsol-ete. How then can we begin to make sense of all this? If history's main category is time, then historians still have a disciplinary purpose. The apparent accelera-tion of time in postmodern culture is also the source of what Jameson[44] regards as a major weakness in postmodern criticisms, namely the absence of any sense of historicity. Cultural studies, by comparison, operates somewhere between the fashionable and the hegemonic; but it often seems weightless, obsessed with image and representation, and either not interested in enquiring into what goes on behind the screen or else unable to do so. In Australia, cultural

---

43   Galbraith 1992.
44   Jameson 1991.

studies needs also to be seen as a development within English departments which belatedly have smuggled in through the back door a diluted form of sociology. Political science, by comparison, seems a little sleepy, perhaps because its object has disappeared, and perhaps also because its traditional bias towards state and nation seems increasingly distant from the process of globalisation itself. Sociology, as Touraine says, needs to maintain its focus on change rather than system if it is to deserve its place among these classical disciplines which in any case have tried to marginalise it. Political economy either sits on the fence, or on the edge of the gutter; part of the problem, it has also claimed rightly to be part of sociology's immanent criticism, and not least because of its capacity to address questions of imperialism and the world-system.

A postmodern (or indeed modern) response to this quick survey might be simply to suggest that we would be better off without disciplines anyway. After Foucault, we identify discipline and policing, as though disciplines, too, could be dismissed or escaped. But the different disciplines also offer different perspectives, optics, vistas or ways of thinking. These various traditions may well be as disabling as enabling, but they facilitate lines of communication in a world of cultural and economic analysis which often resembles Babel. At the same time it seems to me that at least two broad ways of thinking (or social inflexions) may now be worth further investigation. One is anthropology, the other geography; viewed from a different perspective, they may be the same thing or similar.

Much abused and ridiculed as the pith-helmeted handmaidens of colonialism, some anthropologists are nevertheless interesting people. The modern division of labour in the social sciences or liberal arts could be epitomised as follows: sociology looks in at Western modernity, whereas anthropology looks out. Dualisation, however, collapses the hard distinction between 'in' and 'out', for the inner is now also the outer, and vice versa. Viewed in more perspectival terms, I think the strength of urban anthropology lies in its capacity to treat the familiar as the strange, and the normalised as artifice. This strategy was pioneered, arguably, by thinkers like Montesquieu, who parodied European culture by inverting it. To view ourselves, and modernity, as exotic, as the other, is an interesting challenge. Hence the contemporary appeal of intellectual strategies used by ethnologists like Michael Taussig in *Mimesis and Alterity*,[45] which extend such modern devices as juxtaposition or montage of the unfamiliar to induce shocks of recognition.[46]

---

45   Taussig 1993.
46   Taussig 1992.

This kind of strategy is also suggestive for the idea of place, which is of course a generative and explanatory category in geography. If history is governed at least to some extent by chronology or notions of time, then place now becomes more appropriately central also. Where time is compressed, in the globalisation process space is transformed, although not completely, for sometimes the global overwhelms the local, and at other times the local manipulates the global. And if as individuals we now maintain a multiplicity of identities and levels of meaning, we also still need some sense of place, even if it is only adopted or short-term. Nowhere is this more apparent in intellectual culture than in the demise of expatriate culture, or at least of its previous influence. The periphery, as Gramsci understood, may not be central, but nevertheless it offers a perspective. As Edward Said[47] reminds us, if we are to think of imperialism and culture together, then Gramsci and the idea of subalterneity are one obvious way in.[48] Taussig, by comparison, seems in effect to privilege the insight of Walter Benjamin, and not least because his own methodology mimics that of Benjamin and Simmel: it is an anthropological impressionism, a capacity to compare the uncommon, to generate sparks in the dark of a modernity which sometimes seems to have only a dark side, at least as far as the world of power is concerned. And it was Benjamin[49] who said that culture always rests on power, civilisation upon violence.

A Marxist and a Jew, Benjamin knew that history cut both ways: 'There is no document of civilization which is not at the same time a document of barbarism'.[50] We need not seek to authorise Benjamin as the new theorist to understand just how good he is to think with. In a broader perspective, the point may also be that Benjamin's kind of insight is useful because it breaks through some of the mystifications and opacity we ourselves have created. So it is still necessary, after all these years, to speak of imperialism as well as of dualisation, to manoeuvre together the concepts culture and power.

---

47   Said 1993.
48   Said 1993.
49   Benjamin 1969.
50   Benjamin 1969, p. 256.

CHAPTER 27

Thesis Eleven – Editorial Number One (1980)

Marxism as a theory and as a movement is in crisis. Radical theory has become completely undiscriminating. In the movements and parties there are blockages, perhaps decay, but little advance. In the turn of Anglo-American Marxism away from the project of importing Continental theory there is a danger that theory will be allowed to lapse altogether. There is a need for a new 'theoretical' journal attaching a specifically political understanding to 'theory'.

The fundamental tenet of the original Marxian project and its echoes and refractions through the principal representatives of western Marxism is that theory and politics must find their necessary articulation in each other. The struggle for socialism depends on the politicisation of theory and the theorisation of politics. Neither of the dominant tendencies within Marxist theory – those which propagate more theory or more history in isolation from each other – can be adequate to this task. Within the left this division is maintained between activists who carry out the everyday organising and theorists who stand back and survey the general tendencies. Marxist politics can only have meaning if it can begin to bridge this gap.

The intention of *Thesis Eleven* is to provide the framework in which these themes, problematics and struggles might be unified as politics. Marxists have always exaggerated their claims to the workers' movement, typically by denying the actuality of the movement or speaking to its mythical representation. We deny both these theoretical fictions and the accompanying political claims which confuse the particular dominant forms of the movement (party, unions etc.) with the movement itself. Marxism can only *earn* its political authority through the study of and participation in real struggles. The time for the mere *assertion* of this authority is over.

Yet what bourgeois society has sundered is not easily reunited. Marxism now exists within a severe fragmentation of knowledges: knowledge is not only separated from practice, but also internally compartmentalised. As the product of and the response to bourgeois society, Marxism can hardly be unaffected by the extreme specialisation which is functional to it. Marxism now involves at least philosophy: epistemology, method, ethics; political economy, history, labour history; class and world-systems analysis; theories of and studies in ideology and culture: hermeneutics, psychoanalysis, semiology, anthropology, modes of production, philosophy of history; and a critique of 'actually existing' socialism.

Within radical politics itself traditional economic struggles must now be moderated by and combined with new forms of struggle epitomised in feminism.

The emphasis on politics in *Thesis Eleven* accompanies a central theme of the journal: everyday life. Politics takes as its point of departure everyday struggles and common-sense understandings in order that they might be worked up into critical conceptual levels. The generalised communication of theoretically informed good sense is a central prerequisite for the cultural formation of a new order. Failure to address everyday life, the basic unit of bourgeois reproduction, means political failure. A necessary corollary of the everyday is the cultural specificity of Marxisms. Despite the internationalisation of capitalist relations, the site of political and social reproduction is still national which, of course, means that struggle starts at home, or not at all. Feminism, the anti-nuclear movement, the recently proliferating disarmament movement, to mention but a few, are struggles which Marxists cannot ignore.

If Marxism is to escape the clutches and constraints of the 'scientificity' which so many of its acolytes claim for it, then its discourse must allow the possibility of self-reflexiveness; and if Marxism is to be turned onto itself, then other radical critiques should also be taken up. Marxism cannot claim privilege in a situation in which it has lagged behind radical struggles and in which much authoritative critique has been instigated by non-Marxist socialists and substantive contributions to Marxist studies made by 'uncommitted' scholars. *It is the process of political discourse and struggle which establishes the adequacy of positions* and not some fundamentalist determination by the Marxist classics.

Thesis Eleven seeks to promote open, honest and principled debate which considers everything to be the object of critique. We seek a broad diversity. The unity of the materials carried in *Thesis Eleven* will be reflected in their shared commitment to understanding the world with a view to changing it. *Thesis Eleven* is not alone in these aims; it finds certain affinities with other projects aimed at a radical rethinking of Marxist orthodoxies. These include the British Hegemony group, working further along the lines of the Birmingham Centre for Contemporary Cultural Studies, developing the Gramscian problematic on the theme of popular radicalisation in this present period of reaction. In the US it takes heart from the appearance of a new journal, *Social Text*, the manifesto of which (if less the contents of) expresses positions close to *Thesis Eleven*. The new openness which has entered *New Left Review* and Anderson's *Arguments within English Marxism* as well as the radical rethinking evident in the three volume *Issues in Marxist Philosophy* signal a growing acceptance that radical critique is overdue and can only be conducted in the form of debate and not assertion.

If Marxism is neither history nor theory, neither politics nor economics, it is also neither art nor science. Rather, it is all these unified by a central commitment to changing the world. 'The philosophers have only *interpreted* the world in different ways; the point is to *change* it'. Marx's eleventh thesis on Feuerbach, so often misunderstood as mere licence for mindless activism, implies much more. The importance of this pithy little aphorism is as the driving imperative towards a unity of Marxist theory and practice. In the context of the preceding theses on Feuerbach, the interpretative attitude refers to the discourse of crude materialism; the contemplative attitude which it shares with idealist ontologies. Taken as the basis for social change, its results are all too often the tragic authoritarian forms of organisation all too often witnessed (and anticipated in Thesis Three). If Marx was aware of the material force of ideas then we, today – confronted with ideas in the practices of reproduction, consent, consumption, acceptance and incorporation in the circumscription of possibilities, theories of 'human nature', technological necessity – should need even less to confirm their real and coercive power. The point is not that theory needs to be obliterated, only that it needs to be constituted politically.

We invite you to participate as writers and as readers in the spirit of the eleventh thesis.

∴

The first issue contains a number of papers which relate to the crisis of Marxism. It is our intention to have in each issue a theme or themes as well as other papers, notes and reviews. Themes will attempt to stimulate debate: we anticipate not only detailed replies to papers but also shorter letters and comments. For this number we have collected a range of materials in order to avoid the in-house connotations that go with excessive editorial participation in contributions.

Our commitment to the raising of fundamental questions is opened up by Alastair Davidson's morphology of Marxisms presented as an archaeological recovery, a vintage piece dating from 1974 which demonstrates that it is less *theory* than *some theorists* who lag. It is in fact one of several papers written against the structuralist current in these years which, being ahead of their time, were not taken up. Its arguments will fall on more sensitive ears now than then, for the time is yet more ripe for the development of the project of a Marxist analysis of Marxism.

Agnes Heller's considerations, following it, take up problems of a radical philosophy which might be capable of mediating the existing movements with the oft-forgotten goals of a concrete radical utopia. Radical philosophy here articulates the basic values of the end-goal crucial to particular movements and struggles if the latter are not to be integrated into the existing structures. The main task of radical philosophy is seen as the criticism of the movements against capital, and not of capitalism itself, the latter being a separate subject and therefore the scene of a separate critique.

Johann Arnason's paper examines the ground of the crisis of Marxism in Marx's own work. His is not an argument for an 'original Marxian sin', but rather a plea for present disputes to be understood with reference to the tensions and contradictions in the original project of Marx. Explicitly and implicitly, as Arnason shows, recent debates are not particularly new; the examination of more fundamental original tensions is in this regard a centred priority for the reconstruction of Marxism. The necessity of rethinking Marx is no academic claim for a 'return' to the pure source, but a fundamental questioning: because nothing can be taken for granted, and also because recent debates so often have their roots in the older, more sophisticated yet unresolved problems.

With our interest in theoretical recovery goes a dedication to historical recovery. Steve Wright's paper on left communism in Australia recovers a lost chapter of theory and practice. Throughout the forties the publications of the Workers' Literature Bureau represented one veteran's attempt to offer an alternative to the dominant Marxisms in the local labour movement. Jim Dawson's project, culminating in the *Southern Advocate for Workers' Councils* and the first publication of Pannekoek's major relevant study, is located within the context of his life-long search for the society of 'free and associated producers'. Dawson's conciliar perspectives are located within the specificity of the experience of syndicalism, his proposed solutions being understood as predicated on the existence of a type of proletarian no longer prevalent in capitalism. *Thesis Eleven* takes Wright's paper to be a major contribution to the project of doing history theoretically or theory historically, for it not only fills an important gap in the archive but also draws out specific political implications.

The current enthusiasm for political economy has not generally been accompanied by an examination of political economy or its critique, or of Marx's *Capital* in general. George Markus' paper pursues questions of, and approaches to, political economy in Marx's work. Careful philology reveals striking shifts in the attitude to political economy and its critique. We are very pleased to present this paper, particularly because it gives some indication of the lines of argument in the enigmatic but not-to-be-translated collective work which stalks through footnotes here and there, *Is Critical Economy Possible?*

Thesis Eleven then presents the seminal essay of Hans-Georg Backhaus for the first time in English. The pervasive influence of Frankfurt and Althusserian Marxisms has had the effect of polarising interest and denying the existence of alternatives. Within capital-analysis the revived Sraffian position has accentuated this tendency. The most important characteristic of the value-form argument is that it seeks the combination of a rare conceptual rigour with political interests. It disappears neither into empiricism nor into the genuflections of philosophical hierarchy, but seeks theoretical sophistication with substantial political meaning. Later contributions by the translators will take up the political dimensions of value-form theory.

The vulnerability of Marxism to fads and commodifications has its effects in history-writing as well. Spain, politics, history, Vietnam are taken up in an interview with just such a neglected historian, N.W. Saffin. Apart from its historiographical dimensions the interview takes up issues of politicisation and radicalisation. *Thesis Eleven* regards these as central issues and welcomes contributions on new forms of struggle. Subsequent numbers will include some of Saffin's immense labour of historical research, drawing especially from an enormous manuscript on the Victorian working class. It should be added that we see this interview as indicating a general enthusiasm for interviews as a neglected form of discourse which, if raised above hagiography and abuse, can open up new and accessible arenas of dialogue.

Eurocommunism, if dead, is not forgotten. A first translation of a 1924 communist document is presented not innocently but as a provocation: for in it, Gramsci argues for a transitional programme not unlike the principle (if not the actuality) of 'historic compromise'. Some of the issues raised here will be taken up in future numbers in a general debate on eurocommunism and its Leninist sparring partner. Our second issue, focusing on Marxism and history, will also take up some of the problems opened by the *Annales* school and by the recent developments in British Marxism. Conflicting views on the relationships between empirical material and political struggles will be provided by Michael Eldred and Mino Vianello; case-studies of particular strikes will provide a discussion point not only for problems of Marxist history but also for the examination of the relation between economic and political forms of struggle. The projected third issue, reassessing western Marxism, will present conflicting views on Habermas and Gramsci and assessment of Trotsky, Lukács and Korsch; the fourth will take up problems of ideology and culture. We welcome in this regard papers on social reproduction and everyday life: musical forms, their relation to subcultures and resistance; struggles around technology, the technologisation of leisure and its effects on dole-life; cultural phenomena like McDonalds; the peculiar problems of regions and country towns and especially television as ideological forces in social reproduction; the commodification of sport, sexuality and so on. The interrelationship of these cultural dimensions of crisis with more general political and economic crises will also be broached.

CHAPTER 28

Thesis Eleven – Countereditorial, Number 100 (2010)

The overwhelming fact for us, as young Marxists 30 years ago, was the crisis of Marxism. Marxism was widely imagined by its followers to posit some kind of essential and therapeutic or even revolutionary relationship between theory and practice. Sometimes we called this process of mediation *praxis*; I can remember being fond of this idea until Boris Frankel pointed out to me that *praxis* was the word you would see on a German doctor's door. It only really meant practice anyway; *praxis schmaxis*! So there were all kinds of irresolvable antinomies involved here; praxis came from the active immersion in and transformation of everyday life; theory, closer to the classical *Theoria*, came in contrast not from experience but from above, from contemplation or from reading big books like Marx's *Capital*. Yet the point cannot be only to look upon all this with the immense condescension of posterity or middle age. What we did over these years mattered, and we are proud of our achievement.

Anyway, we on *Thesis Eleven* thought that we could do it better. The key words in that first editorial (drafted by me and Julian Triado) were less theory and practice than theory and politics. We were attracted to the work of Gramsci for many reasons, but one of them was that his own thought tilted this way. Marx's great deficit, on this way of thinking, was in the theory of politics. Turning away from civil society to political economy in the 1859 *Preface* to the *Contribution to the Critique of Political Economy*, Marx's subsequent work slipped from the critique of political economy back into the labyrinth of political economy itself. For Marxists of this period, the attendant way of thinking was called structuralism. All these things were attractive to us, then, but they seemed to err on the side of science, to be attracted too remorselessly to the Enlightenment project of telling the truth about bourgeois society, as though this would make us free. In fact, it seemed best to tell the unpalatable truth that the secret of bourgeois society lay in its extraordinary capacity to reproduce itself.

Gramsci, in any case, looked attractive in this setting, as did the earlier Habermas, as critical theory turned to politics and to democracy. But this was also to turn to liberalism, or at least to the warmer stream of social liberalism which aligned itself to social democracy. Only this failed to add up to anything like a Marxist politics, or a robust rather than gently reformist way of proposing to change the world.

This is not the only theme in our first editorial. There is also a conspicuous desire to work out of Marxism in the best sense, for Marxism after the period of its sixties renaissance had something to say about almost everything – as we then claimed, its spread reached from epistemology, method and ethics, to political economy, history, labour history, class and world systems analysis, ideology and culture, hermeneutics, psychoanalysis, semiology, anthropology, modes of production, philosophy of history and the critique of Soviet-type societies, feminism and social movements. Whew! It was a promising moment for Marxism as a radical intellectual culture, even if the crisis of Marxism stubbornly persisted.

Could there then be a new kind of Marxist politics, and were we to be its carriers? Marxism has been many things, not least as traditions, and we already were young but firm carriers of some of these traditions, especially those we then called western Marxism and critical theory. But rather than becoming the agents of transformation, we and others like us became its objects. The world began to change a great deal into the eighties but, as Gramsci had anticipated, this was at the hands of the others. It started with the rise of neoliberalism. The global transformers came from the right, beginning in the USA and the UK. The Labor Party in Australia shifted right, and the left with it. The eurocommunist CPA in Melbourne anticipated the slide by joining the ALP. Our local audience disappeared before our eyes, into the Labor Party. Our critical contempt for the ALP at the moment of its vital reinvention from 1983 meant that we were too far ahead. Our old left friends needed to believe in the ALP, and that was where their futures were.

How then did we fail? And, what might 'failure' or 'success' actually mean? One fundamental task we set ourselves in the first editorial was to engage thoroughly with everyday life. Julian Triado and I began a major paper called 'Theses on Everyday Life', which was consigned to the gnawing criticisms of the local possums. What did happen, as far as I can tell, is that our imperative to take a political turn eventually was confirmed as a cultural turn. This much was entirely consistent with our firmer moorings, in western Marxism and critical theory. After all, Gramsci's signal orientation was towards western culture, in contrast to the disastrous Soviet turn to the east. Yet to take culture seriously would also mean taking our location in Australia or in the antipodes seriously. And this would remain a major creative tension for the journal, dealing with our European and transatlantic roots while seeking to make sense of our own locations and later of other, alternative modernities, from Latin America to Asia. Finally, we wanted to do this in a manner which remained open. We, as the editors, were Marxists, but our journal was conceived as one working at the crossroads of socialism and scholarship. We were then, and remain happy now, to carry the views of various others, not least those we disagree with.

So how did it all look, in the beginning? The first issue of *Thesis Eleven* was cream in colour, with red print on the cover – what else? We had a friend lined up to design the cover; we had a mock-up. She disappeared overseas; the resulting cover, done the day before print downtown, finally looked a bit like the barrel of a gun. We priced it at $4.50. I have no idea where that price came from, rather than $4 or $5; presumably we did a few sums on the back of an envelope guessing setting costs and printers' bills. We took copies in Julian's Renault 12, the vanguard of the intellectual proletariat, to Readings in Carlton and to the International Bookshop in Melbourne. We sent copies to AMS distributors in Sydney, to Carrier Pigeon Boston and to Merlin in London. The layout of the first issue was appalling – all our own work. We learned everything from scratch, galleys – this was BC, before computing – distribution, editing, arguing. The first issue was laid out in the student newspaper office, *Lot's Wife*, at Monash, under the supervision of our friend Ash Fraser, the collective labour consisting of numerous friends, family and assorted ratbags. It was great fun, though the Protestant work ethic overwhelmed. We worked all night and slept all day. It was the best kind of solidarity we could have hoped for. Enduring relationships were built this way, even when folks then moved on.

The first issue was entitled 'Whither Marxism?'; we were already being clever. Its content was more theoretical than political. It brought together papers known to us, from Davidson, Heller and Arnason, Markus and Backhaus. The Budapest School had arrived in the period of its Australian exile from 1978. We had asked Agnes Heller and Ferenc Fehér to join as editors; they had the good judgement to decline, knowing that this was our thing, and that we had to make our own mistakes. But they helped us in a thousand ways. We carried a short document by Gramsci in the first issue, likely more a symbolic than a substantive gesture; and an interview with my teacher, the local labour histor ian N.W. Saffin. We published the Honours thesis of our friend Steve Wright, on J.A. Dawson and the 'Southern Advocate for Workers Councils'; so the Australian content was there, jostling for space with critical theory and western Marxism, and already anticipating our later and stronger sense that the peripheries spoke back to the centres. This was export as well as import work, and we always thought, rightly or not, that our own views, built in Melbourne and for a period with the help of a Sydney group, were as good as anything that we imported from the centres to send back.

The first issue was bagged globally, by *Telos*, and locally, by *Intervention*, and ignored by everybody else, which was probably the right response: to wait and see. We gained some sympathetic coverage in the Melbourne *Age* in 1986, and some astonishing abuse in the culinary column of the magazine *Australian Society*. Some folks on the left thought there were already too many journals, or that theory was bullshit. For the first three issues we carried Marx's Eleventh Thesis on the back cover. After that, we figured folks would know it; we would not need to keep reminding them. We ran the Eleventh Thesis on the inside front until Number 7. This did not work. Some archivally minded types wanted to know if this was Thesis Eleven from the Second Comintern Congress, and some people thought it was (or should be) Thesis 11, Thesis Two. There was at least for a period a Turkish journal of the same name. And at this stage we had yet to discover John Anderson's advice that the real significance of Thesis Eleven was that it was the last thesis.

One serious revolutionary attacked us at a sociology conference (of all places!) for dropping the text of the Eleventh Thesis from the cover: plainly the journal was a reformist Trojan horse. He denounced us as the biggest potential obstacle to the cause of socialist revolution in Australia. A feminist in the audience – in not an entirely predictable intervention – came to our defence, pointing out that this was the usual masculinist tirade – some people do the housework of starting and running journals, others just trash the floor with them and then expect somebody else to clean up. So much for revolutionary politics. We had to be reformists, for we believed in the survival of the present enough to start a journal. This was a practical commitment to be present. So the project built in the memory of our departed friend, Athol, became an institution, a bureaucracy, an organisation with files, habits and office-bearers; and an international reputation.

If the first issue was theoretical, and at least as Germanic as Italian, the second issue of *Thesis Eleven* took us into other territories we were enchanted by, not least those of history. These were the wild days of Althusserians and Thompsonians, calmed sometimes by the gentler and more productive labours of the Annales historians, lifted by controversies over eurocommunism. The third issue was closer in orientation and content to the first, covering western Marxism, democracy and history. The cover to Number 3 is klutzy; the '3' fell off the cover copy work, to be replaced at the last moment by an 'M' turned 90 degrees on its side. The production values were amateurish, but the content was deadly in earnest. The fourth, at the initiative of Ferenc Fehér, addressed the economic crisis east and west. Number 5/6, 336 pages including what looks like some 8-point font, was the blockbuster on culture and ideology. It contained our only spoof review ever, Lawrie Zion masked as Klaus Truggle, reviewing the fictive title by D.H. Myer, *Marx on Down Under*, which we reprint as the final contribution to this special hundredth issue. The most hilarious thing was, nobody got it; nobody noticed when we were silly, or funny, so eventually we gave up trying. Number 7, a very serious issue on labourism, socialism and social democracy, flopped, perhaps because our timing was lousy; we were too enthusiastic in the critique of the New Labor party which was already feeding too many hands on the Australian left. Another joke, perhaps our last explicit effort, appeared in Number 7, an excerpt from a local pizza menu. 'PLEASE TURN OVER. Sir, I write to record my protest at the increasing tendency for sections of an article, to be scattered throughout the newspaper. It is extremely (*Please turn to page 46*)' – this alongside Stuart Hall, Oskar Negt and Ernest Mandel, highly inappropriate. And so it goes. You can see the earlier issues struggling with the creative tensions of centre and periphery, being European in the broad sense, located closer to Asia, looking sideways at Latin America, all this from the antipodes. It was the usual story: whatever appealed in the centres would bore the local audience, and the other way around.

Running a journal is a thankless business. Our collective labours disappeared into the project, just as Marx told us labour disappears into the commodity. A bit like playing the music you love, you have to please yourself, and contribute the best you can to world literature in the process, knowing that all this stuff counts for something, even if you aren't entirely clear what it is. It is for others to judge, and they will. As for us, we are proud to have got this far, and look forward to what comes next. Thank you for joining us, in the spirit of *Thesis Eleven*, then and now.

References

Adorno, T. 1974, *Minima Moralia: Reflections from Damaged Life*, translated by E.F.N. Jephcott, London, UK: New Left Books.

Alavi, H. and Shanin, T. 1988, 'Introduction', in Kautsky, K., *The Agrarian Question*, Winchester: Zwan.

Alexander, P.F. 1992, *Leonard and Virginia Woolf: A Literary Partnership*, New York: St Martins.

Alexander, S. 1988, *Women's Fabian Tracts*, London: Routledge.

Ali, M. 2009, *In the Kitchen: A Novel*, New York: Doubleday.

Ali, T. 1978, *1968 and after: inside the revolution*, London: Blond & Briggs.

Althusser, L. 1969, *For Marx*, Harmondsworth: Penguin Books.

Althusser, L. 1971, *Lenin and Philosophy, and other Essays*, New York: Monthly Review.

Althusser, L. 1972, *Politics and History: Montesquieu, Rousseau, Hegel and Marx*, London: New Left Books.

Althusser, L. 1978, *Le marxisme aujourd'hui*. Unpublished.

Althusser, L. 1993, *The Future Lasts a Long Time*, London, UK: Chatto & Windus.

Althusser, L. and Balibar, E. 1975, *Reading Capital*, translated by B. Brewster. London: New Left Books.

Anderson, P. 1974, *Passages from Antiquity to Feudalism*, London: New Left Books.

Anderson, P. 1976, *Considerations on Western Marxism*, London: Verso.

Anderson, P. 1980, *Arguments within English Marxism*, London: Verso.

Archer, R. 2007, *Why Is There No Labor Party in the United States?* Princeton, NJ: Princeton University Press.

Arendt, H. 1973, *On Revolution*, Harmondsworth: Penguin Books.

Arnason, J.P. 1993, *The Future That Failed: Origins and Destinies of the Soviet Model*, London: Routledge.

Asad, T. and Wolpe, H. 1976, 'Concepts of modes of production', *Economy and Society*, 5 (4), pp. 470–2. doi: 10.1080/03085147600000012.

Avenas, D. and Brossat, A. 1971, *De l'antitrotskyisme: elements d'histoire et de theorie*, Paris: François Maspero.

Aya, R. 1976, 'Pre-Capitalist Modes of Production', *Theory and Society*, 3 (4), pp. 623–29.

Ball, A.M. 2003, *Imagining America: Influence and Images in Twentieth-Century Russia*, Lanham, MD: Rowman & Littlefield.

Barrett, M. 1980, *Women's oppression today: the Marxist/feminist encounter*, London: Verso.

Baudrillard, J. 1975, *The Mirror of Production*, translated by M. Poster. St Louis, MO: Telos Press.

Bauman, J. 1986, *Winter in the Morning: A Young Girl's Life in the Warsaw Ghetto and Beyond, 1939–1945*, London: Virago.

Bauman, Z. 1972, *Between Class and Elite*, Manchester, UK: Manchester University Press.

Bauman, Z. 1973, *Culture as Praxis*, London, UK: Routledge.

Bauman, Z. 1976, *Socialism the Active Utopia*, London, UK: Allen & Unwin.

Bauman, Z. 1982, *Memories of Class: The Pre-History and After-Life of Class*, London: Routledge & Kegan Paul.

Bauman, Z. 1987, *Legislators and Interpreters: On Modernity, Post-Modernity and Intellectuals*, Cambridge: Polity.

Bauman, Z. 1989, *Modernity and the Holocaust*, Oxford, UK: Polity.

Bauman, Z. 1991, *Modernity and Ambivalence*, Cambridge: Polity.

Bauman, Z. 1992, *Intimations of Postmodernity*, London: Routledge.

Bauman, Z. 1995, *Life in Fragments: Essays in Postmodern Morality*, Cambridge: Polity.

Bauman, Z. 1997, *Postmodernity and its Discontents*, Cambridge: Polity.

Bauman, Z. 2000, *Liquid Modernity*, Cambridge: Polity.

Bauman, Z. 2001, *Community: Seeking Safety in an Insecure World*, Wiley.

Bauman, Z. 2003, *Liquid Love: On the Frailty of Human Bonds*, Cambridge: Polity.

Bauman, Z. 2004a, *Europe: An Unfinished Adventure*, Cambridge: Polity.

Bauman, Z. 2004b, *Identity: Conversations With Benedetto Vecchi*, Cambridge: Polity.

Bauman, Z. 2004c, *Wasted Lives: Modernity and Its Outcasts*. Cambridge: Polity.

Bauman, Z. 2004d, *Work, Consumerism And The New Poor*, Maidenhead: Open University Press.

Bauman, Z. 2005, *Liquid Life*, Cambridge: Polity.

Bauman, Z. 2007, *Liquid Times: Living in an Age of Uncertainty*, Cambridge: Polity.

Bax, E.B. 1893, 'The Curse of Civilisation', in *The Ethics of Socialism*, London: S. Sonnenschein & Co.

Bax, E.B. 1988, 'Our German Fabian Convert', in Tudor, H. and Tudor, J.M. (eds) *Marxism and Social Democracy: The Revisionist Debate, 1896–1898*, Cambridge: Cambridge University Press.

Bayertz, K. 1984, 'From Utopia to Science? The Development of Socialist Theory Between Utopia and Science', in E. Mendelsohn and H. Nowotny (eds.) *Nineteen Eighty-Four: Science Between Utopia and Dystopia*, Dordrecht: Reidel (Sociology of the Sciences a Yearbook), pp. 93–110. doi: 10.1007/978-94-009-6340-5_5.

Bebel, A. 1971, *Woman under Socialism*, translated by D. De Leon, New York: Knopf.

Bebel, A. 1976, *Society of the Future*, Moscow: Progress Publishers.

Bebel, A. 1988, 'Speech to Stuttgart Conference', in H. Tudor and J.M. Tudor (eds.) *Marxism and Social Democracy: The Revisionist Debate, 1896–1898*. Cambridge: Cambridge University Press.

Beilharz, P. 1976, 'Book Review: Mandel's Late Capitalism', *Australian Left Review*, 1 (52), 38–9.

Beilharz, P. 1979a, 'Assessing the "Italian road": A review of the materials', *Politics*, 14 (1), 124–30. doi: 10.1080/00323267908401702.

Beilharz, P. 1979b, 'Trotsky's Marxism – Permanent Involution?', *Telos*, 39, 137–52. doi: 10.3817/0379039137.

Beilharz, P. 1980, 'The Legacy of Rosa Luxemburg', *Theory and Society*, 9 (4), 661–4.

Beilharz, P. 1981a, 'Marxism and History', *Thesis Eleven*, 2, pp. 7–22. doi: 10.1177/07255136 8100200102.

Beilharz, P. 1981b, 'The Other Trotsky', *Thesis Eleven*, 3, 106–113. doi: 10.1177/072551368100 300109.

Beilharz, P. 1985, 'Theorizing the Middle Class', *Arena* 72, 9–105.

Beilharz, P. 1986, 'Isaac Deutscher: History and Necessity', *History of Political Thought*, 7 (2), 375–84.

Beilharz, P. 1987, *Trotsky, Trotskyism and the Transition to Socialism*, London, UK: Croom Helm.

Beilharz, P. 1990, 'The Life and Times of Social Democracy', *Thesis Eleven*, 26, 78–94. doi: 10.1177/072551369002600106.

Beilharz, P. 1991a, 'Back To Postmodernity', *Thesis Eleven*, 29 (1), pp. 111–18. doi: 10.1177/07 255136910290010.

Beilharz, P. 1991b, 'Vere Gordon Childe and social theory', in T. Irving, G. Melleuish, and P. Gathercole (eds.), *Childe and Australia*, St Lucia, Australia: Queensland University Press.

Beilharz, P. 1992a, *Labour's Utopias: Bolshevism, Fabianism, Social Democracy*, London: Routledge.

Beilharz, P. 1992b, 'Reviews: Fredric Jameson, Postmodernism, or, The Cultural Logic of Late Capitalism', (Duke/Verso, 1991); Margaret Rose, The Post-Modern and the Post-Industrial (Cambridge University Press, 1991); Alex Callinicos, Against Postmodernism: A Marxist Critique (Cambridge, Polity, 1990), *Thesis Eleven*, 33 (1), 167–71. doi: 10.1177/072551369203300112.

Beilharz, P. 1993a, 'John Anderson and the Syndicalist moment', *Political Theory Newsletter*, 5, 5–13.

Beilharz, P. 1993b, *Transforming Labor: Labor Tradition and the Labor Decade in Australia*, Cambridge, UK: Cambridge University Press.

Beilharz, P. 1994, *Postmodern Socialism: Romanticism, City and State*, Melbourne, Australia: Melbourne University Publishing.

Beilharz, P. 1996a, 'On the importance of being Antipodean and the consistency of being Bernard', *Voices*, 6 (4), 8.

Beilharz, P. 1996b, 'Place, taste and identity', *Art Monthly Australia*.

Beilharz, P. 1997, *Imagining the Antipodes: Culture, Theory and the Visual in the Work of Bernard Smith*, Cambridge, UK: Cambridge University Press.

Beilharz, P. 2000, *Zygmunt Bauman – Dialectic of Modernity*, London, UK: SAGE.

Beilharz, P. (ed.) 2002, *Zygmunt Bauman*, London: SAGE. 4 vols.

Beilharz, P. 2003, 'Budapest Central: Agnes Heller's Theory of Modernity', *Thesis Eleven*, 75, 108–113. doi: 10.1177/0725513603751008.

Beilharz, P. 2005a, 'Postmarxism', in G. Ritzer (ed.) *Sage Encyclopedia of Social Theory*, London, UK: SAGE.

Beilharz, P. 2005b, 'Postmodern Socialism Revisited', in P. Hayden and C. el-Ojeili (eds.) *Confronting Globalization: Humanity, Justice and the Renewal of Politics*, London: Palgrave Macmillan UK (International Political Economy Series), 23–33. doi: 10.1057/9780230598829_2.

Beilharz, P. 2005c, 'Revolution', in *Encyclopedia of Social Theory*, Thousand Oaks: SAGE Publications, Inc., 642–45. doi: 10.4135/9781412952552.

Beilharz, P. 2006a, 'Ends and Rebirths: An Interview with Daniel Bell', *Thesis Eleven*, 85 (1), 93–103. doi: 10.1177/0725513606062952.

Beilharz, P. 2006b, 'Robert Hughes and the provincialism problem', in P. Beilharz and R. Manne (eds.), *Reflected Light – La Trobe Essays*, Melbourne, Australia: Blackink.

Beilharz, P. 2009, *Socialism and Modernity*, Minneapolis, MN: University of Minnesota Press.

Beilharz, P. 2010a, 'Another Bauman: The Anthropological Imagination', in K. Tester and M. Davis (eds.), *Bauman's Challenge: Sociological Issues for the 21st Century*, Basingstoke, UK: Palgrave Macmillan, pp. 62–9.

Beilharz, P. 2010b, 'Modern and Postmodern', in J. Hall, L. Grindstaff, and M.C. Lo (eds.), *Handbook of Cultural Sociology*, London, UK: Routledge.

Beilharz, P. 2012, 'Labour's utopias revisited', *Thesis Eleven*, 110, 46–53. doi: 10.1177/07255 13612450141.

Beilharz, P. 2013, 'Bernard Smith: The quality of marxism', *Thesis Eleven*, 114, 94–102. doi: 10.1177/0725513612455795.

Beilharz, P. 2015, 'Agnes Heller: From Marx to the Dictatorship Over Needs', *Revue internationale de philosophie*, no. 273 (3), 269–77.

Beilharz, P. 2017, 'Non-Russian route to a German thinker', *The Australian*, 11 February, p. 20.

Beilharz, P. 2018a, 'The Budapest School – travelling theory?', in J.F. Rundell and J. Pickle (eds.), *Critical theories and the Budapest School: politics, culture, modernity*.

Beilharz, P. 2018b, 'The Marxist Legacy', in P. Kivisto (ed.), *Cambridge Encyclopedia of Social Theory*, New York: Cambridge University Press.

Beilharz, P. and Hogan, T. 2006, *Sociology: place, time & division*, Oxford: Oxford University Press.

Beilharz, P. and T. Hogan 2012, *Sociology: antipodean perspectives*, South Melbourne: Oxford University Press.

Beilharz, P. and E. Mandel 1983, 'Social Democracy and Social Movements', *Thesis Eleven*, 7 (1), 159–62. doi: 10.1177/072551368300700110.

Bell, D. 1960, *The End of Ideology: On the Exhaustion of Political Ideas in the Fifties*, Glencoe, IL: Free Press.

Bell, D. 1996, *Marxian Socialism in the United States*, Ithaca, NY: Cornell University Press.

Bellamy, E. 1880, *Dr. Heidenhoff's Process*, New York: Appleton.

Bellamy, E. 1898, *The Blindman's World and Other Stories*, edited by W.D. Howells, Boston, MA: Houghton, Mifflin and Company.

Bellamy, E. 1989, *Looking Backward*, Harmondsworth, UK: Penguin.

Bellamy, E. (no date a) 'How many men make a man?', in *Edward Bellamy compositions, 1860–1939*, Houghton Library, Harvard University.

Bellamy, E. (no date b), 'The Religion of Solidarity', in *Edward Bellamy compositions, 1860–1939*, Houghton Library, Harvard University.

Bellamy, E. and Green, M.A. (no date) 'A Biography of Edward Bellamy', in *Edward Bellamy compositions, 1860–1939*, Houghton Library, Harvard University.

Belloc, H. 1913, *The Servile State*, London: Constable and Co.

Benjamin, W. 1969, *Illuminations: Essays and Reflections*, edited by H. Arendt, translated by H. Zohn, New York: Schocken Books.

Berman, M. 1984, *All that is Solid Melts into Air*, New York: Knopf.

Bernstein, E. 1965, *Evolutionary socialism: A criticism and affirmation*, New York: Schocken.

Bernstein, E. 1988a, 'Amongst the Philistines', in H. Tudor and J.M. Tudor (eds.) *Marxism and Social Democracy: The Revisionist Debate, 1896–1898*. Cambridge: Cambridge University Press.

Bernstein, E. 1988b, 'Critical Interlude', in H. Tudor and J.M. Tudor (eds.) *Marxism and Social Democracy: The Revisionist Debate, 1896–1898*. Cambridge: Cambridge University Press.

Bernstein, E. 1988c, 'Problems of Socialism', in H. Tudor and J.M. Tudor (eds.) *Marxism and Social Democracy: The Revisionist Debate, 1896–1898*. Cambridge: Cambridge University Press.

Bernstein, E. 1988d, 'Statement', in H. Tudor and J.M. Tudor (eds.), *Marxism and Social Democracy: The Revisionist Debate, 1896–1898*, Cambridge: Cambridge University Press.

Bernstein, E. 1988e, 'The Struggle of Social Democracy', in H. Tudor and J.M. Tudor (eds.), *Marxism and Social Democracy: The Revisionist Debate, 1896–1898*, Cambridge: Cambridge University Press.

Bernstein, E. 1996, *Selected Writings of Eduard Bernstein 1900–1921*, edited by M. Steger, Atlantic Highlands, N.J.: Humanity Books.

Birchall, I. 1980, 'The Autonomy of Theory: A short history of NLR', *International Socialism* (2) 10, 51–91.

Blackbourn, D. 2006, *The Conquest of Nature: Water, Landscape and the Making of Modern Germany*, London: Jonathan Cape.

Bliss, W.D.P. 1970, *The Encyclopedia of Social Reform*, Westport, CN: Greenwood.

Boggs, C. 1977, 'Marxism, Prefigurative Communism and the Problem of Workers' Control', *Radical America*, 11/12(6/1), 99–122.

Bradley, A.C. 1929, *Shakespearean Tragedy*, London: Macmillan.

Bradley, A.C. 1955a, 'Hegel's Theory of Tragedy', in *Oxford Lectures on Poetry*, London: Macmillan.

Bradley, A.C. 1955b, *Oxford Lectures on Poetry*, London: Macmillan.

Braudel, F. 1974, *Capitalism and material life, 1400–1800*, Glasgow, UK: Fontana.

Braverman, H. 1974, *Labor and monopoly capital: the degradation of work in the twentieth century*.

Brick, H. 1986, *Daniel Bell and the Decline of Intellectual Radicalism: Social Theory and Political Reconciliation in the 1940s*, University of Wisconsin Press.

Britain, I. 1982, *Fabianism and Culture: A Study in British Socialism and the Arts 1884–1918*, Cambridge, UK: Cambridge University Press.

Brossat, A. 1974, *Aux origines de la revolution permanente, la pensee politique du jeune Trotsky*, Paris: François Maspero.

Broué, P. 1988, *Trotsky*, Paris: Fayard.

Buci-Glucksmann, C. 1980, *Gramsci and the State*, translated by D. Fernbach, London: Lawrence & Wishart.

Buick, A. 1975, 'Joseph Dietzgen', *Radical Philosophy*, 10, 3 7.

Bukharin, N.I. and E.A. Preobrazhensky 1967, *The ABC of Communism*, Ann Arbor, MI: Michigan University Press.

Burke, K. 1969, *A Rhetoric of Motives*, Berkeley: University of California Press.

Cahiers Leon Trotsky 1979, 'La delegation de l'Institut a Harvard', *Cahiers Leon Trotsky*, 4, 65.

Cahiers Leon Trotsky 1980, 'Apres l'Ouverture des papiers d'exil', *Cahiers Leon Trotsky*, 5, 3–4.

Calhoun, C. (ed.) 1992, *Habermas and the Public Sphere*, Cambridge, MA: The MIT Press.

Callinicos, A. 1989, *Against Postmodernism: A Marxist Critique*, Oxford, UK: Polity.

Carchedi, G. 1977, *On the economic identification of social classes*, London; Boston: Routledge and Kegan Paul.

Carchedi, G. 1987, *Class Analysis And Social Research*, Oxford: Blackwell.

Carlo, A. 1977, 'Trotsky and the organisation problem', *Critique*, 7 (1), 19–29. doi: 10.1080/03017607708413194.

Carlyle, T. 1857, 'Signs of the Times', in *Critical and Miscellaneous Essays*, London: Chapman and Hall.

Carlyle, T. 1896, *On Heroes, Hero-worship and the Heroic in History*, London: Chapman and Hall.

Carlyle, T. no date, *Sartor resartus*, London.

Carmichael, J. 1975, *Trotsky: An Appreciation of His Life*, London: Hodder & Stoughton Ltd.

Carroll, J. 2007, 'Zygmunt Bauman-Mortality and Culture', in K. Tester and M.H. Jacobsen (eds.), *Bauman before Postmodernity: Invitation, Conversations and Annotated Bibliography 1953–1989*, Aalborg: Aalborg Universitetsforlag.

Castoriadis, C. 1987, *The Imaginary Institution of Society*, translated by K. Blamey, Cambridge, UK: Polity.

Castoriadis, C. 1988a, *Political and Social Writings: Volume 1, 1946–1955*, edited by D.A. Curtis, Minneapolis, MN: University of Minnesota Press.

Castoriadis, C. 1988b, *Political and Social Writings: Volume 2, 1955–1960*. Edited by D.A. Curtis, Minneapolis, MN: University of Minnesota Press.

Castoriadis, C. 1992, *Political and Social Writings: Volume 3, 1961–1979*, edited by D.A. Curtis, Minneapolis, MN: University of Minnesota Press.

Claeys, G. 1987, *Machinery, money, and the millennium: from moral economy to socialism, 1815–1860*. Cambridge: Polity Press.

Claeys, G. 1989, *Citizens and saints: politics and anti-politics in early British socialism*, Cambridge: Cambridge University Press.

Clark, M. 1977, *Antonio Gramsci and the Revolution That Failed*, New Haven: Yale University Press.

Clarke, S. 1980, *One-dimensional Marxism: Althusser and the politics of culture*, London: Allison and Busby.

Cliff, T. 1989, *Trotsky: towards October, 1879–1917*, London: Bookmarks.

Cohen, G.A. 1978, *Karl Marx's Theory of History: A Defence*, Oxford, UK: Clarendon Press.

Cohen, J.L. and A. Arato 1992, *Civil Society and Political Theory*, Cambridge, MA: The MIT Press.

Cole, G.D.H. 1918, *Self-government in industry*, London: Bell. Available at: https://archive .org/details/selfgovernmentioocoleuoft (Accessed: 15 October 2018).

Coleman, P.J. 1987, *Progressivism and the world of reform: New Zealand and the origins of the American welfare state*, Lawrence, KS: University Press of Kansas.

Connell, R.W. and T.H. Irving 1980, *Class Structure in Australian history*, Melbourne: Longman Cheshire.

Cooley, M. 1980, *Architect or Bee? The Human Price of Technology*, London, UK: Hogarth Press.

Corrigan, P.R.D., H. Ramsay and D. Sayer 1978, *Socialist Construction and Marxist Theory: Bolshevism and Its Critique*, London, UK: Macmillan.

Corrigan, P. and D. Sayer 1978, 'Hindess and Hirst: A Critical Review', *Socialist Register*, 15, 194–214.

Crehan, K.A.F. 2002, *Gramsci, Culture, and Anthropology*, London, UK: Pluto Press.

Cutler, T. et al. 1978, *Marx's 'Capital' and Capitalism Today, 2 Vols*, London, UK: Routledge.

Davidson, A. 1968, *Antonio Gramsci, The Man, His Ideas*, Sydney: Australian Left Review.

Davidson, A. 1977, *Antonio Gramsci: Towards an Intellectual Biography*, London: Merlin Press.

Davidson, A. 1982, *The theory and practice of Italian communism*, London: Merlin Press.

Day, R.B. 1973, *Leon Trotsky and the Politics of Economic Isolation*, Cambridge, UK: Cambridge University Press.

Day, R.B. 1976, 'The Theory of Long Waves: Kondratiev, Trotsky, Mandel', *New Left Review*, 99, 67–82.

Deleuze, G. 1994, *Difference and repetition*, New York: Columbia University Press.

Dennis, N. and Halsey, A.H. 1988, *English ethical socialism: Thomas More to R.H. Tawney*, Oxford: Clarendon Press.

D'Eramo, M. 2001, *The pig and the skyscraper: Chicago: a history of our future*, London: Verso.

Deutscher, I. 1953, *Russia after Stalin*, London: Hamilton.

Deutscher, I. 1954, *The Prophet Armed: Trotsky 1879–1921*, Oxford, UK: Oxford University Press.

Deutscher, I. 1966, *Ironies of history: essays on contemporary communism*, London: Oxford University Press.

Deutscher, I. 1969a, 'A Reply to Critics', in *Heretics and renegades; and other essays*, Indianapolis: Bobbs-Merrill.

Deutscher, I. 1969b, *Heretics and renegades; and other essays*, Indianapolis: Bobbs-Merrill.

Deutscher, I. 1970a, *Stalin: a political biography*, Harmondsworth: Penguin Books.

Deutscher, I. 1970b, *The prophet outcast: Trotsky, 1924–1940*, London: Oxford University Press.

Deutscher, I. 1970c, *The prophet unarmed: Trotsky 1921–1929*, London: Oxford University Press.

Deutscher, I. 1977, *The unfinished revolution Russia 1917–1967*, London: Oxford University Press.

Deutscher, I. 1980, '22 June 1941', *New Left Review*, I (124).

Deutscher, T. 1971, 'Work in Progress', in *Isaac Deutscher: the man and his work*, edited by D. Horowitz, London: Macdonald and Co.

Dewey, J. (ed.) 1972, *Not guilty: report of the Commission of Inquiry into the Charges Made Against Leon Trotsky in the Moscow Trials*, New York: Monad Press.

Dews, P. 1992, *Autonomy and Solidarity: Interviews with Jürgen Habermas*, London: Verso.

Dietzgen, J. 1906, 'The religion of social democracy', in *Some of the Philosophical Essays on Socialism and Science: Religion, Ethics, Critique-of-reason and the World-at-large*, Chicago, IL: C.H. Kerr.

Dobb, M. 1976, 'Review of Hindess and Hirst, Precapitalist Modes of Production', *History*, 61.

Dosse, F. 1997, *History of Structuralism*, translated by D. Glassman, Minneapolis, MN: University of Minnesota Press.

Draper, H. 1977, *Karl Marx's Theory of Revolution, 4 Vols*, New York: Monthly Review.

Dubiel, H. 1992, 'Domination or Emancipation? The Debate over the Heritage of Critical Theory', in *Cultural-Political Interventions in the Unfinished Project of Enlightenment*, edited by A. Honneth et al., Cambridge, MA: The MIT Press.

Dunayevskaya, R. 1982, *Marxism and Freedom*, Sussex, UK: Harvester.

Eastman, M. 1925, *Leon Trotsky: The portrait of a youth*, New York: Greenberg.

Elliott, A. (ed.) 2013, *The Contemporary Bauman*, London: Routledge.

Engels, F. 1880, 'Socialism, Utopian and Scientific', in K. Marx and F. Engels, *Selected Works*, 1970 reprint. Progress.

Engels, F. 1892, *The Condition of the Working-class in England in 1844*, London: Swan Sonnenschein.

Engels, F. 1959, *Correspondence: Frederick Engels, Paul and Laura Lafargue*, London: Lawrence and Wishart.

Fehér, F. 1979, 'Toward a Post-Machiavellian Politics', *Telos*, 42, pp. 56–64. doi: 10.3817/127 9042056.

Fehér, F. 1984, 'The French Revolutions as Models for Marx's Conception of Politics', *Thesis Eleven*, 8 (1), 59–76. doi: 10.1177/072551368400800105.

Fehér, F. 1987, 'In the Bestiarium', in *Eastern Left, Western Left*, F. Fehér and A. Heller (eds.), Oxford, UK: Polity.

Fehér, F. 1988, *The Frozen Revolution: An essay on Jacobinism*, Cambridge, UK: Cambridge University Press.

Fehér, F. 1991, 'The Status of Postmodernity', in F. Fehér and A. Heller (eds.), *The Grandeur and Twilight of Radical Universalism*, Piscataway, NJ: Transaction Publishers.

Fehér, F. and A. Heller 1981, 'Equality Reconsidered', *Thesis Eleven*, 3, pp. 23–40. doi: 10.1177/072551368100300103.

Fehér, F. and A. Heller 1983, *Hungary 1956 revisited: the message of a revolution – a quarter of a century after*, London: Allen & Unwin.

Fehér, F. and A. Heller 1987a, 'Class, Modernity, Democracy', in *Eastern Left, Western Left*, F. Fehér and A. Heller (eds.), Oxford, UK: Polity.

Fehér, F. and A. Heller 1987b, *Eastern Left, Western Left: Totalitarianism, freedom and democracy*, Cambridge, UK: Polity Press.

Fehér, F., A. Heller and G. Márkus 1983, *Dictatorship Over Needs: An Analysis of Soviet-type Societies*, Oxford, UK: Basil Blackwell.

Fleischer, H. 1973, *Marxism and History*, London: Allen Lane.

Fletcher, R. (ed.) 1987, *Bernstein to Brandt: A Short History of German Social Democracy*, London: Hodder Arnold.

Foucault, M. 1977, *Discipline and Punish: The Birth of the Prison*, translated by A. Sheridan, New York: Pantheon.

Frankel, B. 1983, *Beyond the State?: Dominant theories and socialist strategies*, London, UK: Macmillan.

Freud, S. 1939, *Psychopathology of everyday life*, Harmondsworth: Penguin.

Frevert, U. 1987, 'Women Workers, Workers' Wives and Social Democracy in Imperial Germany', in R. Fletcher and W. Brandt (eds.), *Bernstein to Brandt: A Short History of German Social Democracy*, London: Hodder Arnold.

Furner, J. 2011, 'Marx's sketch of communist society in The German Ideology and the problems of occupational confinement and occupational identity', *Philosophy and Social Criticism*, 37 (2), 189–216.

Gabriel, M. 2011, *Love and Capital: Karl and Jenny Marx and the Birth of a Revolution*, New York: Little Brown.

Gadamer, H.G. 1975, *Truth and Method*, New York: Seabury.

Gay, P. 1962, *The Dilemma of Democratic Socialism: Eduard Bernstein's Challenge to Marx*, New York: Collier.

Geras, N. 1976, *The Legacy of Rosa Luxemburg*, London, UK: New Left Books.

Geras, N. 1981, 'Classical Marxism and Proletarian Representation', *New Left Review* (1), 125, pp. 75–89.

Geras, N. 1986, *Literature of revolution: essays on Marxism*, London: Verso.

Gill, G. 1979, 'The Signs of Consumerism', *Arena*, 53, pp. 28–39.

Gilligan, C. 1982, *In a Different Voice*, Cambridge, MA: Harvard University Press.

Godelier, M. 1972, *Rationality and irrationality in economics*, New York: Monthly Review.

Goethe (no date), *Faust Part One*.

Goodwin, P. 1979, 'Razor Sharp Factional Minds – The Fourth International Debates', *International Socialism*. (2), (5).

Gori, F. (ed.) 1982, *Pensiero e azione politica di Lev Trockij Vols. 1 and 2*, Firenze: Olschki.

Gouldner, A.W. 1980, *The two marxisms*, New York: Seabury.

Gramsci, A. 1971, *Selections from the Prison Notebooks*, edited by Q. Hoare and G. Nowell-Smith, New York: International Publishers.

Gramsci, A. 1972, 'The Southern Question', in L. Marks (ed.), *The Modern Prince and Other Writings*, New York: International Publishers, pp. 28–51.

Gramsci, A. 1975, 'The Revolution Against Capital', in P. Cavalcanti and P. Piccone (eds.), *History, Philosophy and Culture in the Young Gramsci*, St Louis, MO: Telos.

Gramsci, A. 1977, *Antonio Gramsci: selections from political writings*, London: Lawrence and Wishart.

Grandin, G. 2009, *Fordlandia: the rise and fall of Henry Ford's forgotten jungle city*, New York: Metropolitan Books.

Grosz, E. 1989, *Sexual subversions*, Sydney: Allen & Unwin.

Habermas, J. 1970, *Toward a Rational Society: Student Protest, Science, and Politics*, translated by J.J. Shapiro, Boston, MA: Beacon Press.

Habermas, J. 1971, *Knowledge and Human Interests*, translated by J.J. Shapiro, Boston, MA: Beacon Press.

Habermas, J. 1973, *Theory and Practice*, translated by J. Viertel. Boston, MA: Beacon Press.

Habermas, J. 1975, *Legitimation Crisis*, translated by T. McCarthy, Boston, MA: Beacon Press.

Habermas, J. 1979, *Communication and the Evolution of Society*, translated by T. McCarthy, Boston, MA: Beacon Press.

Habermas, J. 1981, 'Modernity versus Postmodernity', *New German Critique*, Translated by S. Benhabib, 22, 3–14. doi: 10.2307/487859.

Habermas, J. 1984, *The Theory of Communicative Action, Volume 1: Reason and the Rationalization of Society*, translated by T. McCarthy, Boston, MA: Beacon Press.

Habermas, J. 1987a, *The Philosophical Discourse of Modernity: Twelve lectures*, translated by F.G. Lawrence, Cambridge, MA: The MIT Press.

Habermas, J. 1987b, *The Theory of Communicative Action, Volume 2: A Critique of Functionalist Reason*, translated by T. McCarthy, Boston, MA: Beacon Press.

Habermas, J. 1988, *On the Logic of the Social Sciences*, translated by S.W. Nicholsen and J.A. Stark. Cambridge, MA: The MIT Press.

Habermas, J. 1989a, *The New Conservatism: Cultural Criticism and the Historians' Debate*, edited by S.W. Nicholson, Cambridge, MA: The MIT Press.

Habermas, J. 1989b, *The Structural Transformation of the Public Sphere: An Inquiry into a Category of Bourgeois Society*, translated by T. Burger, Cambridge, UK: Polity Press.

Habermas, J. 1990, *Moral Consciousness and Communicative Action*, translated by C. Lenhardt and S.W. Nicholson, Cambridge, MA: The MIT Press.

Hallas, D. 1979, *Trotsky's Marxism*, London: Pluto Press.

Hardt, M. and A. Negri 2000, *Empire*, Cambridge, MA: Harvard University Press.

Haupt, G. 1986, 'The Role and Influence of Social Democracy in South-East Europe', in *Aspects of International Socialism, 1871–1914: Essays by Georges Haupt*, edited by E. Hobsbawm, translated by P. Fawcett, Cambridge: Cambridge University Press.

Hegel, G.W.F. 1956, *The philosophy of history*, New York: Dover Publications.

Hegel, G.W.F. 1976, *Hegel's Philosophy of right*, London: Oxford University Press.

Hegel, G.W.F. 1980, *Lectures on the philosophy of world history*, Cambridge: Cambridge University Press.

Heimann, H. and T. Meyer 1978, *Bernstein und der demokratische Sozialismus: Bericht über d. Wissenschaft*, Berlin: Dietz.

Heller, Á. 1972, 'Towards a Marxist theory of value', *Kinesis*, 5 (1).

Heller, Á. 1976, *Theory of Need in Marx*, London: Allison & Busby.

Heller, Á. 1978 *Renaissance Man*, London, UK: Routledge & Kegan Paul.

Heller, Á. 1982a, *A Theory of History*, London, UK: Routledge & Kegan Paul.

Heller, Á. 1982b, 'The Emotional Division of Labour Between the Sexes: Perspectives on Feminism and Socialism', *Thesis Eleven*, 5, 59–71.

Heller, Á. 1984a, 'Marx and Modernity', *Thesis Eleven*, 8, pp. 44–58. doi: 10.1177/072551368 400800104.

Heller, Á. 1984b, *Radical philosophy*, Oxford, UK: Basil Blackwell.

Heller, Á. 1993, *A Philosophy of History in Fragments*, Oxford, UK: Wiley-Blackwell.

Heller, Á. 1996, *An Ethics of Personality*, Oxford, UK: Blackwell.

Heller, Á. 1999, *A Theory of Modernity*, Oxford, UK: Wiley-Blackwell.

Heller, Á. 2001, *The Three Logics of Modernity and the Double Bind of the Modern Imagination*, Budapest: Collegium Budapest.

Heller, Á. 2007, 'What is Postmodern: A Quarter of a Century After?', in *Moderne begreifen: Zur Paradoxie eines sozio-ästhetischen Deutungsmusters*, C. Magerski, R. Savage, and C. Weller (eds.), 2007 edn., Wiesbaden: Deutscher Universitätsverlag, 37–50.

Heller, Á. and F. Fehér 1988, *The Postmodern Political Condition*, New York: Columbia University Press.

Herf, J. 1986, *Reactionary Modernism: Technology, Culture, and Politics in Weimar and the Third Reich*, Cambridge, UK: Cambridge University Press.

Hilton, R. (ed.) 1976, *The Transition From Feudalism to Capitalism*, London, UK: New Left Books.

Hindess, B. and Hirst, P.Q. 1975, *Pre-capitalist Modes of Production*. London: Routledge & Kegan Paul.

Hindess, B. and Hirst, P.Q. 1977, *Mode of Production and Social Formation: An Auto-Critique of Pre-Capitalist Modes of Production*, London: Macmillan.

Hirsch, H. 1977, *Der 'Fabier' Eduard Bernstein*, Bonn: Dietz.

Hobson, J.A. 1902, *Imperialism*, London.

Hogan, T.L.F. 1995, *Modernity as revolution: Thomas Carlyle and the absent centre of British social theory: a study of the writings of the young Carlyle as text and context*. Thesis. Available at: https://trove.nla.gov.au/version/26499515 (Accessed: 22 March 2019).

Holub, R.C. 1991, *Jürgen Habermas: Critic in the Public Sphere*, London, UK: Routledge.

Honneth, A. 1991, *The Critique of Power: Reflective Stages in a Critical Social Theory*, translated by K. Baynes. Cambridge, MA: The MIT Press.

Horkheimer, M. and Adorno, T.W. 1973, *Dialectic of Enlightenment: Philosophical fragments*, translated by J. Cuming, London, UK: Allen Lane.

Howard, D. 1977, *The Marxian Legacy*, London, UK: Macmillan.

Hussain, A. 1977, 'Crises and tendencies of capitalism', *Economy and Society*, 6 (4), 436–460. doi: 10.1080/03085147700000011.

Hussain, A. 1980, 'Symptomatology of revolution', *Economy and Society*, 9 (3), pp. 348–58. doi: 10.1080/03085148008538604.

Jacobson, J. 1972, 'Isaac Deutscher: The Anatomy of an Apologist', in *Soviet communism and the socialist vision*, New Brunswick: Transaction Books.

Jameson, F. 1991, *Postmodernism, Or, The Cultural Logic of Late Capitalism*, Durham: Duke University Press.

Jameson, F. 2011, *Representing Capital: a commentary on volume one*, London; New York: Verso.

Jay, M. 1973, *The Dialectical Imagination: A History of the Frankfurt School and the Institute of Social Research, 1923–1950*. Boston, MA: Little Brown.

Jessop, B. 1982, *The Capitalist State*, London, UK: Martin Robinson.

Johnson, R. 1982, 'Reading for the best Marx', in R. Johnson (ed.), *Making histories*, London: Hutchinson.

Kautsky, K. 1889, 'Der Jungste Zukunftsroman', *Die Neue Zeit*, 7.

Kautsky, K. 1895, 'Die Intelligenz und die Sozialdemokratie', *Die Neue Zeit*, 13 (2).

Kautsky, K. 1896, 'William Morris', *Der Wahre Jacob*, 268.

Kautsky, K. 1901, 'Die Revision des Programmes der Sozialdemokratie in Oesterreich', *Die Neue Zeit*, 1 (3).

Kautsky, K. 1907, *Ethics and the Materialist Conception of History*, Chicago, IL: C.H. Kerr.

Kautsky, K. 1909, *The Road to Power*, translated by A.M. Simons, Chicago: S.A. Bloch.

Kautsky, K. 1910, *The Social Revolution and the Day After the Revolution*, translated by A.M. Simons and M.W. Simons, Chicago, IL: Kerr.

Kautsky, K. 1920, 'Demokratie und Demokratie', *Der Kampf*, XIII.

Kautsky, K. 1925, *The Labour Revolution*, London: G. Allen & Unwin.

Kautsky, K. 1927, *Thomas More and his Utopia*, translated by H.J. Stenning, London: A.C. Black.

Kautsky, K. 1971, *The Class Struggle*, New York: Norton.

Kautsky, K. 1988a, *The Agrarian Question*, London: Zwan.

Kautsky, K. 1988b, *The Materialist Conception of History*, New Haven: Yale University Press.

Keane, J. 1988, *Democracy and Civil Society*, London: Verso.

Kennedy, B. 1995, *A Passion to Oppose: John Anderson, 1893–1962*, Carlton South, Australia: Melbourne University Publishing.

Kidron, M. 1974, *Capitalism and theory*, London: Pluto Press.

Kleinknecht, A. 1981, 'Innovation, Accumulation, and Crisis: Waves in Economic Development?', *Review*, 4 (4), 683–711.

Knei-Paz, B. 1978, *The Social and Political Thought of Leon Trotsky*, Oxford, UK: Oxford University Press.

Kolakowski, L. 1978, *Main Currents in Marxism*, Oxford: Oxford University Press.

Konrád, G. and I. Szelényi 1979, *The intellectuals on the road to class power*, Hemel Hempstead, UK: Harvester Press.

Korsch, K. 1936, *Karl Marx*, New York: Chapman and Hall.

Kuhn, T.S. 1962, *The structure of scientific revolutions*, Chicago: University of Chicago Press.

Labedz, L. 1988, 'Deutscher as Historian and Prophet', *Survey*, 30 (1–2).

Laclau, E. and C. Mouffe 1985, *Hegemony and socialist strategy: towards a radical democratic politics*, London: Verso.

Lafargue, P. 1907, *The Right to be Lazy and Other Studies*, translated by C.H. Kerr, Chicago: Kerr.

Lafargue, P. 1975, *The Evolution of Property and Social and Philosophical Studies*, London: New Park.

Laplanche, J. and J.-B. Pontalis 1973, *The language of psycho-analysis*, London: Hogarth Press. Available at: http://books.google.com/books?id=wLxrAAAAMAAJ (Accessed: 2 October 2018).

Law, D. 1982, 'Trockij and Thermidor', in *Pensiero e azione politica di Lev Trockij Vols. 1 and 2*, edited by F. Gori, Firenze: Olschki.

League for the Revolutionary Party 1979, 'Myth and Reality of the Transitional Program: "Workers' Government" vs. Workers' State', *Socialist Voice*, pp. 16–32.

Lecourt, D. 1975, *Marxism and epistemology*, London: New Left Books.

Lenin, V.I. 1899, *The Development of Capitalism in Russia*, Moscow: Progress Publishers.

Lenin, V.I. 1902, *What is to be done?* Moscow: Progress Publishers.

Lenin, V.I. 1977a, 'Speech in the Name of the RSDLP at Lafargue's Funeral', in *Collected Works*, Moscow: Progress Publishers.

Lenin, V.I. 1977b, 'State and Revolution', in *Collected Works*, Moscow: Progress Publishers.

Lenin, V.I. 1977c, 'What is to be done?', in *Collected Works*, Moscow: Progress Publishers.

Levine, A. and E.O. Wright 1980, 'Rationality and Class Struggle', *New Left Review*, (1), 123, 47–68.

Lidtke, V.L. 1985, *The Alternative Culture: Socialist Labor in Imperial Germany*, New York: Oxford University Press.

Liebersohn, H. 1988, *Fate and utopia in German sociology, 1870–1923*, Cambridge, MA: The MIT Press.

Lipow, A. 1982, *Authoritarian Socialism in America: Edward Bellamy and the Nationalist Movement*, Berkeley, CA: University of California Press.

Lipset, S.M. 1971, *Agrarian Socialism: The Cooperative Commonwealth Federation in Saskatchewan: a Study in Political Sociology*, Berkeley, CA: University of California Press.

Lipset, S.M. and G. Marks 2001, *It Didn't Happen Here: Why Socialism Failed in the United States*, New York: W.W. Norton & Company.

Lloyd, H.D. 1900a, *A Country Without Strikes: A Visit to the Compulsory Arbitration Court of New Zealand*, New York: Doubleday, Page & Co.

Lloyd, H.D. 1900b, *Newest England*, New York: Doubleday, Page & Co.

Lowith, K. 1957, *Meaning in History: The Theological Implications of the Philosophy of History*, Chicago: University of Chicago Press.

Löwith, K. 1982, *Max Weber and Karl Marx*, London: Allen & Unwin.

Lubasz, H. 1976, 'Marx's Initial Problematic: The Problem of Poverty', *Political Studies*, 24 (1), 24–42. doi: 10.1111/j.1467–9248.1976.tb00091.x.

Lukács, G. 1971, *History and Class Consciousness: Studies in Marxist Dialectics*, translated by R. Livingstone, London: Merlin Press.

Luxemburg, R. 1971a, *Selected political writings of Rosa Luxemburg*, edited by D. Howard, New York: Monthly Review Press.

Luxemburg, R. 1971b, 'Social Reform or Revolution', in *Selected political writings of Rosa Luxemburg*, edited by D. Howard, New York: Monthly Review Press.

Luxemburg, R. 1988, 'Tariff Policy and Militarism', in *Marxism and Social Democracy: The Revisionist Debate, 1896–1898*, H. Tudor and J.M. Tudor (eds.) Cambridge: Cambridge University Press.

Lyotard, J.-F. 1984, *The Postmodern Condition: A Report on Knowledge*, translated by G. Bennington and B. Massumi, Minneapolis, MN: University of Minnesota Press.

Macherey, P. 1966, *A Theory of Literary Production*, London: Routledge & Kegan Paul.

MacIntyre, S. 1980, *A Proletarian Science: Marxism in Britain 1917–1933*, Cambridge: Cambridge University Press.

Mandel, E. 1969a, *A socialist strategy for Western Europe*, Nottingham: Institute for Workers' Control (10).

Mandel, E. (ed.) 1969b, *Fifty years of world revolution, 1917–1967*, New York: Merit Publishers.

Mandel, E. 1969c, *The Inconsistencies of 'State-Capitalism'*, London: International Marxist Group.

Mandel, E. 1969d, 'The New Vanguard', in *New Revolutionaries – Left Opposition*, edited by T. Ali, London: Peter Owen.

Mandel, E. 1969e, *The Revolutionary Student Movement: Theory and practice*, New York: Merit Publishers.

Mandel, E. 1970a, *Revolutionary Strategy in the Imperialist Countries: The Speech Nixon & Mitchell Tried to Ban*, New York: Pathfinder.

Mandel, E. 1970b, 'The Rise and Decline of Stalinism', in *The Development and Disintegration of World Stalinism*, New York: SWP Education Series.

Mandel, E. 1971a, *An Introduction to Marxist Economic Theory*, New York: Pathfinder.

Mandel, E. 1971b, *The changing role of the bourgeois university*, London: Spartacus League.

Mandel, E. 1971c, *The Formation of the Economic Thought of Karl Marx*, New York: Monthly Review.

Mandel, E. 1972, *Der Spätkapitalismus. Versuch einer marxistischen Erklärung*, Frankfurt: Suhrkamp Verlag.

Mandel, E. 1973a, *On Bureaucracy: A Marxist analysis*, London: IMG Publications.

Mandel, E. 1973b, 'Workers' Control and Workers' Councils', *International*, 2 (1).

Mandel, E. 1974a, *Marxist Economic Theory*, single volume ed., London: Merlin Press.

Mandel, E. 1974b, 'Ten theses on the social and economic laws governing the society transitional between capitalism and socialism', *Critique*, 3 (1), pp. 5–21. doi: 10.1080/03017607408413128.

Mandel, E. 1974c, 'Workers Under Neocapitalism', in *The Revolutionary Potential of the Working Class*, edited by E. Mandel and G. Novack, New York: Pathfinder.

Mandel, E. 1975a, *Late Capitalism*. London: New Left Books.

Mandel, E. 1975b, 'Self-Management: Dangers and Possibilities', *International*, 2 (4).

Mandel, E. 1976a, 'Althusser corrige Marx', in *Contre Althusser*, edited by J. Vincent, Paris: Union Générale.

Mandel, E. 1976b, 'Introduction', in *Capital, Volume I*, Harmondsworth, UK: Penguin.

Mandel, E. 1977a, 'The Leninist Theory of Organisation', in *Revolution and Class Struggle: A Reader in Marxist Politics*, edited by R. Blackburn, Glasgow, UK: Fontana.

Mandel, E. 1977b, 'The Nature of the USSR, Socialism, Democracy', *Inprecor*, December, 4–9.

Mandel, E. 1978a, *From Stalinism to Eurocommunism: The Bitter Fruits of 'Socialism in One Country'*, London: New Left Books.

Mandel, E. 1978b, 'On the Nature of the Soviet State', *New Left Review*, 108, 23–45.

Mandel, E. 1978c, *The Second Slump: A Marxist analysis of recession in the seventies*, London: New Left Books.

Mandel, E. 1979a, 'Behind Differences on Military Conflicts in Southeast Asia', *Intercontinental Press*.

Mandel, E. 1979b, *Introduction to Marxism*, London: Ink Links.

Mandel, E. 1979c, *Revolutionary Marxism Today*, translated by J. Rothschild, London: New Left Books.

Mandel, E. 1979d, *Trotsky: A Study in the Dynamic of His Thought*, London: New Left Books.

Mandel, E. 1979e, 'Why the Soviet Bureaucracy Is Not a New Ruling Class', *Monthly Review*, 31 (3).

Mandel, E. 1980a, *Long Waves of Capitalist Development: A Marxist Interpretation*, London: New Left Books.

Mandel, E. 1980b, 'Once again on the Trotskyist definition of the social nature of the Soviet Union', *Critique*, 12 (1), 117–126. doi: 10.1080/03017608008413264.

Mandel, E. 1980c, 'Report on the World Political Situation', in *1979 World Congress of the Fourth International. Major Resolutions and Reports*, New York: Inprecor/Intercontinental Press.

Mandel, E. 1981, 'Introduction', in *Capital, Volume III*, Harmondsworth, UK: Penguin.

Mandel, E. 1983a, 'Economics', in *Marx: The First Hundred Years*, D. McLellan (ed.), London: Fontana.

Mandel, E. 1983b, 'Social Democracy and Social Movements', *Thesis Eleven*, 7, 159–162.

Mandel, E. and G.E. Novack 1974, *The revolutionary potential of the working class*, New York: Pathfinder.

Mannheim, K. 1936, *Ideology and utopia: An introduction to the sociology of knowledge*, New York: Harvest.

Marcuse, H. 1964, *One-Dimensional Man: Studies in the Ideology of Advanced Industrial Society*, London: Routledge & Kegan Paul.

Marie, J.-J. 1980, *Trotsky, le trotskysme et la Quatrième Internationale*, Paris: Presses Universitaires de France.

Marinetti, F.T. 1909, *The futurist manifesto*.

Márkus, G. 1978, *Marxism and Anthropology: The Concept of 'human Essence' in the Philosophy of Marx*, Assen: Van Gorcum.

Marx, K. 1852, *The Eighteenth Brumaire of Louis Bonaparte*, 1948 reprint, Moscow: Foreign Languages Publishing House.

Marx, K. 1964, *Pre-capitalist economic formations*, edited by E.J. Hobsbawm, London, UK: Lawrence & Wishart.

Marx, K. 1965, *Capital, Volume I*, Moscow: Progress Publishers.

Marx, K. 1970, *A Contribution to the Critique of Political Economy*, Moscow: International Publishers.

Marx, K. 1973, *Grundrisse: Foundations of the Critique of Political Economy*, Harmondsworth, UK: Penguin.

Marx, K. 1975, 'Economic and Philosophical Manuscripts', in *Marx: Early Writings*, edited by L. Colletti, Harmondsworth, UK: Penguin.

Marx, K. 1978, *Das Kapital, 1*, Frankfurt [Main]: Verl. Neue Kritik.

Marx, K. and F. Engels 1848, *The Communist Manifesto*, 1970 reprint, Peking: Foreign Languages Press.

Marx, K. and F. Engels 1961, *Marx/Engels: Werke*. Berlin: Dietz Vlg Bln.

Marx, K. and F. Engels 1975, *Marx-Engels Selected Correspondence*, Moscow: Progress Publishers.

Marx, K. and F. Engels 2004, *Collected Works* (50 vols), London: Lawrence & Wishart.

Marx, L. 1964, *Machine in the garden*, New York: Oxford University Press.

Mathiez, A. 1955, 'Bolshevism and Jacobinism', *Dissent*, (Winter). Available at: https://www.dissentmagazine.org/article/bolshevism-and-jacobinism (Accessed: 11 October 2018).

Mattick, P. 1981, 'Ernest Mandel's Late Capitalism', in *Economic Crisis and Crisis Theory*, London: Merlin Press.

McBriar, A.M. 1962, *Fabian Socialism and English Politics: 1884–1918*, Cambridge: Cambridge University Press.

McMurtry, J. 1978, *The Structure of Marx's World-View*, Princeton, NJ: Princeton University Press.

McQueen, H. 1970, *A New Britannia*, Ringwood, Australia: Penguin.

Mehlman, J. 1977, *Revolution and repetition: Marx/Hugo/Balzac*, Berkeley: University of California Press.

Meier, P. 1978, *William Morris: the Marxist dreamer*, Sussex: Harvester Press.

Meyer, T. 1977, *Bernstein's Konstructiver Sozialismus*, Berlin: Dietz.

Miller, R.F. and F. Fehér (eds.) 1984, *Khrushchev and the communist world*, London: Croom Helm.

Minson, J. 1985, *Genealogies of morals: Nietzsche, Foucault, Donzelot and the eccentricity of ethics*, London: Macmillan.

Mommsen, W.J. 1984, *Max Weber and German Politics, 1890–1920*, Chicago: University of Chicago Press.

Mommsen, W.J. and J. Osterhammel (eds.) 1989, *Max Weber and His Contemporaries*, London: Unwin Hyman.

Montag, W. 2003, *Louis Althusser*, Basingstoke, UK: Palgrave Macmillan.

Moore, B. 1978, *Injustice: The Social Bases of Obedience and Revolt*, New York: Random House.

Morgan, A.E. 1944, 'Edward Bellamy', in Arthur Ernest Morgan papers concerning Edward Bellamy, 1912–1944, Houghton Library, Harvard University.

Morgan, A.E. (no date), 'The Philosophy of Edward Bellamy', in Arthur Ernest Morgan papers concerning Edward Bellamy, 1912–1944, Houghton Library, Harvard University.

Morris, W. 1962a, 'News from Nowhere', in A. Briggs (ed.) *William Morris – Selected Writings*, Harmondsworth, UK: Penguin, pp. 183–301.

Morris, W. 1962b, *Selected Writings*, edited by A. Briggs, Harmondsworth, UK: Penguin.

Morris, W. 1984, 'Looking Backward', in A.L. Morton (ed.) *Political writings of William Morris*, London: Lawrence and Wishart.

Mouffe, C. (ed.) 1977, *Gramsci and Marxist Theory*, London: Routledge.

Mouffe, C. and E. Laclau 1981, 'Socialist Strategy – Where next?', *Marxism Today*, January, 17–22.

Mouffe, C. and A.S. Sassoon 1977, 'Gramsci in France and Italy – A review of the literature', *Economy and Society*, 6 (1), pp. 31–68.

Müller, H. 1892, *Der Klassenkampf in der deutsche Socialdemokratie*, Zurich: Verlags-Magazin.

Murphy, P. 1988, 'Agnes Heller', in *Social Theory – A guide to central thinkers*, edited by P. Beilharz, Sydney, Australia: Allen & Unwin.

Murphy, P. 1990, 'Socialism and Democracy', *Thesis Eleven*, 26, 54–77. doi:10.1177/072551369002600105.

Nield, K. and J. Seed 1981, 'Waiting for Gramsci', *Social History*, 6 (2), 209–27.

Nolan, M. 1994, *Visions of Modernity: American Business and the Modernization of Germany*, New York: Oxford University Press.

Nove, A. 1980, *The Economics of Feasible Socialism*, London, UK: Routledge.

Nye, D.E. 1994, *American technological sublime*, Cambridge, Mass.: MIT Press.

Pablo 1974, 'From the Third to the Fourth World Congress', in *Towards a History of the Fourth International: Pt. 4*, Pathfinder Books.

Parsons, T. 1937, *The Structure of Social Action*, New York: The Free Press.

Parsons, T. 1951, *The Social System*, New York: The Free Press.

Payne, R. 1977, *The life and death of Trotsky*, New York: McGraw-Hill.

Peukert, H. 1986, *Science, Action, and Fundamental Theology: Toward a Theology of Communicative Action*, translated by J. Bohman, Cambridge, MA: The MIT Press.

Poggi, G. 1993, *Money and the Modern Mind: Georg Simmel's Philosophy of Money*, Berkeley: University of California Press.

Poulantzas, N. 1978, *State, power, socialism*, London: New Left Books.

Prawer, S.S. 1978, *Karl Marx and world literature*, Oxford: Oxford University Press.

Projekt Klassenanalyse 1971, *Leo Trotzki: Alternative zum Leninismus?* Berlin: Verlag für das Studium der Arbeiterbewegung.

Pusey, M. 1991, *Economic rationalism in Canberra: a nation-building state changes its mind*, New York: Cambridge University Press.

Rabinow, P. 1992, 'A Modern Tourist in Brazil', in S. Lash and J. Friedman (eds.) *Modernity and identity*, Oxford: Blackwell.

Rader, M.M. 1979, *Marx's Interpretation of History*, New York: Oxford University Press.

Rakovski, M. 1978, *Towards an East European Marxism*, New York: Palgrave Macmillan.

Rée, J. 1984, *Proletarian Philosophers: Problems in Socialist Culture in Britain, 1900–1940*, Oxford: Oxford University Press.

Riley, P. 1994, 'Introduction', in *Fénelon: Telemachus*, Cambridge, UK: Cambridge University Press.

Ritzer, G. 1993, *The McDonaldization of society*, Thousand Oaks: Pine Forge Press.

Ritzer, G. 1995, *Expressing America: A Critique of the Global Credit Card Society*, Los Angeles: Pine Forge.

Robrieux, P. and P. Broué 1980, 'Les derniers secrets des Archives de Trotsky', *Le Monde*, 4 May.

Rogers, H.K. 1983, 'Eduard Bernstein Speaks to the Fabians: A Turning-point in Social Democratic Thought?', *International Review of Social History*, 28 (3), pp. 320–38. doi: 10.1017/S0020859000007720.

Rosemont, F. 1988, 'Bellamy's Radicalism Reclaimed', in D. Patai (ed.) *Looking Backward, 1988–1888: Essays on Edward Bellamy*, Amherst, MA: University of Massachusetts Press, 147–209.

Rosemont, F. 1990, 'Introduction', in *Apparitions of Things to Come: Edward Bellamy's Tales of Mystery & Imagination*, Chicago, IL: Charles Kerr.

Ross, G.D. 1979, *Marx and History: From Primitive Society to the Communist Future*, Austin, TX: University of Texas Press.

Roth, G. 1963, *The Social Democrats in Imperial Germany: A Study in Working Class Isol-ation and National Integration*, Totowa: Bedminster.

Rundell, J.F. 1989, *Origins of modernity: the origins of modern social theory from Kant to Hegel to Marx*, Cambridge: Polity Press.

Ruskin, J. 1901, *Unto This Last*, 1901 reprint, London: George Allen.

Said, E.W. 1993, *Culture and imperialism*, London: Chatto & Windus.

Salvadori, M. 1979, *Karl Kautsky and the Socialist Revolution 1880–1938*, London: New Left Books.

Salvadori, M. 1989, 'Reinterpreting Kautsky', *International Review of Social History*, 34 (1), 110–116. doi: 10.1017/S0020859000009081.

Samuel, R. 1980, 'British Marxist Historians 1880–1980, Part 1', *New Left Review* (1), 120, 21–96.

Sartre, J.P. 1969, *The Communists and Peace*, London: Hamish Hamilton.

Sassoon, A.S. 1980a, *Gramsci's Politics*, London, UK: Croom Helm.

Sassoon, A.S. 1980b, 'The Gramsci "Boom": A reflection on the present Crisis?', in *Power and Politics*, London: Routledge & Kegan Paul, 203–211.

Sassoon, A.S. 1988, *Gramsci's Politics*, 2nd edn, Minneapolis: University of Minnesota Press.

Sassoon, D. 1996, *One Hundred Years of Socialism: The West European Left in the Twenti-eth Century*, London, UK: Tauris.

Sawer, M. 1977, *Marxism and the Question of the Asiatic Mode of Production*, The Hague, Netherlands: Martin Nijhoff.

Scaff, L.A. 1987, 'Fleeing the Iron Cage: Politics and Culture in the Thought of Max Weber', *The American Political Science Review*, 81 (3), pp. 737–55. doi: 10.2307/1962674.

Schivelbusch, W. 1979, *The railway journey: trains and travel in the 19th century*, New York: Urizen Books.

Schlosser, E. 2001, *Fast food nation: what the all-American meal is doing to the world*, London: Allen Lane.

Schön, D.A. 1979, 'Generative Metaphor: A perspective on problem-setting in social policy', in A. Ortony (ed.), *Metaphor and thought*, Cambridge, UK: Cambridge University Press, pp. 254–83.

Seabrook, J. 1985, *Landscapes of poverty*, Oxford: Blackwell.

Seabrook, J. 1988, *The leisure society*, Oxford: Basil Blackwell.

Seddon, D. 1978, *Relations of production: Marxist approaches to economic anthropo-logy*.

Segal, H.P. 1988, 'Bellamy and Technology', in *Looking Backward, 1988–1888: Essays on Edward Bellamy*, edited by D. Pataim Amherst, MA: University of Massachusetts Press, pp. 91–105.

Segal, R. 1979, *The tragedy of Leon Trotsky*, London, UK: Hutchinson.

Shakespeare, W. (no date a), *As You Like It*.

Shakespeare, W. (no date b), *Hamlet*.

Shaw, W.H. 1977, *Marx's Theory of History*, Stanford, CA: Stanford University Press.

Simmel, G. 1978, *Philosophy of Money*, translated by T. Bottomore and D. Frisby, London: Routledge.

Sinclair, K. (ed.) 1961, *Distance Looks Our Way: The effects of remoteness on New Zealand*, Auckland, New Zealand: The University of Auckland.

Singer, P. 1980, *Marx*, Oxford, UK: Oxford University Press.

Slaughter, C. 1974, *Trotskyism versus Revisionism: A documentary history*, London: New Park Publications.

Smith, B. 1962, 'The rebirth of Australian painting (Second Macrossan Lecture)', in *Australian Painting Today*, edited by B. Smith, St Lucia, Australia: Queensland University Press.

Smith, B. 1984, *The Boy Adeodatus: The Portrait of a Lucky Young Bastard*, Ringwood, Australia: Penguin.

Smith, B. 1988, *The Death of the Artist as Hero: Essays in History and Culture*, Melbourne, Australia: Oxford University Press.

Smith, B. 2002, *A Pavane for Another Time*, London, UK: Macmillan.

Smith, B. 2007, *The Formalesque: A Guide to Modern Art and Its History*, Melbourne: Macmillan.

Sombart, W. 1951, *The Jews and Modern Capitalism*, translated by M. Epstein, New York: The Free Press.

Sombart, W. 1976, *Why is there no Socialism in the United States?* New York: M.E. Sharpe.

Sontag, S. 1978, *Illness as metaphor*, London: Penguin Books.

Spriano, P. 1975, *The occupation of the factories: Italy 1920*, London: Pluto.

Stedman Jones, G. 2017, *Karl Marx: greatness and illusion*. Cambridge: Belknap.

Steenson, G.P. (ed.) 1981, *'Not one man! Not one penny!': German social democracy, 1863–1914*, Pittsburgh: University of Pittsburgh Press.

Steger, M.B. 1997, *The Quest for Evolutionary Socialism: Eduard Bernstein and Social Democracy*, New York: Cambridge University Press.

Steinberg, H.J. 1972, *Sozialismus und deutsche Sozialdemokratie*, Bonn: Neue Gesellschaft.

Steinberg, H.J. 1976, 'Workers' Libraries in Germany before 1914', *History Workshop*, translated by N. Jacobs, (1), 166–180.

Tarbuck, K. 1977, 'Ten Years Without Deutscher', *International*, 4 (1). Available at: https://www.marxists.org/history/etol/writers/tarbuck/1977/xx/deutscher.htm (Accessed: 10 October 2018).

Taussig, M. 1993, *Mimesis and alterity: a particular history of the senses*, London: Routledge.

Taussig, M.T. 1992, *The nervous system*, New York: Routledge. Available at: http://site.ebrary.com/id/10603829 (Accessed: 15 October 2018).

Taylor, J.G. 1975, 'Review Article: Pre-Capitalist Modes of Production, Part 1', *Critique of Anthropology*, 2. doi: 10.1177/0308275X7500100406.

Taylor, J.G. 1976, 'Review Article: Pre-Capitalist Modes of Production, Part 2', *Critique of Anthropology*, 3. doi: 10.1177/0308275X7500100406.

Taylor, J.G. 1979, *From Modernization to Modes of Production: A Critique of the Sociologies of Development and Underdevelopment*, London: Macmillan.

Terray, E. 1972, *Marxism and Primitive Societies*, New York: Monthly Review.

Tester, K. and M.H. Jacobsen 2005, *Bauman Before Postmodernity: Invitation, Conversations and Annotated Bibliography 1953–1989*, Aalborg: Aalborg Universitetsforlag.

Thatcher, I.D. 2003, *Trotsky*, London, UK: Routledge.

Theophanous, A.C. 1980, *Australian democracy in crisis: a radical approach to Australian politics*, Melbourne: Oxford U.P.

Thomas, H.R. 1983, *Nietzsche in German Politics and Society, 1890–1918*, Manchester, UK: Manchester University Press.

Thomas, J.L. 1983, *Alternative America: Henry George, Edward Bellamy, Henry Demarest Lloyd and the Adversary Tradition*, Cambridge, MA: Harvard University Press.

Thompson, E.P. 1963, *The Making of the English Working Class*, London: Victor Gollancz Ltd.

Thompson, E.P. 1967, 'Time, Work-Discipline, and Industrial Capitalism', *Past & Present*, 38, 56–97.

Thompson, E.P. 1977, *William Morris: romantic to revolutionary*, London: Merlin Press.

Thompson, E.P. 1978a, 'Peculiarities of the English', in *The Poverty of Theory*, London, UK: Merlin Press.

Thompson, E.P. 1978b, *The Poverty of Theory and Other Essays*, London, UK: Merlin Press.

Ticktin, H. 1980, 'The ambiguities of Ernest Mandel', *Critique*, 12 (1), 127–137. doi: 10.1080/03017608008413265.

Tiersky, R. 1983, *Ordinary Stalinism: Democratic Centralism and the Question of Communist Political Development*, London, UK: Allen & Unwin.

Tomba, M., P.D. Thomas and S.R. Farris 2013, *Marx's temporalities*, Leiden: Boston: Brill. Available at: http://booksandjournals.brillonline.com/content/9789004236790 (Accessed: 22 March 2019).

Tönnies, F. 1974, *Community and Association*, translated by C.P. Loomis, London, UK: Routledge & Kegan Paul.

Touraine, A. 1987, *Return of the Actor: Social Theory in Postindustrial Society*, Minneapolis, MN: University of Minnesota Press.

Touraine, A., M. Wieviorka, and F. Dubet 1987, *The Workers' Movement*, translated by I. Patterson, Cambridge, UK: Cambridge University Press.

Trotsky, L. 1925, *Literature and Revolution*, New York: International Publishers.

Trotsky, L. 1937, *The Revolution Betrayed. What is the Soviet Union and where is it going?* translated by M. Eastman, London: Faber and Faber.

Trotsky, L. 1970a, *Nos tâches politiques*, edited by B. Fraenkel, Paris: Belfond.

Trotsky, L. 1970b, *Rapport de la delegation Siberiane*, Paris: Cahiers Spartacus.

Trotsky, L. 1970c, 'Unsere Politischen Aufgaben', in *Schriften zur revolutionären Organisation*, Reinbek bei Hamburg: Rohwohlt.

Trotsky, L. 1971, *The Struggle against fascism in Germany*, New York: Pathfinder Press.

Trotsky, L. 1973a, *1905*, Harmondsworth, UK: Penguin.

Trotsky, L. 1973b, *The age of permanent revolution: a Trotsky anthology*, New York: Dell.

Trotsky, L. 1973c, 'The USSR in War', in *In Defense of Marxism*, New York: Pathfinder Press. Available at: http://books.google.com/books?id=VqPaAAAAMAAJ (Accessed: 11 October 2018).

Trotsky, L. 1974a, *The Permanent Revolution and Results and Prospects*, New York: Pathfinder.

Trotsky, L. 1974b, *Trotsky's Diary in Exile, 1935*, New York: Atheneum.

Trotsky, L. 1975, *My life: an attempt at an autobiography*, Harmondsworth: Penguin.

Trotsky, L. 1978, 'Stalinism and Bolshevism', in *Writings of Leon Trotsky, 1936–1937*, New York: Pathfinder Press.

Trotsky, L. 1979, *Our political tasks*, London: New Park Publications.

Trotsky, L. 1986, *Trotsky's notebooks, 1933–1935: writings on Lenin, dialectics, and evolutionism*, edited by P. Pomper, New York: Columbia University Press.

Tudor, H. and J.M. Tudor (eds.) 1988, *Marxism and Social Democracy: The Revisionist Debate, 1896–1898*, Cambridge: Cambridge University Press.

Vollmar, G. von 1891, *Über die nächsten Aufgaben der deutschen Sozialdemokratie*, München: Ernst.

Waters, M. 2002, *Daniel Bell*, Routledge.

Webb, S. 1916, *Towards social democracy?* Westminster: Fabian Society. Available at: http://books.scholarsportal.info/viewdoc.html?id=/ebooks/oca3/28/towardssocialdemoowebbuoft (Accessed: 15 October 2018).

Webb, S. and B. Webb 1978, *The Letters of Sidney and Beatrice Webb: Volume 1, Apprenticeships 1873–1892*, edited by N.I. MacKenzie, Cambridge, UK: Cambridge University Press.

Weber, M. 1958, *The Protestant Ethic: Spirit of Capitalism*, edited by T. Parsons, New York: Charles Scribner & Sons.

Weber, M. 1988, *Max Weber*, New Brunswick: Transaction.

White, H.V. 1973, *Metahistory: the historical imagination in nineteenth-century Europe*, Baltimore: Johns Hopkins University Press.

Wiener, M.J. 1985, *English Culture and the Decline of the Industrial Spirit*, Cambridge, UK: Cambridge University Press.

Wiggershaus, R. 1994, *The Frankfurt School: Its History, Theories, and Political Significance*, translated by M. Robertson, Cambridge, MA: The MIT Press.

Williams, R. 1977, *Marxism and Literature*, Oxford, UK: Oxford University Press.

Williams, R.H. 1990, *Notes on the underground: an essay on technology, society, and the imagination*, Cambridge, Mass.: MIT Press.

Wright, A. 1979, *G.D.H. Cole and Socialist Democracy*, Oxford, UK: Oxford University Press.

Wright, A. 1986, *Socialisms: Theories and Practices*, Oxford, UK: Oxford University Press.

Wright, A. 1987, *R.H. Tawney*, Manchester, UK: Manchester University Press.

Wright, S. 2002, *Storming Heaven: Class composition and struggle in Italian autonomist marxism*, London, UK: Pluto Press.

Wyndham, F. 1972, *Trotsky: A documentary*, London: Allen Lane.

Yeo, S. 1977, 'A New Life: The Religion of Socialism in Britain, 1883–1896', *History Workshop Journal*, 4 (1), 5–56. doi: 10.1093/hwj/4.1.5.

Žižek, S. (ed.) 2002, *Revolution at the Gates: Selected Writings of Lenin from 1917*, London, UK: Verso.

Index

www.ingramcontent.com/pod-product-compliance
Lightning Source LLC
Chambersburg PA
CBHW070859030426
42336CB00014BA/2251